# James' Introduction to English Law

| First Edition | December 1950 |
| *Second Impression* | January 1952 |
| | |
| Second Edition | August 1953 |
| *Second Impression* | September 1954 |
| *Third Impression* | November 1954 |
| | |
| Third Edition | June 1955 |
| *Second Impression* | July 1976 |
| *Third Impression* | January 1957 |
| *Fourth Impression* | February 1958 |
| *Fifth Impression* | January 1959 |
| | |
| Fourth Edition | September 1959 |
| *Second Impression* | February 1961 |
| *Third Impression* | August 1961 |
| | |
| Fifth Edition | June 1962 |
| *Second Impression* | December 1963 |
| *Third Impression* | August 1965 |
| | |
| Sixth Edition | June 1966 |
| *Second Impression* | April 1968 |
| | |
| Seventh Edition | April 1969 |
| *Second Impression* | October 1969 |
| *Third Impression* | May 1970 |
| | |
| Eighth Edition | July 1972 |
| *Second Impression* | July 1973 |
| *Third Impression* | May 1974 |
| | |
| Ninth Edition | June 1976 |
| *Second Impression* | September 1977 |
| | |
| Tenth Edition | September 1979 |
| *Second Impression* | November 1982 |
| | |
| Eleventh Edition | April 1985 |
| *Second Impression* | May 1987 |
| *Third Impression* | June 1988 |
| | |
| Twelfth Edition | May 1989 |
| *Second Impression* | August 1994 |
| *Third Impression* | June 1995 |

# James' Introduction to English Law

Thirteenth edition

**Peter Shears**  BA, LLB, LLM
Director of Legal Studies, University of Plymouth

*and*

**Graham Stephenson**  LLM, Solicitor
Principal Lecturer in Law, University of Central Lancashire

**Butterworths**
London, Dublin, Edinburgh
1996

| United Kingdom | Butterworths a Division of Reed Elsevier (UK) Ltd, Halsbury House, 35 Chancery Lane, LONDON WC2A 1EL and 4 Hill Street, EDINBURGH EH2 3JZ |
| --- | --- |
| Australia | Butterworths, SYDNEY, MELBOURNE, BRISBANE, ADELAIDE, PERTH, CANBERRA and HOBART |
| Canada | Butterworths Canada Ltd, TORONTO and VANCOUVER |
| Ireland | Butterworth (Ireland) Ltd, DUBLIN |
| Malaysia | Malayan Law Journal Sdn Bhd, KUALA LUMPUR |
| New Zealand | Butterworths of New Zealand Ltd, WELLINGTON and AUCKLAND |
| Singapore | Reed Elsevier (Singapore) Pte Ltd, SINGAPORE |
| South Africa | Butterworths Publishers (Pty) Ltd, DURBAN |
| USA | Michie, Charlottesville, VIRGINIA |

A CIP Catalogue record for this book is available from the British Library.


ISBN 0 406 02445 6

Printed by Clays Ltd, St Ives Plc

# Preface

The first edition of this book was published in 1950. In the preface Philip James described the work as 'intended primarily for the serious student of the law in the early stages of his study, whether he be a university student or a candidate for a legal or other professional examination'. He added the hope that it would also prove digestible to the 'man in the street'. In taking over this book we share his intention and hopes. It has been some seven years since the last edition was published. Like it or not, the law moves on daily. In a book which seeks to cover as broad an area as this one it is inevitable that many points have required reconsideration and updating. We have sought to include mention of significant developments in such areas as statutory interpretation, criminal justice and procedure, public order, the continuing 'privatisation' of major utilities, social security, legal aid and advice, civil and criminal consumer law and the considerable movements in the common law of negligence. Space has always been a problem for this book. The first preface included the admission that in such a vast field it is difficult to know what to include and omit and which points to stress more than others. We have taken the view that this is undoubtedly true and that we cannot please everyone. Finally we acknowledge that we owe huge debts of gratitude to our families and to the publishers for their patience.

We have stated the law as we believe it to be in September 1996.

October 1996                                                                            PS, GS

# Contents

# List of statutes

# List of cases

# Part I
## Introductory

# Summary of Part I

# Chapter 1

# The nature, classification and sources of law

This book is intended for law students who are starting their studies and for others who wish to have a general idea of the general nature of our law. It has therefore been thought appropriate to open with a discussion of the elementary topics indicated in the title to this chapter. The rest of Part I will be devoted to a description of the courts which administer justice, a brief survey of legal procedure and evidence, and a discussion of the basic concepts of legal personality, status and capacity.

Let us first consider what is meant by 'law'.

## 1 The nature of law

Many books have been written and continue to be written about the nature of law; here we must be brief. All will agree that it is a set of rules which form the pattern of behaviour of a given society. And they will agree, too, that the laws with which we have to deal differ from the 'laws' of nature which are 'rules' derived from observation of the physical universe (eg the rule that the tides ebb and flow): for 'law' in our sense is normative (pattern-setting), a *prescription* rather than a *description* of behaviour. Go further than this, however, and there is general disagreement, dictated much, perhaps, by the predilections of each particular jurist.

One school of thought which has persisted through the ages, and which was epitomised by the work of John Austin (1790–1859) – a follower of Jeremy Bentham (1748–1832) has it that law has nothing to do with justice or morality because it is a *command* of political superiors ultimately backed by a 'sanction', an unpleasant consequence (such as imprisonment), in case of disobedience. This theory (like the Marxist theory, which sees law as the will of a ruling class) is attractive, if only because it is simple: it derives ultimately from the image of imperial Rome and is connected with the work of Jean Bodin (1530–1596) who saw in the emergent structure of nation states and absolute monarchies of the post-reformation a social structure based upon the '*sovereignty*' of the monarch, whose word was law – '*L'état*', said Louis XIV, '*c'est moi*': and that was true. But this was

3

an inadequate picture: for not only may laws be broken without anything in the nature of punishment (as, for instance, the rules which prescribe the forms for making a will) but in a complex modern State, with its political checks and balances, it is by no means easy to detect a 'sovereign' in anything more than a formal sense. We shall return to the concept of sovereignty when legislation comes to be discussed.

Another, and an older, school of thought envisages two sorts of laws. One sort is unconnected with morality: such as the legal rule of the road 'left' or 'right'. Such a rule is neutral and unchallengeable, whether decreed by a tyrant or enacted by a democracy. The other sort is concerned with matters which have a moral bearing; so that in relation to them the context of legal rules (enforced by the state) becomes coincident with that of moral rules: the *must* of the law and the *ought* of morality meet on common ground. 'Thou shalt not steal' is, in our society, at least, both a legal and a moral rule. Where rules do thus have a double context the school in question (the 'natural law' school) contrasts 'natural' law with civil (state) law and asserts that the latter must accord with the demands of the former; or, at least, must always strive to do so.

This school derives from Plato and Aristotle and beyond, and it has had its triumphs. Embedded in stoic philosophy and propagated by Cicero, it provided much of the inspiration for the work of the superlative jurists of the classical period of Roman law whose works became enshrined in the *Corpus Juris Civilis*, and thence became the basis of the 'civil' law of Europe (p 13). And, indeed, 'natural' law, as taught by Saint Thomas Aquinas (1224–1273), in the guise of divine law revealed to man by human reason, underlay much of the stability of the middle ages; for, as Bracton (p 21) had it, even the King himself was subject to it. (A doctrine, of course, to be violently repudiated during Machiavelli at the reformation.) And 'natural' law did more: it underlay the thesis of the Dutch jurist, Hugo Grotius (1583–1645) in his *De Jure Belli ac Pacis* ('The Law of War and Peace') which founded modern international law.

But this theory has a serious shortcoming. Neither Plato, nor anyone else, has ever given a satisfactory definition of 'justice', nor has anyone ever been able to say, beyond the repetition of platitudes – such as 'do as you would be done by' – what the ultimate 'ought' of any given situation really is. And, indeed, the concept of 'natural' law can be, and often has been, a dangerously emotive instrument in the hands of extremist politicians who seek to twist the content of the law to suit their ends. For example, was John Locke (1632–1704) right, in propounding 'natural' law, in regarding the protection of private property as a basic function of the law, or was Karl Marx (1818–1883) right in urging just the opposite?

If the reader cares to embark upon the study of Jurisprudence it will be found that there is much more to be told about the nature of law than this; but this is not a work on Jurisprudence. For our purposes it may suffice to think of law as a set of rules which are generally obeyed and enforced within a politically organised society.

## 2 The classification of law

Municipal law, ie state law, as opposed to international law, is commonly divided into categories. The chief of these categories is the distinction between public law on the one hand, and private law on the other.

*Public law* consists of those fields of law which are primarily concerned with the State itself. Thus constitutional law, which regulates the functioning of the organs of the central government, and the relationship of the individual to them, is a branch of public law. Criminal law is also 'public' law because crimes are wrongs which the State is concerned to prevent; and so is most of the law created by modern statutes designed to promote social security, for these statutes cast special duties upon the State.

*Private law* is that part of the law which is primarily concerned with the rights and duties of individuals. Thus the branches of the law which govern private obligations – such as the law of contract and of torts – are all aspects of private law. So too, is the law of property, which determines the nature and extent of the rights which people may enjoy over land and other property, and the law of succession which governs the devolution of property upon death, and in certain other events.

These are only examples of sub-divisions of public and private law; many others might be given. Here it must suffice to explain that both the main division and the sub-divisions are, to some extent, arbitrary and that they are made primarily for the purposes of convenient exposition; each field of law tends to overlap with that of its neighbours and no one field can be fully understood in isolation from the rest. Further the sub-divisions may themselves often be sub-divided; for example, the law of agency and the law of employment are branches of the law of contract, but they are commonly subjected to independent treatment; constitutional law also, in its widest sense, includes many special branches, such as the law of local government, electoral law and administrative law.

Mention should here be made of a special subject which cannot receive further notice in this book; this is private international law (also called the 'conflict of laws'). The 'international' law referred to above, which governs the mutual relationship of states, is 'public international law'. 'Private' international law governs a different field; its rules are primarily concerned with determining what system of state law should properly be applied by our courts in cases which contain some 'foreign' element. Suppose, for instance, that A, in England, makes a contract by correspondence with B, a French person, in France and that by the terms of this contract B is to perform services for A in America. Suppose that B breaks his contract and that A sues him in England. It will be clear that *English* law is not necessarily the correct law to be applied to *all*, at any rate, of the facets of this case. In order to determine which is the correct system to apply, the court will consult the rules of private international law.

Another important division of the law, the difference between 'substantive' and 'adjective' (ie procedural) law, will be mentioned at a later stage (p 58).

# 3   The sources of English law

The courts are the interpreters and declarers of the law; the 'sources' of law are therefore the sources to which the courts turn in order to determine what it is. Considered from the aspect of their sources, laws are traditionally divided into two main categories according to the solemnity of the form in which they are made. They may either be *written* or *unwritten*. These traditional terms are misleading, because the expression 'written' law signifies any law that is formally *enacted*, whether reduced to writing or not, and the expression 'unwritten' law signifies all *unenacted* law. For example, as will appear, judicial decisions are often reduced to writing in the form of law reports, but because they are not formal enactments they are 'unwritten' law.

Since the fashion was set by the *Code Napoléon* many continental countries have codified much of their law, public and private; on the Continent, therefore, the volume of written law tends to preponderate over the volume of unwritten. But in England unwritten law is especially important, for much more of our law derives from judicial precedents rather than from legislative enactment. This does not, of course, mean that none of our law is codified, for many parts of it are; such as the law relating to the sale of goods (Sale of Goods Act 1979) and the law relating to partnership (Partnership Act 1890). All that is meant is that, as yet at least, although Parliament casts increasing multitudes of statutes upon us, we have not adopted the system of wholesale codification which prevails in many continental countries.

Two principal and two subsidiary sources of English law must be mentioned. These principal sources are Legislation, and Judicial Precedent; the subsidiary sources are Custom and Books of Authority.

## A   THE PRINCIPAL SOURCES

### 1   LEGISLATION

Legislation is enacted law. In England the ultimate legislator is Parliament, for in our *traditional* constitutional theory Parliament is sovereign. The composition of Parliament and the nature of the legislative process will be discussed below (Chapter 5); here we are only concerned to explain the significance of the doctrine of '*parliamentary sovereignty*'. It means first, that all legislative power within the realm is vested in Parliament, or is derived from the authority of Parliament – Parliament thus has no rival within the legislative sphere – and it means secondly that there is no legal limit to the power of Parliament. Parliament may therefore, and constantly does, by Act delegate legislative powers to other bodies and even to individuals (p 129), but it may also, by Act, remove these powers as simply as it has conferred them. By Act, moreover, Parliament may make any laws it pleases however perverse or 'wrong' and the courts are bound to apply them. The enactments of Parliament are not subject to question, for our constitution knows no entrenched rights similar to the fundamental liberties guaranteed by the Constitution of the United States and safe-guarded by the Supreme Court. It will have been noted that we have referred to the 'traditional' theory. This is intended to serve as a warning that when constitutional law falls to be discussed the effects of membership of the European Union upon that theory will have to be considered. It is proper to add that when we speak of Her Majesty as 'Sovereign' we use the word in a different, and symbolic, sense: whatever may have been the position of Henry VIII, the Queen is not now the supreme law-maker. Her Majesty is 'sovereign' only in the affection of (most of) her people and as the embodiment of national unity.

In the legislative sphere Parliament is thus legally 'sovereign' and master, but this does not mean that the courts have no influence upon the development of enacted law; for, in order to be applied, every enactment, however it be promulgated, has to be interpreted (or *construed*), and the courts are the recognised interpreters of the law. The meaning of words is seldom self-evident; they will often bear two, or even more, possible interpretations and hence the courts must always exercise a considerable degree of control over the practical application of statutes (enactments of Parliament). The difficulty of interpretation may be illustrated by a simple example. Suppose that Old King Cole, who is an absolute despot, com-mands that all 'dogs' in his kingdom are to be killed. Suppose that Jack Sprat, one of his subjects, who has an alsatian wolfhound, applies to the courts for a decree that it shall be spared, alleging that it is a 'hound' and that the royal command is only concerned with 'dogs'. The court will have to decide whether the word 'dogs' is to be taken to embrace 'hounds': whichever way it decides, it will influence the practical application of the King's command (and the life expectancy of Jack Sprat's pet).

The interpretation of enactments is primarily a matter of seeking to ascertain the intention of the legislator in relation to a given set of facts and of applying the enactment accordingly. This 'intention' may be discovered, in theory if not in law, in at least three ways. First, in case of doubt, the legislator himself may be consulted. But apart from the simplest case of an absolute dictator, this method is impracticable because large bodies like modern legislatures cannot easily be consulted and, in any case, could hardly find time to give decisions: and it is also undesirable because if the maker of a rule of law be permitted to apply it to particular circumstances he will become a judge in his own cause and may bend the rule to suit his inclination. 'Legislation reference', as this method has been called, was, nevertheless, the original abortive plan of the *Code Napoléon* (1800). In the second place, the interpreter may examine the words of the enactment and consider their meaning broadly in the setting and circumstances of their promulgation in order to discover the general intention of the legislator (the *ratio legis*) which lies behind the words and to give it effect. In the third place, the words and phrases of the enactment may be closely examined upon the supposition that the legislator has given perfect expression to his will.

The third of these methods of interpretation is the established approach of English law and the second is the approach of continental courts. Both methods must now be examined because, although the first is still the standard English approach to interpretation, there are now circumstances in which our courts must employ the second.

## (a)  The traditional interpretation
The traditional English interpretation concentrates upon the wording of the statute and construes it narrowly: this keeps the statute to its word and allows it to have force not an inch beyond. The reason for this approach, just like the reason, as will appear, for the continental approach, is to be sought in the evolution of the legal stystem. Primarily our 'common law' (p 23) is 'case' law which has been constructed from the decisions of the *courts* in particular cases; and legislation, though it is true that it is treated as the ultimate master, has been regarded by the courts as an interloper in the organic development of the common law. Indeed, one of the greatest of our judges, Sir Edward Coke (1552–1634), even found it possible to maintain that an Act of Parliament contrary to the reason of the common law was invalid. Thus, though they have respected Parliament as sovereign, the courts have kept the influence of legislation within bounds. They have restricted it to the letter of its word.

This attitude has much to commend it. It tends to eliminate the risk that the judiciary will make new law under pretence of interpretation, and it casts upon the Legislature the burden of making its intention explicit so that the laws it passes may be clear guides to conduct. Certain rules ('canons') have been evolved, many of which are designed to ensure that this form of interpretative method is maintained; and some leading examples of these rules must shortly be given.

But first the inexperienced interpreter must be informed that his task may be lightened if he be careful to consult the enactment itself to see whether it contains (as modern Acts often do) an 'interpretation' section which defines the meaning of the words used in that particular statute for the purposes of that statute: for example, at random, the Olympic Symbol etc (Protection) Act 1995, s 18(1) informs the interpreter that 'Olympic motto' – something that may not be on everyones's lips - unsurprisingly means the motto of the International Olympic Committee and further that the motto itself is 'Citius, altius, fortius'. [And... subsections] Here we are referring to s 18(1). The intended meaning of the expression 'infringing goods' is stated to be as given by s 7(4). Now s 7(4) is itself further divided into s 7(4)(*a*), (*b*) and (*c*).

It may be well here to add that in modern statutes, which tend to embrace matters of detail, the *detail* of many matters contained in the 'body' of the Act is often relegated to Schedules annexed to the Act, and forming part of it. For example, the Environment Act 1995 has 24 such Schedules.

Further, interpretation in general is guided by the Interpretation Act 1978 (re-enacting and consolidating some earlier legislation, in particular, the Interpretation Act 1889) which, as well as containing some basic definitions of standard words and phrases – eg 'the male includes the female gender' – lays down certain general rules about interpretation.

We must now, while warning the reader that there are high authorities – and in particular Lord Denning, formerly a distinguished Master of the Rolls – who believe, it seems, that the English method of interpretation ought to be abandoned in favour of the continental, give the promised examples.

### i  The literal rule

The cardinal rule is that the words of an enactment must *prima facie* be interpreted in their *ordinary, literal or grammatical* sense. And provided that so to interpret them does not give rise to some absurdity, repugnancy, inconsistency or ambiguity the court is not entitled to construe them loosely or fancifully, even if a strict construction appears to it to lead to a wrong result.

### ii  The golden rule

Here we may cite Lord Wensleydale in *Grey v Pearson* (1857) 6 HL Cas 61 at 106: 'In construing statutes', he said, 'the grammatical and ordinary sense of the words is to be adhered to'; in other words, the literal rule is to be applied. This is how a lawyer takes his first look at an enactment. But perforce, for such is often the case, Lord Wensleydale went on to say if this approach proves unsatisfactory as leading to 'some *absurdity*, or some *repugnancy* or *inconsistency* with the rest of (the statute)' then 'the grammatical and ordinary sense of words may be modified *so as to avoid that absurdity and inconsistency, but not further*'. This is the so-called 'Golden Rule': be strict in interpretation, but modify the construction where essential so as to avoid absurdity or inconsistency. How, then, is such modification to be approached?

### iii   Consider the whole enactment

If the use of the 'Golden Rule' leads to the conclusion that the words under consideration produce absurdity, repetitiveness, inconsistency or redundancy the next thing the lawyer must do is to look at the whole of the enactment in question. For what seems absurd or redundant as it stands may take on meaning in the light of the whole context. And in considering the statute as a whole certain matters have to be borne in mind.

*a  The Preamble.*   It is legitimate to consult not only the body of the Act, but where there is one, also the preamble. Statutes used commonly (though they now rarely do) are preceded by a preamble, similar to 'recitals' in a deed, setting out the background and purpose of the enactment: and this may be of assistance in understanding the meaning of any part of it. For instance, the preamble to the famous Statute of Uses (1535) gives a valuable guide to its general intent.

*b  The Title.*   Modern Acts have a 'short' title and a 'long' title. The latter gives a general indication of the purpose of the Act. For example, the Road Traffic (New Drivers) Act 1995 is a short title. The long title of that statute is 'An Act to make provision about newly qualified drivers who commit certain offences, including provision with respect to tests of competence to drive'. The rule is that in interpreting the Act (the 'body' of the Act) the court can have regard to the title of it in order to help to resolve an ambiguity in the body of it; but it is not open to the court to use the title to restrict what is otherwise the plain meaning of the words of an Act.

*c  Punctuation.*   No attention should be paid to punctuation: for in parliamentary, as in other draftsmanship, punctuation is a matter of personal preference.

*d  Marginal notes.*   These are common in modern enactments but, though some find them helpful, they are not, according to the prevailing opinion, to be relied upon as guides. The reason for this appears to be that since they are inserted at the draftsman's discretion, and are not subject to parliamentary debate, they should not be taken to indicate Parliament's intention so much as the *draftsman's* interpretation of it; which is a matter of no legal weight.

### iv   The history of the enactment

The word 'history' is here used in a double sense. In the first sense it signifies the *genesis* of the enactment itself: its progress through Parliament and the debates and discussions which produced it. Nothing would, perhaps, seem more sensible than that the courts should consider these things in order to discover the true intention of the legislators, but the rule was that reference was not to be made to Parliamentary debates. Indeed, this was endorsed by the Law Commission in their work on statutory interpretation, arguing that statements made in Parliament are unreliable for such purposes as this. However, the position has now been modified by the House of Lords decision in *Pepper v Hart* [1993] 1 All ER 42 where it was held that reference to Hansard (the report of Parliamentary debates) would be proper where the statute which falls for interpretation is ambiguous or obscure or a literal interpretation of the words used would lead to absurdity and the statements referred to are those of a Minister or other promoter of the bill and they are clear as to the meaning of the words in question.

This is not to say that the courts will make regular use of Hansard. If the words used in the legislation are clear then, whatever view may be taken of their co-incidence with Parliamentary intention, they will usually be interpreted as meaning what they say.

A second sense of the word 'history' in this context signifies the *background* against which the statute is passed. This may include, for instance, a previous series of enactments in the same field as the Act to be interpreted (often, misleadingly, called the 'parliamentary history' of the enactment) and it may also include such matters as the general social, political and legal background prevailing at the time of the passing of the Act. It *is* permissible and generally desirable for the court to consider the 'history' in these senses; though a House of Lords decision has emphasized that in interpreting a consolidating statute (one which brings together a series of previous enactments), unless the word or phrase in the consolidating enactment is ambiguous, there is to be no recourse to the statutes consolidated.

*v The rule in Heydon's case*

Although perhaps it is no more than a particular illustration of (iv) this rule is important enough to receive special mention. It is as follows. 'That for the sure and true interpretation of all statutes . . . four things are to be . . . considered: (1) What was the *common law before the Act*; (2) *what was the mischief* . . . for which the common law did not provide; (3) what remedy the Parliament hath resolved . . . to cure the disease of the commonwealth; (4) the true reason of the remedy.' (*Heydon's Case* (1584) 3 Co Rep 7a.) This rule is also called the 'Mischief' Rule; and it applies today as much as it did four hundred years ago. For example, in *Gorris v Scott* (1874) LR 9 Exch 125 the plaintiff claimed against the defendant in respect of the loss of his sheep which were washed overboard and drowned while the defendant was engaged in carrying them by sea. The loss was due to the fact that no pens had been provided for the sheep: and this was in breach of a duty imposed by a certain enactment to provide pens for animals carried by sea. The plaintiff asserted that since the loss followed upon the breach of this duty he ought to succeed; but it was held that the purpose of the relevant regulation was not to prevent loss overboard but to minimise the spread of contagious disease, and it therefore followed that the claim did not fall within the 'mischief' of the Act.

It should be added that it is permissible, in order to ascertain the 'mischief' of the statute but *not* in order to determine its true interpretation, to consult reports of committees, commissions, reporting agencies and other bodies which have prepared the background of the legislation.

### vi   Ut res magis valeat quam pereat

('Let the thing stand rather than fall') – It must be presumed that the draftsman intends every word to bear a meaning: to be something which 'stands', so as to be neither repetitious nor redundant. And if a particular clause appears on the face of it to be either of these things then the court must seek to give it a meaning which avoids such a conclusion.

### vii   Expressum facit cessare tacitum

('If something is expressed there is no room for implication') – This may also be rendered: '*Expressio unius, exclusio alterius*' ('If something is expressed it must be taken to exclude something else'). Thus where an Act imposed rates upon 'houses, buildings, works, tenements and hereditaments' but expressly exempted 'land' it was held that the word 'land' (which in normal legal terminology would include 'houses . . . etc') must here mean land alone (in the layman's sense) unencumbered by houses . . . etc'. In other words, the express mention of 'houses . . . etc' excluded the legal implication, which would normally have tacitly arisen, that 'land' would include land bearing 'houses . . . etc'.

### viii   The ejusdem generis rule

('Of the same genus') rule – Frequently enactments refer to a class of things (genus) to which their provisions are to apply, and after the class there follow some general words which imply that other 'like' things are intended to be included. Then the question may arise in the course of litigation whether something which is not one of the specified genus falls within the general words. The issue then becomes whether the thing in question is or is not *ejusdem generis* with the class specified. Let us suppose a statute to embrace 'Any motor car, van, motor cyle or other such thing.' And let us suppose the issue to be (a) whether a motor cycle combination (side car) and (b) whether a pedal cycle, come within the intent of the statute. It may be guessed that (a) would be held to be included but that (b) would not, (a) is clearly of similar genus, (b) is not. Though as to (b) the reader must be reminded that the court must have regard to the Act as a whole; and it is therefore possible that a review of the whole purpose of the Act might lead it, as it were, to open the gate and conclude that (b) is intended to be included: such a conclusion might, for example, be reached if it were plain that the Act as a whole was intended to govern road traffic of any kind.

## ix Burdensome laws

Certain kinds of enactments, including such as create a criminal offence or impose a penalty, statutes having retrospective effect and taxing statutes, are strictly construed. Though, in keeping with changed attitudes to taxation, the latter are not now as strictly construed as they used to be.

These are some of the rules which govern the exercise of the traditional English approach to interpretation. Though it has merits, from time to time the judiciary are critical of it, none more than Lord Denning.

## (b) The European method

Like the English one, the European approach has been dictated by the past. Whereas our common law is a native development almost uninfluenced by Roman law, before the time of the European codes, starting with the *Code Napoléon*, European countries in general were dominated by it. This influence began with the *Corpus Juris Civilis* of the Byzantine Emperor Justinian (reigned 527–565 AD). That *Corpus* was a statutory restatement of the Roman Civil Law published in 534 AD which was intended to be an all-embracing set of laws. During the dark ages Roman law was neglected; but with the emergence of the middle ages it was rediscovered and subjected to intensive study; especially in the Italian law schools. Clearly rules of law promulgated in Eastern Europe in 534 AD were out of line with the needs of mediaeval Europe; consequently though the process was not immediate, jurists began to 'gloss' (ie to put interpretations upon) it; and eventually these interpretations came to be such as to adapt it to mediaeval needs. With the Reformation emergent nation states needed laws to unify them, and there was a general movement (known as the 'Reception') to adopt the much-glossed Roman law. Even in England, Cardinal Pole would, if he could, have persuaded King Henry VIII to replace the common law by its Roman rival. Roman law thus governed in Europe until the time of the modern codes already mentioned. Inevitably, because its reception against a different social and political environment from the Byzantine origin entailed adaption of old words to meet new needs, the method of interpretation was by way of 'gloss' rather than of literal construction.

This method survived the Codes so that the continental lawyer approaches legislation broadly, looking to the intent, purpose or scheme of it, rather than to the literal sense of the words used. Thus, with the courts as midwives, the words of the legislator may be so manipulated that they may go forward to meet new situations; to enlarge, rather than to confine, the scope of the law. It was in this way, for example, that the wording of the *Code Napoléon* was adapted to meet the age of the motor car.

This approach to statutory interpretation is of practical importance to the English lawyer because in two fields at least he must now himself employ it.

*International Conventions*
First, European Conventions adopted by the United Kingdom must be construed in the continental way. And that is so even if (as is often the case) the Convention is embodied as a Schedule to an Act of Parliament. Moreover, where there is an English translation of a French original the French text is to be treated as the authentic one.

*Community Law*
As part of the European Union, the United Kingdom is subject in law both to the European Treaties and to secondary legislation of the Commission and of the Council (p 109). The European Communities Act 1972, s 3 (1) as amended by the European Communities (Amendment) Act 1986, s 2 (*a*), provides that . . . 'any question as to the *meaning or effect* of any of the Treaties, or as to the validity, meaning or effect of any Community instrument, shall be treated as a question of law (and if not referred to the European Court, be for determination in accordance with the *principles laid down by any relevant* decision of the European Court or any court attached thereto)'. What these principles are, or may in the course of time become, is by no means clear but it seems that the Court seeks to synthesize the approaches to interpretation of all the Member States and to invoke the 'spirit' of the Treaties as a whole. There is little doubt that the general intention is that all matters of interpretation should be determined by the Court *itself*, and that they ought to be referred to it by national courts in which they arise. On the other hand, by art 177 of the EC Treaty it is permissible for a national court – provided that it is *not* a final court of appeal (such as the House of Lords) - to undertake the interpretation itself. Where an English court avails itself of this right, as numerous courts already have, it will not follow the traditional English rules of interpretation, but will, as s 3(1) of the European Communities Act 1972, as amended by the Single European Act 1986, provides, be guided by the interpretational practice of the Court of Justice of the European Communities and the Court of First Instance (situated at Luxembourg).

## 2   JUDICIAL PRECEDENT

Under this head will be discussed, (*a*) case law, (*b*) law reporting.

### (a)  Case law
In all countries, at all times, the decisions of courts are treated with respect, and they tend to be regarded as 'precedents' which subsequent courts usually follow when they are called upon to determine issues of a similar kind.

There are probably two reasons for this, the one psychological, the other practical. The psychological reason is that anyone who is called upon to decide a dispute will prefer to justify his decision, if he can, by reference to what has been done in the past rather than to take the responsibility of decision-making. The practical reason is that it is clearly desirable that rulings should be uniform, for it is often asserted that it is more important that the law should be certain than that it should always promote justice in individual cases.

This reliance upon precedent has been both the hallmark and the strength of the common law. Its rules have evolved *inductively* from decision to decision involving similar facts, so that they are firmly grounded upon the actualities of litigation and the reality of human conduct. And new cases lead onwards to reach forward to new rules. Its principles are, to employ a popular phrase 'open-ended'; they are not firm and inflexible decrees. This characteristic of the common law contrasts, again, with the European civil law. There, harking back to the tradition of the *Corpus Juris*, law is characteristically derived from a code; that is, from an enacted body of rules either (as in the case of Justinian's or of Napoleon's legislation) enbodying the whole of, or some considerable part of, the law, or embracing some special aspect of it. Thus the task of the courts is *deductive*: to subsume the present case under the mantle of the generalized and codified rule. The word 'codification' was an invention of the ingenious Jeremy Bentham (1748–1832). In principle this method carries the danger that the encoded rule may be out of touch with actual needs; and certainly, as noted above, in course of time it may become so, and thus may require judicial adaptation to meet changed conditions. But in practice many codes are really restatements of rules previously embodied in the opinions of jurists (as was the *Digest* which formed the most important part of the *Corpus Juris*) or from case law (like the English Sale of Goods Act 1893, consolidated in 1979 and amended since then) or from custom or from some other tried and tested source. So that although the approach to legal decision is on the one hand inductive at common law and on the other hand deductive in the civil law in reality (apart from interpretive method) the two systems are not quite so divergent as might appear. One thing, however, which is distinctive of the English system is that because the English judge has, through precedent, power to make new law, his position in the legal system is central.

Another salient feature of the English system is the doctrine of the *binding* case. By this doctrine the authority of courts is hierarchical; a court which is inferior in authority to another court is obliged to follow ('bound by') a court of superior authority if required to decide upon facts similar to facts already tried by the superior court. The hierarchy of courts, from the House of Lords at the top to the county courts and the magistrates' courts at the bottom will be described in the next chapter. Here, by way of illustrating the operation of the system of binding precedents we may instance its functioning in relation to the courts of civil jurisdiction. Leaving aside for the moment the binding authority of the European Court of Justice in matters of European Law, the House of Lords is the ultimate appeal court, the highest court in the land. All decisions of the House are absolutely binding upon all other courts; this means that they must be followed by courts called upon to determine similar issues, whether they appear to them to be correct or not. Below the House of Lords comes the Court of Appeal; the decisions of the Court of Appeal bind the courts inferior to it, and, generally speaking, it is also bound by its own previous decisions. Below the Court of Appeal comes the High Court of Justice. Here there is a slight, but not very important, departure from the general rule. A judge of the High Court is, of course, absolutely bound by decisions of the House of Lords and of the Court of Appeal, but he is not *absolutely* bound to follow previous decisions of other High Court judges. In practice, however, he will nearly always do so unless he sees some very good reason for departing from the ruling previously enunciated. Beneath the High Court come the county courts; their ('circuit' and 'district') judges are bound by the decisions of all superior courts.

Until recently the House of Lords treated its *own* previous decisions as binding upon *itself*. This produced a situation by which a point of law might, as it were, become tied at the top without hope of change unless the Legislature intervened (as in practice it sometimes does) to abrogate the House's decision. Hence, legislative intervention being a ponderous method of effecting change on particular points, rulings of the House could, either because they were erroneous or because they had become outmoded, unless and until the legislature did intervene, become serious sources of injustice. On 26 July 1966, the Lord Chancellor therefore announced that from that date, though normally – having regard to the danger of disturbing settled principles which have been relied upon as the basis of legal rights – the House *should* continue to follow its own rulings, it should yet for the future *permit* itself to '*depart from a previous decision when it appears right to do so*'. On the other hand, the House has recently stated that it will not review a previous decision unless their lordships feel free to depart from both the reasoning and the decision, and unless they are satisfied that to do so would be relevant to the resolution of the dispute in the case before them, notwithstanding that the previous decision has given rise to grave concern. It must, however, be understood that it is only the House of Lords itself that has been accorded this freedom of action, and that all other courts still remain strictly bound by the hierarchy of precedent. It must also be appreciated that previous decisions are not departed from lightly, nor have there been many examples of them being departed from at all. Few as they are, they include *R v Shivpuri* [1986] 2 All ER 334, over-ruling *Anderton v Ryan* [1985] 2 All ER 355 and *Murphy v Brentwood District Council* [1991] 1 AC 398 over-ruling *Anns v London Borough of Merton* [1977] 2 All ER 492.

Precedents have thus far been described as 'decisions', but this bald statement requires to be amplified. Not everything which a judge says in the course of his judgment creates a precedent, but only his pronouncement of law in relation to the *particular facts before him*. This pronouncement is called the '*ratio decidendi*' of the case. Judges may, of course, and often do, let fall '*obiter dicta*' (pronouncements 'by the way'), in the course of their judgments, upon points of law which are not directly relevant to the issue before them. These *dicta* may be of great assistance to subsequent courts, especially if they are pronounced by judges of high repute, but they are *never binding*; subsequent courts are under no *duty* to follow them.

The precedents formed by decided cases are, thus, as Bacon wrote of the Reports of Sir Edward Coke, the 'anchors of the laws'. A practitioner who is asked to consider a legal matter will therefore look to the reported decisions of the courts; and he will do this even though the point in issue is regulated by a statute, for, as has been explained, statutes are interpreted by the courts, and a decision which is concerned with the interpretation of the statute is just as binding as any other decision. When this much has been said, it must not, however, be imagined that the law is always discoverable by the simple process of looking up, and finding, the right precedent. For facts are infinitely various and by no means all cases are exactly covered by previous authority. Quite the reverse; the facts in issue often resemble two or more divergent authorities. (If the matter were clear then the case would be unlikely to reach the courts.) In these circumstances the courts therefore have freedom of choice in deciding which of the divergent authorities or streams of authority to 'follow' and much of the ingenuity of counsel is directed to 'distinguishing' the facts of precedents which appear to bind the court to decide against him. Further, even today cases of 'first impression' sometimes arise; cases arising upon facts which bear no resemblance to the facts of any previous case. When the judge rules in such a case he legislates, because future courts must usually 'follow' him. A remark which leads to the comment that in 'distinguishing' between previous decisions and 'following' one rather than another the judge, though appearing only to apply existing law, in fact exercises a quasi-legislative discretion: a fact which the system of 'binding' precedent serves to conceal.

The administration of justice is not therefore a slot-machine process of matching precedents. The judges have a field of choice in making their decisions. But they do not exercise their discretion in an arbitrary way; they rest their judgments upon the general *principles* enshrined in case-law as a whole. Case-law does not consist of a blind series of decisions, 'A will succeed', or 'B will fail', but of reasoned judgments based upon rational principles. These principles have been evolved by the courts through the centuries; and, building precedent upon precedent, they have framed them with two ends in view. First, they have sought to formulate them in such a way that their application may be capable of effecting substantial justice in particular cases; second, they have sought to make them sufficiently general in scope to serve as guides to lawyers faced with the task of giving advice in future legal disputes. Thus in a sense the history of the common law (as opposed to statute law – for statutes are sometimes arbitrary and they have often wrought injustice) is the story of the evolution of the judges' conception of justice (a kind of natural law – see above) realized in the form of rules of law intended to be general in their application and as easily ascertainable as possible. The task of attempting to dispense *justice*, while satisfying the essential need for *certainty*, has not been an easy one; in fact the attempt can never achieve more than a compromise; but, on the whole, it has been well performed and the common law of England is no mean rival to the romanistic systems.

It is the duty of the judges to know and to apply these principles, to adapt them to the conditions of the present, and so to mould them that they may be fit to serve for the future. It is also, as was pointed out above, not so much a knowledge of the facts of cases, as a knowledge of legal principle that the student should seek to acquire.

**(b)  Law reporting**
It will be appreciated that the system of case law calls for accurate reporting and publication of all the more important decisions of the superior courts. Consequently there has been *law reporting* of some kind from as early as the thirteenth century. The history of the law reports falls into three main periods: the period of the 'Year Books', the period of private reporting and the modern period.

The *Year Books*, many of which have from time to time been printed with varying degrees of accuracy, and some of which are now available in translation, appear to have been notes, taken by counsel or students upon cases which they considered to be of interest. They were originally written in Anglo-French (the court language of the middle ages) and they cover the period from 1283 to 1535. They are seldom cited today, partly because there is now seldom need to refer to decisions of those early times and partly because, on the whole, they are not, and apparently were not intended to be, accurate records of the decisions of the courts. Although some rulings upon important points of law appear in them, they are more often concerned with matters which seem irrelevant to the modern lawyer, such as arguments between judge and counsel, arguments conducted out of court and occasionally even remarks about the weather. They are, nevertheless, invaluable documents to the historian.

Law reporting proper began with the era of '*private*' reporting. About the second quarter of the sixteenth century practitioners (one of the earliest of them was Sir James Dyer, a Chief Justice of the Court of Common Pleas, whose Reports begin in 1537) began to compile reports of cases which, for various reasons, they or their successors found it convenient to publish. These reports were intended for practical use; hence in the course of time they came to contain the essential matters which practitioners required to know. That is to say, a statement of the facts in issue, the general nature of the pleadings on either side, a brief statement of the arguments of counsel and, above all, the judgment of the court. The technique of these 'private' reports tended to improve as time went on, and by the close of the eighteenth century they had attained a degree of relevance and accuracy approximating to that of the modern reports. The most renowned reports of this type are those of Sir Edward Coke, one of the greatest of our judges (1552–1634). They cover the years 1572–1616 and are to this day accorded the distinction of being referred to as '*The* Reports' by reason of their author's eminence. Sir George Burrow's *Reports* (1756–1772) are also held in high esteem. At about the close of the eighteenth century certain of the reporters became 'authorized'. This meant that the judges who decided the cases noted by these reporters themselves examined and, where necessary, amended the reports before publication. Many of the 'private' reports are still in use, and most of them have been reprinted in a series of 176 volumes, called the *English Reports*.

The *modern* period of law reporting began after 1865, when, as the result of a general demand from the legal profession, the General Council of Law Reporting was set up. This body is constituted as a self-supporting commercial enterprise and it had, and still has, the function of issuing a series of *Law Reports* which are 'authorized' in the sense just explained. The old private reporting ceased soon after this Council came into being.

The Law Reports continue to be issued at the present time and they are now supplemented by a series of *Weekly Law Reports*. But this does not mean that the Council enjoys a monopoly in the field of reporting, for numerous other reports are issued by commercial concerns. The *All England Reports*, a most useful series, first issued in 1936, afford an outstanding example.

The names of most of the Reports, past and current, are commonly abbreviated when they are referred to in legal literature, and the usual abbreviations will be used in this book. A complete key to them is to be found in *Halsbury's Laws of England*, but even without consulting this or any other key, the student who cares to spend some of their time in a law library will find it quite a simple matter to familiarize themselves with the more important of them.

## B  THE SUBSIDIARY SOURCES

### 1  CUSTOM

Customs are social habits, patterns of behaviour, which all societies seem to evolve without express formulation or conscious creation. In a sense custom should be accorded pride of place as one of the principal sources of law for much, if not most, law was originally based upon it. Moreover custom is not solely important as a source of *law*, for even today some customary rules are observed in their own right and they command almost as much obedience as rules of law proper; they only differ from rules of law in that their observance is not *enforced* by the organs of the State. Thus, it will be seen (p 108) that many of the fundamental rules governing the Constitution are 'conventional' (ie customary), rather than legal, rules.

But in modern times most general customs (ie customs universally observed throughout the realm) have either fallen into desuetude or become absorbed in rules of law. For example many of the early rules of the common law were general customs which the courts adopted, and by this very act of adoption made into law. So too, much of the modern mercantile law owes its origin to the general customs of merchants which the courts assimilated during the course of the seventeenth and eighteenth centuries. So also many of the rules of the law relating to the sale of goods originated as customs, were adopted by the courts, and eventually moulded into a statutory code by the Sale of Goods Act 1893. General custom has therefore now ceased to operate as an important source of law. For law, whether enacted or judicially declared, has in most fields superseded custom.

On the other hand customs, prevailing among particular groups of people living in particular localities, are sometimes still recognised by the courts as capable of creating a special 'law' for the locality in question at variance with the general law of the land. For instance in a well-known case the fishermen of Walmer were held entitled, by reason of a local custom, to a special right to dry their nets upon a particular beach. But recognition of such variants upon the general law will only be accorded if certain conditions are satisfied. The following are among the more important of those conditions: The custom sought to be established must, (1) not be unreasonable, (2) be 'certain', that is to say the right which is claimed must be asserted by or on behalf of a defined group of people, (3) must have existed since 'time immemorial'. Literally this means that it must go back to 1189 (by historical accident the terminal date of 'legal memory') (p 375). But in practice the burden upon a plaintiff to establish such a custom – for example a customary duty in his neighbour to fence against a common upon which he has grazing rights – is not so formidable. For if he can prove that such a usage has in fact existed in the locality for a reasonable time a lawful origin for the usage will be *presumed*, provided, of course, that such an origin was possible; and custom itself is such a lawful origin.


## 2   BOOKS OF AUTHORITY

On the Continent the writings of legal authors form an important source of law. In England, in accordance with our tradition that the law is to be sought in *judicial decisions*, their writings have in the past been treated with comparatively little respect. They have been cited in court, if cited at all, rather by way of evidence of what the law is than as independent sources from which it may be derived.

This general rule has, however, always been subject to certain recognised exceptions; for there are certain 'books of authority', written by authors of outstanding eminence, which may not only be cited as independent sources in themselves for the law of their times but which also carry a weight of authority almost equal to that of precedents. Among the most important of these works are Bracton's *De Legibus et Consuetudinibus Angliae* (thirteenth century), Coke's *Institutes* (1628–1641) and Blackstone's *Commentaries* (1765).

When this much has been explained, it must nevertheless be admitted that in modern times the established tradition appears to have been breaking down, because many textbooks are now in practice constantly cited in the courts, though only the best of them are likely to command attention. The reason for this departure from the established tradition is probably that in comparatively recent years a large increase in the popularity of the study of English law in all our major universities has done much to improve the quality of legal writing and to increase the volume of legal literature. Thus, today Salmond's *Law of Torts* is commonly referred to in court and even works of living authors, such as Smith and Hogan's *Criminal Law*, are now often cited, though by a rule of etiquette, counsel who refers to works of the latter category should not cite them directly as authorities, but should request the leave of the court to 'adopt' the arguments which they contain as part of his own submissions. In practice, however, even this latter etiquette is now not always observed.

## 4 Law reform

This is perhaps the most suitable place to mention the machinery of law reform. Traditionally, as has been explained, the development of the law has depended upon parliamentary action in the form of legislation wherever change was desired and upon the slow evolution of rules by the accretion of case law. Change and reform did therefore take place, but very much by fits and starts: as for instance, in the case of the great legislative reforms of Henry II or of Edward I and, in the nineteenth century, of the Judicature Acts 1873–1875. During the present century it has come to be realised that more direction is required in the matter of law reform than the traditional agencies of change could supply. Special committees therefore came into being such as the *Law Reform Committee* and the *Criminal Law Revision Committee* to which specific areas of the law are from time to time referred for reconsideration and suggested amendment by legislative action. Even these have, however, not been successful in giving full impetus to the desire for reform. Consequently the Law Commissions Act 1965 inaugurated a new departure by setting up a full-time *Law Com-*

*mission*. This Commission is appointed by the Lord Chancellor and it consists of a Chairman and four commissioners drawn from the profession and – refreshingly – also from university law teachers. The functions of the Commission include, *inter alia*, the keeping 'under review all the law . . . with a view to its systematic development and reform, including in particular the codification of such law, the elimination of anomalies, the repeal of obsolete and unnecessary enactments and generally the simplification and modernization of the law'. Various kinds of reports have to be made to the Lord Chancellor and annual reports have to be made to Parliament.

The Commission has already sponsored a large number of reforms and it may prove to be an enduring factor in the struggle of the law to keep pace with change.

# Chapter 2

# The administration of the law

In this chapter we will consider the legal system, its background and the present-day court system, and then describe the organisation of the legal profession.

## 1 The background

### A THE COMMON LAW

Our 'common law' was originally derived from the judicial precedents of the old courts of common law and it now consists of the whole body of judicial precedents. The old common law courts consisted of the Court of Exchequer, the Court of Common Pleas (or 'Common Bench') – both dating from the twelfth century – and the Court of King's (or as appropriate 'Queen's') Bench were royal courts set up by the Crown and they superseded a network of local courts which had existed since Anglo-Saxon times. The law which these latter courts administered was local customary law which varied in content in different parts of the country.

Naturally, when the Royal Courts, which were centralized and assumed jurisdiction over all of the country, came into being they evolved and applied a uniform system of law, common throughout the land: hence this law came to be called '*common*' in contradistinction to the older local laws.

The term 'common law' is, however, now used in several different senses as marking special contrasts. For instance, we say that England, the United States (with the exception of Louisiana) and most of the Commonwealth countries are 'common law' countries when we wish to contrast the Anglo-American systems as a whole with those of countries like France whose law ultimately derives from the Roman law: and we call these '*civil* law' countries. The expression 'common law' can also be used to denote our own 'case' law as a whole contrasted with our statute law. And within our own system 'common law', as will appear, is also contrasted with 'equity'.

Having thus explained the primary meaning of 'common law', as that system of principles which was built up by the common law courts we must now consider the basis upon which those principles were evolved. This requires a brief description of the 'Forms of Action' or the 'Writ System' as they, or it, were called.

In these days a civil action starts with the serving of a *writ of summons*: this is a formal document and the purpose of serving it is to give notice to the *defendant* (person sued) upon whom it is served that the *plaintiff* (complainant) intends to bring proceedings against him, and to warn him to defend the action. The formulation of the grounds of the plaintiff's case comes substantially, through the pleadings, at a later stage.

Under the old law the system was different. The standard machinery for starting an action at common law in any of the three common law courts was the *original writ* ('original' because it originated, or started, the action). There was nothing mysterious about a '*writ*': writs were simply concise written orders emanating from high authority – in the case of a royal writ from the King, through the Chancery, the secretarial department of State. The use of writs for administrative purposes goes back to Anglo-Saxon times and was probably a borrowing from Frankish court practice. It echoes the 'mandates' of ancient Rome.

The 'original writs' with which we are here concerned were documents obtained (for a fee) from the administrative offices of the Chancery. There were many variations in form according to what sort of matter was involved, but the general purpose for which most of them were designed was to secure the presence of the defendant before the royal courts, usually through the agency of the sheriff (as the principal royal official) of the county in which the dispute arose. Further, and this is a vital point, each writ contained a brief statement of the plaintiff's ground of claim. If the position had invariably been for the chancery clerks or for the judge at the trial to decide whether these facts (if proved) disclosed a cause of action against the defendant the content of the writs would have been of no *general* importance. We shall see that writs could be of such a nature and that the fact was fundamental in the development of the law, but the first thing to stress is that – as is natural in any administrative system – writs rapidly became stylised. Claims concerning certain types of misconduct came to be recognized and each type of misconduct came to have its own appropriate writ.

Bringing an action at common law thus came generally to consist in selecting the writ appropriate (as he hoped to prove in court) to the facts of a plaintiff's case. For instance, there was the ancient writ of Right by which the 'demandant' (plaintiff) claimed from the 'tenant' (defendant) that the latter 'unjustly' and without a 'claim of right' deprived him of his land. There was the ancient writ of Debt, alleging that the defendant owed (*debet*) him so much money, and the writ of Detinue stating that the defendant detained (*detinet*) from the plaintiff something which was his. Into one or other of the accepted forms, such as these, the facts of the case had to fit; if they did not fit, however just the claim, the plaintiff must fail.

But though writs thus became stereotyped there had to be a means of creating new ones, otherwise the law could not have developed. The agencies of evolution varied. Sometimes Parliament would recognise a new form of action (writ), sometimes the creation would be administrative – as by the Chancery clerks – sometimes, as in the case of the all-important writ of Trespass, we think we can trace it to an innovator – in that case said to be William Raleigh, a thirteenth-century judge, and the teacher of Bracton. However, by the fourteenth century, after much hesitation and political obstruction, a practice emerged by which the *courts* upon the *facts stated*, and upon proof by the plaintiff of actual loss inflicted on him by the defendant, allowed actions '*on the case*' to succeed: in other words the courts were authorized in such circumstances to grant *new* writs. It must not be thought that this task was lightly undertaken, for the mediaeval judges never forgot that in Francis Bacon's words, they were 'lions' *under* 'the throne' and that innovation might displease the Crown. Indeed, cautiously and lawyer-like, the development of new writs through actions on the case was, at first, at least, slow and a matter of development by strict *analogy* from pre-existing writs. Yet, in this way our common law grew. The Register of Writs expanded in the course of time; and at any given time the Register, recording the sum total of available writs, *contained* the *common law*. Within the ambit of the writs lay people's rights: no writ, no right – unless the court *would* grant a new writ.

Thus the stream of the evolution of the common law can be traced in the proliferation of the Forms of Action (writs). This evolution is a long one, extending over more than seven hundred years; and there were times of stagnation, as after the Barons' war in the thirteenth century; and there were times of change, as, strangely perhaps in view of the overweening power of the monarchy, in the early Tudor Period. The recognition of a new right might well be a political matter: there are times of social calm and times of social ferment. Legal conservatism also tells: the fear of departing from the rulings of one's forbears. There were experiments: new forms replaced old. But the story *was* one of expansion: at first few writs and few rights that could be asserted in the royal courts – though it may be that they could, in mediaeval times, be vindicated in the local courts or in the Church (ecclesiastical) courts. But by the time the writ system was abolished by the Common Law Procedure Act 1852 (and, indeed, not entirely until the Judicature Acts 1873–1875) there were many forms of action which, in sum, contained the common law.

The modern procedure based upon the Judicature Acts now prevails and the ancient system has gone. Legal innovation (especially legislative) during the past hundred years has been prolific, so that we have cut away from the roots created by the writs; yet the framework of our civil actions is still based upon them. And it is unwise to forget Maitland's warning that 'the Forms of Action we have buried, but they rule us from their graves'. The common law, as opposed to statute law with its fits and starts, is still an evolutionary creation from its ancient fountain-heads.

It may, perhaps, be added that the principal defect of the writ system was its formalism – a besetting sin of early law paralleled by the *legis actiones* of ancient Rome. While the Forms of Action ruled it was not only true that the plaintiff had normally to find a writ to suit his case but also that if he chose the *wrong* writ his claim must fail. There was no changing of horses in mid-stream (no 'amendment' as we now know it): one rode one's writ to judgment, and if it then turned out to be the wrong writ one could only go back and try another 'horse' – assuming that one had the time, the money and the patience. Finally it is worth remarking that the evolution of the writ system provides a stock example of the fact that law evolves by granting remedies for grievances rather than by formulating abstract 'rights'. The 'right' acquired is the result of the remedy given. So far has modern law departed from this fragmented approach that it took a determined stand by the House of Lords in *Davis v Johnson* [1978] 1 All ER 1132, to insist that where a statute furnished a 'battered bride' with an injunction to re-instal her in her home it followed that the legislature must also have intended to endow her with a legal right to be there. Indeed, in the entire journey of the case through the lower courts it seemed to have been forgotten that the very existence of the *right* to the 'matrimonial home' arose because it was thought equitable to grant an injunction to *protect it*.

## B   EQUITY

Before the Royal Courts of Justice were housed at their present place (in the Strand) they used to sit in Westminster Hall. The three common law courts were on one side of the Hall and the Court of Chancery was on the other. In this court *equity* was administered, and litigants who could not obtain justice in the common law courts would cross the Hall to seek the Chancellor's aid.

The office of Chancellor (more recently 'Lord Chancellor') has an ancient history. Originally the '*cancellarius*' (from Latin '*cancellus*': a bar or lattice) was an usher who served at the bar of a Roman court. In its more illustrious form the office goes back to the court of Charlemagne and had been translated to England by the time of Edward the Confessor. In this form the Chancellor became the King's right-hand man ('Secretary of State for all Departments', as the historian, Bishop Stubbs, put it) and the most powerful official in the realm. He headed the 'Chancery', the royal secretariat, and he was responsible for the use and custody of the Great Seal of the Realm. He was, moreover, closely associated with the administration of justice, for, as has been remarked, the original writs were issued from the Chancery. Further, he was an important member of the

*King's Council* whose duty it became to consider and adjudicate upon petitions addressed to the Council by subjects who sought justice from it as the body most close to the king himself. Petitions might be presented for various reasons. In particular, they were often presented by people who had, in one way or another, failed to obtain justice in the common law courts. This failure was usually due to one of three causes. First, the common law was in some ways *defective*: for example, the early common law remedies for breaches of contract were grossly inadequate. And secondly, the only *remedy* which the common law courts would usually supply was the award of damages, and damages are by no means always a satisfactory form of relief. Third, although the law was adequate to meet the case, *justice might not always be obtainable* in the common law courts because of the greatness of one of the parties, who might, in mediaeval times, often be in a position to over-awe the court itself. The Chancellor could remedy these defects; he was one of the chief royal officials, and being closely associated with the King, he was bound by neither the rules nor the procedure of the common law courts; nor was he likely to be over-awed by any man.

In hearing these petitions (or 'bills' as they came later to be called when the Chancery had become a court) the Chancellors slowly began to evolve a set of rules which remedied the defects in the common law, and to grant new remedies different from, and more effective than, the common law remedies. Thus they redressed breaches of contract, for they regarded them as morally reprehensible breaches of faith; and it must be remembered that the early Chancellors were ecclesiastics. They also decreed *specific performance* and granted *injunctions*. Moreover, in the course of time, they made use of a special writ of *subpoena*, by which they could compel the attendance of parties or witnesses under threat of fine or imprisonment, should they fail to attend.

The Chancellors, therefore, came to administer justice, but at first they had no independent court; and usually acted in consultation with the Council and even with the judges themselves. By the close of the fifteenth century the Chancellor was acting in a judicial capacity upon his own initiative; so that the history of the *Court of Chancery*, as opposed to the more ancient Chancery (ie secretariat of State) itself, really begins then. This court continued to exist until the Judicature Acts abolished it, retaining the memory of its name in the 'Chancery' Division of the High Court of Justice.

The new rules which were thus administered in the Court of Chancery came to be known as the rules of *'Equity'* (derived from the Latin *aequitas*=levelling). There will be further discussion of equity later in this work; especially in the chapters on land law and trusts – the latter being the unique contribution of equity to our legal system. At present four points alone need be noted.

First, it was only gradually that equity developed into a systematic body of rules; indeed, it was not fully developed until systematised under the chancellorship of Lord Eldon (Lord Chancellor 1801–1806; 1807–1827). The early Chancellors administered it according to discretion (Cardinal Wolsey's administration seems to have been conspicuously fair); so much so that John Selden (1548–1554: lawyer, populist and antiquarian) once remarked that early equity varied 'according to the length of the Chancellor's foot'. From the chancellorship of Sir Thomas More (1529–1532), however, it became usual to appoint *legally* trained Chancellors and this, by the nineteenth century, had led the Court of Chancery to rely upon precedent almost as much as the common law. But even today the administration of equity rests upon discretion; and specific performance of a contract, for example, will not be decreed in a case in which it would be unfair to do so.

In the second place, and conversely, before Sir Thomas More's chancellorship, the Chancellors were usually not only administrative officials but also ecclesiastics and chief of the royal chaplains: it followed that in exercising their discretion, and laying the foundation of the rules of equity, they borrowed from the canon (church) and civil (Roman) law from which the former was to a large extent derived.

In the third place, by the very nature of its origin, equity *assumes the law*: it did not come to defeat the common law but to supplement it and to '*fulfil*' it. It is not a rival, but an ancillary system of rules: as Maitland put it, it is a 'gloss or appendix' to the law. Moreover, as another maxim of equity has it, 'Equity *follows* the law', and yet another, that it 'acts *in personam*', upon the conscience (not surprisingly in view of its ecclesiastical origin) of a defendant. These considerations lead to the result that a person who has an *equitable right* to property has something of less validity than one who acquires a *legal right* to the same property ie a right protected by the common law. The rule is that an equitable right will be destroyed if the property be acquired under a legal (ie common law) title by a *bona fide purchaser for value* of the legal right to the property *without notice* of the right of the person entitled in equity. This important limitation upon the validity of the equitable right will appear when the law of property falls to be considered. For the present let us just give a simple illustration of the distinction between the (weaker) '*equitable*' and the (universally valid) '*legal*' right. Suppose that A is a beneficiary in respect of certain property which is held by X in trust for him. Trusts are the creation of equity and the position therefore is that A's right is *equitable*: X, the trustee, has the *legal* title to the property which in conscience he is bound to hold for A, so that A has full use and enjoyment of it – in the old law X was said to hold 'to the use' (or '*ad opus*') of A. Suppose that X, perhaps for his own profit, sells the entrusted property to B. Then *prima facie* B has a legal title to that property, and his title *defeats* A's; so that all A will have is a right of action (for what it may be worth) against X. We assume by that that B is a *bona fide* purchaser for value of what is of course the *legal* title to the property *without notice of* the trust. Thus law defeats equity.

But change the facts and A's equitable right will acquire a strength of its own. It is *only* the *bona fide* purchaser for value of the legal title to the property who will prevail. So that let B have *reason to know* of the existence of the trust or let him *fail* to *give value* for the property: then, in either case his right will cede to A's. In the one case B's conscience will be affected by his knowledge and the chancellors would force him to act conscionably and yield to A; in the other, equity, as another maxim has it, 'will not assist a volunteer', so that B's gratuitously acquired right (even though he has no notice) gives way to A's equitable title.

It is important at the start to understand this difference between legal and equitable rights.

# 2   The modern legal system

## A   THE SUPERIOR COURTS

### 1   NINETEENTH CENTURY REFORMS

The eighteenth century was an age of stagnation in legal affairs, complacently described and accurately mirrored in Blackstone's *Commentaries on the Law of England* (1765). By contrast, the nineteenth century was an age of reform. The reform movement was largely due to the exertions of one man, Jeremy Bentham (1748–1832) who, throughout his long life, set himself the task of publicly criticising legal institutions and of writing books suggesting the means for their reform. His work was enthusiastically assisted during his life, and carried on after his death, by a host of 'Benthamite' followers; and it eventually bore fruit in a series of reforming enactments.

There were five main defects in the administration of civil (as opposed to criminal) justice in the early part of the nineteenth century.

First, law and equity were, as has been noted, administered in separate courts. This meant that *a litigant who felt himself aggrieved by the decision of one of the common law courts, and who wished to seek the assistance of equity, had to institute separate proceedings in the Court of Chancery*; this system was both time-wasting and costly.

Second, although, as has been seen, equity was originally evolved as a subsidiary system to mitigate the strictness of the common law, some of its rules had by this time come to conflict with rules of common law.

Third, the Ecclesiastical Courts and the Court of Admiralty, having developed independently of the other courts, had a special and peculiar procedure and practice of their own.

Fourth, the system of appeals against wrong decisions was both intricate and unsatisfactory.

Fifth, procedure, especially in the common law courts, was cumbersome and antiquated.

An extreme instance of the unhappy state of affairs is provided by the case of *Marquis of Waterford v Knight* (1844) 11 Cl & Fin 653 where it took an unfortunate litigant 14 years to carry an appeal to the House of Lords only to discover then that, because he had originally started his action in the Court of Chancery when he ought properly to have started it in a common law court, he must go back and start again.

The reformers were therefore faced with a threefold problem. First, the system of courts required to be simplified. Second, the administration of law and equity needed to be harmonised. Finally, the system of procedure was ripe for recasting.

We are not here concerned with the third of these problems and the methods by which it was solved.

Apart from the all-important changes effected by the Judicature Acts (below), the first problem was initially tackled by the passing of the Court of Probate Act 1857, which abolished the probate jurisdiction of the Ecclesiastical Courts and set up a new *Court of Probate*. The Matrimonial Causes Act of the same year, also transferred the matrimonial jurisdiction of the Ecclesiastical Courts to a new *Divorce Court*; at the same time so altering the law as to make divorce by judicial decree for the first time possible in certain cases.

The second problem was initially solved by the passing of the Common Law Procedure Act 1854 which gave the common law courts the following powers: (i) To take into account certain defences upon which a defendant would have been entitled to rely had the action been tried in a court of equity; thus in certain defined cases obviating the need for application to be made to two separate courts. (ii) To grant injunctions in certain cases. Further, by the Chancery Procedure Act 1852, the Court of Chancery was empowered to decide points of common law which arose in the course of Chancery proceedings. Finally, by the Chancery Amendment Act 1858 (Lord Cairns' Act), the Court of Chancery was empowered to grant the common law remedy of damages in lieu of, or in addition to, its own remedies of specific performance and injunction.

All these reforms were far less important than the radical changes made by the Supreme Court of Judicature Acts 1873–1875, passed upon the recommendation of the Judicature Commission set up in 1867 (hereafter the 'Judicature Acts').

By these Acts the superior courts were reorganised and were placed substantially upon their present-day footing. One *Supreme Court of Judicature* was set up. The name 'Supreme' Court is a misnomer: it was adopted because, at the time, it was proposed to abolish the final right of appeal to the House of Lords. This Supreme Court consisted, as it now consists, of two branches, the *Court of Appeal* and a lower branch, the *High Court of*

*Justice*. The new organisation came into being on 1 November 1875, and at that time the High Court was made to consist of the following Divisions:

(i)   the Queen's Bench Division;
(ii)  the Chancery Division;
(iii) the Common Pleas Division;
(iv)  the Exchequer Division;
(v)   the Probate, Divorce and Admiralty Division.

The Acts empowered the Crown to make further reorganisations by order in council. This power was exercised in 1881 when the Common Pleas Division and the Exchequer Division were merged in the Queen's Bench Division.

Thus the Supreme Court of Judicature came to be composed of the Court of Appeal and the High Court of Justice; and until 1970 the latter was subdivided into the *Queen's Bench Division*, the *Chancery Division*, and the *Probate, Divorce and Admiralty Division*. When the Acts came into force, the old courts – the three common law courts, the Court of Chancery, the Court of Probate, the Divorce Court, the Court of Admiralty and certain appellate courts were abolished.

Having set up this new and simplified system of courts, the Acts further provided that for the future all branches of the Supreme Court should be empowered to *administer both law and equity*, and to grant both legal and equitable remedies. Further, all Divisions of the High Court were given competence to try any actions; though certain specific matters were reserved for each Division, roughly corresponding with the matters falling with the jurisdiction of the courts they had replaced. Finally, by s 25 of the Act of 1873, *points of conflict* between law and equity were resolved. This section set out a series of specific rules to govern certain specific points; and in its final subsection, (ii), it enacted that for the future 'in all matters not hereinbefore particularly mentioned, in which there is any conflict or variance between the rules of equity and the rules of common law with reference to the same subject-matter, the rules of *equity shall prevail*'. Though it should be noted that this section has now been repealed and re-enacted in a simpler form by the Supreme Court Act 1981, s 49.

It cannot be over-stressed that the Act did *not* purport to *fuse* law and equity into a single system of rules; it only provided that the two systems should for the future be *administered* in the same courts. Nothing short of codifying the whole law could fuse the two systems into one; each set of rules has a different history, they are based upon different principles; and to this day they are separate and independent.

The Judicature Acts were subsequently amended by and consolidated in the Judicature Act 1925, and the structure just described remained intact until the coming into force of two statutes, the Administration of Justice Act 1970 and the Courts Act 1971. The first of these enactments was repealed and substantially re-enacted by the Supreme Court Act 1981, while the other two were partially repealed and re-enacted. The Act of 1981 therefore now governs the structure of the Supreme Court.

## 2   THE SUPREME COURT OF JUDICATURE

This is now divided into the *High Court of Justice* (Civil) and the *Crown Court* (Criminal) from both of which appeals may lie to the *Court of Appeal*.

### i   The High Court of Justice

It will be remembered that the High Court was formerly divided into the *Chancery*, the *Queen's Bench* and the *Probate, Divorce* and *Admiralty* divisions. In 1970 the last of these divisions (once known as 'Wills, Wives and Wrecks') was abolished and its jurisdiction was transferred partly to the newly created *Family Division* and partly to the other two divisions. Moreover, the 1971 Act effected a radical change by abolishing the time-hallowed 'assize' system and making it possible for sittings of the High Court to take place anywhere in England or Wales according to convenience.

*Any* matter *may* be determined in *any* division of the High Court (even though it be assigned by any enactment to some other division). Thus the conception of the unity of the High Court is preserved. But normally each division keeps to its special business: so that the three divisions will require separate consideration.

Technically the High Court (though it never sits as such, but by divisions) consists of the Lord Chancellor (LC), who is president of the Supreme Court (which, again, never sits as such), the Lord Chief Justice (LCJ), the President of the Family Division, the Vice-Chancellor of the Chancery Division (VC) and – at present – not more than 97 Justices of the High Court ('puisne' judges: abbreviated in legal writings as so-and-so J: plural JJ).

The *Chancery Division* is in theory headed by the Lord Chancellor, but in practice, its vice-president, the Vice-Chancellor, presides assisted by a staff of (at present) 18 puisne judges. The Division has both original jurisdiction to try cases at 'first instance' and appellate jurisdiction. In the exercise of its original jurisdiction it is the successor of the old Court of Chancery and although, as has been explained, all divisions of the High Court are empowered to administer both law and equity it is nevertheless still the fact that, as a general rule, matters which formerly lay within the province of the Court of Chancery remain primarily the business of the Chancery Division. Certain matters are, however, expressly assigned to it by the Supreme Court Act 1981 (hereafter (SCA)), Schedule 1. Amongst these are the execution of trusts, the administration of estates and partnership and company matters. Since 1970 the Chancery Division has dealt with all contentious probate business – non-contentions probate is assigned to the Family Division.

It should be added that a specialised *Patents Court* also forms a part of the Chancery Division.

A *Divisional* Court (of not less than two judges) of the Chancery Division, amongst other kinds of *appeals*, hears appeals in bankruptcy matters.

The *Queen's Bench Division* has for its president the Lord Chief Justice assisted by 64 puisne judges at the present time. Its jurisdiction is mainly original (ie devoted to 'first instance' hearings of cases initially tried by it), but it does also have some appellate jurisdiction.

The *original* jurisdiction is for all practical purposes purely civil today. Unlike the county courts which, as we shall see, have only limited powers, the jurisdiction of the Queen's Bench Division (in common with the other Divisions of the High Court) is subject to no limitation in respect of the amount at stake or otherwise; though minor cases within the jurisdictional competence of the county courts will not normally be tried in the Queen's Bench Division.

In the exercise of its original jurisdiction the court consists of a single judge, whether sitting at the Royal Courts of Justice in London or elsewhere. Juries are now very rare in civil actions, so the judge is *usually* judge of both law and fact.

The classes of actions tried in the division are still principally those that used to be tried by the old common law courts which it replaced. For instance, breaches of contract, actions for the recovery of land and claims (eg 'running-down' cases) founded upon tort or upon breach of statutory duty are usually Queen's Bench matters.

In hearing *appeals* the Queen's Bench Division sits as a *'divisional'* court (see above). Its *civil* jurisdiction in this respect is not large; it mainly consists in the hearing of appeals by way of case stated (see below) in certain civil matters heard before magistrates' courts and of appeals from a number of tribunals, such as the Pensions Appeal Tribunal. On the *criminal* side the appellate jurisdiction is more important, consisting of hearing appeals by way of case stated from magistrates' courts and the Crown Court. From these hearings appeal lies to the House of Lords, subject to certain conditions.

Like the old Court of King's Bench, the Queen's Bench Division exercises an important jurisdiction in respect of judicial review through the prerogative orders and writs of *habeas corpus*; in this capacity it also sits as a divisional court.

The above are what we may perhaps be permitted to call the 'regular functions' of the Queen's Bench Division. Two specialised courts which now also form part of it must, however, also be mentioned. These are the *Admiralty Court* and the *Commercial Court*.

The Admiralty Court was created in 1970 when the jurisdiction former-ly exercised by the admiralty side of the Probate, Divorce and Admiralty Division was transferred to it as a specialized court of the Queen's Bench Division. This Court has both '*instance*' and '*prize*' jurisdiction. The first concerns civil cases connected with ships and shipping; in particular with collisions at sea. The second requires explanation. International law has always permitted belligerents to authorize the seizure of enemy or, in certain circumstances, neutral ships and cargoes by way of 'prize'. When a foreign ship is thus captured it must be taken to a port in the captor's country for 'adjudication' before a *Prize Court*. The business of that court is, amongst other things, to decide whether the capture has been a lawful one by the rules of international law. In admiralty matters the judge is usually advised by nautical assessors (Elder Brethren of Trinity House). The Admirality Court is not a very active court, since many shipping cases are settled by insurers and they also tend to go to arbitration. Naturally prize jurisdiction only relates to times of war.

The Commercial Court, set up in 1970, was new only in the sense that it gave official recognition to a long standing practice by which specialist judges had been assigned to commercial cases and by which a special 'commercial list' had been drawn up. Here the aim has always been to conduct commercial business as simply and as speedily as possible.

The *Family Division* has a *President* (in legal writings abbreviated P), at present assisted by a staff of 18 puisne judges. As befits its name, it has original jurisdiction in all matrimonial matters (formerly exercised by the divorce side of the Probate, Divorce and Admiralty Division), proceedings in respect of the wardship of minors, adoption and guardianship pro-ceedings, various claims and proceedings connected with the Family Law Act 1986, the Children Act 1989, the Domestic Violence and Matrimonial Proceedings Act 1976, and so on.

This Division also has *appellate* jurisdiction in certain classes of appeals from magistrates' courts, including a number of matters connected with matrimonial disputes and with minors.

*Appeals* – Appeal from all Divisions of the High Court normally lies to the Civil Division of the *Court of Appeal*, but in order to save cost and delay, the Administration of Justice Act 1969 introduced what is often called 'leap-frogging' procedure by which in most kinds of *civil* cases appeal may be made *direct* from the High Court to the *House of Lords*. This procedure may be used where both parties agree and where the trial judge grants a certificate to sanction it; but the judge may do so only if he is satisfied that a point of law is involved which is of general public importance and which either relates to a matter of construction of an Act or of a statutory instrument *or* else is one in respect of which he considers that he is 'bound' by a previous decision of the Court of Appeal or of the House of Lords. No appeal lies against a grant or refusal by the judge of such a certificate. If it is granted, however, the appellant must then apply to the House of Lords for leave to appeal.

## ii The Crown Court

This was set up in 1971. Like the High Court, this court may conduct its business either in London or in any part of England or Wales; for this purpose the country is divided into 'circuits', groups of centres to be visited. Each circuit has a 'circuit administrator' with a permanent staff whose duty it is to make arrangements for sittings of the Crown Court within the circuit areas, under the general direction of a High Court judge or judges appointed by the Lord Chancellor as 'presiding judges' of the circuit.

The Court has some minor civil jurisdiction, but its main business concerns all criminal proceedings upon *indictment*. Its structure is complicated by the fact that it has three kinds of judges; *High Court* judges, *Circuit* judges and *Recorders*. Which of these judges will sit normally depends upon the gravity of the offence involved according to a classification of offences which will shortly be mentioned. The differences between the circuit judge and the recorder (a new office unconnected with the recorders of former times) is not one of jurisdiction but of employment; Circuit Judges being full-time judges, recorders part-time. Circuit judges are appointed by the Queen on the recommendation of the Lord Chancellor, and they must have been barristers or solicitors of at least ten years' standing (with an 'advocacy qualification' within the Courts and Legal Services Act 1990) or have been recorders or one of a variety of other judicial appointments (such as chairman of the industrial tribunal or stipendiary magistrate) for at least three years. Recorders may be appointed to their part-time office from among barristers or solicitors of ten years' standing (with the same 'advocacy qualification'). It should be added that in most cases, and always upon the hearing of appeals, not more than four nor less than two justices of the peace sit with a circuit judge or recorder.

The *original* jurisdiction of this court consists, as we have seen, of jurisdiction over all *indictable* offences and the work is apportioned according to the following general scheme.

Offences are divided into four classes. *Class* 1 offences include very serious crimes, such as murder and offences under the Offical Secrets Act 1911, s 1: these are normally reserved for trial by a High Court judge. *Class 2* offences, such as manslaughter, abortion and rape must be tried by a High Court judge unless released by or on the authority of a presiding judge for trial by a circuit judge or a recorder. *Class 3* offences: these consist of indictable offences other than those falling within the other classes. They will usually be listed for trial by a High Court judge, but they may, with leave of a presiding judge, be tried by a circuit judge or a recorder. *Class 4* offences include, *inter alia*, all offences which may, in appropriate circumstances, be tried either upon indictment or summarily. They will normally be listed for trial by a circuit judge or a recorder – as opposed to a High Court judge.

From the Crown Court appeal against *conviction* or *sentence* lies to the Criminal Division of the Court of Appeal.

The appellate jurisdiction of the Crown Court consists in the hearing of appeals from magistrates' courts either against conviction or against sentence and it also tries cases of committal for sentence from those courts. In respect of this appellate jurisdiction there is a further right of appeal from the Crown Court to a divisional court of the Queen's Bench Division by way of 'case stated'.

A useful innovation was made by the Criminal Justice Act 1972, s 36; namely that where a trial upon indictment has resulted in an *acquittal* the Attorney-General (the chief law officer of the Crown) may refer any point of law which has arisen in the case to the Criminal Division of the Court of Appeal for its opinion. The latter may then refer the matter to the House of Lords. This is an appeal on a point of law rather than against the acquittal. That remains unaffected no matter what the outcome of this procedure. The point, of course, is to clarify important points of law before they become 'embedded' at the level of the trial courts.

Locations for sittings of the Crown Court have been arranged upon a three-tier system. Major centres are 'first-tier' centres served by High Court judges, circuit judges and recorders, and which have both civil and criminal jurisdiction; 'second-tier' centres are similarly served, but they are only concerned with criminal cases; 'third-tier' centres are served only by circuit judges and recorders, also having criminal, but not civil, jurisdiction.

### iii  The Court of Appeal

Formerly this court tried appeals in *civil* matters only; but since 1966 it has consisted of two Divisions: the one to hear civil appeals, the other to hear *criminal* appeals.

The Court of Appeal at present has a staff of 32 Lords Justices of Appeal (abbreviated LJ, Plural LJJ) – not to be confused with their superiors, the Lords of Appeal in Ordinary (House of Lords). The quorum for a hearing is usually three, and more than one court of three may sit simultaneously; but, exceptionally, under the SCA, a court may consist of two lords justices. If, however, in such a case, there is an equal division of opinion the parties may demand that the case be re-argued before an uneven number. High Court judges may also sit in the Court of Appeal should it be necessary.

*The Civil Division* – Although certain other high judicial officers, including the Lord Chancellor, are ex-officio members of the Court of Appeal, in practice the *Master of the Rolls* (abbreviated MR) is its president. His office dates from the middle ages when the Master of the Rolls was the Chancellor's principal deputy in the Court of Chancery. The office is a judicial one despite its title: the title derives from the fact that the MR was originally the keeper of the royal records ('rolls') and the incumbent of the office does still have duties in connection with the Record Office.

The jurisdiction of the Division includes power to hear appeals from the decisions in *civil* matters (ie non-criminal matters) of all three divisions of the High Court. The court also hears appeals from the county courts. *Bankruptcy* appeals from the county courts form an exception, for they lie, as we have seen, not to the Court of Appeal, but to a Divisional Court of the Chancery Division. Appeals from the Prize Court also form an exception, for they lie to the Judicial Committee of the Privy Council.

The method of appeal is now by way of rehearing; the method which always prevailed in the case of appeals from the Court of Chancery. This does not mean that the Court recalls the witnesses heard in the court below, nor that it will normally admit fresh evidence, not taken at the trial; but that it reviews the whole case from the shorthand notes of the trial and from the judge's notes.

*The Criminal Division* – The Criminal Appeal Act 1966 transferred the powers formerly exercised by the *Court of Criminal Appeal* (set up by the Criminal Appeal Act 1907) to this division of the *Court of Appeal*; and much of this criminal jurisdiction of the Court of Appeal is defined by the Criminal Appeal Act 1968 as amended in January 1996 by the Criminal Appeal Act 1995. The *Lord Chief Justice* is the president of this Division.

The division hears appeals from the Crown Court. In respect of *convictions* appeal used to lie as of right on a question of law alone, and by leave of the Court of Appeal (ie in this context the criminal division) on questions of fact or of mixed law and fact. However, the 1995 Act now provides that leave of the court or a certificate of fitness for appeal from the trial judge will be necessary in all cases. Under the old law the appeal would be allowed if the court thought (i) that the jury's decision was under all the circumstances 'unsafe or unsatisfactory' or (ii) that the decision was wrong in point of law, or (iii) that there was a 'material irregularity' in the course of the trial: but an appeal could have been dismissed if the court considered that 'no miscarriage of justice has actually occurred'. Now that the 1995 Act is in force, and despite heated debate during the passage of the bill, there is a single ground upon which an appeal will be allowed – that it is 'unsafe'.

Appeal against *sentence* lies only with leave of the Court of Appeal; and whereas formerly – in order to discourage frivolous appeals – the Court of Criminal Appeal had power to increase the sentence, the court may now only vary it so that in the result the appellant is not dealt with more severely than he was in the court below. However, under the provisions of the Criminal Justice Act 1988, s 36, the Attorney General can, with leave from the court, refer a case for increased sentence where the trial judge appears to have been unduly lenient. The sentence can be increased to any level that would have been in the power of the trial judge. The court also has power to consider points of law referred to it by the Attorney General.

The 1968 Act provides for a reference by the Home Secretary. For example, in *R v Maguire* [1992] 2 All ER 433 which led to the quashing of convictions stemming from an IRA bomb attack. However, following the report of the Royal Commission on Criminal Justice in 1993 and under the provisions of the 1995 Act, this role of the Home Secretary is to be handed, in due course, to a Criminal Cases Review Commission which will consist of at least 11 people. This Commission is emphatically stated (s 8(2) of the 1995 Act) to be independent of the Crown.

If the Court of Appeal consider it necessary or expedient in the interests of justice, they *may* hear fresh evidence not given at the trial if, *inter alia*, it appears that there is a reasonable explanation for failure to adduce it then. This discretion is retained by the 1995 Act. Further, the power to hear fresh evidence is widened from that which was 'likely to be credible' under the old law to that which 'is capable of belief' under the 1995 Act. Orders for costs may be made; and in particular an order that an un-successful appellant shall pay the costs of the appeal – in some cases at least, a safeguard against frivolous appeals. No judge may hear an appeal in any case in which he was a member of the court of first instance. The decision of the court must be given in a *single* judgment except where the presiding judge states that the question is one of law on which it is convenient that separate judgments should be pronounced. A court usually consists of three lords justices, but (under the SCA) in hearing appeals against sentence two may sit, though if they do not agree the case must be re-argued before not less than three.

There is a further right of appeal from either division to the House of Lords, as will now appear.

3    THE HOUSE OF LORDS

Most people think of the House of Lords as the upper House of Parliament. That is, of course, correct, but if we go back in time we find that in the early mediaeval period what we now think of as the House of Lords in the normally accepted sense was the *Curia Regis* (King's Court), a central governing body which existed before Parliament evolved. This body exercised all the powers of government, including judicial functions. Thus when Parliament became established the Upper House retained *judicial* powers. At times, indeed, these powers were wide; they included the right to adjudicate impeachments made against individuals by the Commons (as in the case of Warren Hastings) and, until comparatively recently, the right to try peers accused of serious offences. Now the House itself retains few of these functions – though there are some left, such as the right to try disputed claims to peerages – and when a *lawyer* thinks of the 'House of Lords' he will normally have in mind not the Upper Chamber, but the *court* of that name which, though technically a committee of the House, is really separate from it.

The 'House of Lords' in this sense is the highest court in the land, and, apart from the jurisdiction of the European Court of Justice, the ultimate court of appeal. It was created by the Appellate Jurisdiction Act 1876 and it consists of a number of between nine and twelve life peers (*'Lords of Appeal in Ordinary'*) appointed from people who have held high judicial office, or from eminent barristers. Its president is the Lord Chancellor for the time being (abbreviated LC). Ex-Lord Chancellors may be required to sit.

On the *civil* side the House, subject also to the leap-frog procedure already mentioned, hears appeals from the civil division of the Court of Appeal; though only if leave of that court or of an appeal committee of the House itself has been granted. The jurisdiction on the *criminal* side consists of the hearing of appeals from the criminal division of the Court of Appeal and from the Courts-Martial Appeal Court: but in either case there is no right of appeal unless the lower court grants a certificate that a point of law of *general public importance* is involved, *and* either that court or the House grants leave. Subject to similar restrictions there is also a right of appeal to the 'Lords' from divisional courts of the Queen's Bench Division in criminal matters.

The House also entertains appeals from the appellate courts of Scotland and Northern Ireland. The quorum of Law Lords (Lords of Appeal in Ordinary) for the hearing of an appeal is three, but in practice five usually sit and exceptionally seven may do so.

It has been explained that House of Lords' decisions are absolutely binding on all lower courts though now it may exceptionally depart from its *own* previous decisions.

## 4  THE JUDICIAL COMMITTEE OF THE PRIVY COUNCIL

The importance of the Judicial Committee of the Privy Council rose with the expansion of the Commonwealth and fell with its decline. Originally this jurisdiction sprang from the right of the King's Council (an inner body of the *Curia Regis*) to exercise jurisdiction under the royal prerogative – including an ancient right, which still exists, of hearing appeals from the Channel Islands and from the Isle of Man. With the fall of the Star Chamber in 1641 no jurisdiction could be exercised by the Council over cases arising within the realm, but as the Empire grew the Privy Council (as it came to be called) became the ultimate court of appeal from the whole of the expanding Commonwealth. Originally this massive power was exercised by lay members of the Council, but the Judicial Committee Act 1833 the jurisdiction was placed in the hands of a *'Judicial Committee'* of professional judges; and it now consists of such Privy Councillors as hold, or have held, high judicial office in the United Kingdom and of certain other members (who must also be Privy Councillors) such as commonwealth judges. In practice a sitting of the 'Judicial Committee' will normally consist of Lords of Appeal in Ordinary assisted by a commonwealth judge or eminent practitioner.

The Statute of Westminster 1931 empowered the countries of the Commonwealth to abolish appeals to the Judicial Committee, and most of them have done so. Consequently this court is now of comparatively little importance, although a few countries (such as New Zealand and Malaysia) have retained the right of appeal.

The Judicial Committee does, however, retain some miscellaneous functions (connected with its origin as a committee of the Council) such as the ancient right in respect of the Channel Islands and the Isle of Man, the hearing of appeals from the ecclesiastical courts concerning faculties and of appeals from the Prize Court. As final repository of the powers of the mediaeval Council it may also determine any disputed question of law referred to it by the Crown. The Judicial Committee is not bound by its own previous decisions. Moreover its decisions do not *bind* lower courts in the United Kingdom; their authority is only *'persuasive'*; though, naturally, the judicial staff of the Committee being similar to that of the House of Lords, its rulings are treated with great respect.

Because the Judicial Committee is still in *theory* a Committee of the Privy Council (though the two bodies are in practice distinct) its decisions are delivered in the form of advice to Her Majesty; only one opinion is usually given. The advice is usually unanimous. However, since 1966 it has been made possible for dissentient opinions to be recorded. This is in contrast with the practice in other appellate courts. In the House of Lords, for instance, all speeches, 'majority' and 'dissenting', are reported; so also are all the judgments of the Court of Appeal.

## B   THE INFERIOR COURTS

Chief among the inferior courts are the county courts, which exercise civil jurisdiction, and the magistrates' courts exercising powers which are in the main criminal.

### 1   THE COUNTY COURTS

There has always been, and there always will be, a need for local courts to determine minor civil disputes. This need was originally supplied by the old county ('shire') courts and the hundred courts which existed in Anglo-Saxon times but fell into desuetude by the close of the middle ages. From the Reformation until 1846 there was no national system of civil courts for minor causes. The County Courts Act of that year, however, set up a new system of county courts, which is still substantially in operation today. The name 'county' court is misleading, for these comparatively new courts have no connection with the old communal 'county' (shire) courts and their organisation is not based upon the geographical division of the country into counties.

For the purpose of the county court system England and Wales are divided into districts and judges' 'circuits' in such a way as to ensure that local courts for minor civil causes are readily available throughout the country according to the needs of population. These courts were formerly served by county court judges, but the Courts Act 1971 abolished that office and replaced the holders of it by *Circuit Judges* who, as has been seen, may also sit in the Crown Court. Recorders may also deputise for the judge.

Under the provisions of the County Courts Act 1984 (and over 150 other statutes!) county courts have a wide jurisdiction including: (i) Jurisdiction in most actions in contract or tort or for money recoverable by statute. (ii) Jurisdiction in actions for the recovery of land. (iii) Equity jurisdiction. (iv) Admiralty jurisdiction. (v) Probate jurisdiction. But it must be noted that in each case the jurisdiction is subject to monetary limits prescribed from time to time by Order in Council; though these may be exceeded where either the parties agree or the case is remitted to the county court from the High Court.

It should be added that *some* county courts also have a limited jurisdiction in admiralty matters and that certain of them designated as *divorce* county courts have jurisdiction in undefended divorce cases: though defended suits must be transferred to the High Court. In order to discourage the conducting of minor litigation in the High Court, which could have been brought in a county court, a party who succeeds in the High Court upon a matter falling within the county court limits may in certain circumstances be awarded no costs or only awarded costs on the county court, as opposed to the High Court, scale.

Beside the types of jurisdiction already mentioned, numerous nineteenth and twentieth century statutes have conferred further duties upon the county courts. Thus, for example, they have been accorded jurisdiction under the Rent Act 1977, the Consumer Credit Act 1974 and the Landlord and Tenant Acts. As a matter of practical importance they may make *attachment of earnings orders* under the Attachment of Earnings Act 1971, to ensure that judgment debtors pay their debts. They may also make *administration orders* upon application of debtors who are unable to pay under a judgment of the court. The effect of these orders is that the court takes over the administration of the debtor's estate.

The functions of the *District Judge* of the county court should also be noted. They are solicitors (of at least seven years standing). They are responsible for court administration but they also have minor, but in practice important, judicial powers including the power to hear any action taken in the county court in which the defendant fails to appear or admits the claim. The Registrar also hears cases in which the amount claimed does not exceed £5,000 (a figure which may be varied), claims by mortgagees for repossession of land and *any* other actions with leave of the judge and consent of the parties.

Procedure is simpler in the county courts, and litigation less costly, than in the High Court. The judge almost invariably sits without a jury; and solicitors as well as barristers have a right of audience.

If the importance of a court is to be assessed from the standpoint of the amount of work it does, rather than from the importance of the issues it tries, the county courts, in the civil sphere, like the magistrates' courts in the criminal, must be regarded as the most important tribunals in the land; for the amount of litigation conducted in them far exceeds the amount conducted in the High Court. From a practical point of view, although not a source of law-making precedents like the superior courts, these are the most important of the civil courts. This is increasingly so where 'small' claims are concerned. There is an arbitration procedure which is quite quick and informal. It is used where the claim is less than £1,000, or where the parties otherwise agree.

There is a right of appeal, as we have seen, from the county courts to the Court of Appeal.

## 2   MAGISTRATES' COURTS

The office of justice of the peace is an ancient one; it goes back to the creation of 'conservators of the peace' in the thirteenth century – gentlemen appointed in the counties to assist the sheriffs in keeping the peace – a 'policing', rather than a judicial, function. The name '*justice* of the peace', however, appears about 1363 when similar people came to be given the function of trying cases of minor crime at quarterly sessions and this practice developed into the 'Quarter Sessions' which remained with us until they were abolished (together with the much older and more important institution of the Assizes) by the Courts Act 1971. In this way a considerable amount of criminal justice in minor indictable offences came to be done by the voluntary services of laymen (non-lawyers). The memory of Quarter Sessions is preserved in the fact that, as has been seen, lay justices now sit with circuit judges and recorders to hear appeals to the Crown Court. It should be added that in modern times Quarter Sessions did usually have legally qualified chairmen.

More to the present purpose, numerous statutes from the sixteenth century onwards empowered these lay 'justices' to try petty offences (less serious than the minor indictable offences triable at Quarter Sessions) *summarily* (ie sitting without a jury). These more frequent and less formal sessions came to be known as 'petty sessions'. Further, from 1554 justices were empowered to conduct *preliminary examinations* of people charged with indictable offences in order to determine whether there was a strong enough *prima facie* case to commit them for jury trial at Quarter Sessions or (in the most serious cases) before the Royal Justices of Assize.

Both the *summary* jurisdiction of the magistrates and the duty of holding *preliminary examinations* ('committal' proceedings) still survive.

*Summary jurisdiction* – trial without jury – has always, through distorted historical memories of the clause in Magna Carta which demanded trial by 'peers' (by which the Barons meant trial of barons by barons, not trial of the man in the hedgerow by the man in the hedgerow), been regarded with suspicion in our law. Its scope is therefore restricted to less serious offences and (although in certain circumstances the magistrates' court may commit an accused person to the Crown Court for more severe punishment) the penalties, whether by way of fine or of imprisonment, which the court may impose are comparatively mild – generally, for any one offence, six months imprisonment and (or) a maximum set fine. Fines are 'scaled' at one of five levels. Thus the maximum penalties can be increased globally by redefining what each 'level' represents. Generally speaking, however serious the offence, 'children' (ie persons under 14) must, except in cases of homicide, *always* be tried summarily, and 'young persons' (ie minors between 14 and 17) *may*, subject to similar exceptions, *always* be tried summarily provided that they consent.

When trying people under 17 the court sits as a 'youth court', consisting of three lay magistrates (both sexes being represented) drawn from a special panel. Youth courts must sit in a separate place from, or at separate times from, the ordinary sessions and they must not sit in a room that has been or will be used by another court within an hour before or after their sitting; parents must normally be present and the public are excluded.

The justices also have a limited civil jurisdiction; and they have power, in certain circumstances, when sitting as 'family' courts of magistrates drawn from a special panel, to hear cases under, for example, the Children Act 1989, or for orders for maintenance, or for protection of spouses and children.

In certain urban areas there are full-time paid '*stipendiary*' *magistrates* appointed by the Crown, upon the recommendation of the Lord Chancellor, from among barristers or solicitors who have had a 'general advocacy qualification' for at least seven years. Stipendiary magistrates *may*, and usually do, sit alone, having all the powers of a bench of two lay magistrates.

The clerk of a magistrates' court is the 'Clerk to the Justices' or, colloquially, 'Justices' Clerk'. Clerks are usually solicitors (though barristers may be appointed) and, as such, they properly have considerable influence over the 'lay' bench.

*Preliminary examinations* – the other judicial function of the justices is, as has been explained, to conduct preliminary examinations in the case of indictable offences, in order to determine whether a *prima facie* case has been made against an accused person and, if so, to decide upon the appropriate court of trial. The nature of the procedure of a preliminary examination will be discussed below

To complete this brief account of the justices of the peace it is, perhaps, proper to add that in bye-gone days their duties were much greater than they are now. From the Black Death (1348–1349) when, by the Statutes of Labourers (1349–1360), they were given the task of enforcing the law governing labour relations, what Lambard (who wrote a classic treatise on the justices in the reign of Elizabeth I) called 'stacks and shoals of statutes' imposed innumerable administrative duties upon them – eg upkeep of highways, rating, licensing of ale houses and administration of the poor law. All these and more, under the general supervision of the Council. When the latter, with the abolition of the Star Chamber (1641), lost its power the great age of the justices began, as mirrored in the activities of the country squires of eighteenth century literature: they were the rulers of the countryside. This state of affairs terminated with the industrial revolution, whereafter administration passed to other hands, and ultimately to local authorities. Today the chief surviving administrative powers of the justices are the issuing of warrants and licensing.

There are two classes of appeals from courts of summary jurisdiction. First, appeal lies to a divisional court of the Queen's Bench Division by way of 'case stated'. Either the *prosecution* or the *defence*, may, under this form of procedure, require the justices to set out their findings of *fact*, and may then apply to a Divisional Court of the Queen's Bench Division for a re-determination of any question of *law* which they dispute. Secondly, the *defence* has a right of appeal to the Crown Court. This is a true right of 'appeal', for the evidence is reheard and questions both of law and of fact may be reviewed. The Crown Court also hears appeals against sentence, which it may, if it sees fit, *increase*. There is a further right of appeal from the Crown Court to a divisional court of the Queen's Bench Division by way of 'case stated'. As has already been noted, subject to strict safeguards there is now a final appeal from the divisional court to the House of Lords.

The office of justice of the peace is now mainly regulated by the Justices of the Peace Act 1979, and the powers and functions of magistrates' courts are contained in the Magistrates' Courts Act 1980.

We noted that, in practical terms, the county court is the most important of the civil courts. Similarly, the magistrates' courts are the most important of the criminal courts. Every year over two million people are convicted of summary offences.

## C   THE COURT OF JUSTICE OF THE EUROPEAN COMMUNITIES

Since 1 January 1973 the United Kingdom has been a member state of the European Community. Accordingly, the English legal system is now affected in a variety of ways by Community law. One of the most significant of these is that the English courts are now subject to the jurisdiction of the European Court wherever it applies. The court sits in Luxembourg and it has (under Art 177 of the Treaty of Rome) jurisdiction to handle references from member states' national courts on the interpretation of points of Community law. It also deals with Community-based matters such as actions between the Commission and member states or between member states for failing to meet Treaty obligations.

The European Court has always regarded Community law as taking precedence over national laws. The UK courts have not always completely shared that view, but since *R v Secretary of State for Transport, ex p Factorame (No 2)* [1990] 3 CMLR 1 established that the obligations of community membership extend to postponing the implementation of an Act of Parliament the room for doubt has been somewhat reduced.

## D   COURTS OF SPECIAL JURISDICTION

The courts which have been discussed so far are the 'ordinary' courts, institutions which have grown from the origins of the common law. Some mention must now be made of the numerous tribunals which fall outside this category.

For the purpose of exposition (but for this purpose only; for there are in practice no clear distinctions in this matter) these tribunals may be divided into three categories. First, there is the huge company of '*administrative*' tribunals, such as the wide powers of certain Ministers to determine disputed issues within their own executive province, or local tribunals under the Social Security Acts, rent tribunals or the powers of the Special Commissioners of Income Tax. These tribunals assume great importance today, but their nature and the constitutional difficulties which their prevalence creates will best be discussed below. In the second place, there are what we may call courts of '*special jurisdiction*'; these are similar to the ordinary courts but they are constituted to exercise jurisdiction within specialised fields or among certain classes of people only, and consequently their staff and procedure often differ from the standard model of the ordinary courts. Finally, there are '*domestic*' tribunals; these are courts of a special nature set up among groups of people engaged in some common pursuit with the aim of regulating the behaviour of the members of the group.

Examples of *courts of special jurisdiction* and of *domestic tribunals* will now be given; but it must be stressed that they are examples and no more, many others might be given under each head.

Four of these courts will be considered: The Ecclesiastical Courts, Courts-Martial, Industrial Tribunals and the Restrictive Practices Court.

# 1   THE ECCLESIASTICAL COURTS

In mediaeval times the jurisdiction of the ecclesiastical courts was as ample as the power of the mediaeval Church itself – as the quarrel between Henry II and Becket displayed. Not only were the ecclesiastical courts special tribunals for the clergy as a class – a very numerous class at that – but they also held sway over the laity, especially in matters of morality (eg swearing, defamation, drunkenness), marriage and death (wills and intestacy). The court structure was correspondingly complex and until the Reformation, as Henry VIII's matrimonial troubles bore witness, there was a final right of appeal, in consonance with the universality of the mediaeval Church, to the *Papal Curia* at Rome.

Except for the abolition of the latter right of appeal, the court structure was little affected by the Reformation and practice in the ecclesiastical courts continued to be an important and specialised business. The law administered was not common law; it was based, like the law of the admiralty courts, upon the romanized civil law of Europe and the 'canon' law of the Church. There was thus a separate Bar for these courts, consisting not of barristers but of 'doctors' ('civilians') who had their own special habitat at 'Doctor's Commons' rather than the ordinary Inns of Court.

In 1857 the matrimonial and probate (wills) jurisdiction of the ecclesiastical courts was transferred to the then-created Divorce and Probate Courts, and the doctors and their 'Commons' ceased to be. As we have seen, these two courts, in their turn, were merged by the Judicature Acts into the (now disbanded) Probate, Divorce and Admiralty Division of the High Court of Justice.

In keeping with the decline in the Church's authority, the jurisdiction of the ecclesiastical courts has diminished, but they still exist. The usual court of first instance in matters which are *not* concerned with doctrine, ritual or ceremonial is the *Consistory Court* of the bishop's diocese which is presided over by a legally qualified 'Chancellor' who is appointed by the Bishop. His jurisdiction includes the granting of 'faculties' (the right to alter the ornamentation or fabric of churches) and the adjudication of *clerical offences* committed by priests or deacons which do not involve doctrine, ritual or ceremonial. Appeal lies to the one or the other of the two *Provincial Courts*, the '*Court of the Arches*' (Canterbury: so named because it used to be situated in the old church of St Mary-le-bow, built upon arches) and the *Chancery Court* of York: these are presided over respectively by the 'Dean of the Arches' and the 'Auditor', both being barristers or judges. A further appeal lies to the Judicial Committee of the Privy Council. *Offences by bishops or archbishops* (not involving doctrine, ritual or ceremonial) are tried by *Commissions of Convocation*, whence appeal lies to a *Commission of Review*, consisting of three Lords of Appeal in Ordinary and of two Lords Spiritual (bishops entitled to sit in the House of Lords).

Matters concerning *doctrine, ritual or ceremonial* are differently treated, whether in relation to the granting of faculties or to clerical offences; they are tried by the *Court of Ecclesiastical Causes Reserved* which consists of two persons who hold or have held high judicial office, and of three diocesan bishops. Thence appeal lies to a *Commission of Review*. Orders of *Certiorari* do not lie to ecclesiastical courts, but orders of prohibition and mandamus do.

## 2   COURTS-MARTIAL

In order to secure the high degree of discipline essential in the armed forces, those serving (although they are in general also amenable to the ordinary law) have always been to some extent subjected to special rules of '*military law*', which apply to them and not to people generally. The constitution, jurisdiction and procedure of the courts martial are provided in a variety of statutes, including the Army and the Air Force Acts of 1955, the Naval Discipline Act 1957 and the Armed Forces Act 1981. These courts consist of military officers assisted in serious cases by members of the Department of an official called the *Judge-Advocate General* (or in naval courts-martial the Judge Advocate of the Fleet). The Courts-Martial (Appeals) Act 1951 set up a special court, the *Courts-Martial Appeal Court* to hear appeals from courts-martial. The composition and jurisdiction of this court is now regulated by the Courts-Martial (Appeals) Act 1968. It is composed of the judges of the Court of Appeal, of such judges of the Queen's Bench Division of the High Court as the Lord Chief Justice (after consultation with the Master of the Rolls) may nominate, and of certain high judicial officers of Scotland and of Northern Ireland. The quorum is three, but a larger number of judges may sit provided that the number is uneven. The jurisdiction is similar to that of the Court of Appeal, except that appeal only lies with leave of the Appeal Court itself, and then only after a petition to the Defence Council (the co-ordinating organ of the combined services) has been unsuccessful. Appeal from the Appeal Court to the House of Lords lies at the instance of either the appellant or of the Defence Council.

## 3   INDUSTRIAL TRIBUNALS AND THE EMPLOYMENT APPEAL TRIBUNAL

Industrial tribunals, which have now become a part of everyday life, were first set up under the Industrial Training Act 1964, and they are rapidly becoming (as F W Maitland once wrote of the justices of the peace) 'maids of all work' for all disputes connected with employment. Their structure, procedure and general administration is now governed by the Industrial Tribunals Act 1996, as is that of the Employment Appeal Tribunal. Among their many duties are the trying of claims arising under the Equal Pay Act 1970, the Sex Discrimination Acts 1975 and 1986, the Race Relations Act 1976 and the Employment Protection (Consolidation) Act 1978. Having a full-time President, they are regionally organised. There are about 75 industrial tribunals sitting in Great Britain every working day. Each hearing is held before a legally qualified chairman and two other people, drawn respectively from a panel representing employers and a panel representing employees who have special knowledge of industrial relations. Appeal on a question of law lies to the *Employment Appeal Tribunal*. This tribunal consists of High Court judges or of lords justices of appeal nominated by the Lord Chancellor, and of a panel of members similar in composition to the panel of members of industrial tribunals. A hearing is presided over by a judge sitting with two representative panel members. Appeal lies on a point of law from the EAT to the Court of Appeal.

### 4    THE RESTRICTIVE PRACTICES COURT

This Court, first set up in 1956, was reconstituted by the Restrictive Practices Court Act 1976. Its function is to adjudicate upon restrictive trading agreements referred to it by the Director General of Fair Trading. It is staffed by five puisne judges of the High Court of Justice, one of whom is its President (there is also a judge from the Scottish Court of Session and one from the Supreme Court of Northern Ireland): and there are also up to ten 'appointed' members qualified by virtue of knowledge or experience in industry, commerce or public affairs. At a normal hearing one of the judges acts as presiding judge with not less than two appointed members. If the issue concerns a point of law *only* the judge may sit alone; but otherwise the decision of the Court is a decision of the majority of all its members, except that the opinion of the judge must prevail on a question of law. The judge has a second or casting vote in the event of an equality of votes.

### E    DOMESTIC TRIBUNALS

There are many domestic tribunals governing the conduct of particular groups of people; and this is natural, for, as Pollock and Maitland wrote in their *History of English Law*, 'there can hardly exist a body of men permanently united by any common interest that will not make for itself a court of justice if it be left for a few years to its own devices'. For example, the disciplinary powers which trade unions exercise over their members by means of district and other committees; or as an example banned by the Restrictive Trade Practices Act 1956, the powers formerly exercised among themselves by traders who combined to form what were in effect domestic courts to ensure that conditions as to resale prices collectively agreed upon should be enforced. And, indeed the domestic affairs of universities, such as examining and the dismissal or appointment of members, are regulated not by the royal courts but by the '*domus*' in the person of the visitor: a legacy of the visitatorial (overseeing) powers of the bishops of the early church.

But here we will confine ourselves to three instances: the Solicitors' Disciplinary Tribunals under the Solicitors Acts, the Disciplinary Tribunals of the Bar, and the Professional Conduct and Health Committees of the General Medical Council.

## 1 THE SOLICITORS' DISCIPLINARY TRIBUNAL

This tribunal was created (in succession to the 'Disciplinary Committee under the Solicitors Acts') by the Solicitors Act 1974, s 46. It consists of solicitors and lay (ie non-lawyer) members appointed by the Master of the Rolls. Its principal functions are to hear applications to strike the name of a solicitor off the roll and complaints about misconduct by solicitors. The quorum for a hearing is three, though there may be more members. There must always be at least one lay member, but the number of solicitors sitting must exceed the number of laymen (ie non-lawyers). Appeal lies from the decisions of the tribunal to the High Court – or, in certain circumstances, to the Master of the Rolls.

Complaints against solicitors are in the first instance investigated by the Professional Purposes Committee of the Law Society which decides whether there is a case to go to the tribunal. The 1974 Act made an innovation (s 45) by empowering the Lord Chancellor to appoint '*lay observers*' whose duty it is to examine any written allegation made by a member of the public concerning the Law Society's treatment of a complaint against a solicitor: in other words, to ensure that the investigation is impartial.

It should be added that the judiciary themselves still retain wide inherent powers over solicitors as officers of the court, including the power to order them to be struck off the roll. The court may also order them to compensate aggrieved persons if they have been guilty of gross misconduct. This power received statutory recognition in s 50 of the Solicitors Act 1974.

## 2 DISCIPLINARY TRIBUNALS OF THE BAR

Ultimately the control of the conduct of barristers lies with the higher judiciary, but this power of control has long been delegated. The duty of investigating charges of professional misconduct at the Bar lies in the *Senate of the Inns of Court and Bar* which consists of representatives of the Inns and of the Bar as a whole. If the professional conduct committee of the General Council of the Bar is satisfied that there is a *prima facie* case the Senate must set up a *disciplinary tribunal* to hear the complaint, and if it is satisfied that there has been misconduct the tribunal will report the offender to his Inn with directions, eg to reprimand, suspend or disbar him. Against the tribunal's decision there is an appeal to the Lord Chancellor who may appoint judges to act as 'visitors' to the Inn concerned and review the case.

## 3   THE PROFESSIONAL CONDUCT AND HEALTH COMMITTEES OF THE GENERAL MEDICAL COUNCIL

*The Professional Conduct Committee* of the General Medical Council is empowered under the Medical Act 1983 to erase, to suspend or to make conditional the registration of a medical practitioner upon the grounds that he has been convicted of a criminal offence or of serious professional misconduct. This Committee replaces the former 'Medical Disciplinary Committee'. The *Health Committee* is empowered to suspend or make conditional the registration of a practitioner on the grounds that his 'fitness to practice is seriously impaired by reason of his physical or mental condition'. There is also a *Preliminary Proceedings Committee* which, effectively, performs the function of preliminary examination in determining whether there is a *prima facie* case to go before either Committee and, if so, before which. Strangely, perhaps, the power of erasure from the register in the case of an entry fraudulently procured or incorrectly entered is accorded to the GMC itself. Appeals from both the Professional Conduct and the Health Committee lie, in certain circumstances, to the Judicial Committee of the Privy Council. Where a doctor's name has been suspended from the Register the 'court' (a High Court judge) may upon application order it to be restored: from such an order there is no appeal.

The Dentists Act 1984 contains similar provisions as to dentists; the General Dental Council having a Preliminary Proceedings Committee and a Professional Conduct Committee: here again, appeal lies to the Judicial Committee of the Privy Council. The Opticians Act 1958 and the Veterinary Surgeons Act 1966 made similar provisions in respect of opticians and veterinary surgeons. The Professions Supplementary to Medicine Act 1960 extended the system to other allied bodies such as the chiropodists' and dietitians' professions.

# 3   The legal profession

## A   THE BAR

In the manner of the mediaeval guilds the Bar was, by the fourteenth century, organised as an association of members of the *Inns of Court*. Although today there are only four of the Inns left (the Inner and Middle Temples, Lincoln's Inn and Gray's Inn) there were originally more of them, including Inns of Chancery and Sergeants' Inns – the latter being associations of *sergeants* ('*servientes*' – the King's servants) who were the most senior barristers, having the monopoly of audience in the Court of Common Pleas, and from whose ranks the judiciary were created. Even to this day no one can practise at the Bar unless he has been 'called to the Bar' and become a member of an Inn. Originally the Inns were like colleges, centres of legal learning and education and, by Shakespeare's time, fashionable training places for young men. Vestigially the remaining Inns still retain something of the atmosphere of colleges, with powers of control over their members, libraries and halls in which the members lunch and dine: and each Inn has its 'Bench' of senior members and judges who are 'Masters' or 'Benchers' of the Inn. But much of the central control of the profession has now passed to the *Senate of the Inns of Court and Bar* and the education of barristers, under the ultimate surveilance of the Senate, is now a matter for the *Council of Legal Education* and the *Inns of Court School of Law*, situated in Gray's Inn, although universities elsewhere in the UK now offer vocational training for the Bar. Moreover, the *General Council of the Bar* ('Bar Council'), created in 1895, now represents the Bar as a profession.

The best way of explaining the functions of a barrister is to call him a 'trial' lawyer and to compare his position vis-à-vis a solicitor with that of a consultant, as opposed to a general practitioner, in the medical profession. The barrister's principal work lies in the oral presentation of cases, for the most part in the higher courts where barristers enjoy a practically exclusive right of audience. He is employed not directly by his client but almost always through the medium of a solicitor. This duality of function between barristers and solicitors is peculiar to the English common law system and, indeed, is even not followed in the United States. It is said to be desirable in that it ensures that the barrister does not become personally involved with the parties to the action and can thus present the case impartially: it also has the advantage that the barrister, being (as opposed to the solicitor) the specialist in 'law', can be used by the solicitor, like a general practitioner uses a consultant, as someone whose opinion can be sought in matters of doubt or difficulty. Further, it is said to serve as a 'quality assurance' mechanism in that a barrister who is not performing well will not be called upon by solicitors.

Although the barrister is primarily an advocate, of necessity he does a certain amount of 'paper' work: for example he draws pleadings and writes 'opinions'. Barristers do their work, when not engaged in court, in 'chambers': sets of rooms in common occupation headed by a senior barrister and managed by a chief clerk. By tradition they may not enter into partnerships. Since the days of James I, after the example of Francis Bacon, barristers of standing who have 'taken silk' become 'Queen's (or King's) Counsel', are entitled to occupy the front bench in court and to wear a silken gown. 'Silk' is obtained on application and the advantage of becoming a QC is that it means almost exclusive concentration upon advocacy. A 'silk' does not usually appear in court without a 'junior' who will prepare the pleadings, although the 'two counsel rule' which dictated this was abolished in 1977. 'Juniors' are barristers who are not 'silks'; and by no means every barrister does take silk, so that the grade is not necessarily an inferior one.

Before leaving the subject of barristers three special offices need mention. The *Attorney-General* is the Head of the Bar and the Chief Law Officer of the Crown. His appointment is political and 'attornies' come and go with governments. He is responsible for answering questions in Parliament and – with the help of counsel to the Treasury – for advising government departments which either he or the latter may represent in civil litigation. He will always represent the Crown in any matter of constitutional importance which has to be litigated, and he has con- siderable power in criminal matters – such as the power to 'enter a *nolle prosequi*', to withdraw proceedings upon indictment by virtue of the royal prerogative.

The *Solicitor-General* is also a political officer who effectively acts as the Attorney-General's deputy. He is a barrister, not a solicitor. Like the Attorney he is a Law Officer of the Crown.

The *Director of Public Prosecutions* is a lawyer (barrister or solicitor) appointed by the Home Secretary who works under the general control of the Attorney-General. He (or she) is, amongst other things, responsible for the carrying on of important criminal proceedings and giving advice in relation to prosecutions.

## B   SOLICITORS

The solicitor may be colloquially described as the 'front of house' man: the person who, like the general practitioner, deals directly with the client and, where litigation is involved, instructs the barrister. The origins of this side of the profession go back to the mediaeval '*attornatus*' (attorney) who was – as the solicitor still is, but the barrister is not – an officer of the court. The attorney's business was originally to help the client in the preparatory stages of cases. In the course of time a similar class of people practising in the Court of Chancery came to be called 'solicitors'. By the close of the middle ages neither class was admitted to the Inns of Court, and the two sub-professions became merged. This meant that inevitably they sought to form a separate organisation of their own and by the eighteenth century such an organisation had appeared, though it was not until 1845 that the *Law Society* as the representative organisation of the solicitor's profession came into being. The 'attorney' disappeared.

The work of a solicitor is too diverse to classify. Solicitors act as personal and family advisers to their clients. They effect conveyances of property, they prepare wills, advise on matrimonial matters and handle the defences of accused people. Solicitors formerly enjoyed a monopoly in conveyancing. This monopoly was, however, taken away. The combined effect of the Administration of Justice Act 1985 Act and of the Building Societies Act 1986 is to inaugurate a new profession of licensed conveyancers under the control of the Council for Licensed Conveyancers. Moreover, these Acts make it possible for institutions (such as banks and building societies) recognised by the Lord Chancellor to offer conveyancing services through the medium of solicitors or licensed practitioners. Many solicitors are active advocates in the lower courts, such as the magistrates' courts and the county courts. Since December 1993 solicitors have had a 'right of audience' in the higher courts too (some require extra formal training before they can 'appear' there). Whatever the 'right' to appear, a solicitor is a businessman and will often find it more 'efficient' to employ a barrister. But this does not mean that the solicitor takes no further interest in the case, for it is his function, acting upon the barrister's 'advice on evidence' to prepare the witnesses and get the case ready for trial. In particular he must take written 'proofs' of evidence from his witnesses so that at the trial counsel knows (or *hopes* he knows) what they will say.

As has been explained, the Law Society is responsible for the solicitors' branch of the profession. It is centred at the Law Society's Hall in Chancery Lane, and it works through a Secretary-General and a permanent staff under the ultimate control of its *Council* of representative solicitors and its (annual) President. It has very wide powers under the Solicitors Acts: the latest of which is the Solicitors Act 1974 (hereafter 'SA'). Thus no one is qualified to act as a solicitor unless he has been admitted by the Society, his name is registered on the Roll kept by the Society, and he has in force a practising certificate issued by it (SA, s 1). The Society (SA, s 2) is also responsible for the examining and training of entrants to the profession; the latter responsibility is in practice, through its Education Committee, undertaken by its own institution, the *College of Law*, and by a number of universities across the country. The Law Society is responsible for the professional conduct of its members and must investigate charges against them and, if necessary, refer them to the Professional Purposes Committee. Further, by the Administration of Justice Act 1985 the Council of the Law Society is accorded wide powers of imposing sanctions upon solicitors – such as depriving them of costs – 'where it appears to the Council that the professional services of a solicitor in connection with any matter in which he or his firm has been instructed by a client were in any respect not of the quality that could reasonably have been expected of him as a solicitor.'

Like the *attornatus*, his prototype, the solicitor is an officer of the Supreme Court. The effect of this is that, whatever the powers of the Law Society or of its Committees, the Supreme Court of Judicature or any judge thereof still has disciplinary powers over solicitors, and applications for striking off may be made to the High Court.

## C   LEGAL EXECUTIVES

With the increase in the volume of legislation in recent years, the need for able and well-qualified legal assistants in solicitors' offices became very great. It is being met by members of the Institute of Legal Executives. The Institute, which developed out of the old Solicitors' Managing Clerks' Association, was founded in 1963 with the object of providing an independent, self-contained educational and professional structure for people working in solicitors' offices in both private and public practice. The Institute's training scheme emphasises the value of practical experience allied to a sound theoretical knowledge of the underlying law. Members of the Institute, who are designated Fellows, must have completed eight years in employment with a solicitor and must also have passed all of the Institute's examinations. The Institute's final, Fellowship, examinations are of a high standard and the Law Society accepts passes in them for the purposes of exemption from the equivalent papers of the solicitors qualifying examination.

The aim of the Institute of Legal Executives is to encourage the emergence of a body of legal specialists who, whilst working under the ultimate authority of their principals, possess a high degree of expertise and who act on their own initiative and, to a great extent, upon their own responsibility.

## D   REFORMING THE FRAMEWORK WITHIN WHICH LEGAL SERVICES ARE PROVIDED

A Royal Commission was set up in 1976 to consider the whole of this picture and report on changes it thought advisable. The Report appeared in 1979. Some of its many recommendations have already been incorporated into 'the system', and we have noted them. (For example, the extension of the 'rights of audience' in the higher courts to solicitors.)

There has been much heated discussion and many White Papers have appeared, containing proposals for change: the Report of the Review Body on Civil Justice (1988), Legal Services: a Framework for the Future (1989), The Workload and Organisation of the Legal Profession (1989), Contingency Fees (1989) and Conveyancing by Authorised Practitioners (1989). A large proportion of these proposals was included within the Courts and Legal Services Act 1990, where the authority to bring many of these changes about was enacted.

As an example of a change marking a real shift of policy, consider the relaxation of attitudes towards contingency and conditional fees. The payment of fees as a reflection of the result of litigation was long held to be unethical and contrary to public policy. However, the Courts and Legal Services Act, s 58, provides that conditional fees agreements can be made between advocates and clients. Certain types of work are excluded (eg some matrimonial matters and others involving children) but agreements can be made where no fee is paid if the action fails and if it succeeds then the fee can be 'uplifted' to reflect the risk the advocate took. These are early days, but it is thought that this innovation will be confined to personal injury claims and perhaps actions in defamation, where legal aid is not available.

# Chapter 3

# Procedure and evidence

## 1 The function of the courts

Adjudication is the principal and proper function of the courts, and the judges are thus known collectively as the *Judiciary*. There are, however, two other aspects of government besides the judicial, namely the *legislative*, by which laws are made, and the *executive* (or 'administrative') by which they are put into operation. The French jurist de Montesquieu in his great book '*L'Esprit des Lois*' (1748) is usually credited with the distinction of being the first to put forward the idea that it is politically desirable that these three aspects, or, as he called them, 'powers', of government should be kept distinct and exercised by separate persons or bodies. The logic of this proposition could not and cannot be denied; for balance of power is a shield against despotism.

This doctrine of 'Separation of Powers', as it came to be called, enjoyed a great vogue among eighteenth and nineteenth century theorists and most constitutional lawyers still consider that separation should be maintained as far as possible. But time and experience have shown that strict adherence to the theory is, for at least two reasons, impracticable. First, rigorous separation hampers effective government; thus our whole system of responsible government, which controls the relationship between the Legislature and the Executive, has been developed in defiance of the doctrine. In the second place, it is not always theoretically easy or practically convenient to assign any particular activity to any one of the three categories of 'powers'. So the Legislature, the Executive and Judiciary, although they are each primarily concerned with their own special functions, often in practice perform acts which ought in strict theory to fall within the province of one or the other of their neighbours. The student of law should not therefore be surprised to learn that officials of the executive often have to make decisions which border upon the 'judicial' and that the courts have some 'administrative' duties to perform. In respect of the courts this divergence of function is most apparent in relation to such matters as the administration of the estates of the deceased and the supervision of the guardianship of minors, but it should be realised that, in almost every case which comes to be tried, some matters have to be settled which might strictly be assigned to the category of 'administration'; for instance in divorce cases orders have to be made about the division of the matrimonial property between the spouses and to ensure the future welfare of the children of the family. Absolute separation of powers is a theoretical ideal and no more.

The cases which the courts have to try may roughly be divided into two main types: civil cases and criminal cases. In a civil action one party (generally called the *plaintiff*) makes a claim against, or seeks a determination of his rights in respect of, another party (generally called the *defendant*). The duty of the court is to determine and declare the rights of the parties and where necessary to grant remedies for securing them. The aim of the criminal process is, on the other hand, not to give relief to an injured party (although many crimes, such as theft may give rise to an independent civil suit), but to determine whether an *offence* has been committed and to make such orders as may be necessary for the punishment or reformation of the offender.

# 2   The methods of legal process

If C undertakes to decide a dispute between A and B he may act in one of two ways: either *he* may take the initiative and examine the parties and their evidence himself, or he may call upon *them* to take the initiative and present their cases to him. Anglo-American law has traditionally adopted the latter method of proceeding, which we may perhaps be permitted to call the 'contentious' or 'adversary' method, as opposed to the former, which is 'inquisitorial'. Clearly the difference between these two methods of proceeding lies only in the degree of initiative taken by the court, and, provided that the court is impartial, the 'contentious' method has no great advantage over the 'inquisitorial'. It is, however, essential to bear in mind that most English trials represent a drama in which the parties, through their champions (counsel), fight a forensic battle against each other: and this may not be entirely an accident, because in the early days of the common law a claim to land upon a writ of right was settled by physical combat between the parties or their hired champions, and the verdict was left to the God of Battles (trial by battle). In a modern trial the role of the judge or jury is to decide upon the evidence which party has the better cause. This method of proceeding is adopted in criminal, as well as in civil trials; the prosecutor, although etiquette forbids him to press for a conviction, appears not as an inquisitor, but as an adversary of the defence.

# 3   Substantive law and procedure

The rules of *substantive* law are legal rules which guide the courts in making decisions, and a description of these will form the main subject-matter of this book. Rules of procedure or *'adjective'* law, as it is sometimes called, are the rules which determine the course of an action; they govern such matters as how the case is to be presented, in what court it shall lie, or when it is to be tried. Procedural rules are, in other words, the rules which govern the machinery as opposed to the subject-matter of litigation. It is a striking fact, much remarked upon by historians, that in the earlier stages of legal development these rules assume paramount importance; form is better understood than substance, and in early law formal requirements, rather than abstract principles, usually determined legal rights. Because the development of the common law has been continuous, this early dominance of procedure has had a lasting influence upon many of the doctrines of the modern substantive law. Generally speaking, however, procedure, though it is of great importance to the practitioner, is today treated as the servant and not the master of substance, and the rules of procedure are now more flexible than they once were. They derive from various sources. Most proceedings in the Supreme Court (that is, most of the more important civil proceedings) are now governed by a code of rules known as the Rules of the Supreme Court ('RSC'). These rules, which were originally authorised by the Judicature Acts 1873–1875, are amended from time to time, under powers first conferred by those Acts, by a committee known as the 'Rule Committee' which is headed by the Lord Chancellor. The RSC are set out in the *Annual Practice* ('The White Book'). Similar rules are laid down for the county courts: these appear in the *County Court Practice.* With some exceptions – such as the magistrates' courts rules – the rules of criminal procedure have not been codified; they are to be found in works such as Archbold's *Criminal Pleading, Evidence and Practice* and *Stone's Justices' Manual*, which deals with the work of magistrates' courts.

# 4   Outline of civil and criminal proceedings

## A   CIVIL PROCEEDINGS

It is of course impossible to outline all the different varieties of procedure in a very short space; actions, for instance, in the Chancery Division or in the Family Division and proceedings in bankruptcy have special rules. The following is a bare sketch of the course of proceedings in an action in the

Queen's Bench Division; a type of action which may, up to a point, be regarded as standard.

The plaintiff (usually through his legal representative) starts the action by obtaining a *writ of summons*: the writ is a printed document containing blank spaces for the inclusion of appropriate particulars. It must be delivered to the Central Office of the Supreme Court (or, outside London, to a district registry) from where it is said to 'issue', and it marks the commencement of an action. It must, in order to warn the defendant of the substance of the claim, be indorsed with a concise statement of the latter – just sufficient to give the defendant notice of the nature of it; but it is in no sense an irrevocable formulation like the original writ in the days of the forms of action. Upon presentation at the appropriate office the writ is stamped and filed, and a copy of it must then be served upon the defendant or his solicitor. Within 14 days of receipt of the writ the defendant must file an acknowledgement of service together with (if he so intends) a notice of intention to defend.

After appearance come the *pleadings*. Pleadings are documents usually drafted by counsel, which (RSC, Ord 18, r 7(1)) must contain, and contain only, a statement in summary form of the *material facts* on which the party pleading relies . . . and the statement must be as brief as the nature of the case admits. They are thus documents which, by stating the *facts* (not the law) as seen by each party, define the issues to which at the trial the evidence will be directed. The first of the pleadings to be delivered is the *statement of claim*: this is delivered to the defendant or his representative on behalf of the plaintiff; it is a summary statement of the material facts upon which the plaintiff proposes to base his case. Within a limited time the defendant must, in turn, deliver his *defence*, together with any *counterclaim* which he may have. Further pleadings, *reply* (plaintiff), *rejoinder* (defendant), *surrejoinder* (plaintiff), and sometimes even more, may follow if they are necessary for the clear formulation of the issue; though, in practice, pleadings now seldom go beyond the reply stage. Where one of the parties does not make his meaning clear in his pleadings the other party is, subject to certain limitations, entitled to demand what are known as *further and better particulars*, that is to say written explanations or amplifications of any of the statements made.

At the close of pleadings there follow the '*interlocutory*' stages, ie proceedings between pleadings and trial. Applications to the court in interlocutory matters must be made to *masters* of the Supreme Court in London or to *District Registrars* in the provinces. These officials have many kinds of powers. Among the more important may be mentioned the power to order one party at the instance of the other to answer upon oath written questions called *interrogatories*: these answers may help to shorten the evidence required at the trial. The master may also order *discovery of documents*: that is, he may at the instance of one party order the other to set out in an affidavit (a sworn and written statement) a list of relevant documents which he has in his possession; the other party may then, unless his opponent gives reason for objection, inspect and take copies of those documents. Again, the master may be asked to sanction *amendments* of the pleadings or to order dismissal of the case for *want of prosecution*; ie undue delay by the plaintiff in prosecuting the claim. The interlocutory proceedings conclude with the taking out by the plaintiff of a *summons for directions* before the master. The latter will then, if previous applications have not been made, make various orders of the kinds already mentioned and will give directions for the trial. The directions will include the determination of the place and mode of trial, whether, for example in London or elsewhere, or whether before a judge alone (more normal) or before a judge and jury. Finally, the plaintiff will be ordered to set the action down for trial within a specified time.

In a High Court action the parties usually appear by counsel, though they may appear in person: experienced solicitors, since 1994, have a right of audience in the High Court, on applying for a qualification entitling them to appear. The plaintiff's counsel opens with a speech in which he outlines his case and lays the issues before the court; he then calls his witnesses and examines them '*in chief*'. Each witness may be 'cross-examined' by the defence and, if necessary, be 're-examined' by the plaintiff. The principal object of *cross-examination* is to test the accuracy of the evidence given in chief by the witness, and counsel must also 'test his case' by putting to the plaintiff's witnesses any points which his own evidence is likely to controvert. The object of *re-examination* is to re-establish belief in that evidence where it has been seriously challenged in cross-examination. Unless there is, on behalf of the defendant, a successful submission of 'no-case' (ie that the plaintiff's evidence discloses no cause of action) the defendant's case will proceed. In the normal case in which there is oral evidence on the defendant's side, his counsel may open the defence (outline his case) and in any event he will call his witnesses, whose evidence is tested in the same way as the plaintiff's: defence counsel then makes a closing address followed finally by a closing address on behalf of the plaintiff. Where the defence calls no oral evidence this procedure varies in that the plaintiff's counsel makes his closing address before the defence counsel makes his: the defence thus having the advantage of the 'last word'. These orders of proceedings may, however, be varied if the judge so directs. Finally the judge, unless he wishes to reserve it for consideration ('reserved' judgment) gives judgment ('extemporary' judgment) though if (as it is now rare) there is a jury he will sum up the evidence to them and direct them upon the relevant law, the actual determination of the issue upon the facts being theirs.

Such, in outline, is the procedure in a civil action in the Queen's Bench Division. County court actions follow very similar lines; though they are, in most respects, less formal than High Court actions. Appeals have already been discussed.

It should be noted that the expense and delay of a High Court action is in practice often avoided by resort to the special procedure authorised by Order 14 of the RSC. By the provisions of this order, if a plaintiff swears an affidavit to the effect that the defendant has no good defence on the merits, and if the defendant is unable to oppose this affidavit by demonstrating that there is some ground of defence, the master may enter judgment for the plaintiff without sending the case for trial; though there is a right of appeal from the master's decision to a judge.

## B   CRIMINAL PROCEEDINGS

Criminal proceedings normally arise either with the arrest of the offender without a warrant or with laying of an information. Powers of arrest without warrant will be discussed below. An *information* is a statement made, usually by the police, to a justice of the peace accusing some person of a crime: this statement is generally reduced to writing. After the information has been laid the justice must, if he decides to act upon it, determine how the presence of the offender is to be secured for trial. He may decide to issue either a summons or warrant. A *summons* is issued in cases where the offence is not serious and the offender is likely to appear if required. A *warrant* is a written command, usually addressed to the police, ordering the person to whom it is addressed to secure the offender.

Until the coming into force of the Prosecution of Offences Act 1985 the instigation of the prosecution was a matter for the police, but that Act brought into being a Crown Prosecution Service under the direction of the Director of Public Prosecutions. Once a charge has been made, prosecution is now the responsibility of that service, which is staffed by professional crown prosecutors (barristers or solicitors). Though in many cases the actual conduct of the trial is usually left to an independent member of the legal profession.

The trial itself may take three possible forms according to the nature of the offence. There are three main categories of offences. Minor offences, which are triable *summarily* (without a jury), serious offences, which are tried upon *indictment* by jury trial and offences which, because in seriousness they fall between the other two categories, are triable, in the words of the Criminal Law Act 1977, s 16(1) 'either way' (ie either summarily or upon indictment). The CLA lays down *what* offences fall within each of these three categories (ss 14–17, 24, Schedules 1, 2, 3). The three possible forms of proceedings call for separate treatment.

## 1   SUMMARY OFFENCES

These are tried summarily before the magistrates. The procedure in a summary trial is as follows. The clerk to the justices reads out the charge and calls upon the defendant to plead to it. If he pleads not guilty, or if he refuses to answer, the trial will proceed. The prosecution, as in a civil action, may 'open' the case, outlining it to the court. The prosecution witnesses will then be called and their evidence tested by cross-examination, as in a civil case. Thereafter, the defence may submit 'no case'. If the submission fails the defence will, in general, open its case and the defence witnesses (as in a civil action) will follow. The defence may, with leave of the court, thereafter address the court a second time, but only if the defendant has himself given evidence and another witness has been called. If the defence does make a second speech the prosecution will have a right to address the court, too, immediately before the defence.

The court then considers its decision. If it finds the defendant guilty it will have to consider the question of punishment; to assist it in this task the prosecution may call evidence as to good character and make a speech in mitigation. If the offence is one which is triable 'either way' and which has been tried summarily and if, on obtaining information as to the defendant's character and antecedents, the court is of the opinion that they are such that greater punishment should be inflicted than it has power to order, the defendant may be remanded in custody so that the case may be considered by the Crown Court. That court may then sentence him to any punishment to which he would have been liable had he been convicted upon indictment. If the defendant pleads guilty at the outset, the proceedings are similar to the proceedings after conviction just explained; except that in this event it is normal for the prosecution to summarise the facts of the case for the benefit of the court. Finally, at any time in the course of the proceedings the court may accept a change of plea of guilty to one of not guilty if justice so requires, and the case will then proceed as upon a plea of not guilty. Formerly even in the case of a summary trial the defendant has always to appear in person, but now in the case of *summary* offences carrying a maximum penalty of three months or less (and not also triable upon indictment) he may avoid appearance by sending the court a written notification that he wishes to plead *guilty*. But provided that the defendant has been notified of the prosecution's intention to refer to it, a previous conviction of a summary offence may then be given in evidence and taken into account in awarding punishment. These rules do not apply to youth courts, except that by s 69 of the Criminal Justice Act 1991 guilty plea by post procedure has been extended to 16 year olds.

## 2   INDICTABLE OFFENCES

Until 1995, as a first step in proceedings upon indictment, it was necessary to determine whether the evidence was strong enough to commit the defendant (hence such proceedings were called 'committal' proceedings) for jury trial. This was the task of magistrates, sitting as *examining justices*, and traditionally the preliminary examination proceeded thus. The prosecutor outlined the prosecution case and called his witnesses who gave their evidence and might be cross-examined in the usual way; this evidence was written down, signed by the witness, and counter-signed by one of the justices. The records of the evidence thus obtained were known as the *depositions*; they were used amongst other things for checking the witnesses' evidence at the trial. Unless the court then decided that the prosecution had failed to establish a *prima facie* case, it would (unless this had already been done) cause the charge to be read to the defendant; and after advising him that he was under no compulsion to do so, would ask him if he wished to make a statement. If he did, the statement would be taken down in writing and might be given in evidence at the trial. The defendant might then himself give evidence and might call witnesses. Most of this evidence was also reduced to writing. Where the defendant was legally represented his counsel or solicitor might then address the court; and they might also do so, with leave of the court, where the defendant gave evidence and called witnesses, *before* the defence evidence; but if they thus addressed the court *twice* the prosecution would have a final right of reply.

The Criminal Justice Act 1967, s 1 (then the Magistrates' Courts Act 1980, s 6 (2)), however, made an important change by introducing what is often referred to as 'short committal'; and this was the common procedure. The effect of it was that if *all* evidence submitted was reduced to writing the court might commit the defendant for trial *without consideration of the contents of the statements*. But this might be done only if the defendant was *legally represented* and *if no submission had been made that the statements disclosed insufficient evidence to put him on trial*. Further (though less important in practice), under s 2 of the Act (then the Magistrates' Courts Act 1980, s 102), written statements of witnesses were – even though the older oral procedure be employed – admissible in evidence, thus dispensing with the need for attendance of the witness. In order to be admitted that statement had to be signed by the witness and it had to contain a declaration (*inter alia*) that it was true to the best of his knowledge and belief; a copy of it had to be tendered to the defence, and the latter must not have objected to its admission.

This procedure was replaced by s 44 of the Criminal Justice and Public Order Act 1994. This Act repealed ss 4–8 of the Magistrates' Courts Act 1980, replacing them with provisions in Sch 4, Part 1 of the 1994 Act. The new procedure was to be known as 'Transfer for Trial'.

As a result of fierce criticism of the 'transfer proceedings' procedure, the Government decided to reinstate the old style committal proceedings in the Criminal Procedure and Investigations Act 1996. The Act abolishes transfer proceedings, but changes the committal procedure by means of lengthy provisions which are not likely to be in force for a while yet. It provides that a magistrates' court enquiring into an offence as examining justices shall on considering the evidence either (a) commit the accused for trial if it is of the opinion that there is sufficient evidence to put him on trial by jury for any indictable offence or (b) discharge him if it is not of that opinion. If the court is satisfied that the evidence falls within the new section 5A to the Magistrates' Courts Act 1980, then the court may commit the accused without the need to consider the contents of the statements unless the accused is not represented or a representative of one of the accused submits that there is insufficient evidence for there to be a trial by jury. There are detailed provisions covering the types of evidence which may be admitted in evidence, including written statements, depositions and other documents. The overall picture is somewhat confused but for the present the form of committal proceedings first introduced in 1967 but now to be found in the 1980 Act are still operational.

After the committal proceedings the justices must send the defendant to the Crown Court for trial and they must decide whether he is to be detained in custody pending trial or whether to release him on bail. The composition of the Crown Court to which the defendant is to be committed will, it will be recalled, vary according to the nature of the offence, but it must here be pointed out, certainly before 1987, that if the justices formed the view, in the case of an offence in class 4, that the trial should be before a High Court judge they had to indicate that view, giving their reasons for holding it. It had, moreover, been ruled that a number of specific considerations should influence them in reaching such a decision: these included, *inter alia*, the fact that the case involved death or serious risk of life, that it involved widespread public concern, or that a novel or difficult question of law was raised. As a result of a Practice Direction in 1987 by the then Lord Chief Justice it is not clear whether this discretion is still vested in the magistrates.

Before the Bail Act 1976 (BA) the essential idea of 'bail' (meaning ultimately 'taking in hand', 'holding' especially in trust) was that by finding someone to go surety for his appearance a person could avoid being held in custody pending his trial: though in practice a surety was often not necessary because the accused could be bound over in his own 'recognizances', ie what was technically a formal contract with the Crown to pay a stipulated sum if he should fail to appear. Before the Act, apart from some guidance provided by (the now repealed) s 18 of the Criminal Justice Act 1967, the court had an unfettered discretion in deciding whether or not to grant bail. The BA made important and controversial changes in this branch of the law which may be summarised: (i) the Act, makes it plain (s 4) that the general assumption is to be that bail ought to be granted: but (ii) in certain specified circumstances set out in the BA, Sch 1, bail may be refused, and the power to refuse is wider in the case of imprisonable than in the case of non-imprisonable offences: (iii) a person can no longer be bound over in his *own* recognizances though he may still be required to furnish sureties for his appearance who may thus, upon his failure to appear, be subject to 'estreat', ie made to forfeit the sum stipulated in their recognizances: (iv) if it appears that a person released on bail will be unlikely to remain in Great Britain he may be required to give *security* for his appearance: (v) the BA, s 6 makes a radical change; if a person released on bail does not surrender to custody (ie appear for trial) he commits an *offence* and a warrant for his arrest may be issued (ss 6 and 7): (vi) it is also an offence to agree to indemnify a surety (s 9): (vii) whenever bail is granted the court must record the fact. It is still the law that a person who is refused bail has a right of appeal to the High Court.

Between committal and trial the *indictment* must be drawn. The indictment is a document which contains a concise statement of the nature of the offence or offences charged; it is usually drawn by counsel who is assisted in the task by having access to the depositions, or the written statements, of the prosecution witnesses. At the start of the trial the defendant is *arraigned*, that is to say the clerk reads the indictment and asks him whether he pleads guilty or not guilty. Upon a plea of guilty the proceedings are similar to summary proceedings. If the plea is one of not guilty the jury must be called and sworn. Thereafter the procedure is again similar to summary procedure; but with two exceptions. First, under the Criminal Procedure (Right of Reply) Act 1964, the prosecutor's right of reply must always be exercised at the close of the evidence for the defence and before the closing speech (if any) by or on behalf of the defendant. Second, the judge, circuit judge or recorder must sum up the evidence to the jury and direct them upon the law. The jury then consider their verdict. After the verdict the proceedings are, again, similar to summary proceedings.

The time-honoured rule of the common law in favour of liberty was that jury verdicts had to be unanimous. This rule has now been modified, and the relevant enactment is the Juries Act 1974, s 17. This section provides (s 17(1)) that in the Crown Court or the High Court (where there are juries of 12) a verdict of a *majority of ten* may now be accepted; though if, through illness or otherwise, the number of jurors has dropped to ten (below which number it must never fall) then a majority verdict of *nine* may be accepted. In a county court it will suffice if *seven* agree (s 17(2)). By s 17(3), however, no *Crown Court* must accept a majority (as opposed to a unanimous) verdict unless the foreman of the jury has stated in open court what the *numbers* of jurors were who respectively agreed and dissented: failure to conform with this provision will render the majority verdict invalid. But despite these reforms the statute agrees with the common law that unanimity is the golden rule; and accordingly s 17(4) enacts that no court shall accept a majority verdict unless it appears to it that, in all the circumstances of the case, there has been reasonable time for deliberation, and in Crown Court proceedings that the jury have retired for at least two hours. In *civil* proceedings the rules may be relaxed (s 17(5)): for the parties may consent to accept any majority verdict and may even agree to proceed with a case in which the jury has fallen below the minimum number.

## 3    OFFENCES TRIABLE EITHER WAY

These, as was explained, are middle category offences neither minor nor yet extremely serious. It is thus reasonable that, subject to the defendant's right to 'put himself upon the country' as the old saying was – to be tried upon indictment before a jury – such offences may, at the magistrates' discretion, be tried either way: either summarily or upon indictment. This matter is now governed by the Magistrates' Courts Act 1980, ss 18–21. When a person who has attained the age of 18 – for below that age summary trial is in general obligatory – appears before a magistrates' court charged with an 'either way' offence the court must, before any evidence is called, and subject to representations by either prosecution or defence, consider which method of trial (summary or jury) is the more suitable. This decision must be governed by reference to the degree of seriousness, likely severity of punishment, etc. In a Practice Direction in 1990, further considerations were set out. The court should never make a decision on the grounds of expediency, should assume that the prosecution version of events is correct, should generally consider trial by indictment in cases involving difficult issues of fact or law and should consider any special features of the case which take it beyond the run-of-the-mill type of case in relation to its sentencing powers. If the court decides in favour of summary trial, then (MCA, s 20) it must tell the defendant that he has the right to opt for jury trial and must obtain his consent before proceeding to try him summarily: it must also warn him that if he is so tried and convicted the court has power to commit him to the Crown Court for severer punishment than it has, itself, power to award. If the defendant does consent to be so tried, the summary trial then proceeds in the ordinary way (as outlined above). If, on the other hand, he does not consent the court will inquire into the information with a view to committal *and* if it then considers that the case is more suitable for jury than for summary trial the accused has no option (s 21) to elect for the latter, and transfer proceedings (as above) will commence. The MCA, however, by s 25 as amended by Schedule 4 to the Criminal Justice and Public Order Act 1994, also empowers the court to change its mind; that is to say, if it has decided in favour of summary trial and (with the defendant's consent) so proceeded, it may at the conclusion of the prosecution case, decide to proceed upon indictment, and to embark upon transfer proceedings on that basis. And, by contrast, during transfer proceedings the court may (but only with the defendant's consent to forego his right to jury trial) decide that summary trial is the more suitable form, and so proceed.

# 5    Evidence

---

Evidence is the means by which facts are proved, and the rules of legal evidence are rules of law concerned with the proof of facts in courts of law. These rules are designed to determine four main problems. First, who is to assume the burden of proving facts. Second, what facts must be proved. Third, what facts must be excluded from the cognisance of the court. Fourth, how proof is to be effected. Let us consider these points in order.

## A THE BURDEN OF PROOF

'He who asserts must prove': that is to say, the plaintiff in a civil cause, and the prosecutor in a criminal, must put before the court facts which substantiate their claim. And those facts must be such that in a civil case the court or jury can regard them as proved upon the *balance of probabilities*, in a criminal case *beyond reasonable doubt*.

In a sense that is all there is to the burden of proof, so that in a criminal case it is said that the onus (or burden) lies upon the prosecution throughout the case to rebut the presumption that *a defendant is innocent until the prosecution has established his guilt*. But this simple statement needs to be qualified because although at the end of the case it is always for the prosecution to persuade the court, upon all the evidence, of the defendant's guilt, yet the prosecution needs only to prove its case: no more. It need not, in the course of the trial, set out to anticipate and repel every defence that the defendant might possibly raise. Thus if the defendant has some special excuse or means of rebuttal he must prove it – ie produce evidence to support it; and thus, *in the course of a trial*, the burden of doing this lies upon him. For example, in a civil action suppose that the defence wishes to establish that the act which injured the plaintiff was the act of some independent person (act of a 'stranger'), rather than his, he must provide the evidence to establish that fact; or in a prosecution, if the defence wishes to reduce a charge of murder to one of manslaughter by reason of provocation he should furnish evidence of provocation. And again, if a statute creates an offence and adds exceptions or exemptions –as eg 'It shall be an offence to keep mice with the exception of white mice' – then it is for the defendant to bring himself within the exception and establish that his mouse is white. Thereafter, of course, if the prosecution is to succeed the prosecution must bring evidence to show that the mouse was *not* white.

Three further points need to be noted. First, where the burden thus lies upon the *defendant*, even in a criminal case all he need do is to establish his point upon balance of probabilities: the prosecution's burden is 'beyond reasonable doubt' throughout. Second, it is the business of the court or jury to decide upon *all the evidence*, thus, although it is true that if a defendant has a special defence (eg provocation or 'white mouse') defence it is up to him to establish it, yet if some evidence appears from some other source – as for example through a prosecution witness – that the defendant was provoked or the mouse was white it will be for the *prosecution* to displace it if the charge is to succeed. Third, it was remarked that the burden of proof lies upon the prosecution throughout the trial in the sense that it must establish every item of the charge in order to obtain a verdict, yet it was also observed that during the course of the trial the burden may 'shift' to the defendant; and if he then establishes his point (eg furnishes evidence that the mouse was white) the onus 'shifts' again to the prosecution who must negate that evidence and prove that the mouse was black or grey. There are thus two senses in which the words 'burden of proof' are used: the first (what the prosecution must do in the end) is sometimes called the 'legal' or 'final' burden of proof, the second, the burden that shifts, is sometimes called the 'provisional' or 'evidentiary' burden. And, of course, the distinction between these two kinds of burden applies to civil, as well as to criminal, cases.

## B   FACTS TO BE PROVED

As a general rule, special defences apart, a proponent must furnish evidence of all material facts upon which he relies to establish his case, but there are exceptions to this rule. Three of these exceptions should be noted.

First, there are certain classes of facts, which need not be proved because the court is entitled to take 'judicial notice' of them. This means that they are facts which are too notorious to require proof. Examples are, events which happen in the ordinary course of nature, Acts of Parliament passed since 1850 (unless there is a special provision in the Act in question that it shall require to be proved), and public matters affecting the government of the country. Thus, for example, if A alleges that B is the father of her child, and it is proved that B was in some remote part of the world at the time when conception must have taken place, the court will not require proof of the fact that B could not have been the father; for the period of gestation is a notorious fact.

Second, where certain facts are established they may give rise to a *presumption* that other facts follow. *Presumptions may be*: *(i) Irrebuttable presumptions of law*. As where a child below the age of ten is incapable of committing a crime. This is a rule which the court is not allowed to deny – however precocious, malicious or wicked the child in question may be: hence, in essence, it is a rule of *law*, rather than a 'presumption'. The former 'irrebuttable presumption' that a boy under 14 years of age was incapable of sexual intercourse and thus not guilty of rape was reversed by s 1 of the Sexual Offences Act 1993. *(ii) Rebuttable presumptions of law*. Conversely there is a rebuttable presumption of law that a child between 10 and 14 is incapable of a criminal intent, but this may be *rebutted* (displaced) by proof that a particular child in fact *is* capable of the intent. *(iii) Presumptions of fact*. These are reasonable inferences arising, as a matter of *fact*, from given facts or circumstances. 'Circumstantial' evidence affords an example. They are inferences which can always be rebutted by evidence which is sufficient to refute them.

In the third place, in civil proceedings in order to obviate the necessity of proving facts which are not in dispute, formal *admissions* may be (and often are) made by the parties, prior to or during the trial. These admissions may be made in the pleadings, or orally in court and in various other ways. At common law admissions, other than 'confessions', could not be made in criminal cases; but the Criminal Justice Act 1967, s 10, authorised the making of them either during or before the proceedings; though in the latter case they must be in writing and approved by the legal advisers of the party concerned. They may be made by either prosecution or defence; and here again, as in the case of civil proceedings, this machinery for admitting non-contentious evidence is useful in saving time and expense.

## C  FACTS TO BE EXCLUDED

It might be supposed that proof of any facts which *might* support the proposition advanced might be admitted. But this is not the case. Partly in order to prevent waste of time, and partly in order to prevent certain classes of facts from being put before juries which might tend to lead them to unwarranted conclusions, English law only permits proof of facts which are *in issue* and of facts which are *relevant* to the issue.

The expression 'facts in issue' requires little explanation: the facts in issue are the facts which are in dispute upon the pleadings of a civil action, or the facts averred in an indictment, and denied by a plea of 'not guilty'. Thus, upon a charge of burglary the fact that X, at a certain time and in a certain building, took Y's watch is clearly likely to be a fact in issue.

'Relevancy', in its legal signification, is a difficult term to define. Broadly speaking any fact which is logically probative of, or which serves to explain, a fact in issue will be treated as relevant to the issue and will therefore be admissible. This is, however, only a very broad and general rule, for evidence of certain classes of facts is, for the reasons explained above, treated as legally 'irrelevant' – and therefore inadmissible – even though it might be considered logically probative of the issue. Facts which are thus inadmissible fall into certain well-known categories. Here there is only sufficient space to make brief mention of two of these categories.

Firstly, in civil actions parties are normally not permitted to give *evidence of their good character*, ie of their general reputation for good character. The reason for this is that evidence of good character might give rise to prejudice. If Tom Jones demonstrates that he is a really good fellow unwarrantable conclusions may be drawn in his favour; if Peter Smith, his opponent, does the same attention may be diverted from a critical examination of the facts as given by the witnesses on either side to a hypothetical counter-balancing of the supposed merits of the parties.

Second, it might at first sight appear relevant, where a certain course of conduct is alleged, to prove that the person so alleged to have conducted himself *had* in fact so conducted himself upon other occasions. For example, where W alleges that X has obtained his ring from him by deception, proof that X had previously obtained Y's chickens and Z's bicycle in a similar way might appear to support W's case. In logic it clearly might; but in law evidence of *conduct on other occasions* is not, as a general rule, admissible (though this rule is subject to recognised exceptions). The object of a trial is as far as possible to ascertain the truth or falsity of the allegations made, and the fact that a man can be proved to have done other acts at other times, similar to those alleged against him at the trial, may well tend to show that he is the kind of person who is *likely* to do the acts alleged, but it affords no proof whatever that he actually has done them.

## D   THE KINDS OF PROOF

The law recognizes three kinds of proof: proof by oral evidence, by documentary evidence and by real evidence.

### (i)  Oral evidence
*Oral evidence* is evidence which is given by witnesses – usually upon oath or affirmation. Each side to a dispute will normally call one or more witnesses to support with their evidence the truth of the story which that side has to tell. The function of a witness is to inform the court or the jury of *the facts* as he actually perceived them, and clearly, unless he is an expert whose opinion on a technical point it may be essential to ascertain, his *opinions* as to how the facts ought to be interpreted are of little value: for, given the facts, the court or jury are the judges and it is for them to assess and interpret. Thus at common law a witness of a street accident might testify that the 'car was driven fast' (an observable fact) but strictly speaking his observation that 'X was driving *too* fast' was inadmissible. And, indeed, at discretion, the court may still exclude such a statement; but because it was found that it is often difficult for a witness to give a truthful account of what he actually did observe without including an element of interpretation (opinion) of it. The Civil Evidence Act 1972, s 3(2) provided that in *civil* proceedings a statement of opinion by such a witness of facts may be admitted 'if made as a way of conveying relevant facts personally perceived by him'. This relaxation only applies to civil cases and leaves room for the court to rule against admissibility of such a statement.

But as Lord Mansfield (1705–1793) once put it, 'The opinion of scientific men upon proven facts may be given by men of science within their own science.' Such people are *expert* witnesses, and in our 'adversary' system of procedure they play a leading rôle – as where the cause of disease is in dispute and doctors are called by either side to give their diagnoses. But there are, or have been, two limitations upon this expert function. First, evidence by an expert on matters within the knowledge of the judge or jury is, strictly, inadmissible: for expert opinion must not usurp the function of the court itself. Thus a psychiatrist may be called to testify about the existence of mental disturbance, but he should not give evidence that a man whose wife has confessed adultery is likely to behave hysterically: a matter of common knowledge. In the second place, at common law an expert witness was not allowed to give his opinion about the main issue in the case – eg 'Was the designer of the aircraft negligent?' Again, that is the issue for the court *itself*. However, here again, the Civil Evidence Act 1972, s 3(1), (3) has relaxed the rule in *civil* cases: for now (subject to the court's discretion) an expert may express his opinion 'on *any relevant matter* on which he is qualified to give expert evidence'. Yet the position of an expert witness is not a happy one for our 'adversary' system pits doctor against doctor and engineer against engineer: and that circumstance leads the lawyers to talk depreciatingly of 'liars, damned liars and expert witnesses' in order of unreliability. There may be much to be said for the 'assessor' system whereby the expert sits with the judge and advises him on technical matters.

It is, perhaps, germane to add that, in a case in which it is necessary to ascertain the law of a foreign country, expert evidence of it must be called: formerly only people qualified to practise in the country in question could be called as experts, but the 1972 Act (s 4) makes it also possible to call people (such as teachers of law) not necessarily so qualified.

As a general rule in our law, unlike the law of many other countries where written evidence is preferred, evidence is *oral* rather than written (though affidavit evidence is common in the Chancery Division). But, by way of exception, in order to save time and expense the Criminal Justice Act 1967, s 9, subject to safeguards, made it possible for the court in criminal proceedings (other than transfer proceedings) to accept a signed and written statement from an absent witness.

*Hearsay evidence* – The following account must be read in the light of the Civil Evidence Act 1995 which abolishes, subject to safeguards, the hearsay rule in *civil* proceedings. As the Act has not at the time of writing been brought into force, what follows is still the law but a brief account of the Act's provisions will be considered at the end of this section. The Act will repeal the Civil Evidence Act 1968 when in force. Witnesses may give evidence about what they have heard, just as they may give evidence about what they have seen; but this proposition is subject to a very important exception. *'Hearsay'* evidence is, in general, not admissible where it is sought to be introduced to prove the *truth* of the matter in dispute. This means that, in general, where it is desired to prove the truth of some disputed fact, evidence of what was said by some person *not called as a witness*, or of what was stated in some document executed by such a person, will not be admitted. For example, in a murder case a witness would not generally be permitted to testify that, 'Percy Jones (some third person not called as a witness) said that he had seen (the accused) do it'. The reason for this rule is said to be that if such evidence were admitted there would be no way of testing its veracity, for the speaker or the writer of the statement was not necessarily upon oath when he made it, and there is no way of testing the credibility of a person who is not present for cross-examination.

Moreover, anyone who has ever participated in any kind of inquiry will realize that such evidence must necessarily often be of little weight and to admit it wholesale would be to introduce much irrelevant matter. Another example may perhaps help to illustrate this: suppose the issue to be what is a fair rent for a house and that a witness seeks to establish this fact by saying that 'Mrs X, my neighbour's cousin who lives two houses away, told me that she pays £2 rent.' If this fact were proved it would plainly be relevant to the issue, but the statement is suspect, for there is no check that the witness heard or remembered correctly nor that Mrs X was telling the truth. Yet the exclusion of 'hearsay' is said to be peculiar to the common law and it must be confessed that, since there is no smoke without fire, a lot of hearsay pointing in one direction may lead a reasonable man to judge that the cumulative effect of it is true; further, if all evidence had to be direct then it would be hopelessly confined. Hence, for a long time past a number of exceptions (too complicated to be examined in detail here) have been engrafted upon the general rule which excludes 'hearsay'.

Thus 'hearsay' will be admitted where it is plainly necessary that it should; but in most, at least, of the instances where it is thus exceptionally admitted, it will be found that there is some particular reason for supposing that the statement was one which the maker really believed to be true. Thus for example statements made by parties to an action, or by their agents, which are *against their interest* may be given in evidence as '*admissions*' (not to be confused with the formal 'admissions' above referred to) – for there is every reason to suppose that when a person makes a statement which is against his interest it will be true: and this rule is confirmed by s 9(2) (*a*) of the Civil Evidence Act 1968 (below). So also, where a person has *died* before the time of the trial, it is sometimes essential to permit 'hearsay' evidence of what he said, for he can no longer be called as a witness. A large category of 'declarations' of deceased persons are thus permitted to be given in evidence, but in each instance falling within this category it will be found that there is some special reason to believe that the permitted 'hearsay' statement was true. For example, declarations made by deceased people in the 'course of duty' may sometimes be admitted to prove the truth of the facts stated; for when people are acting in the course of some duty which is imposed upon them they generally have no incentive to tell lies. Thus, if it is the duty of a clerk to receive payments for his employer and to make entries in a cash book, and he makes an entry 'Mr Thomas paid Mr Smith (the clerk's employer)' such and such a sum upon such and such a day, and if the clerk later dies, and Smith denies the payment, the entry, if proved to be authentic, may be adduced to prove the fact of payment. Further, beside preserving the common law as to admissions (and also various other kinds of evidence too numerous for mention here) the Civil Evidence Act 1968 (hereafter 'CEA'), by s 9 preserves the common law rules which – in the words of the section – make 'admissible as evidence of facts of a public nature stated therein' *published works* dealing with matters of a public nature (eg histories, scientific works, dictionaries and maps), and as 'evidence of facts stated therein' *public documents* (eg public registers) and *records* (eg court records and treaties). So, should the question be, say, whether a certain object is a crystal, dictionaries and scientific works may be consulted even though their authors be alive and reasonably available as witnesses. These provisions are preserved by s 7 of the 1995 Act.

The CEA itself must now be considered. Superficially at least it makes a large inroad into the rule which excludes hearsay; though it must be noted that it applies to *civil* proceedings. Subject to important reservations shortly to be mentioned, s 1(1) of the Act permits 'a statement other than one made by a person while giving oral evidence' to be admissible as evidence of any fact stated therein. And this is confirmed by s 2(1) which in effect only adds the obvious proviso that such evidence must be otherwise – ie apart from the fact that it is hearsay – admissible; eg it must be relevant. Section 2 (3), however, excludes *oral* evidence which is what is sometimes called 'second-hand' hearsay. The effect of this is that if, for example, a witness seeks to testify that 'B said that (C told him) that the elephant was pink' evidence of C's statement is inadmissible; whereas the statement 'B said to me that the elephant was pink' is admissible *under the Act*.

Section 4 of the Act (confirming and enlarging upon the Evidence Act 1938, which the CEA for the most part repeals) makes special provision for the admission of hearsay contained in private documentary records. Assuming that it would be otherwise admissible (eg that it is relevant), it is enacted that 'a statement contained in a document shall . . . be admissible as evidence of any statement made therein . . . if the document is . . . a *record* compiled by a person *acting under a duty* from information which was supplied by a person . . . who had . . . *personal knowledge* of the matters dealt with in that information and which, if not supplied by that person . . . directly, was supplied by him . . . indirectly through one or more *intermediaries each acting under a duty*.' Acting 'under a duty' includes (s 4(3)) 'a reference to a person acting in the course of any trade, business, profession or other occupation in which he is engaged or employed or for the purposes of any paid or unpaid office by him'. Thus, in the case of such records, subject to the *restrictions* (shortly to be mentioned) which the CEA itself imposes upon its admission, hearsay is allowed with a vengeance. By s 5, the provisions of which are complex, certain kinds of evidence contained in documents produced by computers are also available in contravention of the hearsay rule.

Thus far it may appear that the floodgates were opened wide for the admission of hearsay under the Act; but the restrictions which are imposed are formidable. Section 1 provides that unless the parties *agree* to the admission of the hearsay it may only be admitted 'to the extent that it is . . . admissible by virtue of any provision . . . in . . . this or any other Act'. And the provisions 'in this . . . Act' are highly restrictive. By s 18 of the Act (as implemented by Rules of Court) it is provided that a party who wishes to adduce any of the kinds of hearsay evidence mentioned above must, within a limited period (usually 21 days of setting down for hearing) give *notice*, with particulars of the evidence, to *every other party* to the proceedings. The party so served may then serve (within a further period) a *counter-notice* requiring the first party to call the maker of the statement as a witness unless (as is self-evident) he 'is dead' or unless he is 'unfit by reason of his bodily or mental condition to attend as a witness, or cannot reasonably be expected to have any recollection of matters relevant to the accuracy of the statement'. It must, however, be added that the court is given a general discretion to *allow* the statement where the rules as to notice have *not* been complied with; whereas, though there is power to order *exclusion* of the evidence where the rules *have* been complied with, it is narrowly confined. Section 6(3) contains a reminder that hearsay, if admitted, cannot be given the same weight as first-hand evidence by providing that in assessing it 'regard must be had to all the circumstances from which any inference can reasonably be drawn as to the accuracy or otherwise of the statement'. Thus, for instance, the question whether the statement was made contemporaneously with an occurrence in issue or whether it was made some time after must be pertinent in assessing how much weight is to be attached to it. It will be appreciated that the rules as to notice etc apply only to hearsay evidence received *under the Act* and not to the kinds of hearsay exceptionally admissible – whether confirmed by s 9 of the Act or not – at common law. This is important since in practice hearsay usually enters the picture during the trial when a witness unexpectedly introduces it: a situation with which the CEA is not concerned.

The Civil Evidence Act 1972, s 1, in general, permits hearsay statements of *opinion* to be given in evidence upon the same grounds on which hearsay statements of fact were permitted to be adduced under the CEA. This section will be repealed by the 1995 Act.

It is worth repeating that the CEA applies only to *civil* cases; but it should be mentioned that by the Criminal Justice Act 1988, in certain prescribed circumstances, a statement contained in a document may be admissible in *criminal* proceedings as evidence of any fact of which direct oral evidence of the person who made it would be admissible. *Inter alia* the circumstances include the case where the person in question is dead or, by reason of his condition, is unable to attend the trial. In general, and subject to safeguards, by the same Act, a statement in a document may be admissible in criminal proceedings of which direct oral evidence would be admissible if: (i) the document was created or received by a person in the course of a trade, business, profession or other occupation, or as the holder of a paid or unpaid office *and* (ii) the information contained in the document was supplied by a person (whether or not the maker of the statement) who had, or may reasonably be supposed to have had, personal knowledge of the matters dealt with.

It must be stressed that the 'hearsay' rule only operates where the evidence in question is sought to be introduced as proof of the *truth* of the facts stated. There is no objection to its introduction for any other purpose, provided that it is otherwise relevant; as, for instance, to prove the fact that a debated statement was *made*. Thus if in an action for slander A claims that X called him a thief, it will be in order for a witness to testify that he heard X say this: since what is in issue is *not* whether A is a thief, but whether X made the remark: a fact to which, of course, the witness can testify at first hand.

Section 1 of the Civil Evidence Act 1995 states that evidence in civil proceedings shall not be excluded on the ground that it is hearsay, subject to safeguards in ss 2–4. In particular s 4 contains guides as to the weight to be given to hearsay evidence, such as whether it was reasonable and practical to have produced the original maker of the statement, whether the original statement was contemporaneous with the events in issue, etc.

## (ii) Documentary evidence

*Documentary evidence* is, as its name suggests, evidence which is contained in documents. Five points require notice with regard to evidence of this class.

First, as has already been indicated, documents fall into two classes; 'public' and 'private'. Public documents consist of publications made for public reference, such as public statutes, public registers, and maps. Private documents are documents made for private purposes.

Second, all private documents must as a general rule be 'proved' before their contents may be given in evidence; that is to say, they must be shown to be genuine – any other rule would put a premium upon forgery. This 'proof' is effected by showing that the documents were duly executed by the person by whom they purport to be made. Either the maker of the document, or, if it is attested, an attesting witness, or even a person who merely saw it executed, may testify to the authenticity of the writing or signature. If no such person is available the maker's handwriting may be proved by anyone who can show that he had reason to be acquainted with it. The authenticity of handwriting may also be proved by comparing the disputed document with one which has been proved to have been written by the person concerned; but in this case a handwriting expert should normally be called to make the comparison. This rule as to strict 'proof' is, however, subject to exceptions. (a) In most civil actions documents which are not required by law to be attested are usually 'agreed' and admitted as genuine by the opposing party; this dispenses with the need for proof. (b) 'Ancient' documents, ie documents 20 years old or more, are presumed to be genuine provided that they are produced from proper custody, that is, from the custody of some person who would naturally be expected to keep them. (c) By the CEA, s 6(1) (s 8 of the 1995 Act) documents tendered under the provisions of that Act may be proved either by production of the document itself or by a copy of it 'authenticated in such manner as the court may approve'.

Third, in *civil* actions no document which is required by law to be stamped should be allowed to be produced in evidence unless and until it has been properly stamped.

In the fourth place, private documents must *usually* be produced *in the original*. This is an example of what is called the 'best evidence' rule, which insists that proof must always be made by the *best* means possible; for where reliable evidence is available and a party seeks to offer less reliable proof, his motive becomes suspect; he is likely to be doing so because the production of the best evidence will show something inimical to his case. 'Secondary' evidence (ie something other than the production of the original) of a document, either in the form of a copy, or even in the form of oral evidence as to the contents, may, however, be given where it can be shown that for some reason the original cannot be produced, eg where it can be proved to have been lost. And, as has just been remarked, the CEA, s 6(1) (s 8 of the 1995 Act) makes an important exception to the 'best evidence' rule in relation to documents. Moreover, because originals of *public documents* are seldom available, for they are usually too valuable to be released, authenticated copies of them are allowed. It should be added that tape recordings of conversations may (provided that the voices of those concerned are properly identified), subject to considerable caution on the part of the court, be admitted in evidence.

### (iii)  Real evidence

*Real evidence* is afforded by the inspection by the court or the jury of physical objects. The court may, for instance, view the site of an accident or objects of importance in the trial may be produced for inspection – such as the knife which is alleged to have caused the wound – and where a plaintiff alleges that he has suffered physical injuries, the court will often wish to inspect the injuries in order to obtain an estimate of their severity for the purpose of assessing damages. So also, photographs, tape recordings and radio recordings are admissible as real evidence, and rent tribunals and rent assessment committees are in practice required to inspect premises under review. Contrary to the 'best evidence' rule relating to documentary evidence, 'secondary' oral testimony may always be given about the nature of physical objects other than documents; there is no rule which demands their production.

This seems the place to explain the expression *'circumstantial evidence'*. It is evidence, whether oral, documentary or real, of surrounding circumstances from which the existence of facts in issue or of facts relevant to the issue may reasonably be inferred. If the only admissible evidence were direct evidence of those facts themselves the cutting edge of the law would be blunt; for a killing not actually perceived would always go unpunished. Hence evidence of circumstances which *argue* the fact of the deed must be allowed; for instance that a knife bearing the finger prints of the accused was found beside the corpse immediately after the death. The cogency of circumstantial evidence must of course vary according to the closeness of its connection with the fact in issue: thus such a knife found ten days later twenty miles from the scene of the crime provides but weak evidence, requiring further explanation to connect it with the murder.

## E EVIDENCE IN CRIMINAL TRIALS

Before leaving the subject of evidence, very brief mention must be made of some of the special rules which apply in *criminal*, as opposed to civil, cases. Some points of difference have already been noted but the following are of particular importance.

In the first place, there are strict rules as to the admission of *confessions* of guilt, other than , of course, a plea of guilty at the trial. At common law it had to be proved by the prosecution that any confession by the accused was voluntary. This has now been changed to an issue of reliability. By the Police and Criminal Evidence Act 1984, s 76 a confession cannot be admitted if it has been induced by *oppression* or in consequence of anything said or done which would render it unreliable. 'Oppression' includes torture, inhuman or degrading treatment, and the use or threat of violence (s 76(8)).

'Fear or prejudice' means fear of some actual temporal disadvantage, such as fear induced by a threat that 'It will go badly for you if you don't own up' – even if this threat relates to some other offence than the one being investigated or to the well-being of some other person. 'Hope of advantage' means hope of some temporal, as opposed to merely moral, advantage. Thus where the person in authority says, 'If you confess I'll see that you get bail' the confession will not be admissible. Yet it will be admissible if all that is said is 'Come, confess for the good of your soul'. On the other hand the confession will not be rendered inadmissible in the former kind of circumstances if the offer of advantage was made at the suspect's own request: as where he says to a policeman 'Will you see that

I get bail if I confess?' and the policeman agrees to this. The 'person in authority' will usually be a policeman but the expression includes anyone who is, or is believed by the suspect to be, in a superior position to him: such as an employer, a private prosecutor or even a parent.

By s 77 of the 1984 Act if the case against the accused depends wholly or substantially upon a confession by him, and the court is satisfied that he is mentally handicapped, it must warn the jury that they must be especially cautious before convicting. But there will be no need for the court to do this if the confession was made in the presence of an independent person.

Even if, in the light of the above rules, the judge does decide that a confession is admissible the defence may seek to establish that, having been made as the result of inducement or coercion, it is of little probative value and that will be for the jury to assess.

There are two Codes of Practice issued under the 1984 Act which are relevant to the issue of reliability of confessions. They deal with the issues of detention, treatment and questioning of suspects and tape recording of interviews. The Codes are admissible in any criminal or civil proceedings and may be taken into account in determining any relevant question in such proceedings. A breach of the Codes, depending on its seriousness and direct relevance, may be considered in assessing the reliability of any confession.

Mention must also be made of certain rules governing evidence as to the character and previous record of accused persons. It is obviously just that a criminal charge should be tried upon its own merits, and there is much to be said for excluding all evidence tending to show that the accused is a bad character or has a criminal record from the knowledge of the court or jury until after conviction – when the previous record naturally becomes a vital factor in the court's determination of the appropriate *sentence* to award. The general rule is therefore that no evidence which reflects upon the character of the accused may be advanced by the prosecution *during the trial*. This rule is, however, subject to certain exceptions, of which the following are the most important. (a) It has been noted that, as a general rule, the parties to a civil action cannot give evidence of their good character, ie as to their general reputation for good character. In a criminal case the accused may always do so; but, if he does, the prosecution will then be entitled to seek to rebut this evidence by calling counter-balancing evidence as to his bad character. (b) Before the passing of the Criminal Evidence Act 1898, an accused could not be called to give evidence on his own behalf. That Act (as amended by the Criminal Evidence Act 1979) altered the law and permitted him to give it (though he *need* not) and it further provided by s 1(*f*) that if he does choose to do so he may not in general be asked any question, when cross-examined by the prosecution, 'tending to show that he has committed or been convicted of or been charged with any offence . . . or is of bad character'. But this prohibition is subject to important provisos; for questions of the forbidden class may be put at the discretion of the trial judge in the following circumstances. (i) If (as is sometimes the case) evidence of a previous offence, or of previous offences, is admissible to show that the accused is guilty of the offence charged. (ii) If the accused or his counsel has asked questions of the witnesses for the prosecution with a view to establishing his own good character; if the accused has given evidence of his own good character; if the nature or conduct of the defence is such as to involve imputations upon the character of the prosecutor, or of the witnesses for the prosecution; even though these imputations form a necessary part of his own defence, and even though they impute moral obliquity rather than criminal behaviour. (iii) If the accused has given evidence against any other person charged in the same proceedings as himself. In the two last-mentioned cases (ii) and (iii) the accused is said to have put his own character 'in issue' by his conduct.

# Chapter 4

# Personality, status and capacity

## 1 Legal personality

In everyday life when one speaks of a 'person' one means an individual human being, but in legal terminology the word has a different and, as it happens, an older signification. *'Person'* is derived from the Latin *per* ('through') and *sonare* ('to sound'); for in ancient times *'persona'* signified an actor's mask through which the sound of his voice came to the audience.

It has already been suggested that a lawsuit is like a drama, and this is no new idea, for, by a gradual transference, *'persona'* came to mean first the actor himself, as identified with his part, then in a legal sense it came to signify the subjects of legal rights and duties. In the course of this transference the word lost nothing of its original force because it came to denote, not an individual litigant as a *human being* but anybody or anything permitted to assert legal claims or be subjected to legal duties: on a legal 'stage' the mask of personality does not therefore necessarily have to be worn by human beings. Thus in its legal sense the word has come to mean something wider than simply a human individual; it means any individual, group, or even any *thing* which the law will recognise as a bearer of legal rights and duties.

For different reasons at different times different systems of law have thus accorded legal personality (sometimes distinguished from 'ordinary' personality as 'artificial' personality) to many other things beside people and it has sometimes denied 'personality' to human beings. Thus in early Roman Law slaves had no rights which the law would directly enforce; hence although they were 'people' in the ordinary modern sense, just as much as their masters were, they had no legal standing, no legal 'personality'. At various times also non-human entities have been made subject to legal rights and duties and have thus become artificial legal 'persons'. Animals were, for example, tried for crimes in the middle ages and in an Indian appeal to the Privy Council it was recognised that, in keeping with the then existing customs of India, rights could be accorded to an idol and that it could thus be regarded as a legal 'person'.

Even modern English law which, of course, gives legal 'personality' to human beings, also accords it to certain entities that are not human; these entities are known as 'corporations' and they are said to be endowed with 'corporate personality'.

The various classes of corporations known to the law must now be considered. It will be seen that most, although by no means all, of them are composed of groups of individuals (associations). It is proposed first to discuss corporations and then to deal briefly with certain other associations which receive some degree of legal recognition without being endowed with independent legal 'personality'.

## A CORPORATIONS

It is essential to stress at the start that once a corporation comes into being, it acquires, in the eye of the law, a separate existence from the individual members who compose it. The members all continue to have their own private rights and duties, but the corporation also comes to have *its* 'own', apart from theirs. Moreover, corporations differ from their members in one essential way; they are endowed with 'perpetual succession', that is to say, until they are legally dissolved, they never die; they continue to exist regardless of the entrances and exits (by death or otherwise) of the humans who compose them.

There are two main classes of corporations – corporations '*sole*' and corporations '*aggregate*'. A corporation *sole* is composed of one person (ie one human individual) *and his successors*: examples are, the Monarch in her public capacity, symbolized by the 'Crown' and all bishops and parsons. The people who occupy these offices are, of course, in their *private* capacity, with the exception of the Monarch, ordinary individuals, and they are recognized as such in the courts. Thus, for instance, as an individual, a bishop may own land or other property and is entitled to deal with it in every way that other people deal with theirs, and the courts will protect his rights. But in their public capacity, in the performance of their offices, the members of a corporation sole are regarded as one with their predecessors and with their successors, for the corporate office never ceases to be until it is legally dissolved; thus the property which the members hold by virtue of their offices devolves rather upon their *public* than their personal successors; or, to put the matter in its true perspective, the property which they hold in their corporate capacity never really 'devolves' at all: the office, which is deathless, transcends its holders.

Corporations '*aggregate*' consist of groups of people, such as the dean and chapter of a cathedral, the chairman and members of public boards or the members of a trading company.

Since corporate personality is an artificial legal concept a corporation can only come into existence in a manner which the law prescribes. It provides three principal methods. First, corporations may be created *by the Crown*, by virtue of the prerogative, by royal charter; in the past it was in this way that the East India Company and the Hudson's Bay Company were formed, and, as a modern example, universities are generally created by charter. Second, corporations may be created *by a particular statute*. The familiar modern public corporations such as, for example, British Telecom which owes its existence to the British Telecommunications Act 1981.

Third, certain classes of corporations may come into existence *by compliance with statutory formalities* which regulate their creation as a *class*. Corporations created by either of the last two methods are called 'statutory' corporations, by way of contrast with chartered corporations, which are a species of 'common law' corporations. Corporations of the third class are now far more numerous than the others; amongst them are included trading and other companies incorporated under the provisions of the Companies Acts, now consolidated in the Companies Act 1985.

Incorporation in general has the following, amongst other, results:

*(a)* Since the corporation becomes a legal 'person', it may sue and be sued, and may sometimes even be criminally prosecuted, under its corporate name. One of the main objects in according 'personality' to corporations is to effect this result; since it is clearly simpler to treat an undying 'office' or an aggregate group as a single artificial individual, than it is to treat them as a series or group of distinct members.

*(b)* Once a corporation has come into being, it forms a separate entity from the individuals who compose it. This proposition is usually, and aptly, illustrated by reference to the leading case of *Salomon v A Salomon & Co Ltd* [1897] AC 22, where Aaron Salomon, a boot manufacturer, incorporated his business as a limited company. He held practically all the shares in this company and he acted as its managing director. The company borrowed money from him in his private capacity and issued debentures to him. This, as we shall see, meant that he became entitled to a first charge upon the company's assets. The company became insolvent and went into liquidation. An assignee of the debt claimed to be treated as a 'secured' creditor and have his claim satisfied in priority to the company's ordinary creditors. The House of Lords held that his claim was justified. The company was an artificial person, with a *legal* existence of its own, independent of Salomon, and the relationship between it and him was one of debtor and creditor. In *Lee v Lee's Air Farming Ltd* [1961] AC 12, like reasoning was applied to permit the wife of a man killed in an air crash to succeed against a company formed by him upon the ground that at the time of his death he was acting as an 'employee' of the company in spite of his owning 2,999 of the 3,000 shares, with his solicitor holding the remaining one. It must, however, be understood that the courts will not allow the

fiction of corporate personality to be carried so far as to create absurdity or bring about substantial injustice. Thus, for instance, it was held by the House of Lords in *Daimler Co Ltd v Continental Tyre and Rubber Co (Great Britain) Ltd* [1916] 2 AC 307 that in time of war a company incorporated in the United Kingdom but almost wholly owned by alien enemies must be treated as alien; further the Court of Appeal has held that where a company gained a tax advantage by the employment of a wholly-owned subsidiary the theoretical independence of the corporate personality of the subsidiary must be disregarded. And it has also been ruled that where all the directors and shareholders of a company steal from the company their consent to the transaction is not to be imputed to the company so as to form a defence to the charge. By contrast, it has also been held (in favour of a company) that a local authority which acquired land held by a subsidiary could not call in aid the corporate fiction to shield itself from a claim by the company itself for loss of business, which it, rather than the subsidiary, lost: the court 'pierced the veil of corporate personality' to decide the company's claim according to the realities. The fact is that this is a field in which theory must at times yield to expedience: probably the decision in *Salomon's Case* goes as far as theory is ever likely to go in this respect. Yet the House of Lords has held that the corporate veil should only be pierced where special circumstances exist'.

*(c)* Since corporations are recognised as 'persons' they are entitled, within their powers, to carry on activities, such as trading, just like an ordinary person. In doing this, however, they can only act through their properly constituted agents, for they are themselves abstractions, devoid of mind and body.

*(d)* Because corporations are distinct from their members, the common law rule was that they could only make contracts under their corporate seal, which symbolizes their independent existence; but for reasons of practical convenience, this rule was abolished in the case of companies incorporated under the Companies Acts as long ago as 1867.

*(e)* Since corporations are legal 'persons' one would expect them to have the same legal rights and powers, and to be subject to the same liabilities as ordinary individuals. Chartered corporations are treated in this way: generally speaking, subject to any special reservations in their charters of incorporation, they may through their agents do much the same things as adult people. Statutory corporations on the other hand derive their whole being, and with it their rights and powers, from the statute which creates them. Every act done on behalf of a statutory corporation must thus be justifiable by reference to the powers which its parent Act (or, in the case of a company incorporated under the Companies Acts, its memorandum of association) has conferred, and any act which its agents do in

excess of these powers (*'ultra vires'*) will be ineffective to bind it; it exists only for the purpose of exercising them; once we step beyond these, the fictitious personality disappears. At least this *used* to be the case with corporations created under the Companies Act. The policy, of course, was to protect the shareholders against the unexpected acts of the company. However, those trading with the company were at considerable risk. In reality it was unlikely that they would have read the documents, no matter how public they may be. The Companies Act 1989 has considerably altered the situation. The 'objects' clause within the memorandum of association can now be written as widely as 'to carry on any trade or business whatsoever, and to do anything else which is incidental or conducive to carrying on any trade or business whatsoever'. Further, a company with a narrower clause than this can alter the clause for any purpose. Beyond this, the 1989 Act (amending the 1985 Act) distinguishes between the capacity of the company on the one hand and the power of the directors to bind it on the other, thus protecting both those who deal with the company and the shareholders. The capacity of the company to enter any particular contract can no longer be regarded as being *'ultra vires'* either by those trading with the company or by the company itself. Members of the company may take action to restrain activities which are (or would be) beyond the objects clause, apart from those which fulfill existing obligations within transactions which cannot be challenged. Now this inability to challenge on *'ultra vires'* grounds will, of itself, not make the transaction in question *'intra vires'*. That is, the directors may still be acting beyond the objects clause. The 1989 Act further provides, therefore, that those trading with the company do not have to check the ambit of the clause, providing that they trade in good faith. This may assist the company, in that a business opportunity can be grasped despite the fact that it is technically beyond the objects clause.

(*f*) Corporations may in general hold and dispose of land and of other property as if they were ordinary individuals.

Reference will be made to the contractual, tortious, and criminal liability of corporations in the appropriate chapters below.

Corporations, as we have explained, continue to exist until they are 'dissolved'. The dissolution of a chartered corporation may be effected in a number of ways: among the most important are dissolution by Act of Parliament and dissolution by the Sovereign, who may repeal the charter at will or to whom the charter may be surrendered. The method of dissolving a statutory corporation is usually prescribed in the statute which creates it. Trading companies incorporated under the Companies Acts are dissolved by a process called 'winding up'.

The latter corporations are of such importance that they must be separately described.

*The Companies Acts*

The principal Act is the Companies Act 1985 ('CA'), amended and supplemented by a variety of other statutes. The CA consolidated previous legislation, providing a code of company law some of which dates from the nineteenth century and some of which implements EC directives for the harmonization of company law and what follows represents, in briefest outline, the present scheme.

There are two main classes of companies: *public limited* companies (the largest and most important) and *private* companies which may be incorporated under the Acts. Companies are private unless their memorandum states that they are to be public and the nominal value of their allotted share capital is not less than the authorized minimum, at present £50,000. A public company is not permitted to commence business unless the Registrar (below) issues a certificate. To obtain this he must be satisfied that the minimum capitalization requirements have been met. There are very strict accounting rules for public companies.

Generally, by CA, s 1 the minimum number of people who may form a company is two (formerly the number was seven in the case of a public company). However, a private company, limited by shares or guarantee, can be formed by one member, and it can allow its membership to fall to one. The memorandum of a public company must, in stating the name of the company, include the words 'public limited company' (plc), or in Wales, the Welsh equivalent (a formula which replaces the long familiar 'limited' ('Ltd')). A company is formed when its promotors subscribe their names to a *memorandum of association*, and to *articles of association*. The documents must be delivered to an official called the 'Registrar of Companies' whose duty it is, upon examining them, and satisfying himself that they are in order, to retain them and register them, and to certify that the company has become incorporated. This act of certification therefore represents the birth of a new legal 'person'.

The *memorandum of association* contains matters of interest to people who may wish to have dealings with the company; for it sets out the objects of the company and the sort of business which it is empowered to carry on; it states its corporate name and the part of the United Kingdom in which its registered office is to be situated, and it also states the nature of the liability of its members and the amount of its capital. Thus, people who have dealings with the company's agents can ascertain, since the memorandum is registered, what sort of company it is and the *limits of its powers*. The CA provides that companies may, by *special resolution*, alter their memoranda in certain particulars after they have been incorporated: for example, they may change them to enlarge their 'objects'; in order, for instance, to extend the purposes of their business. The resolution must be registered. The memorandum must be in a form set out in the Companies (Tables A to F) Regulations 1985.

The *articles of association* regulate the internal organisation and method of management of the company.

The Registrar of Companies must be sent copies of any resolution which alters the memorandum or articles of a company.

The CA authorises three classes of companies; companies *limited by shares*, companies *limited by guarantee*, and *unlimited companies.* Companies *limited by shares* are the commonest class; in companies of this sort the liability of shareholders for the corporate debts is expressed in the memorandum of association to be limited, and is limited, to the amount, if any, unpaid on their shares. The capital of such companies may consist of different classes of shares; a common distinction being a distinction between *preference* and *ordinary* shares. Preference shares carry fixed rights to dividend, and in many cases to the return of capital when the company is wound up. The rights of ordinary shareholders, on the other hand, are not fixed but depend for dividend upon such part of the profits of the company as is set aside by the directors for distribution, and, for the return of capital, upon what assets are available when the liabilities of the company have been met. A company *limited by guarantee* is one in which the liability of members is limited to the amount which they each undertake to pay in the event of its being wound up. All of these formed in the future must be private companies, as are most existing ones. An *unlimited company* is a company in which the liability of members is unlimited. A company limited by shares *need* not have special articles of association; the other types of companies *must* always have them. But a company limited by shares which does not have special articles will automatically be governed by certain standard articles set out in what is called 'Table A', which will be found in the Companies (Tables A to F) Regulations 1985.

'*Private*' companies, like other companies, may be registered with limited liability. They have to comply with less stringent requirements in relation to the contents of their accounts and the profits they may distribute as dividends, but are not permitted to offer their shares or debentures to the public, and so cannot obtain Stock Exchange listing. Most registered companies are private. The accounting rules are further relaxed for 'small' and 'medium' sized companies as defined by the CA.

The signatories of the memorandum of association are the original 'members' of a company, but other people may, and, of course, usually do, become members subsequently by taking up shares and having their names entered in the *register of members* which a company must keep.

Once in each year every company must hold an *annual general meeting* which all members are entitled to attend. The company's affairs are usually reviewed at this meeting and, unless the articles make some other provision, the directors are normally elected or re-elected at it. Companies *may* also hold 'extraordinary' meetings at other times.

The *directors* are the people responsible for the general control and management of the company's affairs: they are, as has sometimes been said, the 'hands and brains' of its artificial personality, and through them the more important of its activities are carried on. No particular qualifications are required before a person can act as director, but under the Company Directors Disqualification Act 1986, certain persons may be prohibited by the court from so acting; this power can be used to prevent those who have been responsible for the insolvency of previous companies from managing other companies. The CA makes general provisions about the duties of directors. They owe to their company a fiduciary duty not to do, or omit to do, anything which may give rise to a conflict between its interests and their own. They must also refrain from using any of the company's money or other property, from using any information, and from taking advantage of any opportunity acquired or arising in the course of their employment for the purpose of personal gain: and, if they do so gain, the gain – like the gains of any other agents – must be refunded to the company. Directors must also use such care in the performance of their duties as might be expected of a reasonably prudent person, and they must exercise such skill as might reasonably be expected of a person of their own particular knowledge and experience. By s 309 directors are enjoined to have regard in the performance of their duties to the interests of the company's employees, as well as to those of their members, but the fact that this duty can only be enforced by the company itself reduces its effectiveness.

*Debenture holders* must be distinguished from shareholders; they are creditors of the company who have advanced it loans in return for the payment of interest and they are entitled to hold a document, commonly called a 'debenture', certifying the company's indebtedness. This indebtedness is generally secured by a mortgage or a charge upon the company's property which entitles the debenture holders, should the company become insolvent, to receive payment in priority to the other ordinary creditors. This security may take one of two forms; it may either be effected (usually in the case of a series of debentures by means of a trust deed) in the form of a *'fixed charge'* by way of legal mortgage, or by some other means, over some specific part of the company's property; or it may be effected by an equitable *'floating charge'*. The floating charge is a most useful and practical device. It has been judicially defined as a 'charge on the assets for the time being of a going concern (which) attaches to the subject charged in the varying condition it happens to be in from time to time'. Suppose that X & Co is a shipping company and that it wishes to borrow money. If it can find lenders they may be issued with debentures. Suppose that these debenture holders are given a 'fixed' charge over one of the company's vessels. Until the loan has been repaid the charge will attach to the vessel. This may clearly become inconvenient, since the company might wish to sell the vessel in order to make replacements in its fleet, and it might not be easy to find a buyer for a ship which is subject to a charge. Hence the usefulness of the 'floating charge'. If the lenders are given such a charge, their rights do not attach to any particular part of the company's property, but only 'crystallise' upon the whole of the under- taking at the time when they seek to enforce their security – that will of course normally be when, the debt remaining unpaid, the company becomes insolvent. Thus, unless and until such enforcement occurs the company can deal freely with its property.

Companies incorporated under the Act are dissolved by a process called '*winding up*', regulated by the Insolvency Act 1986. There are three sorts of winding up; 'compulsory', 'members' voluntary winding up' and 'creditors' voluntary winding up'.

A company may be wound up compulsorily upon the happening of certain prescribed events, the most important and usual of these events being that it is unable to pay its debts. Proceedings are commenced by the presentation of a petition to the court, generally, in practice, at the instance of an unpaid creditor. Upon the presentation of a successful petition the company's assets fall provisionally into the custody of an officer called the 'official receiver' who becomes provisional '*liqui- dator*'. Normally the court will, in due course, appoint some other person as permanent liquidator; though it may sometimes cast that duty upon the official receiver. The liquidator has control and custody of the company's property, though it is not normally actually vested in him. His duty is, under the general direction of the court, to do everything which may be necessary for winding up the company's affairs, including the realisation (where necessary) and the distribution of its assets. He may, where necessary, bring or defend actions on the company's behalf. He must as far as possible, satisfy the company's liabilities and divide any surplus assets among the shareholders. When, and not until, the entire affairs of the company have thus been settled the court will make an order for its dissolution. The 'court', in this context, will normally be the Chancery Division or, in the case of companies having small assets, a county court.

A members' voluntary winding up may only take place if the company is still solvent. It is used where the members have agreed that they wish to end the life of the company and distribute the assets. They resolve to wind up the company, and the directors make a declaration that it is solvent.

A creditors' voluntary winding up takes place where the members realise that the company is insolvent, and resolve to wind it up so that the creditors can divide the assets between them. In both types of voluntary liquidation, a liquidator is appointed to wind up the company's affairs. His duties are similar to those under a compulsory liquidation, but he is more independent of the court.

## B UNINCORPORATED ASSOCIATIONS

Unlike incorporated associations, unincorporated associations are endowed with no independent legal 'personality': in the eye of the law they are simply groups of separate individuals. But, nevertheless, in order to be such associations they must be bound together for some common purpose in an organisation which has rules which prescribe the mutual rights and duties of the members, and indicate where the control of the organisation lies. Thus, for instance, it has been held that the Conservative Party is too amorphous to be treated as an unincorporated association.

There is an enormous variety of unincorporated associations; they range from small informal groups of people united together for the enjoyment of some sport or pastime, such as bird-watching societies, through the more formal cricket, golf and social clubs, to vast and highly influential groups, such as trade unions and unincorporated employers' associations.

Subject to certain important reservations shortly to be made, the general rule is that the law disregards the existence of these associations as independent groups. It treats their property as the joint property of all their members, it treats contracts made on their behalf as the contracts of the particular individuals who make them, or authorise their making, and it holds their members *individually* responsible only for such torts as they may themselves have committed – or authorised – in the course of the combined activities of the group. Thus, for example, in *Brown v Lewis* (1896) 12 TLR 455 the committee of a football club employed a person to repair a public stand; this person repaired the stand so ineffectively that it collapsed and a member of the public was injured. The committee who had authorised the work, not the members of the club generally, were held responsible.

To this general rule there are four important exceptions which, nevertheless, in no way affect the general theory that unincorporated bodies themselves have no independent legal existence.

The first exception is this: RSC Ord 15, r 12 provides that: 'Where numerous persons have the same interest in any proceedings . . . the proceedings may be begun, and, unless the court otherwise orders, continued, by or against any one or more of them as representing all. . .'. Thus, for example, the fruit vendors of Covent Garden were once held entitled to be represented by certain of their number in an action to vindicate preferential rights which they enjoyed in respect of their stalls.

The second exception is that although they are not recognised as legal 'persons', the courts and Parliament have for reasons of convenience in some instances allowed unincorporated associations to sue and be sued. Thus at common law trustee savings banks may (particularly because the relevant statutes governing these institutions contain implications to this effect) be sued as such.

The third exception is that in some cases where unincorporated groups of people have interests in property it is sometimes held by trustees on their behalf. The nature of trusteeship will be explained in a later chapter; here all that need be noted is that the trustees are, as such, the legal owners of the property; actions in respect of it may therefore be brought by and against them.

The fourth exception is that the law recognises that unincorporated associations may make rules binding upon their members and may confer powers of governance upon some of their number; for example powers of expulsion are often conferred upon committees, such as the stewards of the Jockey Club. Such committees and similar bodies therefore form a species of *domestic tribunal* and the law accepts their powers and it will not usually interfere with their exercise. But abuse will be restrained, and the decisions of a tribunal may be successfully attacked in the ordinary courts, where the tribunal has acted ('*ultra vires*') in excess of the powers conferred upon it – as by delegating a decision where no power to delegate exists – or has made a decision which contravenes the rules of natural justice; even though the decision be an administrative rather than a judicial one. Further, the rules which bind these associations and their tribunals may sometimes be challenged. For instance a rule that the members of the committee 'shall be the sole interpreters of the rules' and that the committee's decision 'shall be final' has been held to be contrary to public policy and void in so far as it constituted an attempt to oust the jurisdiction of the courts by making the committee final arbiter between itself and its members upon a point of law; which can never be done.

Unincorporated associations may cease to exist – rendering the joint property distributable among those who are members at the time of cessation – in a number of ways. Thus an association's rules may provide for dissolution in certain events; all the members may agree to its termination; the court may make an order that it shall cease to exist; it may terminate simply by inactivity; and it may also be dissolved when the purpose for which it came into being – the 'substratum' of its existence – has gone. A good illustration of a dissolution of the latter kind is to be found in the Irish case of *Feeney and Shannon v MacManus* [1937] IR 23, where it was held that a dining club which met in the building of the Dublin General Post Office automatically ceased to be when that building was destroyed.

So much for the general rules relating to unincorporated associations. It must now be explained that there are certain classes of unincorporated associations which, for one reason or another, are so important and common that the law has been forced, without according them full legal 'personality', to make some special rules in relation to them. Two classes of associations of this type are, indeed, so important that they must be mentioned here; these are trade unions and unincorporated employers' associations on the one hand and partnerships on the other.

TRADE UNIONS AND UNINCORPORATED EMPLOYERS' ASSOCIATIONS

Originally regarded as common law conspiracies, *trade unions* now enjoy a special status. This is governed by the Trade Union and Labour Relations (Consolidation) Act 1992. Unions are not corporate bodies, but the Act provides that their property shall be vested in trustees to hold on their behalf, that they shall be capable of suing and being sued in their own name and that they shall not be treated as unlawful by reason of being in restraint of trade. *Unincorporated employers' associations* have similar status (s 127(1) – although they can become incorporated).

Contracts made by unions are usually governed by the general law of contract. However collective agreements with employers are normally presumed not to be intended to be legally binding, unless they are reduced to writing and the document contains a term expressly to rebut the presumption, stating that the agreement is intended to be legally binding. To say just that the parties intend to be 'bound' might be taken to mean that they intended to be 'bound in honour only'.

The 1992 Act provides that in an official strike the union can be liable in tort where a claim is brought for inducing breach of contract (including interference with performance), threatening breach of contract, or conspiring to commit a tort unless they hold a ballot (by a prescribed procedure) before authorising a call for a strike. This immunity is removed if the ballot is held more than four weeks before the industrial action begins (unless the union was prevented, say by an injunction, from calling action during that period). Virtually all forms of 'secondary action' (ie not against the employer) are unlawful, and thus there is no immunity. Where the action is unofficial the union is still responsible for those calling for it unless the action is repudiated and a proper effort is made to give individual written notice to those involved that the action is not supported. Any union member who claims that his union has authorized industrial action without the support of a ballot can apply to the court for an order, *inter alia*, to require the union to withdraw the authorisation. The Act also gives members a right not to be denied access to the courts under union rules and not to be unjustifiably disciplined by his union for certain specified kinds of conduct, eg failure to participate in, or to support, a strike. The latter right may be asserted before an industrial tribunal.

PARTNERSHIPS

The law relating to partnership is codified in the Partnership Act 1890. A partnership is there defined as the 'relationship which subsists between persons carrying on a business in common with a view of profit'. Thus, a partnership is a 'relationship', and it may therefore come into existence without a formal agreement though, in practice, it will usually be constituted by the conclusion of formal 'articles of partnership'. Such a relationship will not, however, exist unless partnership is the common intention; so that where two people are working together with the aim of forming a company as yet not formed their relationship is not one of partnership.

Although a partnership is not a legal 'person', because it is a joint enterprise all partners are taken to be each others' agents in respect of all acts done in or about the partnership business, and for convenience they may sue and be sued in the name of the 'firm'. Thus as a general rule, any act done in furtherance of the business by one partner binds the rest, even though he has done it without their authority. This rule is subject to certain exceptions: for example, where the partners have agreed that none of them shall alone have power to bind the firm in relation to certain matters, if one of them purports to do so *and the person with whom he deals knows of the agreement*, the firm will not be bound.

A further important rule of the law of partnership, which derives from a general rule of law and of common sense, must also be noted. In order to protect strangers to the firm, wherever a man holds himself out as a partner by acting as if he were one, although he is not – for example by permitting his name to appear upon the firm's note-paper – he may generally be held liable to anyone who gives the firm credit in reliance upon this false representation, just as though he really were a partner.

A partnership firm may be made liable for torts committed, as well as for debts incurred, by any partner acting in actual or apparent furtherance of the business.

In their mutual dealings, the law requires all partners to observe the utmost good faith; they must disclose all profits they make in relation to the business, so that they can be shared in common by their fellows according to their respective rights. Should one partner compete with the firm upon his own account he may be compelled to disclose, and to share, his profits.

Unlike the liability of the members of companies, the liability of partners for the partnership debts is generally unlimited. It is, however, possible to create a 'limited' partnership under the provisions of the Limited Partnerships Act 1907: in these (uncommon) partnerships the liability of some of the partners may be limited to the amount of the capital which they supply; but at least one of the partners must be a 'general' (as opposed to a 'limited') partner and as such his, or their, liability will be unlimited.

Under the provisions of of the Companies Act 1985, the maximum number of partners in a trading firm cannot exceed 20. Certain 'Professional' firms, such as solicitors, accountants, stock brokers, patent agents, surveyors, and so on, are exempted from this restriction by the Act and DTI regulations.

# 2　Status and capacity

'Status' signifies membership of a particular class or group to which special legal capacities, liabilities, or immunities adhere. It will be found that in all societies at all times some people have been endowed with special powers and capacities peculiar to themselves or to their class, while others have been subjected to special incapacities. Thus the Head of the State invariably has certain pre-eminent privileges and immunities which, in the eyes of the law, place him or her upon a different standing ('*status*') from ordinary citizens: with us, for example, the Queen cannot be tried in her own courts for any crime, nor, in her private capacity, may she be sued in tort. Foreign sovereigns and foreign States (under the State Immunity Act 1978) and their ambassadors and diplomats (under the Diplomatic Privileges Act 1964) are entitled to certain legal immunities. On the other hand, some sorts of people, such as minors and persons of unsound mind are for their own good subjected as a class to legal *incapacities* which make their rights and duties different from those of the sane adult.

It is interesting to note that in the laws of early societies differences of status were greater than they are in most civilised countries today. Anyone who cares to read the institutional books on Roman Law will quickly be able to assure himself of this; he will find that a large amount of space is devoted to discussion of the Law of Persons, which describes the different classes in society, such as the slave, the son under his father's 'power', the freedman, and the married woman. In England also in mediaeval times the status of an overlord differed greatly from that of a villain, and even the fact that a man was a craftsman belonging to a particular guild would give him special rights.

The course of history in the West has, under the influence of christianity and humanism, shown a general decline in the importance of status; for it has gradually come to be felt that it is right that everyone should as far as possible receive equal treatment under the law. Nevertheless, some kinds of special status still remain; it is therefore still necessary for some reference to be made to the legal position of certain classes of persons, and to examine their special rights and duties, capacities and immunities.

Here we must content ourselves with a very brief discussion of three matters affecting status: nationality (to which we will append mention of immigration), minority and unsoundness of mind.

## A　NATIONALITY

It need hardly be explained that nationality is a matter which affects a person's relations with the outside world, and that it is not usually of much concern in municipal law; for municipal law normally has to deal with its own nationals. But nationality is clearly a matter of such importance that it must be discussed. In any event, even under municipal law, 'nationals' may in a sense be regarded as having a special status by way of contrast with non-nationals, who are subject to special incapacities. The comparative position has become less clear now that the Treaty of European Union 1993 (the Maastrict Treaty) has provided a formulation of rights for a citizen of the European Union. The first, and probably the most important in the present context, is the right to move and reside freely throughout the member states of the Union.

The law relating to British nationality is now governed by the British Nationality Act 1981. In respect of their political status people are divided into six classes: British citizens, British Dependent Territories citizens, British Overseas citizens, British subjects, certain citizens of the Republic of Ireland, and British protected persons. (The former category of Citizens of the United Kingdom and Colonies has been abolished.) All these categories (except British protected persons) are also designated 'Commonwealth' citizens. All people who are neither Commonwealth citizens nor British protected persons, nor citizens of the Republic of Ireland, are 'aliens'.

BRITISH CITIZENS

A person may become a British citizen in a number of ways:

*(a)* By *birth* in the United Kingdom to a parent who is a British citizen or who is settled (ie ordinarily resident) in the United Kingdom. He may also become a British citizen by *birth* in the United Kingdom to a parent who *becomes a British citizen* or *becomes settled* in the United Kingdom. Such a person must, however, make or have made on his behalf, an application for registration; and this will only be successful if he is over ten years of age, and (normally) in each of his first ten years of age he has spent no more than 90 days outside the United Kingdom.

*(b)* By *adoption* by a British citizen.

*(c)* By *descent*. This applies to a person born outside the United Kingdom to a person who is a British citizen by birth, adoption or naturalisation – but *not* by descent. The last qualification means that the child of a British citizen living, say, in Brazil becomes a British citizen by descent, but the child of such a person will not become a British citizen.

*(d)* By *registration*. The provisions governing acquisition by registration are set out in ss 3–5 of the Act but they are too detailed for description here.

*(e)* By *naturalisation*. Any person of full age may apply for naturalisation provided that, in some circumstances, certain requirements – like knowledge of the language – are satisfied.

BRITISH DEPENDENT TERRITORIES CITIZENS

These are citizens of certain countries set out in Schedule 6 of the Act: the list includes places such as Gibraltar, Anguilla and Bermuda.

BRITISH OVERSEAS CITIZENS

These are certain people who were formerly citizens of the United Kingdom and Colonies who are neither British citizens nor British Dependent Territories citizens. They may have passports, but they have no rights of entry.

BRITISH SUBJECTS

These include people who were formerly British subjects without citizenship under the British Nationality Act 1948 and women registered as British subjects under the British Nationality Act 1965. They may hold passports but they are not citizens and have no automatic rights of entry.

CITIZENS OF THE REPUBLIC OF IRELAND

Citizens of the Republic of Ireland are not aliens but they are also not British citizens. However (s 31) certain Irish citizens may be British subjects if either they had formerly claimed to be such under the British Nationality Act 1948 or, being born before 1 January 1949, and citizens of both the Republic of Ireland and British subjects immediately before 1 January 1949, they now claim to be such.

BRITISH PROTECTED PERSONS

These are people from places which were formerly protectorates or United Kingdom trust territories. They are entitled to a passport.

THE SPECIAL CASES OF THE FALKLAND ISLANDS AND HONG KONG

After the war the British Nationality (Falkland Islands) Act 1983 was passed. This provides that those born in the Islands to parents who were settled there have become British citizens. When Hong Kong is 'handed' to China in July 1997 a special category of British Nationals (overseas) will be created under the provisions of the Hong Kong Act 1985. There is to be no general right of residence in Britain, although a small category of Hong Kong citizens have been granted British citizenship as a form of security in that they will remain in Hong Kong, but they can leave for Britain if their treatment by the Chinese is 'unfavourable'.

IMMIGRATION

Formerly the law of immigration differed according to whether an immigrant was a member of the Commonwealth or whether he was an alien unconnected with Britain or the Commonwealth. It was, however, remodelled by the Immigration Act 1971 ('IA') – as now amended by the British Nationality Act 1981. Section 1 of the IA provides that anyone who has the *right of abode* in the United Kingdom shall be free to come to, live in, and come and go from it without let or hindrance (this, of course, has no reference to customs regulations). Anyone who *lacks this right* may only live, work and settle here subject to permission and control (see below).

For immigration purposes the 'Islands' – ie the Isle of Man and the Channel Islands – and the Republic of Ireland are treated as a 'common travel area' so that immigration restrictions do not apply as between them.

Having distinguished between persons having the right of abode and those who lack it, the Act provides that the first class of persons shall consist of British citizens and of certain categories of Commonwealth citizens. The latter include Commonwealth citizens who immediately before the British Nationality Act 1981 were (and had not ceased to be) Commonwealth citizens having the right of abode in the United Kingdom for three reasons. First because they were born to or adopted by a parent who had citizenship of the United Kingdom and Colonies by birth in the United Kingdom or the Islands. Second, because they were born to or adopted by a parent who had, at the time of birth or adoption, citizenship of the United Kingdom and Colonies. Third, because, being women, they are married to a man falling within either of the above two categories. But by the Immigration Act 1988 women who are polygamously married to such a man are denied the right of abode if there is another woman living who: (a) is the wife or widow of the husband, and who has, at any time since her marriage to the husband, been in the United Kingdom; or (b) has been granted a certificate of entitlement to the right of abode.

By s 3 of the IA any person who *lacks* the right of abode must have leave to enter the United Kingdom, and this leave may be granted conditionally, eg as to time of stay, or employment, or registration with the police. Such people are, moreover, liable to *deportation* if they outstay the period of leave or break some condition of it, or if the Secretary of State deems their deportation to be, for certain reasons, conducive to the public good (s 3(5)). They may also be deported by court order if, being over seventeen, they are convicted of an offence punishable with imprisonment (s 3(6)). Further, members of the family – a wife (or wives), husband or children under eighteen – of the deportee may be deported with him or her. By way of exception, the 1988 Act provides (s 7) that the requirement of leave to enter or remain in the United Kingdom will be dispensed with in the case of any person who is entitled to enter or remain by virtue of any enforceable European Community right, or of any provision made under s 2(2) of the European Communities Act 1972.

ALIENS

As has been noted above, all people who are neither Commonwealth citizens nor British protected persons nor citizens of the Republic of Ireland are 'aliens': aliens are, therefore, foreigners. They are subject to certain incapacities under English law: for instance, they cannot own British ships, nor can they normally act as masters of British ships, nor can they be Members of Parliament, nor vote at elections.

## B MINORS

Formerly 'infants' were people under the age of 21, but the age of majority was altered to 18 by the Family Law Reform Act 1969, s 1; and although this section does not apply retrospectively in respect of references to 'majority' in private documents, such as wills executed before 1970, it does so apply to such references in statutes. The effects of minority in so far as it affects the family will be considered in Chapter 14 and its effect upon criminal and civil liability will receive mention in the appropriate places. Here it is proposed to mention only certain general matters.

Broadly speaking, it may be stated that a minor may hold *property* in the same way as an adult; but this principle is subject to such important exceptions and reservations that, as a matter of practice, it might perhaps be better left unstated. In the first place, although a minor may own personal property, such as money, a car or a pony, which is given or sold to him by some living person, he may, in general repudiate any disposition he makes of it. This right to repudiate is, however, subject to the limitation that if the minor has received something (as by way of sale or exchange) in return for the disposition, he will not be entitled to exercise the right unless it is possible to restore the parties to their original position at the time when he seeks to do so. In the second place, no minor may now hold a legal estate in land (Law of Property Act 1925, s 1(6)). The meaning of this will be explained later in the chapter on the Law of Property. Third, any property which comes to a minor by way of settlement, or *upon the death* of some other person, will now usually be held on his behalf by trustees or by personal representatives until he attains his majority. A minor can therefore only enjoy an *equitable interest* in land, or in any property which comes to him upon the death of another person. The meaning of this will also be explained later in this book.

Although the matter was formerly in doubt, it has now been decided that a minor may be made *bankrupt*; but the circumstances in which this may occur will necessarily be rare.

There is an extensive and amorphous code of legislation giving protection and assistance – for the most part under local government control – to 'children' (for most, but not all, purposes people under 14 years of age) and 'young persons' (people between 14 and 17 years of age). Much of the law is now to be found in the Children Act 1989. The Act was designed to clarify and codify the extensive legislative provision that had developed over the years. The Act has over 100 sections and 5 schedules. It is divided into ten Parts, covering such areas as: 'Orders with respect to Children in Family Proceedings', 'Local Authority Support for Children and Families', 'Care and Supervision', 'Community Homes', 'Voluntary Homes and Voluntary Organisations', 'Registered Children's Homes', 'Private Arrangements for Fostering Children', 'Child Minding and Day Care for Young Children', and so on.

It would be neither profitable nor possible to describe this legislation here; but it should be mentioned that the scope of the law is both considerable and detailed, and that much of its purpose is to secure special protection for juveniles in respect of such matters as cruelty, exposure to danger, and to ensure for them special forms of trial and treatment.

Minors may not conduct *litigation* in person. Plaintiff minors must always be represented by their '*next friend*', and defendant minors by their '*guardian ad litem*'. These representatives will usually be one of the minor's parents or his or her guardian.

## C  MENTALLY DISORDERED PERSONS

Insanity is a thing which affects a person's legal capacity in many ways and the law has always had to take account of it. Such aspects of it as concern contractual capacity, matrimonial law (Chapter 14) and criminal law are discussed in the appropriate places. Here, after some general remarks about unsoundness of mind, it is proposed to confine attention to the provisions of the Mental Health Act 1983 (MHA) concerning the care and treatment of mentally disordered persons and the protection of their property.

Unsoundness of mind affects a person's power to understand the nature of his dealings with others, and the law must therefore recognise this fact and make allowance for it. It follows that, for instance, deeds executed or gifts made by people found by a court, through unsoundness of mind, to be incapable of understanding their nature or effect will be void, and the wills of such people will only be valid if it can be proved that the testator was capable of appreciating their import at the time of executing them. Further, in equity, transactions of people of low intelligence (though not necessarily amounting to unsoundness of mind) may be set aside by the court where there is evidence that the other party to the transaction has taken advantage of their weakness. Moreover, a person who by reason of mental disorder is incapable of managing his property or affairs must as a general rule be represented in a civil action by a next friend or guardian *ad litem*.

Passing now to the MHA, it must be stressed that its object is only to make 'provision with respect to the treatment and care of mentally disordered persons with respect to their property and affairs'. It thus seeks to achieve only this and provides only for '*mentally disordered persons*', a class which for its own purposes it defines. It therefore replaces the common law rules as to insanity *only* within this field and in respect of this particular kind of mentally afflicted people. In summarising the law which falls under this Act we must first ascertain the nature of this special class, then consider first the provisions as to their care and treatment and next those relating to their property and affairs.

Section 1 of the MHA defines 'mentally disordered patients' in the following terms. '*Mental disorder* means mental illness, arrested or incomplete development of mind, psychopathic disorder and any other disorder or disability of mind.' '*Psychopathic disorder* means a persistent disorder or disability of mind (whether or not including significant impairment of intelligence) which results in abnormally aggressive or seriously irresponsible conduct on the part of the person concerned.'

The special class being thus defined, we may turn to the provisions concerning care and treatment.

The Act is concerned with regulating the compulsory admission to hospitals of mentally disordered people and providing compulsory guardianship for them; but it must be noted that it also envisages that a 'patient' (ie a person 'suffering or appearing to be suffering, from mental disorder') may wish to be admitted to hospital voluntarily and informally, and it places no obstacle in the way of his obtaining such admission.

Compulsory admission may be required for two purposes: for assessment or for treatment. Whichever of these two reasons for admission is in view the admission must be founded upon an application to the hospital managers by the patient's nearest relative or by a mental welfare officer of a local health authority, and this application must be supported by written recommendations of two medical practitioners made in specified form.

Where a patient has been admitted for assessment he must usually be discharged from hospital after 28 days of admission unless some further application or order has been made within that time. Where the admission is for treatment, the patient may be detained for six months, but authority for his detention may then be renewed for a further six months and is thereafter renewable at yearly intervals.

The Act provides for *Mental Health Review Tribunals*, and it is the main function of these tribunals – consisting of lawyers, doctors and certain other people – to protect the liberty of the subject by considering applications by the patient and others, such as his nearest relative, for his discharge.

Subject to certain limitations these applications may be made at any time during the patient's detention.

The Act also provides for a *Mental Health Act Commission*, consisting of doctors, social workers and others who are charged with visiting mental establishments and making themselves available to patients who wish to see them.

It is now generally believed that it is in the best interests of the mentally infirm that they should be permitted, as much as possible, to live in the community like other people; consequently compulsory admission to hospital is a last resort. In many cases the mentally afflicted may reasonably be left free to mix with their fellows provided that they seek the help and advice which is now available to them; as through the services of mental welfare officers. But there are intermediate cases in which neither hospital treatment nor entire freedom are indicated. For these cases the Act provides machinery for *compulsory guardianship*.

The implementation of the provisions of the MHA as to compulsory guardianship, like the provisions as to hospital detention, is under the ultimate control of the Department of Health and Social Security, but in practice future responsibility in relation to guardianship falls upon local health authorities. These authorities have the duty, through their appropriate officers, of considering applications in respect of people suffering from mental illness. The formalities governing such applications are in most respects similar to those which govern applications for hospital admission. The effect of successful application for guardianship is that the patient will be placed by the local health authority under the supervision of a guardian. In most respects the rules governing renewal of and discharge from guardianship are similar to the hospital treatment rules appertaining to the same matters, and mental health review tribunals also exercise powers of review over guardianship.

Another way in which compulsory admission and compulsory guardianship may be brought about is by *court order*. The Crown Court and, within limits, magistrates' courts may, in lieu of sentencing accused persons make 'hospital orders' or 'guardianship orders' in respect of them, if they are satisfied upon specified medical evidence that they are mentally disordered. In general the rules governing the duration of treatment or guardianship thus imposed are similar to the rules relating to treatment or guardianship arising as the result of application, and resort may be had to mental health tribunals.

The Crown Court also possesses another special power: where it is satisfied that it is necessary for the protection of the public so to do it may, upon making a hospital order, make a further order in respect of an *offender* containing special statutory restrictions; and in particular restricting the time of his discharge either to such time as may be ordered or without limit as to time. The general effect of these orders is that the patient will remain in hospital detention until the specified time or indefinitely, and applications for discharge, and the ordinary powers of review of mental health tribunals, are excluded. But where the court thus authorises this special kind of detention, power of review and discharge passes to the Home Secretary who may exercise his discretion irrespective of the court's directions; and there is special machinery by which he may be forced to consider the advice of a mental health tribunal. Magistrates' courts have no power to impose restrictions, but they are authorized to commit offenders found to be suffering from mental disorder to the Crown Court which may then do so.

It must be added that if, upon a plea of insanity, a jury find that an accused person was insane at the time when he committed the crime alleged he must be ordered by the court to be detained during Her Majesty's pleasure. It is then the duty of the Home Secretary to direct that he be detained in a hospital. Under the MHA this direction has similar effect to a hospital order restricting discharge without limitation of time. The same applies in the case of a like direction made by the Home Secretary in respect of a person who is found unfit to plead on account of insanity at the time of trial.

It should finally be noted that disordered people are sometimes *incapable of managing their own property and affairs* whether or not their condition is such that they need special care and treatment. In such cases the law must provide a method by which other people can do these things on their behalf. This is the second main concern of the MHA.

The Act reconstituted the *Court of Protection* which now consists of a master, a deputy master and other officers. It is the business of this court to supervise control over the property and affairs of mentally disordered people who have been found after consideration of medical evidence to be incapable of managing these things for themselves. (It will be noted that this court is rather an administrative body than a 'court' in the strict modern sense.) In practice, under the powers of the Act, the court delegates the actual control exercisable over the patient's property, business dealings, and other affairs, to a person called a 'receiver' who may be a near relative of the patient. The receiver then acts as the patient's agent under the general direction of the court.

There are, however, certain powers of supervision which can only be exercised by special judges of the Chancery Division; these include such important matters as authorising proceedings for divorce or for judicial separation on the patient's behalf and the power (provided that the patient is adult) to authorise someone to make a will for him where there is reason to believe that he is incapable of making one for himself. Such wills must be in special form and their validity is subject to special rules. Moreover in theory the MHA places ultimate responsibility for the control of the patient's property and affairs upon the Lord Chancellor, although the only function that he is in practice required to perform is that of exercising the right of patronage on behalf of patients who happen to be patrons of ecclesiastical benefices.

# Part II
# Public law

# Summary of Part II

Chapter 5

# Constitutional and administrative law

Constitutional law defines the principal organs of government and determines their relationship to one another and to the individual. Administrative law controls the use, and checks the abuse, of governmental power. It is treated in this chapter (as, for instance, in relation to the powers of judicial review) as an integral part of constitutional law. The chapter will be divided into six parts: (1) the development of the constitution; (2) the nature of the constitution; (3) the conventions of the constitution; (4) Europe and the future; (5) the institutions of government; (6) the individual and the State.

## 1  The development of the Constitution

The Norman and Plantagenet kings ruled through the *curia regis* (the 'King's Council'); this was the grand council of the realm consisting of the great feudal vassals, the earls, the bishops and the barons. This Council (which is today represented in Parliament by the House of Lords) was in origin the king's 'feudal' court, though this description is misleading if one thinks of it as a 'court' in the modern sense; for it was not purely a judicial institution, but a governing body for the nation in which any kind of business might be transacted. Though it should be added that those meetings of the Great Council which were first given the name of 'Parliaments' were probably principally meetings of a judicial nature. In the course of time a momentous development occurred. The King's ordinary revenues were 'feudal' revenues which his vassals were bound to pay him as such, but he often needed more money than these revenues sufficed to supply. When he thus required 'extraordinary' revenue it was clearly impolitic to attempt to raise it without obtaining some semblance of assent from the nation as a whole, upon whom the burden of payment fell. For this reason it slowly became customary for the king to summon to his great assemblies, in addition to the magnates of the realm, representatives of the shires and boroughs of England. The object of these meetings then became, on the king's part, to obtain money, on the part of the representatives of the nation (the 'Commons') who now attended, to obtain redress of grievances in the form of legislation. The king, with the consent of the magnates, granted rights and liberties to his people by means of solemn enactments; in return the Commons granted him the money he needed. Thus gradually *Parliament* as we know it emerged, consisting of Queen, Lords and Commons. But it must not be imagined that this development was a sudden one; for the 'Model Parliament' (1295) of Edward I is now regarded by historians as a myth and it is thought that Parliament did not begin to emerge in something akin to its modern form until the latter part of the fourteenth century.

The rise of Parliament brought about a fundamental change in the constitution, for in the course of time it became settled that Parliament was the sole 'sovereign' Legislature. But this change was not effected quickly or without a struggle. The kings did not lightly relinquish their powers and it was not until after the physical victory of the Parliamentarians over the king in the civil war of the seventeenth century that the royal claim to legislate without Parliament was dropped. With the flight of James II and the Glorious Revolution (1688), which set William and Mary upon the throne, Parliament finally triumphed and the king lost the power to legislate in England.

The victory of Parliament did not, however, mean that the sovereign had lost *all* power. If it was for Parliament (or rather the 'King in Parliament'; for the Legislature is a trinity of monarch, Lords and Commons) to legislate and for the courts to adjudicate, someone still had to *govern*, and that someone was clearly the king, acting through his ministers.

With the fall of the Star Chamber in 1641 the judicial functions of the Council were, as has been noted, abolished within the realm. Nevertheless, the Council (by then the 'Privy Council') continued to exist for the purpose of advising the king on matters of government. By the Restoration (1660) this body had, however, become too large to be an effective advisory body; so Charles II selected a small group of able men to advise him in matters of policy and to carry on the business of government: the famous 'Cabal' typifies this new institution. These men were both in theory and in practice the king's servants but by the end of the eighteenth century it had become apparent that no government could rule unless it enjoyed the confidence of Parliament which, as we have seen, had already become the ultimate and sovereign source of power. Thus it became the normal practice for these advisers – the king's ministers – to be members of one or other House of Parliament, and, as such, to be responsible to Parliament for the administration of the Departments of State, which many of them controlled, and for the policies pursued by the government. Nevertheless, at first the monarch continued to be in fact, as well as in name, head of this group of ministers which came to be called the '*Cabinet*' (a name derived from the fact that it customarily met in a small room) and hence of the Executive.

But the whole course of constitutional development was against the monarchy retaining the actual power of governing in any of its aspects. In the first place, due to the historical accident that the first two Georges were foreign to England and had little taste for politics, they absented themselves from cabinet meetings (a convention that has been followed by subsequent monarchs). In the second place, and more importantly, causes were at work which made it inevitable that the country should be governed through elected representatives rather than an hereditary monarch. These causes included the new wealth born of the industrial revolution, the increased political awareness of the nation as a whole and, after the great Reform Act of 1832, the widening of the electorate. Even in the eighteenth century George III's surreptitious attempts at personal government were an anachronism. Thus in due course, especially under the impetus of the growth of the modern party system, the actual work of government came to be done by the king's ministers. Ministers were, and are, answerable rather to Parliament than to the monarch, and the latter lost all actual power and responsibility for the control of the nation's affairs.

## 2   The nature of the Constitution

Because the rules of a constitution are laws of fundamental importance, it is not surprising that they are often embodied in a single written document. Thus, for example, the Constitution of the United States was reduced to writing in 1787 and the document which comprises it (as subsequently amended) lays down the fundamental law of America today. Further the US Constitution, like many other written constitutions, cannot be altered easily. A constitutional amendment can only be carried if a very substantial majority, both in Congress and in the individual States, approve it. Such an amendment would require either initiation by both Houses of Congress and the ratification of three quarters of the State legislatures or (more unusually) initiation by two thirds of the States and ratification by conventions in three quarters of the States (eg the repeal of the 18th amendment – on prohibition).

Our constitution is just as important to us as the US Constitution is to the Americans. Nevertheless, it is not 'written'; that is to say, it has never been wholly reduced to writing. Further, since Parliament is 'sovereign' it can, without any special procedure, and by simple Act, alter any law at any time, however fundamental it may seem to be. Although our courts have always been astute to safeguard the rights of the subject and although certain legal remedies, such as *habeas corpus*, are designed to protect him, under our constitution, there are no *guaranteed* rights similar to the fundamental liberties safeguarded by the US Constitution.

The statement that our constitution is not 'written' does not mean that we possess no important constitutional documents; it merely means that the constitution is not embodied in any single document, or series of documents, containing our essential constitutional laws. Thus we have many enactments which either have been or still are, of great importance. One need only cite as examples the Magna Carta (1215), the Bill of Rights (1688) – which sets out the principal rights gained by Parliament and the nation as the result of the seventeenth century constitutional struggles – the Act of Settlement (1700), and the Parliament Acts 1911 and 1949.

## 3   The conventions of the Constitution

Many constitutional rules, such as, for example, the provisions of the Act of Settlement (below), are 'laws' in the ordinary sense, that is to say, they will be recognized and enforced by the courts. But there are certain other rules which govern the working of the constitution, which are not laws in this sense. They are called *'conventions'*. They arise from usage, or agreement, tacit or express, and they are adhered to, once they have developed, not because the courts will enforce them but because political expedience and respect for tradition demand their observance.

Many of the rules which govern the functioning of the central government and the relationship of the executive to the legislature are thus conventional. The convention relating to ministerial responsibility and certain other conventions, will be mentioned below; here it must suffice to give only a few general examples.

The cabinet came into being purely by convention: no statute created it. The Monarch's practice of abstaining from attending cabinet meetings started, as we have seen, as an historical accident and became a convention; no monarch would now claim the right to attend. By convention, when it becomes necessary to form a new Government, the monarch must invite the leader of the party or group commanding a majority in the House of Commons to form it; the Queen will not in practice invite any other person, though 'legally' she could do so. The person so invited will become *Prime Minister* of the new Government. This, the most important of all political offices, grew up by convention, and it was not until the present century that it received recognition in any statute. The Queen *could* refuse her assent to an Act of Parliament, but there is now a long established convention that she will not do so.

There is also the fundamental convention that the Queen acts on the advice of her ministers. By convention a Prime Minister may (though usually he or she will not) seek a dissolution of Parliament without consulting the cabinet. Indeed, the very keystone of democracy that the government must command a majority in the House of Commons is conventional. By convention Parliament must be summoned at least once a year, though *legally* it need only meet once in three years (Meeting of Parliament Act 1694 – generally known as the 'Triennial Act'); this convention is, as we have seen, grounded firmly upon political expedience; for Parliament alone can grant the Government the funds it needs annually for the public administration. Finally, the fact that the courts treat themselves as bound to apply Acts of Parliament is conventional, and so is the doctrine of judicial precedent itself.

Beside conventions, there are certain other important constitutional rules which are not 'laws' in the sense that the courts will enforce them. These are the rules which regulate the internal affairs of Parliament, such as the rules governing the process of legislation and the conduct of debates. Many, but not all, of these 'customs' of Parliament are now contained in the Standing Orders of the two Houses.

# 4 Europe and the future

In this part we shall consider the impact of the European Communities Act 1972 and its effect on the constitution of the UK.

## A  THE EUROPEAN COMMUNITIES AND THE CONSTITUTION

The UK signed the Treaty of Accession in 1972. This, of itself, had no impact upon UK law. It was brought into effect by the European Communities Act 1972 (hereafter 'ECA'). Similarly, the Single European Act 1986 was reflected in the European Communities (Amendment) Act 1986 and the Treaty of the European Union 1993 (otherwise known as the Maastrict Treaty) was given domestic effect by the European Communities (Amendment) Act 1993.

The coming into force of the ECA started a radical new departure in our constitutional affairs. Without attempting to embark upon the specialized subject of European Community law we must try to give some indication of the scope of this change.

The European 'Communities' are (i) *The Economic Community* (EC). This was established by the Treaty of Rome (1957). Its far-reaching 'task' is, *inter alia*, 'the establishing (of) a *common market* and *progressively* approximating the economic policies of Member States'. Its 'activities' include, *inter alia*, the elimination of customs duties; the establishment of a common customs tariff; the abolition of obstacles to freedom of movement within the Community for persons, services and capital;

common agricultural and transport policies, thus ensuring that competition within the common market is not distorted and '*the approximation of the law of Member States to the extent required for the proper functioning of the common market*'. By the Single European Act 1986 a number of further activities and powers were added to the European Community. (ii) *The European Coal and Steel Community* (ECSC). This was established by the Treaty of Paris (1951). Its objects are to set up a common market in coal and steel and to harmonize the development of those industries among the Member States. (iii) *The European Atomic Energy Community* (Euratom). This was established by a second Treaty of Rome (1957). Its main object is to foster the co-ordinated growth of nuclear industries throughout the Community. (iv) *Maastrict*. This is the 'Community' of interests established by the The Treaty of the European Union 1993. The Treaty contains, *inter alia*, an agreement on monetary and economic union, common security and foreign policies and a separate 'protocol' which the UK did not sign, on social policy called the 'social chapter'. Where a reference is being made to all the 'early' treaties together, or just to the 'Maastrict' collection, then it is appropriate to refer to the European Union. Otherwise, when referring to just one of the 'early' treaties, the relevant 'Community' should be named.

Provisions of the Treaty and of Community legislation impose obligations upon Member States and companies and some expressly give rights to subjects. The European Court of Justice has held that many provisions of the EC Treaty and of Community legislation which impose obligations upon Member States and others give rise to rights which are enforceable in the ordinary national courts. Section 2(1) of the ECA seeks to take account of this situation. It provides that where the Treaty imposes obligations or gives rise to rights or liabilities which under Community law must be given effect in the United Kingdom, such rights must be recognized in the United Kingdom, be available in it, and be enforceable in the ordinary municipal courts. Where, therefore, the British Government (or, indeed, a UK company) breaks a binding obligation the government, or company, may lay itself open to an appropriate action in the British courts.

It is, however, for the British courts – and ultimately for the House of Lords – to determine what the appropriate action is. Although breach of Community law by a trading company has thus been held to give rise to liability in damages as a breach of statutory duty, breach of Community law by a government department may not necessarily give rise to liability in damages; judicial review may be the only remedy in the United Kingdom.

Community legislation, that is legislation issued by the Council of the European Communities or by the Commission of the European Communities, is of two types, the Regulation and the Directive. Upon promulgation a Regulation is immediately law within all the Member States. A Member State need not and must not re-enact any of the provisions of a

Regulation or in any other way interfere with its application; and a Regulation, like an Act of Parliament, can impose obligations and confer rights on individuals.

A Directive, on the other hand, can and normally must, be re-enacted in appropriate terms by municipal legislation (by Act or by statutory instrument). It is, therefore, binding on Member States, but not on their subjects. This is not to say, however, that a Directive cannot give rights to a private subject vis-à-vis the State; for it has been held by the European Court of Justice that if municipal law or a State practice conflicts with the provisions of a Directive a private person may plead the Directive in national litigation, and the national court must resolve the dispute by disregarding the inconsistent national law. If, for example, a Directive requires a Member State to abolish sex discrimination as regards retirement, and the Member State fails to give effect to the directive by altering its national employment law, the government itself and all its agencies (including, for example, a regional health authority: see *Marshall v Southampton & South West Hampshire Area Health Authority (Teaching)* [1986] 2 All ER 584) should be required by British courts to cease to discriminate in respect of its own employees. A private employer would not, however, be under any such obligation until the municipal law was altered.

A third type of Community instrument is the *Decision*. This differs from the Regulation and the Directive, in that it is particular, rather than general, in character. It is used primarily where a State must ask permission from the Community in order to depart from the terms of the Treaty. It may also in certain circumstances, confer rights on private subjects.

Section 2(2) of the ECA, which is concerned with the *methods* of implementing such Community legislation as does require implementation, prescribes that it may be brought into force within the United Kingdom by *Orders in Council* or by *departmental regulations*. This subordinate legislation is, however, subject to parliamentary control and to certain limitations contained in Sch 2 of the Act. Control is secured by requiring that it must (by positive or negative procedure) be laid before Parliament. The limits include, *inter alia*, a ban upon the imposition of taxation and upon the creation of major criminal offences. Objects such as these are thus reserved for Parliament itself unless the government already has the necessary powers under some other enactment. Further, in order to ensure conformity with Community law, s 2(4) enables such subordinate legislation (subject to similar safeguards) to amend existing or future Acts of Parliament themselves. It also provides that any enactment must be construed and have effect subject to enforceable Community rights. It has already been noted that questions of interpretation of Community law are ultimately reserved (ECA, s 3) for the European Court of Justice.

The remaining sections of the ECA are concerned with detailed provisions intended to bring United Kingdom law into line with the laws of the Communities which were already in force at the time of its enactment.

The effect of this legislation is thus to bring the people of the United Kingdom *under the laws of the Communities within the ambit of the Treaties* and we are now thus partially governed by a new form of law: 'Community' law. As a people we thus look two ways: for the most part we are at present governed, as we always have been, by common law and statute; but in matters, such as the economic ordering of the community of Member States, within the scope of the Treaties we fall, whether directly or indirectly, under the general law of the Communities. The indications are that the field of the latter is likely to increase at the expense of the former.

So the question now arises 'What of parliamentary sovereignty?' Puristically, technically and theoretically the form of the ECA in fact preserves it: for the Act, in the exercise of the supreme power of Parliament requires our courts to recognize European Community law, including the principle that that law is supreme over State law. Realistically, and practically, however, we now have two 'sovereigns' situated at Westminster and Brussels respectively: just as the peoples of the United States look both to State law and to Federal law. Realistically, therefore, the traditional view of parliamentary sovereignty must be modified. And this poses the further question – given that the future trend is likely to be towards greater integration with the Communities, would it be possible to reverse the process and to return to isolation from Europe? Despite certain practical objections, that would be legally possible. There is no bond with the Communities which, politically, we could not break, and it is to be noted that no attempt was made in the ECA to limit the freedom of future parliaments – indeed, any such attempt would be futile, for present laws and present politicians have no power to bind their successors.

## B   THE STRUCTURE OF THE COMMUNITIES

Although it is not germane to English law something should, perhaps, be added about the internal structure of the Communities. Their principal organs are now: (a) the *Council of the European Communities.* The Council is composed of the Foreign Ministers of the Member States but it may occasionally be composed of other ministers, eg the Ministers of Agriculture. When, at least twice a year, it meets at the level of Heads of Government and the President of the Commission it uses the style 'European Council' but so long as it is dealing with matters within the competence of the Council of European Communities, it is *in law* simply itself. As a 'European Council' it may also discuss matters outside the framework of the European Communities; in particular, political co-operation: and this is now confirmed and recognized in the Single European Act 1986. (b) *The Commission of the European Communities.* The Commission is a collegiate body consisting of 14 members appointed by joint decision of the Member States. Although appointed by the Member States, it cannot be discharged by them, but only on a motion of censure by the European Parliament. Each member of the Commission takes an oath of independence. (c) The *European Parliament*. In form this is a consultative, rather than a legislative body. Most important draft legislation must be put before the European Parliament for its opinion and it may pass resolutions to the Council or the Commission, yet it has also a suspensory veto over questions of major expenditure which may in time give it an effective control of legislation, just as our Parliament once gained control of the Crown by the power of the purse. Further, there has now been created a 'co-operative procedure' by which the Council, the European Parliament and the Commission of the European Communities may make joint decisions. Election (governed in the United Kingdom by the European Assembly Elections Act 1978) of members to the European Parliament is now direct, in the sense that they are elected by the peoples of Member States themselves. Larger States are accorded more members, smaller States less.

*The legislative process* – Most important Community legislation has to be adopted by the Council (normally by a qualified majority) but, in general, the Council cannot make any legislation unless the Commission has first placed it before it in draft. At any stage before the Council has adopted the proposed legislation, the Commission may amend its proposal. In practice, therefore, there is a considerable amount of exchanging drafts between the two institutions.

## C   THE COUNCIL OF EUROPE

As organizations proliferate, names become snares. The Council of the European Communities must be distinguished from the *Council of Europe*. That organization was inaugurated in 1949. It is situated at Strasbourg, and it consists of a *Committee of Ministers* (the foreign ministers of States participating in its activities) and of a *Parliamentary Assembly* consisting of members appointed by the respective governments. Its function is to encourage unity among European States and to promote common action in cultural, legal and economic matters. One of its best known achievements was the European Convention for the Protection of Human Rights and Fundamental Freedoms (1950) which led to the establishment of the *European Commission on Human Rights* and of the *European Court of Human Rights*. Unlike the Community, the Council of Europe has no legislative powers; it operates principally through the formulation of conventions which States are free to adopt or reject. The European Court of Human Rights (situated in Strasbourg) was set up under the Convention to determine all cases concerning the interpretation of the latter which proclaims the recognition of certain fundamental human rights and freedoms by all States (such as the United Kingdom) which are signatories to it. Any person who alleges a violation of any of these rights may apply to the European Commission of Human Rights, and any State which is a signatory may refer to the Commission any alleged breach of the Convention by any other signatory. In turn, the Commission may then refer the complaint to the Court. A State found by the Court to be in violation of the Convention must then enforce the decision. The Court may also order the violator to pay 'just satisfaction' to the person aggrieved. The Convention is not part of English law, but the Court of Appeal has ruled that, in applying our law the courts should 'have regard' to it. The Convention confers no rights of direct enforcement by individuals in the English courts.

# 5   The institutions of government

The Judiciary has already been described in Chapter 2. The remaining institutions with which we must now deal are therefore the monarchy, the Legislature and the Executive.

## A   THE MONARCHY

Ours is now, as has been seen, a 'constitutional' or 'limited' monarchy. The Queen and the Crown (which represents not only the Queen herself, but also her Government) are symbolic of the whole might and unity of the State; but, for all practical purposes, the Queen is herself powerless. The business of government which is carried on in her name is done by her ministers – Her Majesty only acts upon their 'advice' and they are, as we shall see, responsible to Parliament. But, as against this, it must be borne in mind that both in practice, and under the Royal Titles Act 1953, the Queen is Head of the Commonwealth. And this means that in matters affecting Commonwealth affairs the Queen may, in appropriate circumstances, act upon the advice of Commonwealth ministers.

The monarch's duties are thus now for the most part ceremonial, though they are innumerable: the Queen makes State visits abroad, signs endless documents, confers honours, receives foreign ambassadors, and performs many other duties. Individual monarchs may, too, exercise considerable *personal* influence in State affairs, for the prime minister is by convention bound to report the conclusions of cabinet meetings to the Sovereign.

The succession to the throne is regulated by the Act of Settlement (1700). By that Act the Crown was vested in Princess Sophia (Electress of Hanover – grand-daughter of James I) 'and the heirs of her body, being Protestants'. The rules governing this descent are, roughly, the old rules which used to govern descent to real property and the effect of this is in particular that the throne passes to the eldest son to the exclusion of older daughters. It is, however, to be noted that Roman Catholics, and those who marry Roman Catholics are barred from the succession. Further when, as at the time of the accession of our present Queen, there are two or more surviving females *only*, of equal degree, the eldest succeeds in preference to the younger.

By the Royal Marriages Act 1772 no descendant of George II may as a general rule (unless he be the issue of a princess married into a foreign family) marry without the Sovereign's formal assent.

The Regency Acts 1937 to 1953 make special provisions to cover the event of minority or incapacity. A monarch is deemed to attain majority at 18 years of age. Should a monarch under this age succeed to the throne, then the person next entitled in line of succession who has attained the age of 21 will become *Regent*.

The Queen and the Royal Family are provided with annual payments to cover their personal expenses and the expenses of the royal household are defrayed by means of the 'Civil List', a permanent charge upon the Consolidated Fund. A Civil List Act is passed at the beginning of each reign.

The Queen has private property, eg the Sandringham estate, but 'Crown lands' are not the Queen's private property; they belong to the Crown in its *public* capacity, ie to the State. In her private capacity the Queen cannot be sued in tort, though it seems that it may still be possible, as a matter of grace, for Her Majesty to consent to be sued in respect of contractual or property claims by an antiquated process known as Petition of Right procedure.

## B   THE LEGISLATURE

It has already been remarked that the 'sovereign' Legislature is a trinity, composed of Queen, Lords and Commons. Since the monarchy has been discussed above, and it has been pointed out that the royal assent to an Act of Parliament is by convention never refused, it now remains to describe the nature and functions of Parliament as a whole. This topic will be considered under four heads: (1) the meetings of Parliament, (2) the composition of Parliament, (3) the functions of Parliament, (4) the machinery of legislation.

### THE MEETINGS OF PARLIAMENT

The period between the time when Parliament is summoned and its termination by dissolution or by lapse of time is called a '*a parliament*'. Parliaments are summoned and dissolved by Royal Proclamation. By convention the Queen will not dissolve Parliament upon her own initiative but will act upon the advice of the Prime Minister. In the unlikely event of a Prime Minister not seeking a dissolution before the full period has expired, a parliament will 'die' when it has been in existence for five years from the date of its summoning; for the Parliament Act 1911 provides that a parliament shall not endure for more than five years. This period is, however, sometimes extended in emergencies by special Act, as in the Second World War.

Each parliament is divided into *sessions* which usually last for about a year. The Queen *summons* Parliament at the beginning of a session and *prorogues* it at the end. A session is thus a formal thing, and is something like a little parliament in itself; public bills in progress at the end of a session have to be introduced *anew* when the next session begins.

Prorogation affects both Houses, but either House may *adjourn* of its own motion during a session. There may thus be adjournments from day to day, or for a week, or for a month or more.

### THE COMPOSITION OF PARLIAMENT

The two Houses of Parliament are the House of Lords and the House of Commons.

The members of the *House of Lords* are the Lords Spiritual and Temporal. The Lord Chancellor presides at meetings of the House. The 26 Lords Spiritual are the two Archbishops, the Bishops of London, Durham and Winchester, and 21 other diocesan bishops, who are entitled to seats according to seniority of appointment. The Lords Temporal comprise the peers and peeresses in their own right of the United Kingdom and Scotland and the Law Lords. The temporal peerage is either *hereditary* or for *life*. Formerly only United Kingdom peers were entitled as such to an hereditary seat, Scottish and Irish peers being elected from the respective hereditary peerages upon a representative basis only. The representation of Irish peers has, however, now lapsed and by the Peerage Act 1963 all Scottish peers are accorded seats.

Life peerages came into being under the provisions of the Life Peerages Act 1958. That Act empowered Her Majesty to confer *life* peerages by letters patent; and appointment to a life peerage carries with it a right to attend the House of Lords and to sit and vote therein. A further important change was also made by ss 1–3 of the Peerage Act 1963. Before that Act an hereditary peer could not disclaim his title, but he may now do so for the period of his own life, provided that he disclaims within 12 months of succeeding to the title. Disclaimer once made is irrevocable and another hereditary peerage may not later be conferred, though a life peerage may. The same rules apply to peeresses in their own right, so that by disclaimer peers and peeresses may now make themselves eligible for the Commons, being treated as commoners in every respect. During the life of a disclaimant the title is not accelerated so as to let in the next in line, but is in abeyance.

The *House of Commons* is composed of Members of Parliament who are the elected representatives of the nation. Electoral law forms a large and complicated branch of law which cannot be described here. Voting has, since the Ballot Act 1872, been by secret ballot. All adults (ie since the coming into operation of the Representation of the People Act 1969, s 1, everyone aged 18 or more), not subject to special disqualification, now possess the right to vote; but they can only exercise it if they are registered in an electoral register. The right to be registered depends, under the provisions of the Electoral Registers Act 1953, upon residence in a particular constituency upon a 'qualifying' date (10 October). Much of the machinery governing elections is to be found in the Representation of the People Act 1983 as amended by many later Acts.

Most British subjects are now eligible for election to the House of Commons as Members of Parliament provided they have attained the age of 21. The following classes of people amongst others, are, however, not eligible. (a) Peers, and peeresses in their own right. (b) Clergy of the established churches of England and Scotland, roman catholic clergy and all episcopally ordained priests and deacons. (c) Full-time judges of the superior and inferior courts, including some judges of courts of special jurisdiction, such as the Chief National Insurance Commissioner. JPs do not come within this category. (d) Members of the regular armed forces of the Crown. (e) Offenders convicted indefinitely or for more than one year, whether detained or unlawfully at large (the Representation of the People Act 1981). (f) Members of the civil service. This is of vital importance: the essence of the civil service is that it is a non-political and permanent institution. Political heads of departments change as governments come and go, but the civil servants who staff the departments act as permanent advisers to all governments, whatever their political colour.

## THE FUNCTIONS OF PARLIAMENT

Parliament still retains its two original functions. In the first place, it is still generally true to say that no public money may be expended without the sanction of Parliament. In the second place, the most conspicuous of its functions is legislation.

Besides these two functions, modern parliaments have a third. They are, in theory, the 'watch-dogs' of the nation, having the power and the duty of controlling the government. This comes about as the result of the principle of '*Responsible Government*'. The government must, according to this principle, command a majority in the House of Commons and if it fails to do so must resign or seek a dissolution. Hence, in theory, the government can only continue in office as long as it retains the goodwill of the House. In theory, therefore, the House is master of the government, especially because there is a constitutionally recognized Opposition Party ready to take advantage of its mistakes. In modern practice, however, this ultimate power of control is seldom exercised. The reason for this is that modern governments are usually able to retain their majority, once they have gained it, by means of their party organization. The government usually represents a single party, and members will seldom vote against it – both for reasons of loyalty and because they fear a general election which will certainly put them to expense and may lose them their seats.

Parliament is thus seldom able to exercise its power of control over the government directly, but it does exercise it indirectly in at least two ways. First, a salutary check is kept upon the doings of ministers and departments during the daily 'question time' in the House of Commons: an unsatisfactory answer, given due publicity in the Press, may have a material effect upon the popularity of a government (and the career of a politician). Secondly, debates, whether in the Commons or in the Lords, may show weaknesses in the administration. Debates are published – in particular in *Hansard's Reports* – and their substance is transmitted by the media to the nation; it is through debates that the electorate appraises political personalities and governments, and modern governments generally are sensitive to feeling in the constituencies.

THE MACHINERY OF LEGISLATION

It has been explained that, in order to become law, Acts of Parliament require the threefold blessing of Queen, Lords and Commons. It has also been explained that the royal assent is now a formal matter, being signified by letters patent under the Great Seal signed by Her Majesty and pronounced either in the House of Lords in the presence of the Commons or separately in either House.

Until it has received the royal assent an inchoate Act is called a *'Bill'*. Bills are divided into 'clauses', which subsequently become 'sections' in the Acts of which they form the basis. Most Bills may be introduced in either House, but Bills seeking to impose a charge upon the public revenue *must* be introduced in the Commons upon the responsibility of the government.

Bills fall into two main categories, *'Public'* Bills (which deal with matters of public importance) and *'Private'*, or *'Local'* and *'Personal'* Bills (which deal with local matters or matters affecting individuals). The latter must not be confused with a third category, *'Private Members''* Bills, ie Bills, whether public or private which are introduced by ordinary members. Due to pressure of business in recent times, and to the control which the government exercises over parliamentary time, Bills of this third class now seldom succeed in passing into law unless they are adopted by the government and accorded government time. Since there is no substantial difference in procedure between these Bills and Public Bills they merit no separate discussion.

Public Bills may be sub-divided into 'ordinary' Public Bills and *'Money Bills'*. The following, in brief outline, is the procedure for passing an ordinary Public Bill through the Commons. Upon its introduction the Bill receives a *formal* 'first reading'. It is then printed. A 'second reading' follows: this raises a debate upon the general merits, but no specific amendments may be moved. After the second reading the bill reaches the 'committee' stage, that is to say, it is referred to one of two classes of committees for detailed discussion and amendment. The two classes are: (a) *Standing Committees*. These are appointed at the beginning of each session by the Committee of Selection. Formerly there could only be five of them, but this limitation has now been abandoned. Each may consist of between 16 and 50 members, but the Committee of Selection may add as many as an extra 30 for the consideration of a particular Bill. The Committee for Scottish Bills consists of all the Scottish members and of not less than 10, nor more than 15, other members. (b) *Committees of the Whole House*. Important legislation is referred to the House as a whole, sitting as a Committee. When the House 'goes into Committee' the Speaker, the normal chairman of the House, vacates the chair and an official called the Chairman of Committees (the Chairman of 'Ways and Means'), or his deputy, takes the Speaker's place. Since 1967, non-controversial bills may go straight into Committee for their second reading and report stage (see below), if 10 days' notice has been given and 20 or more members do not rise to object.

In 1992 the 'Rippon Commission' recommended a new committee procedure of a 'preliminary briefing' stage and a 'formal committee stage' with a view of addressing what is perceived to be widespead dissatisfaction with the effectiveness of the current system. There seems to be a general acceptance of the fact that it is the government rather than parliament that actually makes the law, but that parliament should at least have a proper system for scrutinising proposals for change. It may well be that the next few years wil see reform here.

After the 'committee' stages the Bill is 'reported' to the House ('report' stage). The House reconsiders it, and may debate any amendments that have been made, or new clauses that have been inserted in committee; where necessary it may also return it to the committee for further consideration. After the report stage the Bill is 'read' for a third time. During the debate on the third reading only *verbal* alterations are allowed to be proposed.

Once the third reading has been completed the Bill is ready to be passed to the House of Lords. Assuming that the Lords do not reject it, it passes through stages in the Upper House similar to the stages just described. If the Lords decide that amendments are required it is returned to the Commons for their concurrence in the proposed amendments.

Formerly the Lords had a general power to reject Bills sent to them by the Commons, and thus to prevent them from being submitted for the royal assent and becoming law. This general power of rejection is now severely limited by the important provisions of the Parliament Act 1911, as amended by the Parliament Act 1949. These Acts give effect to the ever-growing constitutional principle that, as between the two Houses, the House of Commons, which represents the electorate, is the senior partner.

The Act of 1911 provides that any Public Bill which has passed the Commons, and which has been *certified by the Speaker* as a 'money' Bill (ie a Bill proposing financial measures) must be passed by the Lords *without amendment* within *one month* of the time when it is received by the Lords. If the Lords fail to pass such a Bill without amendment within this period of time if may receive royal assent and become law without their concurrence. For these provisions to operate the Bill must not, however, be submitted to the Lords less than a month before the end of a session.

The Act of 1949 (amending similar provisions of the earlier Act) provides that, subject to an exception to be noted immediately, if *any* Public Bill is passed by the Commons in two successive sessions (whether or not they are sessions of the same Parliament) and is rejected by the Lords in each session, it may be presented for the royal assent without the concurrence of the Lords. It is, however, provided that this result will only follow if *one year* has elapsed between the second reading of the Bill in the Commons in the first session and the third reading in the second session. The Bill must, moreover, be submitted to the Lords at least one month before the end of each of the two sessions. The Lords can therefore delay the passage of a Public Bill (other than a money Bill) for a maximum period of one year, but they can do no more. The one exception to this rule, contained in the 1911 Act and left unamended in the 1949 Act, relates to Bills designed to extend the maximum duration of Parliament – which is fixed, as was explained above, at five years, by the 1911 Act: the Lords still have an absolute discretion to reject Bills of this nature, and also Private Bills.

In modern times Private Bills have usually taken the form of enactments granting special powers to local authorities or other public undertakings. For example, Private Acts are often invoked by local authorities to make further provision for 'the health, improvement, local government and finances' in their areas. Various stringent requirements have to be satisfied before a Private Bill can be laid before Parliament, eg its purposes have to be advertised, and various plans and other documents have to be deposited in Parliament. Moreover, though Private Bill procedure is similar in many respects to Public Bill procedure, Private Bills are allocated to special small committees, and these committees (unlike committees on Public Bills) conduct an inquiry into the merits of the Bill rather in the nature of a *judicial* inquiry. Both the promoters and the opposers of the Bill may appear before the committee, and they will usually be represented by counsel.

## C   THE EXECUTIVE

It is proposed, under this head, first to describe the constituent parts of the central Executive, then to explain the sources and nature of executive powers, and finally to examine the ways in which their exercise may be reviewed.

THE COMPOSITION OF THE CENTRAL EXECUTIVE

The Central Executive is traditionally divided into three main groups of institutions, the Privy Council, the Ministry, and the Departments of State: to these there must now be added a fourth class of institutions which may be termed 'governmental agencies' for want of a more precise name.

## (i) The Privy Council

Historically the Privy Council is the last remaining vestige of the *curia regis* from which, as we have seen, all our central institutions, the Legislature, the Executive and the Judiciary, originally sprang. It is now substantially a formal body which gives legal sanction, by *Order in Council* or Royal Proclamation to government policies. The source of the Council's authority is either the Prerogative (below) or powers delegated to it by Parliament.

The responsible head of the Privy Council is a minister called the Lord President of the Council, but the Queen herself still attends its meetings including meetings to approve Orders in Council (usually four or five members).

The office of Privy Councillor is now, in the main, honorary: privy councillorships are conferred in the honours lists, and the rank of privy councillor carries with it the right to use the title 'Right Honourable'. Certain officials are always made privy councillors; these include all cabinet ministers and the Lords Justices of Appeal.

Though the Privy Council has thus become largely a formal body certain committees of it – such as the Judicial Committee, which has already been mentioned – still have active functions: these committees are, however, in practice, separate from the Privy Council itself.

## (ii) The ministry

The 'ministry' is the government of the day. The head of the ministry is the Prime Minister. It has been explained that by convention he or she must normally be the leader of the political party which commands a majority in the House of Commons; and it may be regarded as a twentieth century convention that he or she must be a member of the House of Commons, as opposed to the House of Lords. As well as being Prime Minister – an office which, as we have seen, was until recently purely 'conventional' – he or she also holds the essentially titlular offices of First Lord of the Treasury and Minister for the Civil Service.

Upon accepting office the Prime Minister's first duty is to form a government; that is to say to select (normally from his or her own party) a suitable *cabinet* and *ministry*.

The *Cabinet* is the nucleus of the government. It is usually composed of about 20 of the principal ministers. Cabinet ministers are, as we have seen, always Privy Councillors and as such they take to Her Majesty an oath of secrecy. That this oath is binding there is no doubt, but the fact that in *A-G v Jonathan Cape Ltd* [1976] QB 752 (the '*Crossman Diaries Case*') it was held that information about discussions at cabinet meetings ten years back could, in the circumstances, be published indicates that the rule which prohibits disclosure of such discussions does not rest upon the oath. Nor does it, it seems, rest upon what was formerly supposed to be a rule of absolute secrecy that cabinet papers only become publishable after 30 years. But it does rest upon the *confidentiality* which collective responsibility (see below) requires if discussion is to be uninhibited. All the major decisions of the government are taken by the cabinet, and all policy is ultimately directed by it. Much of its work is prepared by committees – whether 'cabinet' committees, consisting of ministers, or committees consisting of other high officials – and it is assisted in its work by a Cabinet Secretariat under the control of the Secretary of the Cabinet – a civil servant.

We have seen that in constitutional theory the government is 'responsible' to Parliament because no government that fails to maintain a majority in the Commons ought to remain in office. It ought to 'go to the country' (ie to seek a dissolution of Parliament and call for a general election) if it is out-voted on a major issue, and it must do so if it finds itself placed in a minority upon a vote of censure. It will be explained shortly that individual ministers are also 'responsible'. The principle of 'responsibility', however, goes further than this because cabinet 'solidarity' has become an established convention. This means that the cabinet makes its decisions *as a whole*; it is thus '*collectively*' responsible to Parliament and it must face Parliament with a united front. Every minister, whether he be present or not at a cabinet meeting when particular decisions are made, must accept and act upon the policy of the cabinet as a whole. If, therefore, some minister, who is informed of the cabinet policy, expresses views upon some important matter contrary to the expressed views of the cabinet, he ought, at least in strict constitutional theory, to resign; for since ministers are *jointly* responsible they cannot be permitted to remain in office while professing separate and individual policies. It must, however, be admitted that in recent times there has been a growing tendency for ministers to flout this important convention: indeed, in the *Crossman Diaries Case*, though he upheld the convention, Lord Widgery CJ remarked 'I find overwhelming evidence that the doctrine of joint responsibility is generally understood and practised and equally strong evidence that it is on occasion ignored'.

When the Prime Minister has selected the cabinet, his or her next duty is to select the rest of a *Ministry*. Numerous ministers have to be appointed who are not cabinet ministers. Most of these ministers are the political heads of important government departments and they are, in normal times, members of one or other of the Houses of Parliament. As members of Parliament they are individually *responsible* to Parliament, both in the sense that they are deemed to speak and act for the government on all matters of policy within the province of their duties, whether they have previous cabinet authority or not, and in the sense that they must be prepared to answer for the acts of their departmental and other sub-ordinates. '*Ministerial responsibility*' has, however, another, and independent meaning. There is an old maxim that the 'King can do no wrong'; both for that reason and because the Queen is now a constitutional monarch who normally acts only through her ministers, ministers can be made *legally* responsible in person for any wrongful acts which they do in her name. In order to secure this responsibility, every executive act which is done on behalf of the Crown must be authenticated by a document, either countersigned by a particular minister or ministers, or bearing a seal or seals for the custody of which he, she, or they, are responsible.

The cabinet and the other ministers who are not members of the cabinet (together with certain less important office holders, such as Parliamentary Secretaries and Under-Secretaries) compose the Ministry. But there is nothing static about the nomenclature or composition of ministries. Ministries and their functions, departments and their titles appear, dis-appear and merge bewilderingly from time to time, vary from government to government and change even during a single parliament. It must also be added that at present there is a marked tendency to confer the rank of Secretary of State upon senior ministers who are heads of large depart-ments.

Further, most ministers are members of the Commons rather than of the Lords, and this is particularly true of the more important ministers such as the Home Secretary. But necessarily some ministers must be in the Lords; this is partly because there is a statutory limit (at present 95 under the Ministers of the Crown Act 1975) to the number of ministers who may be in the Commons, and partly because every government must have some responsible spokesmen in the Upper House.

### (iii) The government departments

Most of the ministers of the Crown are, as we have seen, the *political* heads of the more important departments. The departments themselves form the real executive organs of the central government; for they, with their staffs of permanent officials (civil servants), are responsible for implementing the policy of the government. All the important departments are headed, subject to the general control of a minister, who comes and goes with the rise and fall of his ministry, by a senior civil servant, called a Permanent Secretary, who has a staff of civil servants.

Space forbids a discussion of the names and functions of the multi-farious departments; many of them, such as the Home Office, the Department of Trade and Industry, the Ministry of Defence and the Department of the Environment, are, in any case, known to everyone. It can only be remarked here that the members of their permanent staffs are 'servants of the Crown'; this means that they may in legal theory be dismissed at any time by the Crown (ie by their superiors acting on behalf of the Crown); for the Crown cannot be bound by contracts it makes with *its servants*, and this position is not affected by the Crown Proceedings Act 1947 (below). But in practice, as opposed to theory, as might be expected, the position of civil servants is secure; for their terms and conditions of service are regulated by Orders in Council and Treasury minutes, and in practice they will usually only be dismissed for gross misconduct or inefficiency.

One department, the *Treasury*, does require mention because it is the most important of all. Before 1714 there was a Lord High Treasurer, but this office was then put into 'commission', that is to say, its control was vested, not in one official, but in several – the 'Board of Lords Commissioners of HM Treasury' (a body which in practice never meets). It has been noted that the *Prime Minister* holds the office of First Lord of the Treasury. The *Chancellor of the Exchequer* (Under Treasurer – the next senior member of the Board) is the real head of the Department; he is at present assisted by the *Chief Secretary to the Treasury*, the *Parliamentary Secretary* (chief government whip), the *Financial Secretary*, the *Economic Secretary* and the *Paymaster General*. Beside the Prime Minister and the Chancellor of the Exchequer, the 'Board' consists of five '*Junior Lords*'. The functions of the 'Junior Lords' are primarily political and parliamentary: they are the principal assistant govenment whips in the House of Commons, responsible for ensuring party discipline in Parliament.

Below these *political* officers comes the *Permanent Secretary to the Treasury*. He is a civil servant, and, although the political office holders are technically his superiors, he is in fact one of the most important members of the Executive. As *permanent* head of the Treasury, he is the head of the Civil Service.

The Treasury is the Finance Department of the State; subordinate only to Parliament, it controls the economy of the nation, for, as will be explained below, all other departmental 'estimates' have to be submitted for Treasury approval before they are laid before Parliament. It is this power of the purse which makes the Treasury the most important of the departments. Formerly the Treasury was also responsible for the civil service establishment; that is for the control and management of the staff of the Civil Service as a whole. These responsibilities, however, now lie with the *Management and Personnel Office* which is nominally headed by the Prime Minister (as Minister for the Civil Service) and in practice a cabinet minister. The *Civil Service Commission*, which has existed for well over a century, is now also a part of the Civil Service Department, but it continues to carry independent responsibility for civil service recruitment.

## (iv) Governmental agencies

By no means all government is carried on by the central executive; an important tendency has been to devolve large areas of public activities upon governmental agencies, usually in the form of *public corporations*. Ever since modern governments have sought to pursue active policies they have turned to the corporate entity (whether aggregate, sole, chartered or statutory) as an instrument. An early example was the Poor Law Commissioners who were incorporated in 1834; a much later one is the British Broadcasting Corporation incorporated by royal charter in 1926.

After the Second World War, however, the use of the public corporation greatly increased. These corporations possessed a wide range of statutory powers, designed by parliament to ensure that the activity flourished. Sometimes the government took a major shareholding, sometimes the corporate structure itself contained regulatory mechanisms. The move towards 'public ownership' was probably more inspired by ideology than efficiency. Overall characteristics such as judicial scrutiny and ministerial accountability operated, but there was little or no coherence in the systems of monitoring or regulation of the nationalised industries.

By the time the 1978 White Paper 'The Nationalised Industries' appeared, the ideology had changed. Financial and productive efficiency was required and its attainment was to be audited. Day to day autonomy was retained, but overall ministerial 'steer' was imposed. Gradually, changing ideology, cloaked in the name of efficiency, caused the move to be taken towards privatisation. First the smaller activities like Jaguar, Sealink and British Aerospace were 'privatised'. Then, in the 1980s, British Telecom, British Gas and electricity followed. Now water, the railways and the nuclear power industry have been (or are in the process of being) thrown open to the 'shareholding democracy'.

The legal structure first used in the Telecommunications Act 1984 has been used as a model in later instances (such as those involving water, electicity and gas). There is an independent regulator (in this case OFTEL) appointed by the Secretary of State, a licensing system for those operating within the industry, a formula for price regulation and an overall supervisory role for the Director General of Fair Trading to ensure that no unpleasant anti-competitive activity is taking place.

The position is constantly shifting. The focus on law and a legal framework has been blurred by the introduction and operation of the concept of a 'Citizens' Charter'. Detailed legislative provision is being dismantled in the move towards 'deregulation'. There is not space enough in a book of this nature to consider the detail of this developing story, but its impact upon the daily lives of UK individuals should not be underestimated.

## The sources

Executive power derives either from enabling Acts of Parliament or from the Royal Prerogative.

## 1 Statutory powers

Most of the powers of the modern executive are derived from statutes: for instance, most local government powers are statutory. Such powers are conferred by a number of devices, some of which entail acts of 'subordinate' legislation (see below). The following are examples of ways by which they are acquired.

*(a)* Powers of subordinate legislation may be conferred upon the *Privy Council* by Act of Parliament ('statutory' Orders in Council). Thus, during the Second World War, the Privy Council was, by the Emergency Powers (Defence) Act 1939 accorded vast powers for the making of Defence Regulations by which it could control not only the whole life of the nation but could also confer powers on other branches of the Executive. These statutory Orders in Council must be distinguished from the 'prerogative' Orders in Council which will be mentioned later. Statutory Orders derive their authority from statute, Prerogative Orders from the Prerogative.

*(b)* Acts of Parliament sometimes authorize ministers to make 'provisional orders' in certain fields. A provisional order is an order which acquires legislative force by *subsequent* parliamentary confirmation in a Provisional Order Confirmation Act. The normal procedure is for departments to combine numbers of these Orders in batches, so that a single Act may be used to sanction several of them at once. Provisional Order procedure is most frequently employed, under the authority of various Acts, to authorize the execution of public undertakings by local and other authorities. The minister concerned is generally under a duty to cause a public local inquiry to be held before he makes an order.

*(c)* Ministers are also authorized by many statutes to make *statutory instruments*, ie orders and regulations, having statutory force. These require no subsequent confirmation by Act: they need only be laid before Parliament and will usually become law if they are confirmed by a simple resolution ('affirmative' resolution) of each House. In some cases, however, they will become law after they have merely been 'laid' for a prescribed period unless they are annulled by resolution of either House ('negative resolution'); and in certain cases subordinate legislation will even be valid if it is simply laid before Parliament immediately after being made.

## 2 Prerogative powers

In his *Law of the Constitution,* Professor A V Dicey defined the 'Prerogative' as the 'residue of discretionary or arbitrary authority which, at any given time, is legally left in the hands of the Crown'. Prerogative powers are called 'prerogative' because they were originally special overriding rights of the Sovereign and, indeed, certain of them still are: for example the conferment of the Order of the Garter and the Order of Merit is within her Majesty's sole discretion. However, most prerogative powers are now exercised by the Executive. Formerly they were extensive:

the Stuarts, after all, claimed the 'divine' right of Kings. But with the emergence of parliamentary sovereignty they have necessarily become less extensive than once they were and, since they derive from the common law, it is for the *courts to define their nature and extent*. They may be exercised directly by the Executive or through the machinery of prerogative (as opposed to statutory) Orders in Council. The exercise of some of them may be subject to question in Parliament while the exercise of others may not. For instance it is a rule that the Prime Minister may not be questioned about advice that has been given to the Queen as to the conferment of honours.

While stressing that far more executive power now derives from the authority of statutes than from the prerogative it must be admitted that prerogative powers are many and various and a few examples of them must suffice: (a) By right of the prerogative, the Queen summons, prorogues and dissolves Parliament. (b) Because criminal proceedings are conducted in the name of the Queen, and because crimes are wrongs against the State (the Crown), the Crown has the prerogative of mercy. First, there is the royal power of pardon. Pardons may be granted by the Queen, acting upon the advice of the Home Secretary. The Crown (in practice the Home Secretary) may also remit or reduce sentences. Secondly, the Attorney-General (the chief Law Officer of the Crown), acting on behalf of the Crown, has power to enter a *nolle prosequi* in criminal proceedings, ie he has a discretion to prevent a criminal prosecution. (c) The Queen is the sole source of honours. She alone, generally acting upon the advice of her ministers, may create peers and confer other honours. Interestingly, in recent years the ministers have acted, to an extent, upon the advice of the general public as to the award of honours to 'deserving' fellow citizens. (d) The Crown, though it has long since lost all legislative power in England – other than powers delegated to it by Parliament – may legislate by Order in Council for certain territories abroad, such as conquered or ceded territories, provided that they have been accorded no representative (ie elected) legislature of their own. (e) The Crown has exclusive control of the disposition and equipment of the armed forces. (f) The Crown has exclusive power to make war or peace (though it would now be unlikely to exercise it in the face of an unwilling Parliament) and of concluding treaties with foreign States, and its exercise of this power cannot be questioned in any court of law. Thus in *Blackburn v A-G* [1971] 2 All ER 1380 it was held by the Court of Appeal that a declaration could not be sought to prevent the government from acceding to the Treaty of Rome even though such accession must impair the national sovereignty. (g) During a war or in contemplation of war the Crown may, whether at home or abroad, order the destruction of, or damage to, private property as a necessary warlike measure. Formerly it was thought that this prerogative right was subject to a corresponding right to compensation on the part of the subject aggrieved, and in *Burmah Oil Co v Lord Advocate* [1965] AC

75 (where the company claimed compensation in respect of oil wells destroyed by HM Forces in face of the Japanese advance into Burma in 1942) the House of Lords – though with some doubt – so held. The War Damage Act 1965, however, reversed the effect of that decision in respect of government action 'during or in contemplation of the outbreak of war'; but the decision has since been confirmed as regards action taken in time of peace. (h) The Crown is also privileged to refuse disclosure of documents relevant to judicial proceedings on the ground that to disclose them would be against the national interest. But here again the courts will be prone to vindicate private against public right: for in *Conway v Rimmer* [1968] AC 910 – where the Crown claimed privilege in respect of certain reports upon the conduct of a police constable in the course of a suit by him for malicious prosecution – the House of Lords held that a minister's certificate claiming privilege of non-disclosure is in general not conclusive against disclosure and that the courts may demand it at their discretion. The disclosure of confidential police files was refused to the applicant in *Halford v Sharples* [1992] 1 WLR 736, but the use of material contained within them was also denied to the other party in the case. Much will depend, however, upon the class of document in question: for example an application for disclosure of cabinet minutes could not be entertained. (i) In the absence of specific definition by Act of Parliament it is within the prerogative for the Crown to determine the limits of British territorial waters.

All these and many other powers may still be exercised by the Crown by right of the prerogative. But since prerogative power is the antithesis of the rule of law it is necessarily subject to limits; for any act of prerogative must be ascribable to a prerogative right recognized as such by the *courts*. Thus the Executive cannot generally claim that its actions are immune from question in the courts by pleading that they are '*Acts of State*', above the ordinary law; it must justify them by reference to a recognized prerogative, to a statute or to a rule of common law. But the word 'generally' is important; for although it is not permissible for the Crown to put its actions beyound question by pleading 'Act of State' in respect of any act done which affects a British subject or even a subject of a foreign State resident *within the jurisdiction* (unless of course there be a state of war between this country and his) yet the plea is valid as against an alien subject in respect of acts committed abroad. Thus, in *Buron v Denman* (1848) 2 Exch 167, a British naval officer had been ordered to release some slaves detained upon foreign territory. He did release them, but in the heat of the rescue he exceeded his orders by burning a 'barracoon' (shed) belonging to a Spanish slave trader. The Spaniard sued the officer for the loss; but when it was found that the Crown had ratified the excess of authority it was held that it became an 'Act of State' and hence unquestionable. More than this – in *A-G v Nissan* [1970] AC 179, a case of a claim by an hotelier (who was a British subject by naturalization) arising from British army occupation of his Cyprus hotel, the House of Lords indicated that though 'Act of State' would not in general be available to the Executive as against British subjects in respect of acts done *abroad*, it did not exclude the possibility of circumstances in which it might be.

It remains to be seen how far the exercise of an Act of State may become challengeable by reference to Art 13 of the European Convention on Human Rights which provides that 'Everyone whose rights and freedoms as set forth in this Convention are violated shall have an effective remedy before a national authoritiy notwithstanding that the violation has been committed by persons acting in an *official capacity*'.

## The nature of executive powers

In relation to the powers of the Executive, the theory of the separation of powers appears now to have little practical effect. It is true that the various organs of the Executive do administer the laws enacted by the Legislature, and this, according to theory, is their proper function; but it is equally true that they do much else beside. Ever-increasing powers of *subordinate legislation* and of *adjudication* are now cast upon the Executive. Remembering that there are some powers (other than powers exercised by statutory order in Council) which are purely prerogative in nature, let us consider these two classes of powers in turn.

### Powers of subordinate legislation

It has been explained that powers of legislating are often conferred by the Legislature upon the Executive. These powers which the Executive thus wields are therefore referred to as a class as powers to make 'subordinate' or 'delegated' legislation. Although Parliament does not delegate legislative powers *soley* to the Executive, the various organs of the Executive are undoubtedly by far the most active 'subordinate' lawmakers. By innumerable statutes Parliament confers powers of legislating by statutory instrument upon ministers and departments, and at the bottom of the scale it also permits local authorities to make bye-laws. Extreme examples of statutes thus conferring huge powers of subordinate legislation upon the Executive (effectively upon the civil service) are the Health and Safety at Work etc Act 1974 and the Consumer Credit Act 1974. Further the process of delegation may extend to sub-delegation. For example, an Act may provide that Her Majesty may, by Order in Council, make regulations empowering such-and-such a minister to make further regulations. And this process may go on indefinitely; sub-sub-delegation is quite common.

The volume of subordinate legislative activity is enormous, and in any given year the number of statutory instruments (around 3000) far exceeds the number of Acts of Parliament. This being so, many people have felt that we are in the clutches of a 'New Despotism' (the title of a book written by the late Lord Chief Justice Hewart) of the Executive, as arbitrary and as serious as the Tudor despotism. This has led to demands for greater control of the legislative powers of the Executive than at present exists. Under the existing law both the courts and Parliament do, however, have *some* degree of control. Some of the methods of *parliamentary* control may be mentioned here:

*(a)* As we have seen, Acts which confer legislative powers upon ministers and departments often provide that statutory instruments made by virtue of these powers shall be laid before Parliament, and where they are so laid, special rules are prescribed by the Statutory Instruments Act 1946 and the Laying of Documents before Parliament (Interpretation) Act 1948. Each House defines 'laying'. In the Commons the instruments are usually laid at the Votes and Proceedings Office. In the Lords they are laid at the Office of the Clerk of Parliaments.

*(b)* The Statutory Instruments Act 1946, also provides that all statutory instruments must be published by the Queen's Printer. This provision ensures that much of the vast mass of subordinate legislation is at least available to the public. But on the other hand the definition of a statutory instrument is unfortunately narrow: it includes, amongst other things, Orders in Council and rules made by ministers under Acts empowering them to legislate by statutory instrument, but it does not include many other forms of subordinate legislation.

*(c)* By the Statutory Orders (Special Procedure) Acts 1945 and 1965, a special parliamentary procedure is prescribed for the making and confirmation of orders declared by any future Act to be subject to 'special parliamentary procedure'. The object of this procedure is to secure maximum publicity and maximum control by Parliament. It *only* applies where the authorizing Act requires 'special procedure' to be employed.

*(d)* In 1944 a House of Commons Select Committee on Statutory Instruments (the 'Scrutiny' Committee) was set up, which, since 1973, usually meets with the Lords' Committee as a Joint Committee on Statutory Instruments. It is charged with the duty of deciding whether subordinate legislation, required to be laid before parliament, should be brought to the attention of either House, upon certain specified grounds: eg that it imposes a charge upon the public revenues, or that it is made in pursuance of an Act which excludes it from challenge in the courts (see below).

NOTE – It should be noted that we have here been concerned to discuss powers of subordinate legislation, conferred upon the *Executive*. Such powers are not, however, *only* conferred upon the Executive; they may be, and often they are, conferred upon other bodies: thus professional organizations, such as the Law Society and similar bodies, are empowered by statute to make rules binding upon their members.

## *Powers of adjudication*

During the past 50 years there has been an enormous increase in the number of tribunals, falling outside the system of the ordinary courts, entrusted with exercising powers of a judicial or administrative nature and many of these tribunals are closely connected with the Executive. Indeed, many and very wide powers are entrusted to particular ministers, as for instance the powers of a Secretary of State for the Environment to grant or refuse planning permission under the Town and Country Planning Acts; and other similar powers and tribunals have been mentioned in Part I, Chapter 2. It must now be explained that the nature of the powers exercised by these tribunals varies. Some have '*quasi-judicial*' power to determine the facts of a case and to decide, not according to fixed rules of law, but according to the dictates of expedience; others have 'judicial' powers, ie power to determine the facts of a dispute and to decide it according to law. Further, in some cases there is a full right to appeal from the tribunal concerned to the courts; in other cases there is a right of appeal upon points of law only; in other cases still, there is no right of appeal, and the only right of redress which an aggrieved party possesses is by way of challenge by prerogative order.

The decisions of these administrative tribunals are, of course, as important in their own sphere as are the decisions of the ordinary courts in theirs, and, together with those of the ordinary courts relating to administrative matters and the vast mass of delegated legislation, they form the bulk of administrative law.

REVIEW OF EXECUTIVE ACTION

It has already been mentioned that Parliament has some degree of control over the exercise of executive powers, but more effective control – though, as will appear, also limited in scope – is kept by the courts and by the Parliamentary Commissioner for Administration.

A JUDICIAL REVIEW

The object of judicial review must be clearly understood. Although the courts are often empowered by statute to hear appeals from administrative decisions on points of law their principal means of control of them is by judicial review. When exercising this power they do not re-examine the decision but review the *manner* in which it is made. Fundamentally, the purpose of review is to ensure that, in a broad sense, the decision is a fair one. A further object is to ensure that any administrative action is *warranted by law*.

It will be convenient to divide this subject into three parts. The first we will call the 'principles' of judicial review, the second the 'machinery' of judicial review, the third the 'limits' of judicial review.

**The principles of judicial review**
These principles were authoritatively defined in *Council of Civil Servants Unions v Minister for the Civil Service* [1985] AC 374. But before outlining

them mention must be made of three fundamental concepts: namely, the Rule of Law, the principle of Natural Justice and the '*Ultra Vires*' doctrine.

## (i)  *The rule of law*

This concept has always occupied an important position in English law, though it only came to be popularized when enunciated by Dicey in his '*Law of the Constitution*'. The origin of the doctrine is very remote: as far as Western thought is concerned it is probably to be found in the notion, taken by the Romans from the Greeks, that over and above all actual laws there is, if only it could be correctly interpreted, a system of 'natural' law, capable of achieving absolute justice in all cases, which is deducible from fundamental and unchanging moral principles.

The first clear expression of this idea in England is to be found in the thirteenth-century work of Bracton, who wrote, '*Ipse autem rex non debet esse sub homine sed sub Deo et sub lege, quia lex facit regem.*' ('The King himself ought not to be subject to any man, but he should be subject to God and the law; for the law makes him King.') The mediaeval notion was that rulers and ruled alike were subject to the commandments of God and to 'the law'. When the temporal power of the Church declined no more was heard of the Divine Law in this connection, but the notion of the ultimate supremacy of 'the law' persisted. Moreover, if (though this is uncertain) what was originally meant to be denoted by 'the law' was natural law this denotation did not persist in England. 'The law' became identified – especially in the imagination of the redoubtable Sir Edward Coke in the early seventeenth century – with the common law of England. Parliament, it was true, became the recognized 'sovereign', and it could therefore alter the law; but, apart from legislation, the common law, according to this theory, ruled all men equally. The first two Stuarts, imbued with the concept of the divine right of kings, challenged this principle and tried to override the law without the sanction of Parliament. As everyone knows, their challenge failed.

The classic modern exposition of the doctrine is to be found in Dicey's book: he explains that it now denotes three things. First, that the regular law of the land predominates over, and excludes, the arbitrary exercise of governmental power. Second, that all classes of people are equally subjected to the ordinary law of the land, administered by the ordinary courts. Third, that the law of the constitution itself is not to be found in a code (as is the case in many foreign countries), but is derived from the rights of individuals, as declared by the *courts*. Writing, as he did, at the close of the nineteenth century. Dicey then proceeded to demonstrate the truth of these propositions. Generally speaking they remain true today, but the second one has in the present century been eroded by the increase in the number of administrative tribunals to which we have already referred.

As long ago as 1932 the Report of the Committee on Ministers' Powers, chaired by Lord Donoughmore, stressed the fundamental importance of the doctrine, and the members of the Committee were unanimously agreed that 'no considerations of administrative convenience, or executive efficiency, should be allowed to weaken the *control of the courts*, and that no obstacle should be placed by Parliament in the way of the subject's unimpeded access to them'. This is really the crux of the matter; whatever may be the modern practice, the doctrine of the rule of law proclaims that the subject *should* always be entitled to assert his rights in the ordinary courts, and this is especially true when he is imperilled by the acts of an overbearing Executive. It is an old doctrine and it is a sound one.

A further Committee (the Committee on Administrative Tribunals and Enquiries) was appointed in 1955 to consider and report, amongst other things, on the constitution and working of tribunals other than the ordinary courts; and this Committee, under the chairmanship of Sir Oliver Franks, reported in 1957. The result was the passing of the Tribunals and Inquiries Act 1958, and the law on the subject was consolidated in the Tribunals and Inquiries Act 1971. This statute has itself been replaced by the Tribunals and Inquiries Act 1992. The 1971 Act created a *Council on Tribunals* which is charged with the duty of keeping under review the constitution and working of certain specified tribunals and of other tribunals to be specified by appropriate authorities, and to make reports thereon. The Council is also empowered to consider and report upon certain administrative procedures generally, such as the holding of ministerial or statutory inquiries. Second, the Act provided for rights of *appeal* on points of law to the High Court from certain tribunals where previously no such right had existed. In the third place the Act prescribed that no provision in any previous enactment which purports to oust the jurisdiction of the High Court should have effect so as to prevent resort to *certiorari* or *mandamus*. Lastly, the Act ensured that in general the decisions of certain tribunals, and the decisions of ministers after the holding of statutory inquiries, must, if required, state *reasons* for the decision made.

This Act went some way towards meeting the dangers created by the conferring of arbitrary discretions upon administrative tribunals; but as will be seen, there are still very considerable limitations upon the control which the courts can exercise over administrative authorities generally.

## (ii) Natural justice

The courts have always insisted that where any person has to make a judicial decision he must comply with the dictates of 'natural justice'; and this requirement has now been extended to the exercise of administrative discretions. A great judge once stigmatized the expression natural justice as 'sadly lacking in precision'; and so it is, but most people will probably agree that the rules which the courts require those who are entrusted with the duty of deciding disputes to observe in the name of 'natural justice' are rules which every ordinary reasonable man would consider to be fair. For example:

*(a)   No man may be a judge in his own cause.* The application of this principle was strikingly illustrated in the case of *Proprietors of the Grand Junction Canal v Dimes* (1852) 3 HL Cas 759, where the House of Lords set aside a decree of Lord Chancellor Cottenham's – by which he had granted relief to the respondent company – upon the ground that he was a shareholder in the company. No doubt in fact his Lordship's decision was quite unbiased; but, as Lord Campbell said in his speech, it is essential that every tribunal should avoid even giving the appearance of having an interest in the subject-matter of an action before it. Although this principle will not be pressed to extremes it has been held that a chairman of magistrates will be disqualified from hearing a case if he is a member of a local education committee and the question is whether food contracted to be supplied on the order of that committee to certain schools is short-supplied.

*(b)   'Audi alteram partem.'* A court or tribunal charged with deciding a dispute must give a *fair hearing to both sides.* The case of *Ridge v Baldwin* [1964] AC 40, illustrates this principle. There the appellant (a chief constable of police) was dismissed by his watch committee after he had been involved in certain criminal proceedings: the dismissal took place in his absence and he was given no opportunity to state his case. The House of Lords held that this procedure (even though the decision had been confirmed by the Home Secretary) was contrary to natural justice and the dismissal was therefore void. A similar decision was reached in *Crompton v General Medical Council* [1982] 1 All ER 35 where it was held that the professional conduct committee of the Council were bound to disclose psychiatric reports about a doctor to the doctor before erasing his name from the register.

The same principle applies where a defendant is denied an opportunity to know the evidence against him, or not allowed enough time to prepare his case, or prejudiced by the fact that extraneous evidence influences a decision against him – as where, after a public inquiry, an inspector discovers and acts upon fresh evidence without disclosing it to the parties. On the other hand, in a number of court cases concerning dismissals of teachers and students it has been stressed that a fair hearing does not necessarily involve the holding of an inquiry exactly on the lines of a formal prosecution. It is enough if the inquiry is thorough and impartial. In the case of administrative tribunals it has long been held (as in the leading case of *Local Government Board v Aldridge* [1915] AC 120) that there is no need for the hearing to be *oral* if a fair view can be formed from written representations. Further, *audi alterem partem* governs the conduct of the trial itself: a defendant has no right to be heard during the process of investigation before the issue is put to trial.

What is 'fair' must vary according to the nature of the proceedings and more stringent standards will be imposed where a person is in danger of punishment than where he is not – as where a complaint is made to a county court by the Commission for Racial Equality which can only result in civil proceedings. Further it has been held that it is not contrary to natural justice that professional misconduct (as where a barrister is tried before a disciplinary tribunal consisting of a judge, three barristers and a lay member) should be judged by a mainly professional body: quite the contrary, a body composed of fellow professionals is often better equipped to judge in professional matters than a body composed of non-professionals.

*(c) Right of expectation.* Where a person has a legitimate expectation that something, such as prior consultation, will take place before an administrative decision is made he has a right to have that expectation fulfilled.

*(d) The reasons for decision.* It is sometimes said to be a rule of natural justice that every tribunal should make known to the parties the *reasons* for its decision. It has always been the practice of the ordinary courts to do this, and they will, as far as possible, insist that other tribunals follow suit. Moreover, as has just been seen, the legislation makes the giving of reasons by many administrative tribunals (including ministers) compulsory in many cases.

## *(iii) Ultra vires*

This doctrine has already been mentioned in respect of its application to the powers of corporations; it was, indeed, in relation to the powers of railway companies that it was first formulated. In the constitutional field it has a wide application. Since Parliament is 'sovereign' and its legal competence is supreme and unlimited the courts, as we have seen, can never question the authority of a statute (however stupid or perverse it may be); but they can, and *will*, if called upon to do so, question the competence of any other person or body, and will ascertain the limits of his or its own powers. All legal powers – save, perhaps, the authority of Parliament itself, which may probably be said to rest upon the greatest of all constitutional conventions, namely that Parliament must be obeyed – are derived either from the common law or from statute. They may, therefore, only be exercised within the limits which the common law or an enabling Act prescribe: once these limits are exceeded the courts will intervene if called upon to do so, and will adjudge any act done in excess of them unlawful and void.

The '*ultra vires*' doctrine has many applications. Thus it may apply to a special power conferred by statute upon a person or body to do some act which, apart from the statutory sanction, would be unlawful. It may apply to powers of subordinate legislation; as in the case of a minister who is empowered by statute to make regulations for a certain purpose, and purports to make them for some other purpose in excess of the authority conferred upon him. It may apply to powers of adjudication; as where a tribunal exceeds the lawful limits of its jurisdiction, or, being empowered by statute to make certain decisions after compliance with certain prescribed formalities, it fails to comply with those formalities.

The applications of the doctrine are as various as the powers that may be conferred; but the principle which underlies it is clear and simple; no power must ever be exercised beyond the limits which the law places upon its exercise: those who exercise powers must not trespass beyond their authority. A well-known application of the *ultra vires* doctrine is *A-G v Fulham Corpn* [1921] 1 Ch 440. The Fulham Borough Council established a municipal laundry. The Council was empowered, by certain Acts, to establish, amongst other things, baths, wash-houses and bathing places. The laundering activities were challenged by a ratepayer. The court had little difficulty in deciding to grant an injunction to restrain the Council from continuing them; they were clearly '*ultra vires*', beyond the powers conferred by the Acts. Again where a minister was authorized by statute to make an order himself where a council acted 'unreasonably' it was held that such an order was unlawful and void when he took it upon himself to make it in the absence of evidence that the council had in fact acted unreasonably; he had exceeded his powers.

NOTE – *Bye-laws* are subject to a further test, beside the '*ultra vires*' test. The courts insist that they must not only be '*intra vires*' (ie within the competence of those who make them) but that they must also be *reasonable*.

The three classic principles just described are still relied upon to control abuse of administrative powers, but in *Council of Civil Service Unions v Minister for the Civil Service* [1985] AC 374, without intending to erode them, the House of Lords formulated certain broader grounds for judicial review. These are: (1) The ground of '*illegality*'. The decision-maker must correctly understand the law that regulates his decision-making power and must give effect to it. Thus, for example, he must not act *ultra vires*. (2) The ground of '*irrationality*'. His decision must not be so outrageously unreasonable that no sensible person who had applied his mind to the question to be decided could have arrived at it. (3) The ground of '*procedural impropriety*'. Under this head the principle of natural justice is expressly included. But the ground also covers the case of failure by an administrative tribunal to observe procedural rules laid down in the legislative instrument by which its jurisdiction is conferred, even where such failure does not involve a denial of natural justice.

## The machinery of judicial review

Applications for judicial review of administrative decisions are applications for review by prerogative order. They must be made, by leave to the High Court (Queen's Bench Division) under special procedure governed by the Supreme Court Act 1981 and RSC Ord 53. As well as being empowered to make the prerogative order the court may also grant an injunction or a declaration if it would be just and convenient for such a grant to be made. Further a claim for damages may be joined with the application. The court may refuse an application if it considers that the claimant has been guilty of undue delay and upon certain other grounds.

The nature of the prerogative orders must now be explained and it is also convenient here to describe declarations.

## Prerogative orders

These orders constitute a main bulwark of the right of a subject to challenge excess or abuse of power by public authorities, courts, tribunals and the central executive itself. Like *habeas corpus* the orders were originally writs of ancient origin and the procedure associated with them was archaic and complex. The procedure has now been simplified and their scope widened.

*Mandamus* is a peremptory order commanding the performance ('*mandamus*' – 'we command') of a public duty which will be made if no other remedy is available. It not only goes to command the performance of an administrative act; it will go to enforce the exercise of a discretion. It has thus been obtained to force a borough council to hold an election of aldermen which it was *bound* to hold, and to compel a local authority to perform a legal duty imposed upon it to produce its accounts for inspection: for both these were positive *duties* which *had* to be performed. It will certainly not be available to dictate a particular course of action to a court during the actual course of a trial; though, of course, it may be that after the trial *certiorari* may go if the wrong course of action (such as a refusal to hear evidence) was taken.

*Mandamus* will not lie against the Crown.

The traditional rôle of *prohibition* is to prevent excess of jurisdiction by an inferior court; but its scope has been considerably widened in modern times, and it will now go to prevent excess of jurisdiction by any *public* body or person, exercising a *public* duty, entrusted with judicial or quasi-judicial powers.

Unlike *mandamus*, *prohibition* and *certiorari* will lie against the Crown.

The purpose of *certiorari* is to bring before the High Court any matter decided in, at issue in, or pending in, an inferior court in order that the High Court may 'certify' itself that no excess of jurisdiction has occurred or is about to occur, or in order to ensure that the principles of natural justice have been complied with.

As in the case of prohibition, so in the case of *certiorari*, the word 'court' has in modern times received an extended interpretation. The order goes to any person or body having jurisdiction to determine the rights of subjects whether judicially or quasi-judicially. *Certiorari* has thus been granted, for example, to review an order of the then London County Council which licensed the opening of a cinema on a Sunday in contravention of a statute forbidding that practice.

But there are limits to the scope of the orders. *Certiorari* has never gone to the ecclesiastical courts; though they are subject to *prohibition*. Further, neither *prohibition* nor *certiorari* will go to restrain the actions of private arbitrators (though they will go in respect of arbitrators acting under powers conferred by Parliament), nor to restrain officials in the exercise of purely disciplinary powers – such as the powers conferred upon chief fire officers and police officers in respect of their brigades or forces or upon prison visitors in respect of prison discipline. Nor yet will they be used to intervene in private or domestic matters; so they will not go to proceedings of committees of clubs and societies. Further, it cannot be used to prevent abuse of *legislative* powers. Moreover, though the Supreme Court Act 1981, s 29(3) provides that the three orders may be directed to the Crown Court, just as much as to any other court or body it exempts from their scope 'matters relating to *trial on indictment*'.

In practice applications for *certiorari* and *prohibition* are often made together: by *certiorari* proceedings in the lower court are brought to the High Court for review; by *prohibition* the lower court is forbidden to exceed its powers.

*Declarations*. A declaration is a judicial declaration of the rights of a party, carrying with it no order for enforcement. This may seem a pointless remedy, but in practice where the courts have declared the existence of a right, officials, such as ministers, as much as other people, will usually be constrained – if only from respect of public opinion – to act in accordance with the declaration. It should be noted that this remedy is not usually available *in vacuo*: people are not permitted to seek a court ruling upon hypothetical matters. In order for a declaration to be invoked there must be an actual dispute on an issue of law of a substantial nature. Relief will not, however, be refused merely because a dispute (substantial at the time when the claim arises) has ceased to be of practical importance at the time of trial.

It has been held that the procedure just described is the only procedure available for judicial review of administrative action. But from that it must not be supposed that where wrongs (such as breaches of contract or torts) are committed by public authorities they will be immune. Since the Crown Proceedings Act 1947 they may be sued in the ordinary way, just like private people. Actions against public authorities lie against them in their designated name (eg the Secretary of State for the Environment); though in certain prescribed circumstances the Attorney-General, who represents the Crown in matters of litigation, may be the nominal defendant. Further, it is important to note that fairly recently a *tort* of 'misfeasance in a public office' has come to the fore (*Bourgoin SA v Ministry of Agriculture, Fisheries and Food* [1986] QB 716). The essence of this tort is that a public officer will be liable if he does an act which he knows he has no power to do, that this act will injure the plaintiff, and it does injure him.

## The limits of judicial review

These must be considered in relation to powers of administrative decision conferred by Parliament on the one hand and powers derived from the prerogative on the other.

## Powers conferred by Parliament

Since it is 'sovereign' Parliament can do anything it wishes. By the use of appropriate words it can thus confer arbitrary and unchallengeable powers which cannot be questioned by the courts. An extreme example of such a power arose in the much-discussed wartime case of *Liversidge v Anderson* [1942] AC 206. The appellant was detained by orders of the respondent (the Home Secretary), under powers conferred by the Defence (General) Regulations 1939, made under the Emergency Powers (Defence) Act 1939. The regulation in question empowered the respondent, *inter alia*, to detain people whom he had reasonable cause to believe to be of hostile origin or associations. The appellant sought leave to apply for particulars of the respondent's grounds for believing that he was of such an origin or that he had such associations. The House of Lords held that he was debarred from seeking the assistance of the courts to obtain these particulars. Provided that, in ordering the detention, the respondent had acted in good faith (which was not denied), the grounds of his belief could not be questioned by the courts. The discretion conferred upon him was absolute.

This case occurred in wartime when it was clearly necessary that the Home Secretary should be allowed a wide discretion in ordering the detention of suspected people. But a similar result may sometimes be reached where the courts decide that the wording of an enactment is so phrased as to confer an absolute discretion. More recently, however, the tendency has been for the courts to act upon the presumption that parliament has no intention to exclude judicial review, and words which may appear to express such an intention will be strictly construed. Thus in *Padfield v Minister of Agriculture, Fisheries and Food* [1968] AC 997, where the House of Lords held that where the Minister, being charged with a statutory duty 'if the minister in any case so directs' to set up a committee of investigation to consider certain kinds of complaints failed to set up such a committee upon political grounds unconnected with the purposes for which the statute had created the duty, *mandamus* would go requiring the minister to consider the complaints in question according to law.

Further, even the words 'any determination' by (such-and-such) a person or body 'shall not be called in question in any court of law' will not exclude judicial review where the decision in question is not a proper one in the sense that some irrelevant factor has been taken into account. Hence in *Anisminic Ltd v Foreign Compensation Commission* [1969] 2 AC 147 it was held that a clause in s 4(4) of the Foreign Compensation Act 1950 so framed did not prevent a determination of the Foreign Compensation Commission, upon which the power of determination had been conferred, from being questioned where the Commission had so misconstrued the statute as to deprive the company of compensation upon the irrelevant ground that its successor in title (an Egyptian company) happened to be a foreign firm.

*Prerogative powers*

Judicial review of prerogative powers was discussed by the House of Lords in *Council of Civil Service Unions v Minister for the Civil Service*. It was ruled that as a matter of general principle the exercise of these powers is as much subject to judicial review as the exercise of statutory powers; but that there are certain exceptions. The issue in the case was whether a decision of the Prime Minister to deprive certain civil servants of the right to union membership without prior consultation could be reviewed. Clearly, as a matter of general principle such a decision was reviewable but it was made under the prerogative right of the Crown to take necessary action in the *national interest*. It was held that since it had been *established* that the action was taken in the national interest the decision could not be reviewed. The question whether it was or was not in the national interest to override individual rights was not justiciable: it was an issue for the executive to decide. The case is therefore authority for the proposition that the Crown's prerogative right to take action in the national interest – once it is established that that was the purpose of the action – cannot be subject to judicial review. No more than that was actually decided, but it was indicated that there may be other prerogative powers which are equally unsuitable for review. These include the prerogative of making treaties, the Crown's duty to take action in defence of the realm, the prerogative of mercy, the grant of honours, the dissolution of Parliament and the appointment of ministers. Clearly there may be other powers within this category. The power to recognize foreign States would seem to be one.

It may be of interest to note that at common law it was long ago established that a private individual has a right, even if his action does infringe the rights of others, to take drastic action in defence of the realm. In such a case the court would have to consider whether, in all the circumstances, such action was justified.

It should be added that statute overrides prerogative and that which is governed by statute cannot be done by show of prerogative. Thus in *Laker Airways Ltd v Department of Trade* [1977] QB 643, where the Secretary of State purported to cancel the plaintiff's transatlantic licence under cover of prerogative, his action was held void upon the ground that such cancellation was governed by a statute.

It must not be forgotten that judicial review is not the only bridle of executive action. As has been remarked above, public officials are now subject to the ordinary remedies (such as damages) available against those who commit wrongs. Further, as has also been remarked above, most executive decisions are subject to *question in Parliament*. In practice this fetters the exercise even of the most absolute prerogative powers. No administration would now go to war without consulting Parliament. Though, of course, nothing in government is certain. In the face of an immediate threat of nuclear war the administration might well be forced to act at once and leave questions until afterwards.

## D THE PARLIAMENTARY COMMISSIONER FOR ADMINISTRATION

This office was created in imitation of the Scandinavian *Ombudsman*, though the English version differs from its prototype. It was set up by the Parliamentary Commissioner Act 1967, and the function of the Commissioner is to investigate complaints by members of the public who claim to have suffered injustice in consequence of maladministration in connection with action taken in the exercise of administrative functions by government departments and certain public authorities. Complaints must be made in writing and be addressed to a *member of the House of Commons*; and it is then for the *member*, and not the aggrieved person, with the consent of the latter, to forward the complaint to the Commissioner. The Commissioner then has a discretion whether or not to make an investigation; if he does decide to do so he must inform the branch of the Executive concerned, and when the investigation is complete must report both to the latter, and the member; if he decides that no investigation is warranted he must still report to the member, giving his reasons for refusing one. It is to be noted that this function is purely *investigatory*; the Commissioner has no executive powers; but if he considers that injustice has been done and that, despite his inquiry, it remains unremedied, he may lay before both Houses of Parliament a special report on the case.

The creation of such an office, while preserving the rôle of members to act as the guardians of their constituents, is clearly much to the good; and injustices have been revealed and remedied. But the limitations upon the Commissioner's powers are considerable. In the first place, he is concerned with '*maladministration*', not with misguided decision (although the House of Commons Select Committee on the Parliamentary Commissioner made a useful contribution by suggesting that the term '*maladministration*' should extend to include harsh decisions based on the over-vigorous application of departmental policies, a suggestion accepted by the Commissioner). He is not a court of appeal from the exercise of administrative discretion, though he may question any administrative act if it appears biased, irrelevant, negligent, inept or dishonest. This is probably a necessary limitation for there is no reason why the Commissioner should know the business of departments better than the departments themselves; yet it has been much criticized and it seems not to be imposed upon the foreign prototypes. In the second place the areas to be investigated were seriously circumscribed by the 1967 Act. Although most departments fell within the Commissioner's province a formidable number of public authorities and services were exempt from investigation – including the Cabinet Office, local authorities and the police, the health service and public corporations. Since 1973, however, there have been National Health Service Commissioners and Local Commissioners for Administration. The former may receive complaints about health authorities (on matters other than diagnosis and treatment) direct from members of the public. The latter will receive complaints, usually channelled through the authorities themselves, about acts of maladministration by local authorities, joint boards, police authorities and water authorities.

Further, by the Parliamentary and Health Service Commissioners Act 1987 the powers of the Commissioner have been extended to cover a large number of non-departmental bodies (such as the Charity Commission, the Countryside Commission, the Arts Council – even Tourist Boards) listed in Sch 1 of the Act.

# 6   The individual and the State

It has already been remarked that under the British constitution there are no such things as 'guaranteed' rights – as there are in the US Constitution – expressly safeguarded in a document of peculiar sanctity. Since Parliament is all-powerful it may do anything by a simple Act, and it may certainly deprive the individual of his rights – indeed, a Tudor Parliament once condescended to pass a special Act to sanction the boiling to death of one Richard Rose, the Bishop of Rochester's cook (alleged to have been guilty of poisoning).

This being the case, the citizen must look, for the protection of his rights, not to any constitutional document but to the general rules of law enforced at any given time by the courts; his rights derive from the ordinary law of the land.

There are, however, certain basic rights which may be termed 'constitutional'. They are the right to personal liberty, to property, to free speech, assembly and association, and to equal treatment.

## A   THE RIGHT TO PERSONAL LIBERTY

Everyone is entitled to personal freedom. This implies two things – first, that no one may lawfully be arrested except upon specified grounds; secondly, that if anyone is arrested or detained, otherwise than upon lawful grounds, the writ of *habeas corpus* may be invoked to set him free and he may sue the person who detained him for assault or false imprisonment.

### ARREST AND DETENTION

The following are the principal grounds of arrest and detention recognized by the law – arrest and detention in pursuance of the criminal law; detention of mentally disordered people; detention by order of the court or of either House of Parliament, upon the ground of 'contempt'.

## (a) Under the criminal law

Arrest and detention of course occur most commonly in furtherance of the criminal law; but those who seek to arrest criminals must be careful not to exceed their lawful powers.

Arrest may always be lawfully effected by anyone authorized to make it by a *warrant* lawfully issued and signed by a justice of the peace or other judicial authority, naming the person to be arrested; though it should be noted that the person who makes the arrest must have the warrant in his possession at the time of the arrest, or at least be in a position to produce it immediately upon request. In some cases, however, people have the power, and may even be under a legal duty, to arrest other people without first obtaining a warrant.

Formerly the law relating to powers of arrest *without warrant* was detailed, obscure and complicated, built up over the ages by an amalgam of common and statute law. It has now, however, been clarified by the provisions of the Police and Criminal Evidence Act 1984 (Part III) – repealing and re-enacting s 2 of the Criminal Law Act 1967. This Act gives powers of *summary* arrest (without warrant) in the special case of *arrestable* offences and also where there are *general* grounds of arrest.

### Arrestable offences

These include offences for which the sentence is fixed by law (eg murder), offences for which a person (not previously convicted) may be sentenced for a term of five years and certain other specified offences.

It is provided that *any* person may arrest without warrant anyone *in the act of committing* an arrestable offence or anyone whom he has reasonable grounds for suspecting to be committing an arrestable offence. Where an arrestable offence *has been* committed any person may arrest without warrant anyone who is guilty of the offence or anyone whom he has reasonable grounds for suspecting to be guilty of it. Where a *constable* has reasonable grounds for suspecting that an arrestable offence has been committed he may similarly arrest anyone whom he has reasonable grounds for suspecting to be guilty of the offence. Further, a *constable* may arrest without warrant anyone who is *about* to commit an arrestable offence.

### General grounds for arrest

If certain 'general arrest conditions' are satisfied a *constable* may arrest anyone whom he has reasonable grounds for suspecting to have committed or attempted to commit *any* offence if it appears to him that service of a summons is impracticable or inappropriate. The *general arrest conditions* are too complex to be examined in detail here; they include the fact that the name of the person concerned is unknown to the constable, that the constable has reasonable grounds for doubting whether a name furnished by that person is his real name; the fact that the person has failed to furnish an address for service; and the fact that the constable has reasonable grounds for believing that arrest is necessary to prevent the person from causing physical harm, damage to property, an affront to public decency or an obstruction of the highway. Also the fact that the constable has reasonable grounds for believing that arrest is necessary to protect a child or other vulnerable person.

Subject to certain other statutory powers of arrest without warrant under certain statutes set out in Sch 2 of the Act there are no other such *statutory* powers.

## Common law powers

It would seem that the Act does not have the effect of abolishing certain powers of arrest conferred by the common law. These include the right of *any* person to arrest anyone whom he sees committing or about to commit a *breach of the peace* for sufficient time to stop the commission of the offence; and the power of a *constable* to arrest such a person in order to secure him for trial. Further, it is probable that similar power exists in the case of *anyone* who sees any person doing, or about to do, *bodily harm*. At common law, also, a *constable* may arrest anyone who is, or whom he has reasonable grounds to believe to be, obstructing him in the execution of his duty; provided that the obstruction is, or is believed by him to be, wilful and of a nature likely to lead to a breach of the peace.

It should be added that by the Criminal Law Act 1967, s 3, anyone is empowered to use '*such force as is reasonable in the circumstances*' in the '*prevention of crime, or in effecting or assisting in the arrest of offenders or of persons unlawfully at large*'. This is merely confirmatory of the common law.

Where a constable makes an arrest without a warrant he must make the true cause of arrest known to the person arrested and he must, in cases where no question of resort to force arises, use such words as 'I arrest you' or make his intention to effect the arrest plain; for example, it is not enough merely to say 'I propose to charge you with theft'. It should also be noted that the police have power to call upon any able-bodied person to assist them in making an arrest; and it is the duty of any person so called upon to assist. In arresting a suspect a constable need not necessarily take him immediately to a police station or before a magistrate, but may lawfully detain him in order to take such reasonable steps as are necessary to assure himself that his suspicions are well founded (for instance he may take the suspect to his home to see whether there is stolen property there). However, after reasonable investigations have been carried out, the arrested person must be taken to an appropriate police station within six hours. Further it has long been established that if after arrest the constable or his superiors decide that there is insufficient cause for detaining the suspect they may lawfully release him without taking him before a magistrate and will not then – provided that the suspicion was reasonable – be liable to an action for false imprisonment.

It may be worth adding that, quite apart from the special disciplinary powers conferred upon naval commanders, a *master of a merchant vessel* has, by the common law, the power and duty of arresting and detaining anyone aboard his ship when he reasonably believes such detention to be necessary for the preservation of order, or for the safety of the ship.

NOTE – This may be the place to note that: (i) By Part I of the Police and Criminal Evidence Act 1984 police are given powers to *search* any person or vehicle found in a public place for stolen or prohibited articles. The latter include such things as offensive weapons: (ii) Part IV makes the important provision that people may only be kept in police detention for 24 hours without being charged unless: (a) An officer of superintendent rank or above authorizes such detention up to 36 hours, or, (b) A magistrates' court issues a warrant authorizing such detention up to 36 hours: (iii) By s 56 of the Act an arrested person detained in custody is in general entitled, if he so requests, to have some other person told that he is under arrest.

## (b) Committal for contempt
There may be contempt of court and contempt of Parliament.

## 1 Contempt of court
The essence of contempt of court is that it is intended to safeguard the proper administration of justice by prohibiting or punishing conduct which prejudices or abuses it. There are two main kinds of contempt of court, 'civil' contempt and 'criminal' contempt.

### Civil contempt
This consists in failure to conform with an order of a superior court. A civil judge may commit to prison any person who disobeys his orders; such as refusing to obey an injunction. The disobedient person may also be fined or the judge may order sequestration of assets. Civil contempt is peculiar in that the Crown may not grant a pardon in respect of it.

### Criminal contempt
This comprises conduct calculated to *interfere with the due administration of justice*. It gives rise to proceedings criminal in nature, but the power to punish it may be exercised by civil, as well as by criminal, judges. It takes a number of forms.

*(a) Contempt in the face of the court* – This controls the behaviour of people in court, including violent, unruly or insulting behaviour. For example, in 1631 Chief Justice Richardson, sitting at the Salisbury assizes was the target of a 'brickbat' thrown by a felon. It missed, unlike the equipment of the enforcement authorities who cut off his hand, fitted it to a gibbet, and followed it with the rest of his body (73 Eng Rep 416). This form of contempt also embraces disregard of a judge's ruling; such as a

refusal to give evidence, to answer questions or to disclose a source of information demanded by the court, even of a journalist to 'disclose his sources'. This latter power to demand information was, however, restricted by the Contempt of Court Act 1981 which provided that such a demand may only be made if it is necessary in the interests of justice, national security or the prevention of disorder or of crime. This jurisdiction is a power inherent in superior courts and such contempt may be punished by fine or imprisonment. Inferior courts have no such inherent power but by the above Act they may impose penalties upon people who misbehave in court, as by interruption of the proceedings.

*(b) Publications prejudicial to a fair criminal trial* – It is contempt to publish anything which may be prejudicial to a fair criminal trial. Thus, for example, when such a trial is in progress or imminent it is contempt to publish allegations about the accused which may have the effect of prejudicing the jury against him.

*(c) Publications prejudicial to fair civil proceedings* – These may also amount to contempt: but there is a difference of emphasis. In a criminal trial liberty is at stake and juries may be influenced, but that is not the case in a civil trial. Nevertheless, publications while a civil trial is in progress or pending may amount to contempt if they are prejudicial to a fair trial. This was the issue in *A-G v Times Newspapers Ltd* [1974] AC 273 (the famous 'thalidomide' case). Claims were pending against the manufacturers of the dangerous drug thalidomide and the *Sunday Times* published an article urging the manufacturers to make a generous settlement, and also postponed publication of another article about the lack of effectiveness of the precautions they had taken in the course of manufacture. The House of Lords held that both articles were in contempt as prejudicial to a fair trial. The one as seeking to constrain the manufacturers to settle the case on terms other than their own and to expose them to public criticism for defending their rights in court. The other as seeking to air one of the central issues of the trial. This decision, however, exposed the difficulty of defining what is prejudicial. *The Sunday Times* challenged it before the European Court of Human Rights which, under Art 10 of the Convention, decided that the suppression of these publications was *not* 'necessary . . . for maintaining the . . . impartiality of the judiciary'.

*(d) Scandalizing the court* – It is contempt to challenge the integrity or impartiality of a judge on the ground that such challenge may undermine confidence in the administration of justice. Thus it was once held to be contempt to publish an article about a particular judge alleging that he was so biased that there was no hope of a fair trial before him. It is not, on the other hand, contempt to criticize the legal, moral or social merits of a

decision. It may be thought that in a modern democratic society this privilege afforded to the judiciary is questionable.

There are also certain other kinds of contempt beside the above.

There has never been doubt that *intentional* contempt is punishable. Formerly, however, contempt was an offence of 'strict liability', punishable without proof of intent. This was altered by the Contempt of Court Act 1981 which, by s 1, confined 'strict liability' to *publications* (written, broadcast or otherwise) which create a *substantial risk* that the course of justice in particular proceedings will be *seriously impeded or prejudiced*. But, even then, those proceedings must, under the Act, be 'active'. Criminal proceedings come to be 'active' under this provision when a person is arrested, orally charged, or when a warrant has been issued for his arrest. Civil proceedings become 'active' when the writ in the action is issued. It is, however, a defence to strict liability if the accused, having taken reasonable care, did not know that the proceedings were active. Strict liability seems harsh, but the damage that such publications may do must be weighed against the burden it casts upon the publisher.

## 2 Contempt of Parliament

The House of Lords, being in origin, the core of the *curia regis* (the King's Court) of early mediaeval times, was from the start, and has always remained, a court – and as has been noted above, to this day it exercises judicial functions as the ultimate appeal court. It was once, indeed, usual to speak of the High Court of Parliament. When the Commons, from being a body of elected representatives assembled to provide money for the Crown, became associated with the Lords as the lower House of Parliament it, too, took upon itself the powers of a court in respect of its own interests. In consequence, both the Commons and the Lords have power to commit for contempt anyone, whether a member or anyone else who, in their opinion, obstructs them in the conduct of their proceedings. Parliamentary 'contempt' is thus a vague (and, perhaps, unsatisfactory) concept. It includes obstruction of parliamentary proceedings, obstruction of members seeking to attend the House, a false statement made by a member to the House; but, more controversially, it has been held to include newspaper criticisms of the perquisites of members and even disruption by students of a meeting of a sub-committee of a select committee.

The power to commit is, however, sparingly used and the last time it was exercised was in 1880. Contempt is in practice curbed by less drastic means; such as admonition by the Speaker or, in the case of a member, expulsion. The Commons cannot impose a fine (a surprising rule in view of the fact that many less august bodies, such as universities, empower themselves to do so) and can only imprison for a period when the House is in session. The Lords, however, have power to impose fines and to imprison for a definite period.

## HABEAS CORPUS

It is one thing to say that the law does not permit unlawful arrests; but it is quite another thing to prevent them from being made. It will be cold comfort for the prisoners to be told that they will have a right to damages when, and if, they escape.

This is where the importance of the historic writ of *habeas corpus* lies. The principle underlying the issue of this writ cannot be better expressed than in the words of Blackstone: 'The King', he wrote, 'is at all times entitled to have an account why the liberty of his subjects is restrained'. Anyone who is detained, or any person with an interest in his liberty *acting on his behalf*, may apply in term time to a divisional court of the Queen's Bench Division or in vacation to any judge of the High Court, for the issue of the writ. If the court or judge order it to issue, it will be served upon the person having custody of the person detained who, upon a named day, must appear before the court or judge to show legal cause for the detention: if he cannot do this the person detained will at once be freed. The writ goes against the Crown as well as against private individuals, and any form of detention, may be challenged whether it be upon a criminal matter (such as extradition) or upon a civil matter (such as deportation on the detention of a mental patient).

The Administration of Justice Act 1960 made important amendments to *habeas corpus* procedure and clarified certain obscurities. The following points should be noted. Where an application is made to a single judge he may not *refuse* the order, and should he consider that it ought to be refused he must refer the case to a divisional court. Not more than one application may be made unless fresh evidence appears to support a second one.

In the case of all applications, whether civil or criminal – save an order of *release* in a criminal matter made by a single judge – there is a *right of appeal* against an order for release as well as against refusal. Appeal lies from the divisional court direct to the House of Lords; but in *criminal matters*, if the divisional court has ordered release without requiring bail or ordering interim detention, the discharged person will be entitled to remain at large whatever the final decision on appeal. Further, in criminal matters the right to appeal is subject only to leave of either the divisional court or the House of Lords and is not restricted by the ordinary requirements as to public importance which apply to criminal appeals.

Apart from this, the general form of *habeas corpus* procedure, unlike the form of procedure on the other prerogative writs, has been little altered since ancient times; *habeas corpus* remains a writ while the others have now become orders. It should be added that in these days *habeas corpus* is often used as a means of challenging administrative decisions which involve custody.

## B  FREEDOM OF PROPERTY

In days gone by the common law treated the right to property as sacrosanct: it was considered to be almost as inviolable as the right to personal liberty. Now this is no longer true. Although the courts will construe a statute which purports to destroy rights of property with the utmost strictness – especially if it gives no right to compensation – so many statutes have empowered public authorities and other bodies to acquire private land, and now even other property, compulsorily, that it is no longer true to say that our constitutional law safeguards the right to property. The principal restrictions upon property rights will be considered below.

## C  FREEDOM OF SPEECH, ASSOCIATION AND ASSEMBLY

The law does not prescribe what people *may* say or write or publish: the general rule is that anyone is free to express any views he likes; provided that he does not contravene the laws of defamation, sedition, obscenity, or blasphemy. Since 1695 there has been no censorship of the Press, though the government has at times (as in the Second World War) been given limited powers of censorship during national emergencies.

Thus, generally speaking, people are free to say or publish whatever they like; but there are certain statutory exceptions to this rule. The following examples may be given. The Official Secrets Acts 1911–1939, and 1989, amongst other things, make it an offence for anyone to divulge any official information which he has received from an officer of the Crown. The Incitement to Mutiny Act 1797, and the Incitement to Disaffection Act 1934, both create offences in connection with words or behaviour calculated to seduce members of the Forces from their allegiance, and the Police Act 1964, s 53, makes it an offence to act so as to cause disaffection amongst the members of any police force.

The Theatres Act 1968 – which abolished stage censorship – makes it an offence to give an obscene performance of a play unless the giving of such a performance can be justified as being for the public good on the ground of literary or other artistic merit. There is also a common law crime of indecency, ie of doing publicly anything which ordinary people would consider disgusting or shocking. Obscene publications are controlled by the Obscene Publications Act 1959 which makes it an offence to publish anything which tends to 'deprave and corrupt' people likely to read, see or hear it. As in the case of the Theatres Act, it is a defence under the 1959 Act to justify the publications upon the ground that it is for the 'public good on the ground that it is in the interests of science, literature, art or learning or other objects of general concern'. This defence has brought forth numerous cases in which surprising people have volunteered surprising 'expert' evidence about the nature of the 'public good'. But the courts have at least made it clear that sex is not *ejusdem generis* to 'science, etc' so as to come within the umbrella of 'objects of general concern'. By the Indecent Displays (Control) Act 1981 it is also an offence to display indecent matter in a public place.

Just as people are, in general, free to say and write what they like, so they are permitted to associate with whom they will. But there are also limits to the general right of free association. For instance, a combination of two or more persons may be an unlawful conspiracy.

Further, as in the case of freedom of speech, there are certain *statutory* limits to the right of free association. For example (in general), a combination of 20 or more persons for the carrying on of any trade or business will be unlawful unless they become incorporated, and 'monopolies' may now be restrained under certain circumstances. It may be added that, by the provisions of the Public Order Act 1936, s 1(1) it is unlawful at any public meeting or in any public place to wear a uniform signifying association with any political organization. This was framed to meet the menace of Sir Oswald Mosley's 'blackshirts' but it was more recently used against the Irish 'Provisionals' when it was held that the wearing of a black beret specifying allegiance to that cause amounted to the wearing of a uniform. By s 2(1) of the same Act it is, amongst other things, an offence for anyone to take part in the control or management of any association which is trained or equipped for the purpose of enabling its members to usurp the functions of the police, or of the armed forces of the Crown.

It cannot be said that there is any such thing as a general 'right' of *public* meeting. People who assemble upon the highway without permission will always be technically guilty of trespass to the owner of the highway (now usually a local authority); for the only *right* which the public have upon the highway is a right of passage. Moreover, people who assemble or process upon the highway will usually be technically guilty of causing an 'obstruction': and if they create a nuisance by picketing people's premises (otherwise than in contemplation of furtherance of a trade dispute) they may be liable to a claim in nuisance.

The Public Order Act 1986 created a number of new offences in the field of public disorder.

By s 1 a new offence of riot is brought into being. The section provides that '(1) Where 12 or more persons who are present together use or threaten unlawful violence for a *common purpose* and the conduct of them (taken together) is such as *would cause a person of reasonable firmness present at the scene to fear for his personal safety*, each of the persons using unlawful violence *for the common purpose* is guilty of riot. (2) It is *immaterial* whether or not the 12 or more use or threaten unlawful violence *simultaneously*. (3) The common purpose may be inferred from conduct. (4) No person of reasonable firmness need *actually* be, or be likely to be, present at the scene. (5) Riot may be committed in *private* as well as public places.' The requirement that the violence must be 'unlawful' means that there must be no legal justification for it – such as, for example, self-defence.

Section 2 creates an offence of 'violent disorder': '(1) Where *three or more persons* who are present together *use or threaten unlawful violence* and the conduct of them (taken together) is such as would cause *a person of reasonable firmness present at the scene to fear for his personal safety*, each of the persons using or threatening unlawful violence is guilty of violent disorder. (2) It is *immaterial* whether or not the three or more use or threaten unlawful violence *simultaneously*. (3) No person of reasonable firmness need *actually be*, or be likely to be present at the scene. (4) Violent disorder may be committed in *private* as well as in public places.'

Section 3 creates a new offence of 'affray': '(1) A person is guilty of affray *if he uses or threatens unlawful violence* towards another and his conduct is such as would cause *a person of reasonable firmness present at the scene to fear for his personal safety*. (2) Where *two or more persons* use or threaten the unlawful violence it is the conduct of them *taken together* that must be considered . . . (3) For the purposes of this section a threat cannot be made by the *use of words alone*. (4) No person of reasonable firmness need *actually be, or be likely to be present at the scene*. (5) Affray may be committed in private as well as in public places.'

Section 4 creates an offence of 'fear or provocation of violence'. '(1) A person is guilty of an offence if he: (a) uses towards another person *threatening, abusive or insulting words or behaviour*, or (b) distributes or displays to another person *any writing, sign or other visible represent-ation* which is threatening, abusive or insulting, *with intent to cause that person to believe that immediate unlawful violence will be used* against him or another by any person, or *to provoke the immediate use of unlawful violence* by that person or another, or whereby that person is likely to believe that such violence will be used or it is likely that such violence will be provoked. (2) An offence under this section may be committed in a public or a *private place*.' The offence will not, however, be committed where both parties are inside a dwelling.

Section 5 deals with the causing of harassment, alarm or distress. '(1) A person is guilty of an offence if he: (a) uses threatening, abusive or insulting words or behaviour, or disorderly behaviour, or (b) displays any writing, sign or other visible representation which is threatening, abusive or insulting, within the hearing or sight of a person likely to be caused harassment, alarm or distress thereby. (2) An offence under this section may be committed in a public or a private place . . .' Here there is the same exception as to dwellings as in s 4. 'It is a defence for the accused to prove (a) that he had no reason to believe that there was any person within hearing or sight who was likley to be caused harassment, alarm or distress, or (b) that he was in a dwelling and had no reason to believe that the words or behaviour used, or the writing, sign or other visible representation displayed, would be heard or seen by a person outside that or any other dwelling, or (c) that his conduct was reasonable.'

Section 6 defines the necessary *intents* to support a prosecution. *Riot* can only be committed if the accused intends to use violence or is aware that his conduct may be violent. In the cases of violent *disorder* or *affray* the accused must intend violence or be aware that his conduct may be violent. In the case of an offence under s 4 the accused must intend the words, etc, to be threatening etc or he must be aware that they may be threatening, etc. In the case of an offence under s 5 the accused must intend the words, etc, to be threatening, etc, or he must be aware that they may be. By s 6(5) 'A person whose awareness is impaired by *intoxication* shall *be taken to be aware* of that of which he would be aware if not intoxicated, *unless* he shows *either* that his intoxication was not self-induced *or* that it was caused solely by the taking or administration of a substance in the course of medical treatment.' 'Intoxication' for this purpose is (s 6(6)) 'any intoxication, whether caused by drink, drugs or other means . . .'

Sections 11–16 of the Act govern rights of *assembly*. In respect of *processions* it is provided that written notice must normally be given to the police of any proposal to hold a public procession. If the senior police officer reasonably believes that a particular procession may result in serious public disorder, serious damage to property, or serious disruption to the life of the community, or that the purpose of the procession is intimidation of others he may impose such conditions on the holding of it as appear to be necessary. Further, if the chief officer of police reasonably believes that, because of particular circumstances existing in any district the imposition of conditions will not be sufficient to prevent the holding of public processions in that district from resulting in serious public disorder he may apply to the council of the district for an order (for a period not exceeding three months) prohibiting the holding of all public processions in that district. In respect of public *assemblies* if a senior police officer reasonably believes that the assembly may result in serious public disorder, etc, he may impose conditions as to the place at which the assembly may be held, its maximum duration or the number of persons who may constitute it. A 'public' assembly means for this purpose an assembly of 20 or more persons in a public place which is wholly or partially open to the air.

Sections 30–38 of the Act make provisions about 'exclusion orders'. These are orders which the court may make upon convicting a person of certain offences connected with football matches. These offences include any offence committed at a prescribed football match, offences involving violence (or the threat of it) while the accused was on a journey to or from a football match, and certain other offences committed on such a journey. The matches concerned are matches prescribed by the Home Secretary. The effect of an order is to make it an offence for the person concerned to enter any premises for the purpose of attending a prescribed match. But no such order may be made unless the court is satisfied that the making of it would help to prevent violence or disorder in connection with the prescribed match. It is also to be noted that s 37 gives the Home Secretary power to extend such orders to sporting events other than football.

Section 61 of the Criminal Justice and Public Order Act 1994 is designed to strenghten the provisions of the 1986 Act in that a policeman can now direct people to leave land where the occupier has unsuccessfully taken steps to ask them to do so, and any of them has caused damage, or if they have been threatening, abusive or insulting, or if, between them, they have six or more vehicles on the land. It is a crime to refuse to leave and it is also a crime to return as a trespasser within three months. Plainly the targets here are 'hippies' and 'travellers'. Other newsgatherers' targets are affected by the 1994 Act too: those preparing for or attending a 'rave' can be removed and those trespassing on land in order to disrupt or obstruct a lawful activity can be charged with the crime of 'aggravated trespass', so 'hunt saboteurs' and those who seek to obstruct road-building bulldozers face new hazards.

The Public Order Act 1986, apart from codifying the offences of 'riot' 'violent disorder' and 'affray', contains, as we have noted, a number of offences connected with the control of public meetings and processions in general and the stirring up of racial hatred in particular. 'Racial hatred' in this context means 'hatred against a group of persons in Great Britain defined by reference to colour, race, nationality (including citizenship) or ethnic or national origins'. It is an offence to use 'threatening, abusive or insulting words or behaviour' or to display 'any written material which is threatening, abusive or insulting' if the user 'intends thereby to stir up racial hatred, or . . . racial hatred is likely to be stirred up thereby'.

## D  EQUALITY

As well as liberty, equality has of late become a headstone of the constitution. In theory, at least, the common law has always treated all men alike; the courts have been open to everyone without distinction. In recent years, however, a universal movement towards the recognition of 'equal rights' for everyone has taken place. This movement found powerful support in the United States and, more important, it underlies the basic philosophy of the Treaty of Rome and prompted the creation of the European Court of Human Rights. In England it also gave rise to legislation, which must now be considered, in the fields of equal pay, sex discrimination and race relations. This field of the law is rapidly becoming increasingly complex – mainly on account of the impact of Community law – and only the briefest account can be given of it here.

**Equal pay**
This is the offspring of the Equal Pay Act 1970 (hereafter 'EPA') – as amended by the Sex Discrimination Act 1975. The EPA ensures equal pay for women and men who are engaged upon 'like work'. As amended, it requires that, whether expressly or by implication of law, every contract of employment at an establishment in Great Britain must have an 'equality clause' (s 1(1)). The essence of this clause is that *pay* shall be equal as between the sexes *and* (as amended) that no term in the contract shall be *'less favourable'* to one sex than to the other. 'Equal pay' means equal pay for work of *equal value* in the same employment; but it need not be work of the same kind. Disputes about equality clauses are tried in the first instance by *industrial tribunals*.

It is, however, very important to note that Art 119 of the Treaty of Rome provides that 'each Member State shall . . . maintain the application of the principle that men and women should receive equal pay for equal work' and goes on to define 'pay' and 'equal pay without discrimination of sex'. The article creates 'enforceable Community rights' so that to any extent that it conflicts with the English legislation it rewrites it by virtue of the European Communities Act 1972, s 2(1). Thus an individual who complains of inequality can claim direct enforcement of any rights he has under it.

**Sex discrimination**
The Sex Discrimination Act 1975 (as amended by the Sex Discrimination Act 1986) inhibits *'sex discrimination'*, discrimination by reference to *marital status*, and *'discrimination by way of victimization'*.

'Sex discrimination' includes treating people *'less favourably'* than others *on the ground of sex* (s 1(1)(*a*)), and it also (indirect discrimination) prohibits the imposition of requirements or conditions upon people which are such that the proportion of members of one sex who can comply with them are 'considerably smaller' than the proportion of members of the other (s 1(1)(*b*)(i)). This might, for example, be the case where applications for employment are limited to the age of between 17 and 28: for, so it has been argued, during that period women are busy rearing children. But s 1(1)(*b*)(i) which applies whether the condition is *intended* as discriminatory or no (though in the absence of intention no damages can be claimed – s 68(3)), is qualified by the provisions that such conditions may be *justified* and that they must be such as to be *to the detriment* of the complainant. Where a person is *treated differently according to marital status* (eg married man/bachelor) the treatment of people of the opposite sex is to be comparable (eg married woman/spinster) (s 1 (2)). Section 2(2) archly rules that it is not discriminatory to give special treatment to a woman on the grounds of pregnancy.

'Discrimination by marital status' (s 3) is only prohibited within the field of *employment*: in that area there must be no discrimination on the grounds of *marriage*. 'Discrimination by way of victimization' (s 4) means discriminating against people because they have (amongst other things) brought *bona fide* proceedings to vindicate their rights under the Act.

Such are the statutory definitions of 'discrimination'. We must now consider the circumstances in which it is rendered unlawful. These are prescribed in Parts II and III of the Act.

Part II of the Act makes it unlawful to discriminate in the field of *employment* from the moment of application to the moment of dismissal; though employment requiring *occupational qualifications* is exempted; thus the role of Don Juan may be reserved for men. Partnerships of *six* or more are caught, and trade unions and qualifying bodies (eg the Law Society); also the police. And now it has even become discriminatory to refuse to let a woman work below the ground in a mine.

Part III applies the discrimination law to *education (Birmingham City Council v Equal Opportunities Commission* [1989] 1 All ER 769) – with exemption for 'single sex' establishments – and to the *public supply of goods, facilities and services* (eg restaurants, transport, etc). Thus in *Gill v El Vino Co Ltd* [1983] QB 425 it was held that there had been discrimination at a restaurant where female customers were excluded from the area of the bar. House disposal is caught, with exemption for sales which are unadvertised and without an agent. Section 33 contains a self-interested exemption of the constitutions, organization and administration of political parties. Other exemptions include hospitals, places of worship and services (*sic*) which are such that a person 'might be seriously embarrassed by the presence of someone of the other sex'. Discriminatory *advertising* is banned and s 38(3) contains the well-known statement that 'use of a job desciption with a sexual connotation (such as . . . "salesgirl") shall be taken to indicate an intention to discriminate'.

The Act brought into being the *Equal Opportunities Commission* ('EOC') which is empowered to work towards equality, to keep under review the working of the Act and to make investigations and reports. Discrimination is made unlawful but its enforcement is solely a matter for remedies prescribed by the Act. In the field of *employment*, enforcement (after conciliation procedures) is through *industrial tribunals*, in other fields through *county courts*: compensation may be obtained in the former and the ordinary common law remedies in the latter. Moreover, after a 'non-discrimination' notice has been served by the EOC upon an offender it may, for a period of five years, be used as a ground for an injuction.

### Race relations

The Race Relations Act 1976 ('RRA') follows the SDA so closely that it may be described briefly by reference to the latter. The RRA creates two sorts of discrimination: '*racial discrimination*' and '*discrimination by way of victimization*'.

*Mutatis mutandis,* s 1 of the RRA defines 'racial discrimination' in much the same way that the SDA defines sex discrimination (see above).

It makes it unlawful to treat people *'less favourably'* on *'racial grounds'* – ie on grounds of *'colour, race, nationality or ethnic or national origins'*. In *Mandla v Dowell Lee* [1983] 2 AC 548 the House of Lords held that the Sikhs form an 'ethnic' group, principally because they have a shared history and a cultural tradition of their own. On the other hand, in *Crown Suppliers (PSA) v Dawkins* [1993] IRLR 284 it was held that Rastafarians are not a goup defined by ethnic origin within the terms of the RRA. By s 2(1) *segregation* is made a form of 'less favourable' treatment, save that 'racial grounds' replace grounds of sex. Section 1(i) (*b*) of the RRA follows s 1(i)(*b*) of the SDA exactly – so that, eg a condition requiring a certain average height (which could not, for example, be attained by people of the smaller races) might be discriminatory. Section 2 of the RRA makes *discrimination by victimization* unlawful exactly on the lines of s 4 of the SDA.

Part II of the RRA (employment) follows Part II of the SDA closely and, in general includes similar *exemption* (see above), and employment of seamen recruited abroad (s 9) is exempted. Part III, again, contains similar forbidden fields and similar exemptions: though the important s 25 bans discrimination in *all* associations of *not less than 24 members*: this, contrary though it would appear to be to the very nature of such associ- ations, catches clubs. But, curiously, s 26 permits 'associations designed to enable the benefits of membership (whatever they may be) to be enjoyed by persons of a *particular racial group* defined otherwise than by reference to *colour*'. Thus, it seems, an American 'Negro Club' would be lawful, but not a 'Black American Club'. Advertisements, again, fall within the ban, including advertisements for employment abroad; except that it is lawful for such advertisements to solicit *nationals*: thus 'British' for India would be lawful, 'Asiatics' not. *Foster parents* (s 23) are exempted (s 39) so are promotors of *sport*, but *only* if they discriminate by reference to nationality, place of birth (eg *Yorkshire born* for Yorkshire cricket) or residence.

It should be noted that the question to be decided is not necessarily whether the discrimination is aimed at the complainant. There may still be discrimination if it is aimed at someone else. Thus there was held to be discrimination where an employee was dismissed because he *refused* to discriminate.

The enforcement provisions are similar to those of the SDA (see above) except that the relevant Commission is the *Commission for Racial Equality*.

# Chapter 6

# Criminal law

In this chapter we will first consider the general principles of criminal responsibility, then outline the elements of a number of specific crimes, and finally discuss the law relating to compensation for criminal injuries.

## 1 The general principles of criminal responsibility

### A THE NATURE OF A CRIME

Crimes are offences against the State; in this, as we shall see, they differ from breaches of contract or of trust and from torts, which are all either solely or primarily wrongs to individuals. The object of criminal proceedings is to punish the offender or to ensure, by some means other than punishment, that he does not repeat his offence: the object of civil proceedings is to satisfy the claim of the party injured.

Since crimes are offences against the State, the State takes the initiative in prosecuting criminals: the Crown is in theory, though usually not in practice, always responsible for conducting prosecutions, and criminal proceedings are conducted in the name of the Queen. Thus if Jones commits a murder the ensuing trial will be called the case of *R* (an abbreviation of '*Regina*'=The Queen) *v Jones*. On the other hand if Jones merely breaks his contract with Smith, who sues him, this civil action will be called *Smith v Jones*, for in this case the Crown has no interest in the matter beyond seeing that justice is done between the parties.

It must not be imagined that because crimes differ from civil wrongs the same set of facts can never constitute both a crime and a civil wrong, for criminal law and civil law overlap at many points. Thus if X takes Y's motor car without his consent X's act may, in many kinds of circumstances, constitute both the crime of theft and the tort of conversion.

## B   CRIMINAL RESPONSIBILITY

Since criminal proceedings may result in punishment it is only just that the mere doing of a prohibited act should not generally be held to constitute a crime. The common law always insisted that there shall be no conviction unless the accused had a 'guilty mind' ('*mens rea*'). This requirement is commonly expressed in the words of the ancient maxim: '*Actus non facit reum nisi mens sit rea*' ('The mere doing of an act will not constitute guilt unless there be a guilty intent').

The term 'guilty mind', or 'guilty intent', when used in this context, is not capable of precise definition; for the courts have, from the earliest times, applied common sense rules in determining when such a state of mind exists. Thus, if a person commits a criminal act, such as poisoning another person's food, and there is evidence from the surrounding circumstances, or from his declared motives, that he *intended* to kill the other person his guilty state of mind may reasonably be inferred. So too, an act in itself comparatively innocent may argue a 'guilty' state of mind if it is one which is clearly calculated to lead to evil consequences. For instance where a prostitute buried her child beneath a pile of leaves and a kite soon afterwards struck at it and killed it, it was held that she was guilty of murdering the child; for kites were common in England in those days, and the risk that the child would be attacked was so great that it was clear that the woman intended the death (*The Harlot's Case* (1560) Crompton's Justice, 24).

It cannot be pretended, however, that the formulation of a test for determining the existence of a guilty intention (as opposed to the formulation of the nature of the required intent itself) is a simple matter. For intention is a state of mind incapable of positive proof; and yet the prosecution must normally establish it. Needless to say, the delicacy of this operation has led to controversy. There are those who believe – and indeed it has at the highest level been ruled – that it ought to suffice to establish *objectively* that what the accused brought about (eg the death of the victim) was a natural consequence of what he did, so that he must be *taken* to have intended the death. But there are also those who believe that the judgment ought to be *subjective*; that it ought to be established that the intent was actually *there*. Since of course the latter task is flatly impossible the conflict between the opposing views is really no more than one of degree of proof. However, for the present at least the argument appears to be settled by the Criminal Justice Act 1967, s 8 in favour of the latter view. The section provides that 'A court or jury, in determining whether a person has committed an offence: (a) shall *not* be bound in law to infer that he intended or foresaw a result of his actions by reason only of its being a natural or probable consequence of those actions: but (b) shall decide whether he *did intend* or foresee that result *by reference to all the evidence*, drawing such inferences from the evidence as appear proper in the circumstances.'

This statutory pontification is calculated to engender further controversies. At present it can be celebrated with an obvious logical corollary. This arises from the controversial decision in *DPP v Morgan* [1975] AC 182 where the House of Lords held that where a belief in some state of affairs is part of the essence of the offence charged, non-belief will negative the intent even if it be wholly *unreasonable*. The case was one of rape in which neither the jury nor anyone else gave the defendant credit for the (unreasonable) non-belief in the woman's lack of consent – or, to put it positively, the unreasonable belief that she had consented: so the conviction stood and no harm was done. And it may be that the ruling should be treated as part of the peculiarities of the crime of rape in which lack of consent must be proved. For the effect of the Sexual Offences (Amendment) Act 1976, s 1(2), see p 182.

Whenever a specific intent forms a part of the offence charged – ie it is the element of *mens rea* in relation to that offence – it must be *proved*: thus where a man dressed up in a cassock, and read through a marriage service in a church because he had been asked to do so by the 'husband' who had told him falsely that he and the 'wife' were already married and merely wished to re-enact the ceremony to please her mother, he was held not to have contravened a statutory provision forbidding the knowing and wilful solemnization of marriages by those pretending to be in holy orders. In the circumstances there was no real pretence and no real intent to act illegally.

This general rule which requires not merely an '*actus reus*' (a 'guilty act') but also '*mens rea*' before a person can be convicted of a crime is, however, subject to qualifications.

First, every man is *presumed* to intend the natural consequences of his act; for, as has already been remarked, it is impossible to prove the existence of a state of mind conclusively. Hence, no one can escape the consequences of committing a cold-blooded murder simply by saying that he did not intend to do it; though, as has just been explained, the question of intention will be judged subjectively (Criminal Justice Act 1967, s 8). But it must, nevertheless, be repeated that the *prosecution must normally prove its whole case beyond reasonable doubt*. Hence if at the close of a case, upon review of all the evidence adduced on either side, the court or jury are left in reasonable doubt whether the accused really intended to commit the criminal act charged, he *must be acquitted*. This proposition may be illustrated by *Woolmington v DPP* [1935] AC 462. In that case W killed his wife by shooting her and he was charged with murder. Some of the evidence at the trial supported the inference that the shooting was *accidental*. The trial judge directed the jury that once the prosecution had proved that the accused had killed his wife, a presumption arose that he had murdered her, and that it was the business of the defence to furnish evidence capable of displacing this presumption. The House of Lords held that the direction was wrong, because, since there was, *inter alia*, evidence before the court from which the inference that the shooting was in fact *accidental* might reasonably be drawn, it was the duty of the prosecution to displace this inference by adducing sufficient evidence of an intent to kill. And it should be added that (as has already been explained: above, p 68) a similar burden will lie upon the prosecution where the evidence as a whole leaves reasonable doubt as to the existence of other grounds of justification or mitigation, such as self defence, automatism (p 166), provocation (p 177) or reasonable doubt as to the validity of an alibi. Thus the harshness of the presumption that a man intends the natural consequences of his acts is often counter-balanced by the cardinal presumption of English law that a man is *presumed* to be innocent until the prosecution have proved him guilty beyond reasonable doubt. It must, however, be noted that where insanity is raised as a defence (p 164) or a statutory defence which expressly or by implication reverses the burden of proof is invoked the burden will lie on the *defendant*.

In the second place, although the common law always insisted upon the presence of '*mens rea*', certain statutes, in creating criminal offences, have dispensed with this requirement and made some offences '*absolute*', ie punishable in the absence of '*mens rea*'. There are many such statutes in force at the present time. The Legislature tends to dispense with the requirement of '*mens rea*' in the case of statutory offences (such as the offence of unlawful possession of firearms under the Firearms Act 1968) for which the penalty is small, the damage to the public occasioned by their commission is great, and the state of mind of the accused would be exceptionally difficult to establish with certainty. Examples of statutory offences of this nature are, or have been, the offence of supplying specified medicinal products without a prescription of a medical practitioner, contrary to the Medicines Act 1968, s 58(2) (*a*), and failure by a bankrupt to account for any substantial part of his estate under the provisions (now repealed) of the Bankruptcy Act 1914, s 157(1)(*c*). In *Sweet v Parsley* [1970] AC 132, however, the conviction of a schoolteacher under s 5 (*b*) of the Dangerous Drugs Act 1965 for having been 'concerned in the management of premises used for the purpose of smoking cannabis' was quashed upon the ground that the accused neither knew nor had the means of knowing of the objectionable habits of her 'beatnik' tenants. The House of Lords stressed that offences must not be construed as 'absolute' unless there is adequate reason to suppose that Parliament intended to make them so.

The principle that '*mens rea*' must normally exist before criminal responsibility can be imputed receives further illustration from the fact that normally, in the criminal law (as opposed to the law of torts) a person will not be held responsible for the acts of his servants or agents if they are carried out without his authority. This rule is, however, subject to one exception, even at common law – the case of public nuisance – and to many statutory exceptions created in the public interest or for some other reason. For example, the Licensing Act 1964, s 161(1) provides that if 'the holder of a justices' on-licence knowingly sells or supplies intoxicating liquor to unauthorized persons he shall be guilty of an offence'. It has been held, more than once under the provisions of this and similar statutes, that a licensee may be held liable where the prohibited acts are committed by his servants or agents without his knowledge; especially where he has delegated the management of the establishment to them. The reason for this strict construction has thus been pithily explained: 'If this were not the rule', said an eminent judge, 'a publican would never be convicted. He would take care always to be out of the way'. It must be added that the general rule that *mens rea* is required may be displaced where a statutory offence concerns an issue of social concern, eg public safety. But even in that case *mens rea* will still be required unless it can be established that the imposition of strict liability would promote the objects of the statute.

Finally, if it is in doubt whether the accused's act or omission *caused* the injury or damage complained of the burden of establishing that it did lies upon the prosecution. See p 180.

## C GENERAL EXEMPTIONS FROM CRIMINAL RESPONSIBILITY

Because the law generally insists upon the presence of '*mens rea*' in order to establish guilt one would expect the presence of certain factors, such as Mistake, Duress, Self-Defence, Necessity and Incapacity to affect criminal liability to a greater or lesser extent. The first four of these factors will be considered in this section; Incapacity will be considered in the next.

### MISTAKE

It will usually be a defence to a criminal charge for the accused to prove that he acted under a mistake of fact. But this rule is subject to three limitations: (a) The mistake must be such that, had the true facts been as the accused believed them to be, he would not have been guilty of the offence in question. Thus it will not be a defence for a man who is accused of stealing a gold watch to prove that he thought it was a silver one or that it was some other valuable object; but it will be a defence, as will appear, for him to prove that he honestly believed, however unreasonably (contrary to the true facts) that the watch was his own. (b) Mistake can only be relied upon where the alleged error relates to some fact or facts essential to the charge. Thus in *R v Hibbert* (1869) LR 1 CCR 184, H seduced a girl of 14. He was charged, under the Offences Against the Person Act 1861, s 55, with the offence of taking an unmarried girl under the age of 16 out of the possession of her parents. There was no evidence to show that he knew that the girl had any parents, and she was in fact at the time in the custody of her father. H was convicted, but the conviction was subsequently quashed (ie annulled on appeal) because on the facts as he believed them to be H had committed no offence; for he did not know that the girl had any parents. In *R v Prince* (1875) LR 2 CCR 154, on the other hand, P's conviction upon a charge under the same section was upheld: he had reasonable grounds for believing that a girl whom he seduced was over 16 (though in fact she was not) but he did, nevertheless, know that she was in the custody of her father. His mistake as to her age had no relevance to the offence charged; he had made no mistake in relation to the crucial fact that he had taken her out of her father's care. (c) In the case of an 'absolute' offence mistake is no defence. Thus in *R v Miller* [1975] 2 All ER 974, it was held that a person charged with driving on the road while disqualified cannot escape liability by proving that he honestly (but mistakenly) believed that he was on private land.

Mistake of *law* is no defence: the general rule is that no man is permitted to excuse himself by asserting that he thought his unlawful act was lawful. The reason for this is similar to the reason for the rule '*ignorantia juris haud excusat*' (ignorance of law is no excuse): in either case knowledge must be presumed, for otherwise people could always escape liability by pretending to the lack of it. Nevertheless, the second rule is sometimes relaxed where ignorance is inevitable: as in a case where a deportation order is made against an individual without publication of any kind. An unpublished law is one which a person cannot possibly know.

## DURESS

It is a defence to a criminal charge to prove that the offence was committed under the compulsion of some other person. The defence of duress is not available to a person charged with *murder*, whether as principal (the actual killer) or as principal in the second degree (the aider and abettor – see p 169). Duress, whether by physical compulsion or by means of threat, is available as a defence only if what is done or threatened is such that it did cause the accused to act as he did and that in so doing he acted as a person of reasonable self-control would have done. It is not essential that the threat should be immediate: thus where a witness committed perjury because a ruffian in court at the time had threatened to 'beat her up' afterwards if she told the truth duress was held to be a good defence. Moreover, if a person joins a gang or organization which he knows may bring pressure on him to commit a crime he will not be excused if, subsequently, he does commit one under pressure. Although it is likely that this rule will be abolished, a wife who commits a crime, other than treason or murder, in her husband's presence and under his 'coercion' may generally escape liability by establishing the coercion. The word probably signifies something less dramatic than the kind of duress by threats just mentioned; it probably includes mere mental domination. It is to be noted that while it is for the wife to prove the coercion, once 'duress' is raised it is for the prosecution to displace the presumption of innocence which it raises.

It seems uncertain how far it will afford a defence to a member of the forces to plead 'superior orders'. The correct rule probably is that this defence will only avail where the act which the accused was ordered to do was not manifestly unlawful. A soldier, for example, who is ordered to shoot a prisoner, otherwise than by way of lawful execution, would therefore be ill-advised to carry out the order.

## SELF-DEFENCE

The reasonable use of force in defence of oneself or of others, or in defence of one's property, may excuse a crime; even homicide. But the success of the defence will depend upon whether the degree of force employed was reasonable in the circumstances: thus if you attack me with a pin I am not justified in retaliating by throwing vitriol at you and if, although your dog is chasing them, my sheep are in no danger of *immediate* harm I am not justified in shooting it. What is 'reasonable' is a question of fact and it may indeed be one which varies with the climate of contemporary opinion: for instance it is doubtful whether the proposition made in *R v Hussey* (1924) 18 Cr App Rep 160 that a man is entitled to kill anyone seeking unlawfully to dispossess him of his home would be accepted today. Yet moments of extreme danger may justify the instinctive taking of measures which, apart from the agony of the moment, would otherwise be unreasonable. Further, if the probability of violence to the defendant is contemplated by him (whether reasonably or not) although not actually imminent, this may provide an excuse for doing some otherwise unlawful act (such as making a petrol bomb) intended to counter the apprehended violence. (See *A-G's Reference (No 2 of 1983)* [1984] QB 456.) On the other hand a mistake as to the degree of force necessary will not excuse if it be induced by voluntary intoxication. A defendant is entitled to rely on a plea of self-defence though he is unable to prove that he demonstrated unwillingness to fight; though such demonstration may well argue that he was acting in self-defence rather than for some other reason. Once this defence is raised it is for the prosecution to prove that the defendant was *not* defending himself, not for him to establish that he was.

## NECESSITY

There is little English authority on the defence of 'necessity', ie compulsion arising from circumstances, as opposed to the intervention of another human being. A man who is pursued by wolves should therefore resist the temptation of killing his companion and delaying the attack upon himself by throwing the corpse behind him; especially since in the one important decision on the matter, the colourful case of *R v Dudley and Stephens* (1884) 14 QBD 273, starving shipwrecked sailors who killed a cabin boy in order to feed upon his body were held to be guilty of murder.

It should finally be noted that in every case where there is some extenuating factor which does not provide a recognized ground of exemption, it is always possible for the court to mitigate the punishment according to the circumstances, and in extreme cases there is always the possibility of commutation or pardon. For instance in the case last cited the sailors were sentenced to death, but the sentence was subsequently commuted to one of six months' imprisonment.

## D   INCAPACITY

Certain persons are treated in law, to a greater or lesser extent, as being incapable of criminal responsibility: People of Unsound Mind, Drunken Persons, Minors and Corporations.

### 1   UNSOUNDNESS OF MIND

This may negative criminal responsibility in a number of ways. There are two main aspects to be considered; either the condition of the accused may be such that it amounts to insanity or it may be that he is suffering from such mental abnormality as to diminish his responsibility.

*Insanity* may excuse at three possible stages. First, during custody before trial: when this happens the Home Secretary is entitled under the provisions of the Mental Health Act 1983, provided that, amongst other things, he considers it in the public interest so to do, to have the accused detained in hospital. In which case of course, unless he recovers, he will not be tried at all. In the second place, although brought to trial the accused may be found unfit to plead. Here the issue is whether he is capable of understanding the conduct of the trial: that question must be tried by a specially empanelled jury. If he is then found unfit the court must either (a) order his admission to a mental hospital, or (b) make a guardianship order, a supervision and treatment order or an order of absolute discharge unless the charge is one of murder where (a) is the only option.

In the third place insanity may be pleaded as a *defence to the crime charged*. In this sense 'insanity' was defined in the well-known rules laid down by the judges in *M'Naghten's Case* (1843) 10 CL & Fin 200. These rules may be summarized thus:

(*a*) Every person is presumed to be sane until the contrary is proved.

(*b*) It is a defence to prove that, at the time of the commission of the act constituting the offence charged, the accused was labouring under such a defect of reason, from disease of the mind, as not to know the nature and quality of his act, or (if he did know this) that what he was doing was wrong.

(*c*) Where a criminal act is committed by a man under some insane delusion as to the surrounding facts, which conceals from him the true nature of the act he is doing, he is under the same degree of responsibility as if the facts were as he imagined them to be.

Normally, as we have seen, the burden of proof lies on the prosecution throughout a criminal trial, but the presumption of sanity creates an exception to this rule; for where insanity is pleaded the *defence* must establish on a *balance of probabilities* that the accused was insane.

When at the trial of an accused person the jury find him to have been insane within the meaning of the *M'Naghten Rules* at the time when he committed the crime charged, a special verdict of 'not guilty by reason of insanity' will be returned. Until 1991, the accused had to be ordered to be detained until the Home Secretary was satisfied he was no longer a danger to the public. The Criminal Procedure (Insanity and Unfitness to Plead) Act 1991 substitutes new provisions in s 5 of the Criminal Procedure (Insanity) Act 1964 and provides that the judge may either (a) order admission to a hospital or (b) make a guardianship order, a supervision and treatment order or order an absolute discharge. If the charge is one of murder, (a) is once again the only available option. Until recently, a finding of insanity being regarded as an acquittal, there was no appeal against the verdict. This was unsatisfactory because not only did the finding condemn the accused to indefinite confinement but it also precluded the possibility of his succeeding upon some other defence (eg alibi) which he might have had. For these and other reasons s 12 of the Criminal Appeal Act 1968, subject to safeguards, now provides a right of appeal to the Court of Appeal and thence to the House of Lords.

*Uncontrollable impulse* is not recognized as a defence in English law. But proof that the accused acted under such an impulse may be a relevant matter to consider because impulsive acts are symptomatic of some forms of insanity. Hence proof of impulsive action may sometimes be relevant to establish such disease of the mind as rendered the accused incapable of knowing the nature and quality of his acts or that they were wrong.

The defence of *diminished responsibility* was introduced in England by the Homicide Act 1957, s 2. It is specifically a defence to a *murder* charge, and if successfully established it has the effect of reducing the conviction from one for murder to one for manslaughter.

This defence will be established where it can be proved on behalf of the accused, on a *balance of probabilities*, that he 'was suffering from such abnormality of mind (whether arising from a condition of arrested or retarded development of mind, or any inherent causes, or induced by disease or injury) as substantially impaired his mental responsibility for his acts and omissions in doing or being a party to the killing'. It is the duty of the jury to consider the issue broadly and without reference to the 'legal' insanity of the *M'Naghten Rules*; in effect, in the majority of cases, they must ask themselves 'Is the accused without being insane, nevertheless on the borderline of insanity?' Medical evidence will be highly relevant but it need not be accepted by the jury as conclusive. Here again, though uncontrollable impulse is no defence, proof of its existence may yet be relevant because it may suggest a state of diminished responsibility. Where, in a murder trial, diminished responsibility is raised as a defence the prosecution may adduce evidence of *insanity*, and where insanity is raised, evidence of *diminished responsibility* (Criminal Procedure (Insanity) Act 1964, s 6). Further, if the defence *pleads* to a *murder* charge that the defendant is a person of diminished responsibility and the plea is supported by medical evidence a plea of guilty to *manslaughter* may be accepted.

Akin to the above defences is the plea of *automatism*. There is no doubt that when a person commits a crime while his mind is in a state of suspense he will not, at least in general, be held responsible for it. Instances are where, at any rate provided that his condition came about through no fault of his own, a man kills another while he is in an hypnotic trance or where he unwittingly assaults another person after insulin has been administered to him. But for this defence to succeed a reasonable foundation for it must be established – such as evidence that the accused was in a trance: normally obviously the mere statement by the accused that his mind was 'a blank' would not be enough. It has recently been stated in *A-G's Reference (No 2 of 1992)* [1994] 4 All ER 683 that a state of 'impaired consciousness' is not enough – there must be a total destruction of voluntary control on the part of the accused. But once such a foundation has been established it will rest upon the prosecution to prove that the act was in fact voluntary if a conviction is to be obtained. The difference between 'automatism' and 'insanity' as defences is that the latter rests upon the fact of *disease*, such as epilepsy, while the former arises from some external factor, such as drugs. Of course it must be observed that where the case is one of insanity the special verdict of 'not guilty by reason of insanity' must be returned, resulting in detention for the public safety, or the making of one of the alternative orders mentioned above.

## 2    DRUNKEN PERSONS

In bye-gone days the law treated drunkenness (provided that it was self-induced) as no excuse for the commission of a crime, but rather as an aggravating circumstance: in the words of Sir Matthew Hale (1609–1676), 'by the laws of England (a drunken person) shall have no privilege by this voluntary contracted madness, but shall have the same judgment as if he were in his right senses'. But in modern times this harsh rule has been relaxed. In the first place, it is now recognized that excessive drunkenness may induce actual disease of the mind, as in the case of *delirium tremens*. Where actual disease is thus proved the accused will be treated in the same way as any other person of unsound mind, and the *M'Naghten Rules* will apply. In the second place, proof of drunkenness which induces a state of mind falling short of insanity may sometimes serve to negative the existence of some particular kind of intent necessary for the establishment of guilt. For instance, malice aforethought (p 176) being an essential element in the definition of the crime of murder, where the accused can be proved to have been so drunk at the time of the killing as not to be able to form any of the intents necessary to establish such malice he cannot be guilty of murder; though such a state of mind induced by the voluntary taking of drink or drugs will be no excuse in the case of a charge – such as one of assault – where no specific intent need be proved; nor will it be an excuse where recklessness, rather than intent, has to be established. But of course, the accused would be guilty of murder, whatever the effects of the alcohol, if he were first to form the intent to kill and then to get drunk in order to carry it out. It must be stressed that, in this defence again, the onus is on the prosecution under the *Woolmington* principle (p 159) – once there is some evidence before the court that the defendant was drunk, the prosecution must establish that, despite the drunkenness, he could form the necessary intent and it is not the duty of the defence to prove the reverse.

On the other hand, where the fact of drunkenness is *of itself* the essence of a charge (as in the case of 'driving under the influence' under s 4 of the Road Traffic Act 1988, or of driving with an undue proportion of alcohol in the blood under s 5 of the Act) it is, of course, useless to call in aid the very thing that constitutes the offence in order to attempt to prove the absence of intention. Further, provided that the accused is capable, at the time of the commission of the crime charged, of forming the appropriate intent it will be no excuse for him to show that alcohol affected his powers of self-control – induced him, for example, to give way to some violent passion to which he would not normally have succumbed. Thus we shall see that in certain circumstances homicide may be reduced from murder to manslaughter where it can be proved that the accused acted under provocation; but it will not avail him to show that, being drunk, he was more easily provoked than he would have been had he been sober.

Although (unlike the taking of alcoholic liquor) the taking of drugs is often *in itself* unlawful, the rules governing the general criminal responsibility of people affected by drugs are in general similar to those governing alcoholic intoxication.

## 3   MINORITY

Up to the age of *ten* no one can be held guilty of any criminal offence. A child of over ten and under *14* is *presumed* to be incapable of forming a criminal intent; but this presumption may be rebutted by evidence which proves that he knew that what he was doing was seriously wrong. The common law presumption that a boy under the age of 14 was incapable of sexual intercourse has been abolished by the Sexual Offences Act 1993, so it is now possible for such a person to be convicted of, for example, rape. It is interesting to note that the age of complete criminal incapacity at common law was seven years: it was raised by statute to eight and then, again, subject to the rebuttability of the presumption noted above, to ten in 1963. By contrast the age of majority, was, as has been seen, lowered by the Family Law Reform Act 1969 from 21 to 18. Up one end, down the other: a paradox?

The rules relating to the trial of juvenile offenders have already been mentioned.

## 4    CORPORATIONS

Under the old common law, when a large number of crimes were punishable by death, it was generally accepted that corporations could not be held liable for crimes committed by their servants or agents; for, as it was said, 'You cannot hang the common seal'. Further, until the passing of the Criminal Justice Act 1925, corporations could not be indicted.

In recent times there has, however, been an increasing tendency to hold corporations criminally responsible for the acts of their servants or agents committed in the course of their employment. They have, for example, been indicted for conspiracy and for infringement of tax regulations. How far the courts will go in thus removing corporate immunity in criminal matters still remains to be seen; it is clear that there must be some limit to the relaxation of the older rules, for the artificial nature of corporations precludes their imprisonment just as much as the hanging of them – indeed, they can only be punished by fine. Moreover, it is unlikely that the intention to commit such crimes as rape or murder will ever be imputed to corporations.

## E    THE CLASSIFICATION OF CRIMES

The distinction between *indictable* and *summary* offences has already been noted. Here it must be explained that until the coming into force of the Criminal Law Act 1967 (CLA) crimes were divided historically into three categories: *treason, felonies* and *misdemeanours* – in descending order of seriousness. Each class had special rules of procedure appropriate to it and certain rules of substantive law peculiar to it.

While making, as has been seen, a new distinction between 'arrestable' and other offences, the CLA (s 1) abolished the dichotomy between felonies and misdemeanours and made the law and practice relating to all offenders (save treason) that which had previously been applicable to misdemeanours. Treason thus remains separate, but, since the Act (s 12(6)) also equiparated trial procedure in treason to that of murder, the only important practical distinction between treason and other forms of crime is that it still retains special rules in relation to the degrees of guilt of those who participate in it. The question of participation now falls to be considered.

## F THE PARTIES TO A CRIME

There are a number of possible degrees of criminal participation. Let us take examples: (i) Suppose A and B combine jointly to commit a crime, eg, B holds C while A assaults him: clearly *both* are *guilty* as 'principals' in the act. (ii) Suppose B, without actually committing the crime, is present at the scene of it encouraging its commission; eg, B connives while A stabs C. (iii) Suppose B, without actually being on the scene, assists A in the preparation of the crime – lends him the knife to do the deed – or 'counsels or procures' the doing of it (Accessories and Abettors Act 1861, s 8, as amended). (iv) Suppose B, after the crime, assists A in concealing it; throws the knife into a pond after A's return. (v) Suppose while doing nothing active to help, and knowing nothing of the deed, B listens to A's story of his exploit after it is done and then takes no steps to expose A to the authorities. In all these cases: (i) actual participation; (ii) connivance; (iii) assistance in preparation; (iv) subsequent assistance; (v) concealment of knowledge of the crime – though less obviously in the remainder than in the first, B has in one way or another been a party to the crime. A's position is clear, but what about B's in every case except the first?

Formerly the law in this field was complicated by the fact that the position varied according to the classification of the crime committed, whether treason, felony or misdemeanour. The CLA having assimilated the law relating to felonies to that of misdemeanours, what we have to consider is what the rule would formerly have been had the crime in question been a misdemeanour. Treason, however, still stands apart.

## 1 CRIMES OTHER THAN TREASON

Referring to the above examples (omitting the first) the misdemeanour rule would have been, and the general rule now is, that where there is *active connivance* (ii) or assistance (iii) in preparation – '*aiding and abetting*' – B will be treated in law, like A, as *guilty of the crime*: except that technically B is not in these cases a 'principal' criminal. Where, however, B merely gives subsequent assistance (iv) or conceals his knowledge of the crime (v) he will now (though this used not to be so in the case of felony) be guilty of *no* crime *unless* he commits an '*arrestable offence*' (p 143) which comes within the following provisions of the CLA.

In the first place the CLA, s 4(1) enacts that 'Where a person has committed an arrestable offence, any person who, knowing or believing him to be guilty of the offence or of some other arrestable offence, does without lawful authority or reasonable excuse any act with intent to *impede his apprehension or prosecution* shall be guilty of an offence.' Thus mere connivance after the act will never be a crime, but the example of throwing away the knife would be – causing grievous bodily harm being an arrestable offence, and the concealing of the knife an act calculated to impede prosecution. There is, of course, no reason why the impeder should know the identity of the criminal. In the second place, the CLA, s 5(1) makes it a crime punishable with not more than two years' imprisonment for a person to accept or to agree to accept any *consideration* (other than making good any loss caused by the offence or making reasonable compensation for that loss) for *not disclosing information* about an arrestable offence which he knows or believes to have been committed. There may, however, be no prosecution for either of these offences without the consent of the Director of Public Prosecutions.

The position of the *aider and abettor* (ii) and (iii) can give rise to subtleties. For example, the abettor may sometimes be guilty of the offence while his principal is not. This position may be illustrated by the case of the man who instigates a 'rape' committed by another person who believes the woman to be consenting – and who thus is *not* guilty of rape while his abettor, who is aware of the lack of consent, is. Again, an abettor cannot be guilty of an offence graver than the offence actually committed by the principal: thus if C instigates B to assault A intending that B shall occasion serious harm to A and B merely commits a minor assault on A, despite C's intent he can only be convicted of unlawful wounding rather than of the more serious offence of wounding with intent to do grievous bodily harm. And finally, an interesting point was raised by *A-G's Reference (No 1 of 1975)* [1975] 2 All ER 684. Can a generous host who 'laces' the drink of a guest be convicted as abettor if the unfortunate guest is subsequently charged under the Road Traffic Act 1988, ss 4 or 5 (above)? The answer is 'Yes' he *may* be: but much must depend upon the circumstances – for instance it may be relevant that the guest is unaware of the fact that the drink has been laced and it must be established that the guest's condition at the time of arrest was in fact the result of the lacing. A further refinement about aiding and abetting is that a person may be guilty of it even if he did not know the exact nature of the crime committed by the principal provided that he did know that the latter intended to commit a crime of a similar kind. Thus in *DPP for Northern Ireland v Maxwell* [1978] 3 All ER 1140 the House of Lords held that where a man guided terrorists to a public house which they bombed it was no defence to him (for he knew that they were engaged in a terrorist activity and that use of explosives was probable) to establish that he did not know that the terrorists had brought explosives nor the exact nature of their abominable plan.

## 2   TREASON

In the case of treason a person present and conniving at the scene of the crime or assisting in the *preparation* or subsequent *concealment* of it is treated in the same way as the person who actually commits it: ie he is a *'principal'* to the crime. Moreover, where anyone knows that treason has been committed (or, possibly, even knows of a plot to commit it) and fails to disclose his knowledge to the authorities he will be guilty of '*misprision*' of treason; an offence for which he may be imprisoned for life.

## G   ATTEMPTS

The law relating to attempts to commit crimes is now contained in the Criminal Attempts Act 1981. A person is guilty of an attempt if 'with intent to commit an *offence* . . . a person commits an act which is *more than merely preparatory*, to the commission of an offence' (s 1(1)). Further, 'a person may be guilty (of an attempt) even though the facts are such that the commission of the offence is impossible' (s 1(2)). In this connexion an 'offence' means an *indictable* offence, but attempts, *inter alia*, to commit conspiracies and attempts to aid and abet are excluded. But a person who aids and abets the commission of an *attempt* to commit a crime, is, nevertheless, guilty of aiding and abetting.

Further, (s 1(3)) a person may be convicted of an attempt to commit an offence if he intends to commit one even though the true facts are such that no offence could have been committed. Thus if Smith has sexual intercourse with a girl of 16 (no offence) he may be convicted of an attempt if he *thinks* she is 15 (had she been, it would have been an offence).

What amounts to something 'more than mere preparation' is a difficult question. Clearly to put a gun in my pocket intending to kill X *is* mere preparation. Equally pointing the gun at X but being physically prevented from firing is 'more than mere preparation'. It should be noted that s 1(2) settles what was formerly a controversial point; it is now plain that the pickpocket who hopefully inserts his hand into an *empty* pocket (an 'impossible' theft) *is* guilty of an attempt.

Section 4(1) provides that where a person is convicted of an attempt under s 1(a) if the offence is murder or any other offence for which the sentence is fixed by the law, the maximum punishment is life imprisonment, (b) in the case of any other attempt, the maximum is the same as is available to the court of trial for the complete offence.

Akin to 'attempt' is *incitement*: as where a man offers, for payment, to give false evidence in another's favour. Here, though the latter refuse the offer, the former has incited him to pervert the course of justice – a crime. But the course of action incited must be a criminal course; hence if a man incites a girl under 16 to have intercourse with him he cannot be guilty of incitement because a girl of that age would commit no offence if she permitted him to do so. (Though this does not apply to incitement of the girl by her grandfather, father or brother because such *incitement* is an offence under the Criminal Law Act 1977, s 54.) If the man *does* have intercourse he commits a separate offence.

It should also be noted that attempts to commit and incitement to commit conspiracy are no longer offences (Criminal Law Act 1977, s 5 (7)).

## H   LIMITATION OF TIME

As regards criminal prosecutions, the common law rule was expressed by the maxim '*nullum tempus occurit regi*' ('time does not run against the King'). A prosecution could be instituted at any time after the commission of the crime. In theory this is still the general rule, but there are statutory exceptions. The most important of these are that prosecutions for *summary* offences must normally be commenced within six months of commission; and, in the case of certain motoring offences unless the accused is warned at the time of detection that a prosecution may be considered, a summons or notice of prosecution must be served within 14 days.

# 2   Specific crimes

For the sake of convenience crimes may be divided into three main categories: offences against the public interest, offences against the person and offences against property.

## A   OFFENCES AGAINST THE PUBLIC INTEREST

There are a number of crimes which fall under this head. The following may be mentioned – treason, sedition, offences against the Official Secrets Acts, conspiracy, riot, violent disorder, affray, fear or provocation of violence, harassment (for which see p 367), and perjury. Some of these have already been discussed in the last chapter. Here space will only permit us to outline the bare essentials of one of them, namely conspiracy.

### CONSPIRACY

*(a) The old law*
The traditional law of conspiracy was the invention of the Court of Star Chamber which, in the early Tudor period, was concerned to buttress the new establishment. Just as, from Caxton, the printing press constituted a threat to the establishment by facilitating the dissemination of pamphlets so did combinations of individuals; Hitlers or Napoleons apart, com-

binations are more dangerous than individuals. To meet the former threat the Star Chamber started the foundations of the law of libel. To meet the latter it created a new law of conspiracy. Literally to conspire is to murmur together (Latin, *conspirare* – to breathe together) and a criminal conspiracy is essentially an agreement to do something unlawful entered into by two or more people who intend to carry out the agreed purpose. What the Star Chamber was concerned to do was to strike down agreements dangerous to the State. Hence although the aim of a criminal conspiracy might be the effecting, in conjunction with co-conspirators, of some object (such as assassination) which was a crime if done by one person alone it might also be, as a matter of policy an agreement to effect some (to the establishment) undesirable political end which of itself, if done by one person, was not unlawful, but only became so by the fact of combination. For it was the combination that was feared: a fear which, perhaps, in a different setting and in later times, the development of trade unionism has borne out. Thus when, after the abolition of the Star Chamber in 1641, the common law courts inconsequently took over its jurisdiction, they inherited the crime of conspiracy, ie the crime of complicity to effect an *unlawful* purpose: and thanks to its history, 'unlawful' did not only mean 'criminal' (a combination to commit a recognized crime) but also whatever the courts might consider 'wrong'; legally, politically or morally. The law of conspiracy could thus be a dangerous instrument in the hands of courts subservient to unscrupulous administrations, for the judges could use the element of combination to create new crimes. In view of the general record of the judiciary in founding the criminal law (perhaps as good as, or better than, that of faction-ridden modern parliaments) perhaps, in settled times, this power was no bad thing; but in times of political friction (as when, in the nineteenth century the courts branded trade unions as criminal conspiracies) it could be undesirable. Shorn, however, of this element of uncertainty about the scope of the 'unlawful', conspiracy could be a useful means of ensuring that where people did agree to commit substantive crimes they could be prosecuted for the *agreement* to commit them if, for one reason or another, the substantive crime were either *not committed* or could *not be proved* to have been committed. Such was the state of the law before the Criminal Law Act 1977 (from now 'CLA', but not to be confused with the 1967 Act).

## (b) The new law of conspiracy
The law of conspiracy now rests upon the CLA. By s 1(1) (as replaced by the Criminal Attempts Act 1981, s 5(17)), in effect, the Act largely confines the crime of conspiracy to agreements to commit *offences*: that is, *crimes*. This is a major change because only shortly before the Act the House of Lords had held that, in certain circumstances, an agreement to trespass on land (a tort, not a crime) could be conspiracy. Thus the statutory crime now only serves the purpose, just described, of ensuring that where there

is an agreement intended to be carried out between two or more people they can be charged with the agreement as well as, or alternatively to, the crime itself.

The CLA, however, contains some exceptions. On the one hand it sets out circumstances in which an agreement to commit a recognized crime cannot be charged as a conspiracy, and on the other hand it recognizes as conspiracies certain agreements to do things which are *not* substantive crimes.

*Criminal agreements which are not conspiracies*: These are (i) Agreements (s 242 of the Trade Union and Labour Relations (Consolidation) Act 1992) to commit a *summary* offence not punishable by imprisonment which are made 'in contemplation or furtherance of a trade dispute'. (ii) By s 2(1) it is enacted that a person 'shall not be guilty of conspiracy to commit any offence of which he is the intended victim'. So that if I agree with you that you shall cut off my nose (a criminal offence) I cannot be charged with conspiracy. (iii) By s 2(2) it is provided that 'a person shall not (be guility of conspiracy) if the only other person or persons with whom he agrees are (a) his spouse; *or* (b) a person under the age of criminal responsibility (ten); *and* an intended victim of (the crime)'. The spouse exception was recognized at common law as being part of the unity of husband and wife: the underage exception is presumably a concession to logic.

*Agreements having non-criminal objects which are conspiracies.* These are contained in s 5(2) and (3) and they remain governed by the common law. They are: (i) Conspiracies to *defraud*; in respect of which people can be prosecuted for such conspiracy even though the agreement does not envisage the commission of a substantive offence – fraud being a wide and general term which embraces objects which would not be criminal, or even tortious, if they were achieved. (ii) Agreements to engage in conduct which (a) tends to corrupt public morals or outrages public decency; and also (b) would not amount to or involve the commission of an offence if carried out by a single person otherwise than in pursuance of the agreement. Thus (wisely or unwisely) leaving public morality within the keeping of the judiciary.

Under the CLA as a general rule – contrary to the former common law – a conspirator cannot be awarded punishment greater than the maximum punishment prescribed for the substantive offence which is the aim of the conspiracy. There can, generally speaking, be no prosecution of conspiracies to commit summary offences without the leave of the Director of Public Prosecutions, or, in some cases, of the Attorney-General (s 4). Further, as has already been noted, the Act (s 5(7)) abolishes the former offences of *attempt* and of *incitement* to commit conspiracies.

## B   OFFENCES AGAINST THE PERSON

The following offences against the person will be selected for discussion: (1) Homicide, (2) Assault and Battery, (3) Rape, (4) Bigamy.

# 1 HOMICIDE

It should be stressed in the first place that it is not necessarily unlawful to kill a man. Thus, death may occur by '*misadventure*' even where some person is instrumental in causing it: an attacker may in certain circumstances, be lawfully killed by a person who is in the act of defending himself; in extreme circumstances a constable making an arrest or preventing an escape, or someone assisting him, may lawfully kill the criminal who offers violence and of course the execution of the death penalty where lawfully inflicted by the judgment of a competent court is lawful.

A common example of death by misadventure occurs where a death happens during the playing of a lawful game. For instance a batsman who kills a fieldsman standing at 'silly point' by driving the ball hard in his direction will not be guilty of any crime, provided that his act was neither intentional nor grossly careless.

The rules relating to self-defence, which apply to a charge of homicide as well as to charges involving non-fatal injuries, have already been mentioned (p 165).

We may now briefly discuss the following unlawful homicides: murder, manslaughter, the aiding and abetting of suicide, and infanticide.

## *Murder*

According to the classic definition, murder comprises the '*unlawful killing of a reasonable creature who is in being and under the (Queen's) peace, with malice aforethought . . . the death following within a year and a day*'. Let us consider the various elements of this definition.

A '*reasonable creature*' signifies a human being, as opposed to an animal.

'*In being*' signifies that there can be no murder of an unborn person. In the eye of the law a child is not 'born' until its body is fully extruded from that of its mother; and it will only then be 'born' if it has acquired an existence independent of its mother. Until these conditions are satisfied there can be no 'murder' of the child. Accordingly it will not be murder to *prevent* it from being born alive. Nevertheless, the Infant Life (Preservation) Act 1929 makes it an offence ('*child destruction*'), punishable with imprisonment for life, wilfully to cause the death of a child which is capable of being born alive – which it is presumed to be after 28 weeks of pregnancy – before it has acquired an existence independent of its mother. For a person to be convicted of this offence it must, however, be shown that the act which caused the death was not done in good faith for the purpose of preserving the life of the mother. And procuration of *abortion* is of course also a crime under the Offences Against the Person Act 1861, s 58. It is committed if a pregnant woman, by any means, does anything with intent to procure her own miscarriage, *or* if any other person does anything – whether or not she be pregnant – with intent to procure a miscarriage. Though, by the Abortion Act 1967 it will be no crime if, under certain conditions, pregnancy is terminated by a registered medical practitioner; provided that two such practitioners are of the opinion that the continuance of the pregnancy would endanger the mother's life or health, or that of her child, or that the child to be aborted would, if born, be seriously handicapped. A second opinion is not necessary in the case of emergency where immediate action is essential to save the life of, or to prevent grave injury to, the mother. As is well-known, this Act has led to many abuses. It should be added that one cannot murder a *dead* person. This may seem obvious but the difficulty is to determine the moment of death: probably the better view is that life ceases when, but not until, the brain ceases to function.

'*Under the (Queen's) peace*' now signifies simply that it is not murder to kill an enemy in war. But it should be noted that, as an exception to the general rule that criminal jurisdiction is confined to crimes committed in this country, murder or manslaughter committed by a British subject anywhere is triable here.

'*Malice aforethought*' is important because it is the element of intent required to establish murder. It may consist of an intent to kill, whether particular or general: for instance X intends to shoot A and does so, or he intends to shoot A and in fact shoots B, or he places a bomb in an aeroplane intending to blow it up in flight with no particular malice against anyone in it, but with a general intent to kill. It may consist of an intent to cause grievous bodily harm, ie really serious bodily harm. But such an intent it must be, no less; furthermore the test of intent is *subjective* ie, not what the state of mind of the accused appeared to be, but 'what *was* it?' In extreme circumstances, where death or really serious bodily harm is a natural and probable consequence of the defendant's act, the jury may be permitted to *infer* that, if he foresaw the consequence, he intended it.

'Malice aforethought' is an archaic term and it is misleading. No ill-will need be involved – as in cases of euthanasia – nor need the act be *premeditated*; intention is all that is required.

'*The death following within a year and a day*'. The mediaeval law wisely prescribed that there could be no prosecution for homicide unless the death followed within a full year of the act alleged to have caused it. Before the development of modern medical science it would have been impossible to be certain, after a greater lapse of time, that the act was the real cause of death. This rule has now been abolished by the Law Reform (Year and a Day Rule) Act 1996.

Formerly the penalty for murder used to be death by hanging, but the Murder (Abolition of Death Penalty) Act 1965 has now substituted life imprisonment for death. At the time of sentencing the court may declare a minimum period which in its view should elapse before the Secretary of State orders release on licence.

People below the age of 18 years at the time of committing a murder cannot be sentenced to life imprisonment, but they must instead be sentenced to be detained during Her Majesty's pleasure.

*Manslaughter*

Manslaughter is the offence of unlawfully causing the death of another, without malice aforethought.

There are two categories of manslaughter: 'voluntary' manslaughter and 'involuntary' manslaughter. *Voluntary manslaughter* is committed when a person causes the death of another in circumstances which would have amounted to *murder* had the act not been done under provocation or in pursuance of a suicide pact. As to diminished responsibility, see p 164. *Involuntary manslaughter* may be committed in three ways. First, by causing death in the commission of an unlawful and dangerous act. Secondly, by gross negligence. Thirdly, with subjective recklessness as to the risk of death or bodily harm.

*(a) Voluntary manslaughter* – In a trial for murder it is for the jury to consider whether there is such evidence of *provocation* either by the victim himself or by some other person as to justify a conviction for manslaughter. And where there is evidence upon which the jury could reasonably so find, the judge must draw their attention to it in his summing up; whether or not the issue of provocation has been raised by the defence. As to the degree of provocation required, the Homicide Act 1957, s 3, provides that 'Where on a charge of murder there is evidence on which the jury can find that the person was provoked (whether by things done or by things said or both together) to lose his self-control, the question whether the provocation was enough to induce a *reasonable man* to do what he did shall be left to the *jury*; and in determining that question the jury shall *take into account everything* both done and said according to the effect which, in their opinion, it would have on a *reasonable man*'. The defendant is thus to be treated as a 'reasonable man' placed in the relevant circumstances. The reasonable man will not, of course, be over-irritable, quick to wrath, or unduly pugnacious but such things as his age or his colour may reasonably affect his reactions: the young cannot be expected to have the same degree of self-control as their elders: and to say 'you damn n****r' to a white man would not provoke him, but it might reasonably provoke a black one.

But it must be stressed that what is 'reasonable' is here solely a question of fact to be decided by the jury in relation to the actual circumstances of the case. Thus even a blackmailer who must expect and accept a degree of provocation from his victim – such as, 'You b**** blackmailing b******' – may yet rely upon provocation if the victim makes a serious physical attack upon him. Provocation may be successfully pleaded even though the accused did (though provoked) form an actual intent to kill.

The Homicide Act 1957, s 4 (as amended by the Suicide Act 1961) enacts that 'it shall be *manslaughter*, and shall not be murder, for a person acting *in pursuance of a suicide pact* between him and another to kill the other or be a party to the other being killed by a third person'. (Italics ours.) The case assumed is of course where the accused has carried out the pact in respect of the other party or parties, or connived at its being carried out, but has failed to implement it in respect of himself. It will be noted that in order for the accused to escape the charge of *murder* he must have been acting 'in pursuance of' the pact; and the section provides that for this to be the case he must himself have had a 'settled intention of dying' at the time of the killing. A suicide pact is not therefore a painless way of committing a murder and escaping with a conviction for manslaughter by changing one's mind in respect of one's own future as soon as the pact is concluded. The section also provides that where the facts of a case do fall within its ambit a conviction for manslaughter may be entered, though the accused has been initially charged with murder.

It remains to be added that where, upon a charge of murder, a plea of *self-defence* (p 163) fails because, for instance, undue force has been used by the accused, it does not necessarily follow that there *must* be a verdict of manslaughter. The position is that, self-defence having failed to exonerate, other issues may arise – for example whether there was provocation or whether, indeed, an intent to murder was in fact present.

*(b) Involuntary manslaughter* – Broadly speaking, this may be taken to include the case where provocation reduces murder to manslaughter (p 177) and the case of murder reduced to manslaughter by diminished responsibility (p 164). But here four other forms of manslaughter must be mentioned, namely, killing as the result of dangerous acts, killing by gross negligence, killing with subjective recklessness and killing during intoxication.

*(i) Killing as the result of an unlawful and dangerous act.* It will be recalled that the malice aforethought of murder requires either an intent to kill or an intent to do grievous bodily harm. There can be no murder without the one or the other of those two forms of intent. But causing death may, nevertheless, be culpable if there is some less specific intent; and it is manslaughter to kill as the result of the intentional doing of some act, such as throwing bricks from a bridge over the motorway, which is both *unlawful* and *dangerous*. Here it is to be noted that what is intended is the unlawful act (of throwing the brick), not the death (of the motorist below). Hence this kind of manslaughter is often called 'constructive' because the intent to kill which, *ex hypothesi*, does not exist, is notionally inferred from the intent to do the unlawful and dangerous act. It follows from this that here the rule of s 8 of the Criminal Justice Act 1967 (p 159) does not apply, and the defendant is judged as regards his state of mind not by his actual intention (because he had no intention to kill) but by the standard of what a reasonable person would consider dangerous. It is thus irrelevant for the brick thrower to prove that *he* did not appreciate the danger of his act. On the other hand, it would be relevant to prove that he was so unintelligent that he was unable to form the intent to throw a brick at all. It should be added that the act *must* be dangerous; hence if a drug addict supplies another addict with a dangerous drug – dangerous only if improperly used – the supplier of the drug will not commit manslaughter if the other man's

death is caused by excessive use of the drug. Further, provided that the dangerous act was intentional it need not be aimed directly at the victim. Thus it has been held that where, in the course of a fight, B knocks down A, who in turn knocks down C in falling, and C dies as a result, B may be guilty of manslaughter.

*(ii) Gross negligence.* A killing brought about by gross negligence has been confirmed in the case of *Adomako* [1994] 3 All ER 79 by the House of Lords as a category of involuntary manslaughter. For this to apply, there must be conduct by the accused involving risk of death and the conduct must have fallen so far below the standard to be expected of a reasonable person.

*(iii) Killing by a reckless act or omission.* Such killing will amount to manslaughter where the conduct of the defendant was such as to create an obvious and serious risk of unlawful physical injury to another, and *either* he has not given any thought to the possibility of there being any such risk *or*, having recognized that there was some risk involved, has none the less gone on to take it. Where such responsibility is based upon an omission to act, rather than upon a positive act, it will only be manslaughter if the defendant was under a duty to act imposed by the criminal law.

*(iv) Manslaughter in relation to intoxication.* It has been noted above that the fact that a person is intoxicated by drink or drugs is not, if his state is self-induced, a justification for causing the death of another. Hence where a man is so intoxicated that he is unaware of doing the act which causes the death he may be charged with *manslaughter*: though conviction for *murder* is out of the question, for there is no malice aforethought.

NOTE – Causing death by the careless driving of a motor car can be manslaughter in a really serious case (and, indeed, how often, one may reflect, has an 'accident' been a murder) but there are, under the Road Traffic Act 1988 as amended by the Road Traffic Act 1991 two special driving offences: (i) *Causing death* by the *dangerous* driving of a motor vehicle on a road: an offence which carries a maximum penalty of ten years' imprisonment: (ii) Driving *dangerously* without causing death: there is also (iii) Riding a cycle on a road dangerously. There are also two minor (summary) offences: (a) Driving a motor vehicle on a road without due care and attention or without reasonable consideration for other people: (b) Riding a cycle on a road or bridleway in a similar manner. Although they are outside the scope of this book, as is well-known, there are also offences – applying both to motor vehicles and cycles, of driving a motor vehicle or riding a cycle under the influence of drink or a drug.

## Aiding and abetting suicide
Since the passing of the Suicide Act 1961 suicide of itself is no longer a crime; but the Act made it an offence punishable with a maximum of fourteen years' imprisonment to aid, abet, counsel or procure the suicide, or attempted suicide, of another. For the offence to be committed there

must be actual aiding and abetting. Hence where a philanthropical society issued a booklet designed to encourage euthanasia by describing the most effective ways of committing suicide it was held that the society would only be contravening the law if the booklet were issued to people known by the distributor to be contemplating suicide. It would not be an offence to distribute it to ordinary people not known to be doing so. Where the facts warrant it, a person charged with murder or manslaughter may be convicted of this offence. The consent of the Director of Public Prosecutions is necessary for prosecution under this Act.

## Infanticide

This is a statutory crime. It is now governed by the Infanticide Act 1938, which provides that where a woman wilfully causes the death of her child, being *under the age of 12 months*, in circumstances which amount to murder, she will not be guilty of murder. Instead, she will be guilty of *'infanticide'*, if, at the time she did the act causing death, the balance of her mind was disturbed by reason either of her not having recovered from the effects of the birth, or by reason of the effect of lactation consequent upon the birth. Infanticide is punishable in the same manner as manslaughter.

## Causation

Although the problem is universal and it arises in tort (p 322) as well as in the criminal law, brief mention must be made of its bearing on homicide cases. If a person is to be found guilty it must be established that his act or omission *caused* the death; if the cause lay in some other extraneous factor he cannot be held responsible. Thus in *R v Jordan* (1956) 40 Cr App Rep 152 it was held that where the accused stabbed a person who was later subjected to treatment which was both abnormal and dangerous the death was caused by the maltreatment rather than by the initial stab: so the accused escaped responsibility. But the situation was different in *R v Malcherek* [1981] 2 All ER 422. There the accused also stabbed the victim and she was also taken to hospital: after normal treatment she had to be put on a life support machine and the machine was disconnected because the case had become hopeless. It was held that the cause of her death was the defendant's act rather than the fact that the machine was disconnected. The question to be posed is does the intervening act constitute an independent cause in itself? If it does the act of the accused ceases to be operative: if it does not it remains operative.

It should be added that where death occurs from a number of causes, all equally operative and attributable to the defendant (as where a man pushed a woman headfirst down a staircase, then dragged her up with a rope round her neck, then cut her throat) the prosecution does not have to single out any one of them as being *the* operative cause.

## 2 ASSAULT AND BATTERY

The word 'assault' is commonly used to signify the two offences of 'assault' *and* 'battery', which are normally committed together. An assault *may*, however, be made without a battery and *vice versa*.

A 'common' assault consists in attempting, or offering, to apply physical force to another person in such a way as to cause reasonable fear in the mind of the person that the wrong will be committed. A battery consists in the actual application of force to the person of another.

Common illustrations of assault without battery are the act of shaking a stick at a person who is close enough to be hit, or of pointing a gun at him: according to the better view this latter act will constitute an assault even if the gun is not loaded, *provided* that the person threatened does not know that it is not; if he does, of course, there is no assault because he does not reasonably apprehend the infliction of a battery. Provided that it is hostile or unwanted any degree of force suffices for the commission of a battery, however trivial, even a mere touch.

Mere accidental contacts which inevitably occur in the course of everyday life, such as unintentional jostling in a crowd, are not assaults. Moreover, where there is consent there can normally be no assault or battery; hence, provided that the dentist acts with proper care, his patient cannot sue him for battery. Further, it has been ruled that it is in the public interest that injuries caused in the proper conduct of lawful sports (such as football) shall not – in the absence of intention or negligence – be actionable. But, on the other hand, it has also been ruled that where people engage in a fight intending to cause bodily harm to each other there is no such immunity; and even though the injured party may have expressly or impliedly consented to injury, the other party may be prosecuted. As in homicide so, *a fortiori*, in the case of assault, self-defence may justify. In order to obtain a conviction for an assault it is not essential to establish that the defendant actually intended it if he behaved recklessly.

When a person has been summarily convicted of assault or battery no civil proceedings in respect of either – for they are both civil wrongs as well as crimes – may be brought subsequently. Common assault is a summary offence and it is punishable by a fine, a maximum of six months' imprisonment, or both.

Besides 'common' assault there are various forms of aggravated assaults and certain other kindred offences prescribed by the Offences Against the Person Act 1861. All of these carry a higher maximum penalty than common assault. They include such things as unlawful and malicious wounding, and the infliction of grievous bodily harm.

The law relating to many sexual offences, including assaults, was consolidated in the Sexual Offences Act 1956. And it should be added that the Sexual Offences Act 1967, legalized homosexual practices among consenting males over 21 in private – though seamen serving on merchant ships of the United Kingdom are excluded from the benefit of this parliamentary indulgence.

## 3   RAPE

By s 1 of the Sexual Offences Act 1956 (as amended by the Sexual Offences (Amendment) Act 1976 and as substituted by the Criminal Justice and Public Order Act 1994), a man commits rape if: (a) he has sexual intercourse with a *person* who at the time of the intercourse does *not consent* to it; and (b) at the time *he knows that victim does not consent to it*, or he is reckless as to whether he or she consents or not. Section 1(2) declares that 'the presence or absence of reasonable grounds' for the defendant's belief is to be taken into account in considering whether 'he so *believed*': so that *Morgan's Case* (p 159) seems to be confirmed, at least to the extent that it is the defendant's *actual* belief that matters.

Because free consent negatives the offence there can be no rape where there is consent; and formerly it was held that a husband could not therefore normally be guilty of raping his wife, because, as Sir Matthew Hale put it, 'by their mutual matrimonial consent and contract the wife hath given up herself in this kind unto her husband, which she cannot retract'. Where, however, a husband and wife were living apart under judicial separation or a separation order, this logic ceased to apply and the husband might then be guilty of rape; so likewise after decree *nisi* though before decree absolute for divorce. Since a House of Lords decision in 1991, it has been the case that a husband could be convicted of raping his wife if she did not consent, whether or not they were living together, separated or divorced.

The 'consent' must, of course, be a real consent. Thus, consent induced by fraud (as where a man induces a married woman to have intercourse with him by impersonating her husband) will not form a defence; and it will also amount to rape if a man has intercourse with a woman while she is unconscious, for then she is incapable of giving or of withholding her consent.

Rape carries a maximum penalty of imprisonment for life.

## 4   BIGAMY

Bigamy is a statutory offence; governed by the Offences Against the Person Act 1861, s 57. It is committed by anyone who, being married, 'marries' any other person during the life of his or her husband or wife.

The first essential is that the defendant must be *married* to a living person at the time of the 'marriage' which constitutes the offence. 'Married' means lawfully married and, for this purpose, monogamously married; a polygamous marriage will not suffice to support the charge. Hence, if the first marriage was *null*, as for example where it was a marriage within the 'prohibited degrees' a second marriage will not be bigamous. This rule will not, however, apply in the case of a merely '*voidable*' marriage, eg a marriage which is liable to be set aside on the grounds of impotence. No second marriage can lawfully be contracted until a decree *absolute* has been obtained annulling the first.

The statute further provides that a second marriage will not be bigamous if, at the time it is contracted, a previous marriage or marriages have been dissolved by a competent court. Moreover, since it has been possible, where a husband or wife has reason to believe that his or her spouse is dead, for him or her to obtain a judicial decree of 'presumption of death' and dissolution of marriage, the effect of this decree will be to dissolve the marriage and enable the person concerned to contract a second marriage lawfully.

The second essential of the offence is that the defendant shall '*remarry*'. The essence of bigamy lies in the profanation of the marriage ceremony. Hence, as regards the *second* 'marriage', provided that a legally recognized ceremony has been conducted, either according to our law, or, if the 'marriage' is contracted abroad, according to some foreign law which we recognize, the offence will be committed even though the second 'marriage' is in other respects a nullity; eg because the parties to *this* 'marriage' were within the 'prohibited degrees'.

By the proviso to the Offences Against the Person Act 1861, s 57, it is a defence to a charge of bigamy to show that the first husband or wife has been continually *absent* for a minimum period of seven years, and has not been known by the accused to have been alive during that period. Of course, if under these circumstances, and without having obtained a decree of presumption of death, the accused does 'remarry', although he or she cannot be charged with bigamy, the second 'marriage' will be a nullity if the other spouse reappears.

Apart from the Act, it is also a defence for the defendant to show that he or she had reasonable grounds for supposing that his or her spouse was *dead* at the time when the second marriage was contracted. Thus, in *R v Tolson* (1889) 23 QBD 168, where Mrs T was deserted by her husband in 1881, and she heard from reliable sources that he had drowned, it was held that her remarriage in January 1887 was not bigamous, though the husband reappeared in the December of that year. Further, by parity of reasoning, it is also a defence to prove that the accused honestly believed on reasonable grounds that the previous marriage was annulled or dissolved, even though in fact it was not. This decision was left undisturbed by the decision in *Morgan's Case* (p 159); as well it might be. A person who 'marries' another knowing that he or she is already married will be guilty of bigamy as principal in the second degree, provided that the act of the other party is itself bigamous. Of course this act might be apparently bigamous, but not really so: for example, the man who 'married' Mrs T could not have been guilty as principal in the second degree, even if he had known that the husband was alive, for Mrs T, the principal, was herself not guilty.

Bigamy is punishable with a maximum of seven years' imprisonment.

## C   OFFENCES IN RELATION TO PROPERTY

The most important offences of this kind are offences connected with theft and with criminal damage to property.

### 1   THEFT AND ALLIED OFFENCES

The law concerning theft, formerly contained largely in the Larceny Act 1916, was refashioned by the Theft Act 1968 (hereafter 'TA'). There is space here to consider the following offences only – (i) Theft; (ii) Robbery; (iii) Burglary; (iv) Obtaining by Deception; (v) Blackmail; (vi) Handling Stolen Goods. And it will also be necessary to mention (vii) the law relating to restitution of stolen property.

#### i  Theft

The old law of larceny (stealing) – a word which is now no longer used – was bedevilled by the fact that though it had been for the most part codified in a number of Larceny Acts it ultimately sprang from the common law which, in former times, was for a variety of reasons obsessed by the need to protect *possession*. Thus larceny was defined by reference to the observable fact of 'taking and carrying away' the stolen goods, rather than by reference to the dishonesty of the thief's conduct.

This approach to the matter, necessary though it originally was in a loosely organized society where breaches of the peace arising from criminous taking were much to be feared, proved in the course of time to be unduly circumscribed, for it meant that the law of theft did not embrace many types of dishonest dealing with property which did *not* involve a taking out of the owner's possession. Thus a patchwork of statute law had to be superimposed upon the law of simple larceny (theft) creating special offences of dishonest dealing with property which were not within the technical confines of larceny. For instance 'embezzlement' was not larceny, but was a special offence; this was necessary because it was committed where a clerk or servant appropriated property received *by him* on behalf of his master, and this meant that the appropriation (he having himself the possession of the property until he gave it to the master) was not an attack upon the *master's* possession. Many other instances of the patchwork quality of the former law could be given.

Hence the TA started from the standpoint of widening the definition of stealing and focusing rather upon the dishonesty of the thief than upon the element of disturbance of possession. Section 1(1) of that Act therefore provides that 'A person is guilty of theft if he *dishonestly appropriates property belonging to another with the intention of permanently depriving the other of it* . . .' All the italicized words are significant.

'*Dishonesty*' is not defined because the intention is that all forms of 'dishonesty' shall be embraced in the sense of the word familiar to the layman: thus, for instance, where someone takes money from another person and asserts that he intended to return it, it will be for the jury to decide whether in the circumstances his behaviour was 'dishonest'. Though if he overdraws his giro account (which is not permitted), knowing that there will be no funds to meet his cheque, such behaviour is clearly 'dishonest'. On the other hand it has been ruled that where the accused gives evidence of his own state of mind the jury may give some weight to what he says in reaching their own conclusion. Moreover, the test is subjective to the extent that there can only be a conviction if the accused, though protesting his honesty, knew that ordinary people would regard what he did as dishonest. Certain kinds of appropriation are, however, specifically excluded by the definition: (a) appropriation by a person 'in the belief that *he has in law the right* to deprive the other of it' (TA, s 2(1)(a)) – eg the case of the taker who honestly believes that the umbrella is his own; (b) appropriation by a person 'in the belief that he would have the (owner's) *consent* if the (owner) knew of the appropriation' (TA, s 2(1) (b)) – eg Jones tells Smith that he may take and keep his (Jones') bicycle at any time, Jones being absent Smith takes it; Jones had in fact, however, changed his mind; (c) appropriation where a person appropriates property 'in the belief that the person to whom the property belongs cannot be discovered by taking reasonable steps' – eg where A finds a jewel in the street and it does not appear that reasonable steps, such as informing the police, are likely to disclose an owner. Needless to say, it is 'dishonest' to take property from the owner knowing that his consent is only apparent. Thus in *Lawrence v Metropolitan Police Comr* [1972] AC 626 the House of Lords upheld the conviction of a taxi driver who accepted the wallet proffered by a foreign tourist and extracted from it an extortionate 'fare'. It was also pointed out that the accused could equally have been charged under s 15(1).

'*Appropriates*'. This is defined (TA, s 3(1)) thus – '*Any assumption by a person of the rights of an owner amounts to an appropriation*, and this includes, where he has come by the property (innocently or not) without stealing it, any *later* assumption of a right to it by keeping or dealing with it as owner.' This disposes of one of the defects of the former law (Larceny Act, 1916, s 1(11)) by which the intent to steal had to exist *at the time of taking*: so if X's sheep were intermingled with Y's and Y drove the flock away in the belief that it was entirely his own, but later upon discovering his mistake, appropriated X's sheep, there was doubt under the old law whether Y was guilty of larceny; but now he certainly will in such a case be guilty of theft. (It should, perhaps, be noted that the restrictive nature of the old law, which was to some extent codified common law, was partially due to the fact that stealing, unless trivial, being originally a capital offence, the courts did all they could to restrict its scope.) The Theft Act, s 3(2), however, contains a special safeguard for the case of a person who, having acquired an interest in property for value and in good faith later discovers that there was a defect in the title – eg a man buys a book and afterwards learns that the seller was not the owner of it but had borrowed it. Under this sub-section such a person will not be a *thief* if he retains the property (though he may be open to a civil claim at the suit of the owner). Whether this accords with common morality is perhaps questionable, but it must be stressed that apart from this special exemption the new law is much wider than the old, which was concerned primarily with the act of 'taking and carrying away'; for the TA, s 3(1) forbids '*any* assumption by a person *of the rights of an owner*'. And it has been held that there is such an assumption where a person, at a supermarket, switches price labels in order to obtain the goods at a lower price than the price intended.

'*Property*'. By the TA, s 4(1), this includes '*money and all other property, real or personal, including things in action and other intangible property*'. The meaning of 'things in action' will be explained below: 'real' property is land. Section 4(2) provides that land *cannot be stolen* except (i) where a part of it is *severed* and appropriated by a person not in possession of it – eg X takes a load of soil from Y's land; (ii) where a tenant appropriates a 'fixture'; (iii) where someone in the position of a trustee or the like, being authorized to dispose of the land on behalf of another person appropriates it in breach of confidence. Again, in law vegetable matter growing on land is regarded as a part of the land (technically it is 'land' not 'goods') and it therefore receives the same treatment as land under s 4(2): ie under (i) above, it is stolen when wilfully severed by someone who does not possess it. But the TA, s 4(3), makes some commonsense exceptions to this rule: thus the picking of *wild mushrooms* and the *flowers, fruit* and *foliage* of *wild plants, trees* and *shrubs* is not theft *unless done for commercial purposes*: but the *uprooting* of such things, as opposed to the mere picking of them is. (Further, by the Wildlife and Countryside Act 1981, s 13, quite apart from any question of theft it is an offence (s 13(1)(a)) intentionally to pick, uproot or destroy certain wild plants listed in Sch 8 of the Act. And also (s 13(1) (a)) it is an offence intentionally to *uproot any* wild plant without the authorization of the owner of the land on which it grows – even, it would appear, a dandelion.) The appropriation of untamed wild creatures (eg wild rabbits) not ordinarily kept in captivity is also excepted (TA, s 4(4)) provided that they are not in possession of another person and that he is not in the course of reducing them into possession. For example, you appropriate a grouse which I have shot but not as yet retrieved. What amounts to being 'in the course of reducing into possession' has given rise to factual disputes in other contexts from Roman times to ours (eg claims by rival hunters or whalers) and it will doubtless continue to do so.

'*Belonging to another*'. This includes the case of a person who has possession or control of the property (such as a bailee with whom property has been deposited) on behalf of another, as well as the case of the person who has a proprietary interest in it as owner or otherwise (TA, s 5 (1)); and a co-owner or partner who appropriates the co-owned or partnership property is also a thief; for he takes what 'belongs to another'. It also embraces the case where the owner has entrusted the property to the thief to deal with in a particular way; as where a club member gives property to the treasurer to be used for specified purposes and it is used for some other purpose (TA, s 5(3)): formerly appropriation of this sort would not have been theft but 'fraudulent conversion'. It also includes the case of a person whose property comes into the hands of the thief by mistake, the latter being under an obligation to restore it or its value.

'*With the intention of permanently depriving*' the other of it. Intending '*permanently to deprive*' is in most circumstances essential; and it follows that a mere conditional intent is not enough – as where, for example, a person picks up a handbag and, having examined the contents, decides that they are not worth taking and leaves the bag where it was.

In general our law knows no such crime as the Roman '*furtum usus*' (the theft of the use of a thing). There are, however, important exceptions to this proposition. First, the TA, s 12, makes it an arrestable offence, *without consent*, to *take* anyone else's conveyance, or to drive it or drive in it *knowing that it has been taken without authority*; though the taking or riding of a pedal cycle in similar circumstances is only a summary offence. It has been held that 'taking' implies movement, not just possession. Thus if I get into your car and simply sit in the driver's seat I cannot be guilty of the offence (and it seems that this is so even if I turn on the ignition) but once I get the car moving, even by taking off the handbrake on a downward slope, by ever so little, I am guilty. It must be noted that in general the 'consent' will be valid for the purposes of this section even though it be obtained by some degree of misrepresentation: eg that the taker wants the car to drive to a nearby destination when he really intends to take it to a distant one; though it is possible that a misrepresentation of a more fundamental nature might be held to invalidate the consent. Second by the TA, s 11, any person who, without authority and without believing that he has authority, removes any article (such as a picture) kept for display to the public in any building or in the grounds of any building commits an offence. And the TA, s 6, also contains further qualifications. First it provides that even though no such intention exists, an intent on the part of the thief to treat the thing as his 'own regardless of (the owner's) rights' will amount to an intention 'permanently to deprive': thus an unauthorized borrowing or a lending of it by the thief may be stealing if, though only if, the period and the circumstances are such as to make the act equivalent to an outright appropriation – eg X retains a library book for such an indefinite period that the retention amounts to treating it as his own. Second, where a person having control of property parts with it under a condition as to its return which he may not be able to perform – and does this for purposes of his own and without the owner's authority – the act of parting may be held to constitute treating the property as his own 'regardless of (the owner's) rights'. Thus if B, without A's permission, pledges A's watch with C, a pawnbroker, without any serious probability that he (B) will be able to redeem the pledge he may be guilty of theft.

The maximum penalty for theft is seven years' imprisonment.

## ii *Robbery*

By the TA, s 8, a person will be guilty of robbery 'if he *steals*, and immediately before or at the time of doing so, and in order to do so, he *uses force on any person* or *seeks to put any person in fear of being then and there subjected to force*'. Everyone knows that the man who points a pistol at the bank cashier and takes the money from the till is a robber; but it should be noted that the same applies to the gunman who, while using no force against the cashier, points his weapon at the security guard. The reader is reminded that – contrary to common usage – 'I have been robbed!' meaning 'My wallet has disappeared' – robbery and theft are different things: for robbery is *violent* theft.

The maximum penalty for this crime or for an assault with intent to rob (eg the gunman who holds up the cashier but is frustrated in his intent to steal by the emptiness of the till) is life imprisonment.

## iii *Burglary*

By the TA, s 9, a person will be guilty of burglary if (a) he *enters any building or part of a building as a trespasser and with intent* to steal anything in the building *or* of inflicting therein grievous *bodily harm or* of *raping* any person therein *or* doing *unlawful damage* to the *building*, or (b) *having* entered any building *or part of a building as a trespasser*, he *steals* or *attempts* to steal anything therein *or* inflicts or attempts to inflict *grievous bodily harm* on any person therein.

It will be noted that (a) involves various kinds of intent *at the time* of the trespassory entry and that (b) involves *commission* of specified crimes *after* entry in the absence of intent at the time of entry. 'Trespass' is of itself a tort; not a crime. The trespasser for the purposes of the crime, must be a trespasser *at the moment of entry*; so that he cannot be guilty of the offence if he is invited to enter by the owner or some authorized person who subsequently changes his mind and tells him to go; but, on the other hand, where a person has general permission to enter, but, at the time of the relevant entry, knows that he is exceeding the limits of that permission (eg by entering with intent to steal) he commits burglary. It has been ruled that it is not essential to the offence that the trespasser entering with intent to steal should intend to steal any particular thing: it is enough if he has a general intent to steal, even though there is nothing in the building or part thereof to be stolen.

In the public mind burglary is probably solely connected with *stealing* in a building (though sometimes one may also hear 'My watch has been burgled in the street': to which our readers must of course retort, 'That is impossible'); but it will be realized that it may also be connected with the other offences (such, inconsequently, as rape). By TA, s 9(3), 'building' in this context includes 'an inhabited vehicle or vessel' and the offence may be committed 'at times when the person having a habitation in it is not there . . .'.

Section 9 has simplified the law. Formerly there was a distinction between burglary (a nocturnal offence) and 'housebreaking' (a daytime offence) and the details of these and other similar, but separate, offences were complex in the extreme.

The maximum penalty for burglary in a dwelling is 14 years' imprisonment, otherwise it is ten years (Criminal Justice Act 1991 s 26); but the TA, s 10, also provides for the case of '*aggravated*' burglary which will be committed if the burglar has with him any firearm, imitation firearm, weapon of offence (any article calculated to cause injury or incapacity) or explosive. The maximum penalty for the aggravated offence is life imprisonment.

*iv Deception*

There are two offences of obtaining property by deception: the one under the TA, s 15, the other under the TA, s 16. Certain allied offences were also created by s 16 but they proved to be unsatisfactory: they were consequently redefined by the Theft Act 1978 which, *pro tanto*, replaces the original s 16. We will first discuss s 15, which defines 'deception' and creates an offence, and then consider the s 16 offences and, finally, the allied offences under the Theft Act 1978.

(a) The TA, s 15 defines 'deception' (s 15(4)) as – '*any deception (whether deliberate or reckless) . . . as to fact or law, including a deception as to the present intentions of the person using the deception*'.

The essential nature of 'deception' under the Act was explained by Lord Diplock in *DPP v Stonehouse* [1977] AC 55 (a case in which the defendant took out insurance policies in favour of his wife and then faked his own death): 'The physical acts', he said, 'of the accused that are an essential element of any offence under s 15 must amount to a "deception", ie the making to the person from whom the property is obtained *a representation* of fact, law or intention that is *false*. The essential state of mind of the accused *at the time of doing* those physical acts is his *knowledge of the falsity* of the representation or his indifference as to whether it is true or false, and his intentions (1) that the false representation should be *communicated* to the person from whom the property is to be obtained; (2)

that such person should *believe the representation to be true*; (3) that this belief should *induce that person* to part with ownership, possession or control *of property to the accused himself or to some other person*, and (4) that the accused himself or that other person should assume the rights of *owner of the property* so obtained.'

The false representation may be verbal, written or by means of imposture; and it may be express or implied. It need not necessarily be made to the person who is disadvantaged: thus where B, knowing that her bank would dishonour her cheque, paid a full rail fare by cheque upon presentation to the *booking clerk* of her cheque card (which obliged *the bank* to pay the railway authority) she was guilty of deception; though it was the authority (through the clerk) rather than the bank who had been deceived. It should also be stressed that the representation may be implied: thus where a person orders a meal at a restaurant he impliedly represents that he will pay for it, and if he does not he will be guilty of deception (under s 16, as amended); moreover, the person who intends to pay for the meal at the time of ordering, but changes his mind (as sometimes, by reason of the poor quality of the food and service even a reasonable citizen certainly might!) and, having consumed the meal, quits the restaurant, also commits deception because, unless the contrary is indicated, the representation continues to be implied until the moment of leaving.

The first offence (s 15(1)) is committed where '*a person by any deception (whether deliberate or reckless) dishonestly obtains property belonging to another with the intention of permanently depriving the other of it*'; and (s 15(2)) '*a person is to be treated as obtaining property if he obtains ownership, possession or control of it*'. It has been held that a person who purchases goods with a credit card when he has exceeded his credit limit is guilty of deception because, in tendering the card, he falsely represents that the card company will honour the payment. It will be appreciated that facts which constitute this offence may often also support a charge of *theft* under s 1(1). But sometimes the s 15(1) offence may be easier to prove than theft. For instance, suppose B borrows A's horse intending to appropriate it: the mere fact of B's acquiring control of the horse under the false pretence of borrowing it will suffice to establish the s 15(1) offence, whereas an 'appropriation' in the sense described above (eg behaving in such a way as to pose a challenge to A's title) will be necessary before *theft* can be proved. Section 15 is the more serious of the two crimes, and it is punishable with a maximum of ten years' imprisonment. It replaced the former crime of 'obtaining by false pretences'.

(b)  The second offence is committed (TA, s 16(1)) by any person 'who by deception dishonestly obtains for himself or another any *pecuniary advantage*'; and, (s 16(2)), 'the cases in which a "pecuniary advantage" . . . is to be regarded as obtained . . . are where . . . (b) (any person) is allowed to borrow by way of overdraft, or to take out any policy of insurance or annuity ... or (c) (any person) is given the opportunity to earn remuneration or to win money by betting'.

(c) The offences under the Theft Act 1978 are: (i) *dishonestly obtaining services* by deception (s 1), ie services rendered upon the expectation of payment; (ii) *evasion of liability* by deception, comprising (s 2): (a) dishonestly securing the remission of any legally enforceable liability, eg a debt; (b) with intent to make permanent default dishonestly inducing a creditor to wait for or forego a payment. Thus, for example, it has been held that where a man told a waiter in a restaurant that he had paid another waiter for his meal (when he had not) he had induced the waiter to 'forego' a payment; (c) dishonestly obtaining exemption from liability to make a payment; (iii) *making off without payment* (s 3) which is committed by any person 'who, knowing that *payment on the spot* for any goods supplied or service done is required or expected of him, dishonestly makes off without having paid ... and with intent to avoid payment'. An intent to delay or defer payment is not, however, enough. By s 3(2) 'payment on the spot' includes payment at the time of collecting goods on which work has been done or in respect of which service has been provided.

## v Blackmail

This offence formerly consisted of a number of separate crimes under the Larceny Act 1916, but here again the TA simplified the law by making it a single offence which is committed by a person who '*with a view to gain for himself or another or with intent to cause loss to another, makes any unwarranted demand with menaces*' (s 21(1)). And such a demand is 'unwarranted' unless the person making it does so in the belief: '(a) that he had reasonable grounds for making it *and* (b) that the use of the menaces is a proper means of enforcing the demand'. Thus if X says to Y (whether or not Y in fact has one) 'I will reveal your criminal record unless you pay me £100' this will *prima facie* be blackmail: but the state of X's mind is material, and if he really thinks that he is justified in demanding the money because, for example, it is money Y already owes him, *and* if he also thinks that a threat to reveal a criminal record is a proper way of extracting a debt, X will not be guilty. But it will be realized that it would be difficult to establish such an ingenuous state of mind to the satisfaction of a jury.

The maximum penalty for blackmail is 14 years' imprisonment.

## vi Handling stolen goods

This was a new offence created by the TA, s 22(1). Previously it had been an offence only to *receive* goods knowing them to have been stolen, but by the subsection the scope of this kind of criminality is widened, for 'A person *handles* stolen goods if ... knowing *or* believing them to be stolen ... he *dishonestly receives* the goods, *or* dishonestly *undertakes or assists in their retention, removal, disposal or realization* by or for the benefit of another person . . .'. This of course embraces much more than actual receiving and the section would, for instance, cover the case of a person who assists a thief to convey the stolen goods to a hiding place knowing or believing it to be stolen property. Here again the word '*dishonestly*' is important because an honest motive may negative a dishonest intent. Thus if Williams steals Walters' car and takes it to Wright who knows it has been stolen and accepts delivery of it, Wright will not be guilty if his purpose in doing so is to restore the car to Walters. Here the courts load the dice in favour of the criminal, for the proof of guilt must be positive: it has been held that it is not enough to establish that a reasonable man would, in the circumstances, suspect that the goods in question were stolen, it must be shown that the accused did believe them to have been or that he deliberately closed his eyes to the obvious.

A person does not 'assist in the retention of stolen goods' merely by using them when they are in the possession of another; he will only do so if he does something active to 'assist' – as by concealing them or concealing the fact that they are stolen. Thus where a husband brought home stolen goods and his wife (knowing that they were stolen) used them in the home it was held that the mere use was not an 'assistance', but when the wife lied to the police and said she had bought them this did amount to 'assistance'. A person 'assists in realization' if he buys the property himself; so that 'handling' is not confined to the normal case of the 'fence' who disposes of it to others.

It should be added that by the TA, s 24(3) it is enacted that 'no goods shall be regarded as having continued to be stolen goods after they have been restored to the person from whom they were stolen or other lawful possession or custody'. Thus where a person receives goods knowing that they were stolen he will not be guilty if in fact, unknown to him, they have passed into the possession of the police.

The maximum punishment for this offence is 14 years' imprisonment.

## vii  Restitution of stolen property

Where a person has been deprived of his property by means of a criminal act it is only right that, if possible he should recover it. Satisfaction can always be had by resort to a civil action and it may be (and often is) effected by administrative action on the part of the police – though, in order to safeguard themselves against a civil claim for conversion the latter should apply for a court order under the Police (Property) Act 1897. This Act provides that where property has come into the possession of the police in connection with *any criminal charge,* magistrates' courts may order it to be delivered to any person appearing to be the owner: and after the expiry of six months from the delivery claims to it by third parties are barred. Yet in some circumstances it may assist the owner to have the active help of the court which convicts the thief. The TA, s 28, therefore empowers any court which has convicted a person of any offence *with reference to theft* – an expression sufficiently wide to embrace, for instance, a case of handling – to order any person in possession of the stolen property to restore it to the person entitled to it. And, reasonably enough, an order may also be made in respect of any goods which represent the stolen goods – eg B steals A's horse and then exchanges it for a cow. Moreover, since in such a case B might rather sell than exchange the horse, the court may also order payment to the owner of any money taken out of the convicted person's possession at the time of his apprehension, not in excess of the value of the thing stolen.

Finally, in order to afford some protection to third parties who may suffer by reason of the theft, it is provided that where the thief has sold or pledged the goods to such people (being in good faith and ignorant of the theft) and the owner has obtained an order for the return to him of the goods, these people may themselves obtain an order for payment – up to the value of the price they paid or the loan they gave – of any moneys taken out of the possession of the miscreant at the time of his apprehension. Thus Jasper steals Tom's car and sells it to Fred (who knows nothing of the theft): Tom obtains an order against Fred for the return of the car to him; then Fred may, if by good fortune Jasper has the cash upon him at the time of his arrest, obtain an order for the repayment to him of the purchase price out of Jasper's ill-gotten gains. Such an ideal solution – Jasper behind bars, all property rightfully restored – must of course in practice seldom be achieved, for money does not stick to the fingers of thieves; and as likely as not Jasper will at least appear upon arrest to be penniless.

## 2   CRIMINAL DAMAGE

The law in respect of damage to property was formerly mostly contained in the Malicious Damage Act 1861 – and it was fragmented, detailed and complicated. That Act has now been substantially repealed and replaced by the Criminal Damage Act 1971 (hereafter 'CDA'); a statute containing generalizations which seem less complicated, but have proved to be more difficult to apply.

Under the CDA there are now three main offences:

(*i*) The offence of *destroying* or *damaging property* (s 1). This is committed (s 1(1)) where 'a person . . . *destroys* or *damages any* property *belonging to another intending* to destroy or damage *any such property or being* reckless as to whether *any* such property would be destroyed or damaged'. It is to be noted that the destruction of the offender's *own* property is *not* here included, and that it has been held that, however unjustified the belief, it is a defence to establish that the defendant *thought* that the property was his own. The intention or recklessness need not necessarily be directed to the property *actually* affected: thus if I shoot at your pet pigeon and hit your neighbour's by mistake the offence will be committed. This offence (s 1(2)) also takes an aggravated form where the intent (or recklessness) in relation to the destruction of or damage to the property is linked with an intent to *endanger the life of another person*, or with reckless disregard of such danger. The test of the intention is whether a prudent bystander would have envisaged an obvious risk that the property would be damaged and life thereby endangered. But, for this offence to be committed the danger to life must arise from the damage to the property. Thus if I fire at a window of a room when there is someone in the room the offence may be committed because of the danger from broken glass. If, however, I fire at a wall (which is unlikely to disintegrate), even though the shot may endanger life, I cannot be charged under s 1(2). The property destroyed *may* be the miscreant's *own* – as for example where Ned blows up his garden shed, reckless to whether he endangers the life of Ted, his neighbour. In the case of an offence under either s 1(1) or s 1(2) if the agent of destruction is *fire* the charge will be one of '*arson*' (s 1(3)) (which, with the coming into effect of the CDA ceased to be a common law offence).

'Recklessness' in the case of criminal damage has the same meaning that it has in relation to manslaughter.

It should be noted that a person will be guilty of arson if, having started a fire by accident, he takes no steps to put it out. Thus, where a man in a boarding house set fire (by accident) to his mattress with a cigarette and then left the fire to spread while he calmly removed himself to another room, he was held guilty.

Whereas drunkenness is no excuse for a charge under s 1(1) it may be a defence under s 1(2) because that sub-section requires a specific intent to endanger life, etc which may be negatived by drunkenness.

*(ii)* The offence of *threatening* to destroy or damage property (s 2). This will be committed by anyone who 'makes to another a *threat*, intending that the other would fear it would be carried out: (a) to *destroy* or *damage* any property belonging to *that other* or *a third person*; or (b) to destroy or damage *his own* property in a way which he knows is likely to *endanger the life of that other or a third person*'.

*(iii)* The offence (s 3) of *possessing* anything with intent to destroy or damage property. This crime will be committed where a person 'has anything in his *custody* or *control*' intending . . . to *use it* or cause or permit *another to use it*: (a) to destroy or damage any property *belonging to some other person*; or (b) to destroy or damage his *own* or the *user's* property in a way which he knows is likely to endanger *the life of some other person*.

None of the offences under these sections will be committed if the accused has some '*lawful excuse*' and it is, as always, for the prosecution, *if doubt arises*, to establish the *absence* of 'lawful excuse'. In the case of infractions of ss 1(1) and 2(a), however, this phrase – besides its ordinary meaning, as embraces, for example, mistake or self-defence – is given an extended meaning (s 5) so as to include two special kinds of circumstances. The first of these (s 5 (2)(a)) is where the perpetrator believes that he has (in doing what he does) the consent of any person who is, or whom he believes to be, entitled to *give consent* to the act. The second (s 5(2)(*b*)) is where the perpetrator causes the destruction or damage while using reasonable means to protect property of his own or of another which he believes to be in immediate need of protection (for instance the case of the sheep-worrying dog). But the need must be immediate; and it is no answer to setting fire to a house that the arson was committed in order to draw attention to the defectiveness of its fire alarm. Whether the belief is justified or not is irrelevant provided that it is honestly held (s 5(3)). Hence if drunkenness (so prominent in relation to this crime) induces an honest, though mistaken, belief that the property damaged belonged to X (who would have consented to it) rather than to Y (who would not) the offence will not be committed.

For the purposes of the CDA '*property*' means (s 10) 'property of a *tangible* nature whether real or personal, including *money*': *wild* mushrooms and the *flowers, fruit* and *foliage* of wild plants, trees and shrubs are, however, excluded. Here there is no proviso as to commercial purposes (see TA, s 4(3)). Perhaps the rambler who picks a wild flower should bear in mind the judgment of Portia and refrain from taking any of the *stem*. The severing of branches of holly would certainly appear to fall foul of the TA, s 4 and of this section.

A person guilty of *arson* or of an offence under the CDA, s 1(2) may receive life imprisonment; offences under the CDA carry a ten-year maximum.

# 3 Compensation

For a long time past, and, indeed as early as the Criminal Law Act 1826, it has been possible for courts to award compensation to people who suffer loss as the result of the commission of crimes. By that Act, which is still in force (in an amended form) the court may order payment *out of public funds* to anyone active in the apprehension of people who have committed an arrestable offence by way of compensation to the former for his exertions and for any expenses he may have incurred in the course of them. Moreover, the Riot (Damages) Act 1886 provides for compensation for property damaged or destroyed by rioters; and the Merchant Shipping Acts contain similar provisions in respect of the plunder of wrecked ships by rioters, while modern legislation has similar provisions in respect of aircraft. More important than any of these particular statutes are, however, the provisions of the Powers of Criminal Courts Act 1973 as to compensation, and the awards made by the Criminal Injuries Compensation Board.

By the 1973 Act (as amended by the Criminal Justice Act 1988), s 35(1) it is provided that 'a court by or before which a person is convicted of an offence . . . may . . . make an order (in this Act referred to as a 'compensation order') requiring him to pay compensation for any *personal injury, loss or damage* resulting from that offence . . . or to make payments for funeral expenses or bereavement in respect of a death resulting from any such offence, other than a death due to an accident arising out of the presence of a motor vehicle on a road'. By s 1(3) – as amended – it is provided that 'a compensation order may only be made in respect of injury, loss or damage . . . which was due to an accident arising out of the presence of a motor vehicle on a road' in certain circumstances of which the most important is, in effect, where the offender was uninsured. Of course if he was insured the injured party will be compensated thereby. An order in respect of bereavement may only be made for the benefit of those entitled to damages for bereavement under the Fatal Accidents Act 1976 (p 314).

It is to be noted that s 35(4) provides that 'In determining whether to make a compensation order . . . the court shall have regard to the means (of the offender)'. And it has been held that no order should be made if it would be likely to have the result of inducing the convicted person to resort to further crime in order to discharge his obligations under the order. Where an order has been made (s 38), and the aggrieved person later brings a civil action against the criminal in respect of the loss, the damages are to be assessed in the normal way, as if no order had been made; but the award itself must not exceed the amount (if any) by which the assessment exceeds the amount of the compensation order. Thus the aggrieved person cannot be compensated twice – in all, he will only receive the amount assessed by the civil court.

By the Criminal Justice Act 1988 the *Criminal Injuries Compensation Board* was placed on a statutory basis. In due course, the Criminal Injuries Compensation Act 1995 will govern the payment of damages to victims of crime (see below). It is composed of legally qualified members and determines claims for compensation in respect of criminal injuries in accordance with a scheme set out in Sch 7 of the Act. The Act defines a 'criminal injury' as 'any *personal injury* caused by – (a) conduct constituting –' (i) certain specified offences (including, *inter alia*, rape, assault and arson): *or* (ii) any other offence 'which requires proof of intent to cause death or personal injury or recklessness as to whether death or personal injury is caused' (manslaughter, for example) or (b) (any personal injury caused by) 'any of the following activities: (i) the apprehension or attempted apprehension of an offender or suspected offender; (ii) the prevention or attempted prevention of the commission of an offence; or (iii) assisting a constable engaged in either (i) or (ii). 'Personal injury' includes any disease, any harm to a person's physical or mental condition and pregnancy. But 'harm to a person's mental condition is only a criminal injury if it is attributable – (a) to his having been put in fear of immediate physical injury to himself or another; or (b) to his being present when another sustained a criminal injury other than harm to his mental condition'. The injury must, however, be a 'qualifying injury'. This means principally, that it must have been sustained in Great Britain, in United Kingdom territorial waters or on board a British ship, aircraft or hovercraft. And also that the injury must not have been sustained in circumstances in which compensation for it is payable by means of compulsory insurance in relation to the use of a motor vehicle on a road. The Board may pay compensation to any person who has sustained a qualifying injury or to any dependant of a person who died after sustaining a qualifying injury. In the case of death the award may include payment of funeral expenses and people for whose benefit damages for bereavement may be awarded (see above) may be given compensation. There is a right of appeal on a question of law from the Board to the High Court. It the person who has caused the injury has been convicted the Board may, in certain circumstances, obtain reimbursement from him. Compensation, once received, cannot be assigned to anyone else and the award cannot pass to the trustee in bankruptcy of the person who receives it.

When it comes into force, the 1995 Act will repeal the 1988 Act. The new Act provides that the Secretary of State shall make arrangements for the payment of compensation to or in respect of persons who have sustained one or more personal injuries as a victim of a crime. The arrangements shall include the establishing of a scheme dealing with the circumstances in which awards are to be made and the categories of persons eligible. Provision is to be made for a standard amount of compensation, determined by reference to the nature of the injury and may include an additional amount for loss of earnings, special expenses, and in fatal cases, such additional amounts as may be specified. A tariff is to be prepared by the Secretary of State to cover the standard amounts. The scheme in particular may set maximum figures for compensation. Reviews of decisions on claims and rights of appeal will be provided for. The jurisdiction of the Parliamentary Commissioner is extended to the scheme.

# Chapter 7
# Welfare law

There has always been something that could be called 'Welfare' law, even (or, perhaps, especially) when all it comprised was the feudal overlord observing duties of protection of his underlings. The roots of social security go back to the Elizabethan poor law and beyond; but modern statutes have proliferated vast fields of law, rules and regulations designed to promote the safety, happiness and well-being of the individual and of society itself.

A thorough survey of welfare law would be a vast undertaking which cannot be attempted here; all that can be done is to indicate, in general terms, some aspects of it and then to discuss in more detail a number of them which seem to demand particular attention.

One may first mention the field of *public health*; starting with nineteenth century statutes the main bastion of protection of public health is now the Public Health Act 1936 which provides a code governing the manifold duties of public health authorities: these include such matters as the prevention of epidemics, the treatment of disease and the abatement of nuisances which endanger health.

Concern about *housing* was reflected in nineteenth century statutes, and, under the many Housing Acts local authorities are charged with assessing needs in their areas, the building of new houses and flats, dealing with areas of bad housing by clearance, improvement or re-development, the encouragement of new house building by other agencies, the re-housing of displaced persons, the abatement of overcrowding and the control of houses in multiple occupation, the making of loans to assist owner-occupation and grants for the improvement and modernisation of houses and the administration of schemes of rent rebates and allowances for tenants in both the public and private sectors. However, when money is to be borrowed or land compulsorily acquired, then central approval is necessary. The central authority is the Secretary of State for the Environment, assisted by a Minister for Housing and Construction and the Secretaries of State for Wales and Scotland. Under the provisions of the Home Energy Conservation Act 1995 local authorities are now required to prepare reports, setting out their plans for the significant, practicable, cost-effective improvement in the energy efficiency of residential accommodation.

The Town and Country Planning Acts are designed to protect the environment as a whole by prohibiting unseemly or unsuitable property development. *Rural amenities* are protected by such statutes as the Countryside Act 1968 which gives to local authorities and to other bodies, such as the Forestry Commission, wide powers to open the countryside for public recreation. As to the protection and conservation of the *environment* in far more general terms, the various Clean Air Acts (consolidated in 1993) have enforced smoke control while the Control of Pollution Act 1974 and the Control of Pollution (Amendment) Act 1989 deal with river pollution, control and transport of waste, noise abatement and many other such matters. An ambitiously global measure was enacted in 1995, simply called the Environment Act. Everything around us is affected, from the land to the air, including the water and fisheries in between.

Under the heading of 'welfare' many other matters could be mentioned, such as the legislation which governs education and the national health service; but space forbids. The following aspects of welfare law have been selected for detailed consideration – social security, legal aid and advice and consumer protection.

# 1  Social security

Social security legislation in its modern form, rests ultimately upon the Beveridge Report which was published in 1942. That Report engendered the National Insurance and the National Insurance (Industrial Injuries) Acts 1946 which – although they are now superseded – set the pattern for the present social security law which is now principally governed by the Social Security Act 1973, the Social Security Pensions Act 1975, the Social Security Contributions and Benefits Act 1992, the Social Security Administration Act 1992 and the Social Security (Consequential Provisions) Act 1992.

The Social Security Act 1973 and the Social Security Pensions Act 1975 set out the requirements for an occupational pensions scheme and, given an approved scheme, the conditions for contracting out of part of the state pensions scheme.

The measures enacted in 1992 are consolidations of earlier statutes, with consequential amendments. These provide the basic scheme of earnings-related national insurance contributions and both contributory and non-contributory social security benefits, together with a number of other social security benefits which are not directly linked with national insurance.

Benefits within the scheme which depend upon contributions (made or credited) include: maternity allowance, unemployment and sickness benefit, category A and B retirement pensions, widow's benefit and child's special allowance. Benefits which do not depend upon contributions include: attendance allowance, invalid care allowance, severe disablement allowance, disability living allowance, category C and D retirement pensions (and age addition payable in addition to any retirement pension), and guardian's allowance. There are various other benefits integrated with all these. They include: invalidity benefits, industrial injuries benefits, child benefit, statutory sick pay, statutory maternity pay, income support, family credit, disability working allowance, housing benefit and social fund payments.

The conditions under which these benefits are payable vary considerably. The many rules and regulations cannot be dealt with adequately here, within the space available, and the picture is constantly developing. For example, from October 1996, jobseekers' allowance will replace unemployment benefit and income support for unemployed people. There are nearly 30 telephone 'helplines' to guide claimants around the system. It is administered by the Benefits Agency which was established in April 1991, employing 63,000 people to process 12 million claims each year, totalling more than £70 billion (about 35% of all public expenditure).

# 2    Legal aid

The provision of legal aid is now governed by the Legal Aid Act 1988, and the regulations made under it, which to a large extent continues a system which was already in existence before it came into force. The Act is designed to make provision in England and Wales for legal advice and assistance and legal representation in civil and criminal proceedings to be provided from public funds to help people who might otherwise be unable to obtain advice, assistance or representation because their means are insufficient. (North of the border the system is governed by the Legal Aid (Scotland) Act 1986.) The legal aid scheme in England and Wales may be considered under four heads: (i) the administration of the scheme; (ii) legal advice and assistance; (iii) legal aid in civil cases; (iv) legal aid in criminal cases.

## (i)  The administration of the scheme
Formerly the provision of legal aid was entrusted to the Law Society; but the 1988 Act transferred this duty to the Legal Aid Board, an incorporated body, which it brought into being. This body consists of members, headed by a 'lay' chairman, who have special knowledge of the provision of legal services, the work of the courts, social conditions and management. Representation of the legal profession is confined to two solicitor and two barrister members. The Act requires the Board to establish a Legal Aid Fund comprising contributions by legally aided people and public funds.

The scheme is financed by monies supplied by this Fund. Since 1994 the Board has delegated some of its powers, and amended the procedures for paying solicitors for advice and assistance and within both the civil and criminal legal aid systems by setting up a franchising structure. This entails making contracts for specified work with firms of solicitors who meet and maintain set standards. These franchisees can then claim larger amounts on account and receive higher hourly rates from the fund.

### (ii) Legal advice and assistance

This advice and assistance may be provided where it is required in respect of the application of English law to any circumstances, whether they involve civil or criminal matters. Normally the kind of advice or assistance in question concerns such matters as giving general advice, writing letters, negotiating settlements, agreements or other documents and advising upon the desirability of bringing or defending legal proceedings. There are certain areas of work which are specifically excluded from the legal advice and assistance scheme (by the Legal Advice and Assistance (Scope) Regulations 1989). They include many (but not all) aspects of both conveyancing and the drawing of wills. The legal advice and assistance scheme will not usually include representation in actual legal proceedings because such representation is supplied by civil and criminal legal aid. The person who provides the advice or assistance will, at least in the first instance, normally be a solicitor.

The rule that the provision of advice and assistance does not extend to representation in litigation is, however, subject to an exception. Assistance '*by way of representation*' may be provided in relation to certain specific kinds of proceedings. At present, however, these, generally, only include domestic proceedings before magistrates' courts and certain specified tribunals.

A person who seeks advice and assistance must, in the first place, consult a solicitor or go to a legal aid office which will direct him to one. It is the first duty of the solicitor to require him to complete a form (the scheme is known as the 'green form' scheme) setting out details of his income and capital. The purpose of this is to enable the solicitor to ascertain whether his or her resources are such as to make the applicant eligible for legal aid under the scheme. The regulations regarding eligibility are too complicated to be discussed here, but the gist of the matter is that in order for the applicant to be eligible his resources must not exceed certain amounts prescribed by regulation from time to time. Moreover, if the resources do not exceed these amounts the legal aid will not necessarily be entirely free because, unless the resources fall below a prescribed minimum amount, *contribution* by the applicant may be exacted.

There is an important further limitation upon the right to advice and assistance under the Act; namely, that the solicitor is required to estimate the costs which are likely to be incurred in giving the advice and assistance and if this estimate exceeds a prescribed amount the aid cannot be provided.

The solicitor himself has a first charge for his costs on any money or property recovered by the applicant as the result of advice and assistance given. This he may exercise if he has not been remunerated by any contribution the applicant has made. If his costs have not been met by contribution or the exercise of the charge they will be defrayed from the Legal Aid Fund.

The 'green form' scheme has now been with us for some years and those who operate it claim that it has been a success. Its limitations, however, are obvious; both because the prescribed limits of eligibility are low and because the services must not exceed a very low cost.

This is the place to note that the limitations of the green form scheme are to some extent met by the fact that a number of agencies do provide free legal services. These include *local law centres*, *staffed by solicitors*, *legal advice centres* and *neighbourhood law centres*. Many *citizens' advice bureaux* offer the free services of solicitors on a rota basis.

### (iii)  Legal aid in civil cases

In this sense 'legal aid' signifies the provision of free or contributory representation in court proceedings. It is available in respect of most proceedings before the ordinary courts, the Employment Appeal Tribunal, the Lands Tribunal, Commons Commissioners appointed under the Commons Registration Act 1965 and the Restrictive Practices Court. In order for an applicant to obtain it his resources must come within currently prescribed *financial limits*, and in the case of married people joint resources are taken into account. As in the case of advice and assistance, so here there are regulations governing contributions payable in cases where, though the applicant is financially eligible, the aid will not be entirely free. Below a prescribed limit, however, no contribution will be required. Beside satisfying the regulations concerning resources the applicant must also show that he has *reasonable grounds* for taking, defending or being a party to the proceedings in question.

The right to aid depends upon the obtaining of a *legal aid certificate*. In order to do this the applicant must satisfy the Legal Aid Board (through a legal aid office) that he is financially eligible and he must also satisfy a *legal aid committee* (barristers and solicitors) that his case is not trivial and that he has reasonable grounds for bringing or defending the proceedings. Where the litigation is between an assisted person and an unassisted person the latter is clearly at a disadvantage. If he loses his case he will have to pay the costs of it: if he wins he can recover no costs from the assisted person. The Act meets this difficulty by providing that, in prescribed circumstances, the court may order payment of these costs by the Legal Aid Board. These circumstances include the fact that the court must be satisfied that, unless it makes the order, the unassisted party will suffer 'severe financial hardship' (this may, perhaps, seem an inequitable fetter upon his rights) and the court must also be satisfied that it is 'just and equitable' that the order should be made.

It remains to be added that the Legal Aid Board is given a first charge upon any money or property recovered in an action by an assisted person in respect of any sums paid by it for which any contribution from the assisted person is due.

#### (iv) Legal aid in criminal cases

In criminal cases it is the *court* before which the proceedings take place which determines whether aid by way of representation in the proceedings is to be provided. This is because in criminal cases an immediate decision is often essential. The court may only grant aid if the accused can show that his financial resources are such that he is (within the prescribed limits) eligible for free or contributory aid. The court must also be satisfied that it is desirable in the interests of justice to grant the aid and it must take into account certain other criteria. For example, it must consider whether the offence is such that, if proved, a sentence would be likely to be imposed which would deprive the accused of his liberty, lead to loss of his livelihood, or to serious damage to his reputation.

The proceedings in question are proceedings before: (a) a Magistrates' Court; (b) the Crown Court; (c) the criminal division of the Court of Appeal or the Courts Martial Appeal Court; and (d) the House of Lords in the exercise of its jurisdiction in relation to appeals from either of those two courts.

Mention should be made of the Duty Solicitor Scheme by which 'duty solicitors' are available in magistrates' courts to advise and assist defendants who are eligible for advice or representation. And they must also represent them if they elect to plead guilty.

It should also be noted that solicitors and barristers against whom complaints are made to their respective disciplinary tribunals may be excluded from legal aid work or have their fees reduced.

# 3  Proposals for change

As part of its 'overall strategy to improve access to justice' (which prominently features the work of Lord Woolf) in July 1996 the government published a White Paper, summary documentation, and many leaflets collectively entitled 'Striking the Balance, The Future of Legal Aid in England and Wales'. It was pointed out that the cost of legal aid in 1995–96 was £1.4 milion – twice as much as in 1990. The cost cutting practice in the past involved 'adjusting' financial eligibility, but now the scope for this is much reduced, given that the number of people who are eligible has fallen from 70% of households in the 1980s to about 50% now. The government asserted that radical change is needed: to control overall costs effectively, to encourage efficiency while maintaining quality, to target the available resources on the most appropriate and cost-effective services and the most deserving cases and to promote fair treatment for all concerned, and discourage irresponsible behaviour. To meet these laudable objectives five core reforms are suggested: replacing the present open-ended approach to resources with pre-determined budgets that can be allocated to meet local demand within national priorities, extending the scheme to new types of providers and services (such as advice agencies and mediators), introducing contracts between providers of services and the Legal Aid Board for specified services of defined quality at an agreed price, setting a new test for deciding whether civil cases should be given legal aid and changing the rules governing financial conditions to increase the potential liability of assisted persons to contribute to their own and, in civil cases, their opponents' costs.

The day before the White Paper was published the Law Society weighed in with their own set of proposals for reform which, it is claimed, would save £130 million and include an extra 8 million people within the scheme. These reforms also include tightening the legal aid 'merits' test to stop money being paid for unjustified cases or for cases which are pursued after a reasonable settlement has been offered. In addition a Conditional Legal Aid Fund is proposed, in line with the conditional 'no win, no fee' arrangements which have been recently adopted by the Profession, and a Test Case Fund for broader matters which might easily result in complex and expensive cases (such as taking action against tobacco companies).

Lord Denning wrote: '...since the Second World War the greatest revolution in the law has been the system of legal aid'. Over the past decade or so the costs of the system have risen while those eligible have fallen. There have been individual instances where the apparently rich have slipped under the barriers while many others are left outside. It is yet to be seen whether the structure will hold. Sometimes the cracks are too wide to be papered over.

# 4   Consumer protection

There is nothing new about 'consumer protection'; only the phrase. The idea of it is older than the ancient law of Rome which implied warranties of title into conveyances of land and forced slave dealers (whose repute was as bad as, or worse than, that of second-hand car dealers) to warrant the qualities of their wares. It is as old as the Assize of Bread and Ale (1266) which decreed elaborate policing of false measure; as old as the Eyre of London in 1321 of which it is recorded that the Justices approved the arrangements of the hatters to enforce the labelling of caps of inferior quality, and having fixed the prices for the poulterers, upon their plea that such low prices would be their ruin, were forced to raise them again.

What is new about consumer protection is that it has become an obsession with individual consumers, politicians and legislatures: and it is spawning institutions and laws. Put together (like 'environmental law') it presents a mountainous hotchpotch of laws, and can be taken to embrace almost anything that is connected with trade, consumption or even personal safety. A number of topics which may properly be regarded as 'consumer protection' will be treated elsewhere; they include the law relating to exemption clauses to implied terms in sale, and to consumer credit. Here, briefly as we must, it is proposed first to examine the institutional machinery of consumer protection, and then to discuss selected fields of consumer protection legislation.

## 1   THE MACHINERY OF CONSUMER PROTECTION

The central institutional machinery designed to protect the consumer is headed by the Secretary of State for Trade and Industry whose Department is responsible, *inter alia*, for consumer protection legislation in general (though other departments, such as the Home Office and the Department of Agriculture, Fisheries and Food also play a part) and is also responsible for the work of the Office of Fair Trading, the Monopolies and Mergers Commission, the National Consumer Council, the Consumer Protection Advisory Committee and Nationalized Industry Consumer Councils.

Much of the central impetus for promoting and policing consumer protection, however, lies in the *Office of Fair Trading* ('OFT') headed by the *Director General of Fair Trading*, a post created by the Fair Trading Act 1973 (hereafter 'FTA'). The Director General's functions are, in general, to keep under review the carrying on of commercial activities in the United Kingdom which relate to goods or services supplied to *consumers*, to collate information about commercial malpractices, to give information and assistance to the Secretary of State in respect of such matters, and to monitor any commercial activities detrimental to consumers (FTA, s 2). 'Consumer' is defined (s 137(2)) as a *person, himself not acting by way of business, who receives goods or services from a person who is*. In particular, the Director, the Secretary of State, or any other minister is empowered to make *references to the Consumer Protection Advisory Committee*, a body constituted by s 3 of the FTA, upon the question whether 'a *consumer trade practice* . . . adversely affects the interests of consumers' (s 14(1)) and the Committee must report on this issue to whoever made the reference. 'Consumer trade practice' is defined in s 13, and it covers such matters as the conditions of supply of goods or services, methods of sale, methods of packing, etc. By s 17 the *Director* may, in making a reference to the Committee under s 14, where the reference concerns a consumer trade practice which is likely to have certain specific effects (eg to mislead consumers or to impose inequitable terms), include in the reference proposals that the Secretary of State should take action to suppress the practice. The Committee must then consider, and report to the Secretary of State upon the proposal as well as the reference. Their report must then be laid before Parliament and thereafter the Secretary of State may, by statutory instrument, make, at his discretion, such regulation as may be thought by him to be appropriate to inhibit the malpractice. Unfortunately, this procedure has in practice been abandoned as it was decided not to appoint any new members to the CPAC on the retirement of existing members. By s 34, where it appears to the Director that a person is carrying on business in a manner detrimental to the interests of, or unfair to, consumers he may seek an assurance from that person that he will refrain from that practice. In the event of refusal or subsequent continuance of the practice the Director may refer the matter to the Restrictive Practices Court. Section 124(3) contains a provision which has proved to be both popular and important: it enacts that 'the Director (shall) encourage relevant (trade) associations to prepare, and disseminate to their members, *codes of practice*': a number of these codes, regulating such matters as methods of supply, promptness of delivery and execution, treatment of customers, etc are in operation. They are outside the general law, being voluntary and contractual as between association members; but they have already had a limited  beneficial effect upon the conduct of traders and suppliers of services.

Besides the Department of Trade and Industry ('DTI') and the OFT there are a number of other bodies designed to promote consumer protection. Briefly, these include the well-known (but none-too-effective) *consumer councils* – such as the Domestic Coal Consumers' Council or the Post Office Users' National Council – set up with the nationalized industries and services; and now controlled by the DTI. They also include the *National Consumer Council*, created in 1975, which is mainly concerned (though not too effectively) with representing consumer interests at the policy level. At local government level the Local Government Act 1972 empowered local authorities to provide advisory services on consumer matters: this has resulted in the creation locally of many *consumer advice centres* to assist consumers generally in making enquiries and airing complaints. It should also be noted that most of the actual *enforcement* of consumer protection – in such fields, for example, as weights and measures or food and drugs – lies with the Trading Standards or 'Consumer Protection' (formerly Weights and Measures) Departments of County Councils.

Voluntary associations, such as the Consumers' Association and the British Standards Institute – the former the promoter of *Which?*, the latter the setter of standards of production and design – fall outside this work. But a final word about the impact of the EC is necessary. As will appear below, EC directives are already affecting the common law in the consumer field, and there is an Environment and Consumer Protection Service within the Commission responsible for promoting consumer policy. There is also the Bureau Européen des Unions de Consommateurs, which is a federation of consumer associations, and which supplies information and advice to the European Commission. Moreover, even the Council of Europe has influenced the consumer field; as, for example, by promoting a Convention on Products Liability (1976). Further, both the EC and the Council of Europe have treated consumer protection as an integral aspect of the promotion of human rights: the former by its Consumer Protection and Information Programme (1975); the latter by its draft Charter on Consumer Protection (1973). EC competence in the area of consumer protection has been independently established by means of the Treaty on European Union on the 1 November 1993.

## 2   FIELDS OF CONSUMER PROTECTION LAW

The following topics are selected for examination: monopolies and mergers, restrictive trade practices, trade descriptions, weights and measures, food safety, consumer safety and investment business.

### (a)  Monopolies and mergers

Monopolies and mergers may be detrimental both to the public interest and to the consumer; and legislation designed to prevent monopolies in the making or vending of products is not new. In particular, the Statute of Monopolies 1623 rendered monopolies (which, like the monopoly for the sole right to import playing cards, had been granted to favourites by royal patent) 'utterly void'. The modern law on the subject is based upon the Fair Trading Act 1973 ('FTA') which replaces the former Monopolies Commission by the *Monopolies and Mergers Commission*. Upon a reference by the Director General of Fair Trading or of the Secretary of State for Trade and Industry, or of a minister, it is the duty of this Commission 'to investigate and report on any question . . . with respect to the existence of a *monopoly situation*' (FTA, s 5). Generally speaking (ss 6–11) such a 'situation' arises as to the *supply of goods or services within the United Kingdom* if: (i) at least *one quarter* of all the goods or services of that description are supplied by or to one person or group: (ii) 'one or more agreements are in operation, the . . . result of which is that goods (or services) of that description are not supplied in the United Kingdom at all'. In respect of *exports* of goods of any description a 'monopoly situation' exists if: (i) 'At least *one quarter* of the goods of that description which are produced in the United Kingdom are produced by one and the same person (or group): (ii) if one or more agreements are in operation which in any way *prevent or restrict, or prevent, restrict or distort competition* in relation to the export of goods from the United Kingdom', and the agreement or agreements 'are operative as to at least *one quarter* of all the goods of that description which are produced in the United Kingdom'; (iii) where agreements similar to (ii) exist in relation to the supply of export goods of any description from the United Kingdom to *any particular market* – with the difference that, in this case, the prevention, restriction etc is to be considered in relation to the supply of goods as a whole to that market, not confined to United Kingdom exports.

Normally references about monopolies are made by the Director General; and he may (s 48) request the Commission to investigate the situation referred, and report the facts; but usually (s 49) the reference will contain a request not only to investigate but also to report whether the matter referred 'operates . . . *against the public interest'*. Various matters to be considered in determining whether the public interest is so affected, including the promotion of consumer interests and of free competition, are set out in s 84. If the Commission *does* consider that there is a 'monopoly situation' and that it does adversely affect the 'public interest' there may be a hearing of interested parties; and eventually the Commission will report to the Secretary of State, who will then lay the report before Parliament. Thereafter, if the report is adverse, either the Secretary of State may make such orders (subject to laying before Parliament) as may be necessary to remedy the situation – and his powers are drastic – or the Director General may seek to take such undertakings from the affected parties as may lead to voluntary elimination of the monopoly.

Monopoly situations are often presaged by *mergers*; and accordingly (FTA, s 5) the Commission has the duty, at the instance of the Secretary of State, of investigating *transfers of newspapers*, or of *newspaper assets* (transfers likely to lead to press monopoly in one or more proprietors) and of *merger situations generally*. The Secretary of State (s 64) may make a 'merger' reference where it appears that enterprises have ceased to be distinct *and* he considers that a monopoly situation has thus arisen *or* where it appears that the assets taken over exceed a certain (large) amount. Upon receipt of the reference the Commission must consider (a) whether a 'merger situation' exists, and if it does, (b) once more, whether it operates against the 'public interest'. The procedure thereafter is similar to the procedure in the case of monopoly situations: either remedial action by order of the Secretary of State or (more usually) by the Director obtaining undertakings.

## (b)  Restrictive trade practices

Monopolies may be harmful because concentration of economic power prevents competition, engenders inefficiency, indifferent service and uncompetitive prices: agreements in restraint of trade are also often detrimental both because they may have similar effects and because, on principle, they limit output – and they are often presumed at common law to be contrary to public policy. Restrictive trading agreements are now under the statutory control of the Restrictive Trade Practices Act 1976 (hereafter 'RTPA'), as amended by the Restrictive Trade Practices Act 1977.

The RTPA (ss 6, 7, 11, 12) enacts that *restrictive trading agreements* and agreements for the provision of *information* (intended, of course, to be acted upon) between people carrying on business within the United Kingdom are, in general, to be presumed to be contrary to the public interest and void. These embrace agreements concerning the supply both of *goods* and of *services*.

As to the supply of *goods* – the inhibited categories are, as to 'restrictive trading agreements', *inter alia*, 'agreements under which restrictions are accepted in respect of the *prices* to be charged, the *terms* on which the goods are to be supplied and the quantities of goods to be produced' (s 6): as to 'information agreements', *inter alia*, agreements 'in respect of the *prices* to be charged, the terms (of supply), the *quantities* of supply and the *areas or places* of supply' (s 7).

As to the supply of *services* – the inhibited categories are, as to 'restrictive agreements as to services', agreements which have been designated by the Secretary of State by statutory instrument for control under the Act *and* which are of certain specified kinds including agreements as to the *charges* to be made, the *terms* (of supply), the *persons* to whom the services are to be made available (s 11): as to 'information agreements', such agreements which have similarly been designated and which are also of certain specified kinds (s 12).

Agreements which fall within these provisions must – normally within three months – be *registered* at the Office of Fair Trading in the Register of Restrictive Agreements. They are, as has been noted, deemed (ss 10, 19) to be *against the public interest* and void (unenforceable but if acted upon to someone's detriment, actionable by him) but they may, if referred by the Director General of Fair Trading to the Restrictive Practices Court, be made valid by that court if it considers them justified by reference to the existence of certain specified circumstances (often called 'gateways') *and* if it is *also* satisfied that they are 'not unreasonable having regard to the balance between those circumstances and any detriment to the public likely to result'. The 'gateways' include the fact that the relevant agreement is reasonably necessary to protect the public against injury, that its avoidance would deny the public of substantial benefits, that it does *not restrict competition* to any material degree (ss 10, 19).

By the Restrictive Trade Practices (Services) Order 1976 as amended the Secretary of State exercised his powers under s 11, and designated many forms of services as coming within the control of the Act; but a formidable list of agreements as to services are *exempted*: they include services in respect of road, sea and air transport, the services of building societies and, above all, professional services listed in Sch 1 of the RTPA (eg legal, medical, architectural, accounting and surveying services: which must, to some degree, be restrictive in order, through their professional institutions, to ensure the exclusion of unqualified practitioners). Moreover, by Sch 3 certain classes of agreements are, in general, exempt; including 'know-how' agreements and agreements concerning patents and designs – trade secrets must, for the common good, be protected. There are also further exemptions contained in ss 29–33 both absolute and qualified – agreements which are important to the national economy, agreements to enforce maximum prices and agreements as to marketing and other matters between agricultural, etc associations.

Trading agreements affect the economy: it follows that they are of concern to the EC, and the Treaty of Rome contains provisions relating to commercial competition. Article 85 renders void agreements between undertakings which affect trade *between member states* and which have, as their object or effect, the 'prevention, restriction or distortion' of competition within the common market. (Article 86 strikes at monopolies – and prevents undertakings from acquiring 'dominant' positions.) Where an agreement does fall within Article 85 the European law is, of course, overriding; but the RTPA, s 5 provides that, subject to discretions exercisable by the court or by the Director General, the Restrictive Practices Court may assume jurisdiction over an agreement even if it contravenes Article 85. It must be stressed that it is only agreements which are inter-community (which affect trade between member states) that are avoided by Article 85: internal agreements remain unaffected. By ss 9(2) and 34 of the RTPA agreements between coal and steel undertakings – controlled under art 80 of the ECSC Treaty – will normally be exempt from registration as falling under community, rather than under national, law. The reader should be warned that, in view of the increasing encroachment of EC law, the signs are that the restrictive trade practices legislation will, before long, be recast.

### (c)  Trade descriptions

The Trade Descriptions Act 1968, as amended by Part III of the Consumer Protection Act 1987, continued the policy of the Merchandise Marks Acts 1887–1953 (which it repealed) – to discourage misdescription of commodities supplied in the course of business.

The cardinal offence under the Act is committed by '*any person who, in the course of a trade or business, (a) applies a false trade description to any goods; or (b) supplies or offers to supply any goods to which a false trade description is applied*' (s 1(1)).

It is to be noted that the offence can only be committed '*in the course of a trade or business*': private transactions (though they may be unlawful on account of fraud or misrepresentation at common law) are not affected: hence it has been held that a sale by a club to a member is outside the section. The meaning of '*trade description*' is set out at length in s 2: it is 'an indication, direct or indirect' of a number of matters particularized in the section; these include – quantity, method of manufacture, composition, fitness for purpose, physical characteristics, testing (eg 'these goods have been tested by So-and-So'), approval (eg 'Department of Trade approved'), place or date of manufacture, name of manufacturer, previous ownership. A description is *'false'* (s 3) if it is 'false to a material degree'. Thus under modern law it would be 'false' to sell a mixture of cotton and linen as 'linen' just as, under the mediaeval law, it was false to vend a mixture of flock and wool as 'wool', and under the modern law to sell tarragona as 'port' just as, under the Roman law it was to sell vinegar as 'wine'. Consumer protection, as we have remarked, is by no means new. 'False' includes 'misleading'. A statement which is not a trade description may be treated as though it were one if it would be likely to be taken for one.

The trade description must be *'applied'* – as by advertisements, including catalogues, circulars and price lists (s 39(2)) – or by affixation or annexation to the goods themselves (eg stamping an article 'soap') or to anything in (eg a tin), on (eg a tray) or with (eg a label or notice) which they are supplied; or by placing them in, on or with anything (eg on a shelf so marked) to which the description is affixed (s 4(1)). An *oral* statement (eg 'This car is fast') may be a false description (s 4(2)). It is to be noted that the offender need not be a 'supplier', he may also be someone who *'offers to supply'* the goods, and that includes (s 6) 'a person exposing goods for supply *or* having goods *in his possession for supply'*. Thus the exposer, as in a shop window, is not the only person affected, but also the one who, eg keeps in *store* for supply tins of milk marked 'Nissly' produced by a manufacturer other than the well-known firm of Nestlé – a misleading description.

Part III of the 1987 Act (s 20(1)) makes it an offence for a person 'in the course of any business of his (to give) by any means whatever to any consumer any indication which is *misleading as to the price at which any goods, services, accommodation or facilities are available.'* And (s 20(2)) if the giver of the indication has failed to take all such steps as are reasonable to prevent the consumer from relying on the indication, the offence will be committed even though the indication has only *become* misleading *after* it was given and the consumer might be expected to rely on it at a time after it was given.

By s 12 it is a special offence to give a false indication (in the course of a trade or business) that goods or services are of a kind supplied to or approved by Her Majesty; and s 13 applies this principle to statements that they are of a kind supplied to any other person or personage (eg the President of the United States).

Section 14 (most of the foregoing being largely reproduction of the Merchandise Marks Acts) introduces a new principle – namely the application of trade description law to *services*, rather than to goods. The section (s 14(1)) provides that 'it shall be an offence for any person in the course of trade or business – *(a)* to make a statement which he knows to be false or *(b)* recklessly to make a statement which is false as to . . .'. Then follows a list of 'matters', including – the provision in the course of trade or business of services, accommodation or facilities, the time at which services are to be provided, the location and amenities of any accommodation, the effect of any treatment, process or repair. (It has been held that to put a notice falsely advertising a 'closing down' sale in a shop window is not to make a false representation as to a 'facility'.) By s 14(4) it is decreed that '"false" means false to a material degree' *and* 'services' does not include a contract of employment; thus, as in much recent legislation, the employee becomes privileged; apart from the law of deceit in seeking employment he may make what false statements he pleases. It must be noted that the liability is akin to liability for misrepresentation at common law, and that the false statement, must, therefore, be an assertion as to a present fact, rather than as to a future state of affairs. This was illustrated in *Beckett v Cohen* [1973] 1 All ER 120 where a builder, having undertaken to build a garage 'within ten days' (not surprisingly) failed to do so; it was held that the statement fell outside s 14(1) because it related to the future. The ruling seems just because future performance can be guaranteed by means of a term in the contract: but it is not easy to see to what s 14(1)*(b)*(iii) (making a false statement as to 'the time at which services are provided') could apply: presumably, to the waitress who slams down the tea tray at 3.30 pm, announcing that it is 4.30 pm. Under this section the mind boggles at the charges which might be brought in respect of statements by ladies of ill-fame (presumably in 'business', though for the purposes of this Act perhaps they might escape as professionals) as to the nature of their services.

Generally speaking the matters within this enactment are policed by former weights and measures authorities now known as trading standards or consumer protection departments who have wide enforcement powers – eg test purchasing and entry of premises – and by proceedings brought by local authorities.

### (d) Weights and measures

This matter is now governed by the Weights and Measures Act 1985 ('WMA'). The prime purpose of the Act is age old: namely, for the stability of trade and the protection of the consumer, weights and measures must be standard and false weight and false measure must not be given.

Part I of the Act (as amended) sets the standards. These are more of scientific than of legal interest. There are international 'primary' standards kept at the International Bureau of Weights and Measures at Sévres; but for the United Kingdom the *primary* standards (WMA, s 2: Sch 2) are – for the yard, Baily's bronze bar, cast in 1845; for the pound (weight) a platinum cylinder (authorized copies of these are deposited at various places, including the Royal Greenwich Observatory): the UK primary standard for the metre and the kilogram are copies of primary international standards. The Department of Trade and Industry is directed (s 3) to maintain 'secondary' and 'tertiary' standards for most weights and measures (copies from the primary standards) and that Department (s 4) is also responsible for ensuring that local weights and measures authorities (county councils) maintain derivative local standards. The Department also maintains coinage standards. Weights and measures are thus physically derived from national and international prototypes. Moreover, the authorities (s 5) must not only keep local standards but must also provide weights and measures inspectors ('trading standards officers') with (derived) 'working' standards.

Part II of the Act governs weighing and measuring for trade; and operates only in relation to 'use for trade' (s 7); that expression means 'in connexion with, or with a view to, a transaction . . . for the transferring or rendering of money or money's worth . . .' Section 8 makes it an offence to use for trade any unit or measurement which is not included in the authorized list of measures contained in Parts I to V of Sch 1 of the Act. Section 11 secures the proper use of measures by enacting that it is unlawful for any trader to use weighing or measuring equipment for trade unless it has been tested and stamped by an inspector – though certain equipment having EC approval and so marked is now exempted from this section. By s 16 it is an offence to counterfeit, remove, alter, etc any such stamp; and it is also (s 17) an offence for anyone, for the use of trade, to have in his possession false or unjust weighing or measuring equipment. Part IV of the Act makes provisions, supplemented by regulations, which are designed to ensure that certain classes of specified goods are sold by quantity, rather than by package or by container, and that most goods in containers must bear an indication of weight or quantity, etc. Section 28 deals with the important matter of 'short weight'; making it an offence to deliver a shorter weight or lesser quantity than the seller purports to sell; and it makes it a statutory offence (and it is also deceit at common law) to make a false representation as to quantity.

It remains to be added that this is an area in which EC law has had considerable impact. Already by EC Directive (76/211/EEC) a new testing procedure has come into force for many pre-packed goods whereby testing is done in relation to the average contents of selected packets rather than by testing particular packages; moreover, under powers conferred by the Act, the Secretary of State may by order prohibit the use in trade of all imperial (ie traditional) units of measurement except the mile, the foot, the inch, the gallon and the pint, and substitute metric units.

Though the Department of Trade and Industry is ultimately responsible for weights and measures, enforcement is local – through the weights and measures authorities. By the WMA, s 83(1) prosecutions for weights and measures offences can normally only be instituted by or on behalf of a local weights and measures authority or by a chief officer of police.

## (e) Food safety

The basic statute law on this subject which goes back over 100 years, now resides in the code laid down in the Food Safety Act 1990 (hereafter 'FSA'). Only the salient features of this Act can be mentioned here.

The Food Safety Act 1990 creates a number of offences in relation to food. Section 7 provides for an offence of rendering food injurious to health with intent that it should be sold for human consumption. There are a number of ways of committing this offence, namely, (a) by adding an article or substance to the food, or, (b) using any article or substance as an ingredient in the preparation of food, or, (c) abstracting any constituent from it, or, (d) subjecting food to any other process or treatment. 'Injurious to health' includes 'any impairment, whether permanent or temporary' and the probable cumulative effect of consuming ordinary quantities of food of substantially the same composition must be taken into account.

Arguably, the most important offence falls within the remit of s 8 which makes it an offence to sell, deposit or consign to anyone for the purpose of sale, food which fails to comply with safety requirements. This includes (a) food rendered injurious to health, (b) food unfit for human consumption, or, (c) food so contaminated (whether by extraneous matter or otherwise) that it would not be reasonable to expect it to be used for human consumption. The Act contains a presumption that if any food is found to be in breach of the food safety requirements, then, until the contrary is established, all food of the same class or description in the batch, lot or consignment will also fail the requirements. Enforcement officers are given wide powers under s 9 of the Act to inspect for and seize food not satisfying the requirements. Magistrates have power to order its destruction.

The Act also contains further regulatory powers for enforcement officers to issue improvement notices (s 10) where it is believed that there is non-compliance with regulations. In addition, the court has power under s 11 to impose a prohibition order, and under s 12, emergency prohibition notices and orders can be served and made in cases of imminent risk of injury to health. Section 13 gives the Minister the power to make emergency control orders in similar circumstances.

The above are the public controls in relation to public safety, but the Act also contains provisions which are less concerned with safety issues, rather with quality issues and consumer protection matters. In particular, s 14 provides that it is an offence to sell to the prejudice of the purchaser food not of the nature, substance or quality demanded by the purchaser. 'Prejudice' has been broadly construed; it is enough if the food sold is merely of inferior quality. 'Nature' relates to what is *demanded*; hence in *Meah v Roberts* [1978] 1 All ER 97 it was held that an offence was committed when a customer asked for lemonade and received caustic soda – a 'food' of obviously different nature. The meaning of 'substance' in this context must turn upon the degree of difference between what is demanded and what is supplied; thus, if, as in *Tonkin v Victor Value Ltd*

[1962] 1 All ER 821, food is served as a 'mock salmon cutlette' (an article considered superior to a fish cake) and the 'cutlette' contains less fish content even than the standard content for a fish cake, an offence has been committed. By s 14(2) it is no defence that the purchaser bought the food merely for analysis or examination. Further, s 15 makes it an offence to label food with a false or misleading description.

The Act provides for the defence known as the 'due diligence' defence in s 21(1) which is similar to that contained in other pieces of consumer legislation. Enforcement officers have wide powers of entry and seizure of documents (s 32) and for procuring samples (s 29).

### (f) Consumer safety

There are two main sources of law for the protection of the health and safety of consumers, the Consumer Protection Act 1987 Part II and the General Product Safety Regulations 1994, the latter implementing a European Directive on Product Safety. The two schemes of control are not co-extensive and present a confusing picture.

Under the 1987 Act Part II, the Secretary of State has the power to make safety regulations which are aimed at specific products with specific set standards, for example, oil heaters, babies' dummies, hood cords in children's' anoraks. Failure to comply with the regulations amounts to a criminal offence and is also a breach of statutory duty in the civil law. There is also the power vested in the Minister to issue Prohibition Notices, Notices to Warn and Suspension Notices.

The 1987 Act (s 10) also contains the general safety requirement – a general offence of supplying consumer goods which are not reasonably safe. There is in addition a general safety requirement contained in the 1994 Regulations which prohibit producers from putting unsafe consumer goods into circulation and places certain duties on distributors of those goods. This requirement in practice seems to replace almost completely the general safety requirement in s 10 of the 1987 Act.

### (g) Investment business

Experience of recent years has shown that there are few fields of activity in which the consumer needs protection more urgently than in the conduct of investment business. This was brought under control by the Financial Services Act 1986. Its provisions are far-ranging and complex and no more than a general indication of their effect upon consumer protection can be given.

The Act created a regulatory body for investment business – the Securities and Investments Board Ltd. No firm may, in general, carry on investment business unless it is authorized to do so by the Board, a recognized self-regulating organization, or a certified professional body: though certain insurance companies, registered friendly societies and operators or trustees of recognized collective investment schemes have automatic recognition. Provision is also made for authorization of firms, by the Secretary of State, to carry on investment business in Member States of the European Community which do not operate from a permanent place of business in the United Kingdom. There are, however, certain exemptions from authorization: amongst other associations these include the Bank of England and Lloyd's.

The Board is given power to regulate the conduct of business by authorized persons, as by imposing capital adequacy requirements, securing indemnity of authorized persons against claims by investors, and setting up a compensation fund to satisfy such claims. It is also empowered to disqualify operators who break the rules it imposes, and investors themselves may bring a civil action against such people in respect of a breach, *inter alia*, of the rules. Further, it may impose restrictions upon the business authorized persons may undertake, prohibit them from disposing of assets or require them to maintain them in the United Kingdom. The imposition of such restrictions is, however, subject to appeal to the Financial Services Tribunal – a legally qualified chairman and two suitably qualified panel members. Again, investors who suffer loss as the result of the breach of any such restriction are accorded a right of civil action.

In general the insurance business is not affected by the Act but life assurance marketing and pension fund activities come within it. Special rules are applied to friendly societies.

It is important to note that s 163 enjoins a general duty of disclosure in company prospectuses of unlisted securities, namely, that 'a prospectus shall contain all such information as investors . . . would reasonably require, and reasonably expect to find there, for the purpose of making an informed assessment' of the standing of the company. 'Insider dealing' is extended to include abuse of information held by public servants and the Secretary of State is empowered to appoint inspectors to investigate cases of insider dealing.

# Part III

# Private law

# Summary of Part III

# Chapter 8

# The law of contract

## 1  The nature, formation and validity of a contract

### A  THE NATURE OF A CONTRACT

At this stage we enter the field of private law which, as has been noted, is administered by the civil courts and is concerned with rights and duties of individuals between each other, rather than rights and duties vis-à-vis the State.

The duties embraced by the law of torts are imposed by *general rules* of law and they are owed to *all and sundry*. Contractual duties are imposed and defined *by the contract* itself and they are owed to the *other party* to the contract. Thus, as has been pertinently remarked, contractual obligations, though they are restricted by many legal rules, are a kind of law peculiar to the parties and only enforceable, by means of an action for damages or otherwise, between *them*.

Historically, the essence of contractual liability is that it rests upon the notion that someone who suffers a loss in reliance upon the *promise* of another ought to receive compensation for the loss.

Contractual obligations may arise in three ways. *First*, it may, (and normally does) rest upon an *agreement* ('consensual' contract). *Second*, it may rest upon the fact that A has done some act in reliance upon a *promise* by B. This is often treated by writers as though it were an anomaly, and there is a tendency to regard it as if it were something rare. The stock illustration of it is the case of the finder of a lost dog who takes the dog home in response to an offer of reward, or the case of the person who supplies information to the police in similar response. But it is doubtful whether it is really rare. Take the case of the publisher who supplies a book upon a letter of request: he simply supplies the book, he makes *no promise* to do so: he supplies the book in reliance upon the promise to pay implied by the request. *Third*, contractual obligation may rest upon the mere execution of a deed or 'specialty' which contains a promise. Here the mere fact of execution of the deed renders contractual a promise which, without it, need not necessarily have been contractual. Thus a gratuitous promise

– such as a promise of a gift – may become actionable in contract if it is enshrined in a deed. But where the contractual obligation in fact arises from a consensual contract there is of course in general no need to go to the trouble of executing a deed. However, in law, practices are more important than theories and in *practice* a number of such commercial transactions are regularly entered into by deed. Further, the creation of obligations by deed has been simplified by the Law of Property (Miscellaneous Provisions) Act 1989 which provides that it is no longer necessary to use a seal to execute an instrument as a deed by an individual (s 1(1)(*b*)). The intention must be clear, the signature added and attested and the document delivered.

Technically, the first two kinds of contracts are called '*simple*' contracts, the third is called a '*specialty*'. Due to the predominance of the first kind of contract it has often been stated that a contract is a 'legally binding agreement'. In fact, due to the recognition of the other two kinds of contract, that is only a part-truth and the repetition of it has often caused confusion. Though, in the following pages the reader will note that most of the discussion turns upon agreements, the most usual form of contract.

It should be added that the second kind of contract is sometimes called a 'unilateral' contract. A meaningless word, because there must always be two parties to a contract. It has crept in, on account of the erroneous assumption just mentioned, because the 'unilateral' contract is contrasted with the 'bilateral': ie the first kind of contract. What tends to be forgotten is that 'contract' derives from the Latin '*contractus* ' (a 'drawing together of two people') not from the Latin '*consensus*' (agreement). And to the Romans, as to us the 'consensual' contract was only one species of contract. Further, most modern writers tend to dismiss contract under seal (by deed) as if it were not a contract. That is nonsense. The essence of the obligation is contractual, but since it rests upon the formal way in which the contract arises it requires no 'consideration' to support it and it *may* – as was remarked above – be employed to enforce a purely *gratuitous* promise.

Perhaps, too, the reader should be warned of something. Normally a tort (such as a trespass) is committed by a single act or omission done or made in a moment of time. When one enters into a contractual obligation, however, one binds oneself for the *future*: either for a short or for a long (in the case of a 100 year lease, for example, or a purchase of shares) period of time. This explains many of the complexities of contract law. Unexpected things can happen after the contract is made: it may, for instance, be found that it was entered into by a mistake, or as the result of a misleading statement (misrepresentation), or it may even be that its continuance is 'frustrated' by some unexpected event (say a landslide or an earthquake).

The more one thinks the more one is led to realize that 'contract' is a very complex concept.

## B  THE FORMATION OF A CONTRACT

Contractual obligation, excluding the case of the specialty, starts, in legal analysis by the acceptance, by word or conduct of an *offer*. One party is called the 'acceptor'('offeree' or 'promisee'), the other the 'offeror' (or 'promissor'). Though since in the case of a unilateral contract acceptance does not import a 'promise' one cannot in that situation talk about a 'promisee'. There are legal rules which govern both offer and acceptance.

*Offers* – An offer may be made to a particular person or to the world at large: in neither case, however, will there be an agreement until a particular person or persons accept. Not only must the offer be made; but it must be *communicated* to the acceptor. What amounts to communication is a question of fact. In the absence of revocation, an offer, not under seal and without consideration is assumed to be open for a reasonable time, unless it is expressed to be an offer of limited duration. Nevertheless, if the acceptor delays acceptance beyond a reasonable time he may be met by the plea that though the offer was once intended it has now lapsed. What does amount to a reasonable time for acceptance is again a question of fact. The death of either party, however, creates an automatic lapse; moreover, if the offeror himself fixes a time-limit for acceptance, it is clear that the offer lapses if no acceptance is made within that time. Further, unless a subsidiary binding agreement to the contrary has been made, it is always open to the offeror to *revoke* his offer; but the rule is that *revocation must be communicated before acceptance* is made. Thus in *Byrne & Co v Leon Van Tienhoven & Co* (1880) 5 CPD 344, B, in Cardiff, posted a letter containing an offer to A, who was in New York, asking for a reply by cable. This was on 1 October. A received the letter on 11 October and at once accepted, as requested, by cable. On 8 October B had posted a letter in which he revoked the offer; this letter of course reached New York *after A had accepted by the prescribed method*, and *the revocation was thus inoperative*. Here A did not know of the attempted revocation at the time of acceptance; had he known of it, through the medium, for instance, of some third party, there is authority for saying that, at least in equity, he would not have been able to keep B to his bargain, for his conduct would have been virtually fraudulent.

In order to become legally binding an offer must be *clear and unequivocal*; a statement made in the course of negotiation will thus not necessarily amount to an offer. So in the well-known decision of the Judicial Committee of the Privy Council, *Harvey v Facey* [1893] AC 552, the plaintiffs were seeking to buy property called 'Bumper Hall Pen'; they telegraphed to the defendant owners, 'Will you sell us Bumper Hall Pen? Telegraph lowest price'. The defendants replied, 'Lowest cash price Bumper Hall Pen, £900'. The plaintiffs then sought to clinch what they thought was a bargain by answering, 'We agree to buy Bumper Hall Pen for £900 asked by you'. It was held that the defendants' statement was merely a statement of price and not an offer to sell; consequently no contract had been formed. But an unequivocal statement, may in similar circumstances amount to an offer. Thus in *Bigg v Boyd Gibbins Ltd* [1971] 2 All ER 183 where one party wrote 'For a quick sale I would accept £26,000' and the other replied 'I accept your offer' there was a binding contract. Moreover, the content of the contract must be certain; so that where a contract for the sale of land was to be completed in phases, but there was no indication of what parcel of land was to come within each phase, the contract was held to be inoperative for uncertainty.

It is clear on principle that *the acceptor must know of the offer* at the time when he accepts. This would apply in the case of a finder of a lost dog: according to what is probably the better view, he must know of the *offer* of the reward. On the other hand, in the case of a *unilateral contract* acceptance need not be *communicated*. Mrs Carlill did not have to notify the company before using the 'smoke ball'. But in the case of a *consensual* contract it would seem that acceptance must be communicated. Thus, in *Felthouse v Bindley* (1862) 11 CBNS 869, after some argument as to price, an uncle wrote to his nephew 'If I hear no more about him, I consider the horse is mine at £30 15*s*.' There was held to be no contract because, although the nephew had intended to set the horse aside from a sale, having failed to do so, he had not signified acceptance to his uncle. Hence, at the sale, the title to the animal passed to the buyer and the uncle had no claim.

In this area difficulty has been caused by 'high pressure' salesmanship. What of the case where B sends goods to A unsolicited and indicates that unless A returns them he will expect him to pay for them? In the past this had been a source of irritation to many, and the law was uncertain, especially if A appropriated the goods. The Unsolicited Goods and Services Act 1971 provides that where goods are sent to a person unsolicited by him (and he having no reasonable cause to believe that they were sent with a view to his acquiring them for business purposes) they are to be considered to be an *unconditional gift* to him upon certain conditions. These conditions are that *either* (a) during the period of *six months* from the day that they were received the sender did not take possession of them and the recipient did not unreasonably refuse to permit him to do so; *or* (b) not less than *30 days* before the end of the six month period the recipient gave notice to the sender (in a form prescribed by s 1(3) of the Act) and that within 30 days from the sending of this notice the sender did not take possession of the goods, nor the recipient unreasonably refuse to permit him to. So, in summary here, silence cannot constitute acceptance in such circumstances as *Felthouse v Bindley* and if unsolicited goods arrive they become the property of the recipient after six months if he does nothing or after 30 days if he informs the sender that they are available for collection and they remain uncollected. Incidentally, here we are dealing with the formation (or not) of contracts, not performance. Most book and record clubs will send the 'editor's' choice if you fail to tell them not to within a defined time. These are not unsolicited goods, unless you did say 'no' in time.

It may sometimes be relevant, as we saw in relation to *Byrne v Van Tienhoven*, to determine the *exact moment at which acceptance is made*. Usually the answer to this question will depend upon the facts of the case; but there are situations in which the courts have been forced to lay down arbitrary rules. So in the case of contracts concluded by correspondence where the offeror designates no particular time or mode of acceptance, the rule is that acceptance is made *when the letter of acceptance is posted* (this is sometimes called the Rule in *Adams v Lindsell* (1818) 1 B & Ald 68); if therefore the offeror wishes to withdraw his offer he must do so before that time. Naturally, however, if it is stipulated that acceptance must be communicated in order to be effective mere posting will not be enough to conclude the contract. Moreover, apart from the special rules relating to postal contracts, a contract is concluded *where and when acceptance is made*, and modern means of communication, such as telephone, fax or 'e-mail', where offer and acceptance are practically instantaneous, have produced some striking results. Thus in *Entores Ltd v Miles Far East Corpn* [1955] 2 QB 327 a London company offered, by telex, to buy goods from a company in Amsterdam and the offer was instantaneously accepted. It was held that the contract was concluded in London. By contrast, in *Brinkibon Ltd v Stahag Stahl und Stahlwarenhander GmbH* [1983] 2 AC 34 where, by telex, London buyers accepted an offer from Austrian sellers it was held that the contract was made in Vienna.

Auction contracts have also given rise to difficulties. Where goods are sold by auction at what time are the offer and the acceptance respectively made? It has been decided that normally, in the absence of contrary expressed intention, the highest bid constitutes the offer, the fall of the hammer constitutes the acceptance: this rule is statutory (Sale of Goods Act 1979, s 57(2)). In the familiar case of the sale of articles displayed in shops – such as books in a bookshop – in the absence of special circumstances the rule is that the display is only an invitation to treat (like an advertisement) and the customer's act of selecting the article and taking it to the shopkeeper constitutes an *offer to buy*, not an acceptance of a general offer. Accordingly, until he has accepted this offer by agreeing to sell the article the shopkeeper is under no obligation to sell.

It remains to be added that if there has been both offer and acceptance a consensual contract can only be complete if *all essential terms have been agreed*; for there can be no agreement if any such terms remain to be settled. This does not, however, mean that everything must be completely finalized; it suffices that the *essentials* are agreed. Thus for instance in *Sweet and Maxwell Ltd v Universal News Services Ltd* [1964] 2 QB 699, the Court of Appeal held that an agreement for a lease was not to be treated as incomplete only because one of its clauses contained a provision that, beside certain terms specifically set out, there should be 'such conditions as shall reasonably be required' by the lessor; for the court could, and courts often do, determine in this context what is or is not reasonable; and hence the agreement was not too indeterminate to be enforceable. By contrast in *Courtney and Fairbairn Ltd v Tolaini Bros (Hotels) Ltd* [1975] 1 All ER 716 where one party wrote to the other that he would be happy to contract if the other would get a third party to 'negotiate fair and reasonable contract sums' there was no contract. For the vital element of price remained unascertained and at the discretion of the third party.

## C   THE LEGAL VALIDITY OF CONTRACTS

For the formation of a *legally binding* contract certain requirements must be satisfied. First, there must be an intention to contract. Second, the parties must have legal capacity to contract. Third, certain legal formalities may have to be complied with. Fourth, there must usually be 'consideration'. Fifth the objects of the contract must not be illegal.

### 1   INTENTION TO CONTRACT

We have seen that most contracts are agreements. It should now be noted that it is by no means true to say that all agreements are contracts. Many agreements fall outside the scope of the law of contract, either because they concern matters of moral, rather than legal obligation or because the parties agree that they are not to be treated as enforceable contracts, or because they are not intended to be binding. A familiar example is the case of a person who drives a friend somewhere in return for payment of the petrol. On the other hand, there have been a number of cases where 'friends' have found themselves contractually bound by agreements argued (by the losing party) to have been purely social arrangements. In September 1995 a pools winner was held by a county court judge to be bound to share a £1.8 million win. In March 1994 another county court held that a £43,000 jackpot bingo win had to be shared. The courts have, moreover, repeatedly declined jurisdiction over agreements which are expressed in a way which shows an intention to exclude their jurisdiction. On the other hand, what appears on the face of it to be a business transaction will not lightly be treated as a merely moral obligation, and it should be noted that expressed *intention* may sometimes have the effect of turning into a binding contract an agreement which might otherwise have been regarded as non-contractual. A famous example of this situation was provided by *Carlill v Carbolic Smoke Ball Co* [1893] 1 QB 256. The defendants manufactured 'carbolic smoke balls' which they advertised as miraculous cures for many ailments and a preventative for influenza. (Incidentally, there was a 'flu epidemic' at the time.) The advertisement stated that £100 reward would be paid to anyone who contracted influenza after having used the ball as prescribed. It was further stated that £1,000 was deposited with a bank to show the sincerity of the company's intention. The plaintiff, Mrs Carlill, used one of these balls, but nevertheless contracted influenza. She sued for the promised reward. It was held that she was entitled to recover. Normally such advertisements are mere 'puffs' which are not intended to create legal relations, but in this instance taking into account, amongst other circumstances, the reference to the deposit at the bank, the court found that the company had intentionally made a binding offer which the plaintiff had accepted.

## 2   CAPACITY

Generally speaking any legal 'person' may be a party to a contract; but there are exceptions to this rule. Thus, for reasons of policy, in time of war an enemy subject cannot sue upon a contract in our courts and, by a rule of professional etiquette, a barrister may not sue for his fees. Two classes of incapacity call for special mention.

### (a)  minors

As has already been noted, a minor is a person under 18 years of age. Such people are inexperienced and, like other legal systems, the common law has always sought to protect them in the matter of making contracts. The general rule is that their contracts are voidable at their option. They may treat them as a nullity if they so wish, but may notify (affirm) them upon attaining majority.

There are, however, three exceptions to the general rule that minors cannot be bound by their contracts. First, where under any contract a minor receives '*necessaries*', he is bound to pay a *reasonable* price for them. 'Necessaries' include anything required by the minor, not in order to keep body and soul together, but to keep him suitably provided according to his particular standard of living at the relevant time; a question to be decided upon the facts of each case. In the second place, there are certain types of contract, such as a covenant to pay rent under a lease or the purchase of shares in a company, which require *continuous mutual relations* between the parties. Contracts of this type are binding upon the minor unless he repudiates them during minority or within a reasonable time of attaining majority. In the third place, *contracts of apprenticeship* and *service* which appear to the court *beneficial* to a minor are generally enforceable both by and against him. But this does not mean that a minor will always be liable upon a contract just because it is likely to be beneficial to him: the *general* rule is that he is not liable. For instance, if he engages in trade he cannot be sued upon contracts relating to his business.

Exceptions apart, minor contractors are therefore the pampered favourites of the law. So far is this true that the courts have refused to permit their immunity to be circumvented by allowing actions against them, which ought properly to be framed in contract, to be framed in tort: thus where a minor is guilty of fraud in inducing a person to contract with him by misrepresenting his age, he cannot be sued in the tort of deceit; for if this were permitted the minor's *contract* would be indirectly enforced.

This leniency of the law towards minor contractors is subject to certain restrictions which justice demands. Thus where, under a contract, a minor has transferred property to the other party, he will not be allowed to recover the property unless he can show a total failure of consideration; that is, unless he can show that he has received *nothing* in return for the property.

Moreover, there are two ways in which the rules of equity mitigate the inequitable lot of those who contract with minors. In the first place, the one-sided remedy of specific performance will not be granted at the suit of a minor. In the second place, the court may sometimes force the minor, at least where he has acted fraudulently, to restore any gains which he has acquired under the contract. This equitable right to restitution is, however, a proprietary right, and it follows that the other party to the contract cannot normally recover *money* which he has paid, for in the nature of things money is not easy to earmark as one's own; though where the plaintiff has delivered goods to the fraudulent minor, and the latter has sold them, there is some authority for saying that if the purchase money received by the minor can be earmarked as such the plaintiff can recover it. What the courts will not do is to allow a personal judgment against the minor, simply for a sum of money; for that would amount to enforcing the void contract.

To this it must now be added that the Minors' Contracts Act 1987, s 3, enlarges the powers of the court to order restoration of property by a minor. It provides that where a minor has acquired property under a contract which is unenforceable against him, or which he has repudiated, he may be ordered – if the court considers it 'just and equitable' to make such an order – to return that property or other property representing that which he acquired.

Section 2 of the same Act renders a guarantee of a minor's contractual obligation enforceable against the guarantor even if the obligation itself is not enforceable against the minor.

### (b) Mentally disordered and drunken persons

It will be recalled that mentally disordered persons may be subject to the control of the Court of Protection and that, if they are, contracts may be made by their receiver on their behalf. Apart from this, the rule is that their contracts will be voidable at their option if, and only if, it can be established that they were wholly incapable of understanding the nature of the contract at the time of contracting *and* that the person with whom they contracted *knew* of their condition.

It is generally accepted that a similar rule applies to contracts made with drunken persons. In *Hart v O'Connor* [1985] 2 All ER 880 the Judicial Committee held that, even though the condition of a mentally disordered person is *not* known to the other contracting party, the former may avoid the contract if there is an element of 'equitable fraud'.

In this context that expression means unfair or unconscionable conduct, such as victimization or taking unfair advantage. This rule would presumably also apply in the case of a drunken person.

Like minors, mentally disordered and drunken persons are bound to pay a reasonable price for 'necessaries' (Sale of Goods Act 1979, s 3).

## 3 FORMALITIES

Generally speaking no particular form is required for the making of a contract. A simple contract may be made in words and/or in writing. Its formation may even be inferred from conduct. But there are some exceptions to this rule.

### Contracts which are valid only if made in writing

Some contracts are not made at all unless they are made in writing. The list includes bills of exchange, share transfers, marine insurance contracts and consumer credit agreements which are 'regulated' by the Consumer Credit Act 1974. However, probably the most important examples within this category are contracts relating to land. The Law of Property (Miscellaneous Provisions) Act 1989, s 2, came into force on the 27 September of that year. It provides that a contract for the sale (or other disposition) of an interest in land can only be made in writing such that all the agreed terms must be within one document, signed by (or on behalf of) both parties. This is unless contracts are to be exchanged. Here the agreed terms must be in both contracts but each contract can be signed by a separate party. The contractual terms can be incorporated by reference to other documents, but where contracts are to be exchanged, such a reference must be made in both contracts (*Record v Bell* [1991] 1 WLR 853).

Some contracts are exempted by the Act from this writing requirement, such as those to grant leases for less than three years and contracts made in the course of public auctions. Others fall outside the Act altogether such as the kind of 'lock out' contract which was upheld in *Pitt v PHH Asset Management Ltd* [1993] 1 WLR 327 as a mechanism for avoiding 'gazumping' in the housing market.

There is a difference between requiring a contract to be *made* in a special form and requiring it to be *evidenced* in a special form: in the one case failure to adopt the prescribed form affects the validity of the contract itself, in the other it affects only the *proof* of its existence and failure to produce that proof only renders it *unenforceable*; so that its existence may yet be used as a defence to a claim, though the required evidence be lacking. Section 4 of the Statute of Frauds 1677 once required six categories of contract to be evidenced in writing. These have gradually been eroded to just one:

## Promises to answer for the debt, default, or miscarriage of another person

This provision has been construed so as to cover contracts of guarantee, but not of indemnity. The distinction requires explanation. In both classes of contract one person undertakes to accept responsibility for the obligation of another, but whereas the guarantor *only accepts responsibility if the principal defaults*, the *indemnifier* undertakes to discharge the obligation *in any event*. Thus, to adopt a time-worn illustration, where A and B come into a shop together and A agrees to buy goods, but A has no money with him, and B undertakes to pay the shopkeeper at a future time in the event of A's default, B is a guarantor of A's debt. If, on the other hand, B undertakes to be responsible whether A pays or not he is an indemnifier. In the former instance only will the contract – being one of guarantee (or 'suretyship') – fall within the statute and require written evidence. It should, however, be noted that by the Consumer Credit Act 1974 (ss 105 and 106) regulated suretyship *and* indemnity agreements *require* a written 'security instrument', as defined in s 105, and unless this instrument is properly executed they can only be enforced by court order.

The writing which the statute requires is, as has been explained, purely evidentiary. It follows that there need be no one document containing the whole contract; it suffices if a series of documents are produced and connected the one to the other by oral evidence; though these documents, when so connected, must tell the whole story in its essentials. But the story they tell must be one of a contract; so that if, for example all they disclose is an agreement 'subject to contract' or to 'formal exchange of documents' they probably do not constitute a sufficient memorandum. Further, the courts have gone as far as to hold that the requirements as to signature may be satisfied by an authenticating mark or even by the imposition of a rubber stamp.

The statute (which if it is relied upon as a defence must be specially pleaded) was passed in order to prevent frauds by requiring strict evidence of the contracts to which it applied; but it was soon found that rogues could evade their obligations by ensuring that the requisite evidence was *not* supplied. Hence the courts did all in their power to prevent the statute from thus being turned into an 'engine of fraud'. They attacked the problem in two ways. First, they sought to achieve justice by straining the interpretation of each section to bring particular facts within or beyond the scope of it as the merits of the case before them might require. It is for this reason that a complex web of case law was woven around the statute. In the second place the Court of Chancery evolved what is known as the equitable doctrine of *part performance*. The basis of this doctrine is that where, in the case of a contract which is rendered unenforceable by reason of non-compliance with the statutory requirements, one party has *partly performed his part of the agreement*, the other party will be forced to perform his.

For it would plainly be inequitable to allow him to evade his obligations by pleading the statute in such a case.

However, in the instances we have discussed, the statutory requirement is now that certain contracts be made in writing if they are to exist at all. Where there is no contract there can be no part performance.

## 4  CONSIDERATION

### The nature of consideration

Despite the dissent of the great Lord Mansfield in the eighteenth century, the courts have insisted that no contract (other than a contract under seal) can be enforceable in the absence of 'consideration'. This element in a contract was defined in *Currie v Misa* (1875) LR 10 Exch 153 thus '*A valuable consideration in the sense of the law may consist either in some right, interest, profit, or benefit accruing to one party, or some for-bearance, loss or responsibility, given, suffered or undertaken by the other*'.

'Consideration' is also now often more concisely described as the 'price of the bargain'. But this requires amplification. Consideration is the essential requirement that a person who makes a promise in the case of a consensual contract or does an act in pursuance of a unilateral contract must have promised or done something in return for the promise of the other party. The promisor must, by his promise, have undertaken to confer a benefit upon the other party or to suffer a detriment as the result of his promise, and the actor must have conferred a benefit or suffered a detriment by his act. (Both parties gain and both parties lose. That is the deal that they made.) Consideration marks the border-line between an obligation arising from a consensual or a unilateral contract and an obligation arising upon a contract under seal: for the latter can arise from a *gratuitous* promise – the promise of a gift. The beneficiary of a promise made by deed need furnish no consideration.

Consideration may be of two kinds; 'executed' or 'executory'. Consideration is said to be *executed* when the plaintiff who claims to have furnished it can show that he has actually performed his part of the bargain. *Executory* consideration is consideration which the plaintiff has promised to furnish, and is ready and willing to furnish, if the defendant will perform his part.

Consideration must be '*real*', ie, it must be something of some ascertainable value in the eye of the law. This does not necesarily mean the market price, just *some* value.

The meaning of this may best be illustrated by giving some examples of acts which have been held to be of insufficient value to form consideration. In the first place, a promise to do something which is obviously *impossible* (such as a promise to touch the sun) is clearly valueless. Second, a promise of a *vague and indefinite* nature will not constitute sufficient consideration. For example, in *White v Bluett* (1853) 23 LJ Ex 36, a son sued his father's executors, alleging that the father had promised to pay him some money if he would cease, which the father alleged he had done, from complaining to him that he had been unfairly treated. The court held that this was no more than a promise to stop 'boring' the father, and that it was therefore too vague to form a 'real' consideration. Third, a promise to do something *unlawful* cannot constitute consideration.

One question has given rise to difficulty. It is this: can the performance of an *existing duty* be treated as consideration for a fresh promise, made by the person to whom the duty is owed, or by some third party? The law on this subject is a little uncertain, but the present position may be summarized in the following way:

*(a)* Where A is already under contract to do something for B, and B makes a fresh promise on condition that A performs his duty, the performance will not amount to consideration for the fresh promise, and therefore A cannot sue upon it. For instance, where in *Stilk v Myrick* (1809) 2 Camp 317 two members of a crew deserted their ship during a voyage the master promised the rest that, if they worked the ship to port, the deserters' pay would be split between them. It was held that the crewmen could not sue upon this promise. The reason was that, at the time when it was made, they were already under an obligation to work the ship to port. However, there are limits to this. In *Hartley v Ponsonby* (1857) 7 E & B 872 the desertion was 19 out of a crew of 36. The voyage had become dangerous. In continuing, having been promised extra pay the sailors had provided valuable consideration. Much more recently in *Williams v Roffey Bros and Nicholls (Contractors) Ltd* [1991] 1 QB 1 the Court of Appeal upheld the principle in *Stilk v Myrick* and yet found there to have been the provision of valuable consideration where sub-contractors were promised extra payment if they completed work on time. The benefit held to have been received by the other party (thus making the promise binding) was that penalty clauses for late work were avoided.

*(b)* A promise to perform a public duty can be no consideration. Thus a policeman cannot claim a proffered reward for stolen property which he recovers *in the course of his duties*.

*(c)* If B contracts to do something for A, can B rely upon the doing of it as consideration for a promise made to him (B) by C? This point has been much disputed and it is one upon which the House of Lords has not as yet pronounced; but in *New Zealand Shipping Co Ltd v A M Satterthwaite & Co Ltd* [1975] AC 154 a majority of the Judicial Committee of the Privy Council decided that such an act is valid consideration.

One very important application of rule *(a)* is the rule in *Pinnel's Case* (1602) 5 Co Rep 117. It was there laid down that payment of a lesser sum than the amount due, cannot normally be treated as a satisfaction for an existing debt. Thus if A owes B £100, and B promises to discharge him if he pays £50, B can break his promise and sue for the whole £100. But this rule will not apply if there is a material alteration in the mode of payment. Thus if A's debt of £100 were due in London and B, to suit his own convenience, agreed to discharge the debt in return for a payment of £50 at York, B's promise of discharge would bind him. The discharge would also be binding if A, instead of making a part payment, were to give B some article (however small) in return for it. It would also, of course, be binding if it were made by deed.

'Composition' agreements form an exception to the rule in *Pinnel's Case*. Where a debtor, by agreement with his creditors, undertakes to pay so much in the pound none of them may sue for the full debt; for if any one of them were to do so, he would be defrauding the others.

## The rules governing consideration

Three important rules require mention:

(1)  although consideration must be real, it need not be adequate;
(2)  consideration must move from the promisee;
(3)  consideration must not be 'past'.

*(1)  Adequacy of consideration.*  For the purposes of the law of contract the common law regards the ordinary man as a commercial man. He must stand on his own feet, and make his own bargains. *Caveat emptor* ('buyer beware') is a maxim of importance. Equity apart, in the absence of fraud or misrepresentation, the courts will not assist a man who complains that he has made a bad bargain. Hence, provided that the plaintiff has given some consideration, it will be no defence for the defendant to plead that it was disproportionate to the value of the promise. At common law consideration need not be *'adequate'*. Where, however, there is inequality of bargaining power between the parties equity may re-open the bargain and by statute (the Consumer Credit Act 1974), ss 137–139 'if the court finds a credit bargain (eg a loan) extortionate it may re-open (it) so as to do justice'.

*(2)  Consideration must move from the promisee.*  In order to sue upon a broken contract the promisee (the plaintiff, to whom the promise has been made) must normally show that *he* has furnished the consideration: it will not suffice for him to prove that someone else has done so. This rule does not, however, apply to actions brought upon negotiable instruments.

*(3)  Consideration must not be 'past'.*  Consideration may, as has been noted, be 'executory' or 'executed' but it must not be 'past'. The meaning of 'past' consideration was illustrated by the case of *Roscorla v Thomas*

(1842) 3 QB 234. A bought a horse from B. Some time *after* the sale, B affirmed that it was sound; it was not. A sued B upon this affirmation; the action failed. The reason was that although A had furnished consideration in the form of payment at the time of the sale he had furnished none for the affirmation. The consideration which a plaintiff alleges must normally be given *in respect* of the promise made by the defendant. Where a benefit is conferred, either gratuitously or in return for a previous promise, a subsequent promise made in respect of this past benefit is not actionable; it is unsupported by consideration. Consideration, as we have seen, is the hallmark of *mutuality*, so that it must be 'present'.

There is at least one exception to this rule; namely that 'past' consideration may support an action upon negotiable instrument.

NOTE – The doctrine of consideration has often been criticized. In 1937 it was the subject of a report by the Law Revision Committee (Sixth Interim Report). Amongst other recommendations, the Committee suggested that the requirement of consideration should be dispensed with in the case of written contracts, and that 'past' consideration should be rendered actionable. The legislature has not, however, acted upon these recommendations.

It must be added that more modern decisions, starting with *Central London Property Trust Ltd v High Trees House Ltd* [1947] KB 130, have shown that, as a principle of justice and equity the courts will not permit a person who has made a clear and unambiguous promise or assurance by which he intentionally modifies his existing contractual rights against another person to resile from that promise or assurance once the other person has taken him at his word and acted upon it. For instance, suppose that X & Co let a block of flats to Y & Co at a ground rent of £2,500 *per annum*, and suppose that, later, X & Co promise in writing to accept only £500, and suppose that Y & Co accordingly reduce the rents due to them from the tenants in actual occupation of the flats. X & Co will not be permitted to invoke the absence of consideration for their promise in order to support a claim for the full £2,500.

This doctrine (sometimes called '*promissory estoppel*') which was substantially novel, though it is a development from older authorities may go some way towards mitigating the rigour of the rule in *Pinnel's Case*: but at present it is not possible to assess the full implications of it. The potentialities of the doctrine are, however, fundamental; so further comments should be made. First, in order for it to operate, the person sued must have *acted in reliance* upon the promise made to him; if he has not done this, no injustice will have been occasioned by the plaintiff's lack of good faith. Thus in *D & C Builders Ltd v Rees* [1966] 2 QB 617, the doctrine could not be invoked where a debtor offered a lesser sum in discharge of a greater debt *under threat* that unless the creditor accepted the offer nothing would be paid at all. In paying the lesser sum the debtor suffered no loss in reliance upon anything; for he had himself forced the transaction upon the creditor. In the second place, the doctrine has been judicially described as a 'shield' and not a 'sword'; it cannot by itself be used to *found* a claim, but only to *avert* one, or to rebut a defence that might otherwise be available. Thus, in *Combe v Combe* [1951] 2 KB 215, where a husband, after *decree nisi* for divorce, promised gratuitously to pay his wife £100 *per annum* by way of maintenance, and the wife in consequence (though not at the husband's request), forebore to apply to the court for an order for maintenance, it was held that the wife could not invoke her voluntary forbearance in order to force the husband to keep his promise. In the third place, although *obiter*, Lord Denning, MR, the progenitor of the doctrine in the *High Trees Case*, has expressed the view that it is not confined to cases in which a contractual relationship between the parties pre-exists the statement relied upon by way of estoppel (ie by way of barring the claim); so that, for example, where an employer makes a promise to a *prospective* employee which the latter relies upon in taking up the employment the employer will be bound by it. Finally, the doctrine is suspensive, not permanent. Thus in one case a licence for the use of a patent provided that the licensees should pay compensation if they manufactured more than an agreed number of articles covered by the patent. The owners of the patent agreed to suspend their right to compensation while a fresh agreement was being negotiated. And this they did. But it was held that, upon conclusion of the negotiations, they were entitled to renew their claim to compensation.

Beside the doctrine of promissory estoppel recent decisions have also focussed upon another old, similar, yet distinct, equitable doctrine, usually called 'proprietary estoppel'. This relates to cases where one person leads another to suppose that he is granting, or will grant, the other rights over his property (usually, at least, land) and the other acts to his detriment in reliance upon the real or supposed grant. Thus, for example, in *Inwards v Baker* [1965] 2 QB 29 a father (without consideration) encouraged his son to build, at the son's expense, a bungalow on his (the father's) land; which the son did. The father's executors sought to evict the son. It was held that they were not entitled to do so: the son had spent money on the bungalow and, thus having acted to his detriment, the executors were estopped from evicting him. There have recently been many similar decisions.

Both these doctrines are as yet indeterminate in their scope. But it can be said that there are certain clear differences between them. First, proprietary estoppel is confined to cases where one person encourages another to use his *land* (or, possibly, other property) – promissory estoppel is not so confined. Second, in proprietary estoppel the person acting on the promise must have acted not only in reliance on it, but also (as in *Inwards v Baker*) to his *detriment*; in promissory estoppel there is no requirement of detriment, only reliance. Third, in proprietary estoppel the reliance may depend upon a promise which is merely *implied*: in promissory estoppel the promise must be clear and unambiguous. Fourth, whereas promissory estoppel cannot of itself ground a claim (see above), but can only act as a defence, in proprietary estoppel the plaintiff can *support a claim* on the basis of the defendant's behaviour. Thus in *Crabb v Arun District Council* [1976] Ch 179, where the defendants allowed the plaintiff to make use of a right of way over their land, and then blocked it up, it was held that the plaintiff was entitled to an injunction to restrain them from doing so.

One should add, for clarity, that 'estoppel' (which is primarily a rule of evidence) means refusing (stopping) to permit a person who has made a promise, or acquiesced in a state of affairs, to go back on his promise or withdraw his acquiescence.

## Illegality

No action will lie upon a contract which involves the doing of something *illegal* if the plaintiff has to rely upon illegality as a necessary part of his claim ('*ex turpi, causa non oritur actio*' – 'there can be no cause of action upon a base ground'). And though it is true that where no part of the illegal purpose has at the time of action been entered upon, property conveyed under the contract may be recovered (a *locus poenitentiae*, pause for repentance, is said to be afforded), yet the presence of an illegal object is regarded as so serious that a defendant sued upon a contract involving such an object may set up his own conscious participation in the illegality as a defence to the plaintiff's claim. But it must be noted that the courts will not carry principle so far as to make the presence of an illegal object an excuse for confiscation. Thus, if in pursuance of an unlawful conspiracy (for instance, to evade some statutory requirement) the property in goods be transferred from A to B and these goods be then sold by C (a thief) to some fourth party, B (despite the illegal origin of his title) may sue the latter. For if he cannot who can?

Some transactions are rendered unlawful by statute, others are unlawful at common law. Examples of contracts which are illegal at common law are contracts to commit crimes, contracts contrary to public policy, and contracts which offend the accepted rules of morality.

'Illegality' is, however, a vague and indefinite term and the effect of it varies according to the nature of the unlawful element. Some things are so clearly 'wrong' that the courts will refuse to enforce contracts that have the barest connection with them. Thus it has even been held that a person in possession of smuggled property cannot claim against his insurers if it is stolen. And in *Pearce v Brooks* (1866) LR 1 Ex Ch 213, for example, the plaintiffs hired out an attractive-looking brougham to a lady (the defendant), knowing that she wished to use it in order to assist her in her profession – prostitution. It was held that the contract, although innocent on the face of it, was tainted with illegality; and that therefore the plaintiffs could not recover the hire money.

Prostitution is an extreme example of an activity of a morally reprehensible kind; the effect it has upon contracts in any way connected with it is therefore extreme. There are, however, other things which, for one reason or another, are 'illegal' without being clearly 'wrong'. For instance, wagering contracts are rendered 'void' by the provisions of the Gaming Act 1845. Normally, therefore, no action may be brought in respect of a wager. The Act does not, however, render wagering *unlawful,* nor does betting offend the general sense of public morality. Hence, in some circumstances, the courts will enforce wagers. Where, for instance, a bet is made abroad in some country where a bet of the nature concerned is entirely lawful it may sometimes be enforced here. Further, in *City Index Ltd v Leslie* [1992] QB 98, wagers on stock market movements were enforceable because of the provisions of the Financial Services Act 1986. On the other hand an arrangement which is not a 'bet' is not void. To be a bet one party must stand to lose. So gambling on the 'Tote' or entering the National Lottery is not 'betting' because neither of the operators stands to lose.

Contracts in contravention of *public policy* require fuller discussion.

The term 'public policy' is here used in a special sense. In one sense, all the principles of common law and of equity which have been evolved through the centuries are rules of public policy, for they have been created by the judges in the light of what they deem to be for the public good. But this is not the sense in which the term is used here. In relation to the law of contract it refers to certain restrictions which the courts place upon the right to make contracts which they believe to be contrary to the public interest. It has been held, for example, that an agreement made by a married person to marry a third party in contemplation of the termination of the marriage by death or dissolution is, if the facts be known to the third party, invalid; for it is in the public interest that the sanctity of marriage should be maintained. Contracts which tend to injure the State, to pervert the course of justice, or to undermine the public service, are also held to be contrary to public policy. Thus it is unlawful to make a contract with an alien enemy in time of war, or to perform such a contract during the continuance of a war, even though it was entered into before the war began. So too, agreements aimed at 'stifling' prosecutions are invalid. So also, where a person in a position of influence contracts with another to use that influence in order to secure for the other some special advantage from the government, the contract will not be upheld; as, for example, where a person agrees to obtain a public honour for another in return for a gift to charity.

One of the most important kinds of agreement which are considered to be against the public interest are contracts 'in restraint of trade': agreements which inhibit unrestricted enterprise by restraining economic competition. Social and judicial attitudes towards such agreements have altered from time to time with changes in the structure of society. The history of these changes of structure and of attitudes is an instructive and absorbing one. The current structure of our acquisitive society has given rise, both in

England and in Europe, to a basic assumption that it is imperative to foster free economic enterprise by encouraging competition.

Yet there is a paradox here. One man's freedom may remove another man's incentives. To take a simple example: if, upon leaving my employment, my employee is at liberty to take advantage of knowledge he has acquired during his employment, and contacts he has made with my customers, he will be free to ruin my business and to leave me with no incentive to carry it on. Thus my interests require to be protected for the very same reason that his do – namely the general interest in free enterprise. So economic considerations themselves demand that justice should strike a precarious balance between freedom to compete on the one hand and restriction of competition on the other.

That is the problem here. It is for the courts to seek a reasonable equilibrium which will best promote the general interest in freedom of enterprise. What we now have to consider is how the courts strike this balance. Being courts, they do it by the formulation of rules. The first rule is that when a contract in restraint of trade falls to be considered it is to be regarded as '*prima facie void*'. This phrase tends to be misleading. It does not mean that every such contract is, like the contract in *Pearce v Brooks*, necessarily void from the start.

If that were so, as will shortly appear, the countryside would be littered with void contracts involving public houses and petrol stations. Of course, if carefully framed, so as to be reasonable, these contracts are as valid as any others. '*Prima facie void*' means only then when their validity if *challenged in court the court is to proceed upon the assumption* ('presumption') that they are void. But the economic balance has to be struck. So the next rule is that the party who seeks to persuade the court that the contract is valid must *establish* that, in all the circumstances, it is no more than a necessary and reasonable protection of *his* interests (eg the case of the employer and his employee) and that, for that reason, it should be upheld. The accepted formula at this stage is that the court must be satisfied that the restraint is reasonable 'as between the parties': but again, for a reason that need not detain us, this formula is misleading. The interest to be considered is that of the person who seeks to impose the restraint. If the court is persuaded that the protection thus afforded by the contract *is* reasonable, it will conclude that the restraint is to be declared *valid*. Yet, in this convoluted process there is still another possible step. It may then, if he can do so, be up to the party seeking to rid himself of the restraint to persuade the court that, though it has thus been established that it is *reasonable*, the contract should yet be declared void as being inimical to 'public policy'. The restricted meaning of this expression will be explained below.

In this brief account this leaves us with three points to highlight. First, what kinds of restraints commonly fall to be considered. Second, what is meant, in this context, by 'reasonableness'. Third, what is here meant by 'public policy'.

*Examples of restraints* – Everyone knows about the 'tied' public house: the brewery exacts from the publican a covenant that he is to supply only *their* products. This, of course, is aimed at restricting competition from other breweries: though the contract will usually also confer advantages upon the publican. The 'tied' house is nothing new. Most people are now also aware that many service stations only supply one brand of petrol. That is because, like the publican, they have (in return for advantages) covenanted with a particular oil company to vend only that company's brand. A 'solus' agreement, as this is often called. Again, this agreement restricts competition by securing a monopoly in respect of the particular outlet involved. Again, as long ago as the early seventeenth century it has been accepted that when a person buys a business he may exact from the seller a reasonable covenant not to undermine his new business by setting up in opposition. Clearly the seller is in a position to do so if the buyer had previously acquired 'goodwill' in respect of the business: a 'name' for himself. It may well be that his former customers or clients will return to him, and he will thus have been paid for the sale and yet, by setting up in competition, destroy the buyer's business. So that here the buyer is entitled to protect his own interests by exacting the covenant. Similar considerations apply, as has been noted, in the case of an employee who leaves his employer and sets up on his own (eg a solicitor's clerk who has formed his own relationships with clients, a milk roundsman, an estate agent's clerk, etc). It is thus fair to *protect the employer's business* by permitting him to place a reasonable restraint upon the activities of his ex-employee.

It is, perhaps, pertinent here to note that the principle we have just been considering has its counterpart in patent and copyright law. Patents and copyright are intended to ensure that an inventor or an author may protect the economic advantage arising from his originality from being exploited by others. And, by contrast, discouragement of monopolies is based upon the need to encourage free enterprise.

*Reasonableness* – Whether a covenant is reasonable is a question to be decided in the light of the facts of each case. This means that all the circumstances have to be considered.

But there are certain questions which commonly have to be answered:

*(a)* Has the person who seeks to enforce the covenant in question a *legitimate interest* of his own to protect? If so, the covenant may be upheld as reasonable: but only to the *extent* that it does protect that interest, and *no further*. In *Vancouver Malt and Sake Brewing Co Ltd v Vancouver Breweries Ltd* [1934] AC 181 A & Co were brewers of 'sake'. They sold their business to B & Co and covenanted, for a period, not to brew 'beer'. Since the only goodwill A & Co had acquired was in respect of what they had actually brewed, namely 'sake', the covenant was unnecessarily wide, so they were held to be free to brew 'beer' *other than* 'sake'. Again, as we have seen, an employer has a legitimate interest in restraining the activities of his ex-employee. But if he seeks to do so by means of a covenant in the

latter's contract the restraint must (in this case, very strictly) be such, and only such as is absolutely necessary to protect the interest.

*(b)* How *long* is the restraint to last? In an extreme case a permanent restraint may be held reasonable: but what is a reasonable period of time will, once more, vary with the facts. For example, in *Esso Petroleum Co, Ltd v Harper's Garage (Stourport) Ltd* [1968] AC 269 the House of Lords regarded five years as a reasonable time for a solus agreement (a 'tie') between a service station and an oil company to run. Fifteen years or more may be reasonable between the buyer and the seller of a business, but more than five years, or less, may be held unreasonable in the case of a covenant restraining an employee.

*(c)* What is the extent of the *area* within which the restraint is to operate? Again what may be reasonable in this respect must vary. Certainly, for example, it may be reasonable to restrain a clerk who is leaving a solicitor's firm from practising within the town in which the practice is situated. But, in cases which involve business competition a much larger area may, and usually will, be admissible. It used to be thought that all restraints which were *general* in point of area were void. This rested upon an eighteenth century assumption that a person in Newcastle could not seriously compete with another in London. But as early as the late nineteenth century this assumption was exploded in the leading case of *Nordenfelt v Maxim Nordenfelt Guns and Ammunition Co Ltd* [1894] AC 535 in which it was held that the inventor, Nordenfelt, upon giving up the management of his business, could be restrained from competition *worldwide*. Since the eighteenth century the means of communication had improved and the scope of commercial enterprises had enlarged.

Special points arise in relation to restraints upon the activities of ex-employees. In the first place, as has already been indicated, such restraints are much more strictly scrutinized than covenants between buyers and sellers of businesses. In the second place all employees owe duties of *fidelity* to their employers. Thus the employee may be in breach of a legal duty (arising from his status as such) if he works on the sly for a rival firm. He is similarly under a duty not to divulge the employer's trade secrets; and this duty subsists even after he has left his employment. He also has a duty not to solicit his employer's customers while his employment continues.

*Public policy* – It has been explained that a covenant in restraint may be considered reasonable, and provisionally valid, by the court, but yet held void because its implementation would be against the public interest. But it has often been asserted that the onus of establishing that the covenant does contravene 'public policy' is a 'heavy one'. *Kerr v Morris* [1987] Ch 90, CA affords an example. A firm of national health service practitioners sought to restrain one of their number, who had left the practice, from practising in the vicinity of their town. The doctor subjected to this restraint claimed that it was contrary to 'public policy'. The Court of Appeal held that it was not. They reasoned that, although the patients in the area had a lawful interest, arising from the objects of the national health service (public policy), in the services of a doctor, yet they had no interest in the services of that particular doctor. In this context it must be pointed out that the aspect of 'public policy' invoked must necessarily be one *other* than the public interest in freedom of enterprise because, *ex hypothesi*, that issue must already have been decided in the covenantee's favour before 'public policy' is invoked to override the primary decision that the covenant was valid on the ground of 'reasonableness'.

Finally, it must be added that a covenant may always be held to be void on the ground that it is *oppressive or unconscionable*.

It should here be noted that membership of the EU has had an impact on this area of UK law. Article 85 of the EC Treaty renders void 'agreements between undertakings, decisions by associations of undertakings and concerted practices which have as their object or effect the prevention, restriction or disruption of competition within the common market' (unless especially exempted by the EU authorities). It follows that agreements made outside the EU and those made entirely within one member state can be affected if free competition within the EU is undermined.

Where restraint seriously limits freedom of choice, freedom of action, or personal liberty it can seldom be upheld. This may be illustrated by *Greig v Insole* [1978] 3 All ER 449 in which it was held that the cricket authorities were not entitled to restrain players who joined Kerry Packer's World Series Cricket from test and first class matches; for such a restraint would seriously affect their means of livelihood. Yet in extreme circumstances it may even be reasonable to restrain personal liberty; thus in *Denny's Trustee v Denny and Watt* [1919] 1 KB 583 a settlement was upheld between father and son by which the former paid the latter's debts, and in return imposed, *inter alia,* an embargo upon the son's going within 80 miles of Piccadilly Circus without consent.

It should also be explained that the courts will sometimes enforce a contract although some part of it is admittedly contrary to public policy. This is done by 'severing', ie cutting out, the invalid part and enforcing the rest. Such an operation will not be embarked upon where the contract as a whole is clearly unlawful, and in practice it is for the most part applied only to contracts in restraint of trade. Even in relation to these, however, severance will only be permitted if the part of the contract which will remain, after the invalid part has been struck out, contains all the elements of a valid contract in itself. This may occur, for instance, where one or two alternatives may be disregarded while leaving another unaffected. Thus where an estate agent had two offices in different places some miles apart and employed an assistant in one of them, the assistant agreed that if he should leave the agent's employment he would not practise for a period of three years thereafter in *either* place. It was held that this was reasonable in respect of the other place; and there was no difficulty in enforcing the restriction in respect of the one office and declaring it invalid in respect of the other.

Although many restraints are *contractually* imposed this need not necessarily be so – they may, for example, be imposed within a profession by dint of a professional code – but this does not alter the right of the courts to scrutinize them if they are challenged. Indeed, it was held that the Pharmaceutical Society was not entitled to insist that chemists sell only their 'traditional' wares (eg drugs) as opposed to their more modern ones (eg wines and spirits).

NOTE – It is important to remark that the common law governing restraint of trade, which has just been examined, has been eroded in relation to contracts which come within the Restrictive Trade Practices Act 1976 by the provisions of that Act.

## 2   The terms of a contract

### A   THE NATURE OF TERMS

The terms of the contract are the promises of the parties: in the simplest form the term 'I will drive your car to Rome' might be answered by the term 'Then, I will pay you £250'. Unlike conveyances (such as the transfer of land) contracts and promises are 'executory'; they relate to the future. Yet a term, though its implementation must relate to the future, may often take the form of a statement of fact; for example, in a contract for the sale of a house the vendor may affirm 'The drains are sound', and this statement will become a term of the contract, being treated as a promise. More rarely, moreover, though it is normally the very reverse of a promise, a statement of opinion may be treated as a term (a promise): this may, for instance, be the case where, upon the sale of a business, the seller gives an estimate of its assets, or where, as in *Esso Petroleum Co Ltd v Mardon* [1976] QB 801, the representative of an oil company about to lease a filling station to a tenant makes an estimate of the throughput of petrol to be expected of the relevant site. In circumstances like these where one party gives an opinion upon a matter which is basic to the contract, and which is peculiarly within his own knowledge, it is something which the other may expect to rely upon when the contract is executed: and it may thus be treated as importing a promise (term).

## B  THE KINDS OF TERMS

By tradition terms are of two kinds; they are either conditions or warranties. *Conditions* are terms of major importance which form the main basis of the contract and breach of a condition gives the party aggrieved a right to damages or (though subject to an important qualification which will be noted shortly) a right, at his option, to repudiate the contract. *Warranties* are terms of minor importance and breach of warranty gives a right only to damages. Traditionally the question whether a particular term is *a condition or* a warranty is referred to the intention of the parties themselves to be gleaned either from any statements they may make as to the comparative importance of the term in question of from the general tenor of the contract as a whole.

This general statement, however, needs to be qualified. In the first place, once the contract is executed, that is to say substantially entered upon, a condition becomes an '*ex post facto*' warranty; this means that it is treated as if it were a warranty and its breach gives rise only to a claim to *damages*. The reason for this is that repudiation is only really practical as long as the parties have not done anything under the contract to alter their position. In the second place it must be noted that the terminology is comparatively new and that until comparatively recent times the words 'condition' and 'warranty' were used interchangeably; further even in present day usage 'condition' may be used to mean something somewhat different, namely a stipulation which either *suspends* the implementation of the contract ('suspensive' condition or condition 'precedent') or *resolves* the contract after it has come into force ('resolutive' condition or condition 'subsequent'). The important rule that upon a conveyance (eg of a house) where, as in *Eccles v Bryant* [1948] Ch 93, according to the usual practice, the completion of the contract is made 'subject to exchange of documents' either party may withdraw until the exchange has actually been effected illustrates the operation of a condition precedent. On the other hand, if I sell you my car in March subject to a proviso that if my Uncle Tom dies before 10 April you are to return the car to me, the contract is defeasible by the condition subsequent that if Uncle Tom dies it will be at an end. In the third place, the dogma that the nature ('condition' or 'warranty') of a particular term is determined by reference to the parties' intention is generally no more than make-believe; and this is inevitably so because people seldom do intimate the comparative importance of the terms of their agreements. As a number of recent appellate decisions have shown, the truth is that, although some terms (whether express or implied by statute or otherwise) are in their nature conditions which will give rise to a right of repudiation, yet it is for *the court at the trial* to determine, *taking into account the extent of the alleged breach*, whether that breach is sufficiently fundamental to allow repudiation. Thus where a contract between two companies stated that it was to be a condition that stipulated frequent visits should be made on behalf of one of them to customers of the other it was held that a claim to repudiate because a few visits had been omitted could not be upheld.

Perhaps an understanding of the difference between conditions and warranties may be helped by two simple illustrations. In *Poussard v Spiers and Pond* (1876) 1 QBD 410, a singer contracted with an opera company to perform in a new opera: the period of the projected run was uncertain, but at the best it was thought likely that it would not be a long one. The singer fell ill and was unable to perform for the first week. It was held that this unwelcome lapse was fundamental and that it amounted to a breach of condition which entitled the company to repudiate the contract. In *Bettini v Gye* (1876) 1 QBD 183, the facts were similar; but with a distinction. There another singer was engaged by a producer for the better part of a year 'to undertake the part of first tenor in the theatres, halls and drawing-rooms of the United Kingdom' (a nostalgically Victorian contract!). He also failed through illness to meet the exact requirement of the contract in that he missed all the rehearsals prior to the first night of the whole engagement, which was a theatre performance. The court saw this as a minor lapse and treated it as a breach of warranty: it was stressed that the rehearsals and the theatre engagement itself were only part of a considerably larger agreement.

## C  IMPLIED TERMS

Thus far it may have been assumed that terms must be express, oral or written declarations of the obligations undertaken. Although contracts may arise solely by implication from conduct most contracts do in fact rest upon statements made by the parties and hence most contracts do contain *express* terms, however few. But terms may also be implied. All agreements are made in the light of circumstances known to the parties and these circumstances may bear upon the agreement as being a tacitly accepted part of it; terms that are understood but not declared.

Terms may be implied for any number of reasons, the basis of the implication being that the parties may be taken to have tacitly agreed to them. There are, however, certain common sources of implication. One such source is usage: where a contract is made between people of the same trade it may usually be assumed that it is to be conducted against the accepted background of that trade (for instance the 'baker's dozen' = 13) or where a contract is made in a particular locality it may be assumed that it is made in the light of the customs of that locality: hence the usage may be treated as being incorporated into the contract. Further, there is doctrine known as the rule in *The Moorcock* (1889) 14 PD 64, by which the courts will at times imply a term where it is necessary to do so in order to give the contract business efficacy. For example, in *The Moorcock* itself the plaintiff's ship was berthed under contract at the defendant's wharf; at low tide she settled on some rock which lay under the river bed and she was damaged. There was nothing in the contract about the safety of the berth but it was held that it must be assumed as a business proposition that the parties had contracted upon the basis that it was sound. This doctrine is, within limits, clearly a reasonable one but current judicial practice is to apply it with caution, since the courts shrink from making people's contracts for them after the event. Hence, today it is probably true to say that *The Moorcock* doctrine will only be called into use where what has been omitted from the express terms is something which anyone would have assumed to be basic to the agreement, and which the parties them – selves would clearly have expressly agreed to had they thought about it. Moreover, no such term will be implied if it contradicts the *express* terms of the contract.

Again, terms may be implied *by law*, either by general rules of the common law itself or by statute. Among outstanding examples are the implied terms contained in the Sale of Goods Act 1979 many of which were incorporated in the Act from pre-existing case law.

## D EXEMPTION (OR EXCLUSION) CLAUSES

These may be discussed under three heads. First, the position at common law. Second, the law established by the Unfair Contract Terms Act 1977, and untidily altered by the Unfair Terms in Consumer Contract Regulations 1994. Third, the relationship between the common law and statute law on the subject.

### 1 THE POSITION AT COMMON LAW

The dogma that by contract people should be free to create rights and duties between themselves, much favoured by the *laissez faire* philosophy of the nineteenth century, has always concealed a paradox: if people are free to contract, they are also free to 'contract out', to place restrictions upon the nature and extent of their obligations: to agree, for example, that one of them shall be exempt from liability for defective performance of the obligations he has undertaken. As between two parties in positions of equal bargaining power (the nineteenth century myth) it seemed logical and just that terms thus excluding liability should be permitted. There was some-thing to be said for this. For instance, a seller who exempts himself as against a buyer from liability for defects in his goods may sell them more cheaply than one who does not. Yet this doctrine was fallacious. For one thing, buyers and sellers are by no means always on equal terms. Selling is often done on a 'take it or leave it' basis, and the customer is often at the mercy of the seller.

While to some extent recognizing the fallacy by, for example, introducing implied terms in the customer's favour (eg those contained in ss 12–15 of the Sale of Goods Act 1979), the courts, nevertheless, clung to the paramount policy of freedom of contract and enforced contracts as a whole, including exemption clauses. So much so that people were, and to some extent still are, permitted, by means of a term in their contract or by means of giving notice to the other party, to free themselves from liability even for their own *negligence*, whether it arose contractually in the form of careless performance of their contract or tortiously, independent of contract. There were, and are, two conflicting interests: freedom of contract on the one hand – the courts are not there to make people's bargains for them – and protection of the weaker party on the other. While accepting the right to exclude, the courts developed techniques designed to make it difficult to do so.

A brief account of some of these techniques must be given. In the first place, every exclusion clause will be construed (*contra proferentem*) against the proponent, the party seeking to benefit by it; and the onus is on him to establish its validity. Further, at common law the court would, and still does, insist that the proponent establish that the exempting clause he relies upon *is* in fact a term of the contract. Thus, for example, in *Olley v Marlborough Court Ltd* [1949] 1 KB 532, it was held that, as against a guest, the hotel could not rely upon a notice purporting to exempt it from liability for the safety of his property because, instead of displaying it at the time of registration at the office, it displayed it in the bedroom and, since the contract had already been made at the reception desk, the notice could not be treated as a term. Moreover, if an exemption clause is to be upheld, the common law insisted (and does insist) that everything reasonable has been done by the proponent to bring the *existence of the clause* to the attention of the other party. For instance, in *Chapleton v Barry UDC* [1940] 1 KB 532, it was held that where a man hired a defective deck chair which collapsed and injured him the hirers could not rely upon a notice on a ticket which he had been given which purported to exempt them from liability. You are entitled to look upon a ticket as a receipt, rather than as a contractual term, and to put it in your pocket unread. The contract will be looked at *as a whole*; so that if, though there is a valid written exemption clause, the person seeking to rely upon it makes some verbal variation, the clause will be treated as void: thus in *Curtis v Chemical Cleaning and Dyeing Co Ltd* [1951] 1 KB 805, it was held that where cleaners, by written notice, purported to exempt themselves from liability for damage to materials cleaned, but the assistant at the counter assured the plaintiff customer that the notice covered only damage to 'beads and sequins' on a dress, the plaintiff (the dress, upon return, being ruined) was entitled to recover, despite the exemption clause. There is a long line of cases which illustrate the fact that exemption clauses are *strictly construed*: thus if a clause excludes liability for breach of *express* terms in the contract the courts will sanction recovery for breach of *implied* ones; if it excludes liability for breach of warranties it will enforce liability for breach of *conditions*; and if it simply excludes 'liability' the court will enforce liability for *negligence*.

Despite all this, until recently the courts had developed a mysterious doctrine called 'fundamental breach'. The argument ran that if the defendant had committed a very major breach of contract the contract came to an end; with the result that all its terms, including any exemption clause, came to an end, thus leaving the defendant liable for the breach. In one case, for instance, it was held that, where a defendant who had agreed to sell a car to the plaintiff and delivered what was, in effect, a total wreck, a broadly drafted term absolving the defendant from all liability simply went by the board upon the basis of 'fundamental breach'.

This doctrine of 'fundamental breach' has now, however, since the decision in *Photo Production Ltd v Securicor Transport Ltd* [1980] AC 827, been emphatically rejected by the House of Lords. The position now is that the traditional position has been restored; namely, that statute apart – as in the case of the important Unfair Contract Terms Act 1977 (below) – parties are, within limits, once more free to make whatever terms of exemption they wish and the question whether the defendant is exempt is purely one of *construction of the contract*. This does not mean, that, as has just been explained, the courts will lightly permit the defendant to escape his obligations; for they lean heavily against exempting terms, but it does mean that where the exemption clause is clear and unambiguous he may do so – and this the more easily where he seeks only to *limit* his liability rather than to *exclude* it altogether. But the exemption clause may, nevertheless, be allowed to prevail. A striking example of this is to be found in the House of Lords decision in *George Mitchell (Chesterhall) Ltd v Finney Lock Seeds Ltd* [1983] 2 AC 803. In that case the defendants, seed merchants, sold to the plaintiff farmers 30lbs of 'Dutch winter cabbage seed' at the cost of £201.60. This the plaintiffs sowed over 63 acres. The seed was not, however, what was ordered, and the crop was a total failure, causing a loss of £61,513. It was a term of the contract that the defendants' liability should be restricted to replacing defective seed or returning the purchase price. This the House of Lords upheld, though what the layman might conceive to be justice was in fact achieved by resort to certain statutory provisions which rendered the defendants fully liable. It is, however, noteworthy that in the leading speech by Lord Bridge of Harwich it was made plain that an exemption clause, however widely drafted, will not excuse a defendant if his performance steps wholly out of the four corners of the contract: as where, having given himself the widest possible exemption, he fails to perform the contract at all – as by contracting to sell a motor car and delivering a bicycle.

## 2   THE UNFAIR CONTRACT TERMS ACT 1977

This statute (hereafter 'UCTA') does not abrogate the major premise of the common law that people are free to contract out of their obligations, because its scope is not universal and in many respects its application is limited; but in a practical sense it goes a long way towards it.

First, as to the limits of its operation. It does not apply to *international supply contracts*, as defined in UCTA, s 26, which are governed by the Uniform Laws on International Sales Act 1967. It does *not* apply (UCTA, s 1(2)) at least in its entirety, to a number of contracts – including, *inter alia*, insurance, land contracts and certain contracts connected with companies – set out in UCTA, Sch 1. Above all, it *only* applies in general to 'business liability', ie to liability for things *done in the course of business* or from the *occupation of premises* used for *business* purposes of the occupier (s 1(3)). So it is possible to exclude liability for undertakings made in private life: but what is meant by 'business' is left unclear: s 14 provides that 'business' includes a profession and the activities of any government department or public authority. Are schools, clubs, universities, cathedrals or trade unions in 'business'? There is little case law on the meaning of the word, and a large field is left for litigation. The 'business liability' limitation to the scope of the Act is thus not a minor one. However, the provisions of s 1(3) were clarified by the Occupiers' Liability Act 1984 (s 2) to the extent that where a person (such as a rock climber entering farm land) obtains the access for recreational or educational purposes the occupier is not subject to a 'business liability' – and hence can exclude liability for loss or damage to the entrant – *unless* the granting of the access was for the occupiers' business purposes: as, for instance, might be the case if the climber were to be invited by the farmer to survey the land.

Having stressed its limitations, we must now examine the relevant provisions of the Act. It concerns (*within the business liability field*): *(i)* exclusion of liability for negligence; *(ii)* exclusion of liability arising from contractual obligation; *(iii)* unreasonable indemnity clauses; *(iv)* guarantees of consumer goods; *(v)* exclusion of liability in sale, hire-purchase and certain allied contracts.

*(i)  Exclusion of liability for negligence* – Section 2 is concerned with exclusion of liability for negligence, whether tortious or arising from careless performance of the contract (UCTA, s 1(1)). In the first place, it is enacted that no one may 'exclude or restrict his liability for *death or personal injury* resulting from negligence by any contract term or notice' (UCTA, s 2(1)). Though this rule is draconian, there is one, perhaps typical, exception (Schs 1, 4), that an employee may so exempt himself as against his employer. The word 'notice' is important because a person may seek to exclude *tortious* liability by a notice (such as 'beware of the machinery') in circumstances in which the relationship between the parties is not contractual. In the second place, the Act (s 2(2)) provides that where the

loss complained of is *other than* death or personal injury (ie damage to property) liability for negligence cannot be excluded unless the term or notice *satisfies the 'requirement of reasonableness'*. This means (s 11(1)) that the *term* relied upon must be 'fair and reasonable' in view of the circumstances known to the parties at the time when the contract was made; or (s 11(3)) that the *notice* was 'fair and reasonable' in view of the circumstances obtaining when the liability arose. The requirement of reasonableness is one for the court to decide, and (s 11(5)) it is for the person who seeks to establish the validity of the term or notice to satisfy the court that it is reasonable.

*(ii)  Exclusion of liability arising from contractual obligation* – That is to say, from contractual obligation other than the obligation not to be negligent in performance. This is governed by UCTA, s 3 which applies 'as between contracting parties where one of them *deals as consumer* or on the other's written *standard terms* of business'. Standard terms are common; everyone is familiar with documents which contain printed (and often lengthy) terms: such documents, forced upon the consumer, are often pistols at his head, and, under the common law, courts have always been quick to invalidate exclusion clauses contained in them if they could find a way. It is important to appreciate the meaning of the words 'deals as a consumer' (UCTA, s 12). They mean that s 3 applies to a contract made between a person who is *not* contracting in the *course of business*, and one who *is* (the latter, of course, having a bargaining advantage over the former, the former needs protection). *But*, auction contracts and contracts by tender (s 12(2)) are not 'consumer' dealings (hence s 3 does not apply to them), and contracts of sale of goods, hire-purchase, exchange, hire and certain similar contracts come within the category (s 12(1) *(c)*) if the goods involved are of a type *ordinarily supplied for private consumption*. Subject to these exceptions, the onus lies upon the person who seeks to establish that the transaction is *not* a consumer dealing (and hence outside the controls created by s 3) that this is the case (s 12(1)).

Within the restricted field of contracts thus defined s 3 provides that – unless *the person who seeks to uphold the clause* can prove that it was *fair and reasonable* (see above) he *cannot*: – (a) by means of a contract term *exclude or restrict* any liability of his in respect of the whole or any part of his contractual obligation; (b) claim to be entitled, as to the whole or any part of his obligation, to render *no performance* at all; nor (c) *to be entitled* to render performance *substantially different* from what was expected of him.

*(iii)  Unreasonable indemnity clauses* – By s 4 of UCTA contract terms in consumer dealings cannot, unless they satisfy the test of reasonableness, be made (as in the case of an indemnity sought by a carrier against a customer) which purport to oblige the consumer to indemnify some other person against that person's negligence or breach of contract.

*(iv) Guarantee of consumer goods* – By s 5 of UCTA, in the case of goods ordinarily supplied for private use or consumption where a defect caused by negligence on the part of the manufacturer or of a distributor of the goods arises while the goods are in use (otherwise than by way of business) by the consumer, the manufacturer or distributor cannot exclude or restrict liability for loss arising from the defect by reference to any 'contract term or notice contained in ... a *guarantee* of the goods' (s 5(1)). 'Anything in writing is (for this purpose) a *guarantee if it contains* ... some promise or assurance ... that defects will be made good by ... replacement, or by repair, monetary compensation or otherwise' (s 5(2)(*c*)). The object of this section is to meet the common practice whereby manufacturers have tended to take back, repair or give compensation for, defective products (such as cars) upon the terms that the customer foregoes his legal rights of action. It is to be noted (s 5(3)) that s 5(1) does not apply to contracting parties: ie those in direct contractual relationship: buyer and distributor, for instance, as opposed to buyer and manufacturer. This appears to be because ss 6 and 7 and s 2(2) safeguard the rights of the consumer who is in direct contractual relationship with the distributor, seller, hirer, etc.

## 3   GENERAL EFFECT OF THE 1977 ACT

This is one of those enactments which seems to achieve justice at the expense of simplicity. So its effects should be summarized.

Outside the scope of the Act the common law, as outlined above, remains. That is, outside 'business' liability (above); for the Act to control the transaction one party at least, must usually be in 'business'. The Act does:

*(a)* (s 2) within the 'business' field, make a further inroad into the common law right, which had already been abrogated by various enactments in a number of fields (such as carriage by rail), by contract or notice to avoid liability for *negligence* (tortious or contractual) resulting in *death or personal injury* and, also, the Act modifies the previous law (within the 'business' field) by subjecting clauses excluding liability for negligence resulting in damage to *property* to the 'reasonableness' test.

*(b)* Again, (s 3) in the case of *consumer or written standard form* dealings, it subjects all terms which purport to exclude or restrict the liability of the person who contracts with the consumer, or who contracts upon his written or standard form terms, to the same test. And, also, by the same section, it ensures that if that person, as against the consumer, seeks to rely upon a term which purports to entitle him to render performance substantially different from the performance envisaged by the contract (eg to deliver plastic rather than leather) or to render no performance at all, that term must also be 'reasonable'. Moreover, UCTA s 9, enacts that a term may be given effect to if *it does* satisfy that test even

though the contract has been terminated by breach, has been lawfully terminated by one of the parties, or has been affirmed by a party who is entitled to repudiate it. It is to be noted, moreover, that s 11 is not confined to contracts which involve 'business' liability.

*(c)* The Act (s 4) makes less important reforms in the sphere of indemnity (consumer) contracts and (s 5) 'guarantees' of consumer goods. [For the important effects of the Act upon implied terms in the contract of sale of goods, etc see below.]

Thus (disregarding the absolute prohibition of exemption clauses in relation to negligence causing death or personal injury and the minor changes of ss 4 and 5) within the areas of its operation it would seem that the Act adds to the common law the test of reasonableness: it is thought that it only 'adds' and that all the familiar common law tests (eg the *contra proferentem* rule) still apply. It is even questionable how much is substantially 'added' because the common law tests themselves are based upon reasonableness'; and Sch 2 of the Act, which offers 'guidelines' to the 'reasonableness test' in relation to s 6, adopts criteria, such as whether the complaining party knew or ought to have known of the existence or extent of the relevant term, which are also employed at common law. Nevertheless, where the courts have tested exclusion and limitation clauses for 'resonableness' in recent years the results have often seemed comfortingly 'just', at least for individuals. In *Smith v Eric S Bush* [1988] QB 743, a surveyor hired to do a 'building society valuation' was unable to rely on a general disclaimer for liability in negligence in circumstances where the prospective purchaser of a house at the 'low' end of the market would not buy the 'Rolls Royce' survey, and in St Alban's City and *District Council v International Computers Ltd* ([1995] FSR 686) software was supplied on standard terms including a limitation clause. It produced figures resulting in the Community Charge being set too low. The company was held liable to pay rather than the local charge payers.

## 4  THE UNFAIR TERMS IN CONSUMER CONTRACTS REGULATIONS 1994

These regulations constitute the implementation by the UK of a directive adopted by the Council of the European Communities in April 1993. They came into effect in July 1995. The broad thrust of the new law might seem to be to introduce an underlying principle of fairness into consumer contracts, since it removes the binding force of terms which, contrary to a 'requirement of good faith' cause 'significant imbalance' of rights and detriment to consumers, given the nature of the goods and/or services in question, the circumstances of the parties when the deal was made and whether the terms are written in plain, intelligible language. However, only contracts which have not been 'individually negotiated' are affected, such as pre-formulated standard forms. Further, there are several excluded categories, such as contracts of employment and those involving succession rights or rights under family law. Moreover, the 'core' of the contract, such as the price and the terms defining the subject matter, are unaffected. In Sch 3 of the regulations there is an indicative (but not exhaustive) list of terms which may be regarded as unfair – but it is important to note that this notion of 'unfairness' is not the same as that of 'unreasonableness' within the Unfair Contract Terms Act, no matter how similar the effect of applying the two 'tests' may prove to be. The practical realities of this new law have been that the Director General of Fair Trading (one of whose many areas of responsibility this is) has already taken a number of businessmen to one side and caused various terms in their standard contracts to be 'adjusted'.

# 3   Void and voidable contracts

Sometimes an agreement may be legal and may apparently contain all the elements of a valid contract and yet certain factors may in reality be present which render it void or voidable. A *void* contract is a nullity, there is no contract. Logically, no rights or obligations are acquired. A *voidable* contract is one which is valid, but may be treated as ineffective by one of the parties, subject to certain conditions. Two such factors which have to be considered are mistake and misrepresentation.

## A   MISTAKE

This is a difficult and controversial branch of the law of contract. Where an operative (ie legally effective) mistake is established the result is that the contract is *void*. It will be appreciated that this is a very serious consequence since, amongst other things, third party rights may be jeopardized. Thus, if I obtain goods from you by means of a fraudulent misrepresentation our contract is *voidable* by you as long as I have not parted with the goods to a *bona fide* purchaser; but, provided at least that you have not taken steps to set the contract aside, once I have done this the goods will become his, not yours. If on the other hand, whether induced by fraud or not, you can prove that you contracted under some mistake which the law treats as operative, the contract being *void*, I can give no title to the purchaser – with the unhappy result that, however innocent he is, you will have a claim in *conversion* against him.

Such a state of affairs, threatening (as it may) the security of completed transactions, is not therefore easily to be inferred and it will be seen that in consequence the ambit of operative mistake is restricted. Two points need notice at the start. First, in order to be legally operative a mistake must be as to some material or fundamental matter going to the *essence* of the contract. If a party makes a mistake as to some minor matter the law will not heed his complaint: for instance if I buy your cow under the mistaken impression that she answers to the name of 'Daisy' and it turns out that her name is really 'Primrose' I am not entitled to force you to take her back; that is, of course, provided that the mistake is only in the name and not as to the identity of the cow. In the second place, people who allege that they have contracted under the influence of a mistake must necessarily be judged rather by their actions than by their innermost thoughts: thus, as Blackburn J, said in *Smith v Hughes* (1871) LR 6 QB 597 'If whatever a man's real intention may be, he so conducts himself that a reasonable man would believe that he was assenting to the terms proposed by the other party, and that other party upon that belief enters into the contract with him, the man thus conducting himself would be equally bound as if he had intended to agree to the other party's terms.' So, no one can escape his obligations simply by stating that he was mistaken about the terms of the contract: he can only escape if he *proves* that he was mistaken, and even then the mistake must be one which relates to some *material* particular. If it were not for these two rules all contractual transactions would be in danger of being set aside at the whim of a party who alleges that he did not appreciate the nature of his undertaking.

Before analysing the various kinds of operative mistake it may be helpful to revert to a matter already touched upon. Mistake and misrepresentation have different effects in law, but the one is often induced by the other: eg my statement that I am the Prince of Richitania may induce you to give me credit for the purchase of a Rolls-Royce. True, you may sue me for damages upon my fraudulent misrepresentation; but you will also have been led to make a material *mistake*, and this is important from your point of view because if there were merely *fraud* and no mistake you could not claim the Rolls (or its equivalent in money) from third parties – and in practice, of course, I should take good care to go and hide somewhere so that your claim for damages from *me* would be likely to be worthless.

We may now turn to a consideration of the various kinds of operative mistake. The subject will be discussed under three heads. First, mistake at common law; second, mistake in equity; third, the *non est factum* plea.

## 1  MISTAKE AT COMMON LAW

At common law mistake may have one or the other of two effects: it may be such as to nullify what appears on the face of it to be a valid contract, or it may so operate as to destroy *consensus* by producing a situation in which the offer given does not correspond with the acceptance made; thus preventing any contract from coming into being.

*i  Mistake which nullifies an apparently valid contract*
Of this we may give four examples; though, as will appear, the fourth is a
category of doubtful validity.

*Mistake as to the existence of the subject matter* – If at the time when
the contract is made, unknown *to both parties*, the subject matter of it does
not exist the contract will be void. Thus in *Couturier v Hastie* (1856) 5 HL
Cas 673, where corn was sold while in transit by sea from Salonica to
England and it transpired that at the time of the contract the ship's master
had in fact (owing to its serious deterioration) disposed of the corn at Tunis,
it was held that the buyer was absolved from payment of the price.

Obviously mistake as to the very existence of the subject matter is
fundamental; what appears to be a contract about something is really a
contract about nothing, and such a transaction must therefore generally
be void. But this will not necessarily be so, for it is possible for a person
to contract upon the terms that he will be liable whether or not the subject
matter exists. Clearly such situations are rare; but *McRae v Commonwealth
Disposals Commission* (1951) 84 CLR 337 (an Australian case) affords
an example. Here the defendants, having 'disposed' to the plaintiffs of a
wreck believed by both parties to be lying on a named reef – when in truth
not only the wreck but also the reef were non-existent – were held liable
to the plaintiffs for the cost of an expedition by the latter to retrieve the
'wreck'; for the situation was such that the defendants must have been
taken, in view of the very nature of their business, to have warranted the
existence of the thing they purported to 'dispose' of.

*Mistake as to physical possibility* – Where *both parties* think that they
are contracting about something which is physically possible the contract
will be void if what is contracted for turns out to have been a physical
impossibility. Thus in *Sheikh Bros Ltd v Ochsner* [1957] AC 136 a contract
was held void where it was agreed that one of the parties should deliver to
the other a quantity of sisal growing on a certain piece of land which,
unknown to both parties, was incapable of producing the stipulated amount
of sisal.

*Mistake as to title* – Mistake of *law* will never avoid a contract, but a
common mistake as to private title may. Thus is *Cooper v Phibbs* (1867)
LR 2 HL149 (a case in equity, though the result would have been similar
at common law) where A took a lease of a fishery from B and it transpired,
unknown to both parties, that A was really the owner of the fishery, the
contract was held to be void.

*Mistake as to the quality of the subject matter* – This is the doubtful
case. In Roman law there was, it seems, a doctrine of *'error in substantia'*
by which – to adapt a dictum of Lord Atkin's in *Bell v Lever Bros Ltd*
[1932] AC 161 – if the thing contracted for was *essentially* different in
*quality or attributes* from the thing as it was believed by both parties to
be the contract would be void. In theory this notion is sound: there is a
world of difference between, say, a genuine diamond and a counterfeit

one. But in practice it is difficult to draw the line between what is 'essential' and what is 'non-essential' – vinegar is sour wine, what if it be mistaken for wine? Thus though some writers support the view that mistakes of this kind, if they are as to the *essence* of the subject matter, may avoid a contract, the actual decisions appear to go the other way, and to suggest that no such category of 'mistake' is accepted as operative at common law. *Bell v Lever Bros Ltd* (above) and *Leaf v International Galleries* [1950] 2 KB 86, afford extreme instances in support of this conclusion. In the former case two employees of the respondent company were sued by the company for the return of certain large payments which had been made to them as compensation for terminating their service agreements. The facts were such that unknown to all parties, owing to certain previous trans-actions by these employees, the agreements could have been terminated without compensation; and upon discovering this the company made their claim. It was held that the mistake was *not* 'essential' since the subject matter of the contract was in essence the *service agreements* and the fact that they might have been terminated without compensation was only a side issue. Yet, if anything could have been regarded as 'essential' surely it was the *validity* of the agreements? In the latter case a picture believed by both parties to be a Constable was sold by the one to the other; it turned out not to be a Constable and, when the buyer sued, the Court of Appeal intimated that the mistake was not one which would avoid the contract. Surely, again, in all common *sense* the assumption that the picture was a Constable was as vital a factor in the transaction as anything could be? These decisions and others therefore lead to the conclusion that the *common law* may not treat a mistake as to the quality of the subject matter, however essential, as operative.

## ii Mistake which nullifies consensus
Here the mistake produces the effect that the parties are not *ad idem* (agreed in the same terms upon the same subject matter); A is making one kind of offer, B is accepting another. This may occur in two sorts of situations. Either *both* parties may be mistaken (this may be called '*mutual*' mistake: though the word is not a term of art) or only *one* party may be mistaken (this may be called '*unilateral*' mistake). In the latter situation the rule is that the mistake will not be operative unless the party not mistaken *knows of the other party's mistake*. Three examples of mistake which thus nullifies '*consensus*' may be given.

*Mistake as to the terms of the contract* – Suppose (taking the facts from *Smith v Hughes* – above) A and B contract for the sale of some bags of oats. A (the buyer) believes them to be old oats, B (the seller) believes or knows them to be new oats: A seeks to repudiate the contract on the ground of mistake. We have seen that even if the mistake is common – in the sense that the oats are new and both parties believe them to be old – it is one as to quality only, and therefore probably not operative. Therefore, in general, A cannot repudiate. But suppose that B knows them to be new and *also knows* that A thinks he is selling them *as old*, then there is room for *unilateral* mistake to operate. For B knows that he is selling A new oats, and A thinks he is buying old ones; the offer and acceptance do not therefore correspond.

*Mistake as to the identity of the subject matter* – Where there are two things in existence and one party is thinking of one of them while the other is thinking of the other the contract will be void for mistake. The parties are at cross-purposes: there can be no consensus, and in the nature of things, the mistake will be mutual. Thus in *Raffles v Wichelhaus* (1864) 2 H & C 906, there was a contract of sale for the consignment of cotton '*ex Peerless*, Bombay' and two ships called *Peerless* were due to sail from Bombay within a short time of each other. One party had one in mind, the other had the other. The contract was held to be void.

*Mistake as to personal identity* – It must not be supposed that this will always go to the validity of a contract: for example, our law accepts the doctrine of the undisclosed principal, and the shopkeeper who sells me apples for cash cannot claim that the sale is void solely because in buying them I have impersonated someone else to whom he might have been equally willing to sell. The identity of a person may, however, be so relevant to the particular contract that a mistake in relation to it will avoid it.

For mistake as to personal identity to be operative the identity of the party concerned must therefore be *relevant* to the formation of the contract; moreover the position must be such that the party mistaken believes the other party to be some real person other than the person with whom he is actually contracting. For if a person is willing to contract with a non-existent entity he presumably does not regard the personality of his co-contractor as a matter of importance.

The following cases may serve to illustrate the law as to mistakes of this kind. *Cundy v Lindsay* (1878) 3 App Cas 459, a fraudulent person called Blenkar signed a letter in a way which made the signature look like 'Blenkiron & Co' which was a reputable firm; in this letter he asked the plaintiffs to send him some goods at his address which was in the same street as Blenkiron's premises. The plaintiffs thus having mistaken Blenkarn for Blenkiron & Co sent the goods to Blenkarn on credit, and needless to say without paying for them Blenkarn sold them to the defendants. It was held that the contract between the plaintiffs and Blenkarn was void for mistake and that the plaintiffs' claim in conversion was therefore sustainable. In *Ingram v Little* [1961] 1 QB 31, the facts were rather similar; a person called at the plaintiffs' house and offered to buy their car; he proposed to pay by cheque, and upon the plaintiffs demurring, gave his name as 'P G M Hutchinson'. Mr Hutchinson was a real person, and upon consulting the phone book, the plaintiffs found his name and address in it as given to them by the caller. Thus satisfied, they accepted a cheque and parted with the car: the cheque was dishonoured and the car disposed of to the defendant. Again, the mistake was operative and the defendant was here held liable to the plaintiff in conversion. In both these cases reliance had been placed upon the assumed credit of an identifiable person or firm. By contrast in *King's Norton Metal Co Ltd v Edridge, Merrett & Co Ltd* (1897) 14 TLR 98, a rogue called Wallis pretended to be an imaginary firm which he called 'Hallam & Co' and had pretentious notepaper bearing that name printed. He ordered goods from the plaintiffs by writing to them on this notepaper and they sent them to him; he then sold them to the defendants. It was held that the defendants were *not* here liable in conversion; for Wallis' personality could not have affected the minds of the plaintiffs – if they were willing to give credit to 'Hallam & Co', a non-existent entity, they were willing to give it to anyone. So, though there was fraud, there was no operative mistake and the defendants to whom Wallis had sold the goods were not liable. Further if the parties are present together at the time of the transaction there is a *prima facie presumption* that, whoever the rogue holds himself out to be, the person who alleges that he was mistaken did intend to contract with the actual person (the rogue) thus present to sight and hearing. So, in *Phillips v Brooks Ltd* [1919] 2 KB 243 it was held that a jeweller who made a sale to one North, who represented himself as 'Sir George Bullough' was not in a position to recover from an innocent third party to whom the jewel was sold; and the same applied to the plaintiff in *Lewis v Averay* [1972] 1 QB 198 who sold a car to a man who, in his presence, purported to be Richard Greene, a famous actor. This being so, *Ingram's Case* must, from this angle, be regarded as a special one in which, on the facts, the presumption was displaced. (Special or not, it is certainly a criticised one.)

Such being the various kinds of operative mistakes recognized at common law, it remains necessary only to repeat that the effect of such mistake is to make the contract *void* (there is no contract); with the result that it may be repudiated entirely and no rights or liabilities can arise under it.

Note – It is often suggested that mistake is a category which could, as a matter of pure analysis, be dispensed with entirely. This is because all the categories we have considered can be explained on other grounds: for instance as cases of *initial* impossibility – which was in fact the way Roman law treated them – similar to *subsequent* impossibility, or as cases turning solely upon non-correspondence of offer and acceptance. This may be true, but the fact remains that the courts, which make the law, do treat Mistake as a special category.

## 2 MISTAKE IN EQUITY

When equitable relief is sought, as by way of specific performance, rescission or rectification, the grant of it is discretionary and in exercising this discretion the courts will take the effect of mistake into account upon grounds wider than the grounds recognized by the common law. Thus *Solle v Butcher* [1950] 1 KB 671 is authority for the proposition that in *equity* a contract may be *voidable* (not void, thus leaving room for the protection of third party rights) where the mistake is one as to the attributes rather than the essence of the subject matter. In that case the landlord and tenant wrongly thought that the house let was outside the Rent Act limits, whereas in fact it was within them; it was held that though this mistake was not one which would operate to make the tenancy void at common law, it was nevertheless voidable in equity; and a similar conclusion was reached in another case where the parties thought the premises were subject to planning permission when they were not. Yet it was ruled in *Riverlate Properties Ltd v Paul* [1975] Ch 133 that in the absence of knowledge of the mistake by the other contracting party even equity will not give relief in the case of a purely unilateral mistake – as where a person mistakenly inserts in a lease a lower rent than he had intended to demand.

This equitable jurisdiction is discretionary and it cannot be prescisely defined: moreover, where equity does grant relief it will impose its own terms. Thus, for instance, in *Cooper v Phibbs* (1867) LR 2 HL 149, the plaintiff was only allowed to obtain the surrender of the lease from the defendants upon the terms that the latter should have a lien on the fishery for the payment of money which he had spent on making improvements during his occupation of the property.

## 3   NON EST FACTUM

*'Non est factum'* ('I did not make it'); is an ancient plea. Originally it applied to a case where a man denied liability arising under a document which bore his signature upon the ground that the signature was not his. Later the defence came to be applied to people who were blind or (as used often to be the case) illiterate, and who had been persuaded to sign away things which they did not intend through misrepresentations by others as to the nature of the document. It is a defence which may still be relied upon, but in *Saunders v Anglia Building Society* [1971] AC 1004 the House of Lords limited its availability strictly.

In that case it was made plain that a *prima facie* burden lies in such a case upon the signer to establish that in signing as he did he was not negligent, in the sense that he used all reasonable care in all the circumstances of the case to ascertain the nature of the document. Hence, those who sign things in reliance upon the statements of others *without reading* them, or who sign them in blank, can seldom be protected by the plea. On the other hand, the issue being one of fact, the courts will not now necessarily limit the defence to the case of blind or illiterate people. The question is, 'Did the signer, having taken proper care to ascertain the purport of the transaction, know *substantially* what the effect of his signature would be?' Was the document *substantially, seriously* or *fundamentally* different in its purport from what the signer believed to be the case? What constitutes the 'substantial' etc must again be a question of fact (a former distinction between mistake as to 'content' on the one hand and 'character' on the other being now discarded). Thus, for example in *Saunders' Case* it was held that where an old lady, who had broken her spectacles, was persuaded to assign the lease of her house – with the result that a companion of her nephew's was enabled to raise a loan from a building society upon the security of it – was *not* entitled to demand the lease back from the Society. Her mistake had been that she was transferring the house by way of gift to the nephew in order to help him to secure a loan; whereas in fact she had been persuaded (for the nephew's own supposed convenience) to make a purported sale to the companion who, having obtained the loan from the Society, absconded with the money. In either event, as Russell LJ had put the matter in the Court of Appeal, the 'object of the exercise' was substantially the same: the deed was knowingly put into circulation by the signer as a security for money. It is asserted that you would now have to be blind, illiterate and without a friend from whom to ask advice before this doctrine could be called in aid.

## B  MISREPRESENTATION

It has been explained that the terms of a contract are promises or statements which are intended to form its framework, and which define the mutual obligations of the parties. It often happens, however, that, before or at about the time of the making of a contract, one of the parties makes a statement of fact which, though it is not intended to be a *term* of the contract, nevertheless induces the other to contract. Statements of this sort are called representations.

Whether a statement is a term, or a representation, is technically a question to be determined by reference to the intention of the parties; but as in the case of the distinction between conditions and warranties, so here, since people do not always express their intentions, all the surrounding circumstances have to be considered. Thus such factors as whether the statement was reduced to writing, whether the situation was such that one of the parties might be expected to have placed special reliance upon it, and even the time that it was made, all have to be taken into account. The distinction may be illustrated by contrasting the case of *Harling v Eddy* [1951] 2 KB 739, with the old case of *Hopkins v Tanqueray* (1854) 15 CB 130. In *Harling's Case* the defendant put up an unpromising-looking heifer for sale at an auction. There being no bids, the defendant then declared that there was nothing wrong with her. The plaintiff then bought her in reliance upon this statement made *during the auction*. The heifer's condition at once proved unsatisfactory (it had tuberculosis) and it died shortly afterwards. It was held that the defendant's statement formed a term of the contract, and that accordingly the plaintiff was entitled to damages. In *Hopkins' Case* the defendant was going to sell a horse at

Tattersall's, and on the day *before* the sale the plaintiff was examining it when the defendant said 'I assure you he is perfectly sound'. The plaintiff bought it the next day in reliance upon this statement which was held to be a *representation* rather than a term.

When a representation is untrue it is called a *misrepresentation*. Just as parties are free to make whatever terms they like, so also they are not *bound* to make representations. Only *active* misrepresentations will therefore normally give rise to a cause of action; mere silence, even as to known defects, does not normally amount to misrepresentation. Thus in *Ward v Hobbs* (1878) 4 App Cas 13, where a man sold pigs 'with all faults' it was ruled that, though to his knowledge they had typhoid, he could not be held liable: he had made no misrepresentation. This rule is, of couse, another application of the *caveat emptor* principle: in theory, at least, the prudent buyer should safeguard himself by exacting terms from the seller (asking questions).

The effect of misrepresentation varies according to whether it is fraudulent or innocent. We must therefore first consider fraudulent and innocent misrepresentation separately, and then mention must be made of the 'collateral warranty' doctrine, of exclusion of liability for misrepresentation and of certain special contracts which do require a *positive* duty of disclosure.

## 1   FRAUDULENT MISREPRESENTATION

A fraudulent misrepresentation is one which constitutes the tort of *fraud* (or 'deceit'). This tort is committed when a person makes a *false representation of fact, knowing it to be false, or without believing it to be true, or recklessly, careless whether it be true or false*. The false representation must, further, be made with the *intention that it is to be acted upon* by the party deceived; and if his claim is to succeed this person must prove that he actually did *act* upon it *to his detriment*. These elements of the tort may be considered in turn.

*(i)   The representation must be a representation of fact* – Thus a mere statement that something '*will be*', cannot form a ground for an action of deceit. For instance, if I say to you, 'My car will win the Monte Carlo Rally', and you buy it in reliance upon my statement, you will have no claim against me, even though the car fails to cross the start-line. I have not deceived you as to an existing fact. It must also be noted that although it has been convenient thus far to treat representations as if they were always verbal statements, this is not always the case. Acts, as well as words, can deceive. For example, a person who, not being a member of the university, dresses up in a cap and gown in a university town, and thus obtains credit from a shopkeeper, is guilty of deceit. Further, a mere statement of *opinion* is not normally a statement of fact.

*(ii)* The representation must be made with a knowledge of its falsehood, or recklessly, without a belief in its truth – This proposition was illustrated in the leading case of *Derry v Peek* (1889) 14 App Cas 337. The directors of a company issued a prospectus stating that the company was empowered to run steam trams in Plymouth. This was not really true, because authorization had to be obtained from the Board of Trade and it had not actually been granted. The directors, however, honestly believed that it was certain to be. It was eventually refused; but meantime the plaintiff had bought shares on the faith of the prospectus. As a result of the refusal the company had to be wound up, and the plaintiff thus suffered loss. When he sued the directors for fraud the House of Lords held that his action failed: the directors might have been stupid, but they *honestly* believed in the statement they had made.

Today the duties of directors or promoters who issue company prospectuses have been made more stringent than they used to be, but the proposition of law laid down in *Derry v Peek*, that an *honest* statement cannot be fraudulent, still holds good.

*(iii)* The representation must be made with the intention that it shall be acted upon by the party deceived – Thus the *mere* telling of a lie will not make the liar responsible to the world at large, for the liar does not always intend that people shall act upon what he says.

*(iv)* The plaintiff must show that he acted upon the representation to his *detriment* – Thus, suppose that Peter offers Graham a stamp and asks him for £10, asserting that it is a particularly valuable one. If Peter knows that it is not, and Graham is deceived into paying £10, Peter is guilty of deceit. If, on the other hand, Graham knows that it is really quite common, and offers Peter 50p which Peter accepts, Peter's attempted deceit has failed, it is not actionable; for Graham has not been induced to act upon it, and has lost nothing.

*Remedies for fraudulent misrepresentation* – Where a misrepresentation which is fraudulent in the sense above defined induces a person to make a contract, the contract will be *void* if the effect of the fraud is to induce an operative mistake; hence no property can pass under it and the plaintiff may claim from the fraudulent person or from third parties anything that has been transferred. As has already been explained, however, by no means do all frauds induce an operative mistake and the more usual effect of fraudulent (like innocent) misrepresentation is to render the contract *voidable* at the option of the person defrauded. In other words, the contract is *valid but voidable*. The effect of this is that that person may:

*(i)* Recover damages for fraud (or deceit); ie in tort, in respect of any loss.

*(ii)* He may, upon discovering the fraud – and within a reasonable time he must – make an decision whether to affirm or to repudiate the contract; then the result will depend on his choice: (a) if he affirms, the contract remains valid and he may insist upon its performance; (b) if he repudiates

within a reasonable time the contract is avoided and he may take back anything he had lost under it. Repudiation may take the form of actual notification to the other party or of taking such steps to bring it to his attention as is reasonable in the circumstances. It is essential that repudiation should be communicated as soon as possible, since delay may mean that innocent third parties may acquire rights over the subject matter of the contract (eg, by its resale by the rogue); once such rights are acquired in the absence of reasonably prompt repudiation the right to avoid is lost. It should be added that sometimes it may be advisable for the plaintiff to institute an *action* for rescission of the contract instead of relying purely upon his right of repudiation.

## 2   INNOCENT MISREPRESENTATION

Any misrepresentation which is not 'fraudulent' in the sense defined above is 'innocent', whether negligently made or not. The law governing such misrepresentations has much in common with that which governs fraudulent ones. First, as in the case of fraudulent misrepresentation so in the case of innocent; unless the effect of the statement is to produce operative mistake the contract is voidable at the plaintiff's option; not void. Second, the party aggrieved may affirm the contract either by words or conduct, and although mere lapse of time after knowledge of the misrepresentation will not normally amount to an affirmation in itself, it may be treated as evidence of it. Lapse of time beyond the appropriate limitation period will of course, *per se* form a bar. Third, once third parties have acquired rights (as for example in goods sold, and bought for value and in good faith) the contract cannot be avoided.

Formerly, however, in the case of innocent misrepresentation it was *not* possible either to obtain rescission of the contract once it was executed, ie, once performance had been entered upon, *or to obtain damages* for loss arising from the misrepresentation; though equity gave a limited right of compensation.

The Misrepresentation Act 1967, however, altered this position. By s 1 it is provided that neither the fact that the misrepresentation has been incorporated into the contract and become a term of it, nor the fact that the contract has been performed, will preclude a claim for *rescission*. But rescission is an equitable remedy governed by discretion rather than by rule, and the court must therefore take all circumstances and equities into account. For instance, apart from the former rule which made the bare fact of execution of the contract a bar to rescission, rescission in equity must depend upon the power of the court in all the circumstances to effect '*restitutio in integrum*' – put things back where they were when the parties entered upon their bargain – and lapse of time and intervening events may make this impossible. Hence the Act (s 2(2)) provides that the court may refuse rescission at its discretion and award *damages in lieu* of it wherever it would *'be equitable to do so, having regard to the nature of the misrepresentation and the loss that would be caused by it if the contract were upheld, as well as the loss that rescission would cause to the other party'*.

Section 2(1) of the Act provides that a person who enters into a contract as the result of innocent misrepresentation and *suffers loss* thereby may recover damages against the misrepresentor provided that damages would have been recoverable had the statement been fraudulent; *but* the defendant will *escape* liability if he *'proves that he had reasonable ground to believe and did believe up to the time the contract was made that the facts represented were true'*. Thus, in effect, damages may be obtained *under the Act* for *negligent*, though *not* for what might be called entirely innocent, misrepresentation. The two different grounds for awarding damages must, however, be kept clearly apart: damages *in lieu of rescission* are one thing, damages claimed for *loss suffered* are another. Thus in a particular case damages might be awarded under both heads; rescission *and* damages having been claimed. Where this happens s 2(3) operates: this provides that if both are awarded the court must take into account in assessing liability in respect of damages in lieu or recission any award made (under s 2(1)) in respect of damages for loss arising from the negligent misstatement.

## Liability in tort
It must be added that it is now clear that a *negligent* misrepresentation which induces a contract may *also* be actionable in tort under the *Hedley Byrne* rule (as developed, eg, in *Caparo Industries plc v Dickman* [1990] 2 AC 605) which governs careless misstatement generally: but that doctrine ought not normally to need to be invoked in the case of contractual misrepresentation because it is easier for the plaintiff to sue under the Act (thus casting the burden of proof upon the defendant) than to assume the burden of proving negligence – which he must do in the tort action.

## 3   COLLATERAL WARRANTY (COLLATERAL CONTRACT)

A 'collateral warranty' (or 'contract') arises from the legal obligation which is imposed when a person makes an assertion which is relied upon by another as an inducement for him to enter upon a contract. If the assertion is false, and the person who relies upon it suffers loss, by reason of entering the contract, he will have a cause of action against the person who had made it. The word 'collateral' implies that this kind of obligation can only arise where the person who places the reliance is contemplating entering upon a *contract*. The obligation itself is thus 'collateral' to that contract. It is an interesting question whether such a form of obligation is better called a 'warranty' or a 'contract'. The former is probably the more precise word because the warrantor himself is not intending to create a contractual obligation. But, in a sense he may be said to be 'contracting' because the circumstances are such that his assertion may be regarded as implying a promise that if the other party binds himself by entering into *his* contract the assertion will be true. To *imply* a promise is, however, to employ a fiction of a contract where really there is none; and the use of fictions (if they be taken seriously) may often lead to confusion of thought. On the other hand, it has to be admitted that the word 'warranty' has more than one meaning in law, and is used in a number of differing contexts (eg 'guarantees') by laymen.

A collateral warranty (or 'contract') may take two forms. Either the contract contemplated may be one between the warrantor himself and the other party, or it may be between the other party and some other person. The former situation may be illustrated by *Mardon's Case* where, it will be recalled, a misstatement about the potential of a petrol station was made before the parties agreed to terms and it was held that it was actionable; thus treating what was essentially a representation as if it were a term. The latter situation may be illustrated by *Shanklin Pier Ltd v Detel Products Ltd* [1951] 2 KB 854, where the plaintiffs, under a contract with a third party to paint their pier, were entitled to designate the paint to be used, and selected the defendants' paint in reliance upon a false statement by the latter's agent that it was suitable for such an undertaking: again, the defendants were held liable. It should be added, however, that such statements will only be actionable if it is clearly intended that they are to be acted upon. For example, a mere statement in an advertisement that a product is 'foolproof' is not a statement of such a nature.

It should be noted that reliance upon a collateral warranty is preferable to reliance upon the Misrepresentation Act 1967 in the first kind of situation and upon the *Hedley Byrne* doctrine in the second because the liability is imposed even if the warrantor's assertion is in no way negligent.

## 4    EXCLUSION OF LIABILITY FOR MISREPRESENTATION

It is enacted by the Unfair Contract Terms Act 1977 s 8 (replacing the Misrepresentation Act 1967, s 3) that any term which purports to exclude or restrict liability for misrepresentation in a contract or which seeks to exclude any remedy for misrepresentation shall 'be of no effect except in so far as it satisfies the *requirement of reasonableness* as stated in s 11(1)' – of the 1977 Act.

## 5    CONTRACTS IN WHICH DISCLOSURE IS REQUIRED

The duty which the law in general imposes upon people negotiating a contract is, as we have seen, the purely negative duty to refrain from making misrepresentations. But there are two special classes of contracts in respect of which such people are required to make positive disclosure of facts known to them, but unknown to the other party.

First, where the parties are in a confidential relationship, equity requires the person in whom confidence is reposed to make full disclosure of all material facts in respect of any contract he may make with the other party. This is a general rule, and it is not limited to particular classes of relationships. The solicitor–client relationship, however, forms a stock example.

Second, there are certain classes of contracts in respect of which one party has means of knowledge which, in the nature of things, the other cannot be expected to possess. These contracts are called contracts *uberrimae fidei* ('of the utmost good faith'). Here the person having the special means of knowledge must make full disclosure of all material facts known to him which might influence the other person's decision to enter into the contract or to continue to perform it once it has been entered upon. Failure to disclose such facts will give the other party an option to rescind, even though *restitutio in integrum* is no longer possible.

By far the most important of the contracts *uberrimae fidei* are contracts of insurance. A person who applies for insurance must disclose all facts known to him which would be likely to affect the decision of the insurer to underwrite the risk. But it should be noted that the applicant need only disclose facts *known* to him. Thus, if a person applies for a policy of life insurance and is asked, 'Do you suffer from any known disease?' and he replies 'No', and it subsequently appears that, without knowing it, he had cancer, he will not be guilty of non-disclosure. In practice, however, insurance companies tend to evade this rule by so framing the terms of policies that the statements of the assured become the basis of the contract; thus his knowledge becomes irrelevant.

There are several other classes of contracts in which a degree of disclosure is required; and they are therefore in some respects similar to contracts '*uberrimae fidei*'. The degree of disclosure varies, and is not usually so strict as that required in the case of contracts of insurance. As examples, promoters of companies are bound, by the provisions of the Companies Act 1985 to disclose certain specified matters in their prospectuses and under various sections of the Financial Services Act 1986 extensive duties of disclosure are imposed upon those who apply for stock exchange listings and those who issue prospectuses for unlisted securities.

# 4 Privity of contract

A contract creates a special legal relationship for the parties who enter upon it. It follows logically that only such people as are 'privy' (parties) to a contract can normally be affected by it. This aspect of the law of contract is often epitomized in the Latin maxim '*res inter alios acta aliis neque nocere neque prodesse potest*', which may be loosely translated, 'An agreement can only bind the parties; it can neither impose *obligations* upon other people, nor confer *rights* upon them.'

This general rule is, however, subject to exceptions. The two branches must be considered separately.

## A   A CONTRACT CANNOT IMPOSE OBLIGATIONS UPON PEOPLE WHO ARE NOT PRIVY TO IT

The courts have generally been disposed to uphold this principle, and have refused to countenance attempts to evade it. Thus in *Scruttons Ltd v Midland Silicones Ltd* [1962] AC 446 a firm of *stevedores* whose servants damaged some *cargo* were held not entitled (in an action by cargo owners) to rely upon a clause which limited liability for damage and was contained in the bill of lading, which of course represented the contract between cargo owners and *ship* owners. And this was so even though it had been agreed between the stevedores and the shipowners that the former should 'have such protection as is afforded by the terms' of the bill of lading; for that agreement could not prejudice the rights of the cargo owners. It would have been otherwise if the shipowners had contracted on behalf of and as *agents* for the stevedores: for then, through the agency of the carriers, the cargo owners would have been in a contractual relationship with the stevedores, who could thus have taken advantage of the exemption clause.

But there are exceptions to the general rule. In the first place, although the Resale Prices Act 1976 (substantially re-enacting earlier legislation) makes collective arrangements – by the imposition of 'stop lists' and otherwise – among traders unlawful, and also inhibits the imposition of *minimum* resale price conditions, yet by s 14 it permits the latter practice in the case of 'exempted goods'; eg goods which have, after reference to the Restrictive Practices Court and upon grounds specified in s 14, been exempted from the general ban upon minimum resale price conditions. And, where a class of goods is thus exempted under s 14 a minimum price condition may be enforced (s 26) by 'a supplier against any person – *(a)* who is not *a party to the sale*, and *(b)* who subsequently acquires the goods *with notice* of that condition,' provided that the person concerned acquires the goods in the course of business. Thus, by way of exception to the privity rule, the statute enables a manufacturer who sells exempted goods which he has subjected to a minimum price condition to a wholesaler who, in turn, has sold the goods to a dealer, to enforce the condition directly against the dealer though there is no privity of contract between the manufacturer and the latter.

It should be added that for the sake of simplicity the only parties mentioned have been manufacturer, wholesaler and dealer: in practice of course there may be other parties (to whom the same rules will apply) in the sale 'chain'.

In the second place, where a contract creates an *interest of an enduring nature*, the subsistence of this interest will sometimes be permitted to have an adverse effect upon the rights of third parties. An obvious example of an interest of this sort is to be found in the case of a lease of land. Suppose that A leases land to B for seven years, and that A sells the land to C while five years of B's lease remain unexpired. At any rate since the middle ages, it has never been doubted that C takes the land subject to B's right under the lease. In this case C is therefore adversely affected by the contract between A and B. Moreover, restrictive covenants run with the land and their effectiveness is not limited to the original covenantor and covenantee.

Further, there is authority – though a later decision has exposed the matter to considerable doubt – for the proposition that where shipowners sell a *ship* which is subject to at least some kinds of charter (ie is let out to a charterer) the buyer may, if he has full notice of the charter and its terms, be restrained by the charterer from using the ship in a manner inconsistent with the charter until the charter period expires.

## B   A CONTRACT CANNOT CONFER RIGHTS UPON PEOPLE WHO ARE NOT PRIVY TO IT

The effect of this rule may be illustrated by *Tweddle v Atkinson* (1861) 1 B & S 393 where, a son being about to marry, his future father-in-law agreed with his *father* to pay the son a sum of money, which he (the father-in-law) failed to do. It was held that since the son was not a party to the contract between the two older men he could not bring a successful claim against the father-in-law's estate.

The rule that third parties cannot be adversely affected by contracts made between other people is both logical and practically just. The rule that strangers to a contract cannot acquire benefits under it rests upon logic alone, and it is subject to a considerable number of exceptions. The following are among the more important of them:

*(i)* Where one of the parties to a contract enters into it as trustee for a third party, the third party acquires an equitable right which is in the subject matter of the contract. He may therefore force the trustee to insist upon the performance of the contract on his behalf.

*(ii)* A principal may acquire the benefit of a contract made by his agent.

*(iii)* Certain statutes permit third parties to acquire rights under contracts made by other people. Two of them may be mentioned. First, by s 151 of the Road Traffic Act 1988 insurers who issue a policy which

covers third-party risks are in some cases made liable to people, other than the assured, for whose benefit the assured has taken out the policy. Second, by the Third Parties (Rights against Insurers) Act 1930, third parties who have claims against an assured in respect of a motor accident may claim direct against the insurers if, amongst other things, the assured becomes bankrupt. They thus receive a benefit as the result of the contract between the assured and his insurers. Perhaps more important still is the agreement of 1945 between the Minister of Transport and the Motor Insurers' Bureau whereby the latter undertakes to indemnify anyone in whose favour judgment is given in an accident claim if the judgment has not been satisfied in respect of any liability required to be covered by the Road Traffic Acts. There have been subsequent agreements, and it is now a condition of authorisation to transact motor insurance business that the motor insurer is a member of MIB Ltd (RTA 1988, s145(5)).

*(iv)* The so-called 'collateral warranty' doctrine may also sometimes form an exception to the rule where (as in the *Shanklin Pier Case*) a third party to the relevant contract is entitled to sue upon it.

*(v)* One practical way of circumventing the harshness of the rule in some cases rests upon the fact that where A contracts with B in favour of C, though C cannot sue B for breach of the obligation, A can. And if he does, he may recover damages in respect of any loss to C. An example is *Jackson v Horizon Holidays Ltd* [1975] 3 All ER 92 – where a father recovered on behalf of himself and the family in respect of a very disappointing holiday. Moreover, where the equitable remedy of *specific performance* is available A may obtain it in favour of C. Thus in *Beswick v Beswick* [1968] AC 58, a man assigned his business to his nephew (the defendant) upon condition that after his (the assignor's) death the defendant would pay an annuity to the assignor's widow. After the latter's death, the nephew having failed to carry out his promise, it was held that the widow, as personal representative of the deceased, though not of course in her own right – for she was not a party to the contract – could claim specific performance in her own favour against the defendant. This exception to the rule is, however, necessarily limited to cases in which specific performance is an available remedy.

NOTE – The rule that a third party can acquire no rights under a contract has long been subject to criticism (see the Report of the Law Revision Committee: (1937) Cmd 5449) and was the subject of adverse comment by the House of Lords in *Woodar Investment Development Ltd v Wimpey Construction (UK) Ltd* [1980] 1 All ER 571.

# 5   Assignment of contractual rights and liabilities

## A   ASSIGNMENT OF RIGHTS

An 'assignment' of a right is a transfer of an existing right from one person to another. At common law *choses in action* were not assignable. The nature of choses in action will be explained later. For the present it need only be noted that they have been authoritatively defined as '*all personal rights of property which can only be claimed or enforced by action, and not by taking physical possession*'. Contract rights, such as the claim of a creditor against a debtor, are therefore 'choses in action'. It follows that, at common law, contract rights were not assignable. In respect of choses in action generally, the rule as to non-assignability has long since been eaten away by exceptions. Negotiable instruments became freely assignable by the custom of merchants, and most other choses in action have been made expressly so by various statutes, such as copyright and patent rights.

The legislature has also been active in making *contract* rights other than negotiable instruments assignable. Thus the assignment of life insurance policies is governed by the provisions of the Policies of Assurance Act 1867, and policies of marine insurance are assignable under the provisions of the Marine Insurance Act 1906. By far the most important enactment, however, in this regard, is s 136 of the Law of Property Act 1925: this section re-enacts s 25(6) of the Judicature Act 1873. It provides that: '*Any* absolute assignment by writing under the hand of the assignor (*ie transferor*) . . . of any debt or other . . . thing in action, of which express notice in writing has been given to the debtor . . . is effectual in law . . . to pass and transfer from the date of such notice . . . the . . . right to such debt or thing in action.'

The above enactment governs contract rights generally. Therefore, if B owes A £100 and A wishes to transfer the debt to C, he may do so by making an out and out transfer in writing and giving *written* notice of the transfer to B. The transfer may be either voluntary or for value.

This being so, the question arises, 'What happens if A wishes to make the assignment, but fails to comply with the *statutory* provisions?' Suppose for example that A fails to comply with the requirement as to writing. The answer to this is that the assignment may still be valid. Although assignment of contract rights was not possible at common law, it could, from comparatively early times, be effected by the operation of the rules of equity. 'Equitable' rights, eg the rights of a beneficiary to funds in the control of his trustee, were always and still are, freely assignable. Further, the Court of Chancery would support the claim of an assignee of a purely 'legal' right, such as a claim to a money debt. This was done by forcing the assignor (the creditor) to bring an action at law against the debtor and to transfer the fruits of the action to the assignee. Since the Judicature Acts have combined the courts which administer law and equity this cumbrous procedure need no longer be adopted; but '*equitable assignments*' can still be made according to rules which are less exacting than the rules laid down in the Law of Property Act.

No formalities are required for an *equitable assignment*. It is sufficient for the assignor to transfer his right to the assignee by any appropriate means. Two rules which govern assignments generally, whether statutory or equitable, require attention.

First, apart from the provision as to written notice in s 136, it is always wise for an assignee to give *notice* of the assignment to the debtor. If the assignee fails to do this, the debtor will be entitled (since he knows nothing of the assignment) to discharge his liability by paying the assignor himself, or by paying any other assignee who gives him notice. For example: W, for value, assigns to Y X's debt to him. W is a rogue. He goes to Z, receives value, and re-assigns the same debt to *him*. If Z gives notice to X before Y gives notice, Z will be entitled to payment and Y will have lost his right. Where the right assigned is an equitable right, such as the claim of a beneficiary to a trust fund, the notice to the trustee must be *written* if it is to be effective (Law of Property Act 1925, s 137(3)).

In the second place, an assignee always takes subject to any rights (such as rights of set-off) which the debtor may have against the assignor. *Nemo dat quod non habet* ('No one can give what he has not got'). The assignor cannot give the assignee a better right than he himself has.

Finally, even at the present time there are certain classes of contract rights which are not assignable. The most important of these are bare rights of action (eg mere claims to damages upon a *broken* contract) and rights of a personal nature (eg rights to the performance of personal services): though this statement must be qualified at least to the extent that, provided that the requirements of the LPA, s 136 are complied with, an insurer who has paid his insured in respect of loss arising from the commission of a tort or breach of a contract may sue the wrongdoer in his own name in order to recoup himself.

## B   ASSIGNMENT OF LIABILITIES

As a general rule liabilities are not assignable. This is common sense. If, for instance, A were to commission B to paint his portrait A would be surprised if, without consulting him, B were to transfer his obligations to another artist.

The rule is well illustrated by *Robson and Sharpe v Drummond* (1831) 2 B & Ad 303. D hired a carriage from S for a period of five years. S undertook to keep it painted (an operation which required skill) and in good repair. Unknown to D, S was in partnership with R. When S retired from business, while there were two years of the contract still to run, R claimed to be entitled to continue with the contract. It was held that he could not, and that D could treat it as terminated by S's retirement.

There are three exceptions or qualifications to the general rule that contractual liabilities cannot be assigned.

First, the parties to a contract may *agree* that the duties of one of them shall be assignable; there is nothing to prevent this. Thus, if Drummond had agreed, Sharpe might have stipulated that his duties should be transferable to Robson in certain events. Second, liabilities may be transferred by '*novation*', ie by the termination of an existing contract and the formation of a new one, under which a third person undertakes to perform the duties of one of the parties to the old contract. Third, although liabilities are not *assignable*, they may sometimes be *vicariously performed* by a third party on behalf of the person bound.

For instance, if I employ a man to repair a common article, such as a table, as long as the table is repaired I cannot complain if someone else does the job. As *Robson's Case* shows, however, there are limits to this rule, and there can be no vicarious performance of a contract which requires any special personal skill.

Since 'assignment' denotes the *transfer* of an *existing* obligation the last two, at any rate, of the above-mentioned 'exceptions' are more apparent than real.

# 6 Discharge of contract

Contractual obligations may be discharged by performance, by agreement, by frustration, and by breach.

## A PERFORMANCE

It is obvious that a party to a contract who has performed his obligations will be discharged from further liability. He will also normally be discharged if he makes a valid offer (or 'tender') of performance which the other party rejects. Mere tender of a *money* debt will not, however, operate as a discharge. In order to escape liability a debtor must show, not merely that he tendered the correct sum upon the date on which it was due, but also that he was ready and willing to pay up to the time that the creditor brought his action for the recovery of the debt.

## B    DISCHARGE BY AGREEMENT

Discharge by agreement may take four forms. First, the contract may be discharged by mutual agreement. (They agreed to be bound, so they can agree not to be.) In this case the agreement of one party forms consideration for the agreement of the other. But if one party, having performed, or being ready and willing to perform, his part of the contract merely waives performance by the other (eg agrees to postpone the time of performance) he can always retract the waiver by reasonable notice unless it has been supported by fresh consideration.

In the second place, an existing contract may be mutually discharged, and a *new one substituted* in its place: this is a form of novation.

In the third place, the contract may be subject to a *condition subsequent* in which case failure of the condition may give rise to discharge. In the fourth place, a contract may be discharged by *accord and satisfaction* – as where B owing A £500, the latter agrees to accept a motor cycle in satisfaction of the debt.

But it will be remembered that payment of a *lesser sum of money* would not discharge B unless the doctrine of promissory estoppel were to come into play or unless there were novation by way of varying the terms of the contract. Further, many kinds of contracts are not intended to be of indefinite duration, and either expressly or by implication they depend upon appropriate notice for their discharge. Agreements for periodic leases afford an example, but perhaps the commonest contracts of this kind are contracts of employment. These are subject to the Employment Protection (Consolidation) Act 1978.

## C    FRUSTRATION

It sometimes happens that, in the course of the performance of a contract which is intended to last over a period of time, unforeseen events occur which render further performance impracticable or impossible. Examples of such events are sickness, accident, war, the interference of third parties and legislation which renders further performance illegal.

This raises the question of what is to become of the contract. Originally the law was strict: it took the view that the contract would remain in force because the parties could have made express provision against the possibility of the event. Thus in *Paradine v Jane* (1647) Aleyn 26 the plaintiff sued the defendant for rent. The defendant pleaded that 'a German prince, Prince Rupert, an alien born' had entered the land and expelled him from it 'from July 1642 until Lady Day 1646', whereby he (the defendant) had had no profit from the land and ought to be excused the rent. The plea was of no avail: the defendant, it was held, should have made express provision against such a contingency.

This state of the law continued until *Taylor v Caldwell* (1863) 3 B & S 826 where A agreed to hire out a music hall in Vauxhall Gardens to B. Six days before the letting the hall was accidentally destroyed by fire. It was held that the continued existence of the hall was a basic assumption upon which the contract was founded and that it was therefore discharged when the hall was destroyed. The contract was thus, as we now put it, 'frustrated' by the fire. This was a case where the frustrating event rendered further performance physically impossible. But the doctrine of frustration received considerable extension in *Jackson v Union Marine Insurance Co Ltd* (1874) LR 10 CP 125 when it was applied to circumstances which rendered the contract no longer viable rather than physically impossible. The case was one of a ship which was stranded on a reef and was put out of action for a length of time which rendered its voyage commercially impracticable, though, since the ship was ultimately repaired, not actually impossible. This extension of the doctrine of frustration is usually called 'commercial frustration'.

A person who seeks to avoid a contract on the ground of frustration must show not merely that the event has rendered the contract more onerous than he had expected, but also that it has destroyed the whole foundation of it; or as it has sometimes been put in relation to commercial contracts, that it has destroyed the whole 'basis of the venture', made continued fulfilment something radically different from what was originally contemplated, or rendered its continuance positively unjust. Thus, for example, if an artiste dies or is taken seriously ill so as to be unable to perform, or if an employee who holds a key position in a business is sentenced to a long term of imprisonment or becomes chronically sick, either contract may be frustrated. By contrast, where on account of a criminal charge, the head of a school was suspended for a time until the charge was dismissed, it was held – especially in view of the fact that his staff continued to run the school in his absence – that the suspension did not frustrate the contracts for the education of the pupils so as to enable the latter to be withdrawn from the school without the customary term's notice. And again something which merely adds to the length of a voyage does not *necessarily* frustrate a contract the fulfilment of which depends upon the voyage. So in *Tsakiroglou & Co Ltd v Noblee and Thorl GmbH* [1962] AC 93 a contract for the sale of groundnuts which was elastic in its terms as to the date of delivery in Hamburg (the port of destination) was held by the House of Lords not to have been frustrated by the closure of the Suez Canal in 1956, which forced the carrying ship to take the longer Cape route rather than the normal, and shorter, Suez route from Port Sudan to Hamburg. Had the delivery date been a matter of importance the result might have been different.

Further, the element in the contract which the supervening event destroys must be something which both the parties, not merely one of them, must be taken to have regarded as basic. Thus in *Blackburn Bobbin Co v*

*Allen* [1918] 2 KB 467, the seller agreed to supply the buyer with Finnish timber. Unknown to the buyer, the seller held no stocks but customarily shipped orders direct from Finland. War broke out and the seller's supplies were cut off. It was held that this event did not frustrate the contract because the *method* of supply was irrelevant to it. For all that the buyer knew, the seller held stocks of Finnish timber, or obtained it indirectly from some other country.

The doctrine of 'frustration' is also subject to three major limitations. In order for it to operate the following conditions must be satisfied:

*(i)* The supervening event must not normally be one which the parties expressly allowed for in the contract. Thus, if I contract to build a house beneath the Matterhorn and agree to do so expressly in the face of the risk of avalanches, I cannot claim to be discharged from my obligations if an avalanche destroys the house when it is all-but finished. The event was one which the contract itself envisaged. On the other hand the mere fact that a subsequent event is foreseeable or even foreseen at the time of the contract does not mean that its occurrence *cannot* result in frustration. Thus in *W J Tatem Ltd v Gamboa* [1939] 1 KB 132, a ship was let on charter to the Republican Government to evacuate refugees during the Spanish Civil War. It was clear that there was risk of capture by the Nationalists but no provision was made to cover the event. Despite the obviousness of the risk, capture was held to frustrate the contract.

*(ii)* The frustration must not be 'self-induced' by one of the parties. For example in *Ocean Tramp Tankers Corpn v V/O Sovfracht The Eugenia* [1964] 2 QB 226, it was held that when the charterers in 1956 allowed the *Eugenia* to enter the Canal Zone in face of the obvious danger of closure they could not treat her detention in the Canal as frustration, for they themselves brought it about.

*(iii)* The event relied upon must destroy the very root of the contract. Thus in *Krell v Henry* [1903] 2 KB 740 a contract for the hire of a room to see King Edward VII's coronation procession was held to have been frustrated when the procession was cancelled due to the King's illness. *But* in *Herne Bay Steam Boat Co v Hutton* [1903] 2 KB 683 a contract for the hire of a ship to see the Spithead review of the fleet by the King *and* to cruise round the assembled fleet was held not to have been frustrated: the fleet was still there, though the King was not able to be.

It seems also that the courts will not permit the doctrine to be invoked so as to allow a party to escape liability for the breach of a minor obligation. Thus it was held that where a tenant left a house without painting it as the terms of the lease provided that he should he could not escape liability to his landlord by proving that wartime regulations had made it impossible for him to obtain a licence to paint. But this does not mean that a lease itself can never be frustrated (as where, for instance, the land subject to it becomes inundated by the sea).

Once it has been proved that a contract has been frustrated, it is automatically avoided. This rule formerly led to unhappy results, because it was held that the supervening event had the effect of leaving matters exactly as they lay at the moment it occurred. Hence, unless there had been a total failure of consideration, money, once paid, could not be recovered even though frustration made further performance of the contract by the recipient impossible. The position is, however, now regulated by the Law Reform (Frustrated Contracts) Act 1943. The Act provides that where frustration occurs sums paid before the happening of the frustrating event are to be recoverable, subject to deduction of expenses incurred by the payee. All subsequent liabilities are extinguished. Further, if one party has conferred a benefit upon the other, as by performing services for him, he may claim the value of this benefit from the other, or, as the case may be, may set the value off against any claim which the other may have against him. Certain classes of contracts are excluded from the operation of the Act: in particular, contracts for the sale of specific goods, which are frustrated by the perishing of the goods, are not included, for they are governed by the Sale of Goods Act 1979, s 7.

## D  DISCHARGE BY BREACH

Where one of the parties to a contract entirely fails to perform his obligation the other may *repudiate* it and he will then be discharged from further performance. He may also claim for any loss he has suffered.

Breach may take one of two forms. It may either be constituted by substantial failure of performance, or by renunciation before or after the time for performance arrives. Whichever of these two forms it may take, it must amount to a *substantial* failure of performance, or of a refusal to perform. Further, where a breach occurs during performance, it it often a nice question whether it can be regarded as fundamental so as to entitle the aggrieved party to repudiate rather than merely to claim damages. Instalment contracts often raise difficulties. A party who claims the right to rescind will seldom succeed if he can only show a failure to deliver one of a series of instalments; for such a failure will seldom indicate that the party in breach will not perform the rest of the contract. He will, however, always be entitled to claim *damages* for any breach, however small.

Where, before a contract is due to be performed, one party renounces his obligations or renders performance impossible by his own act, he is said to have committed an '*anticipatory*' breach. English law, unlike most other systems, gives effect to anticipatory breaches. Thus, in the days when breach of promise of marriage was actionable, where B promised to marry Miss A when B's father should die, and B renounced the contract during his father's lifetime, it was held that Miss A could sue him. It will be noticed that this is an extreme instance of an 'anticipatory' breach, for not only was the time for performance not due, but it might never have arrived at all. Either of the parties to the contract might have predeceased the father.

# 7   Remedies for breach of contract

Having considered the circumstances in which a contract may be discharged (ie terminated) as the result of a breach, we must now consider the nature of the principal remedies which are available to the party injured by the breach. These are damages, *quantum meruit*, specific performance, injunctions, and rescission and rectification.

## A   DAMAGES

Damages are a common law remedy, and they may be claimed by an injured party as of right. They are money compensation for loss suffered. The object of granting them is to put the injured party, as far as money can do it, into the position in which he would have been had the loss not been suffered, ie (as far as concerns us here) had the contract not been broken. Thus, there can be no rule which will prescribe in every case what damages the plaintiff *will* obtain: the amount of damages must always depend upon the 'value' of the loss. There are, however, certain general rules governing damages:

*(i)* The value of the loss (the 'measure' of the damages) is generally assessed, not according to the price the plaintiff puts upon it, but objectively, according to the value that an ordinary, reasonable, person would put upon it. Thus, for example, where a breach of contract consists of failure by the defendant to deliver goods under a contract of sale, the general rule is that the 'measure of damages is *prima facie* to be ascertained by the difference between the contract price and the market, or current, price of the goods at the time when they ought to have been delivered' (Sale of Goods Act 1979, s 51(3)). Note: 'price' here means the 'market' (ie ordinary) price, not, for instance, the price for which the plaintiff may, unknown to the defendant, have himself contracted to re-sell the goods.

*(ii)* Damages may be recovered only in respect of loss arising from the breach of contract itself. There can be no claim for loss which is too '*remote*' from the breach to be regarded as a proximate result of it. The distinction between remote and proximate damage is hard to draw. The courts, however, apply a test which was propounded by Alderson B in *Hadley v Baxendale* (1854) 9 Exch 341 at 354.

'*Where two parties*,' he said, '*have made a contract which one of them has broken, the damages which the other party ought to receive in respect of such breach of contract should be such as may fairly and reasonably be considered either arising naturally, ie according to the usual course of things, from such breach of contract itself, or such as may reasonably be supposed to have been in the contemplation of both parties, at the time they made the contract, as the probable result of the breach of it*'. It will be seen that this really provides two rules. According to *Rule I* damage will be regarded as 'proximate' if it is damage which arises 'naturally' from the breach. Subsequent decisions have shown that, for the purposes of the law of contract, this means damage which the party in breach ought reasonably to have *foreseen*, in the light of the knowledge of the circumstances which he possessed at the time the contract was made as *likely*, in the ordinary course of things, to follow from breach of his obligations. According to *Rule II*, as appeared from later statements in Alderson B's judgment, damage which is not 'ordinary' in the above sense may give rise to a claim for damages (ie may be 'proximate' and not 'too remote') where though it is of an extraordinary nature, the parties did in fact contemplate that it might occur. This will happen, for example, where the plaintiff communicates the likelihood of a *peculiar kind* of loss to the defendant, and the defendant accepts the contract with that likelihood in mind. Though, according to the nature of what is contemplated, the effect of the Rule *may*, of course, be to diminish rather than increase the extent of liability if the harm they *did* both contemplate was something *less* drastic than might ordinarily have been expected.

The operation of Rule I may be illustrated by *Hadley v Baxendale* itself. A crank shaft broke in the plaintiff's mill. This meant that the mill had to stop working because it could not operate without the shaft. The plaintiffs wanted to send the shaft to the manufacturer at Greenwich as quickly as possible, so that it could be used as a pattern for a new one. Speed was essential since, while the mill was stopped, the plaintiffs lost profits which they would otherwise have made from its use. The plaintiffs' servants therefore delivered the shaft to the defendants, who were carriers, and who accepted it for carriage, but were guilty of serious delay in making delivery.

On the above facts, the plaintiffs brought an action for breach of contract by reason of the delay; they claimed, amongst other things, damages for loss of profits which they would have obtained by use of the mill during the period of delay. The court held that this loss of profits was not a 'natural' consequence of delay in delivering a crank shaft, and that the claim therefore failed; for the plaintiffs had done nothing to bring the case within the operation of Rule II (above). All that the defendants knew, when the contract was made, was that the article to be carried was a broken shaft, and that the plaintiffs were millers. There was nothing in this information to suggest that delay in delivery would cause a loss of profits – as far as the defendants knew, the plaintiffs might, for instance, have had a spare shaft.

The case of *Victoria Laundry (Windsor) Ltd v Newman Industries Ltd* [1949] 2 KB 528, provides a contrast with *Hadley v Baxendale*. The plaintiffs were launderers and dyers who required a particularly large boiler, both in order to extend their existing business and in order to provide them with a suitable plant for obtaining certain exceptionally profitable dyeing contracts. The defendants, a firm of engineers, contracted to sell them such a boiler. Through the fault of the defendants' sub-contractors, the delivery of this boiler was seriously delayed. The plaintiffs claimed as damages, first, an amount equal to the estimated loss of *the increased profits* which the use of the boiler would have acquired for them during the period of the delay, second, the amount which they would have earned from the dyeing *contracts* during the same period. Since the defendants knew, at the time of the agreement, that the plaintiffs were dyers and launderers and they were informed that the boiler was required for immediate use the Court of Appeal held that damages were recoverable under the *first head*. Whereas there is no reason to suppose that delay in delivering a mill-shaft will cause a milling business to cease, anyone would reasonably expect that a laundry which requires a boiler immediately will be likely to need it to satisfy the demands of its customers. With regard to the *second head*, the court held that the plaintiffs could not recover upon the basis of the exceptionally high figure contemplated in their contracts – this was something which the defendants could not reasonably have contemplated in the light of the facts known to them at the time of the agreement, and the plaintiffs had not informed them of the contracts: had they done this, of course, they might have recovered this exceptional amount under Rule II.

In *The Heron II, Koufos v C Czarnikow Ltd* [1969] 1 AC 350, the House of Lords reconsidered the relationship of the rules as to remoteness of damage in contract and tort. It will be seen that the test of reasonable contemplation, or foresight, now in the main governs in both fields. But their Lordships stressed that the degree of foresight required under Rule I in *Hadley v Baxendale* is something less than what is required in tort. In the latter, at least in some circumstances, the defendant will be held liable for consequences which are not inherently probable, but which are nevertheless 'on the cards'. In contract the liability depends upon the presumed contemplation of the parties at the time when they made their agreement, and it is to be presumed that they would only contemplate liability for what is usual, normal or not unlikely to *happen*; it is therefore only for events of this kind that the defendant will be made to pay. Thus in *Hadley v Baxendale* though 'on the cards', the loss of profits was something improbable; but in *The Heron II* the House had no difficulty in maintaining that delay in delivering goods at a commercial port was something which would have the *probable* effect of depreciating the re-sale value of the goods by reason of a drop in the market price of them during the period of delay. Thus the owners of the goods could therefore recover their loss of profit from the defendant shipowners.

It must be added that in *H Parsons (Livestock) Ltd v Uttley Ingham & Co Ltd* [1978] QB 791, the Court of Appeal, in ruling that the test of remoteness is whether the relevant loss ought to have been contemplated as a 'serious possibility' also held that in contract, as in tort, if the loss is of a 'type' which ought to have been contemplated it will not be held to be too remote even though the actual *form* it takes could not have been. Thus, the facts of the *Parsons' Case* were that, by the defendants' default, the plaintiffs' pigs ate mouldy nuts from which they contracted a rare and unforeseeable disease of which they *died*. It was held that because it was a 'serious possibility' that such a diet would make the animals *ill* (something thought to be similar in 'type' to death) the defendants were liable for the loss. That may be good law, but the Court of Appeal's further pronouncement that the rules of remoteness themselves are the same in contract and tort – though sound both in theory and upon principle – flies in the face of the *Heron II* (a House of Lords decision), and cannot be accepted.

*(iii)* Parties sometimes include a clause in a contract to the effect that if one of them breaks it he shall pay a sum of money to compensate the other for the breach. If the sum agreed upon is a *genuine pre-estimate* of the value of the loss which one party suffers, he may sue to recover it by way of liquidated (ie quantified) damages from the party in breach.

The sum so assessed must *not*, however, be a *'penalty'*, ie an amount greatly in excess of the loss that is likely to be suffered. Thus it has been held that a clause in a hire-purchase agreement which purported to secure for the owner upon any breach of the agreement, *not merely* repayment of instalments and interest due, but also a sum representing a minimum of *two-thirds of the whole price* as 'agreed compensation for depreciation of the goods' was a penalty and unenforceable. The true object of such a clause is clearly not to secure compensation – for a breach may occur after a single instalment out of many is due – but to ensure the owner a minimum unearned return.

*(iv) Exemplary* damages cannot be recovered in actions based upon contract.

*(v)* It is now settled that, as in tort so in contract, damages are not confined to items of physical loss and may be recovered in respect of inconvenience, frustration, disappointment, anxiety, etc. So that a man who took a holiday in Switzerland through a travel agency and discovered that it in no sense matched up to its description in the brochure was held entitled to damages to compensate for his disappointment.

Finally, it needs to be pointed out that in contract, as in tort, there must be a *causal* connection between the defendant's default and the plaintiff's loss; for the former cannot by any test be held responsible for something which he did not cause. Thus in *Quinn v Burch Bros (Builders) Ltd* [1966] 2 QB 370, the plaintiff was engaged upon some building work as sub-contractor for the defendants who were obliged, when necessary, to supply him with a ladder on request. This they failed to do, so the plaintiff used an unfooted trestle which was clearly dangerous in the circumstances; and he fell and was injured. It was held that, although it was true that they had broken their contract, the defendants were not liable because the plaintiff had brought the injury upon himself.

## B    QUANTUM MERUIT

A claim for damages is a claim for compensation for loss. A claim upon a '*quantum meruit*' (for an amount 'earned') is a claim in respect of unremunerated services.

Where, under the terms of a contract, one person performs services for another, and the other breaks or repudiates the contract, the person who has performed the services may usually, instead of claiming damages, sue upon a *quantum meruit* to recover the amount earned by his labours. Thus, in *Planché v Colburn* (1831) 5 C & P 58, the plaintiff agreed, for £100, to write a book for the defendants, who were publishers. When he had written part of the book the defendants abandoned the project and repudiated the contract. It was held that the plaintiff could recover £50, upon a *quantum meruit*; for, though, in the circumstances, he had never completed the contract, yet, he ought not to lose the fruits of his labour upon the defendants' behalf.

It must also be explained that a *quantum meruit* may be used, not merely as a remedy for breach of contract, but also as a method of recovering a reasonable remuneration for the performance of a contract when no specific remuneration has been agreed upon. Thus, where X renders Y services which are clearly not intended to be voluntary, but in respect of which no price has been fixed, X may sue Y upon a *quantum meruit* for a reasonable sum of money. The same rule applies in respect of goods delivered; where no price is determined, the buyer must pay a reasonable price (Sale of Goods Act 1979, s 8(2)). Though it should, perhaps, be added that the claim in this case is, strictly speaking, upon a *quantum valebat* (for the 'value' of the goods). It must be appreciated, however, that where a person agrees to do something for a lump sum, for example to build a wall, he can normally only sue for payment if the work is *substantially* performed. Frustration apart, he cannot – unless at that stage the other party prevents further performance or repudiates the contract – build half the wall, and then claim upon a *quantum meruit* for half the money. The courts will not *imply* a contract in favour of a plaintiff who has made an express agreement and failed to perform it. This rule is known as the rule in *Cutter v Powell* (1795) 6 Term

Rep 320. In that case the defendant agreed to pay Cutter 30 guineas for acting as second mate aboard a vessel plying between Jamaica and Liverpool. Cutter died when the vessel was nineteen days short of Liverpool. It was held that his widow could recover nothing in respect of the work he had performed during the previous 49 days of the voyage.

The above rule is logical because it is based upon the principle that no one should be entitled to claim payment unless he has done what he has bargained to do: but pushed to extremes it may work injustice, and its rigour is mitigated in two respects. First, as elsewhere in the law of contract, the word '*substantially*' may be subjected to common-sense construction; for example, in *Hoenig v Isaacs* [1952] 2 All ER 176, the plaintiff agreed to furnish and decorate the defendant's flat for £750: he completed the contract, but made some of the furniture so unsatisfactorily that it required alteration. The defendant had paid £400 by instalments in the course of the execution of the contract, but, when sued for the remaining £350, he invoked *Cutter v Powell* on the ground that the plaintiff had not performed his part. The Court of Appeal held that the contract had been *substantially* completed, and upheld the plaintiff, while reducing his claim by £55 18s 2d, the cost of making the necessary alterations. In the second place, in cases where a contract has been frustrated, the importance of the rule in *Cutter v Powell* has now been much diminished by the provisions of the Law Reform (Frustrated Contracts) Act 1943, and, indeed, as the result of these provisions a different result would be reached today upon the facts of the case itself.

## C   SPECIFIC PERFORMANCE AND INJUNCTIONS

Specific performance and injunctions are equitable remedies. They were therefore originally only obtainable in the Court of Chancery. Since the Chancery was a court of 'conscience', they were always, and since the combination of the courts administering law and equity, still are, discretionary remedies. Unlike damages, which are granted as of right, equitable remedies are only granted where, in all the circumstances of the case, it is fair and just that they should be granted. *Specific performance* is a decree of the court ordering a defendant to perform his obligations under a contract. For the purposes of the law of contract an *injunction* is an order commanding a defendant to refrain from breaking his contract.

## 1   SPECIFIC PERFORMANCE

The following rules govern the granting of a decree for specific performance:

*(a)* Specific performance will never be decreed where damages will provide an adequate remedy; for equity '*follows the law*', it is designed to supply the defects in it, not to override it. Thus, though a purchaser may obtain specic performance of a contract to purchase land, there can never be a decree for specific performance in respect of a mere money loan. But it must not be thought that this remedy is confined to land cases; for, in accordance with its purpose of supplying the defects in the law, a decree may (at discretion) be made for the return of specific goods of especial and peculiar value (though normally damages will suffice to recompense non-delivery), and in exceptional circumstances even an order to enforce the supply of non-specific goods – such as the supply of petrol – may be proper if an award of damages would be inadequate. Indeed, perhaps inconsequently, it has even been held that although a decree cannot be made to force a tenant to perform a repairing covenant it may be made to force a landlord to do so.

*(b)* Specific performance will not be granted in the absence of 'mutuality'. In order for a contract to be specifically enforceable, the parties must, in fairness, be on a footing of equality. Thus there cannot be specific performance of a gratuitous promise, even though it be made under seal – equity, as the maxim goes, 'will not assist a volunteer', someone who offers no consideration. Similarly, there will be no specific performance in favour of a minor because the contract cannot be enforced against him.

*(c)* There can be no specific performance of a contract for personal services. This had long been settled by the courts, but now the point is enshrined within the Trade Union and Labour Relations (Consolidation) Act 1992, s 236.

*(d)* By the Chancery Amendment Act 1858 (Lord Cairns' Act), s 2 the court has a discretion to award damages in lieu of or in addition to specific performance if it 'thinks fit'.

## 2   INJUNCTIONS

For the purposes of the law of contract, injunctions are in general 'prohibitory'; that is to say, they are orders commanding a person to refrain from doing something. Thus a man who has undertaken not to do some particular thing may be forced by an injunction to refrain from doing it. Injunctions may, however, also be used as an indirect means of obtaining specific performance where, for some reason, that remedy is unobtainable. For example, if B contracts to obtain supplies only from A the contract cannot be specifically enforced, for enforcement would require continuous supervision; but an injunction may be granted to restrain B from obtaining supplies from elsewhere. In the case of contracts for *personal services* injunctions will only be granted in respect of *express negative* covenants. Thus, in the leading case of *Lumley v Wagner* (1852) 1 De G M & G 604, Miss W undertook to sing at a series of concerts organized by L, and she also undertook *not* to sing elsewhere during the period for which the concerts were to last. It was held that an injunction could be granted to restrain her from singing elsewhere. It is to be noted that in this case the effect of granting the injunction was not necessarily to force Miss W to perform the positive covenant to sing for L; it merely *encouraged* her to do so, by preventing her from singing elsewhere. If the effect of it would have been to force her to do so it could not have been granted; for in the case of contracts for *personal services* injunctions will not be used so as to tie someone to someone else or 'starve' – as it has been said. Again this point is now confirmed by the Trade Union and Labour Relations (Consolidation) Act 1992, s 236.

It should be added that Lord Cairns' Act (above) also permits an award of damages in lieu of an injunction.

## D RESCISSION AND RECTIFICATION

### RESCISSION

Subject to the qualifications already mentioned, the court, in exercise of its equitable jurisdiction, may order *rescission* of a contract where it would, on account of mistake, misrepresentation or otherwise, be unreasonable to uphold it.

### RECTIFICATION

This equitable remedy applies where it is sought to correct, or rectify, a document which purports to embody some prior agreement, whether oral or in writing, and this prior agreement has not – due to mutual mistake – been properly reproduced in the document. It must be understood, however, that the issue is entirely whether agreement and document fail to correspond: and if they do correspond it will be useless for one of the parties to assert that he did not intend what was said or written in the agreement. This may be illustrated by *F E Rose (London) Ltd v William H Pim Jnr & Co Ltd* [1953] 2 QB 450, where the plaintiffs received from the Middle East an order for 'Moroccan horsebeans' described here as '*feveroles*'. In negotiating with the defendants for the supply to them of these articles the plaintiffs asked what they were. The defendants asserted that they were just 'horsebeans'; so in the contract the plaintiffs ordered 'horsebeans', then, having discovered that feveroles are in fact not horsebeans, but beans of a special kind, they sought to have the contract rectified so as to read 'feveroles' for 'horsebeans'. It was held that this could not be done (so as to entitle the plaintiffs to sue the defendants upon the contract) since agreement and document were in accord; both referred to 'horsebeans' and there was therefore nothing to be rectified. This may perhaps seem formalistic; but the logic is plain. It should be added that except in cases of grave injustice the courts will seldom, in the exercise of this discretionary jurisdiction, rectify a contract where the alleged mistake is unilateral.

# 8   Limitation

Rights of action cannot be permitted to endure for ever. People must be made to press their claims with reasonable diligence. Hence rules of *limitation* have to be made, ie rules which prescribe the time within which actions are to be brought.

Most of the rules in respect of limitation are now contained in the Limitation Act 1980.

As regards contract claims the rules are that:

*(i)*  An action upon a *simple* contract (ie a contract other than a contract under seal) must be brought within *six* years of the accrual of the cause of action.

*(ii)*  An action upon a contract under seal must be brought within *twelve* years of the accrual.

*(iii)*  Actions in which the damages claimed consist of or include damages in respect of *personal injuries* to the plaintiff or any other person must be brought within *three* years subject to the same rules which apply to such claims in tort.

The cause of action normally 'accrues' at the time when the contract is broken.

The above rules are subject to certain exceptions.

First, where a person who is liable for a liquidated (ie a quantified) sum either makes a written *acknowledgment* of his indebtedness or makes a *part-payment* of the debt, time will start to run against him afresh from the date of acknowledgment or part-payment. Hence, if X were due to pay Y £100 under the terms of a contract under seal dated 1 January 1990, Y's claim would normally have been barred by effluxion of time on 1 January 2002. If, however, X were to have made written acknowledgment of his indebtedness on, say, 1 January 1994, Y's rights to bring his action would subsist until 1 January 2006. Moreover, an acknowledgment made *after* 1 January 2002, would have the effect of reviving the right for the statutory period.

In the second place, there are certain '*disabilities*', such as minority and unsoundness of mind. Where a plaintiff is under a disability, time normally begins to run against him from the moment when the disability ceases, or from his death, whichever first occurs.

Third, where the plaintiff's action is based upon *fraud*, or where his right of action is *concealed by the defendant's fraud* (or the fraud of his agent or of any person through whom he claims), or where the action is for relief from the consequences of the plaintiff's *mistake*, the period of limitation does not begin to run until the plaintiff discovers the fraud, or the mistake, or could, with reasonable dilligence, have done so. 'Fraud' in the *second* of the above-mentioned contexts ('concealed' fraud) does not bear the usual meaning described above; it embraces as well what is known as 'equitable' fraud, which includes any form of unconscionable *concealment* even though not involving moral turpitude. For example in *Applegate v Moss* [1971] 1 QB 406 it was held that the employee of a builder who covered up bad foundations so that the result of his slipshod work was not discovered until the house collapsed some years later could not rely upon the statute as a bar to the houseowner's claim against him until six years *after the truth had been discovered.*

In the fourth place, as regards actions for *personal injuries* the Act provides specially for injuries (eg slow developing diseases such as silicosis) which may not be discoverable until long after the event which causes them. In these cases time (*three* years) begins to run either from the date of the *accrual of the cause of action* or from the date (if later) of the plaintiff's *knowledge* of the injury: though, at discretion, and subject to exceptions, even the latter period may be extended by the court.

In general, claims to equitable remedies, such as specific performance and injunctions, are not subject to the Act (see s 36(1)). Instead, they are governed by the equitable doctrine of '*laches*' (the application of which is preserved by s 36(2) of the Act). This doctrine is based upon the principle that it is unjust to permit a person to sleep upon his rights: delay may either be evidence of acquiescence in the infringement of the right violated, or may give rise to such changes in circumstances that it may become unfair to keep the other party to his bargain.

Where this doctrine applies the length of time required for it to operate is variable, depending upon the 'equities' arising in each case; though in the case of the particular remedy of specific performance, the time is usually likely to be short, for even a short delay is likely to alter the circumstances of the defendant. In certain cases, however, where an equitable claim is essentially similar to a common law claim, the courts may (under the authority of s 36(1)) apply the statute 'by analogy', disregard the doctrine of 'laches', and permit the full statutory period to run. Thus, for example, a secret profit made by an agent is recoverable as an equitable debt, and yet the plaintiff is entitled to insist upon the full six-year period of limitation; further, in this particular case, time does not begin to run against the plaintiff until the facts are discovered. Moreover, the 'laches' doctrine applies only to the person who sleeps on his own rights, not for instance to a successor in title who claims under him.

And there is one further matter (though it is not strictly a question of limitation), and that is the equitable doctrine of *acquiescence*. Where a person who is entitled to a right, whether legal or equitable, acquiesces in its infringement to such an extent that it would be unconscionable for him to seek to enforce it, equity will not allow him to do so.

# 9    Quasi-contract

The term 'quasi-contract' ('as if a contract') is a misnomer. A misnomer which was due to an accident of history. Paradoxically a quasi-contractual claim is a claim to what is *owed*, *otherwise* than by way of contract. Being a claim to what is 'owed' it is, in ultimate analysis a proprietary claim, like a claim for the recovery of land. The basis of it is broad, for it seeks to prevent 'unjust enrichment' of one party at the expense of another. What is to be thus *legally* treated as 'unjust' has been based upon the ultimate sense of practical morality of the courts. Though, after all, that is a truism because, as was pointed out above, the common law as a whole has been developed upon the basis of the judicial sense of what is socially 'just'.

Very brief mention may be made of some of the classes of quasi-contractual actions in the modern law; they fall, roughly, under three heads.

*i  Actions for money had and received*
Where, for some reason, A pays money to B to which B is not entitled, A may recover it. Thus, money paid upon a *total failure of consideration* must be returned. This may happen, for instance, where, under a valid contract, one party pays money to another who *entirely* fails to honour his side of the bargain. An action will also lie for money paid by *mistake*. This, of course, need not necessarily involve a breach of contract: so that the claim will lie where, for example, money has been paid under a contract which is void by reason of an operative mistake – as where, unknown to the parties, the subject matter of the contract had ceased to exist at the time of the making of the contract. This type of action also covers the case where Smith has paid money to Brown by mistake, thinking that Brown is Jones (the person to whom Smith owed the money). But the mistake involved must be one of *fact*, not of *law*. '*Ignorantia juris haud excusat*'. We are all expected to know the law. Since the 'law' is in a state of continuous evolution this is a counsel of perfection. But, of course, the rule is one of policy. People cannot be permitted to avoid the consequences of their acts simply by saying 'But I did not know the law!'.

## ii Actions for money paid

The full name for this action is 'money paid to the *use* of another'. 'Use' is a mediaeval term and 'for the benefit of another' would now be a more appropriate expression. This kind of claim will lie in favour of Davies where Thomas owes Hughes a debt which Hughes has instructed Thomas to pay to Davies. But it seems that it will only lie if Thomas has notified Davies that he (Thomas) is willing to make the payment to him. Similarly, an action will lie in favour of an assignee of a debt against the principal debtor, or in favour of a surety against the person whose debt he has paid. Though it is to be noted that in the latter case the claim will only normally lie where the surety has been requested by the debtor to act as such: people cannot act as sureties for others without their knowledge and then claim indemnity.

## iii Actions for services rendered and benefits conferred

An action upon a *quantum meruit* where the defendant has broken his contract and the plaintiff claims, not upon the contract, but for the value of the benefit he has conferred upon the defendant, falls under this head. So also, in all probability, does a claim against a minor for a reasonable price for 'necessaries' supplied.

# Chapter 9

# Particular contracts

There will only be space to consider agency, the contract of employment, sale of goods, and consumer credit and consumer hire contracts.

## 1  Agency

Agency, in the present context, is a relationship whereby one person (agent) agrees upon behalf of another (principal) to conclude a contract between the principal and some other person.

As regards the contract between the principal and the third party the agent is normally a mere conduit, or connecting link, for concluding that contract and once that contract is concluded his duties are at an end and he fades, as it were, out of the transaction.

Agency is usually constituted by the principal giving the agent express directions to act for him. It sometimes happens, however, that people lead others to believe that someone is their agent, when in fact they have given him no authority; if they do this, they will be liable for his acts. Thus, if I habitually send my employee to order goods for me at a certain shop, in such circumstances that the shopkeeper comes to look to me for credit, I am not entitled to terminate the agency merely by telling the employee that he is to stop ordering. If I do this, and he continues to make orders, ostensibly for me, but really on his own behalf, I shall be liable to the shopkeeper for the price of the goods he orders. I am '*estopped*', as it is said, from denying that I have given the employee continued authority to act for me, until I inform the shopkeeper that he is no longer entitled to do so. This principle of 'holding out' is not limited to contracts of service; it is an important principle of general application. Anyone who permits another person to act in such a way as to justify other people in thinking that that other person is his/her agent, may find himself/herself held liable as principal; a husband/wife, for example, in respect of purchases made by his wife/her husband. This principle, moreover, goes further, so as to cover the case of such officials as company secretaries who, by the *very nature of their office*, without any actual indication by the company to the plaintiff that it will be responsible for their acts, are the ostensible agents of the company. For this form of estoppel to apply there must, however, be an apparent authority: so that where at an auction the catalogue contained a statement that the auctioneers had no authority to make any representations on behalf of the vendor, and they did make a mis-representation, it was held that the vendor could not be held liable: the purchaser had been warned not to look to the principal.

An agent is subject to certain special duties arising out of the relation-ship between his principal and himself. First, though he is entitled to receive a commission for his services, he must not make a profit from the position he occupies. If he does this without authority the principal may recover the profit from him, by an action for money had and received or, alternatively, if his behaviour causes a loss to his principal, an action for fraud. And if the agent accepts a secret bribe in connection with his work similar claims may be made against the person who makes the bribe as well: this may happen, for example, if the agent, in return for a bribe, makes arrangements with another person to enable the latter to sell property to the principal at an inflated price.

Second, once a man has undertaken to act as agent, he must continue to act as such; he is not allowed to alter his position and step into the shoes of the other contracting party.

Third, since an agent enjoys a confidential position, he may not delegate his duties to another person without his principal's consent.

An agent may either contract with the third party as agent for a named principal, or simply 'as agent' without naming his principal, or, by an anomalous rule of English law, he may, at any rate in making commercial contracts, act for an *'undisclosed principal'*, while purporting to contract on his own behalf; and, unless the contract is by its terms expressly or impliedly confined to the parties to it, the undisclosed principal may both sue and be sued upon it. Where the contract is made on behalf of a named principal, or by a person acting 'as agent', it does not matter if he really has no authority to act at the time that he makes the contract; as long as the principal 'ratifies' (adopts) the contract subsequently. Where, however, the contract is made on behalf of an *undisclosed* principal the agent must have authority to act *at the time when the contract is made*.

Naturally, where the existence of the principal is undisclosed, the third party has special rights. Though an agent normally incurs no liability under the contract he makes, an agent for an undisclosed principal is in a less happy position, for the other party may not only sue the principal when he discovers his identity but also the agent himself. Election to sue the one, however, extinguishes the claim against the other. What amounts to election is a question of fact; it may be made at any time up to judgment.

People sometimes purport to act as agents for others without authority. If they do this, they may either do so by mistake, thinking they have, or will obtain, authority, or dishonestly, pretending to be agents, but knowing that they are not. Where this happens an innocent person may suffer by entering into a contract with the supposed agent, and such a person clearly requires legal protection. If the agent knew he had no authority, and that he could get none, he may, if loss has been incurred, be sued for fraud; but if he acted honestly he cannot be. Accordingly, it became necessary to evolve the doctrine of 'warranty of authority' (effectively a species of collateral warranty) by which everyone who purports to act as an agent may be held liable to the other contracting party upon an implied warranty of authority however innocent he may be, if it turns out that he has no authority from his principal.

## A    THE CONTRACT OF EMPLOYMENT (OR SERVICE)

The contract of employment is now largely regulated by the Employment Protection (Consolidation) Act 1978 (as amended by the Employment Act 1980, the Sex Discrimination Act 1986 and the Trade Union Reform and Employment Rights Act 1993, consolidated in the Employment Rights Act 1996, in force 22 August 1996)). Section 149 of the 1978 Act ('EPCA') defines the contract of employment as a 'contract of service or apprentice-ship' and it is to be contrasted with a contract 'for services', which is a contract by which – as where a doctor contracts to cure a patient – one person agrees to do something for another upon an independent basis. The employer-employee relationship is a special one with special legal con-sequences: for instance, at common law the employer is vicariously liable for wrongs committed to others by his employee in the course of his employment: whereas, of course, the patient is not responsible for the misdeeds of his doctor. And again, as has been noted all employees, from chargehand to managing director owe a duty of fidelity to their employer. It is interesting to note that it has been held that the contract between a presbyterian minister and his church falls in a special category and is not to be treated as a contract of service.

In early law the employment (master-servant) relationship was rather proprietary than contractual; so that the master could claim against others who injured his servant, or could sue them for enticing him away, just as if he were a chattel. But by the nineteenth century the proprietary analogy had disappeared and the contract of service had come to be treated much like any other contract, freed from implications of status. Indeed, this was the paradigm example of Sir Henry Maine's mid-nineteenth century aphorism: 'the movement of all progressive societies has hitherto been a movement from status to contract'.

The 'hitherto' was wise and prophetic because during the past hundred years the employer-employee relationship has taken many steps back towards 'status'. Not only are the factory worker and his employer enmeshed by webs of regulations imposing (as in the case of safety regulations) general duties upon the latter for the benefit of the former but the contract of employment itself is subjected to manifold legal rules which neither employer nor employee can agree to disregard (EPCA, s 140).

It is these general rules, as prescribed by the EPCA that must now be considered.

Part I of this important Act concerns terms of employment: Part II governs the rights which arise in the course of employment: Part III relates to maternity in the course of employment: Part IV deals with termination of employment: Part V governs unfair dismissal: Part VI regulates redundancy payments: Part VII provides for the case of an employer's insolvency.

Before considering the content of the Act as a whole it is necessary to warn the reader that although its provisions are general there are some contracts of service which are either wholly or *partly* excluded (EPCA, ss 141 and 146) from its provisions: these include contracts of employment outside Great Britain, contracts between husband and wife and contracts of police service.

### (a) Particulars of Terms of Employment (Part I)

The EPCA, s 1 provides that an employer must, not later than two months after the beginning of the employment, give his employee a *written statement* containing specified particulars which form the basis of the contract – these include the amount of remuneration, hours of work, holiday entitlement, etc. The statement must also provide information about disciplinary procedures. Further (s 8) the employer must provide a written *itemized pay statement*. Neither of these statements are, however, normally required in the case of employment for less than eight hours per week.

### (b) Rights in the course of Employment (Part II of the 1978 Act and Part III of the Trade Union and Labour Relations (Consolidation) Act 1992)

*(i) Guarantee payments* – Employees are entitled to 'guarantee payments'; payments for any day or days which are 'workless' – days in which there is no work to do. These payments are to be made by reference to scales set out in the Act. But an employee who refuses an offer of 'reasonable alternative employment' is not entitled to a guarantee payment. In order to qualify for such a payment (s 13 of the 1992 Act) the employee must have been in the employment continuously for at least one month.

*(ii) Trade union and other duties* – No action (s 146 of the 1992 Act) must be taken by an employer to *prevent* an employee from joining an *independent* trade union, to *prevent* him from taking part outside working hours in activities connected with such a union, or to *compel* the employee to become a member of any union or of a particular union or one of a number of particular unions. Moreover, employers must permit worker officials

of independent trade unions time off (paid) for their official duties (ss 168–170 of the 1992 Act), and the same applies to the activities of representatives (other than officials) of such unions – though striking is not one of the permitted activities.

The employee must also be allowed time off for enumerated public duties, such as justice of the peace or 'council' work; and he must also, when the employee has been given redundancy notice, allow him paid time off to look for work or to make arrangements for retraining.

### (c) Maternity (Part III)
There are several special rights available to women employees in connection with pregnancy. These are set out in the 1978 Act (as amended) and, in respect of maternity pay, in the Social Security Contributions and Benefits Act 1992:

*(i)* There is a general right to maternity leave of 14 weeks, irrespective of the length of period of continuous employment (s 33 of the 1978 Act as amended). The employee must notify the employer of the date of the beginning of the maternity leave period not less than 21 days ahead of the date, or as soon as is reasonably practicable.

*(ii)* In addition to *(i)* above, the employee has the right to return to work at any time up to 29 weeks from the end of the maternity leave period (s 39), but this right is normally contingent upon her having been continuously employed for not less than two years and the giving of the 21 days' notice as in *(i)* above, but the employee must also give notice that she intends to return.

*(iii)* A pregnant employee has the right to paid time off for antenatal care (s 31A of the 1978 Act).

*(iv)* The right to leave in (i) above, does not give a right to paid leave. The right to paid maternity leave is embodied in ss 164–171 of the 1992 Act. There are a number of qualifications to claiming this benefit, the main ones being that the woman must be an employed earner within the meaning of the national insurance contribution rules and must have been continuously employed normally, to receive maximum benefit, for two years up to the week immediately prior to the 14th week before the expected week of confinement.

### (d) Termination of Employment (Part IV)
When it is necessary for an employer to give *notice* to terminate the employment, provided that the employee has been continuously employed for four weeks or more, the *employer* must: (i) give one week's notice if the period of continuous employment has been less than two years; (ii) give one week's notice for each year of continuous employment if that employment has been more than two but less than 12 years; (iii) give 12 weeks' notice if the employment has been for 12 years or more. The *employee*, for his part, provided that he has been employed for not less

than four weeks, must give his employer not less than one week's notice. Notice, may however, be *waived* by either party and pay may be given and accepted in lieu of notice.

It is important to stress that the EPCA, s 49(5) preserves the right of either party to terminate the contract *without notice* by reason of such conduct on the part of the other, as would justify his terminating it at common law; eg such conduct as destroys the basis of the contract: as for example, a downright refusal to pay on the one part, or to work on the other.

Whether or not notice has been given, an employee who has been continuously employed for two years or more is entitled to be provided, within 14 days of requesting it, with a *written statement of the reasons for his dismissal*: so is a person employed on a fixed term contract which expires and which has not been renewed.

### (e)  Unfair Dismissal (Part V)

Claims for *wrongful* dismissal are nothing new: an employee who thinks that he has been wrongfully dismissed may bring an action for damages at common law and such a claim is justiciable in the ordinary courts. The EPCA, however, sanctions a special form of claim (justiciable by an *industrial tribunal* with appeal to the Employment Appeal Tribunal), for 'unfair dismissal'.

With certain exceptions, this right is available to anyone who has been dismissed. The excepted classes are: (i) normally people above the age of 65; (ii) people who have not been continuously employed for two years; (iii) people who are under a fixed term contract of one year or more who have in writing, during that period, waived the right to treat non-renewal of the contract after its expiry as a 'dismissal'.

'Dismissal' means: (a) termination of the contract by the employer, with or without notice; (b) failure to renew a fixed term contract after its expiry; (c) conduct of the employer (such as calling a secretary 'a bitch') which goes to the root of the relationship and entitles the employee to repudiate the contract without notice; (d) refusal to permit a woman to return to work after maternity absence. (Note – *At common law*, the relationship of the parties being solely contractual, no claim for wrongful dismissal will lie, and the termination of the contract cannot be wrongful, *if due notice has been given*, for whatever reason: nor will any action lie upon non-renewal at the expiry of a fixed term contract.) 'Unfairness', for the purposes of the Act, means dismissal of the employee *for an inadmissible reason*. It lies upon the employer to disclose his reason or reasons for the dismissal, and it must be a reason of a kind specified in the EPCA, s 57: namely, a reason related to: (a) the capability of the employee – 'his skill, aptitude, health or any other physical or mental quality'; (b) the qualifications of the employee – any degree, diploma or professional qualification; (c) the employee's conduct; (d) redundancy; (e) the fact that his work, if he were to continue in it, would contravene an enactment – eg the case of a driver disqualified; (f) 'any other substantial reason'. In this regard it is important to note that there is a Code of Practice drawn up under statutory authority by the Secretary of State for Employment which may be used by employers as a guide to their conduct; and which, though an employer is under no legal obligation to observe it, may be admitted in evidence to act as a criterion of judgment of the employer's behaviour.

So much for the general nature of unfair dismissal. The Act further specifies a number of reasons for dismissal which are, by their nature, to be treated as *unfair*: these include: (i) the fact that the employee joins or proposes to join an independent trade union or, outside working hours, takes part in union activities, or that he refuses to join a particular union or one of a group of particular unions; (ii) the pregnancy of a female employee unless, *inter alia,* she is rendered incapable of her work on account of it. On the other hand there are reasons which are *fair* and automatically admissible; eg that the employee has refused, or proposes to refuse, to join an independent union which has a membership agreement with the employer in respect of the category of employee to which the dismissed person belongs.

Where unfair dismissal is established the industrial tribunal may award compensation to the employee upon a basis prescribed by the Act, or it may make an order for reinstatement or re-engagement. It should be added that provision is made for conciliation by authorized conciliation officers to seek to settle a complaint of unfair dismissal without resort to a tribunal.

### (f)  Redundancy Payments (Part VI)

The Redundancy Payments Act 1965 first introduced the principle that people whose employment ceases on account of redundancy (eg because their factory has been forced to close down) are entitled to compensation in the form of 'redundancy payment'. Part VI of the EPCA now governs this matter.

To qualify for such payment the employee must have been in continuous employment for a minimum of two years, he must not normally be past retirement age (65 for men and women) and he must not have been lawfully dismissed by his employer without notice (ie on account of gross misconduct). He must make a claim to an industrial tribunal within six months after his dismissal. The payments are calculated on the basis of scales prescribed in the Act, and although they are primarily to be paid by the employer he is entitled to a 'redundancy rebate' from public funds in respect of a proportion of them.

### (g)  Employer's Insolvency (Part VII)

When an employer is unable to pay the employee because he has become insolvent the employee may apply to the Secretary of State for Employment for payment of the debt from public funds. Such payments are at the present time subject to an upper limit of £210 in respect of any one week of unpaid wages.

It may be well to repeat that, in keeping with the object of the Act to replace a contractual relationship by one which is governed by the general law (a 'status' relationship), it is provided (s 140) that, in general any provision in any contract which purports to exclude or limit the operation of any provision of the Act or to preclude the presenting of a complaint to an industrial tribunal shall be *void*. The web of legal obligation is thus a vice.

## B  SALE OF GOODS

The law relating to sale of goods used to be governed by the Sale of Goods Act 1893; itself largely a consolidation of the nineteenth century common law. It is now governed by the Sale of Goods Act 1979 (hereafter SGA as amended by the Sale and Supply of Goods Act 1994 and the Sale of Goods (Amendment) Acts 1994 and 1995) as supplemented by the Unfair Contract Terms Act 1977.

It will be simplest to examine this matter under the following heads.

### 1  THE NATURE OF THE CONTRACT

The contract is defined as '*a contract by which the seller transfers or agrees to transfer the property in goods to the buyer for a money consideration, called the price*' (SGA s 2(1)).

Contracts of sale must be distinguished from two other types of contract:

#### i  Exchange (barter)
Here the consideration is goods or other property in exchange for goods or other property, whereas a sale is a transaction whereby property is exchanged for *money*.

#### ii  Contracts for work and labour and materials supplied
It is not always easy to distinguish these contracts from sales, though the distinction may be of practical importance; for if the contract is a sale special rules may apply to it which do not apply to other contracts. The test for drawing the distinction seems to be, 'Was the contract *primarily* intended to result in the transfer of property?' If so, it will be a sale: if not, it will be a contract for work and materials. Thus if A contracts to make a fur coat for B, and himself supplies the fur, the contract will be a sale, even though, clearly, part of the price is determined by the work that A does in making the coat. Where, on the other hand, A contracts to paint B's portrait, it has been held that the contract will be one for work and materials. Here the element of skill is more important than the goods produced.

The expression 'contract of sale' denotes two things, a '*sale*' and an '*agreement to sell*'. There is a 'sale' where, under the contract, the property in the goods is transferred to the buyer (s 2(4)). The contract is an 'agreement to sell' where the transfer of the property in the goods is to take place at some future time (s 2(5)).

## 2   IMPLIED TERMS

In every contract for the sale of goods the following (amongst other) terms are *implied* by the Act.

### As to title
*(i)  A condition* on the part of the seller that in the case of a sale he has the *right to sell* the goods, and in the case of an agreement to sell, that he will have the right to sell the goods at the time when the property is to pass (s 12(1)).

*(ii)*  A warranty that the goods are free, and will remain free until the time when the property is to pass *from charges* or *encumbrances*: such, for example, as patent rights vested in a third party;

*(iii)*  A *warranty* that the buyer will enjoy *quiet possession* (s 12(2)).

Further, in the case of a contract in which it is intended that the seller shall transfer only such title as he himself (or some third party) may have, there is an implied warranty that all encumbrances known to the seller (and not known to the buyer) have been disclosed (s 12(4)). And in such a case there is also an implied warranty that neither the seller nor – where the intention is that the seller shall transfer only such title as a third person may have – anyone claiming through the seller or the third person shall disturb the buyer's quiet possession (s 12(5)).

### As to quality
*(i)*  Where the seller sells goods *in the course of a business*, there is an implied *condition* that the goods supplied under the contract are of *satisfactory quality, except* that there is no such condition: (a) for defects *specially drawn to the buyer's attention* before the contract is made; or, (b) if the buyer examines the goods before the contract is made, for defects which *that examination ought to reveal* (s 14(2)). 'Satisfactory quality' means that the goods must meet the standard that a reasonable person would regard as satisfactory, taking account of any description of the goods, the price (if relevant) and all other relevant circumstances (s 14(2)(A)). The quality of goods includes their state and condition and aspects to be considered (among others) as appropriate are the fitness for all the purposes for which goods of the kind in question are commonly supplied, appearance and finish, freedom from minor defects, safety, and durability (s 14(2)(B)).

*(ii)*  Where the seller sells goods *in the course of a business* and the buyer, expressly or by implication, *makes known to the seller any particular purpose* for which the goods are being bought, there is an implied *condition* that the goods supplied under the contract are *reasonably fit for the purpose*, whether or not that purpose is one for which such goods are commonly supplied: *except* where the circumstances show that *the buyer does not rely*, or that it is unreasonable for him to rely, on the *seller's skill or judgment* (s 14(3)). A useful illustration of unfitness for a particular purpose was the case of a Jaguar car so unfit for the road that its engine seized up after only three weeks' use.

*(iii)*  In contracts for sale by *description* there is an implied *condition* that the goods shall *correspond with the description*, and where the sale is by *sample and description* that the bulk shall correspond both with the *sample and the description*. The fact that goods *exposed for sale* are selected by the buyer does not prevent the sale from being a *sale by description* (s 13).

*(iv)*  In the case of contracts for sale *by sample* there are *implied conditions* that: (a) the bulk shall correspond with the sample in quality; (b) the goods shall be free from any defect *rendering them unsatisfactory* which would not be apparent *upon reasonable examination of the sample* (s 15).

NOTE – Terms similar to the terms implied by the SGA are also now implied by the Supply of Goods and Services Act 1982 in contracts for the *transfer of goods*, such as barter and contracts for the supply of work and materials, which are analogous to sale: they are also implied in contracts of hire.

This may be the best place to add that the same Act also implies special terms in contracts of hire and contracts for services.

As regards contracts of *hire* the following terms, *inter alia,* are implied: (i) an implied condition that the bailor has a right to transfer possession of the goods; (ii) where there is a bailment in the course of business, a condition that the goods supplied are of satisfactory quality.

As regards contracts for the supply of *services*: (i) a term that where the supplier is acting in the course of business he will carry out the services with reasonable care and skill; (ii) a term that where, in similar circumstances, no fixed time has been agreed for the service to be performed it shall be carried out in a reasonable time; (iii) a term that where payment for the service has not been agreed the person dealing with the supplier of the service shall pay a reasonable charge.

*Exclusion clauses* – Originally, it will be recalled, people were free to restrict or exclude their contractual liabilities, whether express or implied, and the law of sale of goods was no exception to that rule. In ultimate theory, at least, that individualistic principle still remains, because by the SGA, s 55(1), all the implied terms contained in the SGA, ss 12–15 *may* be negatived or varied by agreement, by the course of dealing between the parties or by (trade) usage. But, in keeping with current ideas the Unfair

Contract Terms Act 1977 ('UCTA'), following earlier legislation, makes large inroads into this principle.

By that Act, whether the situation be one of 'business liability' *or not* (UCTA, s 6(4)) the following rules apply:

(i) The implied obligations as to title, etc under the SGA, s 12 *cannot* be excluded or restricted by any contract term (UCTA, s 6(1)(*a*)). (ii) The same applies (UCTA, s 6(2) (*a*)) to the implied obligations as to quality, etc under the SGA, ss 13–15 in the case of 'consumer dealings'. (iii) In the case of contracts which are not consumer dealings the *latter* obligations *may* be excluded or restricted subject to the 'reasonableness' test; and here the test must be applied in the light of 'guidelines' as to 'reasonable' furnished by the UCTA, Sch 2: these include, *inter alia*, the relative bargaining power of the parties and whether the person alleged to be bound by the term knew or ought to have known of its existence.

It is proper to add that by the UCTA, s 7 certain other contracts, including hire, exchange and contracts for work and materials (eg repair contracts with parts supplied), in so far as they contain implied terms similar to the terms implied in sale of goods bythe SGA, are subjected to similar rules in respect of the application of exclusion clauses. As to exclusion clauses in hire purchase contracts – see p 301.

## 3    THE EFFECT OF THE CONTRACT

Some of the more important points may be noted.

### *i  The passing of property*

The cardinal rule is that property passes (and the 'agreement to sell' becomes a 'sale') when it is *intended* to pass (s 17(1)). Section 18 lays down rules for ascertaining the intention of the parties where it is not made clear. These rules should be consulted in detail. The most important of them (Rule 1) is that, 'Where there is an unconditional contract for the sale of specific goods in a deliverable state the property in the goods passes to the buyer *when the contract is made*, and it is immaterial whether the time of payment or the time of delivery, or both, be postponed'. It is important to note that the goods may become the buyer's *before delivery*.

Normally no property can pass to the buyer where the goods are still 'unascertained' (s 16) but this rule is now subject to the exception introduced by the 1995 Sale of Goods Amendment Act in relation to unascertained goods forming part of an identified bulk. Goods remain 'unascertained' usually until they are appropriated to the contract. Thus, if I agree to sell 1,000 reels of cotton out of my stock of 50,000, no property can pass to the buyer until a particular 1,000 are singled out and appropriated to the contract. However, where the bulk is reduced to (or to less than) the quantity due to the buyer under the contract, the balance of the goods is to be treated as appropriated to the contract and the property will then pass to the buyer. So, therefore, in the example above, if the bulk is reduced to 1000 reels or less, the property will pass to the buyer. Section 20(A) now provides also that a buyer may in certain circumstances have an undivided share in an identified bulk and be an owner in common.

## ii Conditions and warranties
Where a contract of sale is subject to a condition to be fulfilled by the seller, the buyer may waive the condition or elect to treat the breach of it as a breach of warranty (s 11(2)). Whether a stipulation is a condition or a warranty depends upon the construction of the contract (s 11(2)). Where the buyer has accepted the goods the breach of a condition can only be treated as a breach of warranty (s 11(4)). As to conditions and warranties see above, p 241. Section 15(A) now provides that in cases where the buyer of goods does not deal as a consumer and the breach of condition is so slight that it would be unreasonable for him to reject them, the breach is not to be treated as one of condition but may be treated as one of warranty, thus restricting the buyer's remedy to damages only. The burden of establishing that the breach is slight etc is on the seller.

## iii Effect of the destruction of the goods
Unless it is agreed otherwise the 'risk' of accidental destruction passes to the buyer when the property passes (s 20) but it should be recalled that the new s 20(A) makes provision for property to pass in certain circumstances in cases of unascertained goods. Hence, before *delivery*, the buyer may often both own the goods and be forced to take the risk of accidental destruction. If the goods perish or are damaged, as a result of the seller's negligence, it is another matter.

Where, through no fault of the buyer's or of the seller's the goods perish before sale, but after the agreement to sell (ie before the property has passed to the buyer), the agreement is avoided (s 7).

## iv Protection of third parties
It has been explained that under an agreement to sell, the goods may sometimes be the buyer's, even though they have not been delivered; that is to say, while the seller retains possession of them. Similarly, the seller may sometimes permit the buyer to take delivery before the property has passed to him. Wherever either of these two things happen, the person in possession becomes a source of potential danger to third parties; he appears to be the owner of something that is not really his and he cannot give a title to them to anyone.

In order to avoid the consequences to which this situation might lead, ss 24 and 25 effectively provide that, on the one hand, where a seller is thus in possession he can give a good title to an innocent third party to whom he sells the goods (s 24) and that, on the other hand, a buyer thus in possession may similarly confer a good title. 'Transfer' includes a 'sale, pledge, or other disposition'. This important rule may appear to operate harshly upon the owner, but he has after all, by his conduct, in entrusting the possession of the goods to the other party, permitted him to hold himself out to strangers as the owner. If it were not for this rule, innocent third parties might buy goods, only to find themselves subjected to an action for conversion by an owner of whose very existence they had no reason to suspect.

### v  Unpaid seller's rights

An unpaid seller has a right ('seller's lien') to retain possession of the goods against payment. This right subsists where: (a) the goods have been sold without any stipulation as to credit; (b) the goods have been sold on credit, but the term of credit has expired; (c) the buyer becomes insolvent (s 41(1)).

Further, an unpaid seller may stop the goods 'in transit' ('stoppage *in transitu*') and resume possession of them, after he has parted with them, if the buyer becomes insolvent (s 44). For this purpose 'transit' lasts until the goods are delivered to the buyer or his agent (s 45(1)). The expression 'agent' here signifies 'representative', not an agent in the technical sense, as described in the last section.

Suppose, for instance, that X, in London, sells goods to Y in Sydney. X delivers them to his agent, with instructions to take them to Sydney. Y sends an agent to collect them at the harbour. If X hears that Y has become insolvent, he may, at any time until they are delivered to Y's agent at the quay, stop the goods *in transitu* by ordering his agent to retain them.

## 2    Consumer credit and consumer hire contracts

The Consumer Credit Act 1974 ('CCA') regulates 'consumer credit' agreements. It is a massive statute, which in the manner of paternalistic legislation, has spawned copious regulations.

*Regulated agreements* – The CCA 'regulates', ie contains special rules about, most consumer credit and consumer hire agreements which fall within a prescribed economic range of credit or of payment for hire, and which are made between an individual (or partnership, but not a corporation) and any other person (the 'creditor' or 'hirer') by which the latter provides credit, or, in the case of hire, hires goods, to the former (ss 8 and 15). Certain agreements are, however, *exempt* from regulation (s 16): notably agreements made with local authorities and building societies for the purchase of land or the provision of houses; and, by Order made under powers conferred by s 16(5), 'debtor-creditor-supplier' (see below) agreements of certain categories, including agreements, other than hire-purchase, conditional sale or pledge agreements, which envisage single repayment at regular periods: this exempts credit card agreements (such as Diners Club or American Express) which comply with that requirement.

*Classification* – In order to distinguish between different kinds of agreements in certain defined respects the Act contains cumbersome, and at times overlapping, classifications of them. The main, and simple, differentiation is between *'consumer credit agreements'* (s 8) and *'consumer hire agreements'* (s 15).

First, as to *'consumer credit agreements'*. By s 8(1) the Act distinguishes the generic form of *'personal credit agreements'* from 'consumer credit agreements' which are defined (s 8(2)) in terms of agreements subject to the prescribed financial limits and these 'consumer credit agreements' are thus (as opposed to agreements above that limit) *'regulated'* agreements within the Act. They are divided into the following categories:

*(a) 'Restricted use credit'* agreements and 'unrestricted use credit' agreements. The former include transactions (such as hire-purchase and credit or conditional sale) where the credit is given for a particular purpose; the latter include such things as personal bank loans not restricted to any special purpose.

NOTE – A *'credit sale'* agreement is an agreement, other than a conditional sale agreement, under which the purchase price is payable by instalments.

A *'conditional sale'* agreement is 'an agreement for the sale of goods or land under which the purchase price is payable by instalments *and* the property is to remain in the seller notwithstanding that the buyer is in *possession* until such conditions as to the payment of instalments or otherwise as may be specified in the agreement are fulfilled.' A *'hire-purchase'* agreement is one under which there is no sale, but a bailment by the hirer to the purchaser giving *possession* to the latter until, upon payment of the instalments, the purchaser exercises his option to purchase – see CCA, s 189.

*(b) 'Debtor-creditor-supplier'* agreements. This draftsman's monstrosity includes agreements whereby a supplier himself gives credit to a purchaser, hirer, etc and also agreements between a third party and a purchaser, etc, made under pre-existing arrangements with a supplier – eg the typical case of purchase of a car by hire-purchase through a dealer and a finance company.

Such agreements the Act contrasts with *'debtor-creditor' agreements*, ie all other credit agreements.

*(c) 'Credit token'* agreements. These are agreements 'for the provision of credit in connection with the use of a credit token' (s 189) and a 'credit token' (ss 14(1), 189) is a 'card, check, voucher, coupon, stamp, form, booklet, or other document or thing (a rare opportunity for the application of the *ejusdem generis* rule – p 12) given to an individual by a person carrying on a consumer credit business' who undertakes that he or another person will 'supply cash, goods and service' to the individual.

This includes, typically, credit cards, but not bankers' cheque cards which are tokens of guarantee (and, of course, entail a 'consumer credit agreement') nor the extremely popular debit cards such as Switch.

'*Credit*' includes a cash loan and any other form of financial accommodation (s 9); and it is classified as either '*running account*' credit or '*fixed sum*' credit: examples of the former are bank overdrafts and credit cards, and of the latter loans by banks, pawnbrokers, etc.

Contrasted, as has been mentioned, with regulated 'consumer credit agreements' are regulated '*consumer hire agreements*'. These are agreements, *other than* hire-purchase agreements, for the hire of goods which are *capable* of subsisting for *more than three months* – eg hire of a tractor for four months, even though the agreement may in fact be terminated in two months, but *not* a two months' contract.

The '*total credit charge*'. This vital provision of the CCA, s 20 (which embraces all credit agreements, whether they are regulated or not) must be noted. The section requires the Secretary of State to make regulations to ensure that the creditor makes known to the debtor the '*total*' credit charge, ie the total actual outlay required, including, ie charges, fees, stamp duties, etc. This requirement is now implemented by the Consumer Credit (Total Charge for Credit) Regulations 1980 and no less than fifteen volumes of consumer credit tables.

*General rules of regulated agreements* – In general (but only in general) the following rules apply to regulated agreements:

(*i*) Certain information prescribed by the Secretary of State must be disclosed by the creditor/owner to the debtor/hirer before the agreement is made (s 55).

(*ii*) Where an agreement is only at the prospective stage either party may withdraw by giving notice, written *or oral* (s 57).

(*iii*) A regulated agreement will not be '*properly executed*' unless it is: (a) made in prescribed form; (b) signed by *both* parties or their agents; (c) readily legible (s (1)). If an agreement is '*improperly*' (ie not 'properly') executed the result will be (s 65) that it can only be enforced by *court order*. Which means, for example, that where the debtor defaults in such a way that the creditor would normally have a right of recaption (re-taking) of goods subject to the contract he can only exercise this right by court order.

(*iv*) There are complicated provisions concerning the supply by the creditor/owner to the debtor/hirer of prescribed ('statutory') copies of the agreement under certain conditions. These must be consulted (ss 62 and 63).

(*v*) Regulated agreements are *cancellable* upon the giving of written notice within a defined period – in *general* 14 days from signature by the debtor/hirer – *if* they emerged from *oral* representations by the creditor/hirer or his agent, eg the case of house-to-house canvassing. *But* two classes of agreements are not, in any event, cancellable: namely, agreements secured on *land* and agreements which are signed by the debtor/hirer at the creditor/owner's *business premises* (see also the Consumer Protection (Cancellation of Contracts Concluded Away from Business Premises) Regulations 1987).

It is important to note that s 74 exempts, *inter alia, non-commercial* contracts from almost all of the above rules: purely private loans are thus, for example, not 'regulated'.

*The currency and termination of the agreements* – Parts VI and VII of the Act contain detailed provisions concerning the dealings and rights and duties of the parties during the currency of the agreement and its termination by default or otherwise. These are too complex for discussion here. But it should be noted that the Supply of Goods (Implied Terms) Act 1973, as amended by Sch 4 of the CCA, imposes upon *hire-purchase* contracts implied terms, similar to the implied terms of the SGA, and that the Unfair Contracts Terms Act 1977 (ss 6(1)(*b*), 6(2)(*b*)) applies the same rules about *exclusion clauses* to these contracts as the rules which it applies to sales of goods (above).

*Hire Purchase Act 1964, ss 27 and 28 (motor vehicles)* – These sections (as amended by the CCA, Sch 4) extend to *hire-purchase* and *conditional sale* transactions similar protection to an innocent purchaser from a dishonest hirer or conditional sale purchaser (both of whom have possession, but – unlike the purchaser under a *credit sale* – not the ownership of the car involved) to that enjoyed by an innocent purchaser under the SGA, s 25 (p 297). Section 27 enacts that a hirer who disposes of a motor vehicle to a private purchaser (ie someone other than a motor dealer or a finance house) may give a good title to the purchaser, provided that the latter takes in good faith and without notice of the hire-purchase agreement. Those in the trade (being people who may be expected to be on their guard against that kind of fraud) do not fall within this protection, and still cannot acquire a good title from a fraudulent hire-purchaser; but the *'first private purchaser'* may acquire a good title if he takes from them. This means that if A (hirer) sells to B (dealer) and B sells to C (first *private* purchaser) who is not a dealer and who takes in good faith and without notice, then C acquires the property in the vehicle and may, of course, pass a valid title to anyone else, even to another dealer.

*Liability of creditor for breaches by supplier* – By the CCA, s 75, in the case of a regulated debtor/creditor-supplier agreement the creditor (eg a finance house or the issuer of regulated credit card agreements) may be held liable by the debtor in respect of any claim against the supplier (dealer) in respect of misrepresentation or breach of contract – that is, he may be held legally responsible for the default of the supplier (eg in respect of the latter's breach of condition, express or implied, or misrepresentation (effectively a statutory enforcement of a collateral warranty). The creditor has, however, a right to be indemnified by the supplier. Further, the supplier is deemed by law to be the agent of the creditor for a number of purposes: eg receipt of a notice of cancellation.

*Licensing of credit and hire business* – Under the general control of the Director of Fair Trading, the Act brings into being a system of licensing (local authorities and certain other bodies being exempted) of consumer credit and consumer hire businesses which deal in regulated transactions.

# Chapter 10

# The law of torts

It is proposed first to discuss matters affecting tortious liability in general, then to give some examples of specific torts and to examine the appropriate remedies.

## 1 General matters

### A THE NATURE OF TORTIOUS LIABILITY

The word 'tort' is derived from the French '*tort*' ('wrong'). Torts must be distinguished from crimes on the one hand, and from breaches of contract on the other.

A *crime* is, as has been explained, a wrong which, by means of punishment or otherwise, the State inhibits. A tort is a *civil* wrong which entitles a person who is injured by its commission to claim *damages* for his loss, whether purely by way of reparation or as a way of bringing home to the defendant the anti-social nature of his act. An *injunction* is also a proper remedy in some circumstances.

A breach of contract is, like a tort, a civil wrong; but it is different from a tort. Whereas *contractual duties are imposed by the parties* to the contract themselves, the duty to refrain from committing torts is *imposed by the general law* of the land, independently of the wishes of the plaintiff or of the defendant. In many circumstances, however, alternative claims in contract and tort may arise upon the same facts.

Historically, torts are divided into two main classes: *trespasses* and actions '*on the case*'. A trespass is a 'direct and forcible' injury. This is the most obvious and dramatic of all wrongs. It is not therefore surprising that, in point of time, trespasses were the earliest torts which the law recognized and remedied. Actions 'on the case' were actions for damage caused otherwise than 'directly and forcibly'. They were called actions 'on the case' primarily (although historically the matter is somewhat more complicated) because they were originally granted in circumstances in which there had formerly been no remedy but the plaintiff could show that, upon the facts of his case, he had suffered damage as the result of some act or omission of the defendant.

The difference between 'trespass' and 'case' may be illustrated. If Jones hits Brown, or walks over his land, or kicks the paint off his car, he has committed a trespass. Suppose, however, that Jones carelessly leaves a mat on a slippery floor where Brown is likely to walk and suppose that Brown slips on the mat and is injured. Or suppose again, that Smith negligently permits a fire that has arisen on his own land to spread, and to damage Clark's crops. In both these two latter examples there has been no 'direct and forcible' injury; in the second the injury was neither 'direct' nor 'forcible'. Yet in both instances, the injured party could sue the other by means of an action on the case.

For the purpose of pleading, the vital distinction between 'trespass' and 'case' has long since disappeared. History has, however, left this legacy, that where a plaintiff's claim is founded upon a trespass, he need – except where the trespass is one to the person and arises from negligence – prove no actual damage, he is entitled to compensation (it may be nominal) as of right, upon mere proof of the trespass. In most other tortious actions a plaintiff must prove that he has suffered some *actual* ('special') damage, for damage was nearly always an essential element in the plaintiff's claim in actions on the case.

From mediaeval times, then, trespasses have not been the only actionable torts; for injuries other than trespasses were remediable by means of case. Indeed, most of the modern torts, such as deceit, libel, slander and negligence derive from these. It must not, however, be imagined that, because proof of damage was essential to found an action upon the case, that therefore proof of *any sort of* damage would, or will, give rise to a claim in tort.

There always has been, and there always will be, damage (*'damnum sine injuria'*) which the courts must regard as 'damage without injury'; for there are necessarily some types of loss which the law cannot recognize as giving rise to legally redressable claims. Thus, some harm is too trivial to found an action, while the courts look upon other harm as part of the give and take of life in a world in which people's interests conflict – a circumstance which causes the need for law; a kind of referee. Thus, for instance – in the absence of the limited redress afforded by the law relating to fraud, patents, copyright, trade marks, conspiracy, injurious falsehood, and unjustified interference with contractual relations – damage to business interests and in the course of trade or industrial competition is seldom actionable, even though it be intentionally inflicted.

Although in general – subject, however, to exceptions, as in the case of defamation and liability under the Rule in *Rylands v Fletcher* (p 335) – tortious liability can only arise if the harm complained of was caused by the *fault* of the defendant (in the sense that he acted *intentionally* or *carelessly*), the *motive* which actuates him, whether good or bad, is *in general* irrelevant to legal inquiry. For instance, if I take the Duchess' diamonds intending to sell them for the relief of the poor it would clearly be socially undesirable to allow me to plead my charitable motive by way of defence. And equally a bad motive ('malice') will not usually make that unlawful which, the motive apart, would otherwise be lawful: for instance I am, in general, permitted to cause harm to your business by means of my own competition, and it can normally make no difference to this fact that that competition is actuated by a desire to spite you. To these general propositions, there are, however, exceptions. For example, in tort, as in crime it will *excuse* my assaulting you if I can show that in doing so I was actuated by the respectable motive of seeking to use reasonable force in defending myself. And it will be seen below that '*malice*' may exceptionally create *liability*; as in nuisance, and injurious falsehood. An improper motive may also make that a conspiracy which would otherwise not be one and may negative a plea of qualified privilege in defamation.

There is some harm, too, which, though it arises from unlawful acts, is too far removed from them in point of time, space or circumstance, to be justly visited with legal sanctions. Though in philosophy it may be true that *every* antecedent act is linked with *every* later consequence, the law, to be practical and just, can only make wrongdoers pay for the more *immediate* results of their misdeeds. For example, where Brown carelessly runs down and kills Smith, although, as we shall see, Smith's dependent relatives will in certain circumstances be entitled to claim from Brown compensation for their loss, Smith's employees, who may be thrown out of work and suffer hardship as the result of their employer's death, will have no legal claim against the wrongdoer.

It follows that although the categories of recognized civil injuries have expanded from time to time, and doubtless will continue to expand, this expansion must nevertheless be limited by the practical consideration that not every injury of which people may complain can be regarded as a legal wrong. An early example of this proposition is to be found in the *Gloucester Grammar School Case* (1410), in which the master of an established school tried, without success, to sue another master who had set up a rival school (an early example of fostering the 'policy' of freedom of competition). A tort does not consist simply in the infliction of an injury, but in the infliction of a *legally recognized* injury.

Moreover, the different classes of recognized injuries (or 'torts') have in the course of time each become subjected to special legal definitions, and special rules have come to apply to each of them; so that they will only be actionable within the limitations thus imposed.

## B GENERAL DEFENCES TO ACTIONS IN TORT

There are certain general defences to actions in tort. Inevitable accident, assumption of risk, self-defence, and statutory authority may be instanced. Of these inevitable accident and assumption of risk require mention.

### 1 INEVITABLE ACCIDENT

An inevitable accident is something which cannot be avoided by the taking of ordinary precautions. With some exceptions, as in the case of liability under the rule in *Rylands v Fletcher*, the plea of 'inevitable accident' will form a good defence to actions in tort (p 335). Thus in *National Coal Board v J E Evans & Co (Cardiff) Ltd* [1951] 2 KB 861, it was held that where, unknown to the land owners, the plaintiffs placed an electric cable under certain land, and a firm of contractors employed by the landowners to excavate a trench in the land caused damage to the cable, the latter were not liable to the plaintiffs in trespass; for they did not know of the existence of the cable and they were entirely without fault in permitting their excavator to strike it.

### 2 ASSUMPTION OF RISK

A person who consents to run the risk of injury cannot maintain an action in tort against the person who causes that injury. *'Volenti non fit injuria'* ('Where there is consent there is no injury'). This is a principle of general application. It applies not only in cases where people agree to run the risk of injury, but also in cases where the law presumes that they have consented to do so.

Three points must be noted in connection with 'assumption of risk'.

*(i)* No one will be allowed to consent to run the risk of *illegal* harm. Thus the rule would not apply in the case of a boxing match conducted with bare fists. And it has been ruled generally that consent will not bar a prosecution – and, presumably, a civil claim – where, in a fight the contestants intend to cause bodily harm (*AG's Reference (No 6 of 1980)* [1981] QB 715) .

*(ii)* Mere *knowledge* of a risk need not necessarily amount to *consent* to run it. So in *Smith v Baker* [18 91] AC 325, a workman was employed to drill rock in a cutting. He knew that a crane carrying loads of stones constantly swung over his head, and that there was danger that a stone might drop on him. Due to the negligent manner in which his employers allowed the crane to be operated a stone did drop, and he was injured. The House of Lords held that the man could recover against the employers. His knowledge of the danger did not, under the circumstances, imply that he consented to run the risk of injury. But it must be added that outside the master-servant relationship – where the employee tends to run risks

under compulsion, for fear of losing his job – knowledge of the existence of a risk coupled with a continuation of the activity to which it is incident, may sometimes be treated as equivalent to consent to incur it. Thus, if a harbour authority *notifies* shipowners that a particular anchorage is dangerous, and the owners nevertheless use it, they will not be able to claim for damage resulting from such use.

*(iii)* Where one person creates a dangerous situation, and another tries to avert the danger, the latter is not necessarily debarred from suing the former because he voluntarily took a risk. He will be debarred if he was merely meddlesome or foolhardy, but not if he acted under a clear moral duty. Thus, in *Haynes v Harwood* [1935] 1 KB 146, where a van was negligently left unattended in the street, and a boy threw a stone at the horses with the result that they bolted, it was held that a policeman who rushed from a police station to stop the horses could recover damages from the owner of the van for injuries received in stopping them. The accident occurred in a public street and a woman and children were in danger.

It is not at present clear what situations the courts will regard as giving rise to sufficient moral compulsion to bring this rule into play. It has been extended to cover people who run risks in the protection of the property (as well as of the person) of others, provided, at any rate, that they bear some special relationship to the owner of the property. For instance, a servant is under a duty to protect his master's goods; if, therefore, he sees that they are in danger from, say, fire, he should rescue them. It follows that if the fire has been started through the master's negligence, and the servant is injured in the rescue, he is entitled to claim against his master. The rule has also been extended to the case of a doctor who was asphyxiated while trying to rescue a man from a well which had become filled with fumes due to the defendant's negligence. On the other hand it has been held that a man who is injured in attempting to stop a runaway horse *in the country*, where no one is in danger, will have no claim against the owner. The law encourages the hero, but dislikes the busybody.

## C CAPACITY

Generally speaking anyone of full age may sue and be sued in tort. Let us consider the position of minors, of unborn persons and of corporations.

### (a) Minors

Although, as a general rule, minors enjoy no special exemption from tortious liability, the fact that a defendant is under age may have some effect. For instance, a child who is charged with negligence, or with contributory negligence, will be judged, not according to the standards of a reasonable adult, but according to those of a child. Thus, for example, it was held in a Canadian appeal to the Judicial Committee that a person who negligently sold petrol to a child was liable for injuries caused to the child when the latter set light to the petrol as a part of a game of 'Red Indians'. It is not negligent for a *child* to set fire to petrol.

In one exceptional case minors are exempted from liability in tort, and this is an incident of their immunity from *contractual* liability. A plaintiff will not be permitted to evade the rule which accords contractual immunity by framing his action in tort. Thus, in *Jennings v Rundall* (1799) 8 Term Rep 335, a minor hired a mare and injured her by over-riding. It was held that since his act was substantially no more than a breach of contract, the owner could not sue him in tort for the damage caused by his negligence. But it must be noted that if the wrong is *independent* of a contract, though connected with it, the minor may be liable despite the existence of the contract. Thus in *Burnard v Haggis* (1863) 14 CBNS 45, where another minor similarly hired a mare for riding, but used her for *jumping*, against the express admonition of the owner, and consequently injured the animal, it was held that the minor could be held liable in tort. The act of jumping, though connected with the contract, was outside its terms, and could therefore be treated, independently, as a tort.

Minors have full capacity to *sue* in tort, though (as in the case of all litigation) they require to be represented in the action by an adult acting as 'next friend'.

Formerly the claims of *unborn children* to protection by the law of torts were doubtful; but provisions in their favour have now been made by the Congenital Disabilities (Civil Liability) Act 1976. In the first place an action may lie against a person whose breach of legal duty to a parent results in a child being born disabled, abnormal or unhealthy; though if the breach of duty precedes conception there will be no liability if either or both of the parents knew that there was a risk that the child would be born disabled. Moreover, where a contract with a parent excludes liability the exclusion will also apply to the unborn child, and where a parent shares responsibility with the defendant for the fact that the child is born disabled the damages recoverable against the latter may be reduced.

In general no claim will lie on behalf of the *child when born* if the person responsible for its disabilities is its *mother*. But by the Act 'a woman driving a *motor vehicle* when she knows (or ought reasonably to know) herself to be pregnant is to be regarded as under the same duty to take care for the safety of her unborn child as the law imposes on her with respect to the safety of other people'. Thus if the child be born disabled as the result of her negligence she will be liable to it. It should be added that it is a prerequisite to liability that the child be born alive. This, it may be noted, is contrary to the law of some jurisdictions in the United States which permit claims on behalf of a damaged foetus.

Further, our law, again unlike that of some American jurisdictions, does not permit a claim brought on behalf of a child born disabled. Thus in *McKay v Essex Area Health Authority* [1982] QB 1166 it was held that if a doctor fails to advise an abortion in circumstances in which there is a serious risk that if the pregnancy goes forward the child will be born disabled, and it is born disabled, the child has no cause of action. Public policy precludes such a claim because there is no way of balancing the merits of no life against the benefits or disadvantages of a disabled life.

A somewhat similar situation arises where a child is born as the result of a negligently performed sterilization operation and the mother claims in respect of the expense of rearing it. In *Udale v Bloomsbury Area Health Authority* [1983] 2 All ER 552 it was held that, the birth of a child being a blessing rather than a curse, the mother ought not to have a claim. She should cheerfully shoulder the expense. But the Court of Appeal overruled that decision in *Emeh v Kensington and Chelsea and Westminster Area Health Authority* [1985] QB 1012. It was there decided that the general interests of the family as a whole require that provision should be assured for the upkeep of the child.

## (b) Corporations

Corporations are abstractions; they are incapable of indulging in any activities; consequently they cannot commit torts. It might therefore be thought that they cannot be held liable in tort. This is not, however, the case. A corporation is regarded in law as the employer of its agents – from director to office boy – and employers may, as we shall see, be held 'vicariously' responsible for the torts of their agents acting within the course of their employment.

## D  JOINT TORTS

Torts are sometimes committed, not by one person alone, but by two or more people jointly. For instance, A and B may combine together to defraud C. Moreover, for special reasons, two or more people may be held jointly liable where one of them has only in fact committed a tort; thus, as will shortly be explained, a master is jointly and severally liable with a servant for torts committed by the servant in the course of his employment.

Liability for 'joint' torts is both 'joint' and 'several'. The plaintiff may, at his option, sue *both* (or *all*) of the defendants, or he may recover the full amount of his loss from *one* of them alone. Although it was not usually so at common law, by the Civil Liability (Contribution) Act 1978 one tortfeasor who is jointly liable to a plaintiff with another, or others, in respect of the same damage, may recover contribution from his fellow-tortfeasors where the plaintiff has recovered the whole amount, or more than his fair share, from him (s 1(1) of the Act). The amount of contribution recoverable is such, in the words of the Act, '*as may be found by the Court to be just and equitable having regard to the extent of [the fellow-tortfeasor's] responsibility for the damage*'. Moreover, the court has power (s 2(2)) to exempt a joint-tortfeasor from contribution and also to direct that one of the tortfeasors shall indemnify the other or others.

No contribution can be obtained where the person sued is liable to *indemnify* his co-tortfeasor, or tortfeasors. Liability to indemnify may arise, for example, where one man employs another to do something which is not obviously wrong, but which he (the employer) knows to be tortious. In such a case, if someone is injured and recovers damages from the innocent dupe, the latter will have a right to be indemnified by his employer. Under the Act the employer, if sued alone, will therefore have no right to contribution from the dupe. Where the right to damages is subject to restriction (as, for example, where the plaintiff was guilty of contributory negligence) the liability of any contributor is subject to that restriction – s 2(3).

By the same Act (s 2(3)) a plaintiff who has obtained judgment against one of the tortfeasors is not debarred from suing the other or others (as, at common law he usually was) – provided, of course, that his claim has not been fully satisified.

## E   VICARIOUS LIABILITY

Masters (employers) are held 'vicariously' liable for torts committed by their servants (employees) in the course of their employment, ie they are held liable for the wrong of the servant even though the tort is one which they have not ordered or authorized. This is a common-sense rule, for employees are usually people of slender means and it is fair that an injured plaintiff should be entitled to seek compensation from those who control and profit by the organization in which he is employed. On the other hand, in legal theory (though practice usually parts company with theory, since no one sues a man of straw) there is nothing to prevent the master from making good his own loss by claiming against the servant-tortfeasor.

Before vicarious responsibility can be imposed upon a defendant, it has to be shown that: (a) the person who committed the tort was his 'servant', and (b) that the servant was, at the time when the tort was committed, acting within the course of his employment.

## 1   WHO IS A 'SERVANT'?

According to a time-worn definition a *servant* is any person who works for another upon the terms that he is to be subject to the control of that other as to the *manner* in which he shall do his work. Thus chauffeurs, casual labourers and apprentices are clearly servants. Skilled (self-employed) workers, such as electricians, carpenters and dressmakers, who come to work in people's houses, are *independent contractors* and not the servants of the householder; for though he may give them general directions, he cannot control the actual manner in which they are to set about their work. People who work under contracts of the former type are said to be employed under a contract of '*service*', while people who work under contracts of the latter type are said to work under a contract '*for services*'. Generally, of course, today those classes we have instanced under the second head will be the 'servants' of someone else who will then, himself, be vicariously liable for their misdeeds.

It must, however, be explained that at the present time this branch of the law is being modified in the process of judicial decision. Although no new definition of a 'servant' has as yet gained currency, the modern 'servant' begins to look different from his prototype, the manual or domestic worker. For instance, hospital authorities have been held vicariously responsible for the negligence of nurses, radiographers, and even of whole-time assistance medical officers; and companies are regularly made liable for the torts of their executives. Both 'servant' and 'master' are therefore expanding categories and the policy which underlies this expansion probably springs from a feeling that it is right that large institutions and enterprises should bear the losses incidental to their activities; activities which they can only, in the nature of things, perform through the instrumentality of their staff. To which the student may reflect, 'What's in a *name*?' For present purposes the 'servant', 'employee', 'worker', call him what you will – is a person for whose torts another will at any given time, in accordance with current policy, be held legally responsible.

## 2   THE COURSE OF EMPLOYMENT

Clearly a master cannot be made liable for every wrongful act which his servant commits, but only for wrongs committed about the master's business, and whether any particular act does thus fall within the scope of employment must always be largely a question of fact.

The law may be illustrated by the following example. Smith employs Jones (a 'servant') to drive his lorry from A to B. While on the road, Jones negligently knocks down Thomas. Smith will be liable to Thomas. If, instead of going direct from A to B, Jones makes an unauthorized detour through C, and an accident occurs, Smith will again be liable. If, however, instead of merely deviating from his course, Jones were to drive off to place D, in the opposite direction from B, upon a 'frolic', as a judge once put it 'of his own', Smith could not be held liable for any accident which might occur. The question is, 'Was there a *deviation* or a *departure* from duty?' This question is equally apposite when applied to all forms of employment, not only to deviations made in the course of journeys.

It should be noted that the employer may be held liable even if he has *prohibited* the servant from doing the act in question. Though prohibition may be relevant in determining whether the act was committed in the course of employment, it cannot, of itself, exculpate the master: if the law were otherwise masters could escape liability by the simple expedient of prohibiting their servants from committing any torts during their service. Thus, in *Limpus v London General Omnibus Co* (1862) 1 H&C 526, where a driver caused an accident by drawing his bus across the road so as to obstruct a rival bus, it was held that the Company were liable; even though orders had been given that their drivers were not to race or to obstruct rivals.

It should also be mentioned that difficulty arises in cases where one employer (sometimes called the '*general* employer') lends a servant to another ('*special* employer') for some particular purpose or for a period of time. In such cases which of the two masters should be responsible if the servant causes tortious injury to some third party? On the face of it the answer is simple: 'Whichever of the two had the right of control over the servant's activities at the time the injury was caused'. But the application of this principle is difficult. For instance, in the leading case of *Mersey Docks and Harbour Board v Coggins & Griffiths (Liverpool) Ltd* [1947] AC 1, the facts were these. The appellants hired out a crane to the respondents (a firm of stevedores) for the purpose of unloading a ship. The appellants also provided a driver for this crane upon the terms that he should be for the duration of the contract 'the servant of the hirers'. In fact although the respondents supervised this man's work, they had no power of control over his actual management of the machine. Through negligent handling of it he injured someone. Which of the two masters was liable? The driver himself, little realizing that the effect would be to attract sole liability to himself, stoutly objected in evidence that he was no one's servant. But the House of Lords paid no attention to this. Nor did they heed the terms of the contract; for the parties could not by agreement between themselves affect the legal rights of the person injured. They took the view that the crucial issue was which of the masters had the ultimate control over the driver's management of the crane, and that, since this right remained in the appellants, liability was theirs.

Circumstances alter cases, and it will be appreciated that the determination of this issue must depend upon a consideration of all relevant facts; but in the *Mersey Docks* case the House of Lords enunciated an important rule for the future; namely that it lies upon the general employer to establish that the vicarious responsibility which is initially his has been shifted from his shoulders to those of the special employer; and they stressed that the onus of establishing the change is to be treated as a heavy one.

### Independent contractors

As a general rule people are not liable for the torts of independent contractors, ie people whom they employ to work for them otherwise than as servants. For example, if I commission X & Co to build a ship for me and a fire is negligently caused by one of their servants during the work, if this fire burns down Y's wharf, X & Co will be liable, but I shall not.

This general rule is, however, subject to a number of exceptions. Instances are: (i) Where the contract under which the contractor works is one which, if it is to be properly implemented, is likely to involve the commission of a tort. For example, if A employs B & Co to erect a building in a congested area he may be held liable for nuisances caused by the inevitable dust and vibration incident to the work. (ii) Where an especially high duty of care is imposed upon a person by law he cannot escape liability for its breach by employing an independent contractor. Thus, people who do dangerous things on or near a highway (other than acts such as driving a car, which constitute an ordinary use of the highway), will be liable for any injuries caused to the public; even though they employ an independent contractor for the work. For instance, in *Tarry v Ashton* (1876) 1 QBD 314, the occupier of a house was held liable for injuries caused to a passer-by by the falling of a lamp from a rotten bracket which projected over the pavement from his wall. It was no defence for him to show that he had employed an independent contractor to repair the bracket. (iii) Where liability is 'strict' (independent of negligence), as in the case of liability under the rule in *Rylands v Fletcher*, a defendant will be liable for the acts of an independent contractor.

## F THE SURVIVAL OF ACTIONS

The death of either of the parties may affect rights of action in tort. At common law the general rule – although there were important exceptions to it – was expressed by the maxim '*actio personalis moritur cum persona*' ('a personal action dies with the litigant'). Whether the plaintiff or the defendant died, the right of action died with him.

Since the Law Reform (Miscellaneous Provisions) Act 1934 (as subsequently amended), the above general rule no longer exists. Rights of action in tort now survive both in favour of the estate of a deceased plaintiff and against the estate of a deceased defendant. This proposition is, however, subject, amongst others, to the following qualifications:

(i)   Actions for defamation, do not survive.
(ii)  Exemplary damages cannot be awarded in favour of the estate of a deceased plaintiff.
(iii) Claims for 'bereavement' (below) do not survive.

Beside the maxim just discussed, there was another maxim enshrining a different principle which did, and to some extent still does, affect the survival of actions. This is the maxim that '*In a civil court the death of a human being cannot be complained of as an injury*'. (The 'rule in *Baker v Boulton*' (1808) 1 Camp 493.)

Suppose that Smith has a servant, Tompkins, and that Atkins negligently runs down and kills Tompkins in a street accident. Smith, however great the loss he may suffer as the result of Tompkin's death, will have no claim against Atkins, even though he might have had one if Tompkins had lived. It could be that Atkins may be prosecuted for manslaughter, but, whether he can or not, Smith will have no *action*. Thus, it is sometimes, as has often been said, 'cheaper to kill than to maim'.

The harshness of this rule is mitigated in two ways:

*(a)* The rule forms no bar to an action based, as sometimes happens, not merely upon tort, but also upon breach of contract. Thus, in *Jackson v Watson & Sons* [1909] 2 KB 193, J bought some tinned salmon from W. He gave it to his wife to eat and it poisoned her. In an action by J against W for breach of contract, it was held that the injury he suffered as the result of the loss of his wife's society and services might be taken into account as an element in the assessment of J's damages.

*(b)* By the provisions of the Fatal Accidents Act 1976 (which consolidates a series of Acts, starting with the Fatal Accidents Act 1846 – 'Lord Campbell's Act') as amended and partially re-enacted by the Administration of Justice Act 1982 the *dependants* of a deceased person can claim damages for loss arising by reason of his decease if the death was caused by some default on the part of the defendant which would, had the deceased remained alive, have entitled him to bring an action in tort.

The action should normally be brought by the personal representatives (see below, Chapter 14) of the deceased person, on behalf of the dependants. 'Dependants' for this purpose include the deceased's wife or former wife, husband or former husband, parent or other antecedent, child or other descendant, grandparent, grandchild, step-parent, step-child, brother, sister, uncle, aunt (and the issue of the latter four). Further, a claim may now be made by any person living with the deceased at the time of death, provided that the cohabitation has lasted for at least two years. A claim may be made by any person not the deceased's parent or child but treated by him as such. Illegitimate and adopted children are also included.

In general the loss which the legislation envisages is *pecuniary* loss – the loss of a 'breadwinner'. But the Act (as amended) provides that a wife or husband of the deceased, or if the deceased was a minor, and not married, his parents (if he was illegitimate, his mother) may all claim £7,500 damages – an amount subject to variation – for the mere fact of *bereavement*.

Claims may be brought in respect of the same fatal accident, both under the 1934 Act and the Fatal Accidents Act, but no award may be made which would have the result of giving a dependant a benefit twice over. For instance, if an award is made under the 1934 Act in respect of a deceased husband who has, say, died without making a will and leaving his wife as his sole surviving relative, the benefit which the wife will receive from this award, as sole successor to the husband's estate, must be taken into account in assessing the amount she is to receive under the Fatal Accidents Act.

Money spent by dependants upon funeral or mourning expenses is recoverable.

# 2 Examples of specific torts

There is insufficient space to attempt more than a very brief outline of some of the essential characteristics of a few illustrative torts, and the reader who wishes to make a serious study of the subject is referred to the specialized works.

Two general remarks should, however, be made. In the first place the reason for curtailing discussion of the law of torts is that it is case law *par excellence*; it might be described as a honeycomb of particular instances, resting upon a delusively simple structure of principle. The study of torts can only be based upon the cases, and if we were to stray among their fascinating pastures we should be in danger of leading the reader into a large volume. Thus they must be warned that what appears here as simple in plan is as complex in realization, and little hint can be given of the wealth of this complexity. In the second place, as has been seen, tort law has been built up by the courts in what was once judicially described as 'disconnected slabs': the writer therefore believes that there is no merit in choosing any particular order of treatment and would on the whole be happy to adhere to the traditional method of discussing trespass and its immediate off-shoots first, since they came first in point of time. But if Saturn devoured his children, similar opprobrium falls upon the modern tort of negligence, for it has not only overshadowed trespass, its grandfather, but bids fair to swallow up many of its other less illustrious relatives. In modern practice, therefore, most of 'torts' is negligence. So, to mark this fact and impress it upon the reader negligence will be discussed first.

## 1 NEGLIGENCE

'Negligence', for the purposes of the law of torts, is a word which is used in a dual sense. On the one hand it may signify the attitude of mind of a party committing a tort; thus, goods may be converted intentionally, unintentionally, or 'negligently' – the taker having made insufficient inquiries to satisfy himself as to their ownership. On the other hand, 'negligence' is today also a tort in its own right, independent of other torts; and it is with the independent tort of negligence that we are now concerned.

'Negligence' in this latter sense signifies *the breach by the defendant of a legal duty to take care not to injure the plaintiff or cause him loss*; if such a duty is broken, and the plaintiff can show that he has been injured or that he has suffered loss as a result of the breach he will have a right of action against the defendant.

## The duty of care

The first thing to be considered is, therefore, *in what circumstances does a legal duty to take care exist?* There are, of course, many situations in which it is so clear that a duty is owed that this matter will require no consideration. For instance, it is obvious that drivers of motor cars owe a duty to other road users to drive carefully, and so if they injure people through careless driving they are guilty of negligence, and can be sued. Not all situations in which people claim that they have been injured by the carelessness of others are, however, of such a simple and familiar nature. It is thus at least desirable that there should be some general test by which the existence or non-existence of a *'duty of care'* can be determined. In the leading case of *Donoghue v Stevenson* [1932] AC 562, Lord Atkin propounded such a test in a passage in his speech which became famous. He said, 'The liability for negligence . . . is no doubt based upon a general moral sentiment of moral wrongdoing for which the offender must pay. But acts or omissions which any moral code would censure cannot in a practical world be treated so as to give a right to *every person* injured by them to demand relief. In this way rules of law arise which *limit* the range of complainants and the extent of their remedy. The rule that you are to love your neighbour becomes in law: You must not injure your neighbour, and the lawyer's question: Who is my neighbour, receives a *restricted* reply. You must take *reasonable care to avoid* acts or omissions which you can *reasonably foresee* would be *likely* to injure your neighbour. Who then, in law *is* my neighbour? The answer seems to be "persons who are so *closely* and *directly* affected by my act that I ought *reasonably* to have them in *contemplation* as being so affected when I am directing my mind to the acts or omissions which are called in question".' This test has come to be known by lawyers as the 'reasonable foresight' rule. The only valid criticism of the dictum is that people do *not*, of course, direct their minds to their omissions, and indeed, often not even to their acts. Otherwise, after decades of discussion in the cases, with the exception which will be noted, it represents the modern law.

This test, when applied by Lord Atkin to the facts of *Donoghue's Case*, resulted in a decision in favour of the plaintiff (a decision in which the majority of the House of Lords concurred). The facts were that a friend of the plaintiff at a café in Paisley bought a bottle of ginger beer from the proprietor and gave it to the plaintiff. The bottle was opaque, so that its contents could not be seen: in fact, as well as ginger beer, it contained the decomposed remains of a snail. Upon drinking part of the contents the plaintiff became ill, and sued the manufacturer of the ginger beer in negligence. The House of Lords held that the manufacturer ought to have *foreseen the likelihood* that a person in the position of the plaintiff would consume his wares and that he therefore owed her a duty of care to ensure that the bottle should not contain the objectionable matter it did; hence, if this duty had in fact been broken the manufacturer would be liable.

It will be realized that Lord Atkin's test is a *restrictive*, or *limiting* one. I am only to be held liable for my carelessness ('negligence') in cases where two limiting factors are present. The harm inflicted must be *reasonably foreseeable* and the circumstances must be such that there is a *close and direct relationship* between the parties. What in any given case is 'reasonably foreseeable' and what is a 'close and direct' relationship must inevitably be a variable and it has recently become common for the courts to say that it has to be decided upon the basis of what is 'just and reasonable' in the circumstances.

First, as to the requirement of 'foresight'. If there is no reasonable probability that the harm will ensue from the act or omission 'called in question' liability will be excluded. Thus in a House of Lords decision it was held that no one can be expected to anticipate that if he leaves his dog shut up in his car the dog will jump about and break a window, and that a splinter of glass will injure a passer-by. The event was characterized as a 'fantastic possibility' against which no one could be expected to guard.

Second, as to the requirement of 'directness' (or, as it is usually called, 'proximity'). This is such a variable that the operation of it can only be illustrated by examples. In *Home Office v Dorset Yacht Co Ltd* [1970] AC 1004 the Home Office was sued by the plaintiffs for damage done to their yacht by borstal boys. This had happened because prison officers (for whose conduct the Home Office was, in law, responsible) guarding the boys had left them to themselves on Brownsea Island in close proximity to the plaintiff's anchorage. Needless to say, intent upon escape, the boys boarded a handy yacht and, by incompetent manoeuvring, collided with and damaged the plaintiffs' yacht. The physical relationship between the prison officers and the plaintiffs' yacht was both close and direct, indeed, as Lord Morris remarked, 'the risk of such a happening was glaringly obvious'. Hence there was not only reasonable foreseeability of the damage but also 'proximity'. Thus the Home Office was held to owe a duty of care. It might, of course, have been otherwise had the boys succeeded in reaching the mainland without damaging the yacht and then burgled a house 50 miles away. The relationship between the householder and the prison officers would probably have been held not to be 'proximate' or 'direct'. A 'moral code' might 'censure' the officers, and, indeed, such an event might reasonably have been foreseen by them, but, as Lord Atkin said, 'rules of law must arise which limit the range of complainants'. Though the determination of what is a 'direct' relationship is, as has been remarked, a flexible thing, and some American courts would in such circumstances have held the Home Office liable to the householder. The position in *Hill v Chief Constable of West Yorkshire* [1989] 2 All ER 238 differed considerably from that in the *Dorset Yacht Case*. In *Hill's Case* the claim was by a mother on behalf of the estate of her daughter who had been murdered by Sutcliffe, the notorious Yorkshire killer. The daughter's was the last in the series of murders and the basis of claim against the police was negligence, in that, had they conducted their enquiries properly, the killer would have been arrested before he could ever attack Miss Hill at all. This claim could not be allowed. There was no close relationship between the police and Miss Hill. Of course, with Sutcliffe still at large, it could have been foreseen that *some* young woman in West Yorkshire was at risk, but there was nothing to point to Miss Hill in particular; though perhaps it might have been otherwise, at least with regard to proximity, if she had been personally in receipt of threats.

There is, however, an exception to the rule that, foresight and proximity established, a duty of care will arise. Even when these are established, a claim may yet be denied on the ground that to permit it would be contrary to 'policy'. This nebulous concept was, a very long time ago, compared by a judge to an 'unruly horse'. The essence of it is that sometimes considerations other than the need to do justice between the parties must be taken into account. These considerations include the general public interest ('public policy'), expedience, economic considerations and even the dictates of morality. Such factors may operate so as to outbalance the plaintiff's rights and defeat his claim. This balancing is a delicate matter: so delicate that recent dicta at the highest level have suggested that the determination of what is, or is not, 'policy' should be left to the legislature. (A counsel of despair because ultimately the whole body of the common law is based upon judicial assessment of what is socially just and expedient – therein, in fact, lies its strength.) A stock modern example of the 'policy' exception is to be found in *Rondel v Worsley* [1969] 1 AC 191. That was a claim in negligence against a barrister in respect of his conduct of a case in court. It was held, *inter alia*, that a civil action cannot lie against counsel in the conduct of litigation because public policy so demands. In particular, it was said that it is essential to the administration of justice that all concerned in a trial should be free to speak and act without fear of subsequent civil claims. The granting of such an immunity may be thought questionable and the reasons given for it may seem to some unconvincing. But that only illustrates how 'unruly' the 'horse' may be. In *Hill's Case* it was said that, the lack of proximity apart, 'public policy' would also have barred the claim. The reason given was similar; that police investigations would be hampered if they were to be made under a possible threat of actions. It may perhaps be thought that both these cases serve to illustrate the tendency of officialdom to cast a net of immunity around itself. Indeed, before the Crown Proceedings Act 1947 the Crown enjoyed wide immunity from civil actions. But it is interesting that in the *Dorset Yacht Case* it was held that in exercising its prison functions the Home Office enjoyed no such immunity as that later afforded to the police in *Hill's Case*. More recently, the courts have adopted a cautious approach to the issue of the existence of a duty of care in novel cases. In *Murphy v Brentwood District Council* [1991] 2 AC 398, the House of Lords stated that the courts should use an incremental, analogical approach to deciding this issue rather than a wide-ranging general principle of liability. This was also confirmed by the House in the case of *Caparo Industries plc v Dickman* [1990] 1 All ER 568.

*Careless mis-statement* – The proximity test is now generally accepted as the appropriate criterion for determining whether a duty of care is owed. Yet it has often been criticized for its vagueness, and the question of what a person ought to foresee in given circumstances imports, as often as not, social and moral considerations as well as quantitative judgments in terms of time and space. Moreover, the test cannot be applied to all kinds of situations and in some circumstances its application needs to be modified for practical reasons. Acts and words, and the injury that may arise from them respectively, being essentially different, and a certain social freedom in respect of mis-statement being generally accepted, careless *mis-statement* will by no means always give rise to a claim; even though injury could have been foreseen by the maker of the statement. Indeed, until the important decision in *Hedley Byrne & Co Ltd v Heller & Partners Ltd* [1964] AC 465 it was thought to be the law that no claim could be brought upon a careless (as opposed to a fraudulent) mis-statement (at least so long as it caused non-physical loss) under any circumstances unless the maker of it owed a contractual or fiduciary duty to the person injured. In *Hedley Byrne's Case* – where a firm of bankers gave a misleading reference about the affairs of one of their customers to another bank whose customer relied upon it to his loss – the House of Lords disposed of the fallacy that *no* claim will lie upon a careless mis-statement, but stressed that the mere probability of injury arising from a mis-statement will not always be enough to found a claim.

The exact impact of this decision at present remains to be seen and the *ratio decidendi* is by no means clear-cut, but it would appear that careless mis-statement which causes injury whether in an economic or in any other form, will be actionable if the injury was foreseeable at the time when the statement was made; but *if*, and *only if*, the circumstances were such that either the defendant was someone possessed of a special skill, such as a doctor or an accountant or an architect, who made the statement in the course of his business, or *if* the statement was made by someone not possessed of such a skill but who made it in circumstances such as to mislead the plaintiff into thinking that he had it. It would follow that if in the course of a journey by train a solicitor should find himself in company with a stranger who should ask his legal advice, he would be well advised (*being* a solicitor) to warn the stranger that such counsel as he might give would be extra-professional and without liability. And it also followed that in *Mutual Life Citizens Assurance Co Ltd v Evatt* [1971] AC 793 (a Judicial Committee decision), the appellant company was held not liable to one of its policy holders who suffered loss by investing in another company in reliance upon a mis-statement as to the financial stability of that company made by one of the appellant company's officials. For advice about investments is not part of an insurance business, nor had the officer intimated that he was purporting to act as a stockbroker, but this some-what restrictive approach has not been followed by the English courts, preferring to say that the statement need only be made in a business context to fall within the principle (see *Esso v Mardon* [1976] QB 801). In order for the special relationship criterion to be satisfied, the reliance of the plaintiff on the defendant's statement must be reasonable, ie, highly likely (see *Caparo v Dickman* (above ) and *Smith v Bush* [1990] 1 AC 831).

In order to avoid confusion it must be appreciated that the provisions of the Misrepresentation Act 1967 in respect of negligent misrepresentation apply only to representations made in the course of the conclusion of a *contract*. It must now be added that, as appeared when misrepresentation in contract was discussed, the fact that a mis-statement which induces the making of a contract may (alternatively to a claim under the Act), be actionable under *Hedley Byrne*.

## Breach of duty

The essence of a claim in negligence lies in the assertion that, in all the circumstances, the defendant has omitted to take reasonable care to avoid the injury complained of. It might, therefore, be thought that every claim should be decided on its merits and that there would be no need of prior enquiry as to whether a 'duty of care' had arisen. This is true in most cases: there is not any such need. As has been remarked, for example, every driver is aware that he must avoid collisions – and so is every court. The existence of a duty in that situation has long been established: there is no need to establish its existence, and the sole issue is whether it has been broken. But facts are infinitely various and novel situations arise which, as Lord Atkin said, call for a determination whether, in the circumstances, a duty was owed. It is then, and only then, that it has to be determined whether there is, or is not, a 'duty'. And the prior determination of this issue has the merit that if it alone is concentrated upon, and the decision is that it does *not* exist, time and money is saved because the need to call evidence upon all the matters alleged to constitute the negligence in question is avoided.

Once, however, the existence of the 'duty' is assumed or established, the question is 'Has it been broken?' In all the circumstances of the case 'Has the defendant failed to take such care as he ought to have taken to avoid causing the injury of which the plaintiff complains?' 'Has he been *legally* negligent?' Negligence (carelessness) in its legal sense means *failure to take such reasonable care as a reasonable man placed in the position of the defendant ought to have taken*. So the issue becomes 'Has the defendant's conduct failed to reach this standard?' This question can only be decided in the light of all the facts and circumstances of the case.

*Reasonable care* – What is 'reasonable' varies according to the nature of the risk involved and a considerable number of other factors. The higher the risk, the greater the care required. One has to take greater care in handling a bomb than a pin. Where the risk is great one must be more on one's guard than where it is small. Thus 'reasonable foresight' is normally foresight of *probable* dangers to be guarded against, but where there is a *serious* danger to be avoided it may embrace a need to foresee and guard against an *improbable* event. This was the case in *Overseas Tankship (UK) Ltd v Miller SS Co Pty Ltd (The Wagon Mound (No 2))* 1 [1967] AC 617. There the defendants' engineer released oil into the sea (an illegal act in itself) and sparks falling upon it set the sea alight, damaging the plaintiff's vessels. Liability was held to have been established even though the evidence was that the risk that oil floating on the sea would catch light was by no means great but was, nevertheless, appreciable. In the circumstances it was reasonable to require prescience of such an event. And so, through the gamut; from the custody of banana skins to the custody of mice or tigers; the standard of care demanded must vary. But one must use *some* care even with one's mice. Further as was above remarked, there may be other considerations to be taken into account than the nature of the risk involved. For example, I must take greater care in my dealings with blind people or children than need be taken in my dealings with other adults. In case of *necessity*, such as may arise where I rush to the rescue when a house is on fire, I may be allowed to dispense with normal precautions. The *public interest* may even *require* me to take an obvious risk. The time has long since gone when a flag-man walked in front of a train, and trains are required to go faster and faster. Though this gives rise to serious danger, from expedience, it cannot in itself be treated as a failure to use reasonable care. The *cost*, physical or economic, of preventing the injury may also have to be weighed in the scale of what it is reasonable for the defendant to do. One is not required to close down one's factory merely because circumstances have arisen (such as flooding) which may possibly endanger an employee. And so on with limitless variations of facts.

*The reasonable man* – The care must be judged by the standard of the 'reasonable man', once described judicially as the 'man on the Clapham omnibus' – forsooth the juryman whose duty it used to be to decide the question of 'reasonableness'. This was, however, an over-simplification. In this context the 'reasonable man' of the law is in fact the reasonable man placed in *all the circumstances* of the defendant. Thus the bricklayer will be judged by the standards of the reasonable bricklayer, the driver by those of the reasonable driver, the engineer by those of the reasonable engineer, and the doctor by those of the reasonable doctor. Thus, for example, the modern rule in respect of negligence on the part of a doctor or a surgeon is that the standard of his performance must come up to a standard accepted as proper by a responsible body of medical men skilled in the particular thing he is doing. He will not, on the other hand, be guilty of negligence simply because some other body of medical opinion may require a different standard.

It remains to be added that at common law, as under the old Roman law, *imperitia culpae adnumerator* – lack of experience is a kind of negligence. Thus if an unskilled person undertakes something which requires special skill he will be held responsible if he fails to attain the standard of a person who has such skill. This may seem a harsh rule, but in the civil law the loss to the plaintiff has to be considered as well as the burden cast upon the defendant. Thus it has been held that a learner driver will be held to the standard of care required of a qualified driver. Even here a story may not be amiss. It is said that a visitor from China who was in fact a bricklayer once induced a famous hospital to allow him to perform brain operations. Strangely, he performed them successfully.

## Causation

Assume now that there is a duty of care and that that duty has been broken; one more factor beyond proof of actual damage, remains before the plaintiff's case is established. That factor, the first to be established in point of proof; is that the injury must result from, or be *caused* by, the breach of duty. Whether or not a particular injury is the cause of a wrong is usually an obvious question which can be answered at once; and in all torts the element of *causation* is usually *assumed* either to exist or not to exist, in which latter case there can be no liability. But sometimes, and particularly in negligence cases, the causal element creates difficulty. Thus a '*novus actus interveniens*' (an independent intervening act) or a '*nova causa interveniens*' (independent intervening cause) may, as it were, isolate the defendant's wrong from the damage suffered by the plaintiff – as where, B having carelessly lit a fire, C *intentionally* spreads it to A's land, or an earthquake unforeseeably occurs and brings about a similar result. And the plaintiff's *own* act or fault may similarly prove, upon examination of all the facts, to be the true cause of the injury rather than the defendant's apparent wrongdoing. Thus in *McWilliams v Sir William Arrol & Co Ltd* [1962] 1 All ER 623, a man was killed by falling from a steel tower and it was alleged that the death was due to (ie caused by) the negligence of his employers in failing to supply a safety-belt; whereas examination of all the facts showed that, although it was true that they had failed to supply one, the essence of the matter really was that even if they had done so the deceased would not have worn the belt. So the situation was that it was not the negligence of the defendant employers which caused the death but the behaviour of the deceased himself, which was the real *cause* of his death, and accordingly the employers were not liable.

Where it is doubtful whether the defendant caused the loss the burden of proving that he did lies on the plaintiff.

## Damage

Normally, therefore, in an action for negligence, the plaintiff must prove that the defendant owed a duty, that he breached the duty and that the plaintiff was *damaged* in some way as the result of the breach. 'Damage' includes physical injury, mental suffering , damage to property, etc, but, subject to exceptions, a purely *economic* loss – such as loss of profit – is not recoverable unless it results from some physical damage caused by the negligence. Thus in *Spartan Steel and Alloys Ltd v Martin & Co (Contractors) Ltd* [1973] QB 27, it was held that where the defendants, through their negligence, caused a stoppage of electric power in the plaintiff's mill the latter could recover for loss of profit arising from physical damage to a 'melt' in their furnace (a physical loss) caused by the stoppage, but not for loss of profit arising because the smelting of further steel (a purely economic loss) had to be postponed. This arbitrary distinction is, however, subject to a number of exceptions. For instance, economic loss alone is recoverable under the *Hedley Byrne* principle and it is also recoverable in cases where the relationship of the parties, though not strictly contractual, is closely akin to a contractual one.

## Burden of proof: *res ipsa loquitur*

It is for the plaintiff to adduce sufficient evidence to establish a *prima facie* case of negligence. But there are certain situations in which '*res ipsa loquitur*' ('the thing speaks for itself'). These arise when the facts are such (as where the cause of the injury lies exclusively within the defendant's control) that it is difficult for the plaintiff to prove the negligence, but the facts point so strongly to it that the court may find in the plaintiff's favour unless the defendant can provide some explanation to rebut the presumption of negligence. If, however, the defendant does give such an explanation it is then for the plaintiff to *prove* negligence affirmatively if he can. *Byrne v Boadle* (1863) 2 H & C 722, is a stock example of a '*res ipsa*' situation. The plaintiff was walking along the street when a barrel of flour fell upon him from an open door in an upper floor of the defendant's warehouse. It was held that the proof of these facts raised such a strong presumption of negligence that the case could go to the jury without any evidence being adduced as to how the accident occurred.

## Contributory negligence

Before the Law Reform (Contributory Negligence) Act 1945 it was a complete defence to an action of negligence for a defendant to show that the plaintiff's own negligence had *contributed* to cause the damage of which he complained. For instance, if in a collision between two cyclists it was shown that the defendant was riding with his eyes shut, but that the collision had been partly caused by the fact that the plaintiff's bicycle had defective brakes, the plaintiff could recover nothing. The Act altered the law. It provides (s 1(1)) that '*Where any person suffers damage as the result partly of his own fault and partly of any other person . . . a claim in respect of that damage shall not be defeated by reason of the fault of the person suffering the damage, but the damages recoverable in respect thereof shall be reduced to such extent as the court thinks just and equitable having regard to the claimant's share in the responsibility for the damage.*' Thus, in the example given, the plaintiff's claim might no longer fail entirely, but his damages might be reduced by, say, one third of the sum which he would have obtained had he not been at fault at all.

Having considered the more important of the principles underlying the tort of negligence in general, mention should now be made of special rules which govern its application in two common kinds of situation; first in relation to the employer's obligations to his employees and secondly in relation to the duties owed by occupiers of land, premises and permanent structures to other people who they permit to use them.

## Employers' liability

*Common law* – The *employer's* duty has broadly been judicially defined as requiring him to '*take reasonable care for his servant's safety in all the circumstances of the case*'. But this is a flexible definition and it really tells us no more than that he must not be negligent towards the servant. Consequently the cases show that the obligation can be expressed more specifically, by breaking it down into a threefold aspect; namely, a duty to provide *competent staff, adequate plant and material, a safe system of work*. The employee who is injured as the result of his employer's failure to make reasonable provision in any of these respects will have a right of action. This is a field in which there is prolific litigation and no attempt can be made to summarize the effect of it here – especially because the decision in every case depends upon all the circumstances. But it must be stressed that all that is required of the employer is 'reasonable care'; he is not an insurer of his servant's safety, nor does he even owe him that obviously high degree of care that a teacher owes to a pupil. For instance if the employer supplies a suitable tool for a particular piece of work and an experienced employee chooses to use an unsuitable one, thereby bringing injury upon himself, he will have no claim.

*Statutory* – It is also important to remark that in many kinds of employment special statutory duties are cast upon the employer by statute, eg the Health and Safety at Work, etc Act 1974 and regulations thereunder. While some of these duties are 'strict ' others are based upon lack of care; and which of these things they are depends upon the construction of each enactment. In the former case proof of breach of the duty – assuming that the breach caused the injury – is all that is required to establish liability, while in the latter negligence must be proved. And it is also possible that where injury arises from a breach of duty there was also negligence under the ordinary rules of the common law; so that it is usual to plead alternatively both breach of the statutory duty and common law negligence.

## Occupiers' liability

We must now consider the obligations owed to *visitors* (and their property) by *occupiers* of land or premises or of fixed or movable structures, such as vessels, vehicles or aircraft. The law on this subject is principally regulated by the Occupiers' Liability Act 1957 (OLA).

'Visitors' in this context include people who come upon the property either in the occupier's interest (eg plumbers) or in their own (eg guests) or in the exercise of some right conferred by law (eg users of public parks), and also people who enter as the result of a contract between the occupier and some third party (eg where a landlord retains a common staircase in his own control but contracts to allow his tenant's visitors to use it).

The occupier's obligation concerns '*dangers due to the state of the premises or structures or things done or omitted to be done on them*' (OLA, s 1(1)) and it is a duty to '*take such care as in all the circumstances of the case* is reasonable to see that the visitor will be reasonably safe in using the premises *for the purpose for which he is permitted by the occupier to be there*' (OLA, s 2 (2) – authors italics). This duty the section terms the '*common duty of care*'. The words italicized are important. In the first place what is 'reasonable' may vary according to the visitor: a fence at a particular spot may be necessary to protect a child but not an adult, a warning that a rubber connection is perished may be necessary in the case of a casual guest, but not in the case of a gas-fitter. In the second place the visitor who abuses his invitation by going where he has not been invited (as by breaking uninvited into a locked room) ceases to be a visitor and becomes a trespasser.

Further, what is required of the occupier is no more than 'reasonable' care. Hence he will not be liable for the negligence of an independent contractor (as for instance where such a contractor carelessly fixes a chandelier which falls upon a guest at dinner) provided that he has taken reasonable steps to satisfy himself that the contractor is reasonably competent and that his work has been properly executed. Moreover, the occupier may absolve himself by giving reasonably effective warning of dangers (such as low beams), and he will not be liable for injuries from risks willingly accepted by the visitor – as where the visitor, seeing a rotten floor board, knowingly takes the risk of jumping on it.

Mention must also be made of a special class of people, those who enter for a purpose which *primarily envisages the use* of the premises of structures: hotel patrons, for instance, or users of racecourse stands. Such people enter under *contract* and consequently the particular contract may contain special terms. But the OLA, s 5(1) provides that in the absence of such terms the occupier will owe to such visitors the 'common duty of care'. There are, however, certain exceptions to this rule and the most important of them concerns contracts '*for the hire of, or the carriage for reward of persons or goods in any vehicle . . . or other means of transport*'. (OLA, s 5(3)). Here, apart from special terms in the contract, the occupier's duty remains what it was at common law, namely to ensure that the vehicle is as fit for the purpose for which it is to be used as reasonable care and skill *on the part of anyone* can make it. This is a burdensome duty, for in this kind of case the occupier may, for example, be held liable for the carelessness of an independent contractor though he was himself in no way at fault; yet, on the other hand, he will not be liable if he can prove that *no one* was at fault.

The Act was only concerned with lawful visitors; it did not apply to other entrants, and, in particular, to unwanted visitors – trespassers. There, thus, remained special, rather nebulous, common law rules about the duty owed to them. However, this position has now been altered by the Occupiers' Liability Act 1984 which provides that the occupier owes a duty to such visitors 'in respect of any risk of their suffering injury on the premises by reason of any danger due to the state of the premises or of things done or omitted to be done on them'. But the scope of this liability is limited by the requirements that the occupier must be aware of the danger or have reasonable grounds to believe that it exists, that he must know or have reasonable grounds to believe that the visitor is in the vicinity of the danger, and that the risk is one against which he may reasonably be expected to offer the visitor some protection. The duty is a 'duty to take such care as is reasonable in all the circumstances of the case to see that (the visitor) does not suffer injury on the premises by reason of the danger concerned'. The occupier will not be liable in respect of risks of which he gives proper warning, nor in respect of risks willingly accepted by the intruder.

## 2  TRESPASS

It has already been explained that a trespass is a 'direct and forcible' injury. There are three forms of trespass: trespass to the person, trespass to land, and trespass to goods.

*Trespass to the person* may take the form of an actual battery or of a technical assault (this is assault and battery, coincident with the crime). Until recently all trespasses to the person were, in keeping with the historical development of the law which has been described, like other trespasses, actionable *per se*, ie, without proof of *actual* damage, and the burden of proving that the trespass was justified (as by inevitable accident) lay upon the defendant. But the law on this point has become complicated since the Court of Appeal decision in *Fowler v Lanning* [1959] 1 QB 426. The facts were that (no doubt unintentionally) B shot A during a shooting party and A claimed in trespass, alleging only, as under the pre-existing law he was entitled to do, the fact of the shooting, and leaving it to B to *justify* his conduct – as by proof that it *was* an accident. The court held, contrary to the previous law, that A could have no claim unless he could *establish* in B one of two things; either *intention* or *negligence*. And in a later case the new position was clarified. Where the injury is direct and *intention* is established then the claim will be in *trespass to the person*, with the result that, as before, actual damage need not be proved and the damages (as before) may be merely nominal – though of course if the circumstances so warrant they may be substantial or even aggravated. Where negligence only is established the claim *no longer lies in trespass* and the tort will be *negligence*, not trespass at all; actual damage and *lack of care* having consequently to be *proved* by the plaintiff.

Whether this improves the law is open to doubt; for surely if I hit you, you are entitled to demand that I justify the blackness of your eye? It should be added that, at present at any rate, it is not thought that the *Fowler v Lanning* ruling affects other forms of trespass; it is to be assumed that they remain actionable *per se*, without proof of special damage and that the burden of justifying them remains upon the defendant.

*Trespass to land* is committed when one person enters upon land in the possession of another without lawful justification, or remains upon it after his authority to be upon it has been revoked. It may also be committed by merely throwing or putting things upon the land.

## 3   FALSE IMPRISONMENT

Where one person falsely (ie unlawfully) restricts the physical freedom of another, the other will be entitled to bring an action for the tort of false imprisonment. Imprisonment, in the sense of actual incarceration, is not essential for the commission of this tort; what is required is that there should have been complete restriction of the plaintiff's liberty of action by the defendant. Thus, though arrest may sometimes be lawful, even without a warrant, where an *unlawful* arrest is made, this will amount to a false imprisonment; for while under arrest, even though no physical force be used – but, for example, mere threats or persuasion – the movements of the person arrested are under the control of his captor. But, for the purposes of this action, the control must have been complete, not merely partial. Thus if I prevent you from passing along a path by placing an obstacle across it, this obstruction may be a nuisance, but I shall not be liable for false imprisonment; for, if you wish, you are free to make a detour, or to go back the way you came: your liberty is only inhibited in one direction.

A further restriction upon the competence of this action is that it lies only in respect of the active imposition of restraint. Thus if a man voluntarily imprisons himself the law will not require others – at any rate apart from a contractual or other special duty to do so – to release him upon his demand. For instance, in *Herd v Weardale Coal Co* [1915] AC 67, a miner sued his employers for false imprisonment. After a dispute had arisen, while the man in question was in the pit, he demanded to be taken to the surface before his shift was due to end. The employers' agents at first refused to grant him the use of the cage, and he was thus stranded, idle in the pit for some 20 minutes. His claim for damages for this detention failed: he had entered the pit of his own accord, and his employers were under no duty to convey him to the surface until the end of the shift.

The action for false imprisonment helps to vindicate the constitutional right to personal freedom; but, of course, it is small solace to a prisoner to know that once he is released he may have a right to a civil action, and it will be remembered that everyone who is imprisoned, otherwise than by due process of law, may secure immediate release by means of the writ of *habeas corpus*.

Finally, it should be noted that although assault usually accompanies false imprisonment, the two causes of action are distinct; for it is possible to imprison a person without committing an assault, as where one person locks another in a room.

## 4    WRONGFUL INTERFERENCE WITH GOODS

Formerly there were three torts which inhibited interference with other people's goods. The Torts (Interference with Goods) Act 1977, however, abolished the time-honoured action of detinue, thereby substantially reducing the number to two: namely conversion and trespass to goods. ('Substantially', because the Act (s 1) also recognizes that 'interference with goods' may also include 'negligence so far as it results in damage to goods . . . and any other tort so far as it results in (such damage)'.)

### Conversion

Conversion is in a sense (but only in a sense) the civil counterpart of the crime of theft. But it rests upon a different basis, since it is committed when a person deals with the goods of another in such a way as to show that he calls the *title* of the other in question. Clearly the most obvious form of conversion is therefore the wilful taking of another person's goods. But this is not the only form. For example, a man who innocently acquires goods from a thief (who can give him no title to them) will usually be liable in conversion if he does anything which affects the title. Thus, in *Hollins v Fowler* (1875) LR 7 HL 757, X obtained cotton from F by fraud. X sold the cotton to H (a cotton broker) who re-sold it to Y, receiving only broker's commission for the deal. It was held that H was guilty of conversion; for he had purported to deal in the title to the goods, even though he was ignorant of F's rights.

The person entitled to claim in conversion is the person in possession of the goods or the person who, though not in possession, is entitled to the immediate possession of them at the time of the wrong. This means that anyone in possession can claim, like the chimney sweep boy in *Armory v Delamirie* (1722) 1 Stra 505, who found a gem and claimed against a goldsmith to whom he had entrusted it for valuation. And, by contrast, the owner (such as the bailor of goods to another during the continuance of a contract for the hire of them to the other) may not be entitled to sue.

**Trespass to goods**
This is direct interference with goods in the possession of another (who is the person entitled to sue). Such interference will usually be physical, as by touching or removing the goods: but it may also be a trespass to drive another person's cattle away, without actually touching them. And it is thus possible to commit a trespass to goods without converting them. Thus in *Bushell v Miller* (1718) 1 Stra 128, a porter at a custom house put aside from their proper place some goods belonging to another: he forgot to replace them and they were subsequently lost. Assuming that he had not been negligent, he could not be liable in conversion, but he could in trespass for the mere act of *removing* them.

It should be noted that by the Torts (Interference with Goods) Act 1977, s 11(1) contributory negligence is no defence to a claim in conversion or for intentional interference with goods.

## 5 DEFAMATION

Defamation may broadly be defined as '*the publication of a statement which tends to lower a person in the estimation of right-thinking members of society generally*'.

The tort of defamation is divided into two major categories, *libel* and *slander*. A *libel* is defamatory matter which is published in some permanent form. The usual form is *writing or printing*. Permanence being the essence of the matter, however, writing is not essential: for example, it has been held that the inclusion of defamatory statements upon the sound-track of a film may constitute a libel, and an effigy at Madame Tussaud's has also been held to be libellous. Further, under the provisions of the Defamation Act 1952, words and images broadcast for general reception by wireless or television are now treated as publications in a permanent form, and the Theatres Act 1968, s 4, applies the same principle to verbal statements and gestures in the public performance of a play. *Slander* is the publication of defamatory matter in a transient form, normally in the guise of an oral statement.

It is important to distinguish the two classes of defamation because, whereas a libel is actionable (*per se*) *without proof of special damage*, slander is (subject to exceptions) only actionable if the plaintiff can show that he has actually suffered damage. Moreover, whereas libel is a crime, as well as a tort, slander (except where the words spoken tend directly to create a breach of the peace, or are blasphemous, obscene, seditious, or reflect upon the due administration of justice) is *only* a tort. The exceptional circumstances in which slander is actionable *per se* are: (i) imputations of crime: provided that it is not punishable merely by a fine; (ii) imputations that the plaintiff is suffering from a contagious disease calculated to cause him to be shunned by society; (iii) by the Slander of Women Act 1891, imputations of unchastity in a woman; (iv) by the Defamation Act 1952, s 2, imputations disparaging the plaintiff in any office, calling, trade or business held or carried on by him at the time of publication of the slander.

For the purpose of the law of torts, in order for a defamatory statement to be actionable it must be published not merely to the person defamed, but *to some third party*. The essence of the plaintiff's claim is that he has suffered damage through loss of reputation; and there can be no loss of reputation where the *plaintiff alone* knows of the statement. In the case of the *crime* of libel it is otherwise, for the purpose of punishing libels is to prevent breaches of the peace, and the party defamed is the most likely person to commit a breach of the peace if the libellous statement is communicated to him.

The question whether a statement is defamatory is one for the judge to consider in the first place. If, by the test defined in the first paragraph of this section, he decides that it *cannot* be regarded as defamatory, he must withdraw the case from the jury (defamation being a tort in relation to which juries are still employed). If the judge decides that the statement is *capable* of being regarded as defamatory he must leave the question of 'libel or no libel' for the *jury* to decide.

At common law a defamatory statement is actionable even though it be made entirely innocently. 'Liability for libel', it has been judicially declared, 'does not depend upon the intention of the defamer; but on the fact of defamation'. At common law it was enough for the plaintiff to establish that the defendant made and published the statement and that it was defamatory; if he could do this he did not need to concern himself with the defendant's state of mind. Thus in the leading case of *Hulton (E) & Co v Jones* [1910] AC 20 the defendants published a fictional story about one 'Artemus Jones', described as a churchwarden of Peckham, who, so the story went, indulged in certain undignified frolics at the Dieppe races. A barrister named Artemus Jones sued in libel, alleging that people thought the tale referred to him. The defendants were held liable, though it was assumed that they neither knew, nor had reason to know, of the very existence of the real Artemus Jones. So also in *Newstead v London Express Newspaper Ltd* [1940] 1 KB 377, it was stated in a newspaper that 'Harold Newstead, thirty-year-old Camberwell man' had been convicted of bigamy. The statement was true of a barman in the Camberwell district, but not of the plaintiff, a hairdresser, of the same name and age, to whom the defendants were not adverting, and of whose very existence they did not know. It was held that the plaintiff could recover from the defendants.

This is a harsh rule, and it is now modified by the Defamation Act 1952, s 4, which provides that if the person who publishes (ie makes or otherwise disseminates) an *'innocently'* defamatory statement makes an *'offer of amends'*, in a prescribed form, coupled, amongst other requirements, with an offer to publish an apology, he shall be entitled to the following relief. If the offer be *accepted*, it will form a *bar to an action* by the party aggrieved, though the High Court may award him certain costs and an allowance for expenses reasonably incurred. If the offer be *refused*, provided that it was made as soon as reasonably practicable, and has not since been withdrawn, proof of the 'innocence' of the statement will form a *defence* should the aggrieved party sue. Statements are to be deemed to be *'innocent'* (s 4(5)) if (a) the publisher did not intend to publish them of and concerning the plaintiff, and did not know of circumstances by which they might be understood to refer to him (as in *Hulton v Jones*); or if (b) the words were not defamatory on the face of them, and the publisher did not know of circumstances by virtue of which they might be understood to be defamatory of the party aggrieved.

There are three special defences to an action for defamation:

*(i) Justification* – The defendant may escape liability if he can prove that the statement was substantially 'justified' (true). No one can claim that his reputation has been damaged by the publication of the truth. Here again, the *crime* of libel differs from the tort: it is not usually a defence to a criminal prosecution for libel to prove that the statement was true.

*(ii) Privilege* – A defamatory statement made upon a 'privileged' occasion is not actionable. The reason for this is that the occasion is one on which the need for freedom of expression outweighs the right to an unblemished reputation. There are two main classes of privileged occasions: occasions of *absolute* privilege and occasions of *qualified* privilege.

*Absolute* privilege gives complete freedom of speech, for example, in relation to parliamentary and judicial proceedings. Where it exists this protection from actions for defamation is absolute in the sense that no action will lie in respect of any statement made even if it be made *maliciously* (ie effectively, intentionally). It may be thought that such a privilege is, perhaps, too wide. *Qualified* privilege arises mainly in cases where the maker of a statement is under a duty to make it, and the person to whom it is made has a reciprocal interest in receiving it. The best example of an occasion of this kind is where a person, upon request, gives a reference to a prospective employer. It also covers fair and accurate reports of judicial and other proceedings and certain kinds of reports made in newspapers. The difference between absolute and qualified privilege is that the latter will not avail the defendant if he has acted *maliciously*. That is to say, he has acted for some reason (such as spite) other than a desire to give honest information. For it is only the honesty of the opinion that attracts the privilege.

*(iii)  Fair comment* – Statements of opinion, as well as statements of fact, may be defamatory; yet it is clear that, in the public interest, criticism should be free as long as it is fair. Hence it is a defence to an action for defamation to show that the alleged defamatory statement was a *'fair comment'* honestly made upon a matter of *public interest*. 'Public interest' is a wide term; it covers the behaviour of all public men, such as Minister of State and local officials, or anyone who performs any public function. It also covers the works of people, such as authors and artists, who invite criticism by publication of their works.

In order to acquire protection the comment must satisfy four conditions. First, it must be a statement of *opinion*, not an assertion of fact. Second, it must be *'fair'*, ie it must be an opinion, however misguided, which is honestly held: 'criticism', said Collins, MR, 'cannot be used as cloak for mere invective'. Third, it must *not* be *'malicious'*, ie it must not be *distorted* by reason of some improper motive, such as spite or mercenary considerations. Fourth, it must not reflect upon the *moral* character of the person criticized.

## 6  NUISANCE

The word 'nuisance' is connected with the Latin *'nocumentum'* (harm). Nuisances are divided into two main classes: public nuisances and private nuisances.

A *public nuisance* is a *crime* indictable at common law and it is also restrainable by injunction at the suit of the Attorney-General. Examples of public nuisance are keeping a common gaming-house and obstructing highways and rendering them dangerous . If, however, any person suffers *special* damage as the result of a public nuisance, over and above the harm caused to the public at large, he may bring an action in *tort* against the person who creates the nuisance. Thus, in *Benjamin v Storr* (1874) LR 9 CP 400, B kept a coffee-house in Rose Street, Covent Garden. S, for the purposes of his business, kept horses and vans standing outside the coffee-house all day long. This caused an obstruction to the highway. B complained that he suffered special damage because the vans obstructed the light to the windows of his coffee-house and he had to incur expense in keeping gas lights burning all day. He further alleged that the smell from the excreta of S's horses made the premises objectionable and deterred customers. It was held that these facts amongst others, constituted special damage which would entitle B to maintain an action against S.

A *private nuisance* is solely a *tort*. It is in essence a wrong (other than a direct act of trespass) which incommodes a person in the use and enjoyment of his land, and it also embraces certain injuries and inconveniences caused to users of the highway. There are two classes of private nuisances: (a) Nuisances which damage the plaintiff's enjoyment of an easement (see Chapter 11), such as a right of way, or his enjoyment of a natural right, such as his right to have his land supported by the land of his neighbour. Nuisances of this class are generally actionable by the plaintiff *without the necessity of proving any actual damage*; (b) Nuisances which arise when obnoxious things, such as smoke, water, smell, vibrations, animals or the branches or roots of trees are allowed to escape or obtrude upon the plaintiff's land. Nuisances of this class are only actionable if the plaintiff can prove that they have *actually* incommoded him *in the enjoyment of his land.* These are the commonest form of nuisances, but there are so many others that it would be idle to attempt to enumerate them here.

Further, the law of nuisance is a branch of the law which is preeminently governed by the rule of 'give and take': we must all bear certain reasonable inconveniences from the activities of our neighbours, and the law takes this commonplace consideration into account. The cases, therefore, show that a variety of factors have to be weighed in determining the incidence of liability. The following examples may be given.

First, in nuisance (by way of exception to the general rule – p 305) the presence of '*malice*', in the sense of improper motive, such as spite or ill-will, may sometimes be a determining factor in liability. But an important distinction has to be observed. Where the law gives a person a legal *right* to do something no amount of ill-will in the doing of it will make that right in to a wrong. This was the position in *Bradford Corpn v Pickles* [1895] AC 587. Water percolated in undefined channels beneath Pickles' land and flowed thence to land belonging to the appellant corporation. The corporation used this water for their city supply. Actuated by a desire to force the corporation to buy his land at his own price, Pickles obstructed the flow of water by sinking shafts into it. The corporation sought an injunction to restrain him from his mercenary behaviour. It was held that no injunction would lie, because a previous decision of the House of Lords had laid down that whereas it is a nuisance to obstruct the flow of water when it runs from one's own land to another's in defined channels it is no nuisance to extract merely percolating water – indeed, if this were the law it would provide a disincentive to land drainage. This kind of obstruction was therefore something which Pickles had a *right* to do; as Lord Halsbury, LC said, what he did was 'a lawful act, however ill the motive might be' and he therefore 'had a right to do it'. And yet, it may be asked, 'Suppose Pickles' activity had not (as clearly it was) been prompted by a commercial motive, but by reason of a spiteful desire to deprive the people of Bradford of their water supply? *Should* his 'right' have been protected?' In granting 'rights' the courts should take account of *all* the circumstances. People must be free to bargain on their own terms, but ought they to be free to inflict intentional injuries upon others? That is an issue that Lord Halsbury and his successors have usually tended to evade.

On the other hand the law often concedes to people the *privilege* of doing things without conferring upon them a positive right; as for example the 'right' to shoot on their own land. Here the 'right' is something which *may* be done, but *only* if it *is done lawfully*, and the element of 'malice' may render the activity unlawful (and therefore a nuisance) where, in the absence of 'malice' it would have been lawful. Thus in *Hollywood Silver Fox Farm Ltd v Emmett* [1936] 1 All ER 825, the plaintiffs were awarded damages against the defendant who had ordered his son (on account of differences between him and the plaintiffs) to fire guns on his (the defendant's) land as near as possible to the plaintiff's land in order that, as actually occurred, the plaintiffs' vixen might miscarry. Had there been no evidence of spite, and had the damage been caused without malicious intent – merely as incidental, for example, to a shooting party – the plaintiffs would have had no claim.

In the second place, a person who is abnormally *sensitive*, or who owns property peculiarly liable to damage, must put up with inconveniences which cause harm to him by reason only of this exceptional sensitivity. Thus in *Robinson v Kilvert* (1889) 41 Ch D 88, the plaintiff occupied the upper part of a house and the defendant the lower. For the purpose of his business the defendant had to use a furnace, and the heat thus generated damaged some brown paper which the plaintiff (a paper merchant) had in store. This paper was exceptionally sensitive to heat and ordinary paper would not have been damaged under the circumstances. For that reason it was held that the defendant's activities did not constitute a nuisance.

In the third place, though a single act may probably amount to a nuisance – as where I throw a banana skin onto the pavement and you slip upon it and are injured – the *duration* or *repetition* of an obnoxious activity may sometimes (upon the principle of 'give and take') be relevant in determining whether that activity constitutes a nuisance. This proposition may be illustrated by contrasting the case of *Castle v St Augustine's Links Ltd* (1922) 38 TLR 615, with *Stone v Bolton* [1950] 1 KB 201 (reversed in the House of Lords, [1951] AC 850, upon other grounds). In the former case the plaintiff was a taxi driver who lost his eye when a golf ball was sliced onto the road from a tee on the defendant's course. In the latter case the plaintiff was on the highway near a cricket ground when she was injured by a ball hit out of the ground. In the former case the plaintiff was held entitled to recover in nuisance because balls had *constantly* been driven onto the road at the place; the tee constituted a continuing danger. In the latter case the plaintiff failed to recover in nuisance because balls had *seldom* before been known to be hit onto the road; the playing of cricket in the ground did not therefore constitute a continuing danger.

Private, as opposed to public, nuisance is essentially a remedy for an occupier of land, the right to sue inheres in him *qua* occupier; no one else is entitled to it, save a reversioner (p 355) who has a prospective interest in the land, and may therefore sue if the nuisance be such as to cause permanent injury. Thus, in *Malone v Laskey* [1907] 2 KB 141, where vibrations from an engine upon adjoining premises caused a cistern to fall upon and injure the wife of an occupier, it was held that she had no right of action in nuisance: she had no proprietary or possessory interest, actual or prospective, in the land. But it must be added that as the law *now* stands the wife might have had a claim in *negligence* (see also now *Khorasandjian v Bush* [1993] QB 722).

A person will be liable in an action for nuisance if he either *creates* the nuisance, or, being in a position to abate (stop) it, he *permits it to continue* once he knows that it exists upon his premises. Thus in *Leakey v National Trust* [1980] QB 485 it was held that where the defendants permitted a hillside to collapse through weathering upon the plaintiff's land they were liable for the damage caused. People will not, however, be liable for nuisances which arise upon their land in such circumstances that they could not reasonably be expected to have known of them. Thus, in *Caminer v Northern and London Investment Trust Ltd* [1951] AC 88, an elm tree, growing on land of which the defendants were the lessees, fell onto the highway injuring the plaintiff and damaging his car. The tree was 130 years old and was affected by elm butt rot. While the tree was still growing the defendants could not by reasonable examination have discovered the existence of this disease, it was held that they were not liable.

## 7   THE RULE IN RYLANDS V FLETCHER

Liability under the Rule in *Rylands v Fletcher* (1868) LR 3 HL 330, has been selected for mention because it is an example (there are others) of what is called '*strict*' liability, ie it is an instance of the imposition of tortious liability independent of any 'fault' or negligence on the part of the wrongdoer.

The facts of this case were the following. The defendant wanted to construct a reservoir upon his land. He employed an independent contractor to do the work. Unknown to the defendant there was a disused shaft of a coal mine under the site of the reservoir, which communicated with an adjoining mine belonging to the plaintiff. Through the contractor's negligence, this shaft was not discovered, and as a consequence, when the reservoir was filled, the plaintiff's mine was flooded and he suffered damage. He brought an action against the defendant. It was held that, despite the defendant's innocence, the plaintiff could succeed.

When the case (which eventually reached the House of Lords) came before the Court of Exchequer Chamber, Blackburn, J propounded the doctrine which has now become known as the Rule in *Rylands v Fletcher:* 'the person who for his own purposes brings on his lands and collects and keeps there anything likely to do mischief if it escapes, must keep it in at his peril, and if he does not do so, is prima facie answerable for all the damage which is the natural consequence of its escape' (LR 1 Exch 265, 279–280).

This proposition was accepted by the House of Lords, and it has since been acted upon as a rule of law. Lord Cairns, LC, however, added to it a rider which is now treated as a part of it. He said that, in order for the Rule to apply, the defendant's use of the land must be '*non-natural*'. The courts have found difficulty in defining what is a 'non-natural' user. For example, *Rylands v Fletcher* itself decides that the collection of a large quantity of water upon one's land is 'non-natural'; on the other hand in *Read v Lyons* (below) Viscount Simon doubted whether the making of munitions for the Government in a factory in time of war does amount to a 'non-natural' user. The truth seems to be that the distinction between 'natural' and 'non-natural' user must be one which depends, as Lord Porter said in the same case, upon 'all the circumstances of the time and place'.

Two points require notice. First, the Rule applies to things '*likely to do mischief if they escape*'. Whether a thing is one which is 'mischievous' raises a question. The following things have, among others, been held to fall within the rule: gas, electricity, fumes, rusty wire from a fence, explosions, a flag-pole. But this list is capable of expansion as fresh circumstances arise. Second, in order to give rise to '*Rylands v Fletcher*' liability there must be an 'escape'. This point was made clear in *Read v Lyons & Co Ltd* [1947] AC 156. The plaintiff was an inspector of munitions in the defendant's factory in wartime. While she was on the premises a shell exploded, and she was injured, but the explosion could not be attributed to negligence on the part of anybody. It was held that the plaintiff could not recover under the Rule in *Rylands v Fletcher*, for her injury was not caused by anything that had 'escaped' from the premises. (It was further indicated, though not decided, that, in any event, liability under the Rule ought not to apply in the case of claims for injuries to the *person*; though under the existing law it probably does.)

*Defences* – Though this liability may still be regarded as 'strict' (see below, *Cambridge Water Co Ltd v Eastern Counties Leather plc* [1994] 2 AC 264), and exists despite the absence of intention or lack of care, there are, nevertheless, several defences to an action under the Rule in *Rylands v Fletcher*. The following should be noted:

*(i)* Where the plaintiff has consented to permit the defendant to bring the mischievous thing upon his property there can be no liability under the Rule; though the defendant may of course be liable if he has been negligent. Thus, where a house is divided into flats and water escapes from a cistern in an upper flat, and damages a lower one, the lower owner will normally have no action under the Rule: the cistern being kept for the mutual benefit of both parties, the lower owner will be taken to have consented to the collection of the water.

*(ii)* Where the escape is due to the plaintiff's own fault he will have no action. For instance, if a man were to remove a retaining-wall, so as to cause his neighbour's pond to overflow onto his own land, he could not invoke the Rule.

*(iii)* Where the escape is due to the wrongful act of a stranger there is no liability. Thus in *Box v Jubb* (1879) 4 Ex D 76, a third party caused the

defendant's reservoir to overflow onto the plaintiff's land by emptying his own reservoir into a stream which fed the defendant's. The defendant was not liable.

*(iv)* Whereas it is no defence for the defendant to plead that the escape was 'accidental', it is a defence for him to show that it was due to an 'Act of God' which he could not reasonably have foreseen and provided against. An 'Act of God' is an event, such as a storm, which produces consequences independently of human agency. It is clear that not all Acts of God will excuse, but only such as are exceptional and cannot be guarded against. The defence has only succeeded in one reported case (and that of doubtful authority) where some artificial dams in a stream were washed away by a storm which was described by witnesses as the 'heaviest in human memory'.

*(v)* Where the mischievous substance is collected by the defendant under statutory authority he will not normally be liable in the absence of negligence. For example, where a local authority has statutory power to carry a substance such as water or gas in a main, it will not normally be liable, in the absence of negligence, if the substance escapes and does damage.

These defences have been set out because they show that, though it is 'strict', liability under the Rule can be avoided; but it must not be thought that they would not be available as defences to claims in other torts. Thus the first may be regarded as an instance of assumption of risk, the second and third as depending upon lack of causal connection, the fourth as a case of accident and the fifth (statutory authority) as a universal excuse, since an Act of Parliament can, in law, achieve any result.

## 8 PRODUCT LIABILITY

*Donoghue v Stevenson* (p 316) established that under the 'neighbour' principle a manufacturer of products could be liable to the consumer for defects in them; but the liability was (and, failing resort to the Consumer Protection Act, still may be) in *negligence*. The burden of proving negligence is, however, a heavy one to place upon the shoulders of the plaintiff and the trend of opinion of recent years – actuated particularly by such disasters as the famous 'thalidomide' case (p 146) – has been that it has become necessary to impose 'strict' liability upon manufacturers in respect of defective products. This trend led to the promulgation of the EEC Product Liability Directive (85/374/EEC) upon which our own Consumer Protection Act 1987 (Part I, Product Liability) is based.

This Part introduced a new form of 'strict liability' which, it specifically provides, is to be treated as tortious.

The liability arises '*where any damage is caused wholly by a defect in a product*' (s 2(1)). It may be imposed upon the following: (i) The *producer* of the product. (ii) 'Any person who, by putting his name on the product or using a trade mark or other distinguishing mark in relation to the product, has held himself out to be the producer of the product'. This, it will be noted, includes not only owners of trademarks but also 'own-branders', such as supermarkets or wholesalers who vend items as their 'own'. (iii) 'Any person who has *imported* the product into a member state from a place outside the (European Community) in order, *in the course of business*, to supply it to another person' (s 2(2)). Further, liability may be imposed upon a mere *supplier*: but *if*, and only if, the injured party has requested the supplier to identify any of the above-mentioned persons, if the request has been made within a reasonable time, and the supplier has failed to comply with it (s 2(3)). The damage complained of may be to the person who suffers it, to the producer of any product in which the defective product is comprised (eg a manufacturer of a car which incorporates a defective braking system supplied by another manufacturer) or to any other person (eg the child of a buyer) . However, in keeping with EEC policy, *no* liability is imposed upon producers or suppliers of *game* or *agricultural produce* – defined as 'any produce of the soil, of stock-farming or of fisheries' – provided that it has not undergone an industrial process (s 2(4)). This exempts the farmer but not the baker.

The word '*damage*' in s 2(1) is widely defined. It includes 'death or personal injury or any loss of or damage to any *property* (including land)' (s 5(1)). Damage to the property produced *itself* is not, however, included (s 5(2)). Moreover, (s 5(3)), the property damaged must be 'property ordinarily intended for private use, occupation or consumption' and actually intended for those purposes by the claimant. This is an important reservation: the private car is included but not, it seems, the commercial van. As far as property (as opposed to personal) damage is concerned the property must be worth a minimum of £275. As to '*defect*' (s 5(4)): 'There is a defect in a product . . . if the safety of the product is not such as persons generally are entitled to expect' (s 3(1)). A vague definition which has to be construed in the light of all the circumstances. '*Product*' is also broadly defined as 'any goods or electricity' (s 1(2)). '*Producer*' means: (a) the person who manufactures the product; (b) the person who won or abstracted the product (for instance, by mining); (c) the person who subjects the product to 'an industrial or other process' (again, the baker; though note that the greengrocer who sells unprocessed apples – also an agricultural product – is not caught).

The liability, as has been noted is 'strict', independent of negligence: all the plaintiff need do is to prove the damage and that it was caused by something defective. But s 4(1) provides defences: (a) That the defect is 'attributable to compliance with any requirement imposed by or under any enactment or with any Community obligation'. (b) That the defendant did not supply the product. (c) That the supply was otherwise than in the course of business or with a view of profit – a gift, for example. (d) That the defect did not exist in the product at the time (generally speaking) of supply.

(e) 'That the state of scientific or technical knowledge' (at the time of supply) 'was not such that a producer of products of the same description as the product in question might be expected to have discovered the defect if it had existed in his products while they were under his control'. (This, of course, makes an important qualification of the 'strictness' of the obligation.) (f) That the defect constituted a defect in a product (the 'subsequent product') in which the product in question had been comprised and was wholly attributable to the design of the subsequent product. (We may imagine the case of a racing car fitted with standard tyres unsuitable for a racing car.)

The Act imposes a limitation period of *three* years for claims whether in respect of personal or property damage, though that period may be extended if such factors as fraud or disability are present. Time starts to run from the date of 'knowledge'. But there is an *absolute* and unqualified bar after *ten* years.

Finally, s 1(1) has a potentially important provision. 'This Part shall have effect for the purpose of making such provision as is necessary in order to comply with the product liability Directive and shall be *construed* accordingly'. In other words, the Part must be interpreted in the light of the Directive.

## 9 CONSPIRACY

The modern tort of conspiracy emerged later than the crime, but as early as *Gregory v Duke of Brunswick* (1843) 6 Man & G 205 it was held to be actionable for a group of barrackers to hiss an actor off the stage. The gist of the action is that it is a tort for two or more people to combine to injure another by the doing of some unlawful act. This tort, being originally a form of action on the case, requires that *actual* loss must be inflicted.

During the past century, however, civil conspiracy has usually taken what has been described as an 'anomalous' form. Namely, that of the execution of an agreement which has as its *predominant* object the aim of causing loss to the plaintiff's *business* interests. The tort in this form was finally recognized in *Crofter Hand Woven Harris Tweed v Veitch* [1942] AC 435 and this was confirmed in *Lonrho Ltd v Shell Petroleum Co Ltd* [1982] AC 173. The 'anomaly' lies in the fact that, provided that loss is suffered, the execution of the agreement is tortious *in itself*. It does not rest upon the commission of what would be a tort if it were committed by *one person*: it is no tort for one person to cause wilful economic loss to another unless he does it by the commission of a recognized tort (such as fraud or interference with contract). When a civil conspiracy takes this particular form, often referred to as 'simple' conspiracy, the predominant intent to injure is essential: so that if, as in the *Crofter Case* and the *Lonrho Case*, the *predominant object* of the combination is to further the defendants' *own* interests the tort will not be committed. This need not cause surprise in view of the requirement of public policy which seeks to encourage free competition. But what has often been thought peculiar is that the element of *combination* should make that a tort which, otherwise would not be one. As was remarked above, a Napoleon or a Hitler have in themselves greater power to cause harm than a multitude. But there is another side to this question. May it not seem odd that English law should refuse to allow an action against a single individual who causes economic loss to another, not in furtherance of his *own* interests – the essence of commercial activity – but from sheer disinterested malevolence? The problem is the *Pickles* one (p 333). In the sphere of business competition and the protection of economic interests the courts have often been guilty of confusion of thought.

Doubt has recently been expressed whether, in a case where business interests are attacked by a conspiracy to do something *tortious in itself* (by means of interference with contract, for example), it is necessary that the predominant object must be one of injuring the plaintiff. It has been held by the House of Lords in *Lonrho plc v Fayed* [1992] 1 AC 448 that the predominant aim of causing injury is irrelevant; though in fact (as where the agreement involves fraud) it will usually be present.

Ever since the Trade Disputes Act 1906 the activities of those who indulge in trade disputes have been shielded from claims in conspiracy and certain allied torts. The relevant enactment now is the Trade Union and Labour Relations (Consolidation) Act 1992 which provides (s 219) that 'An *agreement or combination* by two or more persons to do or to procure the doing of an act *in contemplation or furtherance of a trade dispute shall not be actionable* in tort if the act is one which, if done without any such agreement or combination, *would not be actionable in tort*'. Secondary action is excluded from the immunity (s 224). '*Trade dispute*' is defined by s 244 – so as to include, *inter alia*, disputes as to terms and conditions of employment, allocation of work, facilities for officials of trade unions and negotiating machinery.

## 10   INTERFERENCE WITH CONTRACTUAL RELATIONS

Like conspiracy, this tort is one of comparatively recent origin. It began with *Lumley v Gye* (1853) 2 E & B 216 where the defendant induced Joanna Wagner to break her contract to sing for the plaintiff, an impresario: and it was held to be a tort maliciously to induce a breach of contract. Since then the tort has lost its youthful simplicity and has extended well beyond mere inducement to breach of contract.

The requirement of 'malice' was dropped before the end of the nineteenth century, though *knowledge* of the existence of the contract is essential; but the element of 'inducement' has been expanded to include *interference* in other ways, eg X will commit the modern tort if, A having a contract with B which necessitates the use of certain tools, X removes the tools so as to prevent the performance of the contract.

Further, provided that '*unlawful means*' are employed to interfere with the contract, the interference need not now *be direct*. Thus in *Daily Mirror Newspapers Ltd v Gardner* [1968] 2 QB 762 an injunction was granted against officials of a retailers' trade union in the following circumstances. In the interests of their union the officials sought to induce their members (newspaper retailers) to stop taking supplies from wholesalers who were themselves under contract to buy the papers from the plaintiff newspaper proprietors. The officials' action, being *unlawful* as a breach of the Restrictive Trade Practices Act 1956, the Court of Appeal held that this *indirect* attack upon the wholesaler's contract with the plaintiffs – for the ceasing of the retailers' orders to the wholesalers would have forced the latter to break that contract – came within the ambit of the tort. The reader may think that the requirement that where the attack is indirect the 'means' must be unlawful is illogical: and so it is – it in fact crept in because of the close involvement of this tort with the jungle of trade union law.

Further, under the modern law 'interference' need not amount to actual breach. Thus in *Torquay Hotel Co Ltd v Cousins* [1969] 2 Ch 106 union officials threatened to stop fuel oil supplies by Esso to the Imperial Hotel by calling upon tanker men (*in breach of their contracts* with Esso) to refuse delivery to the Imperial. It was held that, had this actually been done, the tort of interference would have been committed (indirectly by the use of 'unlawful means' – breach of the tankermen/Esso contracts) even though the contract *attacked* – the Esso/Imperial contract for Esso to supply the oil – would not have been broken because there was a clause in it excusing them from delivery in the case of labour disputes, the situation which had actually arisen: but it would, of course, have been *interfered* with.

Still more, though *malice*, in the sense of spite or ill-will was, as has been explained, early discarded as an element of the tort, until recently it was thought that the defendant must *know* of the existence of the contract attacked; but even this requirement seems now to have been dropped and it may be enough if the interferer acts recklessly, indifferent whether a breach of contract will result or not.

Where inducement is relevant – which of course it will not be where the interference takes the form of, for example, removing the tools essential to performance of the contract – then some sort of persuasion must be used: mere *advice* is not enough. The distinction between persuasion and advice is not, however, always an easy one to make.

No action lies where the defendant acts with *lawful justification*. But what amounts to lawful justification is not at present clear. On the one hand, by way of contrast with the law of conspiracy, it is no justification for members of an association (such as a miners' federation) to prove that they were acting in the interests of their association, nor is it enough that the defendant was prompted by impersonal and disinterested motives. On the other hand, in *Brimelow v Casson* [1924] 1 Ch 302, it was held that members of an actors' protection association were justified in boycotting a theatrical manager – who persistently paid his chorus girls so little that they were forced to supplement their earnings by immorality – by inducing theatre proprietors not to engage him, and, in cases where they knew that contracts to do so were already in operation, to break them.

Finally, here, as in the case of conspiracy, the 1992 Act casts protection around trade disputes. It provides (s 219(1)) that 'An act done by a person *in contemplation or furtherance of a trade dispute* shall not be actionable in tort on the ground only *(a) that it* induces another person to break a contract or interferes or induces any other person to interfere with its *performance*.' But, by s 222 this protection is removed where the reason for doing the act in question is the fact or belief that an employer has employed, or might employ, a person who is not a member of a particular trade union. A rule directed against the 'closed shop' principle.

It is to be noted that by s 224 of the 1992 Act, immunity is withheld where the act in question amounts to secondary action which is not lawful picketing.

## 11   INJURIOUS FALSEHOOD

This is a compendious term used to denote a group of torts concerned with the making of damaging imputations.

Essentially, injurious falsehood is committed when a person damages another by making false and *malicious* imputations – written, oral, or otherwise – which cause that other person damage in respect of some interest other than his reputation. The damage here envisaged is usually damage to business interests, but the tort is not entirely confined to that sort of damage: for example, in an old case, a lady succeeded in an action against the defendant who wrote to a man she was about to marry falsely alleging that she was married to him (the defendant), with the result, in the phrase of the reporter, that she 'lost her marriage'.

The idea may be illustrated by *Ratcliffe v Evans* [1892] 2 QB 524, the starting point of the modern law relating to this tort. B published in a newspaper a false statement to the effect that A had ceased to carry on business, and naturally A's business declined. Though the statement was clearly no libel, for no one thinks the worse of a man for shutting up shop, there being evidence of malice, it was held to be actionable as *injurious falsehood*. By contrast, in *Drummond-Jackson v British Medical Association* [1970] 1 All ER 1094 it was held that an article in a journal which charged the plaintiff with having practised a dangerous dental technique was *libellous*.

*Malice* is normally an essential ingredient in all forms of injurious falsehood; and 'malice' here seems to mean some indirect or improper motive in the defendant, eg a desire to inflict injury. Further, at common law, proof of special damage (ie proof that some particular loss has been caused) was usually essential; but, by s 3, the Defamation Act 1952 made proof of this unnecessary where either the statement complained of is both calculated to cause pecuniary damage and is published in a permanent form – including broadcast statements – or is calculated to cause damage to the plaintiff in respect of his current business or profession. Since, in modern times, most cases of injurious falsehood have concerned imputations of the latter type, it can now, therefore, be said that proof of *special damage* will *not* normally be necessary.

It remains to mention two special varieties of injurious falsehood: slander of title and slander of goods. *Slander of title* is committed by a defendant who falsely and maliciously disparages another person's title to property in a manner calculated to cause him damage: for example, where Y falsely and maliciously alleges that X is offering certain goods for sale in infringement of a patent vested in Z. *Slander of goods* is committed when a person falsely and maliciously disparages goods manufactured or sold by another, even though his motive be to boost his own sales; but a statement by B that his goods are better than A's will not ground an action because, amongst other things, if the judges were to countenance such actions they would be encouraging the use of the court as a forum for advertising.

## 12   EUROPEAN COMMUNITY LAW

European Community law is now giving rise to the recognition of claims in tort based upon breaches of it. Thus in *Garden Cottage Foods v Milk Marketing Board* [1984] AC 130 the House of Lords held that breaches of Article 85 and 86 of the Treaty of Rome could ground an action in tort brought in the United Kingdom. Again, in *Bourgoin SA v Ministry of Agriculture, Fisheries and Food* [1986] QB 716 the Court of Appeal allowed judicial review of an *'ultra vires'* decision of the Ministry in contravention of Article 30, though the remedy of damages in tort was held inappropriate. There have been other cases in similar vein and such actions are likely to multiply (see, eg, *Frankovich v Italy* [1992] IRLR 84).

For the tort of misfeasance in a public office see p 138. And for deceit see p 258.

# 3   Remedies in the law of torts

The two principal remedies available to a plaintiff in an action in tort are damages and injunctions.

## A DAMAGES

*Assessment* – The main purpose of awarding damages in tort, as in the case of breach of contract, is to compensate the plaintiff for the loss he has suffered. The assessment of the amount (or 'quantum') of the damages is often a simple matter; for instance in a case of conversion a correct assessment can usually be made by reference to the value of the goods converted. Assessment is not, however, *always* a simple matter. For instance, where the plaintiff has sustained physical injuries, damages may be awarded him as compensation for his pain and suffering, and they may also be awarded for loss of amenity (ie for loss of the ability to enjoy the accustomed pleasures of life) and for loss of *future* earnings. Traditionally, and normally, the award under this head is made once and for all at the trial in the form of a lump sum calculated to compensate for all present and *future* loss. In the case of actions for personal injuries, however, where there is a chance (as where epilepsy *may* result at some future time from a fractured skull) that a serious disease may develop after the trial, the Administration of Justice Act 1982 gives the court power to make an initial award on the assumption that such disease will *not* develop and a further award at a later date if it *does*.

*Classification* – Damages are classified in a number of ways. The most important distinction is between '*general*' and '*special*' damages. General damages are damages at large which are not susceptible to exact calculation: eg for loss of a limb. It is for the court or jury to assess the amount. Special damages are awarded for such losses (eg medical expenses or loss of earnings prior to trial) as are exactly calculable and they must be specifically set out in the pleadings.

Damages may be '*nominal*' or '*substantial*'. Nominal damages are awarded when the plaintiff can prove that his rights have been infringed, but is unable to prove any *actual* damage. Thus if X walks upon Y's land he commits a trespass and nominal damages, say ten pence or less, may be awarded against him even though he did no damage. Substantial damages are assessed by reference to the actual loss, whether physical or non-physical (such as loss of amenity) however great or small. Where *actual* damage is the gist of the action, as in an action for negligence, nominal damages can of course never be awarded.

In general, damages are, on principle, *compensatory*, but they may also be *aggravated*: for instance if an act, such as slapping someone in the face, is done wilfully and publicly it may cause greater than normal injury to his feelings and hence the damages required for compensation may be larger ('aggravated') than the act complained of would normally justify. In certain circumstances, however, the courts will depart from the compensatory principle and permit the awarding of damages ('*exemplary*', '*punitive*' or '*vindictive*') aimed at punishing the defendant rather than at compensating the plaintiff. These circumstances (the principle being a deviation from the compensatory rule) are not common and they were defined by the House of Lords in *Rookes v Barnard* (1964). First they may be awarded where – as to John Wilkes in the great constitutional case of *General Warrants, Wilkes v Wood* (1763) Lofft 1 – the plaintiff has been injured by arbitrary action of government servants: second in cases where the defendant's conduct is such as to be calculated to make a profit for himself by his tort which exceeds any compensation which he would usually have to pay the plaintiff: in the third place where statute authorizes their award.

*Remoteness* – The rules as to remoteness of damage in relation to the law of contract have been discussed above; the reader will therefore be familiar with the meaning of 'remoteness'. It will be recalled that in contract damage is 'proximate', or 'direct', under the first Rule in *Hadley v Baxendale*, if it arises 'naturally' from the breach of contract; ie if it is such as the parties must be taken reasonably to have foreseen as likely to follow, in the ordinary course of things, from the breach.

*The Old Rule* – In tort it could formerly have been asserted with reasonable certainty that the rule was different, and that the test of remoteness was one of direct *consequence*. The defendant would of course be liable for all *intended* consequences, whether direct or indirect, but he would also be liable for all consequences *directly* connected with his wrongful act or omission whether or not they were such that he ought reasonably to have foreseen the probability of their ensuing. Establish the wrong to the plaintiff, and the defendant must foot the bill for the consequent harm; what ought to have been foreseen, in the words of the late Lord Sumner, 'goes to culpability' (ie in torts such as negligence where 'foresight' is a relevant element in liability) 'not to compensation'. It should be noted that even this seemingly harsh proposition does not spell compensation without limit, for the defendant would only be held responsible for such damage to the plaintiff as is causally connected with his wrong; he would not, for instance, be liable for such injury as the plaintiff avoidably brings upon himself, nor for injury due to the intervention of other people, nor for extraordinary intervening occurrences such as earthquakes; for the problem was one of causation, and a person should never be held liable for what he has not caused.

The rule so stated was the law laid down by the Court of Appeal in *Re Polemis and Furness Withy & Co* [1921] 3 KB 560. The facts of this case were that a ship was hired under charter and during the voyage some of the petrol containers which constituted her cargo leaked, and her hold became full of petrol vapour. At Casablanca a stevedore in the employment of the charterers negligently let a plank fall into the hold. For some unexplained reason the fall of this plank touched off a spark; there was an explosion, and in the resulting conflagration the ship became a total loss. The owners sued the charterers for the value of the ship – nearly £ 200,000 (a large sum then). It was found as a fact that 'the causing of the spark could not have been reasonably anticipated from the falling of the (plank), though some damage to the ship might reasonably have been anticipated'. The court held the charterers liable for the full amount. Once the stevedore (the servant of the charterers) had been proved to be negligent – as he was, for 'some damage to the ship' might reasonably have been anticipated from his carelessness – all damage directly following upon his act was, under the rule as stated above, recoverable. The limits of the rule may be illustrated by adding a fanciful variation to the facts: suppose that some malevolent stranger had, unknown to the stevedore or to the charterers, placed an explosive charge beneath the plank and that this charge had been detonated by the fall, then the catastrophe would have been caused by the stranger rather than the stevedore, and the charterers would have escaped liability for anything but a nominal sum for such harm as the actual falling of the plank might have been assumed to have caused.

*The New Rule* – In 1961, however, the Judicial Committee in *Overseas Tankship (UK) Ltd v Mort's Dock and Engineering Co Ltd (The Wagon Mound)* [1961] AC 388, decided to depart from the 'direct consequence' test of *Re Polemis* and to adopt in its stead a reasonable foreseeability of type of harm rule. This case arose out of the same occurrence as *The Wagon Mound (No 2)* but the plaintiffs were different, and the two cases also differed on a finding of fact: for in *The Wagon Mound* that evidence was that no one could at that time be expected to know the furnace oil floating on water *could* be set alight. Hence, the Judicial Committee, in *The Wagon Mound,* having decided that 'foresight', rather than direct consequence, was to be the determining test, by no possible means, however long-sighted the 'foresight', could the defendants be held liable. The *Polemis* test would have produced the opposite result, because the ship's engineer was undoubtedly initially negligent – and, indeed, even doing a criminal act by committing a public nuisance – and the damage sustained was the direct consequence of that negligence.

'Foresight' thus rules in tort as well as in contract but whereas, as will be remembered, 'foresight' in contract is limited to such consequences as the parties might have been expected to contemplate as the *probable* result of the breach, in tort, by contrast, there are some kinds of circumstances (as was ruled in *The Wagon Mound (No 2)*) – in which the defendant will be expected to foresee results which are by no means probable and held liable if he fails to guard against them.

Moreover, the decision of *The Wagon Mound* in favour of 'foresight' has to be qualified. In the first place the Judicial Committee were there solely concerned with the tort of negligence and there was therefore some reason to suppose that the new rule was only intended to apply to *that* tort: for one thing, since negligence consists in the infliction of negligent harm, and the concept of negligence itself involves the foresight element, there is logic in maintaining that the defendant's liability ought to cease within the limits of such damage as he has foreseeably caused. The rule has, however, not been so confined; for in *The Wagon Mound (No 2)* it was held that the 'foresight' test (in its tortious guise) also governs in cases of nuisance, whether resting upon a basis of lack of care or not, and whether public or private. Recently, the House of Lords in the *Cambridge Water* case held that the rule applied to cases brought under the rule in *Rylands v Fletcher*. And the Court of Appeal has held that it does apply to the tort of deceit (fraud).

In the second place it has been ruled that where *foreseeable* injury is caused and *unforeseeable* injury of similar *type*, or kind, ensues the defendant will be made to pay not only for the former injury but also for the latter (for the effect of the *Parsons Case* in contract see p 277). Thus, for example, it was held in *Smith v Leech Braine & Co Ltd* [1962] 2 QB 4 05 that where a man received a slight burn on the lip as the result of his employers' negligence and entirely *unforeseeably* this burn produced lethal cancer, a claim could succeed in respect of the man's death; for both injuries, the burn and the cancer (or at least so the court chose to think), were similar in 'type'.

*Double compensation: tax* – It used to be the case that in assessing damages in claims for personal injuries account must be taken of social security and of industrial injury benefits received. And it must be added that in a claim for damages the amount of tax which a successful plaintiff would have had to pay on future earnings is taken into account by way of deduction from the damages he is to receive from the defendant who has deprived him of those earnings. This rule is applicable to claims based upon breach of contract as well as to claims in tort.

## B INJUNCTIONS

Injunctions are the creation of equity, they are orders of the court commanding something to be done ('*mandatory*' injunction) or forbidding something ('*prohibitory*' injunction). As an alternative to claiming damages a plaintiff may, in the case of many torts, seek an injunction to restrain the commission or continuance of the tort.

Injunctions, being equitable remedies, were originally granted only by the Court of Chancery, but they may now issue from any Division of the High Court and, in cases related to land, from a county court. Like other equitable remedies they are discretionary; the court is not bound to grant them, and it will usually refuse to do so if an award of damages will afford adequate compensation. Since the Chancery Amendment Act 1858 (Lord Cairns' Act) the court has had power to award damages either in addition to, or in substitution for, an injunction.

An injunction may be sought, not only where a wrong has already been committed, but also where there is a clear likelihood that it will be committed unless restrained (*Quia timet* injunction – 'because he fears').

For example, if X threatens to build, and is about to build, a structure which will obscure the light to Y's windows (a form of nuisance) Y may sometimes obtain a *quia timet* injunction to prevent this infringement of his rights.

Finally, injunctions may be either *'interlocutory'* or *'permanent'*.

An interlocutory injunction is one which may be granted before the hearing of an action to restrain the defendant's activities and maintain the *status quo* between the parties until the conclusion of the trial. The principles which govern the court's discretion to grant such injunctions were authoritatively (if confusingly) stated by the House of Lords in *American Cyanamid Co v Ethicon* [1975] AC 396. They are: (a) That the court must be satisfied that there is a serious case to be tried. (b) That the court must consider whether the plaintiff would be adequately compensated by an award of *damages* by a refusal of the interlocutory injunction if, at the trial, the plaintiff were to succeed in obtaining a permanent one. (c) If damages would not afford an adequate remedy (eg the defendant were insolvent and uninsured) the defendant would be satisfied by the plaintiff's 'undertaking as to damages' if the interlocutory injunction were to be granted, but a permanent one to be refused after the trial. (d) In general, it is prudent for the court to take such measures as are calculated to preserve the *status quo*. (e) It may not be improper for the court to take into account the relative strength of the parties' *prima facie* cases. The 'undertaking as to damages' is an undertaking by the plaintiff to indemnify the defendant as to any damages which he might sustain by reason of the grant of the interlocutory injunction in the event of failure of the action at the trial.

A species of interlocutory injunction which has recently come to the fore is the *'Mareva'* injunction which originated from a case of that name. This is an injunction to prevent the defendant from 'removing from the jurisdiction of the High Court . . . as sets located within that jurisdiction', whether or not 'he is resident within that jurisdiction' (Supreme Court Act 1981, s 37(3)).

As is well-known, this device has proved to be highly effective. A permanent injunction is one which may be granted after the actual trial of the case.

# 4   Limitation

The law on this matter is principally governed by the Limitation Act 1980. This Act prescribes a period of *six* years 'from the date on which the cause of action accrued' as the normal period within which actions founded upon tort must be brought. Normally, therefore, where the tort consists of one simple act, such as converting a watch, the plaintiff's right of action runs from the day of the act which constitutes the tort. But there are exceptions to the general rule. *Personal injuries claims.* In actions for negligence, nuisance or breach of duty (including trespass or breach of contract), where the damages consist of or include damages in respect of personal injury to the plaintiff or to any other person, the claim must be brought within *three* years of *accrual* or within three years of the *date of 'knowledge'* of the injury; whichever is the later. The date of accrual is the date of infliction of the injury. The definition of 'knowledge' is complicated but, broadly, it means coming to know, or being in a position in which one ought reasonably be expected to know, of the injury: that it is a significant injury and that it is consequential upon the breach of duty alleged. The 'knowledge' period may, subject to exceptions, even be further extended at the discretion of the court. The reason for taking 'knowledge' as an alternative starting point is that some diseases, such as silicosis, may be dormant for some time and their effects may appear long after the breach of duty which causes them. In the case of actions which survive for the benefit of the estate under the Law Reform (Miscellaneous Provisions) Act 1934 time runs from the date of *death* or the time of *knowledge* of the *personal representatives*. In claims under the Fatal Accidents Act 1976 the relevant dates are the date of *death* or the time of *knowledge of the person for whose benefit the action is brought.*

*Damage to property* – Just as a disease may lie dormant so damage to property may be *latent* (as where the foundations of a house are defective and cracks appear in the fabric, or subsidence occurs, only after a period of time). The Latent Damage Act 1986 meets this contingency. It provides that where damage to property is caused by *negligence* the relevant starting points are the date of *accrual* (a *six* year period) or the date of *knowledge* (*three* years), whichever is the later. The date of 'accrual' is, of course, the time when the damage caused by the negligence is done (eg foundations are badly constructed). Here, however, there is an absolute time bar after the expiry of *15* years from accrual. There is no provision for extension by the court of the period of knowledge. A successor in title to the property (such as a purchaser) may take advantage of these limitation periods except that, where the starting point rests upon *knowledge*, knowledge by a predecessor in title bars the successor's claim.

Where a tort consists of a continuing wrong, eg nuisance by continuing vibration, a fresh cause of action arises daily as long as the tort continues to be committed. Thus if a tort of this kind continues for, say, seven years, and the plaintiff then brings an action for the first time, his right of action in respect of damage occurring in the first year (7–6 = 1), but in respect of that year only, will be barred.

In tort actions the provisions as to *disabilities* and *fraud etc* are similar to those which apply to breaches of contract.

# Chapter 11

# The law of property

This chapter will be devoted to a discussion of rights and interests in property, and of the methods by which it may be transferred from one living person to another. The rules which govern devolution upon death will be treated separately in Chapter 14.

In any discussion of the Law of Property it is essential to deal with the land law separately. The reason for this is obvious. Land is, in the phrase of Sir Edward Coke, 'of all elements the most ponderous and immovable'; land endures, all other property perishes, alters or is lost in the course of time. It follows that rights and interests which can be enjoyed in land are necessarily more complex than others.

Further, history set land law apart. Land was the essential pivot of feudal society (see below) and thus had special importance. At common law it alone could be recovered against an intruder by means of a real action (the Writ of Right) which was called 'real' (Latin, *res* – a thing) because it involved a property claim for the return of the thing itself. And land law is often called the law of *Real Property* to this day: Americans speak of house agents as 'realtors'. The legal opposite of land is goods, 'chattels' (from the Latin *cattala* = cattle, the commonest early form of goods). Chattels were not necessarily specifically recoverable by action at common law. Hence chattels (and all property other than land) were called *Personal Property* or 'personalty' as opposed to 'realty'. Leases of land, however, fell historically into the special category of 'chattels real' (contrasted with goods, etc, which were 'chattels personal'). This was because, as will shortly appear, leases were hybrids, with some characteristics of realty and some of personalty.

## LAND LAW

## 1  Introductory

Modern land law is largely founded upon certain statutes enacted in 1925. The most important of these are the Law of Property Act (LPA), the Settled

Land Act (SLA), the Administration of Estates Act (AEA) and the Land Registration Act (LRA). These statutes will be referred to individually by the abbreviations indicated, collectively as the 'Property Acts'. They did not purport to introduce a self-sufficient code, but only to effect far-reaching changes in the land law and in the methods of conveying (transferring) land, and it is therefore still helpful to have some knowledge of the law prior to 1926. Accordingly, by way of introduction, it is proposed first to define the subject of inquiry by explaining what is meant by 'land', then to give a brief account of the old land law, lastly to outline the purposes and general effect of the Property Acts.

## A   THE MEANING OF 'LAND'

The ordinary purchaser of land probably pictures himself as acquiring a visible portion of the earth's surface. In fact the law entitles him to more, for, broadly speaking, in the eye of the law 'land' includes the surface of the land, the earth beneath it and certain rights in respect of the airspace above.

And there is even more to it than this; for the word 'land' in strict law includes all '*hereditaments*' (Latin '*heres*' = heir), that is everything which would at common law descend to the heir at law upon intestacy. And such things included both '*corporeal*' and '*incorporeal*' hereditaments. The former are physical; the land itself and things such as walls or houses adhering to it: the latter are non-physical and include, *inter alia*, rights of way appurtenant to 'land' (in the ordinary sense of the word) and a number of legal notions such as *rent charges* (sums of money charged upon lands). Thus, for historical reasons which cannot here be mentioned 'land' in the legal sense embraces more than a visible plot of soil.

Corporeal things attached to land are known as 'fixtures' and the term *fixture* is a term of art. *Prima facie* anything permanently attached to the land, or to something else which is itself attached to the land, is a fixture; hence it is a part of the land and will pass automatically with the land upon a transfer. The fact of attachment, however, only raises a *presumption* that the thing concerned has lost its quality of being a chattel and has become technically part of the land. This presumption may be rebutted by showing, for instance, that the object is something in itself wholly unconnected with the use of land, and that it has only been 'annexed' (attached) for its better enjoyment as a chattel. Thus, in *Leigh v Taylor* [1902] AC 157, it was held that a valuable tapestry did not become a fixture by being battened to a wall. Again, things beneath the land, such as a buried prehistoric boat (*Elwes v Brigg Gas Co* (1886) 33 Ch D 562) belong to the landowner even if their very existence is unknown to him.

There are, however, certain things which cannot be subject to private ownership and however much they may be attached to the land they cannot pass to a purchaser. Examples are unmined gold and silver and (as a result of legislation) petroleum and coal.

## B   THE OLD LAND LAW

The land law as it existed in 1925 was largely judge-made. It derived from two main sources. First, from principles which had been evolved by the courts of common law in mediaeval times. Secondly, from rules of equity developed by the Court of Chancery (p 26).

Certain peculiarities were inherited from the mediaeval law.

### Tenure

The mediaeval law was designed to meet the needs of *feudalism*. Feudalism was a system of government through the agency of landholders. In feudal theory no man could 'own' land, save the king. All the land in England was divided among tenants (French, '*tenir*' = to hold) some of whom were *free* and others *unfree*.

The *free* tenants held their land either directly, or indirectly, by subgrant from a superior tenant, *de rege*, 'under the king'. Every tenant, whether he was a tenant-in-chief holding directly of the king, or a sub-tenant holding of a mesne lord, owed duties to his overlord; these duties were manifold and were ultimately designed to supply the lack of a central government by ensuring certain basic *services*. For instance, there was *knight-service*, the duty of performing *military* service essential to the king. There was *sergeanty* which consisted of performing services – such as cup-bearer or mace-bearer to the king ('grand' sergeanty) or performing lesser personal services ('petit' sergeanty). There was *socage* tenure, usually taking the form of fixed agricultural services, commuted by the fifteenth century to money payments ('quit rents'). There was *frankalmoign* (free alms), ecclesiastical tenure, by which the clergy might hold land in return for praying for the lord. Further, tenure carried with it certain 'incidents', such as the lord's right to *wardship* and *marriage*, ie the right to enjoy the profits of the land during minority when a tenant died leaving an infant (21 boys, 14 girls) heir, and the right to dispose of infant tenants in marriage – which was valuable since an infant who refused the proffered marriage would forfeit the 'value' of it to the lord. Every tenant who had sub-tenants had rights over them, such as the right to hold a court which they were bound to attend. By this means, with the king as ultimate overlord, the government of the country was carried on by a descending scale of landholders. But the king's overriding interest must not be forgotten: not only was the property of a person who committed a serious crime forfeit to the Crown but, upon the death of a tenant without heirs his land 'escheated' to the overlord, ultimately to the Crown.

Beside free men, however, in mediaeval times there were serfs (or 'villeins') who were *unfree*. Villeins originally held their land by unfree, or 'villein' tenure. This was a form of bondage which obliged them to perform services for the lord of the manor in which they lived. They could not leave their holding; they were 'bound to the soil'. The status of villeinage, however, gradually became obsolete; villeins became free men, and the land which had once been held by villein tenure became subject to *copyhold* tenure. The term 'copyhold' derived from the practice of recording tenancies of this type in the court roll of the manor in which the land was situated, the tenant being given a copy of the record as evidence of his title. The rules relating to copyhold differed in many respects from the rules relating to freehold tenure.

As a political system feudalism fell into decay within two hundred years of its introduction by the Normans. Though the Tenures Abolition Act 1660 converted all military tenures into free and common socage and most of the incidents appertaining to military tenures were then abolished, the idea of tenure remained long after the obligations incident to feudal land-holding had ceased to exist. And even today the theory of it remains in that 'freehold' land (freehold being the basis upon which all land is now held) is historically no more than land held in free and common socage to which, of course, neither services nor incidents have for centuries attached.

## Estates
While the terms of the tenant's holding marked his tenure (ie knight-service, etc) the extent (ie duration, eg life or fee simple) of the interest was known as his '*estate*' – the word is akin to the word 'status'. It survives in the terminology of the modern law.

## Freehold land
Ie the land of a free tenant, called an '*estate of freehold*', was not devisable, that is to say it could not be disposed of by will. The reason for this was, probably, that the feudal overlord was entitled to certain rights upon the tenant's death. He was, for instance, sometimes entitled to a money payment called a 'relief' from the heir. If the tenant were permitted to make a will the lord might be deprived of these rights.

## Terms of years
During the mediaeval period another interest in land, beside the freehold estate, became common. This was the *term of years*, the forerunner of the modern leasehold interest. Terms of years were essentially different from freehold estates. The grant of a term was primarily looked upon as a commercial venture from which the grantor hoped to make a profit, and as such, it fell outside the feudal scheme of land tenure. This ostracism of the term of years had consequences which were important in the subsequent history of the law. These were: (i) that the termor was denied a

real action, and, indeed (though he was later, by the action of *ejectment*, given a remedy against intruders as effective as a real action) at first his only remedy if he were evicted was against his landlord in damages: (ii) that terms of years, like personal property, *could* be disposed of by will: that (iii) upon the tenant's death intestate (ie without making a will) the term descended, like personal property, to the next of kin rather than the heir at law. The lease was thus a hybrid, neither real nor personal property: and it was classified as a '*chattel real*'.

## Defects of the mediaeval law

The mediaeval land law suffered from two major defects. First, as has been explained, freehold land could not be disposed of by will. Secondly, the common law rules governing the limitation (grant) of freehold estates were severely restrictive.

Freehold estates had either to be fee simple estates, estates in fee tail, or life estates.

**Fee simple** – The word fee indicated an estate of freehold. A fee simple estate arose when land was limited (granted) to a man 'and his heirs'. This limitation gave the heirs nothing: the grantee acquired an interest as near to unrestricted ownership as it was possible to acquire under a system governed by the concept of tenure, and he could, subject to feudal restrictions upon alienation (ie transfer), thus sell the land if he chose or give it away; but, of course, if he kept it till the time of his death, it would descend to his heirs.

**Fee tail** – Another form of disposition was a gift to 'A and the heirs of his body' (or to A and certain designated lineal heirs, eg 'To A and the heirs male of his body'). The object of this kind of disposition was to provide 'family' land for a man (or woman) and his (or her) lineal descendants, with the intention that the land should revert to the donor or his successors if the line became extinct. Originally (probably in order to foster the policy of freedom of alienation, and to prevent the land from becoming 'tied' in one line, a policy to which the courts have consistently adhered) just as they construed a disposition 'To A and his heirs' as an out-and-out gift to A, so the courts construed this form of disposition as giving A a fee simple *conditional* upon the birth of an heir of the designated class. Thus the claims both of the designated heirs and of the donor were frustrated. This perverse construction caused discontent which the *Statute De Donis Conditionalibus* (1285) was passed to allay. That Statute provided, in effect, that the future dispositions of this nature should be strictly construed '*secundum formam in carta doni expressam*' (according to the true tenor of the deed of gift). A new form of estate was thus indirectly brought into being, which came to be known as a '*fee tail*' (French, *taillé* = 'cut down') because unlike a fee simple estate which *could* (although, if the fee simple tenant chose to dispose of the land, it need not) descend to the *general* heirs of the donee (lineal or collateral), the fee tail could only descend to the *limited* class of lineal heirs designated in the instrument of gift. Moreover, as a result of the provisions of the Statute, the fee tail differed from the fee simple in that the claims of the successive heirs and of the donor, upon the extinction of the designated line, were protected: when their turn came, they could claim the land, according to the terms of the original gift, whatever the original donee or their predecessors might have done – for example, if the donee sold the land his successor in title could reclaim it from the purchaser after the donee's death.

Moreover, from about 1472, even in the face of the provisions of the Statute, the courts reasserted their policy of fostering free alienation, and again frustrated the intentions of donors, by sanctioning the use of certain legal devices which enabled tenants in tail (ie the original donee and his successors) to bar the rights both of their successors in tail and of the person entitled to the reversion or remainder should the line become extinct; thus enabling the tenant in tail, if he wished, to sell the land free of the claims of the people entitled under the gift. As we shall see, the modern law governing entailed interests – the modern successors to estates in fee tail – has continued this policy .

**Life estates** – A life estate arose when, for instance, land was granted to 'A for life', or to 'A during the life of B' (estate *pur autre vie* – 'for the life of another').

Estates might be granted in *possession*, ie to take effect immediately, or they might be granted in *remainder*. In a grant, for instance, to 'A for life and after A's death to B in fee simple', the grant to B was valid; it took effect in 'remainder' because the land 'remained away' from the grantor after the expiry of A's life estate. Further, estates in *reversion* were recognized. Thus if X, the tenant in fee simple, granted land to Y for life, X held the fee simple 'in reversion' during Y's life; for after Y's death the land would 'revert' to X. For reasons which need not detain us, the mediaeval law hardly ventured to recognize any grants of freehold estates beyond these. In particular, it would not permit estates of freehold to be so limited that they would arise for the first time upon the happening of a *future* uncertain event.

## Developments after the Middle Ages
From the early years of the fifteenth century, the Court of Chancery set to work to remedy these defects of the common law. The remedy was supplied through the instrumentality of the *use* (Chapter 12). By means of this device it became possible to create *equitable* interests in freehold land which were capable of coming into being for the first time upon the death of the grantor.

Thus the prohibition against the devise of freehold land was circumvented. Further, by means of the use, the Court of Chancery permitted *equitable interests*, different in nature from the old common law estates, to be created. In particular equitable *future interests* were allowed to be granted; these were capable of arising in ways which the common law had not permitted.

In respect of wills, the combined effect of the Statute of Wills (1540) and the Tenures Abolition Act (1660) rendered the assistance of equity unnecessary; for it made all land freely devisable. Moreover, as a result of the effect and interpretation of Henry VIII's famous Statute of Uses (1535) – which was not repealed until the Property Acts – a much wider range of *legal* estates became permissible than it had been possible to create in former times; for under the provisions of this Statute, as a general rule, where one person became seised (possessed) of land to the *use* of another (Chapter 12), then, in place of the equitable interest which the former would previously have held, he was for the future to be entitled to a *legal estate* to the extent of the interest granted. Nevertheless, by means of special conveyancing machinery, the Court of Chancery also, in the course of time, continued to enforce the *equitable interests* it had formerly created. And further, every new *legal* estate was permitted an *equitable* counterpart. Thus, for example, there could be equitable interests equivalent to estates in fee simple or in fee tail.

Hence, beside the older divisions of the law, a new division arose. Rights in land might either be *legal* or *equitable*. The nature of this distinction must be clearly understood. The man who has a legal right to property has a right which he can assert against all comers. The man who has an equitable interest in property has something more than the mere 'personal' right which one party to a contract has against the other, for he has a right to the property itself. But the right of the equitable owner will, as has been explained (p 28) be lost if the property comes into the hands of one who is a *bona fide* purchaser of the *legal* estate in the property, provided that he is a purchaser for *value*, and that he has *no notice* of the equitable interest. 'Notice' in this context may be either actual or '*constructive*'. Constructive notice means such notice as the purchaser would have received of the equitable interest had he used reasonable diligence in making enquiries.

## C   THE PURPOSES AND EFFECTS OF THE PROPERTY ACTS

Despite some reforms effected by nineteenth century statutes, the law in force immediately before the passing of the property Acts was unsatisfactory for many reasons. In the first place, the distinction between 'real property', 'chattels real' and 'personal property' produced unnecessary complexity and matters were by no means improved by the fact that real and personal property devolved upon intestacy by different rules. Secondly, the land law was highly artificial. Thirdly, owing to the multitude of interests which might encumber a given piece of land at one and the same time, the transfer of land was rendered, at the best a complicated matter, at the worst, well-nigh impossible.

The principal aims of the Property Acts were therefore:

(1) To minimize the distinction between real property and chattels real, and, as far as the natural distinction between movables and immovables permits, to assimilate the rules of law relating to land and other forms of property.

(2) To simplify the land law. This simplification was to be undertaken mainly with a view to the third object which was –

(3) To make transfers of land as easy as possible.

These aims were achieved in the following manner:

*(i)* The land law was assimilated to the law relating to personal property in two respects. (a) By the provisions of the AEA, the rules governing intestate succession to land and goods have been made uniform. Thus the main distinction which divided real property from chattels real ceased to exist. (b) Formerly when a man died intestate leaving no successors, his goods (*bona vacantia*) became the property of the Crown: his real estate fell, as has been noted, to his immediate overlord, who took by right of '*escheat*' – one of the valuable 'incidents' of tenure to which the feudal overlord was entitled. All property, whatever its nature, now lapses in these circumstances to the Crown.

*(ii)* The Law of Property Act 1922 completed the work of earlier statutes by abolishing copyhold tenure. All land is, therefore, now held by freehold or leasehold tenure. Since the feudal services incident to tenure have long since disappeared, the tenant in fee simple is today in practice, though not in strict theory, the 'owner' of his land.

*(iii)* Conveyancing (ie the transfer of land) was simplified by the application of two principles. First, the categories of legal estates were reduced to a minimum. Second, certain devices were introduced which have made it possible, upon the transfer, to free land from equitable interests to which it is subjected.

The first principle was implemented by s 1(1) of the LPA which provides that the only *estates* in land which are now capable of subsisting as *legal* estates are estates in fee simple absolute in possession and terms of years absolute. Apart from a limited number of *interests* which may still be *legal* (see below), all other interests are *equitable*. When it is recalled that legal rights over land are rights good against all and sundry, the importance of this provision will be understood.

The second principle was applied in two ways. On the one hand machinery was devised which now ensures that, wherever there are interests (which can now only be equitable) over land which are limited to be enjoyed by persons jointly or in succession, the land is either automatically subjected to a 'trust for sale' (LPA) or it becomes 'settled land' (SLA). In either case, as will be explained below, a purchaser may now acquire the land free from many equitable rights.

# 2    Estates and interests in land

## A    LEGAL ESTATES AND INTERESTS

'1 –(1) The only *estates* in land which are capable of subsisting or of being conveyed or created at law are – (*a*) An estate in fee simple absolute in possession; (*b*) A term of years absolute. (2) The only *interests* or charges in or over land which are capable of subsisting or of being conveyed or created at law are – (*a*) An easement, right, or privilege in or over land for an interest equivalent to an estate in fee simple absolute in possession or a term of years absolute. . . .'

The italics are ours, but these are the words of part of s 1 of the LPA. Although there are some other *interests* beside the estates and interests here mentioned, which are still capable of subsisting at law, we need not be concerned with them. For present purposes, it will suffice to examine the nature of fee simple estates, terms of years, and easements. The words '*capable of subsisting at law*' are important, and the force of the word '*capable*', in particular, must be appreciated. The Act does not provide that the above classes of estates and interests *must* be legal in character: they may, and do, subsist as equitable interests, but what concerns us here is that they, and, as far as concerns our present purposes, they alone, are *capable* of being held as *legal* estates and interests.

## 1    THE FEE SIMPLE

### (i)  The nature of a fee simple
The term 'fee simple' survives from *mediaeval* times. The word 'fee' ('*feodum*') signified an estate of inheritance, that is an estate which would descend to the heir of a tenant who died intestate. Thus a life estate was not a fee. The word 'simple' served to distinguish the fee simple from the estate in fee tail which, as has already been noted, descended, not to the heirs generally, but to a particular class of heirs designated in the instrument which created the entail.

It has already been stated that the modern holder of a fee simple estate is to all intents and purposes the owner of his land. He is still technically a *tenant* in fee simple, but his tenancy has no practical consequences. Ownership is, however, as has been remarked, a relative and not an absolute concept. An owner has greater rights than anyone else over his property; but these rights are always subject to some restrictions imposed by the general law of the time and place in which he lives. Formerly the rights of landowners were great. An Englishman's home was his 'castle'. He could do much as he liked with his land provided that his user did not come within the prohibition of the law of torts that he should not injure his neighbour. Considerable limitations, have, however, been imposed by modern legislation upon the rights attaching to land ownership. These will be discussed separately.

### (ii) The creation of an estate in fee simple

Words which define, or delimit, a right in land are known as *'words of limitation'*. Originally the only words of limitation which would suffice in a conveyance *inter vivos* (ie between living person as opposed to disposition by will) to pass a fee simple estate were the words *'To ... and his heirs',* although the Conveyancing Act 1881 permitted *'To ... in fee simple'* as an alternative. But by virtue of the LPA, s 60, the necessity for words of limitation to create a fee simple was abolished in conveyances executed after 1925, and it is now the rule that the grantee will take 'the fee simple or otherwise the whole interest which the grantor had power to convey in such land, unless a contrary intention appears in the conveyance'. Thus where A, the tenant in fee simple, conveys land *'To B'*, B will acquire the whole fee simple unless a contrary intention appears. Wills were formerly treated more liberally than conveyances, *inter vivos,* and ever since the Wills Act 1837 the rule has been that a devise *'To B'* without words of limitation will pass the fee simple in the absence of a contrary intention shown in the will. The result today is that there is no difference between wills and conveyances in this matter.

It may be appropriate to add that 'words of limitation' must be distinguished from their even more technical counterpart, *'words of purchase'*. The former define an estate or interest, the latter confer one; and they are nevertheless words of 'purchase' even though the 'purchaser' gives nothing in return for the benefit received. Thus in 'To A and his heirs' the whole phrase *delimited* A's estate (ie marked it out as a fee simple in A) and also constituted words of 'purchase' in A: but it was construed as conferring nothing upon the heirs. The words 'and his heirs' were therefore *not* words of purchase *qua* the heirs. On the other hand, in 'To X for life, remainder to Y' the words are words of purchase as regards both X and Y: they mean what they say; X is to take for life and after his death the estate will pass to Y.

### (iii) The fee simple as a legal estate

It will have been observed that the LPA defines the species of fee simple which is capable of subsisting as a *legal* estate as a *'fee simple absolute in possession'*. The expressions 'absolute' and 'in possession' require explanation.

'*Absolute*' signifies that the estate must be unqualified. The reason why only an unqualified fee simple is allowed to subsist as a *legal* estate is that it is a major object of the Act to make land freely alienable. The owner of a qualified legal fee simple does not have the whole interest in the land to convey to a purchaser. Hence, for example, in a grant to 'X in fee simple until he shall marry', X's interest, not being absolute, cannot subsist as a legal estate; it can be equitable only, and this will have the desired effect of leaving the land freely transferable under the overreaching provisions of the 1925 legislation.

'In *possession*' signifies that the grantee must be entitled to immediate possession of the estate. Thus, suppose land to be limited 'To A for life and after A's death to B in fee simple'. In such a grant B's remainder is said to be 'vested in interest' immediately the conveyance operates, for nothing remains to complete B's rights except the natural determination of the prior estate upon the death of A. This interest is not, however, at once 'vested in possession', since B is not entitled to immediate enjoyment of the land. It is therefore an equitable interest only.

It must finally be noted that the LPA takes account of the fact that land subject to a lease is in practice freely bought and sold. Thus a man who lets his land may still be 'in possession' of a fee simple estate, for 'possession' is for this purpose defined so as to include, beside actual physical enjoyment, 'the receipt of rents and profits, or the right to receive the same'.

## 2   LEASEHOLDS

### (a)  The nature of leasehold interests

The parties to a 'term of years' or 'leasehold interest' are today known as 'landlord' and 'tenant' (or as 'lessor' and 'lessee') respectively.

Some mention has already been made of the history of leaseholds. The principal feature which distinguishes this class of interest from freehold interests is that the landlord-tenant relationship is usually primarily a commercial one whereby the tenant occupies the land in return for a money consideration (rent). Freehold interests often arise as the result of inter-family dealings which are necessarily of a non-commercial nature, though, of course, the sale of a fee simple generally is.

It was held by the House of Lords in *Street v Mountford* [1985] AC 809 that the essence of a leasehold tenancy is that it is based upon an agreement whereby it has been intended that the occupier of the premises in question should be granted exclusive possession of them for a fixed or periodic term at a stated rent. If the agreement is one of that nature the court will *presume* that the relationship of landlord and tenant has been created. This presumption may, however, be displaced by proof of special circumstances which show that the agreement was *not* designed to create a tenancy. For example, it may be that the parties, by their agreement, had no intention of creating legal relations, or that the possession was granted simply as part of a contract of employment. The Court of Appeal has recently held that, whatever the views of the person in possession, there will be no tenancy if the grantor of the possession did not intend that it should be *exclusive*. It will be appreciated that the question whether a tenancy has been created is of vital importance when a person seeks Rent Act protection: for the Acts only protect *tenants*.

It may often be the case that what has been granted is a mere *licence* to be in possession of the premises or of the land concerned. A licence, unlike a tenancy, is not an interest in land. But, whether it be granted by contract or gratuitously, it has some protection at common law. The licensor must keep to the terms of his contract, and even if the arrangement is gratuitous he cannot evict the licensee without reasonable notice. Moreover, equity will, at discretion, protect a licensee.

The expression 'term of years', which is equivalent to 'leasehold interest', is perhaps misleading. Leases can exist for any *fixed* period (eg five years), but they may also take other forms. For example, there are 'periodic tenancies', such as quarterly or yearly tenancies, which are terms of years though they are determinable upon the giving of notice by either party. There are tenancies at *sufferance* arising where a tenant 'holds over' after the expiry of his lease. And, as well as other forms, there are tenancies *at will*, determinable by either party without notice which are really in essence bare licences, but which have the attribute that if rent is paid periodically they are converted into periodic tenancies.

Unlike fee simple estates, leasehold interests may subsist as legal estates even though the tenant is not to take *possession* at once. A term granted at a rent must, however, be limited *to take effect* within 21 years; any grant which purports to postpone the taking of effect of the term for a longer period is invalid (LPA, s 149(3)).

### (b) The creation of leaseholds
In order to give rise to a *legal* estate a lease must *either* be created by deed *or* be one which takes effect in possession for a term not exceeding three years at the best rent obtainable. All kinds of informal leases other than the latter give rise to equitable interests only.

### (c) The relationship between landlord and tenant
The relationship of landlord and tenant is primarily governed by rules of the common law, but it has been modified to some extent by statute.

*i The relationship of landlord and tenant at common law*
Tenancies are created by contract; consequently at common law their terms might be infinitely various. There are, however, certain obligations which

are usually implied, and certain covenants which commonly occur, in leases.

## (a) Implied obligations

**Landlord's obligations** – A landlord is bound to do all that a reasonable landlord ought to do for his tenants in accordance with the nature of the property: thus, for instance, where the property comprised in the lease is a block of flats he must keep lifts, rubbish disposal equipment, etc, in reasonable order. Further, in the absence of express terms the landlord is under an obligation to ensure that neither he, nor anyone claiming under him, will disturb the tenant in his occupation of the premises. He impliedly covenants that the tenant shall remain in 'quiet enjoyment'. Further, where the premises are let furnished there is an implied warranty that they are reasonably fit for human habitation; for instance, a house infested with bugs has been held to be unfit for such habitation. This warranty does not, however, apply to houses which are let unfurnished, unless they are small dwelling-houses let at low rentals specified in s 8 of the Landlord and Tenant Act 1985 which then imposes a statutory warranty to that effect: but even this has no application where the condition of the premises in question is such that they cannot be made fit at reasonable expense. Section 11 of the same Act imposes implied covenants upon lessors of dwelling-houses for a term of less than seven years: (a) to keep in repair the structure and exterior of the house (including drains, gutters and external pipes); (b) to keep in repair and proper working order the installations in the dwelling-house: (i) for the supply of water, gas and electricity and for sanitation, and (ii) for space heating or heating water. These obligations can only be excluded or modified if both parties consent and an order of a county court is obtained. The obligation to repair only arises if the landlord knows, or reasonably ought to have known of the particular disrepair (eg a faulty floor) in question. Finally as a matter of practical importance, often not observed by landlords, there is a statutory require-ment that the landlord must supply *weekly* tenants with a *rent book* in proper form. Failure to do this is an *offence*. Moreover, the Landlord and Tenant Act 1985, s 1, provides that where a tenant makes a written request to a landlord's agent, the landlord's name and address must be supplied *in writing* to the tenant, and where the premises subject to the tenancy are assigned to another landlord the latter must give the tenant *written* notice of his name and address.

**Tenant's obligations** – Generally speaking the tenant is liable for payment of rates and taxes, except such taxes as the landlord is under a legal obligation to pay. He is also under a duty to refrain from committing *waste*. This means that he is bound to refrain from damaging the property and that, quite apart from agreement, he must generally keep it in a reasonable state of repair.

## (b) Express covenants

Two very common covenants, beside the covenant to pay *rent*, call for mention.

**The covenant not to assign or underlet** – In the absence of contrary agreement a tenant may assign his whole interest in the lease to a third person, or he may sub-let the premises for a term shorter than his own. In either event, if the tenant's interest amounts to a legal estate the third person will also acquire one. Landlords, however, very commonly exact a covenant against assigning or underletting. This may either be framed in the form of an absolute prohibition or as a prohibition against assigning or underletting without consent, and in the latter case the landlord is under a statutory duty not to withhold his consent unreasonably. By the Landlord and Tenant Act 1988 where a lease includes a covenant on the part of the tenant not to assign, underlet, charge or part with possession of the premises comprised in the lease or any part thereof, and the covenant is subject to the qualification that consent is not to be unreasonably withheld, the tenant may make written application for consent to the landlord or any other person entitled to give consent. The consent must then be given unless the tenant is in breach of a covenant in the lease. A lease may also include a covenant on the part of the tenant not, without the landlord's approval, to consent to a sub-tenant, assigning, etc, the premises and it is covenanted that approval is not to be unreasonably withheld. Again, in this case the landlord's consent must be given unless, by giving his own consent to the assigning etc, the tenant would himself be in breach of a covenant in his own lease. There provisions do not apply to secure (p 368) tenancies.

**The covenant to repair** – This may be either a landlord's or a tenant's covenant, though as a rule the landlord is responsible for the fabric of the house and the tenant for other repairs. The standard of 'repair' required is the standard which a reasonable landowner would adopt in relation to his own premises and it is thus a variable standard; a house in Park Lane requires more attention than a house in Poplar. On the other hand, the standard is fixed as at the time of the letting in respect of the particular house and a decline in the neighbourhood will not affect the stringency of the duty.

It has been explained that as a general rule contractual obligations, being personal to the parties, are not assignable, but because of the enduring nature of land certain covenants between landlord and tenant form an exception to this rule. This exception is best described in the time-honoured words that '*covenants which touch and concern the land demised* (leased) *run with the land*'; they will bind the successors in title to either party. The principle is reasserted in the LPA (ss 141 and 142). Whether any particular covenant falls within this category is largely a question of fact. Thus, in *Thomas v Hayward* (1869) LR 4 Exch 311, X who had let a public house to Y was held not to be bound, as against Y's assignee, by a covenant that he would not himself keep another public house within half a mile of the demised premises; for this covenant clearly had no direct reference to the land demised as opposed to the business conducted thereon. On the other hand where, upon the lease of a restaurant, the tenant covenanted that X should not be concerned in the business, it was held that this covenant directly concerned the use of the premises.

Where the covenant does 'run' so as to bind successors, the original parties (ie the landlord and tenant) of course remain liable to one another according to the terms of their contract, but they are entitled to be indemnified by any successor who is in breach. It is of the greatest importance to note that these rules apply only where there is *privity of estate* between the party suing upon the covenant and the party in breach. This means that, in order for the covenant to be binding upon successors, they must take the same interest in the land as that originally created. Thus, covenants may run between landlord and assignee, but not between landlord and sub-tenant. If A leases land to B for a term of three years and B assigns the lease to X after two years, X may be bound by the covenants in favour of A contained in the lease. If, on the other hand, B sub-lets his term to Y for three years less one day, Y cannot be bound by these covenants but he will of course be bound by the covenants in the sub-lease.

## ii  Statutory provisions affecting the relationship between landlord and tenant

Modern statutes have done much to restrict the freedom of the parties to a lease to make their own terms. The following examples may be given.

### (a)  Statutory provisions respecting improvements

Where a tenant increases the value of the premises by making improvements it is unfair that he should lose the results of his industry upon the expiration of the tenancy. Thus even at common law he had a right to *emblements*, that is to say a right to enter, and to take artificially produced crops, such as wheat, when the tenancy had ceased unexpectedly before the harvest. Further a tenant may remove articles ('*tenants fixtures*') used for trade or for ornamental or domestic purposes upon quitting the premises, even though they have been attached to the land, but he must not cause serious damage to the property by doing so. Thus, a tenant who keeps a garage may remove his petrol pumps as 'trade fixtures'. It will, of course, be realized that these rights in practice form an exception to the rule that things affixed to the land become the property of the owner (p 351).

Tenants' rights in respect of improvements are, moreover, greatly increased by the provisions of two statutes; namely the Agricultural Holdings Act 1986, and the Landlord and Tenant Act 1927 (as amended by the Landlord and Tenant Act 1954, Part III). The first Act entitles tenants of agricultural holdings upon the termination of the lease to receive compensation from their landlords for certain specified forms of improvements, such as the erection of farm buildings. The same Act also provides that certain classes of fixtures which have been attached to the land for agricultural purposes shall be removable by the tenant, either during the term or within two months of quitting. The landlord has, however, an option to purchase these fixtures at the end of the lease. The Act moreover, allows the tenant compensation on a prescribed basis to assist him in 'reorganizing his affairs' at the termination of the lease.

The second Act entitles a tenant who uses the premises for *business* purposes (an expression which includes 'a trade, profession or employment') to compensation from the landlord, at the end of the tenancy, for any structural improvements he has made which increase the letting value of the premises. The amount of compensation must be approved by the landlord or, in case of dispute, by the court.

## (b) The Rent Acts
It would be impossible to give an accurate account of this chaotic subject in the space available; yet some mention of it is called for. *Rent protection*, that is to say the control of rents and ensuring for the tenants security of tenure (ie making it difficult for the landlord to evict them) has been in force in one form or another since 1915; and it has been the subject of a series of enactments which almost defy explanation. Matters were, however, improved by the fact that most of the relevant law was to be found in the (consolidating) Rent Act 1977, but further changes have been made in recent years.

Briefly, the history of the subject is that from the time when the First World War caused a housing shortage – which has of course been with us ever since – it became necessary to protect tenants. This has been sought to be achieved by no less than three different systems. The earliest was rent 'control' now abolished by the Housing Act 1980. The next, introduced by the Furnished Houses (Rent Control) Act 1946 created a special form of protection for *furnished* tenancies. The next – introduced by the Rent Act 1965 (*originally* only for *unfurnished* premises but now embracing furnished premises also) intended to replace, as it has now replaced, the 'control' system – is a system of rent *regulation*. The next, originally introduced by the 1964 Act, is what we may call the tribunal system.

All these systems concern, or concerned, only *private* letting, not lettings by local authorities, new town development corporations, certain kinds of housing associations, and certain other similar institutions. The 'public sector' was thus excluded. But the Housing Act 1980 introduced a fifth system to embrace the public sector.

We will now therefore first consider regulation within the private sector and then regulation within the public sector.

### (i)  The private sector
Under this head we need to consider first the *regulated* system and then the *tribunal* system.

*Protected tenancies*
These were originally the creation of the Rent Act 1965 (now replaced by the Rent Act 1977). This scheme came into force on 8 December 1965. Formerly only unfurnished tenancies were regulated, but the Rent Act 1974 brought furnished (other than resident landlord – below) tenancies into the system. The system will gradually die out by virtue of the Housing Act 1988 which provides that no new Rent Act tenancies could be created after the 15 January 1989.

For the system to operate there must be a 'letting'. Tenants, therefore, not licensees or lodgers, are protected. Moreover, the letting must be a letting of a 'separate dwelling'. This does not mean that only lettings of whole houses fall within the system; it merely means that, generally speaking, the letting must be in respect of accommodation which affords a complete home in itself: flats or even a single room, may therefore be subject to regulation, and so may accommodation shared by other tenants.

Where a tenancy satisfies these conditions certain results follow:

*(i)*  The premises become subject to a 'fair rent' assessed and registered by an official called a 'rent officer' from whom there is an appeal to a 'rent assessment committee'. In determining what is a fair rent the 1977 Act provides that 'regard shall be had . . . to all the circumstances (other than personal circumstances) and in particular to the age, character, locality and state of repair of the dwelling house, and, if any furniture is provided for use under the tenancy, to the quantity, quality and condition of the furniture'. But regard must also be had to the fact that the demand for similar dwelling houses in the locality is not substantially greater than the supply: this is commonly known as the 'scarcity' factor.

*(ii)*  The tenant is afforded *security of tenure*: his tenancy becomes a 'protected tenancy'. This has the effect that whereas at common law his right to occupation would end at the expiry of the current term of the tenancy in his case this will not be so. Instead when the term expires he may continue in possession as a 'statutory tenant' with what has been called the 'status of irremovability' upon the same terms as the original tenancy. Further, this right is subject to 'transmission' which means that if the tenant dies his or her surviving spouse may continue in possession as a 'statutory tenant by succession': so, if there be no surviving spouse, may any member of his or her family residing with him or her at the time of death. There

may be two such transmissions: so that, for instance, the widow of the first successor may succeed him in the right to occupation.

*(iii)* The only way in which this 'status of irremovability' may be determined (otherwise than by the tenant voluntarily) is by *order of the court*, and this only upon certain statutorily specified grounds. These include, *inter alia*, non-payment of rent, the causing of nuisance or annoyance, the fact that the premises are required by the landlord for his own use and the right of an owner-occupier who has temporarily let the premises to recover them for himself. The Housing Act 1980 also introduced the new concept of the 'shorthold tenancy': this is a regulated tenancy for a term of not less than one, but not more than five, years: upon its expiry the court may give the landlord a mandatory order for re-possession.

*(iv)* Certain types of letting fall outside the system altogether; these include, *inter alia*, lettings by educational establishments to students, holiday lettings, lettings which fall within the 'tribunal' system and leases falling within the Leasehold Reform Act (below). 'Assured' tenancies (not to be confused with tenancies given the same name under the Housing Act 1988, see below) also fall outside the system. Introduced by the Housing Act 1980, they are residential tenancies granted by approved bodies (such as pension funds) in respect of buildings erected or converted after 8 August 1980. The rents are not controlled but there is security of tenure.

### The tribunal system

This now applies to tenancies (within the same rateable values as those which apply to regulated lettings) which, in the main, are lettings *where the landlord is resident at the commencement of the letting*. They are called 'restricted contracts'.

The determination of the rent (here '*reasonable*' rent) is in the hands of *rent tribunals*, which are composed of a chairman and members drawn from the same panels as rent assessment committees. The rent officer is not involved, and references are made direct to the tribunal; first references may only be made by a tenant or by a local authority. Tribunal decisions are registered in the offices of local authorities and, unless the tribunal confines it to the particular letting, the rent so registered becomes the lawful rent for the premises in future.

As regards *security*, the tenant has no such statutory security as has the tenant under the regulated system; but the tribunal has power to order that the tenant remain in possession for limited periods.

Two further points should be made. *First*, subject to minor exceptions, it is an offence to evict *any* residential *tenant* without a *court order*, and it is also an offence to deprive any residential *occupier* (even a licensee) of his occupation. It is also an offence for a landlord to cause 'harassment' to his tenant (eg by making conditions unpleasant for him) with intent to cause him to quit. *Second*, it is generally illegal for anyone to receive a *premium* in respect of leases of any premises. This rule has been so strictly construed that it has been held to include a case where four guineas had been charged towards the cost of a tenancy agreement. It is also an offence to offer furniture or fittings at an excessive price in connection with the granting of leases.

As the result of the passing of the Housing Act 1988 it is no longer possible to create new protected tenancies, new restricted contracts, or new assured tenancies under the Housing Act 1980. These kinds of tenancies have been replaced by what the 1988 Act calls 'assured tenancies'. Protected tenancies and restricted contracts created before the 15 January 1989 remain governed by the previous legislation as described above; but the former assured tenancies have, in general, been converted into the new type of assured tenancy. This new assured tenancy is defined in the 1988 Act as a tenancy 'under which a dwellinghouse is let as a separate dwelling'; and a 'tenant, or joint tenant', is an individual who occupies the premises as his principal home. The change only affects the private sector and outside its scope are tenancies at low rents, business lettings, lettings of licenced premises, holiday lettings and some lettings by resident landlords.The new assured tenant has no right to challenge the contractual rent he has agreed to pay; but if the tenancy is terminated and the landlord wishes to increase the rent, the matter is referred to a rent assessment committee. The latter must determine whether the rent demanded exceeds the rent which might reasonably be expected to be obtained in the open market by a willing landlord under an assured tenancy on the same terms as the existing tenancy.When a fixed term assured tenancy expires security of tenure is ensured by the fact that, normally, a 'statutory periodic tenancy', will arise. No assured periodic tenancy can be terminated by the landlord without an order of the court which can only be made on specified grounds. Normally a surviving spouse or a person living with the tenant as husband or wife succeeds to the tenancy. The Act also brought into being a new form of shorthold tenancy – the 'assured shorthold tenancy'. These tenancies must be for a fixed term of not less than six months. Before the commencement of such a tenancy the tenant must be notified that it is an assured shorthold and that the landlord can recover possession upon its expiry. The landlord can demand a market rent but, upon the signing of the agreement, the tenant may apply to a rent assessment committee. The committee can only reduce the rent if it is significantly higher than the rent (having regard to the rents payable under other assured tenancies in the relevant locality) which the landlord might be expected to obtain.

### (ii) The public sector
Since the Housing Act 1980 (now also the Housing Act 1988) tenants within the public sector (p 369) also enjoy protection which formerly they lacked. Their tenancies have become 'secure' tenancies. These are tenan-

cies where a dwelling house is let as a separate dwelling by a landlord, such as a local authority, who falls within the public sector. Though certain such tenancies are excluded: these, amongst others, include student lettings and business and agricultural tenancies. The 1980 Act (as amended by the Housing Act 1985) gives the secure tenant a right to purchase the freehold (or, as the case may be, the leasehold) of the premises from the landlord under certain conditions.

The cardinal difference between the secure tenancy and the protected tenancy of the private sector is that there is *no rent control* of the former. But provided that the tenancy is a periodic one or for a fixed term determinable by the landlord it can only be *terminated* by *court order* upon grounds similar to those upon which a protected tenancy may be terminated. But there are also other grounds – for example, that the dwelling was let to a person having 'special needs' and that that person no longer resides in the dwelling.

### The Landlord and Tenant Act 1954, Part II

Subject to certain exceptions (including, amongst other things most tenancies not exceeding six months, agricultural tenancies, and tenancies protected by the Rent Acts), tenants who occupy the demised premises wholly or in part for the purposes of *business* are, subject to certain conditions, granted security of tenure by this Part of this Act (as amended by the Law of Property Act 1969). These provisions are complicated; but their effect is that, in substance, such tenancies can only normally be terminated (even though the period for which they were originally granted has expired) by giving notice to quit. If the notice is served by the landlord the tenant may apply to the court (in most cases a county court) for the grant of a new lease. The landlord may oppose the tenant's application only on certain grounds and the court has power, if such grounds are not established by the landlord, and the parties cannot agree to the creation of a new lease, to order a new tenancy for a period not exceeding 14 years; though, in certain circumstances, while ordering the tenant to quit, it must order the landlord to pay the tenant certain specified compensation. Subject to approval by the court, the LPA 1969, s 5 permits the parties to exclude the operation of Part II by agreement.

### The Leasehold Reform Act 1967

This Act (as subsequently amended) for the first time brings into play the principle of leasehold enfranchisement. Politically this is by no means a new idea and it was mooted as far back as 1885. Basically the notion of the lease as an investment for the landlord, with the corollary that the tenant – however long he continues to pay – can never own the land, is something repugnant to much modern political thought; so enfranchisement (ie the compulsory converting of the tenant's lease into a freehold estate) was certain sooner or later to leave the realm of debate and become a reality.

The particular situation with which the Act is designed to deal is the case of the long lease at a low rental, which was thought by some to bear hardly upon the tenant. Thus, for example, in the latter part of the nineteenth century in certain mining areas long leases of land (usually 99 years' building leases) were granted by landowners to workers at a ground rent representing only the value of the *land* – for the workers to build upon. The effect of the transaction was thus that upon the expiry of the lease the house (being a part of the land) would revert to the owner, even though it had been built by the tenant and continuously inhabited by him or his successors. The Act is thus primarily designed to enable people of his kind, by giving a requisite notice to the landlord, to obtain compulsory enfranchisement. The right is, however, only exercisable within fixed limits. The lease must be one originally granted for more than 21 years; it must be one at a low rent, ie, an annual payment of less than two-thirds of the rateable value (usually the assessment on 1 April 1973); the property in question must be a house (eg flats are excluded); the rateable value of the premises must be not more than £750 (£1,500 in Greater London) or, if the tenancy was created after 18 February 1966, the relevant values are £500 and £1,000 respectively; and at the time the tenant gives notice he must have occupied the house for at least five years or for periods amounting in the aggregate to five years out of the last ten. If all these requirements are satisfied the tenant becomes the freehold owner of the house subject to compensation payable to the landlord upon a somewhat complex basis, this roughly amounts to the market value of the freehold (excluding buildings on the land), upon the hypothetical assumption that it would continue to be let during the remainder of the current term, and for a further 50 years thereafter, at a modern ground rent. It will be realized that this is poor compensation to the landlord.

It must be added that as an alternative to purchasing the freehold, a tenant has a right (upon giving notice) to demand that his lease shall be extended for a further period of 50 years from the date of its expiry. This is not, however, very useful to the tenant since if the extension is granted the rent will be a modern ground rent (reviewable after 25 years) greater than the pre-existing one *and* the landlord will have an over-riding right to claim occupation of the premises if he needs them either for redevelopment or for occupation by himself or by an adult member of his family. The extended lease provisions would therefore seem to be as much weighted in the landlord's favour as the enfranchisement provisions are weighted against him.

### The Landlord and Tenant Act 1987

This Act contains important provisions concerning privately owned flats.

Part I of the Act enables tenants of blocks of such flats to acquire a right of first refusal upon a disposal of the premises by the landlord in certain circumstances. The tenants concerned must be 'qualifying tenants', ie the tenancy must not be a protected short-term tenancy nor a tenancy of business premises. Further, there must be two or more flats held by such tenants and the number of flats so held must exceed 50% of the total number of flats involved. Upon making a proposal for a disposal the landlord must serve notice upon the tenants containing particulars of the terms of the disposal. This notice constitutes an offer by the landlord to dispose of the property to the tenants on those terms. If the 'requisite majority' of the tenants accept this offer the landlord can dispose of the premises to a person nominated by it. The 'requisite majority' means more than 50% of the tenants involved.

Part II of the Act applies in general to premises consisting of the whole or a part of a building if the building or part contains two or more privately owned flats. Subject to certain qualifications the Part gives a tenant the right to apply to the court for the appointment of a manager or a receiver where the landlord is in breach of any obligation owed to the tenant.

Part III enables the court to make an 'acquisition order' enabling a 'qualifying tenant' to acquire the landlord's interest in premises to which the Part applies. Here a 'qualifying tenant' is a tenant of a long lease (ie principally a lease granted for a term certain exceeding 21 years) of a privately owned flat other than one occupied for business purposes. Although there are certain other complicated provisions which cannot be set out here, the premises involved must in the main consist of the whole or a part of a building and contain two or more flats held by qualifying tenants. The first step in applying for an acquisition order is that the 'requisite majority' (ie more than 50% of the tenants) must serve a preliminary notice upon the landlord specifying the grounds upon which the court would be asked to make the order and giving the landlord an opportunity to remedy any specified matters of complaint. Failing such remedial action the court may make the order: (i) if the landlord is in breach of any obligation owed by him under the leases in respect of the repair, maintenance, insurance or management of the premises, or (ii) if, both at the date of the application and for three years preceding it a manager had been appointed under the provisions of Part II of the Act.

Part IV gives to the court a power, upon application, to vary the terms of any long lease of a flat if the lease fails to make satisfactory provision in respect of a number of matters, including repair or maintenance of the flat or necessary installations, insurance and the provision and maintenance of services.

### The Leasehold Reform, Housing and Urban Development Act 1993

Part 1 of this Act gives to qualifying tenants holding leases in blocks of flats a 'right of collective enfranchisement'. The purpose of this is to enable tenants to gain ownership and management of their block of flats. A qualifying tenant must hold a lease of more than 21 years and be at a low rent. The tenant must also comply with strict residence conditions. The premises in question must be a building containing two or more flats held by qualifying tenants and the freehold must be vested in one and the same person and there are other fairly stringent conditions attached. The procedure is also rather complex and the price payable is fixed according to criteria laid down in the Act but is based upon the assumption of a sale on the open market by a willing seller in particular but incorporates elements designed to compensate the freeholder for a share in the value of the merger of the freehold and leasehold interests.

## The determination of leases

*Leases for a fixed period* – These leases normally expire automatically at the end of the agreed term. But there are exceptions to this rule; they include leases of *business premises*, certain leases of *residential* property at low rentals for more than 21 years, and *agricultural* leases. In order to provide farmers with security of tenure the Agricultural Holdings Act 1986 enacts that agricultural tenancies for a fixed period of two years and upwards shall only determine upon the agreed day if either party gives notice at least one year in advance. If this notice is not given the statute operates to prolong the tenancy into a tenancy from year to year, as from the original date of expiry.

*Periodic leases* – In the absence of special agreement (and apart from rent protection) periodic leases (ie leases not expressed to expire on a fixed date but created by reference to a period of determinability – eg from week to week, quarter to quarter, etc) normally expire when one full period's notice is given by either party. Suppose, for example, A grants B a quarterly lease from Lady Day (25 March) and suppose that, in April A decides that he wants to determine the lease at Michaelmas (29 September). A must give B notice on or before Midsummer Day (24 June). Strictly speaking in this example, the notice should be served on the day *before* the quarter day and should be framed so as to require the tenant to quit at midnight on the day before the following quarter day. In practice, however, notices from quarter day to quarter day are allowed. Similar rules apply, *mutatis mutandis*, to all periodic tenancies except tenancies from year to year; but this is now subject to the important provision of the Protection from Eviction Act 1977, s 5(1) that in the case of *all* periodic tenancies (including, eg weekly tenancies) of premises 'let as a dwelling-house' written notice must be given '*not less* than *four* weeks before the date on which it is to take effect' (and this may exclude either the first or the last day of the period, but not both). In the case of yearly tenancies only six months' notice is required, but it must be calculated (like notice of all periodic tenancies) to expire upon one of the anniversaries of the date upon which the lease was granted. Yearly agricultural tenancies, however, normally require at least a full year's notice, which must expire at the end of a current year of the tenancy (Agricultural Holdings Act 1986). The Housing Act

1974, s 123 provides that notices to quit must be in *writing* (in practice they always have been) and they are required to contain certain prescribed information.

## 3 RIGHTS OVER NEIGHBOURING LAND

It has been seen that one of the features of a lessee's interest is that it carries the right to exclusive enjoyment of the lessor's property. The three interests which now fall to be discussed, *Easements, Profits à Prendre*, and *Restrictive Covenants*, confer rights over 'other people's land' (*jura in alieno solo*) of a more limited nature than the lessee's right.

Easements and profits *may* subsist as *legal* interests. Restrictive covenants can only be *equitable*, but they are discussed at this point for the sake of convenience, for they bear a close resemblance to easements.

Before examining these three rights it must be stressed that they are all interests in land. As such they are not personal to the parties who create them, and they accordingly bind third parties and successors in title to the land. This characteristic formerly distinguished such interests from bare *contractual* rights or *licences*, which in strict theory were personal to the parties and did not bind the land; though some of them – such as the right of a theatre-goer to see the performance without arbitrary eviction by the proprietor – did afford some right to remain on the land. It must, however, now be admitted that, under the doctrine of proprietary estoppel, there are forms of licences which are coming to acquire the status of at least something like equitable interests; as for instance where a person who has been permitted to dwell in a house by the owner has relied upon the permission sufficiently to expend money upon improvements.

*Easements* and *profits* are limited rights over the land of another person. The distinction between the two is that, whereas an easement is a bare right over or in respect of the land, a profit carries with it the right to remove something from the land; as, for example, the right of pasturage of cattle.

### (a) Easements

#### i the nature of an easement

Examples of easements are rights of way, the right to have one's buildings supported by the land of one's neighbour, the right to discharge water over another's land, and the right to 'light'. The latter is a right to prevent adjoining owners from obstructing the flow of light to a particular window or windows of one's house.

As a general rule, an interest can only be classified as an easement if the following requirements are satisfied:

*(i)* An easement can only be enjoyed in respect of land – This means two things. First, there must be a '*dominant tenement*' and a '*servient tenement*'; that is, there must be two pieces of land, one (the 'dominant

tenement') to which the benefit of the easement attaches (to which it is said to be '*appurtenant*'), and another (the 'servient tenement') which bears the burden of the easement. Secondly, the easement must benefit the dominant tenement. Thus, although it is possible for X, in Sussex, to grant Y, who has land in Derbyshire, a right of way over X's Sussex land, this right cannot be an easement because it cannot benefit the use of Y's land.

*(ii)* There must be a dominant and a servient owner – Thus, suppose S to have two contiguous estates, and suppose that he habitually uses a footpath over the one to enable him to reach the other, this use does not constitute an easement.

*(iii)* Easements must be capable of forming the subject-matter of a grant – This rule arises from the fact that at common law the normal method of creating easements was by deed of grant. Thus it is possible to acquire an easement to the uninterrupted flow of air to a particular ventilator in a factory. It is not, however, possible to acquire an easement in respect of the flow of air over the whole of one's property; since it would not be possible to interrupt such flow, and therefore the right could not be granted. So also, it is impossible to acquire a right to protection of one's house from the weather by using one's neighbour's house as a shield.

## ii  The acquisition of easements

Easements usually come into existence in one of two ways: they are either acquired by grant, express or implied, or by prescription. *Express grants* require little notice. The rule is that they must usually be made by deed. An *implied grant* may arise where a man who owns two adjoining pro-perties sells one of them. Suppose, for instance, X owns Blackacre *and* Whiteacre. It has been noted above that if he uses a path across Whiteacre in order to reach Blackacre his user cannot be an easement. Suppose, however, that he sells Blackacre to Y; then the law will sometimes presume, quite apart from anything that it contained in the deed of conveyance, that Y has been granted an easement of way over Whiteacre. Consequently such rights – which are capable of becoming easements – are sometimes called 'quasi-easements'. The readiness of the law to imply a grant in such circumstances was strengthened by the LPA (s 62(1)), which enacts that conveyances of land are to be deemed to include *by implication* 'all liberties, privileges, easements, rights and advantages whatsoever, appertaining or reputed to appertain to the land'. And it is to be noted that where it is sought to establish a grant in this way it is not necessarily, as in the case where it is sought to establish a right by prescription, a bar to its establishment that the exercise of the right was consented to by the owner. Further, 'liberties, privileges and advantages' are things which defy precise definition; for instance a customary right to have a wall kept in repair by a neighbour has been held to come within the section.

In the case of prescription, as in the case of custom, the law permits long-continued practice to ground a claim of right. The reason rights can be acquired by prescription is that long and unchallenged user implies as much acquiescence on the part of the servient owner as if he had made a grant. There are two forms of prescription, '*common law*' prescription and prescription *under* the Prescription Act 1832. In order to establish a claim to an easement by '*common law*' prescription the claimant must show that he, or his predecessors in title, has exercised the right which he seeks to establish, continuously for a very long period. The exercise must run from 'time immemorial' and it must be 'as of right'. The limit of legal memory is fixed for this purpose at the year 1189; although all this means is that the right has to be proved to have been exercised for a considerable time and that there is no evidence that it has not been in existence from 1189. The expression 'as of right' means that the exercise must be '*nec vi, nec clam, nec precario*', neither 'forceful' nor 'secret', nor dependent upon the 'permission' of the servient owner. It is thus not easy to prescribe at common law. To take only one simple instance, it would be hard to acquire a right of support for one's house in this way; for few houses date from 1189. As a last resort, however, the difficulty may be avoided by reliance upon the fiction of '*lost modern grant*'. By this doctrine the court may *presume* after the right in question has been enjoyed for a reasonable length of time that a grant by deed was made some time after 1189, and uphold the right by reference to this notional 'deed' which it will conveniently presume to have been 'lost'. Moreover, the presumption will be made where 20 years' (the statutory period for the acquisition of an easement) uninterrupted enjoyment can be established. Though it will not be made if it be proved that a grant would actually have been *impossible*; nor will it be made if there is plain evidence that *no* grant *was* made; nor yet if there is no evidence of acquiescence on the part of the servient owner. The use of such a fiction may seem questionable; but the courts are rightly concerned to uphold established usage without being over-particular as to any exact requirement as to the period of use.

*Statutory prescription* under the provisions of the Act of 1832 was introduced in order to remedy the defects of the older law. In order to establish a claim to an easement under the Act a claimant must show continuous user as of right for 20 years *immediately preceding* the bringing of an action in which his claim is called in question. Further continuous use for 40 years will ground a claim even though the user has been subject to oral permission. If, however, the right is exercised by the written permission of the servient owner no claim can be established, and it makes no difference when the written permission was given. In the case of the easement of light, the Act provides that enjoyment for 20 years without interruption will suffice, even though it is not 'as of right'. The grant of written permission will, however, destroy the claim, even in this case. The words 'immediately preceding' are important: statutory prescription can only – unlike prescription by lost modern grant – be involved if the user relied upon was in active exercise at the time of the claim: it would not be enough (under the Act) to show, say 20 years' user 20 years ago. It may be of interest to add that it has been held that in the case of a right of way prescription will not be defeated by the fact that the actual alignment of the way is varied during the prescriptive period.

The Rights of Light Act 1959 provides that in order to prevent the acquisition of an easement of light, a servient owner may register a notice as a local land charge which will have the effect of an obstruction of the access of light known to and acquiesced in by all the parties concerned. This provision renders it unnecessary to erect screens or boards (which are in any case now subject to planning control) designed to interrupt the access of light.

## (b)  Profits

The essential difference between easements and profits has already been noted. There are certain minor differences. For instance, whereas, as has been noted, easements must be appurtenant to a dominant tenement, profits may be enjoyed *'in gross'* by an owner who has no such tenement. Moreover profits may be *'several'* (enjoyed by one person) or *'common'* (enjoyed by a number of people including the owner of the servient tenement). The prescription periods for profits are 30 and 60 years respectively, corresponding with the 20 and 40 year periods which apply in the case of easements.

These rules apart, the rules governing profits are very similar to the rules governing easements. Examples of profits are fishing rights, grazing rights and the right to enter land to cut turf. An appurtenant profit cannot be granted if it exceeds the needs (eg for grazing) of the dominant tenement.

## (c)  Restrictive covenants

It has been explained that, in defiance of the rule that contractual obligations are personal to the contracting parties, certain covenants which touch and concern land 'run with the land' and are valid not only between the parties, but against other people too (p 363). It will further be remembered that the binding effect of these covenants is limited. In particular, covenants do not bind people, such as sub-lessees, who have no 'privity of estate' with their landlord; moreover the burden, as opposed to the benefit, of vendor and purchaser covenants do not bind the land at common law.

These limitations of the common law rules could give rise to injustice. Consider the following case. T owned Leicester Square, London; T sold the garden in the centre of the square to E, and exacted a covenant from E to the effect that both E and his successors in title would keep it in its existing condition as an ornamental garden. T retained houses surrounding the Square. E resold the garden, and after it had passed through the hands of a series of purchasers, M bought it, knowing of the covenant. M threatened to build upon it. T sought an injunction restraining M from this unconscionable action. The position at common law was that, since the covenant constituted a 'burden' upon the land, it could not bind M. This position was clearly unjust, for T had a legitimate interest in preserving the amenities of the surrounding property which he had retained, and if M could snap his fingers at the covenant, he was in a position to buy 'burdened' land cheap, and then to make a profit by disregarding the burden.

The facts which have just been set out are the facts of the leading case of *Tulk v Moxhay* (1848) 2 Ph 774. Impressed by the rightness of T's claim, Lord Cottenham, LC cast about for some reason for granting an injunction. He found himself able to do so by holding that since M had notice, his conscience was affected by the covenant. In other words, the decision in favour of T amounted to this, that he had an equitable interest in the enforcement of the covenant. Thus a new class of equitable interest was created in order to supply the deficiencies of the common law. This interest, as defined and modified by subsequent authorities, has now become the *restrictive covenant of modern law*.

Lord Cottenham based his decision solely upon the fact that M had notice of the covenant. Today, however, the fact of notice alone will not suffice to make a restrictive covenant enforceable. Such covenants will only run with the land, so as to affect third party rights, if the following requirements are satisfied. *(i)* The obligation must be 'restrictive', ie negative in *effect* (however expressed). Thus the covenant in *Tulk v Moxhay* was restrictive. Although it was framed in positive terms ('To maintain ... uncovered with buildings'), it implied a substantially negative obligation, ie *not* to build: conversely, a covenant may be positive in effect even though framed in negative terms (eg a covenant not to allow a garden to fall into a bad state of cultivation, ie to *keep* it tidy). *(ii)* The covenant must 'touch and concern' an ascertainable area of land which is subjected to it. The meaning of this expression has already been discussed; but it should be added that the covenant must in some way *benefit* the land in respect of which it is created. *(iii)* The land in respect of which the covenant is claimed must belong to the person who seeks to enforce it. In this regard restrictive covenants display some similarity to easements. The reason for their enforcement is that they form a valuable adjunct to what may loosely be termed the 'dominant tenement'. This requirement of 'dominant' ownership does not, however, preclude an express assignment of the benefit of the covenant to a purchaser of part of the 'dominant' land. *(iv)* If the claimant is anyone other than the original convenantee he must, as a general rule, either show that the benefit of the covenant has been expressly assigned to him, or that it was originally 'annexed' to the land, or that it relates to land the subject of a building scheme or a scheme of development. A building scheme is a plan of development of land to be divided into plots for separate occupation and this presupposes, in the words of a famous judicial *dictum*, as between the purchasers of the plots 'community of interest and reciprocity of obligation'; so that, for example, a restriction upon the height of trees or fences imposed upon plot A will be matched by a corresponding restriction upon all the other plots, and thus, though it is restrictive of A, it will inure to the benefit of the estate as a whole. A covenant will usually be held to be '*annexed*' if it indicates the land to be benefited and signifies an intention to benefit that land. It will not be 'annexed' if it is expressed in terms which show an intention that it is to be *personal* to the parties or their successors. Thus there will be no annexation to the land where X covenants simply 'for myself and my assigns', because 'assigns' may include assignees of the covenant as well as assignees of the land.

The provisions of the Land Charges Act 1925 removed the law relating to restrictive covenants further still from its origin in *Tulk v Moxhay*. All restrictive covenants (unless between lessor and lessee) entered into since 1 January 1926, are registrable as '*land charges*'; hence, as will later appear, if registered they are valid against a *bona fide* purchaser for value without notice.

By s 84 of the LPA (as amended by the Landlord and Tenant Act 1954, s 52 and LPA 1969, s 28), restrictive covenants affecting freehold land and leasehold land where the lease was created for forty years or more, and not less than twenty-five have expired, can now, under certain circumstances, be modified or discharged by order of the Lands Tribunal (p 396).

In keeping with general principle, where the dominant and the servient land come into the hands of one owner the restrictive covenant will be extinguished.

## B   EQUITABLE INTERESTS

Preliminary explanation is needed here. In the first place, space will not permit of a discussion of all equitable interests, and only the more important of them will therefore be described. In the second place, the term 'equitable interest' is here used to denote an interest which can *only* be equitable. In this respect, apart from restrictive covenants, the interests about to be described differ from the fee simple, terms of years, and easements and profits, because such interests are capable of subsisting either as legal or as equitable interests. In the third place, all the equitable interests about to be described are 'trust' interests. Trusts will be discussed in a separate chapter. All that need be mentioned here is that where land is conveyed to trustees 'upon trust', the trustees may hold a legal estate in the land, but they hold it on behalf of other people (*beneficiaries*) who have equitable interests only. The nature and extent of these interests depend upon the terms of the trust. Finally, it has already been stressed that one of the major objects of the Property Acts was to render land freely transferable. This object was partially achieved by employing settlements and trusts for sale to over-reach equitable interests. The meaning of '*settlements*', '*trusts for sale*' and '*over-reaching*' must therefore be considered before the modern equitable interest can be described in its proper perspective.

## 1  SETTLEMENTS AND TRUSTS FOR SALE

### (a)  Settlements

#### i  Strict settlements

Much of the history of land law can be epitomized in terms of a struggle between family pride and the law. Landowners consistently endeavoured, with the help of their legal allies, the conveyancers, to 'tie up' the land in their families while the law has striven to keep it freely alienable.

We are first concerned with 'strict', ie traditional, settlements. The strict settlement has been known since the seventeenth century. In its simplest form it arises in the following way. M, who owns land, is about to marry W. He hopes to found a family, and to preserve the land in the family for as long as the law will allow. As will appear below, the law, in pursuance of its policy of championing free alienation, will not permit the land to be 'tied' for a very long period of time. It will, however, allow M to convey his land to trustees upon trust to hold it for him (M) for life, with remainder to his eldest son in tail and successive remainders (should this son die without issue) to M's younger sons in tail. This conveyance, which has the effect of earmarking the land as 'family' land, creates a strict settlement. But it must be noted that (because transfer duty on the whole capital value will today be payable on the death of each limited owner) the usual way of giving effect to the intentions of the parties in such a case would *not* now normally be by way of strict settlement; though since some such settlements still exist it is essential to deal briefly with this machinery.

The history of M must therefore be carried further. Suppose that the settlement is made, the marriage celebrated, and a son (X) is born. X attains his majority and wishes to marry. At this stage it would be normal, for reasons which will be explained when entailed interests come to be discussed, for X and M to agree to make a *re-settlement*. A re-settlement, at its simplest, would take the following form. The land would be reconveyed to the trustees upon trust to hold it for M for the rest of his life (subject to an annual sum of money charged upon the land in favour of X), remainder to X for life, remainder to X's eldest son in tail, etc. Upon M's death X would in due course make a similar re-settlement with his eldest son. So the process of settlement and re-settlement could continue from generation to generation and the land be retained in the family.

This ingenious method of 'tying' the land was satisfactory to the land-proud, but in practice, before the statutory modification which is about to be described, it often had disastrous consequences. The land was so effectively 'tied' that there was never anyone at any given moment with power to dispose of it. Property which might have been sold at a good price often became nothing but a burden to an impoverished family. Further, because there was never anyone with the rights of an owner there was little incentive to make improvements. Consequently in the last century the legislature intervened to strike the shackles from settled land. This branch of the law is now governed by the SLA which made far-reaching changes with the object of facilitating sales of land subject to settlements, of safeguarding the interests of purchasers, and of encouraging improvements. The Act retained and enlarged powers previously conferred upon tenants for life. It further provided that future settlements must be made by two deeds. The one deed, called a '*trust instrument*', declares the trusts upon which the land is to be held. The other deed, called a '*vesting deed*', declares that the legal estate in the land is vested in the person who is for the time being entitled to the enjoyment of it as tenant for life (ie 'M' and 'X' successively in the above illustration). The names of the trustees of the settlement also appear in this deed but there is no mention of the trusts upon which they hold. A new vesting deed is, of course, executed from time to time as each new life tenant becomes entitled to the land.

Under this machinery a purchaser is normally only permitted to examine the vesting deed; thus, as far as he is concerned, the owner of the land is the tenant for life, not the trustees. He must, however, pay the purchase price to the named trustees. The trustees then hold the money in place of the land and they are bound to invest it, and to apply the income according to the trusts of the settlement.

In the ordinary case the effect of the Act is therefore this:

*(i)* The vesting deed makes the tenant for life '*estate owner*' with the result that he may sell the land and has general powers of administration and management, which include the power to lease or mortgage it.

*(ii)* A purchaser can and must (except as to the payment of purchase money – (*iii* below)) deal with the person declared in the vesting deed to be the tenant for life as if he were the owner in fee simple.

*(iii)* The purchase money must be paid to the trustees: it takes the place of the land.

*(iv)* A purchaser never knows the nature of the equitable interests affecting the land. He is thus not affected by notice of them. They lie behind the 'curtain' of the vesting deed. They can therefore be *over-reached* when the land passes to a purchaser, so that he acquires the entire fee simple free from the trusts.

It should generally be remarked that, though it is necessary to understand their history, *strict settlements are now seldom met in practice*.

### Implied settlements

We have seen that the SLA freed land from the dead hand of family settlements. It did more than this, however. It applied the machinery just described to every case in which the free transfer of land is impeded by the absence of an adult owner who holds the fee simple absolute.

Subject to one important exception, to be noted below, wherever the land is *so limited that there is no fee simple owner of full age entitled to dispose of it,* it automatically becomes 'settled land' *by operation of law* under the provisions of s 1 of the SLA. All major interests in land which are neither legal estates in fee simple, nor terms of years absolute, are now equitable interests and they can only exist *behind a trust. Trustees* must therefore be provided to hold this automatically 'settled' land. Beside the trustees, as we have seen, in order for the machinery of the Act to operate, there must also be a *tenant for life* in whom the power of disposing of the land can be vested. The Act therefore provides that anyone of full age entitled to the possession of the land thus 'settled' shall be endowed with this power. Where there is no such person, eg where the land is limited in fee simple in trust for a minor, the powers of a life tenant are conferred upon the trustees as '*statutory owners*'.

Thus the SLA machinery makes it possible to overreach most equitable interests upon a transfer of land, whether or not these interests arise under a strict settlement. This statement must, however, be subjected to one important qualification. Land can never be 'settled land' where it is held upon *trust for sale.*

## (b) Trusts for sale

Settlements and trusts for sale are mutually exclusive.

Land becomes subject to an express trust for sale when it is conveyed to trustees under a trust which imposes upon them an *absolute duty to sell* it. Such a conveyance has the effect of evoking the equitable doctrine of *conversion*. This doctrine is based upon the principle that equity 'looks upon that as done which ought to be done'. Thus, from the moment of the conveyance, whether there has been an actual sale or not, the land is regarded in equity *as if* it were the *purchase money* to be realized from the sale.

The implications of this doctrine will be obvious. If it is desired to make a complicated series of limitations in respect of land, and at the same time to leave the land freely alienable, this object can be achieved by means of a trust for sale. Immediately the conveyance takes effect the rights of the beneficiaries under the grant attach in theory, not to the land, but to the purchase money. The trustees have not only a power, but a binding *duty*, to sell the land itself, and the equitable interests of the beneficiaries do not adhere to it.

Upon this showing it might appear that a trust for sale constitutes a peculiarly perverse method of granting *land*, for the beneficiaries would seem not even to be entitled to equitable interests in the *land*, but only in the proceeds of sale. This, however, is not the case, because although the land is in theory 'converted' from the time of the conveyance, the trustees are usually entitled to *postpone* the sale indefinitely. Hence in practice the beneficiaries may enjoy the land just as though they were entitled to it under a strict settlement. Thus the machinery of a trust for sale is similar to, and simpler than, the machinery of a strict settlement. Indeed, in some instances it may have the advantage of keeping the land in the family; as where the power of sale is only exercisable with the consent of a particular person.

Some further points require elucidation. First, there is no need for a 'tenant for life' where land is subject to a trust for sale: the *trustees* exercise the power of sale: they are the legal owners. Second, by s 28(1) of the LPA, trustees for sale are given all the powers of a 'tenant for life' under a settlement. They may, however, revocably delegate their powers of leasing, accepting surrenders of leases and of management, at any time before sale, to any person of full age for the time being beneficially entitled in possession under the terms of the trust to the rents and profits of the land. This person is, of course, in a position similar to that of a tenant for life; and he is clearly the person to exercise these powers. Third, since the rights which encumber the land are in theory rights only in respect of a share of the purchase money, notice of them will have no effect upon a purchaser of the land: he pays the trustees, the distribution of the money is their business. He takes the land free. It follows that there is no need of machinery to conceal these rights and the trust may therefore be created by one deed; though, in practice, for simplicity, two deeds are generally used.

The trust for sale is thus a straightforward device. It must, however, be stressed that no trust will be treated as a trust for sale unless the instrument which creates it imposes an 'immediate binding' trust. This means that the trust must be intended to take effect at once upon the conveyance, and that the duty to sell (subject to the *power* of postponement) must be absolute. Where land is conveyed to trustees subject to a series of limitations, and the trustees are given only a *discretion* to sell, there is no conversion and no trust for sale; the land becomes 'settled land'. This is a fine distinction, and it is often difficult to determine whether the wording of (eg) a will makes the land 'settled land' or subjects it to a trust for sale.

Finally, just as the SLA created implied settlements in order to facilitate free alienation, so, for the same reason, it imposed 'statutory' trusts for sale in certain circumstances; as where land is held by personal representatives upon an intestacy.

## 2    THE CLASSES OF EQUITABLE INTERESTS

### (a)  Entailed interests

*(i)  The nature of entailed interests*
As a matter of history the idea of the entail derives, though somewhat remotely, from the ancient institution of the *maritagium*. The object of

this was to convey land on the marriage of a daughter so that it should be held for at least three generations in the new family as a kind of starting inheritance. Should the family fail through lack of offspring the land reverted to the donor (father) or his heirs. The modern entail retains this notion, earmarking the property within the family and it is thus essentially connected with family settlements – which are now rare. There are two main classes of entails. Interests *in tail general* – these have the effect of limiting the property entailed in turn to the grantee and then to his heirs successively; including all heirs of any marriage that he may make. '*Heirs*' are the people designated as such by the common law rules of inheritance (which need not detain us here). Interests *in tail special* – these have the effect of limiting the property to the grantee and then to the heirs successively who are descended from a *specified spouse* of the grantee. Both general and special entails may, however, be so limited as to descend to heirs of one *sex* to the exclusion of the other, being then either interests in '*tail male*' or in '*tail female*'.

Before 1 January 1926, entailed interests were known as 'estates in fee tail'; real property alone could be subjected to them, and they were capable of subsisting as *legal* estates. *Any* property, whether land, goods or other personalty, can now be entailed (LPA, s 130(1)) but an entailed interest can only be an *equitable* interest and can only exist behind the curtain of a trust.

### (ii) The creation of entailed interests

There are two main forms of words of limitation (ie words denoting the nature of the interest) for the creation of entailed interests. The first form is 'To . . . in tail (or "in tail male" etc)'. The second form is 'To . . . and the heirs of *his body* (or "the heirs male" etc).' or, in the case of a special entail, 'To . . . *and the heirs (or "the heirs male" etc) begotten by him on the body of* . . . (the specified spouse)'. The word 'heirs', *must*, however, be used, since the essence of the entail is limitation to lineal *heirs*.

Either form of limitation will be permitted whether the grant be by deed or by will, but either the one or the other must be used.

### (iii) The barring of entails

It will have become plain that the entail is the instrument, *par excellence*, of ancestral pride. Its essential purpose is to keep the property in the family by creating, in effect, an endless series of life interests. On principle, therefore, an entail fetters the property and makes it inalienable – except for the period of a particular life interest – until the family becomes extinct. The courts have, however, as has been noted, always striven to prevent this result. With the exception of a period during the middle ages, it has always been, and still is, possible for a tenant in tail to free the property of the interests of his remaindermen (the line of his successors) and, in certain cases, to give himself the fee simple by extinguishing the interest of the reversioner. The 'reversioner' is the person to whom the land would revert should the family become extinct, ie normally the grantor or his successors.

Devious devices have been used in the past for 'barring' entails. The position today is that a tenant in tail in *possession* may turn his interest into a fee simple estate by the easy method of executing a 'disentailing assurance'. This is merely a deed by which the tenant conveys the land to himself absolutely. A tenant in tail in *remainder* can only turn his interest into a fee simple (expectant upon the death of the tenant in possession) if he has the *consent* of the 'protector of the settlement' who will usually, though not invariably, be the tenant in tail in possession. Without this consent, he can only bar his own successors in tail, not the reversioner. It should be added that at common law a tenant in tail could not devise the entail, and if he died without having disentailed, the estate descended to his heirs. This position was, however, altered by the LPA, s 176(1), which armed him with a statutory power – provided that specific reference is made to the property or to the instrument creating the entail, and that he is of full age and in *possession* of the property – to devise or bequeath it. And this testamentary disposition will bar the entail and pass the fee simple to the devisee.

The interest which arises where the above-mentioned consent is not obtained used to be called a '*base fee*' and is now technically an equitable interest equivalent to a base fee. Thus, if the land is limited 'to A and the heirs of his body', A may, if in possession, by executing a disentailing assurance, obtain the fee simple for himself. If, however, A is not in possession, for example where his entail takes effect in remainder, then a disentailing assurance by A without the consent of the protector of the settlement, will entitle A only to a base fee. This is not a valuable interest, because it is always threatened by the possibility that the family may become extinct, when the land will revert to the grantor or his successors. It was this unsatisfactory nature of the base fee that made the practice of re-settlement possible. A father who wished to keep the land in the family could rely upon his eldest son to prefer the offer of an annual sum of money, and the expectancy of a future life interest, to a mere base fee. The base fee, being all that the son could acquire by his own efforts, was unattractive because it was not easily saleable. Like an entailed interest, an equitable interest equivalent to a base fee (LPA, s 173(3)) may now – subject to similar requirements, and especially that as to *possession* – be devised so as to pass a fee simple to the devisee.

## (b)  Life interests

The normal life interest under the modern law is the interest of the tenant for life under a strict settlement. We have already seen how this interest arises; it therefore only remains to consider the rights and duties of the tenant.

The common law treats the tenant for life as if he were entitled to the income, but not to the capital, of a fund of money. He may enjoy the profits of his gift but he must pass on the bulk to his successors. Thus, generally speaking, he is entitled to the produce of the lands but he must not commit 'waste' which damages the inheritance. A tenant for life, for instance, who pulls down the mansion-house (ie the principal house of the estate) destroys something which belongs not to him but to his family.

Under the scheme of the SLA, as has been observed above, the tenant for life now plays a dual rôle: he is both a beneficiary, who owns a part interest in the family property under the trusts of the settlement, and he is also an 'estate owner' for the purpose of conveying the land upon a sale. Beside the *power of sale* (which can only be exercised for the best price reasonably obtainable) the SLA confers further powers upon him. Amongst these are the following:

(a) *The power of exchange* – Instead of selling the land the tenant for life may exchange it for land of equal value.

(b) *The power to grant leases* – Subject to certain conditions, he may lease the land for a maximum period of 50 years. This maximum may be exceeded in the case of certain types of lease, such as building leases (999 years) and mining leases (100 years).

(c) *The power to grant mortgages* – In certain circumstances, as for instance when capital is required for making improvements, the tenant for life may raise the money by granting a legal mortgage over the land.

(d) *The power to make improvements* – It has been explained that the old law discouraged improvements. Few people will spend large sums to benefit posterity primarily and themselves only secondarily. Under certain conditions the SLA therefore permits a tenant for life to charge the cost of improvements upon 'capital'. Capital money under a settlement is any money subject to the trusts of the settlement: for instance, money arising from a sale of part of the land. The money will, of course, normally be in the hands of the trustees. The Act schedules various classes of improvements. Permanent improvements, such as irrigation, are entirely chargeable to capital, for they benefit posterity. Transitory improvements, such as the installation of oil heating, may be paid out of capital, but the tenant for life must refund the expenditure (usually within 25 years). Further, as a result of the amendment of the SLA effected by the Agricultural Holdings Act 1986 a tenant for life of *agricultural* land can claim reimbursement of the cost of repairs out of capital money – this is, of course, important in the case of large landed estates.

Before the tenant for life may exercise any of his powers he must give notice to the trustees of the settlement. Some of the powers, moreover, can only be exercised with the consent of the trustees or by leave of the court. In the exercise of all of them the tenant is acting not for himself alone, but on behalf of the 'family', so that when he exercises them he is himself in the position of a trustee (SLA, s 107) and he must not use them only for his own interests. But, on the other hand, the Act (SLA, s 106) secures for him an absolute right to exercise the powers, by enacting that any provision in any instrument that tends to fetter his right to exercise them shall be void.

### (c)  Future interests

The expression 'future interests' is, perhaps, misleading. It has only been used in deference to tradition. It must not be supposed that we are about to discuss any fresh classes of estates and interests in this section. What we are now concerned to consider is the legal effect of creating any of the interests hitherto described in such a way that they shall arise, not immediately, at the time of the gift which creates them, but *at some time in the future*.

It need hardly be repeated that the only important estates and interests in land which are now capable of subsisting as *legal estates* are the fee simple absolute *in possession* and the term of years absolute. Generally speaking, all interests limited to arise in the future can now only be equitable, whatever their nature. The sole important exception to this rule concerns *terms of years*. These may be legal estates, whether limited in possession *or in the future* (provided that they are to take effect within 21 years). As a general rule, in the absence of a trust for sale, the effect of conveying any other interest so that it shall arise at a future time is to subject the land concerned to an automatic settlement. Thus all future interests except terms of years are capable of being over-reached.

It is necessary, however, to examine the effect of futurity a little further. Though future interests are thus subject to the 'overreaching' machinery of the Property Acts, they are also only valid if they conform with the requirements of the *Rules against Perpetuities*. Since these rules only apply to *contingent*, as opposed to *vested* limitations, the difference between these two classes of limitation must be explained before they can be described.

'*Vested*' rights are of two kinds, they are either vested in 'possession' or vested 'in interest'. A right which is vested in possession is one which usually carries with it the immediate right to the enjoyment of the land. Thus if A grants Whiteacre to B 'in fee simple', B's title vests in *possession*. A right is vested in *interest* where it resides in an ascertained personwhose right to possession merely awaits the natural determination of an existing estate. Thus where land is granted by X to Y for life, remainder to Z, in tail, whilst Y's interest is vested in possession, Z's remainder and X's reversion are both vested in interest. Z's remainder only awaits the natural event of Y's death. X's reversion resides in himself and his successors and only waits the failure of Z's successors. It must be noted that, whether vested in possession or in interest, a vested right actually exists in some holder; and this is nonetheless true if, though it will ultimately become ascertained, its exact extent is not known. Thus in *Beachway Management Ltd v Wisewell* [1971] Ch 610 it was held that a periodic payment imposed by way of rent charge to meet the cost of road maintenance pending adoption of the road by a local authority – by an estate developer upon the purchase of a house – was 'vested' even though the periodic sums to be paid were to vary by reference to the rateable value of the land.

'*Contingent*' rights are rights which *do not come into existence* until some uncertain event takes place. Thus if A grants land to B, a minor, 'if he reaches the age of 21', B has no real interest at all, he has a mere 'contingency'; the hope of an interest which will only vest in him provided that he reaches the age of 21.

If it were possible to grant land contingently in such a way that the interest of the grantee could spring up at any time in the future, upon the occurrence of some uncertain event, it would become entirely 'tied'. No one would buy it. Suppose, for instance, that B were a bachelor and that A, the owner of Blackacre, were permitted to grant the fee simple to 'any great-grandchild of B who shall have ten children at the age of forty'. Clearly in such a case either the land or – if such a grant were possible under modern law – at any rate the proceeds of the sale of the land, would be 'tied up' for a very long time indeed. The law, in its perennial anxiety to foster freedom of alienation, has therefore from time to time devised Rules against *Perpetuities* which aim at restricting future contingent grants within a reasonable period of time; some of these rules have been discarded and others modified. The subject is complex and it must not be supposed that the following outline is intended to provide anything more than a very general guide. Briefly, there are two main rules.

The *first rule* (common law) is time-honoured and it applies to all property, whether real or personal. It prescribes that where a future interest is created the limitation must be such that the interest must vest (if it is ever to vest at all: for a contingent interest may never vest if the contingency fails to occur) *within a life in being and 21 years thereafter*, adding, where appropriate, a period of gestation. 'Life in being' means the life of a person extant at the time when the gift takes effect. In the case of a gift '*inter vivos*' (ie between a live donor and a live donee – as in the case of a conveyance by deed from A to B) the gift takes effect at the time of the *execution of the instrument* creating it; in the case of a gift by will it takes effect at the time of the *testator's death*. The period begins to run from one or other of these points of time, and upon the determination of the 'life', only 21 further years are allowed. Moreover, at common law, at the relevant time the nature of the future gift had to be such that it could be predicted that it *must* vest (if it were ever to vest at all) within the period. Thus a gift to trustees to hold land in trust to convey it to X '20 years after the decease of the reigning Sovereign' was (and is) inevitably valid: Sovereigns (here the 'life in being') are mortal and X's interest (assuming only that X would be alive at the future date) must inevitably vest within the period. On the other hand, a gift dependent upon a future uncertain contingency which *might* (or might not) fall outside the period when viewed at the relevant time was invalid at common law, since it could not be predicted that it *must* vest (if it were ever to vest at all) within the period.

Thus at common law a gift 'To A' (life in being), a bachelor, 'for life, remainder to his first son to marry' was bad because A *might* have a son or sons none of whom would marry until after the period. Common law did not therefore allow the validity of the gift to lie in suspense to 'wait and see' (as it has often been expressed) whether events would prove that the donee would *in fact* qualify within the period.

This position has now in the case of most (but not all) gifts depending upon some future uncertain contingency been altered by the Perpetuities and Accumulations Act 1964, s 3. This provides that 'where, apart from the provisions of this section . . . a disposition would be void on the ground that the interest disposed of might not become vested until too remote a time, the disposition shall be treated, *until such time* (if any) as it becomes established that the vesting *must occur*, if at all, *after the end* of the perpetuity period, as if the disposition were not subject to the rule against perpetuities. . .'. This, in effect, means that now where the future interest in question depends upon an uncertain contingency the disposition will not be invalid simply because the predicted event *may* occur outside the period; it is permissible to await the determination of the period in order to discover whether the event has in fact occurred within it; if it has the gift will be good. On the other hand if during the period it becomes clear that the event *must* fall outside it, from that moment the gift fails. In the nature of things the former situation is likely to be the most common since an exact forecast of the time of occurrence of an uncertain future event is something which cannot often be made; but the latter situation may nevertheless arise in some cases. For instance, if one reverts to the last example one sees that it is a case of 'wait and see' until the end of the period: then and only then can anyone be sure that A will *not* have a son who *will* marry within the period; if he does, of course, the gift will be saved by the section, if he does not it will *then* (and only then) become void. It is possible, however, to imagine a contingency which, as it were, clarifies its date of occurrence during the period and before it actually has occurred. Thus suppose a gift 'To A for life, remainder to his eldest son when the comet White shall have appeared'. Assume that the date of appearance is uncertain, though likely, to occur after A's death: then assume that after the gift has taken effect the date of appearance is accurately predicted and that it will fall outside the period: the gift fails under s 3 from the moment of this prediction.

So much for the common law rule as modified by the 1964 Act. Now as to the *second rule*, which is new, having been introduced by s 1 of that Act. It introduces a period *alternative* to the first one and it is applicable to most (though not quite all) kinds of dispositions. To quote the section: '. . . where the instrument by which any disposition is made *so provides* . . .' the alternative period shall be '. . . a duration equal to such number of years (*not exceeding eighty*) *as is specified . . . in the instrument*'. All that needs to be noted is that the duration chosen must be specified in the instrument; if it is, and is not in excess of *eighty* years, the gift is valid even though it would have been void under the 'life in being' rule.

There is only enough space to add the following remarks. First, the time of *vesting* is all that matters; provided that this falls within one or other of the rules it does not matter that the interest in question will *endure* beyond that period. In the second place s 4 of the Act provides that where a limitation would be avoided by the first rule because its date of vesting depends upon the attainment by someone of an age in excess of 21 the gift will be saved from invalidity by treating the specified age as if it were the age nearest to it which (had it been specified) would have complied with the rule. Thus in a gift 'To A for life, remainder to his first son at 28' if we assume that at A's death there is a son aged 6 the prescribed age of 28 would take the gift out of the period (28–6 = 22); with the result that the figure 28 will be treated as if it were 27 (27–6 = 21); which accords with the rule. Finally, subject to exceptions, any limitations which offend the rules are void, though prior interests (such as 'To A for life') upon which they depend remain valid.

Similar principles apply to '*accumulations*'. Thus if X by will directs that the *income* accruing from his property shall be accumulated for a period of time, and then be given to a named beneficiary, X creates an accumulation. The permitted period of accumulation is governed by special rules in addition to the Perpetuity Rule. These rules are stricter than the Perpetuity Rule. They will be found set out in ss 164–166 of the LPA, and s 13 of the 1964 Act. It has been held that corporations are not subject to the rule against accumulations.

It should also be noted that the courts subject *any* gift which tends to make property inalienable to rules similar to the Perpetuity Rule. Thus a trust directing the income of a certain fund to be perpetually applied to furnishing a cup for yacht racing has been held to be bad. But there is some relaxation of this principle where gifts to charities are concerned (p 425).

# 3 Mortgages

A man who is in need of a loan may raise it in several ways. He may have a rich friend who lends *gratis* or at so much per cent. If he has no such friend he will have to borrow from a stranger; but strangers demand security. There are two principal forms of security, '*personal*' security and '*real*' security. Personal security usually requires a person who will stand surety for the debt. Real security requires some form of property; the borrower may, for instance, secure the loan by giving the lender possession of his watch. If he is lucky, however, the borrower may own land; in this case he will be able to secure the debt upon the land. The best way of securing a debt upon land is by way of mortgage. 'Mortgage' is a strange word. It is said to derive from the ancient practice by which the borrower conveyed the land to the lender with a proviso for reconveyance should the loan be paid by a certain date; if the loan was not repaid on that day the land became a 'dead pledge' ('*mortgage*') forever to the borrower, for it became the property of the lender. The word survives, although mortgages are no longer created in that way.

## A   THE NATURE OF MORTGAGES

The forms of mortgages recognized today are largely the creation of the Property Acts. They fall into two main groups: legal mortgages and equitable mortgages.

### i  *Legal mortgages*
There are two forms of legal mortgage: the mortgage by way of demise (lease), and the charge by way of legal mortgage. The *mortgage by demise* is effected in the following way. A, who is fee simple owner of Whiteacre, wishes to borrow from B. He grants B by deed, a legal term of years (usually for 3,000 years) of the land with a proviso that if the principal loan and interest are paid by a certain date, usually six months from the loan, the term of years shall cease to have effect. A further covenants in the deed to repay the loan and interest upon the agreed date. The effect of this transaction is to give certain rights both to A (mortgagor) and to B (mortgagee). These rights will be described below. For the present it need only be noted that, under the modern law, unlike the earlier law, B does not become absolutely entitled to his 3,000-year term once the agreed date for repayment is past: indeed, in the usual case it is never intended that the loan shall be repaid on the agreed date, and the real purpose of this is to provide a redemption date, the significance of which will appear later. If A only has a *lease* of Whiteacre he may effect a similar result by subleasing the property to B; the sub-demise will usually be for a period of ten days shorter than A's own lease.

The *charge by way of legal mortgage* is the creation of s 87 of the LPA. It is a short deed in which it is stated that a charge is made by way of legal mortgage, though no term of years is thereby created. The important thing to note is that, once executed, it gives rise to the reciprocal rights to which we have referred.

Should A in the example given above, fall into further financial embarrassment, he may wish to execute a further mortgage to C over the same land. He may do this either by granting C a term of 3,000 years plus one day or, if he only holds a leasehold interest, by granting a second sub-demise nine days less in duration than his own lease. In either case he, of course, has the alternative of executing a second charge by way of legal mortgage. He can also grant further mortgages (3,000 years plus two days etc) until he can no longer find a lender because his land is charged to its full value – mortgaged 'to the hilt'.

## ii Equitable mortgages

*(a)* Mortgages of equitable interests can, themselves, only be equitable – by way of contrast with mortgages of legal interests, which may be either legal or equitable. They are made by way of an assignment of the equitable interest concerned, with a proviso for redemption upon payment by the mortgagor of principal and interest. A deed is not required for the creation of these mortgages, but they must – in the absence of part performance – be made in writing.

*(b)* 'Equity looks on that as done which ought to be done.' If, therefore, in consideration of money advanced, X agrees to grant Y a legal mortgage, but fails to do so, provided that this agreement is evidenced in writing or supported by a sufficient act of part performance, Y has a form of equitable mortgage, which the courts will uphold.

*(c)* An equitable mortgage also arises where title deeds are merely deposited with someone, other than the owner, as security for a debt, without any formal mortgage document. It is, however, advisable for the lender (mortgagee) to insist upon the execution of a memorandum under a seal (ie a deed), because, as we shall see, this may give him a better remedy.

Finally, an equitable *charge* arises wherever there is a written agreement to treat property as security for a debt.

## iii Mortgages of registered land

*Registered* land will be discussed below but it is convenient to mention mortgages in respect of it here. Where a holding is registered the two more important ways of mortgaging it are:

*(a)* By way of *registered charge*. This is a legal interest which can only be created by deed. It may take the form of a mortgage by demise (freehold) or by sub-demise (leasehold) or by way of charge by way of legal mortgage. In the deed the land is usually described by reference to the register (see below). Such a charge will *only become* a legal estate by entry on the register. When it is so entered the mortgagee receives a 'charge certificate' and the land certificate (below) is deposited at the Land Registry during the continuance of the mortgage; this machinery gives protection to the mortgagee.

*(b)* A registered proprietor may create a mortgage by depositing the *land certificate* with the mortgagee; this, provided that written notice is given to the Land Registry and an appropriate entry is made on the register, will give the mortgagee an effective lien similar to an equitable mortgage.

## B   THE RIGHTS OF THE MORTGAGOR

### 1   THE RIGHT TO REDEEM

It might appear from the foregoing that once the period fixed for the repayment of the loan had passed the mortgagee obtained an indefeasible right to his lease or to the property. This, indeed, was the way in which the common law looked at the matter. Equity, however, tracing its descent from general morality 'looks to the *intent* rather than the form' and it has always insisted that a mortgage is, in essence, no more than a *form of security* as opposed to a conditional contract of sale. Hence equity disregarded the form of the contract and gave the mortgagor an equitable right to '*redeem*' (recover) the land at any time until sale or foreclosure by the mortgagee. This right is called the '*equity of redemption*'. The mortgagor can, of course, only exercise it if he repays the principal loan with interest to date.

So strictly did equity adhere to this principal that it did not, and does not, permit the right of redemption to be destroyed by expedients which hide what is in essence a mortgage transaction under the mask of some other form. Thus, in one case, B granted A a lease for twenty years, in return for a loan, and his right to terminate the lease was postponed for nineteen years. It was held that the lease being no more than a cloak to cover a mortgage transaction, B could terminate it by repayment of the principal and interest at an earlier date. '*Once a mortgage, always a mortgage*' –the equity of redemption is inviolable.

Further, equity insists that there must be '*no clog on the equity*'. This means two things.

(1)   The court will not countenance any covenant in the contract which purports to postpone the repayment period for an unreasonable time. What will be regarded as 'unreasonable' is a question of fact which must vary according to the relationship between the parties. Thus in *Knightsbridge Estates v Byrne* [1939] Ch 441, it was held that where one company had lent another £310,000 at 5.25% upon a mortgage of some very valuable property in London it was reasonable for the parties to agree to postpone the period for repayment for 40 years. The mortgagors fully realized that the mortgagees required a long-term investment. This, however, was an exceptionally long period; it would not be regarded as 'reasonable' as between private people in the case of a mortgage of property of little value in return for a small loan. If such a long period were agreed upon in a case of this sort the mortgagor would be entitled to disregard it, and to redeem long before it had expired. And he will also be entitled to disregard the contractual period of postponement and redeem where, although the time of postponement might not otherwise be objectionable, the transaction as a whole is illegal as being in unlawful restraint of trade.

(2) Once the money has been repaid and the land 'redeemed' the matter is at an end; the mortgagee must be satisfied with the return of his money together with the interest agreed. He must reap *no other collateral advantage*. This rule was evolved in by-gone days when mortgagors were usually necessitous people and mortgagees unscrupulous money-lenders who tried to secure more than their fair interest by imposing onerous stipulations upon the mortgagor. Like the last rule, it has therefore become modified in modern times and stipulations of this sort will now sometimes be enforced if the parties are on equal terms and the bargain, though a hard one, is not unconscionable, even after the mortgage has been redeemed. Thus, for instance, in *Multiservice Bookbinding Ltd v Marden* [1979] Ch 84 it was agreed between the mortgagors and the mortgagee that capital and interest repayments would be linked to the Swiss franc – which in result meant that the mortgagors would have to repay an amount in sterling considerably more than the actual amount of the loan. It was held that the transaction was valid. There was nothing unconscionable in such an agreement: the mortgagors had entered it fully advised and with their eyes open to its effect. But, once more, the collateral advantage secured must be reasonable. Thus where a loan of £2,900 in respect of the purchase of a house was secured by a charge on the property for the payment of £4,553 (the difference of £1,653 being by way of premium) it was held that, upon the mortgagor's default, the mortgagee could realize no more than the £2,900 at a rate of interest determined by the court.

## 2 THE RIGHT TO GRANT LEASES

Where, as will normally be the case, the mortgagor is in possession of the land, he has a limited right to lease it.

## C THE POWERS AND REMEDIES OF THE MORTGAGEE

The mortgagee cannot 'call in' (ie demand repayment of) the mortgage until the redemption date has passed, and in the case of certain mortgages of properties subject to the Rent Acts, not even then unless the mortgage payments are in arrears or there has been a breach of some other covenant (eg to repair) by the mortgagor. Subject to this, the principal powers and remedies of a *legal* mortgagee are the following:

(i) to take possession;
(ii) to foreclose;
(iii) to sell;
(iv) to sue upon the personal covenant;
(v) to appoint a receiver.

**(i) Entry in possession** – It should not be imagined that the mortgagee will normally take advantage of the lease which is granted to him. The usual position is that the mortgagor remains in possession of the premises throughout the duration of the mortgage. The term of years is granted merely as a security which the mortgagee may use if he wants to. If he does enter into possession the object of doing so is to keep down interest on the loan by paying himself out of the rents and profits arising from the land; but the court will exercise stringent supervision over him, and he is strictly accountable, not only for what he actually receives, but also for what, by the exercise of due diligence, he ought to have received.

**(ii) Foreclosure** – Equity, as we have seen, disregarded the *form* of a mortgage transaction and gave the mortgagor a right of redemption. Even equity, however, found it necessary to impose a limit upon the time for which this right could endure. The unpaid lender must sooner or later have a right to realize his security. Thus, if the debt be unpaid for an unreasonable time beyond the agreed repayment period, the mortgagee may 'foreclose' by obtaining an *order of the court* that the land shall become his unless payment in full is made by a certain date. Once that date is past, the order may be made 'absolute' unless the mortgagor has paid; he then loses all right to the land unless, as sometimes happens, he can persuade the court to 're-open' the order at a later date. Because of this, and certain other considerations, this right has a number of disadvantages and it is rarely exercised.

**(iii) Power of sale** – Under certain conditions, the mortgagee has a statutory power to sell the whole of the mortgagor's interest in the land. He may then recoup himself out of the purchase money, but he is not allowed to keep any *surplus* proceeds arising from the sale. The intervention of the court is not required for the exercise of this power; but although in its exercise the mortgagee does not act as a trustee for the mortgagor he nevertheless owes him a duty of care. For instance he must regard the latter's interests enough to take reasonable care to obtain a reasonable price. Sale is the most usual method of enforcing the security.

Where a mortgage is security for a regulated agreement *the power of sale and the power of entry into possession* can, by the Consumer Credit Act 1974, s 126, only be exercised by court order.

**(iv) Action on the personal covenant** – The repayment covenant is, of course – quite apart from the security over the land created by the rest of the mortgage – an ordinary contract. Hence the mortgagee may, at any time after the expiry of the repayment period, sue for the recovery of the loan.

**(v) The appointment of a receiver** – Under certain conditions, with a view to obtaining repayment of the interest, the mortgagee may exercise a statutory power of appointing a receiver to receive on his behalf the rents and profits arising from the land, with a view to ensuring payment of the interest. The receiver is deemed to be the agent of the mortgagor, and the mortgagee thus avoids the disadvantage of strict accountability to which, if he were to enter into possession, he would be subject.

The remedies of an *equitable* mortgagee whose mortgage is created by *deed* are much the same as the remedies of a legal mortgagee. The sole remedy of an *equitable* chargee is to have the land sold or a receiver appointed by the court.

# 4 Restrictions on ownership

Modern legislation has placed considerable restrictions upon land owner-ship. Compulsory acquisition and town and country planning.

## A COMPULSORY ACQUISITION

In days gone by the common law treated the right to property as sacrosanct: it was considered to be almost as inviolable as the right to personal liberty. Today this is no longer true. Although the courts will construe a statute which purports to destroy rights of property with the utmost strictness – especially if it gives no right to compensation – so many statutes have empowered public authorities and other bodies to acquire private land compulsorily, that it is no longer true to say that our constitutional law safeguards the right to property.

The law relating to compulsory acquisition is complicated. Only two points can be mentioned here. Where a statute authorizes the compulsory acquisition of *land* special procedures and measures of compensation laid down by various Acts including the Acquisition of Land Act 1981, the Land Compensation Act 1961 and the Compulsory Purchase Act 1965 (as amended) usually have to be applied.

Briefly, under the 1981 Act, the position is that an acquiring authority must submit a draft compulsory purchase order and submit it to the appropriate 'confirming authority' (Ministry, Department, etc). There must then be press publicity and the owners of the land in question must be informed. An inspector appointed by the confirming authority must hold an inquiry and consider objections. Thereafter the order may be confirmed or rejected by the authority. Confirmation can, in general, only be challen-ged before the courts if it is *ultra vires*. After confirmation the owners of the land have to be compensated. The basic measure of compensation is the 'market value' of the land, ie the amount which the land, if sold in the market by a willing seller, might be expected to realize. There may also be compensation for depreciation of land retained by the owner as well as for the loss of the land acquired. All disputes about the compensation have now to be submitted, subject to a right of appeal on points of law to the Court of Appeal, to a special tribunal, called the '*Lands Tribunal*', set up by the Lands Tribunal Act 1949. Unlike many other special tribunals, this body must be presided over by a barrister of standing or by a person who has held high judicial office. Its members are members of the legal profession and people experienced in land valuation.

A further important enactment is the Land Compensation Act 1973 as amended by the Planning and Compensation Act 1991 which contains detailed provisions concerning compensation where the activities of public authorities have adverse effects upon interests in land. Two important provisions may be noted.

In the first place s 1 in general gives a right to compensation where the value of the interest '*is depreciated by physical factors caused by the use of public works*'. The '*factors*' concerned are 'noise, vibration, smell, fumes, smoke, artificial lighting and the discharge on to the land of any solid or liquid substance'. The '*public works*' include *(a)* any highway; *(b)* any aerodrome; and *(c)* 'any works on land used in the exercise of statutory powers'. It is to be noted that the claim is not in respect of the construction of, eg the airport, but of its *use*, eg the noise arising from the aircraft or the noise of a motorway. The claimant's interest in his land must be in existence at the time when the work first comes into use (s 2); and there are certain other provisions as to the time in which the claim must be brought. Moreover, except in the case of depreciation caused by the use of a *highway* no claim will lie if (because no special immunity has been provided in respect of it) an action in nuisance will lie against the perpetrator.

In the second place, by s 29 and the following sections of the 1973 Act, provision for extra compensation is made for 'persons displaced from land': these include payment for '*home loss*' – as where a house is acquired for demolition by a local authority – and a reasonable amount becomes payable simply for the injury involved in losing a home. There is similar provision in favour of certain caravan dwellers and the right to 'farm loss payment' for people displaced from agricultural land.

## B   TOWN AND COUNTRY PLANNING

The Emperor Constantine is related to have paced out the confines of the metropolis he founded. Kingston-upon-Hull was officially planned under Edward I. Official planning is not new. But central planning and control of the general layout of the country as a whole only started in England in the present century. The stress of a large population in an island, the need to prevent waste of resources, increased speed of communication, the need to preserve the countryside and – at least one hopes – the desire to make and keep our island beautiful, demanded state planning. This is common knowledge, but it needs to be stressed because planning control curtails the rights of individuals and people often resent it.

This planning and control has been effected by the Town and Country Planning Acts, starting with an Act of 1909 and culminating in what is now the principal Act, the Town and Country Planning Act 1990 and Regulations made thereunder. The main object of this Act is thus to ensure that all development of the land is nationally and sensitively planned under state control. The Act therefore makes provision for positive planning by public authorities under the ultimate supervision of the Department of the Environment. In order to make the planning effective the Act imposes public control of most land development. There are thus two aspects of this branch of the law: planning on the one hand, control on the other.

(1) *Planning.* This is chiefly effected through area authorities ('county planning authorities' – county councils) and local authorities ('district planning authorities' – principally district councils). The system is that the former authorities are enjoined, under the control of the Department, to make and keep up to date 'development plans' which formulate general development policy within their areas. The latter must make local plans which, based upon the structure plans, make detailed provision for planning within their localities. The planning structure in Greater London is, however, different. Since the abolition of the Greater London Council a single 'tier' system of local government for London has been introduced. There is thus only one ('unitary') kind of local authority – as opposed to the 'two-tier' system elsewhere. In consequence the 'unitary' local authorities will shortly be enjoined to make one plan (instead of the two required elsewhere): a 'unitary development plan'.

(2) *Control.* The 1971 Act limits the right of ownership of land in two ways. First by requiring an owner to obtain 'planning permission' from the relevant local planning authority in respect of any development of his land or buildings. Second, by imposing additional control in respect of certain specified matters.

'Development' in this sense comprises, in the words of the Act, 'the carrying out of building, engineering, mining or other *operations* in, on, over or under land, or the making of any material change in the *use* of buildings or other land'. If an owner wishes to perform such an 'operation' or to make such a 'material change' he must therefore obtain planning permission. What amounts to an 'operation' or a 'material change' is a question of degree. An operation is something which comprises a physical change to the surface of the land. Building a house is clearly an 'operation'; but it has been held that placing a mobile hopper and conveyor in a coal merchant's yard is not. As an example of a material change of 'use' the Act specifically provides that converting a house into two or more separate dwellings constitutes such a change. But altering a yard from a coal to a transit depot has been held not to do so. Converting a dwelling house into a shop is an obvious change.

Some kinds of development and change of use are, however, exempted from permission. The Act specifies a number of changes that are not to be treated as 'development' – for instance, improvements which do not affect the exterior appearance of a house. Moreover, under the Town and Country Planning (Use Classes) Order 1987 a number of 'use classes' is listed, and any change of use within each class is exempted from control. Further, s 59 of the Act empowers the Secretary of State for the Environment to make 'development orders' granting overall permission for certain kinds of development. Thus the Town and Country Planning (General Permitted Development) Order 1995 made in exercise of these powers, gives automatic authorization for a number of specified forms of development.

If, without permission, a person makes a development which requires it the local planning authority may serve on him an *'enforcement notice'* ordering him to take steps to remedy his breach of planning control – eg to pull down the unauthorized house.

Additional control is imposed upon things which are deemed to affect amenity and safety – not only a planned country but a beautiful and safe one. *Inter alia*, these things include matters such as tree preservation orders, the designation of conservation areas (eg areas of historic interest), the preservation of 'listed' buildings, the control of advertising, caravan sites and such nuisances as rubbish dumps. As to safety: the Planning (Hazardous Substances) Act 1990 provides that specified 'hazardous substances' (such as dangerous chemicals) are not to be permitted on any land without permission of a 'hazardous substances authority' (a district council).

It should be noted that in certain matters the Secretary of State has *direct* powers of control. And it should also be noted that there is a right of appeal to him against refusal of planning permission and against enforcement notices. His decision to refuse planning permission is final unless he has exceeded his powers. If this should happen his decision may be challenged in the courts as *'ultra vires'*. An appeal against a decision on an enforcement notice lies to the High Court.

# 5    Protection of the right to land

The right to quiet enjoyment of land used to be protected by the Statutes of Forcible Entry (1381–1623) – incursions into other people's land being a common mediaeval occupation – but those statutes were repealed by the Criminal Law Act 1977 (as amended), s 13 and were replaced by the provisions of ss 6–12 of that Act.

By s 6 it is an offence for any person – provided that there is on the relevant premises someone whom he knows to be opposed to it –without lawful authority to use or to threaten to use *violence* for the purpose of entering premises. But the rights of the owner outraged by 'squatting' or 'sit-in' are safeguarded: for it is a defence to a charge under s 6 to prove that the accused is a displaced *'residential occupier'* – or the agent of one – of the premises or of the access to them. 'Residential occupier' means anyone, other than a person who was himself a trespasser on the premises, who has been excluded from them by a trespasser. Thus the person who comes back from holiday may use or threaten to use violence to oust squatters found in his home; but the squatters will commit the offence if they retaliate. 'Violence' is not defined: in principle, however, it is clear that excessive or unnecessary force may not be used, even by the residential occupier.

By s 7 it is an offence for any person who is on any residential premises as a trespasser, after having entered as such, to *fail to quit them* at the *request* of a 'displaced' residential occupier or of a 'protected intending occupier' (ie broadly speaking, a freeholder or a leaseholder of not less than a 21 year term who requires the premises for his own occupation or a person authorized to occupy by a local authority). The request must, however, be in a form specified in the section: and there are certain defences, eg that the premises are not residential. Section 8 makes it an offence for any person who has entered premises as a trespasser, without lawful authority or reasonable excuse, to have with him a *'weapon of offence'*. Section 10 re-inforced RSC Ord 113 and CCR Ord 26 (which make it possible summarily to obtain an order for possession against squatters (named or unnamed) by making it an offence for anyone to resist or intentionally to obstruct any court officer acting in the execution of such enforcement orders).

## 6 The sale of the land

### CONVEYANCE

Land, unlike goods, is not susceptible of physical delivery, yet it is necessary to have a clear indication of the moment when title to it passes from one person to another. In the case of a sale of land this indication is the 'conveyance'. At the time of writing there are still two methods of conveying land according to whether it is *registered* or *unregistered*. The position, however, is that the land of 90% of the population now falls within the former category. The main difference between the two methods of conveyance is that in the case of the former the title to the land is both *officially examined* and officially guaranteed whereas, in the case of the latter, it is for the parties to the conveyance to establish and ascertain the validity of the title (a time-honoured and tortuous process). In former editions of this book both these kinds of conveyances have been described but because, as has just been remarked, unregistered conveyancing is rapidly becoming obsolete it is thought that the time has come to omit discussion of it. The reader who wishes to learn about it is therefore referred to earlier editions of this book or to any standard work on land law or on conveyancing.

In examining the method of conveying registered land it has been considered best to start with a description of the system of land registration. After that mention must be made of the contract of sale of land, of what needs to be done between contract and conveyance, and completion of the conveyance itself.

THE LAND REGISTRATION SYSTEM

This is governed by the LRA (as amended). Under its provisions, once the title to the relevant interest in the land in question has been subjected to official verification it is registered in HM Land Registry in London or in a district registry. It is important to understand the basic principle: it is simple. Registration *constitutes title* and, as will appear, all that a registered proprietor has to do if he wishes to dispose of his interest is to execute a short and simple deed of transfer in a prescribed form and have the transferee's name substituted for his own on the register. He will have been provided with a '*land certificate*', which is *evidence* of his title, and the certificate will be endorsed to the transferee. As was intended by the original promoters of the LRA, this process, as will be realized, is almost as simple as the transfer of shares in a company.

Only two (legal) estates can be registered under separate titles: these are the fee simple absolute in possession (p 359) and the term of years absolute (p 360) – the latter interest only if it has more than 21 years to run. The separate register for each individual title is divided into three parts (confusingly also called 'registers'): (a) a property register; (b) a proprietorship register; (c) a charges register. The register is kept on an individual card index system and the three parts ((a), (b), (c)) are entered on separate cards. The *property* register describes the land concerned and the interest (freehold or leasehold) involved. Other legal interests, such as easements (p 373), may also be entered and the entry will constitute title to them. The *proprietorship* register states the class (below) of title and the name, address and description of the proprietor. It may also contain any entries of matters which affect his right to dispose of the land. For example, where the land is held by a tenant for life under a strict settlement (p 379) a 'restriction' must be entered preventing the registration of any sale or other disposition of the land upon which capital money will arise unless payment is made to the trustees or is paid into court. Further the restriction must prevent the registration of any disposition which is not authorized by the SLA (p 385). While safeguarding the rights of the beneficiaries under the settlement, this, of course, preserves the 'curtain' principle. The purchaser knows that there is a settlement but he has no notice of the interests of the beneficiaries. The *charges* register contains entries of incumbrances (eg restrictive covenants – p 376).

There are four *classes* of title, embracing 'absolute' title, 'good lease-hold title' and two other less common forms of title which need not be mentioned here. An *absolute title* can only be registered if the title has been investigated and officially approved by the Registrar. It should be noted that a leasehold, as well as a freehold, title may be registered as 'absolute': but this will only be the case if the Registrar has approved not only the title to the leasehold itself but also the title to the freehold and to any other intermediate leases. Where a leaseholder cannot produce the title to the reversion he may be registered as the proprietor of a *good leasehold* title.

As has been remarked above, when a title has been registered the important thing to notice is that it is guaranteed by the State. This means that anyone who suffers loss by reason of any error or omission on the register, or by reason of any rectification of the register, may claim indemnity.

The land registered may, of course, be subject to the rights of third parties – eg rights of way. *Some* third party rights are binding – even if they are *not* registered – upon the land, the registered proprietor and upon successors in title. These rights are called '*overriding interests*': they include, *inter alia*, leases for not more than 21 years, profits à prendre, legal easements and local land charges. The latter are charges of a public nature (such as restrictions upon the use of land imposed by a public authority) which are entered in local land charges registers kept by local authorities. The purchaser must thus ascertain their existence for himself – a rule which has been subject to criticism. *Other* third party rights ('*minor interests*') are required to be entered on the register in various ways if they are to bind a purchaser. Examples are restrictive covenants, equitable easements and estate contracts (such as contracts for the sale of land). By way of exception, a minor interest binds a *donee* even if it is not registered.

At the present time the general rule is that no one may inspect the register without the permission of the registered proprietor but, before long, under the Land Registration Act 1988 the register will be open to public inspection.

THE CONTRACT

It will be remembered that by the provisions of s 40 of the LPA, part performance aside, contracts for the sale of land formerly had to be evidenced in writing. Since 1989, such contracts must be in writing and the doctrine of part performance in this context was also abolished then (see the Law of Property (Miscellaneous Provisions) Act 1989). This was not, however, the only way in which they differed from other contracts; the following are examples of the main differences.

In the first place, contracts for the sale of land fall into two classes, they are either '*open*' or '*formal*'. An 'open' contract is one which does not set out the terms of the sale: consequently certain conditions are implied by law. The most important of these conditions is that the vendor shall be obliged to show a good title (see below). A formal contract is one which contains specific conditions. It usually consists of *particulars, special conditions and general conditions*. The particulars describe the property. The special conditions contain stipulations peculiar to the sale in question. The general conditions are standardized: they are usually incorporated into the contract by reference to one or another of a number of set forms. Forms of general conditions are put out by the Law Society and by local Law Societies and there is a commercial publication called the 'National' Conditions of Sale. Where an open contract is concluded by *correspondence* certain Statutory Conditions of Sale, laid down by the Lord Chancellor under statutory authority (LPA, s 46), apply, unless they are expressly excluded. It should be noted that although open contracts are theoretically of great importance they do not, as might be expected, often occur in practice.

In the second place, it is usual to provide for the payment of a deposit by the purchaser (usually ten per cent), which he will forfeit if the sale falls through by his default.

In the third place, the vendor – who, upon conclusion of the contract becomes *trustee of the land in favour of the purchaser*, so that if he sells it to a third party he is accountable to the purchaser for the proceeds – acquires an 'equitable lien' over the property for the amount of the purchase price for the time being unpaid. The effect of this is that, if the purchaser fails to pay, the vendor may apply to the court to sanction a sale of the land in order to recoup his loss. The lien, arising as it does by implication in equity, will terminate if the vendor secures his rights by some other means, such as the creation of an express charge.

In the fourth place, the risk of destruction by fire falls upon the purchaser from the time of the contract.

Finally, in most contracts for the sale of land, unlike most contracts for the sale of goods, both parties have a right to specific performance; not merely to damages. Moreover, a peculiar rule as to damages was sanctioned in *Bain v Fothergill* (1874) LR 7 HL 158; if the vendor finds that he is unable to complete the sale because of a defect in his title the purchaser will only be able to claim the return of his deposit (if any) and damages for expenses incurred, not for the loss of his bargain. This rule is said to have been made because of the difficulty of proving a good title to English land, but the rule was also abolished by the 1989 Act.

## BETWEEN CONTRACT AND CONVEYANCE

Between the time of the conclusion of the contract and the conveyance the vendor must satisfy the purchaser that he has a valid title to convey.

In parenthesis it need hardly be stated that all the operations that have to be performed in relation to the contract and the conveyance will normally be performed, not by the vendor or purchaser in person, but by their respective solicitors or other qualified representatives.

Under the registered system proof of a valid title is reasonably easy. As has been noted, the entry in the register constitutes the title. So what the vendor has to do is – until the 1988 Act comes into force – give to the purchaser authority to inspect the register and, also, to supply him with a copy of any documents or abstracts, or of any filed plans, that are entered on it. But since overriding interests (and certain other third party rights) are, as we have seen, not entered on the register they must be specifically disclosed; and the vendor must therefore supply the purchaser with copies, abstracts and evidence of them. Having received these, the purchaser must peruse them and may find it necessary to make inquiries ('*requisitions*') to the vendor about them and about any defects in them he may observe. He must also satisfy himself that the property described in the contract is identical to that described in the documents. He may further require evidence (such as the production of death certificates) of any events material to the establishment of the title. Moreover, he will have to make *searches*. He must search (examine) the register or apply for an official search. He must also assure himself that there are no undisclosed overriding interests, and, amongst other things, this will mean searching the local land charges register. He must, too, ascertain from the local authority that there is no development planned that may affect the land or its value. When all these things have been done to the satisfaction of the purchaser the final step will be the completion of the conveyance.

## COMPLETION

As has been observed, this is effected by the simple process of execution by the vendor of a simple *deed of transfer*, followed by *substitution* of the name of the purchaser for that of the vendor on the *register*. The land certificate will also be endorsed to the purchaser. The deed of transfer must be signed by the vendor in the presence of a witness. Among other things it will: (a) state the consideration for the sale; (b) be an acknowledgement by the vendor of the receipt thereof; (c) give the file number of the title; (d) state that the transfer is made by the vendor '*as beneficial owner*'. The magic of these words is that in the conveyance of a fee simple estate certain covenants on the part of the vendor are, by operation of the LPA, incorporated in the conveyance.

Briefly, these implied covenants comprise: (i) a covenant that the vendor has a good right to convey the entire interest he has to convey; (ii) a covenant of quiet enjoyment – that the purchaser shall hold his land free from interference; (iii) a covenant that the land is free from incumbrances – all adverse estates, claims and demands; (iv) a covenant for further assurance – that the vendor shall execute assurances and do all that is possible to perfect the conveyance. These covenants, however, only extend to acts or omissions of the vendor himself or of those claiming under him and of those through whom he claims. They do not extend to the acts or omissions of people from whom the vendor has purchased for a money consideration.

# 7   Limitation

It will be recalled that one of the methods of acquiring easements and profits is by means of prescription. The essence of prescription is that long, open and unchallenged use founds a claim of right. It might be expected that not only the right of easements and profits, but the title to land itself might be acquired in this way. English law, however, has confined the principle of acquisition by prescription to 'incorporeal' rights such as easements, which do not carry with them the right to *possession* of the land. Where a person is in possession of something 'corporeal', a physical object, such as land, the law grants protection to his *possession as such*. Thus a possessor has no need to rely upon prescription to constitute a title: the law will protect him against anyone except a person with a better right to possession than his. Thus if 'squatter' A is evicted by 'squatter' B, A may bring an action to oust B, though naturally A may himself be evicted by the rightful owner of the land. Though, since possession is protected, as such, the possessor will acquire a complete defence to a claim *even by the latter* after the requisite period of *limitation* has run in respect of an action by him: so that then the possessor's possession will have become 'ripened' by lapse of time into ownership.

The general rule laid down by the Limitation Act 1980, s 15 is that anyone, including the owner, who is ousted from the possession of land must bring his action to recover it within 12 years from the time when the cause of action first accrued. Once this limitation period is past, the plaintiff's right to sue is lost, and his title itself is destroyed. Thus if X ousts Y, a tenant in fee simple, and after 13 years Y ousts X, X may bring an action to dispossess Y. Y will not be able to rely upon his former title; he will have lost it through his own inertia. But in order for the limitation period to *start* to run against Y the latter must have discontinued his possession; or, to put the reverse, he must be ousted by X. Thus it has been held that the mere fact that a person makes use of another's land (as by ploughing it – a trespass) will not, even though it continue for 12 years, confer upon the former a title by reason of limitation if the reason that the owner raised no objection was that he was only leaving the land alone because he was waiting to build upon it when a projected road should be made.

The period (which, by the provisions of s 18(1), applies to claims by owners of equitable interests as well as to owners of legal estates) runs from the time when the cause of action *accrues*. In the simplest case where B evicts A, who is in possession, this will be from the moment of eviction. Often, however, people are entitled not to immediate, but only to ultimate, possession (as for instance in the case of a fee simple owner whose land is subject to a term of years). The Act provides that those who are in this position must bring their claim either within 12 years of the actual entry of the wrongful possessor or within six years of the time when they themselves become entitled to possession, whichever of these two periods is the longer. Thus suppose that B is the remainderman under a grant to 'A for life, with remainder to B in fee simple' and that X ousts A: B's right to recovery will be barred either 12 years after X's entry or six years after A's death. Landlords form an exception to this rule; their rights of action normally only 'accrue' against someone who evicts their tenants on the date when the tenancy is due to determine. They are permitted the full 12-year period from that time.

Minors and people of unsound mind are exempted from the ordinary rules. They may claim at any time up to six years from the cessation of the minority or disability (subject in the latter case to an overriding period of 30 years). Actions *by* the Crown are also subject to a 30-year period.

The provisions of the Act which govern fraud and mistake have already been considered (p 282).


## PERSONAL PROPERTY

# 1   The nature of personal property

Property is any object which a person may own or possess. Under the modern law '*personal*' property is any property other than land, except that for the purposes of descent leaseholds are treated as personal property (p 350). The main difference, as has been noted, between land and personal property, is that the former, being indestructible, may be subjected to interests of a more complex nature than the latter. Moreover, personal property, unlike land, escaped the hand of feudalism. Hence the doctrine of tenure never applied to it. Personal property may be owned in theory, as well as in fact.

*Leaseholds* (terms of years) have already been discussed. We have seen (p 350) that they came to be classified technically as 'chattels real' because of their assimilation in many ways to land, and it should be borne in mind that, strictly speaking, they will form an anomalous species of personal property.

Personal property is divided into two main categories: *choses in possession* and *choses in action*. These must be considered separately.

## A   CHOSES IN POSSESSION

*Choses* (ie *things*) *in possession* ('chattels') are the familiar tangible movables, such as books, cars or furniture, of everyday life. They are property which can actually be possessed and transferred by physical delivery. Like other forms of property, they may be the subject of a contract or of a gift. The owner's or the possessor's rights to them are protected by the law of torts and by the criminal law.

## B   CHOSES IN ACTION

There are many forms of property which are not tangible physical objects. Debts, for instance, and shares in a company, are 'property', but they cannot be touched or seen. Property of this kind is known as a '*chose in action*'; the owner's right to it cannot be asserted by taking possession, but only by means of an action. There are many such things beside shares; among the more important are negotiable instruments, patents and designs, copyright and trade marks and trade names. For the sake of brevity the first alone will be examined here.

### NEGOTIABLE INSTRUMENTS

It is possible that in the dawn of history men lived in family groups, and that there was no such thing as commerce. Today, however, even the most backward peoples have some form of commerce, even if it only takes the form of barter.

From early times coined money came to be used as a medium of exchange, and the coinage circumvented the obvious defects of barter. Money itself, however, is not always a convenient medium; it is, for example, both difficult and dangerous to transport from place to place. This inconvenience, moreover, as the 'Great Train Robbery' demonstrated, affects large sums of money in the form of notes as much as it affects coined money. Hence, at least by the middle ages, the merchants of Europe had invented *negotiable instruments* as a substitute for money.

A negotiable instrument is a written document embodying a promise usually (not invariably), to pay money. Three requirements have to be satisfied before the courts will recognize an instrument as 'negotiable'. It must be freely transferable, like cash, by delivery so that it can be passed from hand to hand in such a way as to entitle the holder of it to enforce the original promise. Either it must have been made negotiable by statute, or it must be a document which is treated as negotiable by statute, or it must be a document which is treated as negotiable by commercial custom. It follows that there is no closed list of negotiable instruments, for statute and custom may create appropriate new classes of documents from time to time. Custom, however, is never easy to prove, and it should not, therefore, be imagined that new classes of negotiable instruments are constantly being recognized in modern times.

When an instrument has thus acquired 'negotiability' it will be treated as representing money, and it therefore acquires a basic characteristic of money. If I steal your bicycle and sell it to X it will normally remain yours and you can recover it, or the value of it, from X. If I steal your money and buy a bicycle with it from Y the money ceases to be yours from the moment of the sale. In other words, money is not subject to the rule *nemo dat quo non habet* ('no one can give a better title than he himself has'). The same rule applies to negotiable instruments. Provided that a person who acquires a negotiable instrument takes it in good faith, and provided that he can prove that value has been given for it, he obtains a good title to it, even though he acquired it from a thief.

One of the outstanding features of negotiable instruments is that they may be sued upon by a person who has not himself given consideration and by parties who have no privity of contract. And, like money, they may be 'negotiated', ie may pass from hand to hand.

Three of the more common classes of negotiable instruments must now be considered: bills of exchange, cheques and promissory notes.

## (a) Bills of exchange

The law governing bills of exchange, and the other negotiable instruments about to be discussed, is now for the most part codified in the Bills of Exchange Act 1882 (here abbreviated 'BEA').

The Act (s 3(1)) defines a bill of exchange as 'an unconditional order in writing, addressed by one person to another, signed by the person giving it, requiring the person to whom it is addressed to pay on demand, or at a fixed or determinable future time, a sum certain in money to, or to the order of, a specified person, or to bearer'.

The meaning of this definition may be illustrated. A, a London merchant, is going to Paris. He will need money to buy goods when he is there and he does not wish to take currency with him. He has a friend, B, in London who has a debtor, C, in Paris. A pays B, say, £1,000. B then writes out an order for an equivalent amount of money in francs 'drawn' on C, expressed to be payable to 'A or order'. This document is a bill of exchange. A takes it with him to France. When he arrives he can either demand the money from C, or negotiate the bill by endorsing it to D, a third party. D will, of course, pay A; and, since the bill is 'negotiable', he will be entitled to recover from C the sum appearing on the bill. Should C, for some reason, refuse to pay, D will be entitled to recover from either B or A; but, on the other hand, he may 'negotiate' the bill to E; E to F and so on.

The following is a common form for a bill of exchange:

---

£1,000                                            London, 7 November 1989

Three months after date pay to Mr Thomas Smith or order one thousand pounds for value received.

John Johnston

To Mr Peter Roberts

---

John Johnston is the *drawer*. Thomas Smith is the *payee*, Peter Roberts is the *drawee*. Once Peter Roberts accepts he becomes the *acceptor*. When the bill is delivered to Thomas Smith he becomes the *holder*. If Thomas Smith 'indorses' the bill and negotiates it to X, Thomas Smith becomes the *indorser*, X, the *holder*. And every holder to whom the bill is *negotiated* by further indorsement may, as may X himself – provided all the requirements about to be discussed are satisfied – claim against the acceptor, or, failing him, the drawer or some prior holder.

Various points require to be considered:

### Bearer bills
The bill in the above example was made payable to Thomas Smith 'or order'. The effect of this is that if Thomas Smith wishes to transfer the bill to Timothy Transfer he must indorse it. It might, however, have been made payable to Thomas Smith 'or bearer'. In that case Thomas Smith could transfer it without indorsement. Bills may also be made payable simply 'to bearer', and anyone who holds them may then sue upon them (unless of course it can be *proved* that he is a thief). On the other hand, since s 3(1) of the BEA requires that in order to be a bill of exchange the document must demand payment to a 'specified person' or order, or to 'bearer', an instrument requiring payment to 'cash or order' cannot be a bill of exchange; nor (since a cheque is a special form of bill of exchange) can a cheque.

### Delivery
'Delivery' means transfer. No one may claim rights upon a bill until it comes into his possession by delivery. Thus, until delivery to the payee or acceptance, the bill is ineffectual, and the drawer can incur no liability

upon it. The first delivery (ie to the payee) is known as the '*issue*' of the bill.

## Indorsement

Indorsement is effected by signing the bill; usually on the back. It may be '*in blank*' or '*special*'. An indorsement is in blank where the indorser simply signs his own name, eg 'Thomas Smith'. An indorsement is special where the indorser signs his own name, then adds the name of a new payee, eg 'Thomas Smith – pay Timothy Transfer or order'. The effect of an indorsement in blank is that the bill becomes payable to any bearer who may obtain it. The effect of a special indorsement is that the person named ('Timothy Transfer') can only make a new transfer by indorsement.

## Acceptance

A bill is '*accepted*' when it is signed (usually across the face of it) by the drawee. He may do this at any time, even before the drawer himself has signed. Acceptance may be '*general*' or '*qualified*'. A general acceptance is an unconditional acceptance; a qualified acceptance is one which is subject to condition, eg that the acceptor undertakes to pay only a part of the amount of the bill. A bill may be payable 'on demand' (or 'at sight') or it may be payable upon a fixed date (as in the example). This date is known as the date of '*maturity*'. The bill is due and payable on that date unless it is a 'non-business' day, such as a bank holiday; in which case it becomes payable on the next succeeding business day.

## Holder

Any payee or indorsee in possession of a bill, or any bearer of a bill, is called a '*holder*' (BEA, s 2).

## Holder for value

Any holder of a bill, for which *at any time* value has been given, is deemed to be a '*holder for value*' as regards all parties to the bill prior to himself (BEA, s 27(2)–(3)). Moreover, provided that valuable consideration is given *for the bill* the holder is nevertheless a 'holder for value' if he has given such consideration to a person who is not a party to it, or if the person sued upon it has received it from such a person. Thus if A sues B upon a bill drawn by B it is no defence to B that A's consideration for it was supplied by X, nor is it a defence that B received consideration from X rather than from A.

## Holder in due course

A '*Holder in due course*' is any holder of a bill, complete and regular on the face of it, who takes *in good faith and for value* (see below) before the bill is overdue, and who has no notice that it has previously been dis-honoured (should that in fact have been the case), or of any defect (should there be such) in the title of the person who negotiated it to him. A bill will not be 'complete and regular on the face of it' if the payee, when endorsing it, does not make it apparent by his signature that he really is the intended payee. Thus, though the designation used by the drawer need not always be adopted by the indorser, yet, if the bill is to be 'complete and regular on the face of it', he must be careful to avoid a patent discrepancy between the designation he uses and that used by the drawer. For example, a bill drawn in favour of 'Colonel John Brown', and simply indorsed by the person in question 'John Brown', will be 'regular'; but it has been held that where promissory notes drawn in favour of 'X & Y Co or order' (a foreign partnership firm) were indorsed by one of the partners simply 'X and Y', the notes were not 'regular', so as to entitle a subsequent holder to claim the rights of a 'holder in due course' (though he *could* claim to be a 'holder for value'). The reason for this was that the indorsement ought to have led to a reasonable doubt in the mind of the holder whether 'X & Y Co' and 'X & Y' represented two different entities.

'*Value*' has a special meaning in the present context. By way of exception to the ordinary rules concerning consideration, for the purposes of this branch of the law, 'consideration' may include an 'antecedent debt or liability' (BEA, s 27(1)(*b*)). This point should be stressed, for, as has been explained, normally 'past' consideration is no consideration.

### Presumption of good faith and value
Every *holder* of a bill is *prima facie presumed* to be a *holder in due course* (BEA, s 30(2)). This is a most important rule; but it must be realized that it only imports a *presumption*, and that presumption may be rebutted (so as to render his claim invalid) if it is proved that the holder lacked good faith, ie took the bill knowing of a defect in title *or* knowing that the acceptance, issue, or subsequent negotiation was affected by fraud, duress or illegality. The burden of proving such knowledge in respect of defective *title* lies upon the acceptor or other person who seeks to establish that the plaintiff is not a holder in due course, but where fraud, etc is alleged the holder *himself* must *prove affirmatively* that at some time subsequent to the wrongdoing in question, and before the bill came into his hands, *value* was in fact given for it by *someone* (not necessarily himself) who took in good faith, without knowledge of the wrongful act.

### Presentment
There are two forms of presentment: 'presentment for acceptance' and 'presentment for payment'.

**(a)  Presentment for acceptance** – Strictly speaking this is only necessary (and even so, subject to exceptions) in three cases. First, where the bill is payable 'after sight' (ie is expressed to be payable within a certain time after it has been brought to the notice of the drawee) – clearly here it *must* be 'presented' because, until it is, its maturity date remains unascertained. Second, where the bill itself expressly stipulates that it shall be presented for acceptance. Third, where the bill is drawn payable elsewhere than at the place of residence or business of the drawee. Of course these categories do not include cheques.

Where a bill of these kinds comes into the hands of a holder he must either present it to the drawee for acceptance, or negotiate it within a reasonable time. Upon presentment, the drawee must accept the bill within 24 hours. If the drawee fails to do so within that time, or if he repudiates liability, he will have 'dishonoured' the bill. If this happens, the holder must give notice of dishonour to the drawer, or to the person who indorsed the bill to him. Notice of dishonour must not be given prematurely before dishonour. It is effective from time of *receipt* and must be given within a reasonable time of dishonour or in the case of written notice sent by post it must normally be despatched on the day of dishonour or, at least, by the following day.

The effect of giving notice is to fix the drawer, or the previous indorser, with liability for payment. All parties who have signed the bill prior to the holder are sureties for the payment of it. Thus an indorser who receives notice of dishonour will give notice to the person who indorsed it to him, and so forth, until the drawer receives notice. After the acceptor, the drawer is, of course, primarily liable. Moreover, failure to present for acceptance (where this is required) will discharge the drawer and previous indorsers.

Unless a bill is payable on demand it need not normally be presented for acceptance; moreover, if it is so payable, we have already seen that a holder need not present it if he transfers it to another person within a reasonable time.

**(b) Presentment for payment** – All bills must be presented for payment at the proper time. A bill payable on demand must be presented by the holder within a reasonable time of receiving it (unless he indorses it to someone else). A bill payable upon a fixed date must be presented for payment upon that date. If the acceptor refuses to pay, his refusal constitutes '*dishonour*' and the holder must give notice to prior holders, as in the case of dishonour by non-acceptance.

*Dishonour*
The effect of dishonour is, as has been stated, that the acceptor, and all parties who are prior in order of time to the present holder, are liable upon the bill. Any one of these parties who pays has rights against parties prior to him. Thus, suppose that W is drawer, X acceptor, Y indorser and Z holder; X dishonours the bill by non-payment, and Z is paid by Y. Y may claim against W or X. If W pays Y, he may still sue X.

*Discharge of bills*

Bills may be discharged in five ways –

(1) By payment. This is the normal method of discharge.

(2) By renunciation. Any holder may renounce his rights. In order to be effectual, however, the renunciation must be evidenced in writing.

(3) By delivery up of the bill.

(4) By cancellation, ie written cancellation upon the bill itself.

(5) By 'material alteration'. If, for instance, a holder alters the date of payment appearing on the bill, all parties liable up to the time when the alteration was made will be discharged. If, however, the holder later transfers the bill he will be liable upon it himself, as altered.

## (b) Cheques

A cheque is defined by the BEA as a '*bill of exchange drawn on a banker payable on demand*' (s 73). The rules governing cheques are in most respects similar to the rules governing other bills payable on demand, except that, since the Cheques Act 1957, s 1, it is usually unnecessary for the payee to indorse the cheque unless he wishes to negotiate it. There are, however, certain other special rules which govern cheques alone. Some of these rules must be noted.

**Crossing** – In the first place, as everyone knows, cheques may be '*crossed*'. Crossing may be '*general*' or '*special*'. General crossing is effected by drawing two parallel transverse lines across the face of the cheque. The words 'and company' (or some abbreviation thereof) may also be added, though this is not strictly necessary. A cheque which has been crossed generally can only be cashed through a banker. Special crossing is effected by placing the name of a *particular* banker across the face of the cheque; in this case, though they are often also added, lines are not strictly necessary; and the effect is that the cheque can only be paid through *that* banker. The purpose of crossing is the avoidance of fraud. No banker may pay a crossed cheque over the counter; he must credit the amount paid by the bank which has 'accepted' the cheque to his customer's account. Should a banker pay a crossed cheque over the counter, and should it turn out that he made the payment to a thief, he will be liable to the owner for the amount paid.

**'Not negotiable'** – In the second place, if cheques are marked 'not negotiable', although they can still be transferred by the payee, they cease to be negotiable. This means that if I pay you with a cheque so marked, and the cheque is stolen from you and then transferred by the thief to X, X, even though he gave value and took it in good faith, may be liable to you for the amount of the cheque. Other negotiable instruments cease to be *transferable* altogether when marked 'not negotiable'. A crossing containing the words 'account payee' or 'account payee only' makes the cheque non-transferable (Cheques Act 1992).

**Bankers** – In the third place, cheques are governed by certain rules which arise by reason of the special relationship which a banker bears to his customer. For instance, a *banker* must use, in *all* his dealings with his customer, such reasonable care to protect the customer's interests as conforms with the ordinary practice of bankers of repute; though more than this is not expected of him. Thus, for instance, in *Schioler v Westminster Bank Ltd* [1970] 2 QB 719 it was held that the Bank was not in breach of duty in forwarding a dividend warrant from its Guernsey branch to England with the result that the customer who owned it had to pay tax on it; a result which could have been avoided by, for example, forwarding the warrant to Cork; for, without special agreement, banks are not expected to act as their customers' tax advisers. As regards *cheques* a banker is, however, expected to know his customer's signature. If, therefore, he has reason to suppose that the signature on a cheque presented to him for payment is not authentic he should withhold payment until he has made enquiries; but, though he must take reasonable care to guard against forgery, he will not be expected to have such skill as a handwriting expert might be expected to have in detecting it. Moreover the banker must, within reason, warn the customer of any suspicious circumstances relating to any dealing which might suggest the presence of fraud or such like which might be detrimental to the customer's interests. Importantly in *Hedley Byrne & Co Ltd v Heller & Partners Ltd* [1994] AC 465 the House of Lords made it reasonably clear that a banker who gives a reference to *others* about his customers' credit is not under a duty not to be negligent. The *customer* also owes special duties. He must, for example, exercise due care in keeping cheques, and he must also be careful how he draws them. Suppose, for instance, that A signs a bearer cheque and negligently hands it to a creditor to fill in the amount of his debt (say, £10). The creditor writes '£100' and presents it to a banker, who pays him. This means that A's banker will wrongfully debit A's account to the amount of £90. A, nevertheless, cannot complain, since the wrongful payment has been induced by his own breach of the duty of care which he owes to his banker, and he must accordingly submit to having his account debited with the £100. He of course has a right of action against the creditor; though rights of action against knaves are not usually satisfactory forms of property. The decision of the Judicial Committee in *Liu Tai Hing Cotton Mill Ltd v Chong Hing Bank Ltd* [1986] AC 80 may be of special interest. It was there held that, unless he has contracted to do so, vis-à-vis his bank, a customer is not required to check his bank statement so as to enable him to inform the bank of any unauthorised debits. In operating his current account the customer's only duties are to refrain from drawing cheques in such a way as to facilitate fraud, and to inform the bank of any unauthorized cheques drawn on his current account as soon as he becomes aware of them.

Attention must also be drawn to the Cheques Act 1957, s 4, which enacts that 'where a banker *in good faith and without negligence* receives payment for a customer of a cheque crossed generally or specially to himself, and the customer has no title ... thereto, the banker *shall not incur any liability* to the true owner of the cheque by reason only of having received such payment'. Thus suppose Smith to have drawn a cheque in favour of White and suppose Black to have obtained this cheque; suppose Black to have represented himself to the Z bank as White and to have opened an account with them (as White) and then to have drawn out the money for himself and absconded with it. The bank will be protected by s 4 against a claim by Smith *if they can establish* that, in all the circumstances, they took such reasonable steps as are required by current banking practice – by obtaining references or otherwise – to assure themselves that Black was White.

Finally, it should be noted that the relationship of banker and customer, at any rate in respect of a current account, is a relationship of debtor and creditor. But, even in this respect, the relationship is a special one because, although it is normally the duty of a debtor to seek out and pay his creditor, it is in the nature of the banker-customer relationship that the banker shall only have to pay such sum or sums as the customer may happen to require when he is asked to make the payment, and, even then, only at a particular office; hence, before any legal right of action can accrue in favour of the customer, he must, by cheque, or in some other way, make a demand for payment.

**Bankers' commercial credits** – By mercantile custom, which has now become law, if a bank issues a *confirmed letter of credit* it is as strictly liable to the person to whom the credit is given as it would be had it issued a promissory note (below). And a similar rule applies to bankers' *guarantees* ('guarantee bonds'). Thus, in the absence of fraud, it is no defence to a bank sued upon such documents to prove that the person to whom they are issued is in default as against some other person. For example, let a bank guarantee delivery of so many pounds worth of goods by B to A, and let A, who has contracted to buy the goods, for some reason, default in his contractual obligations to B, A may, in the absence of fraud, sue the bank if B does not make delivery to A. B himself will have to indemnify the bank, and will be remitted to a right of action against A. The reason for the strictness of this rule is that the observance of their obligations by bankers is an essential prop of international commercial transactions.

**(c)  Promissory notes**
A promissory note is defined as '*an unconditional promise in writing made by one person to another signed by the maker, engaging to pay, on demand or at a fixed or determinable future time, a sum certain in money to, or to the order of, a specified person or to bearer*' (BEA, s 83(1)).

Promissory notes were made negotiable by eighteenth century statutes. They are very similar to bills of exchange and most of the rules governing bills also govern notes. Notes, however, differ from bills in one important respect. From the above definition, it will be appreciated that there is no *drawer* of a note; though the *maker* corresponds to the acceptor of a bill; and so it follows that, since the maker must necessarily have signed the note from the start, the rules relating to presentment for acceptance cannot apply to notes. The whole object of this form of presentment is to make sure that a drawee who has not already accepted is going to do so. By definition a promissory note must be an engagement to pay at 'a determinable future time': an undertaking to pay 'on or *before*' a certain date cannot therefore be a promissory note.

It should be explained that an 'IOU' is not a promissory note: it is only evidence of a debt. The border-line between the two classes of document is, however, a narrow one, because any addition to an IOU which brings it within the terms of the above definition will turn it into a promissory note.

Bank notes are promissory notes. The following are possible forms for a promissory note and an IOU.

---

£50                                     London, 8 August 1989

One month after date I promise to pay John Brown or order fifty pounds.

                                              Thomas Atkins.

---

                                        London, 8 August 1989

Hugh Dix

IOU £20

                                              Peter Hicks.

---

NOTE – In relation to a 'regulated agreement', at least in respect of transactions confined to the United Kingdom, a creditor or owner is forbidden by the Consumer Credit Act 1974, s 123(1) to 'take a negotiable instrument *other than a bank note or cheque* in discharge of any sum payable'. And by s 123(2) he can only validly negotiate such cheque to a banker. Should he negotiate it to someone else there will be a defect in title (s 125(2)) with the result that if the debtor can establish that the holder knew the circumstances, the latter's claim will be invalidated. By s 123(3) a creditor is forbidden to take *any* negotiable instrument as *security* for a sum payable under a regulated agreement. Section 124 provides that contravention of s 123(1) or of s 123(2) renders the debt or, as the case may be, the security unenforceable save by *court order*.

# 2   Security upon personal property

Personal property, like land, may be used as a means of securing debts. There are various forms of security upon personal property; but we can make no more than bare reference to three of them.

First, personal property may be mortgaged. In the case of a mortgage of goods (other than ships) if the terms of the mortgage are such that the debtor is to retain possession of the goods, while the creditor acquires the ownership, and if the transaction is effected by a *written document*, the document will be a 'security *bill of sale*'. As such, it must be registered at the Central Office of the Supreme Court under the Bills of Sale Act 1882. It must also contain certain particulars, such as the consideration paid by the creditor; and it should be made according to a prescribed form. The particulars and the form are required in order to protect the debtor against usury, while registration is required in order to give the public notice of the transaction. If the document were not registered the debtor would be in a position to hold himself out to the world as a more affluent man than he really is, and thus he might obtain credit on the strength of property apparently, but not really, his own. A bill is void where the amount of the loan is less than £30.

Secondly, goods may be '*pledged*' (or 'pawned'). In this case the pledgee (pawnee) acquires *possession* of them. There is thus no danger that the pledgor will obtain false credit. Further, the pledgee, being in possession, is entitled to bring an action for conversion if the goods are taken from him. Pledges relating to *regulated agreements* are subject to special rules (similar in many respects to the rules previously pertaining under the Pawnbrokers Act 1872 to 1960), but it must be noted that since chattel mortgages and pledges are consumer credit agreements the provisions of ss 60–64 of the Consumer Credit Act 1974 also apply: these relate, it will be remembered, to the form of agreement, the giving of statutory copies and of notice as to cancellation rights. In the case of *pledge* agreements it is an *offence* (s 115) for the pawnee (pawnbroker) to fail to supply the relevant copies and notice or to supply a 'pawn receipt' (formerly 'pawn ticket').

In the third place, personal property (and in some cases real property; as in the case of a purchaser of land – who has a lien over the land in respect of his deposit) may be subject to *liens* which arise by *implication of law*. Liens (if we omit maritime liens, which bind ships to secure the pay of their crews) are of two main kinds: '*possessory*' (or 'common law') liens and *equitable* liens. The essence of the possessory lien is the right to *retain* the property *until payment*, as in the case of the unpaid seller of goods, the *innkeeper* – who may thus retain most property which a guest brings to the inn – the *repairer*, such as the tailor or the motor repairer over goods actually repaired, the carrier over freight for his charges and the auctioneer over the goods for the purchase price. All these are examples of '*particular*' liens. But possessory liens may also be '*general*'. Here the lien is not to secure a particular sum but may cover all claims arising during a course of business: thus a *solicitor* has a lien over his clients' property for his fees, *a banker* over his client's money or securities for his charges and an *accountant* for his.

The equitable lien differs from the common law lien in that it may attach by law *irrespective of possession*: the purchaser's lien, already mentioned, is an example – it attaches before the land is conveyed; and the vendor has a similar right in respect of purchase money which is unpaid. Upon dissolution of a partnership a partner also has a lien over the partnership property for payment of partnership debts.

Possessory liens carry their own sanction; the right to *retain* against payment. Generally the lienor has no right of sale to satisfy his debt. Equitable liens (because they do not rest upon retention) may, however, be enforced by sale if their existence is confirmed by a declaration of the court, and some statutes do confer special rights of sale in certain cases. For instance, the unpaid seller has a statutory power of resale under the Sale of Goods Act 1979, s 48(3). The innkeeper also has a similar power in respect of the guest's property under the Innkeepers Act 1878; though only if the property has been six weeks on the premises and the sale has been advertised for at least a month. Subject to rules laid down by the Torts (Interference with Goods) Act 1977, ss 12 and 13, a bailee may also, in certain circumstances, sell the bailor's goods. A 'bailee' is, of course, someone, such as a person who keeps goods in deposit, who has possession of someone else's goods.

# 3   Gifts

There are two classes of gifts: gifts *inter vivos* (between living people) and *donationes mortis causa* (gifts conditional upon death).

## 1   GIFTS 'INTER VIVOS'

In order for an effective gift of personal property to be made there must be an *intention* on the part of the donor (giver) to give *and delivery* of the gift to the donee (recipient) or to a trustee on his behalf.

The intention to give may sometimes be paramount. For example, in *Dewar v Dewar* [1975] 2 All ER 728 it was held that where a mother gave, and intended to give, her son a sum of money to buy a house the transaction was nevertheless a gift though the *son* intended to treat it as a loan and, in due course, to return the money: a common situation in family affairs. Needless to say, the donor must be capable of forming a proper intention; though it may be that the degree of capacity may need to be greater in the case of more valuable than in that of less valuable gifts.

What will amount to 'delivery', varies according to the nature of the property. A physical object, such as a fountain pen, may be delivered by actual transfer. The title to choses in action is transferred by whatever is the appropriate method of transfer. Thus shares in a company are transferred when transfer is effected on the company register. Mere transfer of the share certificates will not suffice. But even in the case of a physical object it may be a sufficient delivery if the donor indicates his intention to give and informs the donee of the whereabouts of the thing to be given so that the latter can collect it for himself. Thus in *Thomas v Times Book Co Ltd* [1966] 2 All ER 241, the gift of the manuscript of *Under Milk Wood* to a BBC producer was held to be valid when Dylan Thomas, the poet, having indicated his intention to make the gift, and being about to fly to America, told the donee that he had left the manuscript in a Soho public house where the latter then found and collected it. Moreover, if a person indicates a firm and unchanging intention to make a gift to another and then appoints that other as his personal representative the taking out of representation by that other, since it vests the legal right to the property in him, is treated as tantamount to delivery and completes the gift.

Some forms of property, however, cannot be transferred easily, even though they are physical objects. Thus, it may be inconvenient to transfer hay which is stored in a barn. In cases of this sort the law recognizes the transfer of the means of control – as by handing over the key of the barn – as a valid delivery. Further, in certain special cases, where the goods are of a cumbersome nature, the law permits a document of title to 'represent' them. So the right to a ship's cargo may be transferred by delivery of a document called a 'bill of lading'.

Unless delivery is effected in one way or another there can be no gift. Hence, if I promise to give you my motor car and I say that I will deliver it at your house, I may change my mind up to the very moment that I deliver it to you; even on the very doorstep.

*A mere promise to give is not actionable.* This is the hallmark which distinguishes contracts from gifts, and the rule in equity is that 'there is no equity to complete an imperfect gift', ie a gift which has not been perfected (completed) by delivery, actual or constructive, ie notional.

The above rules are subject to two exceptions. First, a promise to give is, as we have seen, enforceable if it is made by *deed*. In the second place, a gift may be perfected without delivery if the donor declares himself *trustee* for the donee. This does not, however, mean that an attempted, but uncompleted, gift will be construed as a declaration of trust. Moreover, except where a donor declares himself trustee of his property for the donee, equity also insists upon delivery to the trustee for the creation of a trust.

Lastly, intending donors should, perhaps, be warned that if there is some inherently dangerous quality in the article given they may sometimes be held legally responsible for any damage it causes; but this rule will only apply if the article is not obviously dangerous (for example, it would not apply in the case of a gift of a gun with a patently fractured barrel) and the donor, knowing of the hidden danger at the time he makes the gift, omits to warn the recipient.

# 2 DONATIONES MORTIS CAUSA

A *donatio mortis causa* is a gift of personal property made by a donor in contemplation of his own death. These *donationes* differ from gifts *inter vivos* in this respect, that, whereas a gift *inter vivos* takes full effect upon delivery, a transaction will only amount to a '*donatio*' if it can be inferred from the words of the donor, or from all the circumstances of the case, that he intended the gift to take effect only in the actual event of his death; and that if he should recover, he should be entitled to resume full ownership of the property. A '*donatio*' is not, therefore, an informal way of making a will.

Most of the rules which apply to gifts *inter vivos* also apply to *donationes mortis causa* and, in particular, '*donationes*', like gifts, must be effected by delivery. A valid *donatio* may, however, sometimes be effected by the transfer of documents of title to a chose in action even though the documents do not fully 'represent' the chose. For instance, provided that the donor shows a present intention to give, a valid *donatio* of money in a Post Office Savings Bank may be made by transfer of the savings book.

If the donor does die, the *donatio* is similar to a legacy; it is liable, like other legacies, to be taken in satisfaction of the donor's debts.

# Chapter 12

# Trusts

We have already had occasion to refer to *uses*. The word 'use' is said to derive from the Latin *opus* ('help' or 'need'). A 'use' arose in mediaeval times where a person conveyed property of any sort to another (*feoffee to uses*) upon the understanding that that other was to become seised of (ie hold) it on behalf of himself (the donor) or on behalf of some third party (*cestui que use*). Clearly the feoffee to uses was in a position of confidence which he might abuse. Consequently the rights of the *cestui que use* required protection. The common law courts refused to recognize uses, and therefore failed to afford this protection; but at an early date the Court of Chancery, acting as a court of 'conscience', intervened to force the feoffee to uses to administer the property for the benefit of the *cestui que use* according to the terms of the grant. In the course of time the *cestui que use* thus came to have a special interest in the property enforced only in the Court of Chancery. This interest, protected as it was by the Chancellor's equitable jurisdiction, became an *equitable* interest (p 28).

For our purposes we may treat the ancient use as the exact counterpart of the modern trust: the *cestui que use* has now become a *cestui que trust* (or '*beneficiary*'), the feoffee to uses has become a *trustee*. Thus, to borrow the late Sir Arthur Underhill's definition (*Law of Trusts and Trustees*) a trust is 'an equitable obligation, binding a person (who is called a trustee) to deal with property over which he has control (which is called the trust property), for the benefit of persons (who are called the beneficiaries or *cestui que trust*), of whom he himself may be one, and any one of whom may enforce the obligation'.

It is impossible to enumerate all the purposes for which trusts are used. Broadly speaking, they enable people to take the benefit of property, who are, for one reason or another, unable to hold the legal ownership in it themselves. Thus, for instance, where land is owned by more than one person it must be held for them in trust: the reason for this is that it was found impracticable for the *legal* ownership of land to be split between a number of people. Moreover, groups of people, such as unincorporated associations, can enjoy the benefit of property held in trust even though the law does not accord legal 'personality' to their group. The 'trust and confidence' imposed in the trustee by the creator of the trust is the core

420

and essence of the matter. Equity will not permit the trustee to depart from his undertaking. The right of the beneficiary arose only as a sidewind of this rule.

Trusts are a peculiarity of English law and have often not been recognized elsewhere. To some extent this has been remedied by the Hague Convention implemented by the Recognition of Trusts Act 1987.

Any form of property may be held in trust.

Trusts may be classified in many ways. The classification here used is not the only possible one – it has been adopted because it is thought to be the simplest.

# 1  The varieties of trusts

Trusts may be divided into two main classes: *private* and *charitable*. Private trusts are enforceable at the instance of beneficiaries, while charitable trusts are 'public' in the sense that they are generally enforced at the suit of the Attorney-General acting on behalf of the Crown, and that in order to be valid they must always be of benefit to the public or to a section of it, as opposed to individuals.

## A  PRIVATE TRUSTS

### i  Express private trusts

An express trust is a trust which is expressly imposed. It may be created in any manner: by deed, by writing, by will, or (except in certain cases) merely orally. Whatever the method of creation, however, the creator must make his intention absolutely plain. It has thus been laid down that in order for a trust to arise there must be three '*certainties*'. There *must be* certainty of *words*, certainty of *subject-matter* and certainty of *objects*.

(a)  **There must be certainty of words.** This means that the words used must show a clear intention that a *trust* shall arise. Thus if X gives Y a ring and says, 'I charge you to hold this ring in trust for Z', X has plainly imposed a trust. On the other hand, when '*precatory*' (praying) words are used, it is sometimes difficult to determine whether the donor has intended to impose a trust or merely to express a wish. In one case, for instance, a man gave property to his wife by his will and added that he did so 'in full confidence' that she would do what was right as to the disposal of this property among the children of the marriage.

It was held that although precatory words of this sort may sometimes give rise to a trust, these particular words in their particular context did not show an intention to create one, for the giving of the property to the wife 'in full confidence' was merely the *motive* for the husband's gift. The wife therefore took the property absolutely, and the children were not entitled to be treated as beneficiaries under a trust. It must be added that *intention* is paramount, so that facts as well as words may furnish evidence of it – as, for example, where intending to create a trust of money a special account is opened in respect of it.

**(b)  There must be certainty of subject-matter.** This requirement speaks for itself: if the subject matter to be held in trust is indeterminate the courts cannot enforce the trust. Thus if A, by his will, were to direct his executor to hold 'some portion of my property' in trust for B the trust would fail.

**(c)  There must be certainty of objects.** Thus if a man were to give a picture to another upon the understanding that it should be held in trust for someone who should be subsequently named, and if the donor were to die without disclosing a name, there would be no express trust and the picture would 'revert' to the donor's estate by operation of law. On the other hand, a trust dependent upon the condition that the beneficiary must be married to a wife 'of Jewish blood and the Jewish faith' will be valid: whether a person has Jewish blood is an ascertainable fact and so is the meaning of 'Jewish faith'. A seeming exception to this rule occurs with discretionary trusts, where the trustees are authorized to select the beneficiaries from a class specified by the settlor. It was held by the House of Lords in *McPhail v Doulton* [1971] AC 424 that such a trust is sufficiently certain if the trustees can say whether or not a potential beneficiary is a member of the class even if it is impossible to make a list of the members of the class.

Beside being 'certain' the trust must be '*completely constituted*'. This may be brought about in three ways. The creator of the trust may declare himself trustee, he may impose the trust in his will, or he may convey the trust property to trustees.

Where the last of the above methods is adopted the trust will not be 'completely constituted' until an out and out transfer to the trustees has been effected. An attempted transfer will not suffice, for '*there is no equity to perfect an imperfect gift*'. Thus, if the property concerned is land there must be a deed of conveyance: if it consists of shares there must be a valid transfer. Until the trust is thus 'completely constituted' by transfer it will normally be ineffectual.

There is, however, one important exception to the rule as to out and out transfer. If the creator of the trust has agreed to convey the property for *valuable consideration*, equity, which '*looks upon that as done which ought to be done*', will enforce the transfer of the property in due course, and thus render the trust 'completely constituted'. 'Valuable consideration' in this sense means not merely consideration, but includes 'marriage consideration'. Thus if John, who is about to marry Joan, settles property upon trustees in favour of Joan and any issue of the marriage, Joan *and the issue* come within the 'marriage consideration'.

If therefore the transfer to the trustees is incomplete – as it will always be where the property within the trust comprises property which the settlor may acquire after the marriage ('after-acquired' property) – this will be no bar to the 'complete constitution' of the trust. Joan and the issue are regarded as 'purchasers', just as if they had given money value in return for the benefits they are to receive. It should, however, be noted that only close relations, who are within the 'marriage consideration' will benefit: thus an unascertained class of next of kin are mere 'volunteers', not furnishers of consideration.

## ii Implied trusts

Implied trusts arise either from presumed intention ('*resulting trusts*') or by the operation of rules of law or equity ('constructive trusts'). (Implied trusts are sometimes called '*constructive trusts*', and then divided into '*resulting*' and '*non-resulting*' trusts.)

**(a) Resulting trusts** – Without expressly creating a trust, people sometimes act in a way which shows that they presumably intended to do so. Human activities being infinitely various, obviously no exhaustive list can be given of trusts which arise in this way, and random illustrations must suffice.

In the first place, where a man settles property upon trustees in a way which makes no provision for the exhaustion of the entire interest in the property, the unexhausted interest will 'revert' to him. Thus if Robinson settles property upon Jones in trust to pay the income to Smith for life, and makes no further disposition, after Smith's death the property will be held by Jones in trust for him (Robinson), or if he is dead, for the persons entitled under his will or upon his intestacy. It is clear that Jones himself is not intended to take since he is designated 'trustee'.

In the second place, where A (otherwise than by way of loan) supplies money for B to purchase property, B will, in the absence of evidence of a contrary intention, be presumed to hold the property upon a resulting trust in favour of A. This presumption may, however, sometimes be counterbalanced by a contrary presumption called the *presumption of advancement*. This arises where a husband or a father advances money for a purchase by his wife or child. In this case it is presumed that the advance is intended as a gift, so that no resulting trust in favour of the donor arises. The presumption of advancement, like the presumption of a resulting trust, may, of course, be rebutted by evidence of a contrary intention. It should be noted that the presumption extends to cover the case of a person in the place of a parent (*in loco parentis*) who supplies money for someone whom he treats as his child. Grandparents or godparents, for instance, may often be in this position. Similarly where matrimonial property stands in the name of one spouse only, but the other has contributed to its acquisition, the courts will, in case of dispute between them about the property, imply a trust in favour of the other (or even in favour of a mistress where the couple have lived together with the same mutual commitment as in marriage) to the extent of his or her contributions, including not only money payments but also the fruits of labour: as where the wife (or mistress) has helped to build the (matrimonial) home. The underlying principle was well expressed by Lord Denning, MR (*Hussey v Palmer* [1972] 3 All ER 744): 'By whatever name it is described (ie "resulting" or "constructive" trust) it is a trust imposed by law whenever justice and good conscience require. It is a liberal process founded on large principles of equity, to be applied in cases where the defendant cannot conscientiously keep the property for himself alone, but ought to allow the other to have the property or a share of it.'

In the third place, when a trust is declared which the law will not permit to be carried out, eg because it infringes a perpetuity rule, there may be a resulting trust in favour of the donor.

**(b) Constructive trusts** – Constructive trusts are imposed by law independently of anyone's intention. A stock example of a case in which a trust of this type arises is where property held in trust is, in breach of trust, conveyed by trustees to someone who had notice of the trust: here equity protects the rights of the beneficiaries and treats the stranger as a constructive trustee, whether or not he consents to act as such. There have been many cases on what amounts to 'notice', with a notable exposition of the present situation by Sir Robert Megarry, V-C, in *Re Montagu's Settlement Trusts* [1987] Ch 264.

A further example of a constructive trust is provided by the rule in *Keech v Sandford* (1726) Sel Cas Ch 61. In that case a trustee held a lease of Romford Market on behalf of a minor. He attempted to renew the lease in the same capacity. The lessor only condescended to grant renewal on the terms that the trustee was to hold the lease for his own personal benefit. It was held that, despite the attitude of the lessor, the renewed lease must be held in trust for the minor. Equity will not permit a trustee to acquire a benefit for himself by reason of his fiduciary position; if he does acquire such a benefit he holds whatever he acquires in trust for the beneficiaries. *Keech v Sandford* therefore illustrates the general principle that a constructive trust in favour of the beneficiaries will always arise where if it were not implied the trustee would benefit from his position. Further, a person who is not a trustee may, where he obtains information which enables him to make a personal profit – which information he would not have had had he not been acting for the trust – be forced to account for such profits to the beneficiaries as being held by him constructively in trust for them. This may be illustrated by *Boardman v Phipps* [1967] 2 AC 46. In that case a solicitor was requested by trustees to advise on the affairs of a certain private company in which the trust had a substantial minority holding. In the course of so advising the solicitor acquired information which enabled him on the one hand to play a positive role in making the trust holding more valuable, and on the other hand to acquire for himself a considerable number of the outstanding shares and the office of managing director. In an action by one of the beneficiaries it was held that the solicitor who held the shares – the capital value of which was now far in excess of what it was originally – was a constructive trustee for the beneficiaries and was furthermore accountable for the profits received by him by way of dividends declared on these shares. The court was not, however, wholly unappreciative of the solicitor's efforts and directed that he be paid a substantial sum by way of remuneration for his services.

This principle has been applied extensively to company directors. They owe a fiduciary duty to their company and must not allow their private interests to conflict with this duty. They must exercise the powers given to them in good faith in the interests of the company. Any profits they make in breach of duty they hold as constructive trustee for the company. This will extend to profits from dealings with the company, unless their private interest has been disclosed and the transaction authorized, and also to profits made by using information or opportunities they obtained as directors, even if the company was not in a position to exploit the information or the opportunities itself.

## B  CHARITABLE (PUBLIC) TRUSTS

No comprehensive definition of a legal 'charity' has been provided either by statute or by the courts. The meaning is, however, not the same as the popular meaning and it has to be determined by reference to the relevant case law. The *classification* of charitable purposes which is most often quoted is the one made by Lord MacNaghten in *Income Tax Special Purposes Comms v Pemsel* [1891] AC 531. According to this classification charitable trusts comprise trusts: (1) for the relief of poverty; (2) for the advancement of education: and this means education, not propaganda. Thus where there was a trust for the advancement of 'socialized medicine' by means of lectures to promote that aim and socialism generally, rather than to educate the public by stimulating thought on the subject, the object was held not to be charitable; (3) for the advancement of religion; (4) for other purposes beneficial to the community. This last category is usually said to be overriding, so that all trusts, if they are to be charitable, must conform with the requirement that they are for the *public benefit*: though it is established that, in the case of relief of poverty, trusts in favour of poor relations or of 'poor' employees (even of a particular firm) as a class are charitable, though clearly they benefit only a fraction of the public. Trusts in favour of needy individuals are, however, private trusts. 'Benefit to the community' is a very indeterminate object and the cases conflict – though an ill-advised parliamentary group once suggested it as the *sole* criterion – but it may be of interest to remark that the Court of Appeal in *Incorporated Council of Law Reporting for England and Wales v A-G* [1972] Ch 73, held that the Council is a charity because reports of judicial decisions serve the community by disseminating knowledge of the law; and it was also suggested that the objects of the Council might fall within Lord MacNaghten's second category.

Any object which falls outside the *Pemsel* rule is not charitable – and cannot obtain the advantages of that status – a gift for 'worthy causes' is a good example: a cause may be worthy, without being charitable in the *Pemsel* sense. And, again, although a gift for the promotion of sport *may* be charitable (under heads (1) or (4)) if it is tied to some charitable institution – such as a school – designed to further physical education, it will not of itself be charitable. For a gift, for example to promote cricket or football might be used for a non-charitable purpose, such as the encouragement of week day, as opposed to Sunday, cricket.

It must be added that the Recreational Charities Act 1958 settled doubts by enacting that – as long as they are for the public benefit – trusts for providing facilities in the interests of social welfare for recreation or other leisure-time occupation are to be deemed 'charitable', although the meaning of 'social welfare' is carefully defined, and has been held to embrace only the welfare of people who are in some way at a disadvantage to others. The same Act makes trusts for 'social welfare activities', as defined in the Miners' Welfare Act 1952, 'charitable'.

The difficulties of definition apart, once it is clear that a particular 'object' is a 'charity' any trust in favour of it will be subject to special rules, some of which were modified and clarified by the Charities Acts 1960 (hereafter 'ChA'), 1985 and 1992: for example:

(a) Most charities have to be registered in a register kept by the Charity Commissioners and charities with permanent endowments have to submit accounts to them. The Commissioners – whose office is in effect a sub-department of the Home Office – have general supervisory powers over trusteeships of charities, and in particular they share with the courts the power of sanctioning 'schemes' for the administration of charitable trusts. The Commissioners have been subject to criticism and there are moves to increase the strictness of their supervision particularly in relation to the examination of charities' accounts.

(b) Legal proceedings in respect of charitable trusts could formerly only be taken by the Attorney-General, either acting *ex officio* or by relation of interested parties. The ChA has now also empowered the trustees and certain other parties to take such proceedings; but only when the authority of the Charity Commissioners has been obtained.

(*c*)  Charitable trusts are to some extent *exempted* from the *perpetuity rules*: although gifts to charities must in the first instance vest within the required periods, a 'gift over' from one *charity* to *another* may lawfully be limited to vest at any future time. This is perhaps a corollary of the further rule that trusts for the benefit of charities, unlike other trusts, may be perpetual.

(*d*)  Charities are to a large extent exempt from *taxation* and premises occupied by charities and 'wholly or mainly' used for charitable purposes have some exemption from rates. But in order to qualify for exemption they must be so used: thus in *Oxfam v City of Birmingham District Council* [1976] AC 126 the House of Lords held that 'Oxfam' *shops* which are directly used for raising funds, and only indirectly for the charitable purpose of relief of poverty which Oxfam espouses, are not exempt for rating purposes. The decision in this case was reversed by the Rating (Charity Shops) Act 1976 but its reasoning still stands. It is the carrot of tax exemption which causes many institutions to seek charitable status: and it is also this crucial attribute of charities that leads to an overwhelming, confusing and conflicting case law on the subject.

(*e*)  A trust with exclusively charitable objects will never fail for 'uncertainty of objects'. Once property has been conveyed upon trust in circumstances which show that the settlor had a general charitable intention (as opposed to an intention merely to benefit some particular charity) the trustees must apply it for the benefit of *some* charity or charities, and if necessary obtain sanction for a 'scheme' ((*a*) above) to that end.

(*f*)  Where in certain ways defined in the ChA, s 13 – as for instance that the original purposes 'cannot be carried out, or not according to the directions given and to the spirit of the gift' – the objects of the trust have become impossible of fulfilment a charitable trust, unlike a private trust, need not necessarily fail so as to create a resulting trust in favour of the donor or his representatives. For the *cy-près* ('as near as can be') doctrine may apply. This means that sanction may be obtained for a scheme to devote the trust funds to some other charitable object as nearly as possible similar to the object which has failed.

But the doctrine only operates in the case of a trust which is *initially* impossible where it can be established that the donor has a general charitable intention or (under ChA, s 14) where the donor cannot be identified – as for example where the fund consists of a cash collection from multifarious donations deposited in collecting boxes, or where the donor cannot be found, or where the donor has made a written disclaimer of his right to the return of the gift. Failing these possibilities the property will revert to the donor in the usual way.

On the other hand where the impossibility arises *after the trust has come into operation* the *cy-près* doctrine applies without restriction unless the settlor or testator has provided for the contingency of impossibility by stipulating a gift over to some other charity or person, or by declaring a resulting trust to himself or his estate. Even here – except in the case of a gift over to some other charity – the perpetuity rules will apply so as to limit the ability of the disponor to do this.

The Charities Act 1985 as amended by the 1992 Act provides a new procedure to deal with problems concerning local charities for the relief of poverty, including changing the objects when the trustees consider that this should be done.

The Race Relations Act 1976, s 34, provides that a charitable instrument which purports to confer benefits upon a class of people defined by reference to *colour* shall 'have effect' as if it provided for conferring the benefits on persons of the class 'which result if the restriction by reference to colour is disregarded'. So a gift to the 'yellow inmates' of Bedlam would have effect as a gift to *all* Bedlam inmates, yellow or not.

# 2    Trustees

The law governing trusteeship was originally evolved in the Court of Chancery. Much of it is now contained in the Trustee Act 1925 (here abbreviated TrA).

## *Appointment and discharge*

Trustees are normally appointed in the instrument which creates the trust. There is no general rule as to the number to be appointed, though it is unusual to appoint a single individual as a sole trustee. Where, however, *land* is settled, or held upon trust for sale, there may not normally be more than four trustees (TrA, s 34(2)). Further, it is laid down (s 14) that not less than two trustees are required to give a valid receipt to a purchaser of such land. (See also Law of Property Act 1925, s 27(2), and Settled Land Act 1925, s 94(1).) This rule is, however, subject to a further exception, namely that a *trust corporation* acting as a sole trustee can give a valid receipt.

'Trust corporations' are corporate bodies empowered by their constitutions to act as trustees. They include any corporation appointed by the court in a particular matter to be a trustee, and banks, insurance companies and charitable bodies which are authorized to conduct trustee business.

The mere fact of appointment does not oblige a trustee to take office. He may refuse to do so, either expressly or by implication, as by refraining from entering upon his duties. If all the trustees appointed under a particular instrument refuse to act their duties devolve upon the person who created the trust, or upon his *personal representatives* (below, Chapter 14).

Where one out of a number of trustees dies his duties devolve upon the rest. Where a sole surviving trustee dies his personal representatives can exercise his powers.

The court has special powers of discharging trustees and of sanctioning the appointment of new ones to replace them (TrA, s 41).

These powers are not, however, normally invoked, because certain provisions of ss 36 and 39 of the Act usually render such an application unnecessary. Under the provisions of s 36 a trustee may be replaced by a new trustee in certain circumstances, eg if he remains abroad for over a year. The section provides that this replacement may be effected by the people (if any) nominated in the instrument creating the trust to appoint new trustees. Where there are no such people the power of replacement falls upon the other trustees. Section 39 provides that a trustee who wishes to retire may obtain his discharge (without need for replacement) provided that two conditions are satisfied: (i) He must obtain the consent of his co-trustees and of any person who is empowered to appoint trustees. (ii) Upon the discharge of the retiring trustee there must remain either at least two trustees or a trust corporation to perform the duties of the trust.

In either of the above cases, though under s 36 this is not essential, the retirement will normally be effected by deed. The reason for this is that when a retirement occurs the trust property must be divested from the retiring, and revested in the remaining, trustees. Section 40 of the TrA provides that if the transaction is effected by deed this divesting and revesting will be deemed to have taken place automatically in respect of any interest in land and certain choses in action (though in the case of *stocks and shares* transfer documents are still necessary).

### Duties

Trustees have two main duties. First, they must administer the trust property prudently. Secondly, they must strictly comply with all the terms of the trust.

For instance, trustees are entitled to invest trust funds only in investments either authorized by statute or by the express terms of their trust instrument. Before the coming into force of the Trustee Investments Acts 1961 (TIA) the investments authorized by statute comprised only the limited range prescribed by the TrA, s 1. Generally speaking, these were restricted to stocks issued by the British Government and by

Commonwealth countries and Colonies, stocks and mortgages issued by British local authorities, stock guaranteed by the British Government, and mortgages of land in Great Britain. The list did not include 'equities', ie the ordinary shares and stock of limited liability companies. Most of the authorized investments were repayable at par, or not repayable at all, and it was felt that this provided no safeguard against inflation or against the continuing fall in the value of the pound. The effect of the TIA is that, subject to detailed conditions, trustees may now invest a proportion of the trust funds in what are described as 'wider-range' investments, including some 'equities'.

In addition to the power of investment, trustees are given other powers by the TrA. For example, s 31 gives a power to apply income of a trust for the maintenance, education or benefit of a beneficiary aged under 18 and s 32 allows up to one half of the capital held on trust for a beneficiary to be advanced for his or her benefit. It must, however, be stressed that the statutory powers (under the TrA and the TIA) are *additional* to powers conferred by the trust instrument. This instrument may, and in the case of most modern trusts does, extend the statutory powers or, indeed, confer unrestricted powers of investment upon the trustees. The trust instrument may, however, also reduce or restrict the exercise of the statutory powers.

If all possible beneficiaries (both present and future) are of full age and capacity they can together authorize the trustees to deal with the trust property in any manner desired. Otherwise, the trustees have no power to vary the trusts, whatever the circumstances, though on behalf of certain specified classes of beneficiaries (mostly persons under incapacity, such as minority or unsoundness of mind) the court has jurisdiction under the general law and by statute (principally the Variation of Trusts Act 1958) to sanction the variation or revocation of trust dispositions where it is satisfied that such variation or revocation is of benefit to the person or persons concerned.

As a general rule trustees may not delegate their duties. Section 23 of the TrA, however, sets out a list of exceptions to this rule. These exceptions include, for instance, the right to employ a solicitor, a banker, or a stockbroker to effect transactions in connexion with the trust property. The charges of these agents are paid out of the trust estate.

*Liabilities*

In the absence of express authorization in the instrument, if any, which creates the trust or by the court, trustees have no right to be paid for their services. They are, however, entitled to be reimbursed out of the trust funds for any expenses properly incurred in the performance of their duties.

Any action by the trustees which is in excess of their powers – as where trust funds are misappropriated – or which contravenes the terms of the trust instrument constitutes a breach of trust, and a trustee will be personally liable to the full extent of any resulting loss. A frequent example is where trust moneys are invested in unauthorized securities and a loss results – if more than one such investment has been made the trustee cannot set off any profits against the losses, and must make good each individual loss.

A trustee who has been held liable for breach of trust has a right to be indemnified by any beneficiary who has directly instigated the breach to the extent to which he has benefited therefrom, and in suitable circumstances the trustee also has a right of contribution from his co-trustees (if any). By s 61 of the TrA the court has power to relieve a trustee from personal liability for breach of trust when he has acted honestly and reasonably and ought fairly to be excused for the breach: the scope of this statutory protection is, however, uncertain (in particular, it is problematical how far it will avail a professional trustee).

Actions by the beneficiaries against a trustee are statute-barred after six years (Limitation Act 1980, s 21). This time begins to run either from the time of the breach or, where the beneficiary suing is not at that time entitled to possession of his interest, then from the time that he becomes entitled. There is, however, no limit to the time in which an action may be brought where a trustee has been guilty of fraud, or where the action is an action to recover the trust property itself or its proceeds and it is either in the trustee's possession or has been converted by him to his own use.

# 3 Beneficiaries

The principal right of beneficiaries is their right to the enjoyment of their interest in the trust property. In the case of a private trust they have a right to force the trustees, by action if necessary, to administer the property according to the terms of the trust.

In the case of a breach of trust the following rights may be open to beneficiaries:

(*a*) they may bring a personal action against the trustees;
(*b*) they may be able to follow the trust property itself or to claim anything into which it has been converted;
(*c*) they may be able to institute criminal proceedings against the trustees.

The personal action needs little comment. Being an action against the trustees in person it has the disadvantage that if they are men of straw, or are already seriously in debt, the beneficiaries may get little or nothing from them. Beneficiaries have, however, one advantage over ordinary creditors, for should a fraudulent trustee become bankrupt, their right to repayment of their claim in full survives his discharge (Insolvency Act 1986, s 281(3)). In the case of a discretionary trust, where the trustees select the actual beneficiaries from a class specified by the settlor, the only remedy of members of the class is that the trustees can be compelled to consider the competing claims before they exercise their discretion. If the wording of the trust instrument requires the trustees to distribute the trust income, then the discretion must be exercised in favour of somebody.

Equity has always permitted beneficiaries to 'follow the trust property'. In this respect they are unlike people whose rights are based upon the common law, who can usually only, as we have seen, claim damages for their infringement. Thus, suppose that X holds a valuable picture in trust for Y, and that X, in breach of trust, gives the picture to Z. Y may, of course, sue X. This, as we have seen, may be fruitless. But Y has a better remedy: he may claim the return of the picture from Z, who is in the eyes of equity a constructive trustee. This right to the property is defeated, like all equitable rights, once a *bona fide* purchaser for value without notice obtains the picture. Thus if Z sells to T, who has no notice of the trust, Y cannot recover the picture from T (but can recover the proceeds of sale from Z).

Equity, however, favours the beneficiary further than this; for it will force a trustee to return not only the trust property, but also anything into which it has been *converted*. For instance, if A holds £50 in trust for B and, in breach of trust, spends the money on a carpet for his house, B will be entitled to the carpet. This claim is not merely personal but a claim to the *carpet* or its full value: thus if A is insolvent B's claim will not be diminished by the rights of other creditors; his right is something like a right of ownership. This rule, however, only applies where there is a direct substitution of one form of property for another. It would not apply, for instance, if A bought an £80 carpet, supplying £30 of his own. In this case B's claim would still be to £50 only – secured, if necessary, by the sale of the carpet: but it would yet be a claim to the full £50 as against other creditors.

There are certain complex rules governing the rights of beneficiaries to trust monies paid into a trustee's personal bank account, but they are not suitable for consideration in an introductory work.

# Chapter 13
# Family law

In this chapter we will consider certain aspects of the law relating to marriage and to children and the family.

## 1 Marriage

It may be appropriate to discuss this subject under five heads:

- (A) Engagements to marry.
- (B) The formation of marriage.
- (C) Nullity of marriage.
- (D) The effects of marriage.
- (E) Dissolution of marriage.

From being a matter of indissoluble status marriage, by the nineteenth century, characteristically came to be treated as a contract. Today, equally characteristically though a fair portion of it is to be found in the Matrimonial Causes Act 1973, it has become enmeshed in copious and incoherent legislation. One of the most bewildering aspects of the matter is that matrimonial law is administered by the High Court, county courts and magistrates' courts. It has been argued that the best thing that could be done – for simplifying the law itself – would be to entrust the matrimonial jurisdiction to a simple set of tribunals, on the model of the industrial tribunals.

### A ENGAGEMENTS TO MARRY

Traditionally the common law looked upon an engagement, as upon marriage, as a contract, and it had the legal effect that a man who broke his engagement could be sued by his ex-fiancée for breach of promise of marriage – a type of action (immortalized by Gilbert and Sullivan in *Trial by Jury*) which was, not unnaturally, discouraged and for which there were special evidentiary requirements. This form of action was, however, abolished by the Law Reform (Miscellaneous Provisions) Act 1970 which (s 1) enacted that 'An agreement between two persons to marry one another shall not under the law of England and Wales have effect as a contract giving rise to legal rights. . . .' This provision, however, could not stand alone because broken engagements sometimes leave not only injured feelings but also, like broken marriages, tangled property relationships: hence, by s 2, the Act applied the same rules of law as apply to property in which a husband or wife has an interest. It enables an action to be brought under s 17 of the Married Women's Property Act 1882, provided that the action is brought within three months of the broken engagement. Thus, for example, where there have been contributions by the engaged couple towards the proposed matrimonial home the parties' interests may be safeguarded after the engagement has been broken off. Moreover, s 3 of the 1970 Law Reform Act settled disputes about the engagement *ring* by ruling that it shall be presumed to be an *absolute gift*; though this presumption may be rebutted (ie proved unfounded) by evidence showing a contrary intent.

## B   FORMATION OF MARRIAGE

The formalities for the celebration of a valid marriage are in general prescribed by the Marriage Act 1949 (as much amended). In broad terms all marriages celebrated in England under English Law must either be solemnised according to the rites of the Church of England in the presence of two witnesses, or they must be solemnised – whatever other religious ceremony there may be – upon the authority of the certificate of a superintendent registrar. Further, Church of England marriages will only be valid if either there has been publication of banns, or a common licence or a special licence from the Archbishop of Canterbury, or the certificate of a superintendent registrar has been obtained. Normally, because it is in the public interest that people should know whether or not other people are married, civil marriages unaccompanied by a religious ceremony are usually celebrated either in a registered building or in the office of a superintendent registrar, although, the Marriage Act 1994 and the Marriage (Approved Premises) Regulations 1995 now provide for the approval of other 'seemly and dignified' premises for the purpose (thus creating business opportunities of various kinds). The Marriage (Registrar General's Licence) Act 1970 permits marriages, under licence of the Registrar General, in cases of very serious illness where one of the parties is not expected to recover and cannot be moved to one of the normal places of marriage. In addition, by the Marriage Act 1983, people suffering from continuing illness and people detained in institutions may be lawfully married upon a superintendent registrar's certificate in the place where, for the time being, they are.

## C NULLITY

Although obviously one of a very special nature, marriage can, as has been remarked, be regarded as a contract; and, in particular, it is like one in that what seems upon the face of it to be a valid marriage may, like a void or voidable contract, turn out not to be so. Marriages may thus either be *void* or *voidable*. They will be *void* :(i) if the parties are *within the prohibited degrees* of relationship (these are set out in the Marriage Act 1949, Schedule 1, as subsequently amended, providing, eg, that a man cannot marry his mother, daughter or grand-daughter and similarly limiting the liberties of women – beyond the obvious, the extent of prohibition can be surprising); (ii) if either party is *under the age of 16*; (iii) if the parties have intermarried in disregard of certain requirements as to the *formation* of marriage – such as wilful neglect to obtain a marriage certificate – contained in the Marriage Act 1949, s 49; (v) if at the time of marriage either party was already *lawfully married*; (vi) if the parties are *not respectively male and female*. This last ground alone needs comment; it concerns trans-sexualism which has posed a problem for the courts: *Corbett v Corbett* [1971] P 110 (also *Rees v UK* (1987) and *Cossey v UK* (1991)). Gender at birth has been held to determine gender at the time of marriage. In English law it is impossible for homosexual or lesbian couples to marry. Marriages falling within the above categories, being void, have no effect because no marriage has ever existed at all; consequently there is theoretically no need for either party who wishes to impugn such marriages to petition the court to declare them null, but such petitions will be entertained, and it may often be desirable to seek them.

Secton 12 of the MCA sets out the grounds upon which a marriage is *voidable*. These are: (i) that it has *not been consummated* due to the incapacity of either party; (ii) that it has not been consummated due to the *wilful refusal* of the respondent to consummate it; (iii) that either party did *not consent* to it, whether in consequence of *duress, mistake, unsoundness of mind* or otherwise (this was once enough to render the marriage void rather than voidable); (iv) that at the time of the marriage either party, though capable of giving a valid consent, was suffering (whether continuously or intermittently) from *mental disorder* within the meaning of the Mental Health Act 1983 of such a kind or such an extent as to be unfit for marriage; (v) that at the time of the marriage the respondent was suffering from *venereal disease* in a communicable form; (vi) that at the time of the marriage the respondent was *pregnant* by some person other than the petitioner.

Of these grounds of voidability there is only space to comment upon the third. This illustrates the consensual and contractual aspect of marriage. Like any ordinary contract its basis lies in consent; consequently an essential *mistake* as to identity, or deceit which vitiates the consent, will make the union voidable: indeed, prior to 1971 it rendered it void. It is the same with *duress*, some factor which draws a person into marriage by force or fear: for instance, a marriage contracted (note the significance of the colloquial use of the word 'contracted') in order solely to escape some oppressive political régime which poses a threat to the life, limb or liberty of the person involved may be annulled. Yet it must not be thought that fear of a merely unpleasant consequence will have so drastic an effect: so if a girl, according to the custom of her people, consents to a marriage arranged by her parents, she cannot treat the custom as a form of duress so as to enable her to escape the marriage. It must be added that where grounds (iii)–(vi) exist no decree may be granted unless the court is satisfied that proceedings were instituted within *three* years from the date of marriage. Further, where grounds (v) and (vi) are involved the court must be satisfied that the petitioner was at the time of the marriage ignorant of the facts alleged. Finally, *no* decree upon the ground that the marriage is voidable may be granted if the respondent satisfies the court that 'the petitioner ... so conducted himself ... as to lead the respondent reasonably to believe that he would not seek' to avoid the marriage *and* that it would be unjust to grant the decree (MCA, s 13(1)).

A marriage which is voidable (as opposed to void) is one which (MCA, s 16) is to be 'treated as if it had existed' up to the time of decree absolute, and the latter now operates 'to annul the marriage only as respects any time after' it. This serves to underline the fact that where a voidable marriage is in issue a *decree of nullity* is not merely advisable, but essential.

## D   THE EFFECTS OF MARRIAGE

At common law the effect of marriage was to make husband and wife 'one'; chiefly to the former's advantage. For instance most of the wife's property, at least during the subsistence of the marriage, became her husband's and she lost contractual capacity, but the husband, who took so much by way of benefit, incurred the burden of becoming liable for her torts. Now after a long and piecemeal process of change, effected by equity and various statutes, married women have become emancipated from their husbands, and they are treated in law for most purposes as if they were single.

Yet inevitably, marriage being a union of the parties, their legal status is affected by it. There is only space here to mention a few of its more important effects; and these may be considered from five aspects – first, as to court proceedings, second, as to mutual duties and obligations, third, as to the effect of marriage upon the property of the parties, fourth, as to domestic violence, and, fifth, abortion.

**Court proceedings** – Though husbands and wives may now sue each other in contract or in tort, in the case of the latter the Law Reform (Husband

and Wife) Act 1962 gives the court power to stay the action if it appears that it is likely to afford no benefit to either party or that the question is one which may more conveniently be settled under s 17 of the Married Women's Property Act 1882, which allows disputes over title or possession of property to be settled by a county court or High Court judge. As regards theft; although since the Theft Act 1968 spouses may be prosecuted for stealing from each other, prosecution will normally require the leave of the Director of Public Prosecutions. Further, although under the old law the legal unity of husband and wife prevented them from being liable for the tort of conspiracy this is no longer so. And under the Police and Criminal Evidence Act 1984, s 80, in criminal cases the wife or husband of the accused is competent and compellable to give evidence for the prosecution or defence. Though where the spouses are charged together neither is competent nor compellable unless he or she is not liable to be convicted of the offence at the trial as the result of pleading guilty or for any other reason. Moreover, by the same section the former rule that in criminal (as opposed to civil) proceedings the spouse could not be compelled to disclose communications – such as the confession of a crime – from the other has been abolished.

**Mutual obligations** – A husband is normally under a duty to maintain his wife and any children of the marriage according to his ability, and under certain circumstances *either* party may be ordered by the court to do so. Thus under the MCA, s 27 such an order may be made against a husband upon the application of the wife in the case of wilful neglect to maintain either the wife or the children; but it must also be noted that – in accordance with the modern policy which seeks to place the sexes upon an equal footing – the *husband* may also now apply for a similar order against the *wife* where through age, illness or disability, and having regard to the respective resources of the parties, it is reasonable to expect the wife to provide such maintenance.

Further, the Domestic Proceedings and Magistrates' Courts Act 1978 (ss 1–3 as amended) empowers *magistrates' courts* in prescribed circumstances to order a party to a marriage to make *financial provision* for the other or the children, either by way of periodical payment or by lump sum. Much debate has centred upon the Child Support Act 1991 which covers the liability to provide for the 'natural' and adopted children of a couple who have parted company (even if unmarried) and removes certain of the powers of the courts to deal with matters of child maintenance to the Child Support Agency.

*Property* of married people presents difficulties. It has been remarked that originally the common law, in the absence of agreement to the contrary, like the ancient law of Rome, endowed the husband with all the wife's worldly goods. This was in keeping with the needs of ancient societies in which the family group, under the protection of the male, needed to face the world as a unit. As society became more cohesive, both in Rome and in England this male supremacy broke down; and, as has been remarked, by the end of the nineteenth century the English wife's property had in general come to belong to her as her own. This separation of property during marriage is, however, a fact more observed in law than in the reality of marriage where 'his' and 'hers' is often meaningless, and both parties treat the contents of their homes as joint. There is thus something to be said for systems of law which neither treat the husband as sole manager nor the property as separate, but see the situation as one of 'community of goods'. This solution, again, however, is not wholly realistic for, should a quarrel arise the partners may well resort to thinking of 'their own' property. It is thus not surprising that modern legislation in this field rests upon no one principle. Thus though, in law, property which clearly belongs to the wife is her 'separate' property, the Married Women's Property Act 1964 makes special provision in respect of money or other property derived from a housekeeping allowance provided by the husband to the wife: it is enacted that this is *prima facie* (ie in the absence of evidence to the contrary) to be treated as belonging to the parties in *equal shares*.

Moreover, in *equity*, property which is jointly acquired belongs to the parties respectively in proportion to the amount of the contribution of each; or where – as will often be so – the amount of the contribution is not determinable, the ownership is divided according to such proportions as the court may consider just. Further, by the Matrimonial Proceedings and Property Act 1970, s 37 where one spouse makes a substantial contribution to the *improvement* of property in which either or both have a beneficial interest he or she will be entitled to such a share in the value of the improvement as may be agreed between the two or, in default of agreement, as the court may deem just. By the Matrimonial Homes Act 1983, s 1(1): 'Where one spouse is entitled to occupy a dwelling house by virtue of a beneficial estate or interest or contract . . . giving him or her the right to remain in occupation, and the other spouse is not so entitled' then the other spouse is entitled to 'rights of occupation' in the matrimonial home. These include the right not to be evicted without a court order and the right, if not in occupation, to enter and occupy the home with leave of the court. Further, by s 1(2) the court may make orders restraining or excluding the rights of occupation of either spouse. These rights are, of course, of great importance to a deserted wife. They apply to valid polygamous, as well as to monogamous, marriages. The expectations of third parties, such as purchasers of the property, are protected by the fact that the 'rights of occupation' are registrable as a land charge, which means that the third party has a means of knowing about the occupancy, nor can the interest impede the rights of creditors in the other spouse's bankruptcy. It should be noted, however, that this only affects the 'home', and not the furniture.

Mention must also be made of the Married Women's Property Act 1882, s 17 (as amended). This provides that in any question between husband and wife as to the title to, or the possession of, property, either party – and certain other people – may apply in a *summary way* to a judge of the High Court or to a circuit judge who may make such order as to the property in dispute as he thinks fit. The judge also has power to order payment by the defendant spouse to the aggrieved one of the value of any property to which the latter was entitled if, at the time of the application, it is no longer in the possession or control of the former. Moreover, the judge may when necessary order the sale of property to satisfy the aggrieved party's claim. The Matrimonial Proceedings and Property Act 1970, s 39 extends these provisions to cover a period of three years after the determination of the marriage by divorce or annulment (but not by death). Upon divorce distribution of property between spouses will normally be effected under the distribution provisions of the MCA, ss 21– 25 rather than by resort to the MWPA. The effect of marriage in relation to wills and intestacy will be considered in Chapter 14.

**Matrimonial violence** – Two statutes are concerned with what the media call 'battered wives' (though they both also protect battered husbands); they are the Domestic Violence and Matrimonial Proceedings Act 1976 ('DVA') and the Domestic Proceedings and Magistrates' Courts Act 1978 ('DPA').

The DVA, s 1 (as amended) empowers the High Court or a county court – for this purpose the more usual forum – upon the application of a party to a marriage or of a man or a woman who are living together or were so living at the time of the molestation, to grant injunctions containing provisions restraining the other party from molesting the applicant or a child living with the applicant, excluding the other party from the matrimonial home, or requiring him or her to permit the applicant to enter or to remain in it. By s 2, moreover, where a judge grants an injunction restraining such molestation or excluding the other party he may, if he be satisfied that the miscreant has caused actual bodily harm to the applicant or to the child and that he (or she) is likely to repeat the attack, attach a *power of arrest* to the injunction permitting arrest without warrant: and if the miscreant be so arrested he (or she) may not be released in less than 24 hours thereafter. He (or she) must also, within that period, be brought before the judge. It has been held, however, that the arrest power should only be attached in exceptional circumstances. Despite doubts, it has also been ruled by the House of Lords that an injunction may be granted to exclude the guilty party from the home even though he or she owns or has some other proprietary interest in it, and even though the parties are not lawfully married. The Act gives no guidance about the length of time for which such injunctions should be operative, but it has been held that they ought not to be continued for longer than it takes the injured party to find a new home.

The DPA, s 16(1) empowers a *magistrates' court*, under prescribed conditions, to make an order, upon application by one party to a marriage that the other (the 'respondent') shall not use or threaten to use violence against the other or against a child of the family. The conditions are that the court must be satisfied that the respondent has used, or has threatened to use, such violence *and* that it is necessary for the protection of the applicant or children to make the order. Further (s 16(2)) under certain circumstances the court may order the respondent to *leave the matrimonial home* or to remain away from it, or order that the respondent shall permit the applicant to enter, or to remain in, the home. The circumstances are that the court must be satisfied that: (i) the respondent has *used* violence against the applicant or a child, *or* that the respondent, having threatened such violence, has *used* it against some other person, *or*, has contravened an order made under s 16(1) by *using* violence: and the court must *also* be satisfied, (ii) that there is danger that the applicant or the child will be physically injured by the respondent.

It is to be noted that, unlike the relief afforded by the DVA, this protection is only given where the parties are lawfully married.

**Abortion** – Since the Abortion Act 1967 abortion is lawful provided that it is performed by a registered medical practitioner and that two such practitioners have certified that the termination of the pregnancy is necessary for the health of the woman. A husband, it has been held, has no right to forbid an abortion.

## E   DISSOLUTION OF MARRIAGE

**Divorce** – Attitudes to marriage have varied in the course of history – looking back, they seem to swing from one extreme to another. Thus in ancient Rome divorce was originally rare, but by the early Empire it became both easy and common: indeed one party could repudiate the marriage by unilateral act. After Constantine (and the advent of Christianity) the pendulum swung back, and divorce came under the ban of the text which prescribes that 'those whom God hath joined together let no man put asunder'. In the main this ostracism of divorce was inherited by the common law and it continued until the nineteenth century when judicial divorce (as opposed to divorce by Act of Parliament) became possible. Judicial divorce, however – though the grounds for it were extended by various statutes – was in general beset by the notion of the 'matrimonial offence': the success of a petition depended upon the 'guilt' of the respondent, upon the respondent having done something 'wrong', eg adultery. In the course of this century public opinion came to two conclusions. First, that, whatever the will of Divine Providence, there can be no point in tying people to what Sir Alan Herbert once called 'holy deadlock'; second, that to base the right to divorce upon the commission of a 'matrimonial offence' was a senseless approach.

The Matrimonial Causes Act 1973 (as amended), which governs divorce, was a compromise between the view of the Church of England that divorce should depend upon 'irretrievable breakdown' of the marriage and the view of the Law Commission that it must depend upon specific grounds. Thus s 1 of the MCA enacted that 'the sole ground on which a petition for divorce may be presented . . . shall be that the marriage has *broken down irretrievably*'. But what the Statute here gives to Peter it takes back from Paul; for s 1(4) provides that 'if the court is satisfied on the evidence of any such fact as is mentioned in subsection (2) above' (which will shortly be examined), then, 'unless it is satisfied on all the evidence that the marriage has not broken down irretrievably, it shall grant a decree'. In other words, prove the grounds and the issue of 'breakdown' is likely to turn on this proof. This is inelegant legislation, but the fact is that if the main issue were one solely of 'breakdown' it would be difficult to establish, and trials would become unduly protracted by the need to examine all kinds of evidence.

The essential elements of divorce thus lie in s 1(2) of the MCA. 'The court hearing a petition for divorce shall not hold the marriage to have broken down irretrievably *unless the petitioner satisfies the court* of one or more of the following facts . . .'. These facts are:

*(a)* That the respondent has committed *adultery* and that the petitioner finds it intolerable to live with him (or her) – *both* these things must be proved; the intolerability may be independent of the adultery and it is not *necessarily* something which springs from it.

*(b)* That the respondent has behaved in such a way that the petitioner cannot *reasonably* be expected to live with him (or her) – this does not mean that divorce can now be obtained simply because the petitioner alleges that the respondent is an incompatible partner; it means that the court must be satisfied that for the petitioner the situation is such that the marriage has, through the behaviour of the respondent, become un-endurable.

*(c)* That the respondent has *deserted* the petitioner for a continuous period of *at least two years* immediately preceding the presentation of the petition.

*(d)* That the parties *have lived apart* for a continuous period of at least *two* years immediately preceding the presentation of the petition *and* the respondent *consents to the grant of a decree*. This, ie *(d)*, for the first time was a recognition by our law of a right of divorce by mutual *consent*, and it is now the commonest ground of divorce. It must be noted that there are two safeguards in this case: for (by s 10(1) of the MCA) where the court finds, between the time of decree *nisi* and decree absolute, that the petitioner *misled* the respondent into giving consent the decree may be rescinded; moreover, the provisions of s 6 (below) apply. Both in this case and in case *(c)* (above), and *(e)* (below), in order to encourage recon-

ciliation, it is provided that in determining whether the prescribed period is 'continuous' no account shall be taken of any consecutive period or non-consecutive periods not exceeding six months during which the parties have cohabited.

*(e)* That the parties to the marriage have *lived apart for a continuous period of at least five years* immediately preceding the presentation of the petition. Here the petitioner may succeed even though the respondent does *not consent*. But there are also safeguards in this case. First, s 2(4), the petition may be opposed upon the ground that dissolution of the marriage 'will result in grave financial hardship to the respondent and that it would *in all the circumstances* be wrong to dissolve the marriage': 'all the circumstances' include such matters as the interests of children of the marriage, and are not confined to financial circumstances. Second (s 10 (2)–(4)) after grant of a decree *nisi* under either *(d)* or *(e)* the court may take into consideration such circumstances as the age and health of the parties and the financial position of the respondent, and refuse to make the decree absolute unless it is satisfied that the petitioner (husband or wife) has, where appropriate, made reasonable provision for the respondent, or has given an undertaking so to do.

It remains to be added that, generally speaking, formerly no petition for divorce could be established during the first three years of marriage; this period was reduced by the Matrimonial and Family Proceedings Act 1984 to *one year*. Further by long practice there is a waiting period, during which the marriage still subsists (now of six weeks) between decree *nisi* ('unless') and decree 'absolute' in order to allow time for the revealing of any cause why the divorce should not be permitted – which corresponds in the twilight of marriage with the Church's banns which may herald its dawn. The Queen's Proctor is the official charged with the duty of intervening if such a cause should appear. The court, in granting the *decree nisi*, may order that it be made absolute in a shorter period than six weeks if grounds for this are shown, eg to enable a woman to remarry before the birth of her expected child.

**Proposals for change** – The publication of a Green Paper in 1993 and a White Paper in 1995 (both entitled *'Looking to the Future')* and the heated debate upon the Family Law Bill during 1995 and 1996 seem to be leading to substantial reform in the law relating to divorce. The three key elements of the Bill are the introduction of a 'period of reflection and consideration' before a divorce will be granted, strengthened protection against domestic violence and increased access to mediation.

**Finances and property** – Upon granting a decree of dissolution of marriage, nullity, or judicial separation it has for some time been the practice for the court to make incidental orders concerning the property of the parties and the welfare of children of the marriage. The MCA, ss

21–25 (as amended by the Matrimonial Homes Act 1983 and the Matrimonial and Family Proceedings Act 1984) contains important provisions to this end. By reason of these the court may make 'financial provision' and 'property adjustment' orders. The former may require periodical payments or the payment of a lump sum, and these may be payable to the spouse of the person ordered to pay or for the benefit of the children of the family. The latter consist, *inter alia*, of orders for the *transfer* of property to the other spouse or for the benefit of the children. In making such orders s 25 sets out a number of considerations to guide the discretion of the court. It must take into account (a) the income, earning capacity, property and other financial *resources* which each of the parties to the marriage *has* or *is likely to have* in the foreseeable future; (b) the financial needs of each party; (c) the standard of living enjoyed by the family before the breakdown of the marriage; (d) the age of each party and the duration of the marriage; (e) any disability, of either party; (f) the contributions made by each of the parties to the welfare of the family, *including any contribution made by looking after the home* . . .; (g) the value to either of the parties . . . of any benefit which . . . that party will lose the chance of acquiring. Further, under the 1984 Act (and under the extensive provisions of the Children Act 1989 and the Child Support Act 1991) in deciding what orders to make the court must give first consideration to the welfare, whilst a minor, of any child of the family. The 1981 Act also empowers the court to order the sale of property belonging to the parties.

There is a massive case law on these sections, but the extent of discretion given to the courts results in a lack of general principles emerging from the cases. Nevertheless, two points can be made. First, following the ancient practice of the ecclesiastical courts, and of the Divorce Court, the *general* guide (or at least a starting point) in cases where the husband is ordered to compensate the wife was provided in *Wachtel v Wachtel* [1973] Fam 72 namely that, as formerly in relation to payments from income, so now in relation to payments in respect of either income or capital, or in relation to division of property, the *normal* rule is that the wife's share should be one third of the spouse's joint income. This is, of course, *not* modelled on 'community of goods' (which entails *half shares*). In the second place, although it is true that s 25 enjoins the court to take into account the 'conduct of the parties' this does not mean that, as under the old law (based as it was upon the concept of the 'matrimonial offence') adultery or other forms of *matrimonial* misconduct will necessarily reduce the amount to be awarded. Finally, the cases constantly stress the essentially discretionary form of this jurisdiction in describing the policy of the Act as arriving at an *equitable redistribution* of the assets of the family following upon the breakdown. It should be added that there are a number of provisions aimed at encouraging reconciliation.

If the MCA and the preceding Acts are far from perfect they are an improvement on the previous law – though one may wonder whether divorce really is a suitable sphere of activity for courts of *law*.

Dissolution of marriage (divorce) must be distinguished from *judicial separation* (separation). Divorce ends marriage, leaving the parties free to re-marry; judicial separation only has the effect of sanctioning a state of affairs in which they live apart. It is now (MCA, s 17) granted upon the same grounds as divorce, *except* that there is no need of proof of 'irretrievable breakdown'.

Since the Matrimonial Proceedings (Polygamous Marriages) Act 1972 the courts have been empowered to grant 'matrimonial relief' – including divorce, nullity and separation – in the case of marriages (whether polygamous or not) entered into under a system of law which permits polygamy. This does *not* mean that polygamous marriages contracted in the United Kingdom are valid nor that polygamous marriages contracted anywhere by people domiciled therein are valid.

## 2   Children and the family

The subjects now to be discussed are legitimacy, legitimation, adoption and the extensive impact of the Children Act 1989.

### A   LEGITIMACY

Legitimacy and legitimation are governed by a number of statutes: the principal Act is now the Legitimacy Act 1976.

A child whose parents are lawfully married at the time when it is conceived or born, or at any time between those two events, is legitimate. Moreover, the issue of voidable marriages born during the subsistence of the marriage are legitimate; and the issue of void marriages are also legitimate provided that at the time of the act of intercourse resulting in their birth (or at the time of the celebration of the marriage, if later) both or either of the parties to the marriage believed that it was valid. And now a child conceived as the result of artificial insemination by a donor is legitimate unless the father did not consent to the insemination.

### B   LEGITIMATION

Any child which is not thus born in lawful wedlock or which is the offspring of a void or voidable marriage under the conditions just considered is initially illegitimate. Before the Legitimacy Act 1926 people so born could not be legitimated (ie made legitimate) unless a special Act of Parliament were passed to make them so. Now, however (1976 Act, s 2) 'where the parents of an illegitimate person marry one another, the marriage shall, if the father of the illegitimate person is at the date of marriage domiciled in England or Wales, render that person, if living, legitimate from the date of marriage'. Moreover, it is no longer a bar to such legitimation that either of the parents was married to a third party at the time of the birth of the child thus legitimated. The effect of legitimation is that, from the date of the marriage, the legitimated person is treated in most respects as though he had been born in lawful wedlock; he may thus, for example, succeed to the property of his relatives should they die intestate.

Formerly an *illegitimate* child was subject to a number of disadvantages; in particular in regard to intestate succession to his relatives. The Family Law Reform Act 1987, however, puts such a child in the same position as legitimate children in regard to intestacy. But some differences remain between legitimate and illegitimate people. An illegitimate person (and, for that matter, a legitimated one) cannot succeed to a title of honour, and his or her entitlement to British citizenship is derived solely through his or her mother.

Although at common law neither parent was originally responsible for the maintenance of an illegitimate child, the rule came to be that this duty was cast upon the mother. But the mother could obtain an order for payment by the father. The position, however, now is that either the mother or the father may apply for an order under the Children Act 1989 for financial relief in respect of the maintenance of the child. Further, the unmarried father formerly had no rights or duties in respect of an illegitimate child; but now, under s 4 of the 1987 Act, he can obtain a court order to vest in him all rights and duties (to be shared with the mother) that he would have had if the child had been born legitimate.

## C   ADOPTION

The effect of adoption is to vest the rights and duties which a parent has in respect of his child in some other person. Adoption was not a recognised legal institution in England until the passing of the Adoption of Children Act 1926. But the law on this subject is now fully regulated by the Adoption Act 1976.

Adoption of children (people under *18* and *unmarried*) may be effected by court order, and particulars of the adoption must be entered in the Adopted Children Register kept at the General Register Office. In making an *adoption order* the court must have regard to the welfare of the child and (as far as possible) it must consult its wishes. Generally speaking, the order cannot be made unless the child has had his home with the adopter(s) (or one of them) for at least twelve months.

Adoption orders may be made in favour of the following: (i) married couples both of whom must have attained the age of *21*, one of whom, at least must be domiciled in the United Kingdom; (ii) one person alone who has attained the age of *21; and who is unmarried*; though a married person may be sole adopter in certain circumstances: eg that he or she is permanently separated. A sole adopter, also, must be resident in the United Kingdom. Where natural parents adopt (as, for instance, in the case of an illegitimate child) an order can only be made in favour of *one* of them if there is some reason (eg the death of the person in question) for excluding the other.

No order may be made unless the child's parent or guardian gives unconditional agreement to the adoption or the child is regarded in law as 'free for adoption' for a variety of reasons including abandonment, neglect, persistent ill-treatment, and so on (LA, s 16(2)). Once the order is made the child will be treated in law for all purposes as though he were the natural legitimate child of the adopter(s). Adoptions are arranged by adoption societies and by local authorities which are now, by statute, bound to work in co-operation; and the former are enjoined to provide 'adoption services' designed to meet the needs of adopted children, their parents or guardians and adopters or would-be adopters.

The Adoption Act (subject to special rules) permits adoptions under the Hague Convention 1965 where all parties to the adoption are habitually resident in the United Kingdom and one of them is a national of some *other country* which is a party to the Convention. Under the Children Act 1989 adoption proceedings are deemed to be 'family proceedings' and thus the court is empowered to make any order available to it under the 1989 Act. Jurisdiction in matters of adoption is usually exercised by magistrates' courts but the Family Division of the High Court also has jurisdiction. There is a right of appeal from the magistrates' courts to a divisional court of the Family Division.

## D   THE CHILDREN ACT 1989

In a book of this length it is not possible to describe all the intricacies and details of the law in this important area. However, we must note that a 'giant leap for lawmaking' was made with this statute. It was designed to clarify and codify the law relating to children. It repealed and replaced a considerable amount of legislation that had developed piecemeal over many years. There are over 100 sections and 15 schedules. Broadly, the Act covers: orders with respect to children in family proceedings, local authority support for children and families, care and supervision, protection of children, community homes, voluntary homes and voluntary organisations, registered childrens' homes, private arrangements for fostering children, child minding and day care for young children and the Secretary of State's supervisory responsibilities and functions. The basic philosophy behind the Act is that a child should be brought up within his or her family and that local authority support should be provided where necessary to support and facilitate this.

# Chapter 14

# Succession

Wherever one person transfers property to another the transferee may be said to 'succeed' to the title of the transferor. For the purposes of this chapter, however, the word 'succession' will be used in a special sense. The type of succession about to be discussed is 'universal' succession. This takes place where, for one reason or another, the whole, or substantially the whole, of one person's estate (property) passes to another or to others. This may happen in a number of ways, but here we can only discuss succession upon death and succession upon bankruptcy.

## 1   Succession upon death

When people die their property does not die with them. It follows that in every legal system there must be rules governing the distribution of property after death. These rules must be designed to solve two main problems. First, 'Who is to receive the property?' Second, 'How is the distribution to be effected?' The first problem is answered by the rules relating to testate and intestate succession. The second problem is answered by the rules governing the administration of estates. These two sets of rules require separate treatment.

### A   TESTATE AND INTESTATE SUCCESSION

#### 1   TESTATE SUCCESSION

Testate succession (Latin, *testamentum* =something attested, a will) arises where the deceased person has expressed his wishes concerning the devolution of his property during his lifetime, in the form of a *will*. Intestate succession arises where there has been no will or where, for one reason or another, a will has failed to take effect, and consequently the people who are entitled to the property have to be designated by rules of law.

## i The nature of a will

A will is a declaration made by a person in his lifetime of his wishes concerning the devolution of his property after his death. Unless there is a clear intention to the contrary it *takes effect from the time of death*, not from the time it is made; it is said to be '*ambulatory*' until death. Thus, if X leaves 'All my property' to Y, Y will be entitled to receive not only such property (undisposed of before death) as X had at the time he made the will, but also any other property X may have acquired between that time and his death. The will '*speaks from*' the death.

## ii Testamentary capacity

The general rule is that anyone (except a minor or a person of unsound mind) may make a will. If it is desired to show that a testator (the deceased person) was not capable, through unsoundness of mind or from any other cause, of forming a proper intention to make his will the fact of his incapacity must be clearly proved.

## iii Formalities

A will is normally a formal declaration of intention. The Wills Act 1837, as amended by the Administration of Justice Act 1982, prescribes the following formalities:

(*a*) The will must be in writing, and signed by the testator, or by some other person in his presence and by his direction; *and* it must appear that the testator intended by his signature to give effect to the will.

(*b*) The signature must be made or acknowledged by the testator in the presence of *two* or more witnesses present at the same time. Acknowledgment will, of course, be necessary if the testator has signed before asking the witness to attend.

(*c*) Each witness must either (i) attest and sign the will (ie witness the testator's signature and sign his own name) or (ii) acknowledge his signature in the presence of the testator – but not necessarily in the presence of any other witness.

Sections 27 and 28 of the 1982 Act and Sch 2 thereof prescribe certain special formalities which, if complied with, give international formal validity to a will.

If anyone to whom, or to whose husband or wife, the testator has left property is a witness he will not be entitled to take under the will; but the Wills Act 1968 provides that if the will is duly executed without the attestation of such a person that attestation must be disregarded. In other words, provided that there are two qualified witnesses the attestation of any other witness may be disregarded and they thus become entitled to take under the will. Similarly, by a rule of public policy (the 'forfeiture' rule) no one who unlawfully kills another person may benefit under his will or intestacy. But because unlawful killings may sometimes be committed under cirumstances where there is little moral blame (eg a 'mercy'

killing of a husband by his wife) the rigour of this rule was mitigated by
the Forfeiture Act 1982. That Act provides that a court may, at its discretion, make an order with regard to any interest in the property devolving
upon the offender which the justice of the case requires. In reaching its
decision the court must have regard to the conduct of the offender and of
the deceased, and to all the circumstances of the case. Further, the Act
makes it plain that the forfeiture rule extends to aiders and abettors of the
killing, at the same time permitting the court to make a modifying order
in respect of claims by them. In the case of a convicted offender it is
provided that no order may be made unless proceedings for the purpose
of modifying the rule are brought within three months of the conviction.

### iv  Soldiers' wills

It was a rule of Roman law that soldiers in the field might make informal
wills; for a soldier may often be in imminent fear of death and far from
advice. This rule has passed into our law. Soldiers, sailors, and airmen
while in *actual military service* (which has been held to include service in
the Northern Ireland emergency) and seamen at sea (under any conditions)
have special privileges. (a) They may make wills even though they are
not of age, provided that they have attained the age of 14 years. (b) They
may make informal wills. Even an oral declaration will suffice provided
that it is a serious statement of intention; thus a soldier about to embark
for France upon active service during the Second World War, took out
his pay book, tapped it, and remarked, 'If anything happens to me,
everything is to be for R'. This was held to be a valid will. A witness to a
'soldier's' will *may* receive benefits under it.

The construction of the words 'actual military service' (Wills Act 1837,
s 11) has often given rise to difficulty and they have been liberally
construed. For example, it was held by the Court of Appeal that an airman
on an instructional course in Canada during the war came within the
privilege afforded by the rule. And further, seamen have been held to be
technically 'at sea' for this purpose while actually ashore between voyages
but under orders to join a ship.

### v  The classes of testamentary disposition

Testamentary dispositions of freehold land are technically called '*devises*'.
Dispositions of personal property (including leaseholds) are called '*bequests*' or '*legacies*'.

A gift may be general, specific, demonstrative or residuary. A *general*
gift is a bequest of some money or thing not distinguished from all others
of the same kind, eg a bequest of '£100' or of 'a horse'. A *specific* gift is
a gift of a specified thing which can be distinguished by the description in
the will from all other things, eg 'I bequeath to X my mare, Daisy'. A
*demonstrative* gift is one of a sum of money to be paid out of a particular
fund, eg '£500 out of my 2.5% War Stock'. A *residuary* gift is a gift of

the residue of the estate, or part of it, left over after all other gifts have been made and debts paid.

These distinctions are important because the nature of the gifts will determine whether they are liable to ademption or abatement. *Ademption* occurs when something which is subject to a specific bequest perishes between the time the will is executed and the death. If, for instance, A bequeaths a specified picture to B and this picture is destroyed by fire before A's death, B is clearly entitled to nothing. The gift is 'adeemed'. This doctrine could not apply to general legacies and it is established that it does not apply to a demonstrative gift, for it is deemed to be the intention of the testator to give effect to such a gift even though the fund from which it is to come has ceased to exist at the time of the death. *Abatement* occurs when there is not enough property to satisfy all beneficiaries after the creditors of the deceased have been paid. In this case some of the beneficiaries must lose their rights, and their gifts 'abate' (ie cease to take effect) in a specified order. 'Residuary' gifts abate first and 'specific' gifts last. If the residue is exhausted, general gifts are resorted to next; they abate proportionately, according to the value of each. Demonstrative gifts will not abate unless the fund out of which they are payable is itself exhausted: if that happens they will be treated for the purposes of abatement as if they were general gifts.

## vi Revocation

A will may be revoked either expressly or by implication.

*Express* revocation can only be effected if the instrument by which the testator purports to revoke is properly executed according to the formalities the Wills Act requires for the making of a will. The same rule applies to alterations or interlineations in the will: they must be signed and witnessed.

*Implied* revocation arises in three ways. (i) By the making of a subsequent inconsistent formal testamentary document which disposes of the whole property embraced by the original will. Thus, though it is usual for solicitors to insert in wills a clause, 'I hereby *revoke* all other wills and testamentary dispositions heretofore made by me', this is not strictly necessary; for provided that the second will does dispose of the *whole property* it automatically revokes the first. If there is only a *partial* inconsistency, the parts of the former not inconsistent with the latter will remain effective. (ii) By 'Burning, tearing, or otherwise destroying' the will (Wills Act 1837, s 20). This, however, only effects a revocation if there is both physical destruction and an intention to revoke by such destruction. Further, the destruction must be effected either by the testator or by someone *in his presence* who acts with his authority. Thus, if you accidentally throw your will into a wastepaper basket, and it is taken away and destroyed, it is not revoked. Evidence of the contents of such a will may be given (if it can be obtained) after your death. Intentional destruction of a will with the object of making a fresh one *may*, if such an intention can be proved, revoke the will from the moment of destruction so as to leave the maker intestate until the new one is executed. (iii) By marriage. Marriage contracted after the execution of the will revokes it automatically for most purposes. This rule does not, however, apply where the will is expressed to be made 'in contemplation' of a marriage: where, therefore, a man made a will leaving everything 'unto my fiancée, MEB', and then married MEB, the will was not revoked; for the form of disposition clearly contemplated marriage with MEB whom the testator did, in fact, marry. Where, after a testator has made a will his or her marriage is dissolved, annulled or declared void any devise or bequest to the former spouse *lapses*; but the spouse may, nevertheless, make a claim for reasonable provision under the Inheritance (Provision for Family and Dependants) Act 1975 (see p 456). In respect of deaths on or after 1 January 1996, in the event of any devise or bequest of property, on divorce or annulment of the testator's marriage the property shall pass as if the former spouse had died.

## 2   INTESTATE SUCCESSION

Intestacy is governed by the Administration of Estates Act 1925 ('AEA'), as amended by various statutes, in particular the Intestates' Estates Act 1952 and the AEA 1971.

Before the rules relating to distribution can be set out the machinery adopted by the Act for effecting it must be explained. Wherever a person dies intestate it is provided that all his property, is to vest in his '*personal representatives*' (p 458), upon trust for sale. It must be realized that this trust for sale is only a practical device which makes distribution possible where there are a large number of beneficiaries. Its imposition does not mean that the property *must* be sold. There is a power to postpone sale indefinitely. Thus there may never be an actual sale; the property *may* remain 'unconverted' when the personal representatives vest it, in its original form, in the person entitled to it.

This may be illustrated by an example. Suppose X dies intestate. All his property becomes subject to a trust for sale in the hands of the personal representatives. If X's sole surviving relation is his wife, the personal representatives need not sell; they only have to vest the entire estate (after payment of debts, etc) in her. The administration is then complete. If, however, there were a large number of people entitled to a share in the property (say, for instance, X had five children), the trust for sale may come into play. The reason for this is that, although it would not be easy or desirable to split up the entire property into many different parts, it is comparatively simple to divide up the money realized from the sale. This does not, however, mean that, even where there are numerous beneficiaries, the property need always be sold if it is possible to distribute it (as by distributing shares comprised in the estate among them) without turning it into money.

For the present that is all that needs to be understood about the machinery of administration. We may now consider the problem of *distribution*.

The statutory rules (contained in the AEA) governing the distribution of intestates' estates are based upon the assumption that people who die intestate would, if they had made a will, have wished to make provision for certain classes of near relations; preferring some of those relations to others. Thus, the primary assumption is that people usually wish to provide for their children equally, and also to make provision for their widows or widowers during the remainder of their lives. Failing surviving children or a surviving spouse, or both, they usually wish to benefit their nearer relations, and only wish to leave their property to remoter relations if there are no nearer ones surviving. It is equally true that after divorce or judicial separation people do *not* usually wish to benefit the divorced or separated spouse, and the law takes this also into account (p 457). The actual rules are complex; but if the reader will bear the principles in mind, their effect should be fairly easy to understand.

Five main groups of people have to be considered:

(1) A surviving husband or wife.
(2) Surviving children.
(3) Surviving parents.
(4) Surviving brothers and sisters of the whole blood.
(5) Surviving relations of remoter degree.

(1) *A surviving husband or wife*:

*(a)* If the intestate leaves *no children and no parent or brother or sister of the whole blood* (categories (2)–(4) above), then (subject to what will appear under (2)*(b)*(i) below), the surviving husband or wife will be entitled to the whole residuary estate absolutely. For deaths after 1 January 1996, the spouse must survive the intestate for 28 days to qualify.

'*Residuary estate*' here means the entire property of the deceased, less the funeral and administration expenses, and any debts or other liabilities incurred by the deceased during his or her life.

Further, it must be understood that sometimes even though children or brothers and sisters *do* survive the intestate, the spouse may still become solely entitled. The reason for this is that the survival of these classes of people will ultimately only affect the rights of the surviving spouse if they acquire a 'vested interest' in the property; this will only happen if they attain the age of 18 years or marry before that age. The surviving spouse will therefore become absolutely entitled to the estate if all children and brothers and sisters alive at the time of the intestate's death in fact die minors and unmarried; though unless (and *until*) these events occur, the income of the estate will be distributed upon the assumption that they will become entitled according to the rules set out below, and the rights of the surviving spouse are provisionally curtailed accordingly.

(*b*) If the intestate *leaves children* as well as the surviving spouse, then (subject to what has just been explained about the acquisition of vested interests), he or she has an absolute right to receive *the sum of* £125,000 (duty free and bearing interest until payment) from the estate, or from the proceeds of its sale. Of course the payment of this sum, or indeed, of only a part of it, will often exhaust the entire estate; and there will be nothing for the children. Further, in all circumstances the surviving spouse is absolutely entitled to the '*personal chattels*' of the deceased. These include all articles of a personal nature, such as jewellery, motor cars, furniture, pictures, collections of stamps acquired by way of hobby, etc, but exclude chattels used at the death of the intestate for business purposes, money and securities for money. Thus in *Re Crispin's Will Trusts* [1975] Ch 245 it was held that for this purpose a clock is a clock: so that even a valuable collection of clocks may be 'personal chattels' provided that it has not been collected for commercial purposes. Moreover, the surviving spouse has a right to have the matrimonial home appropriated as part of his or her share of the residue. Apart from the absolute right to what has sometimes been called the 'statutory legacy' of £125,000 (this figure may, however, be altered by statutory instrument), and the other rights mentioned, the surviving spouse is also entitled to the *income produced by half the remainder* of the residuary estate during his or her lifetime. The capital of this half of the remainder of the residuary estate, and the *other* half of it are, as we shall see, held on the '*statutory trusts*' (below) for the children. By s 2 of the Intestates' Estates Act 1952 a surviving spouse may, upon giving notice to the personal representatives, have the life interest converted to a lump sum. Exercise of this right often, as will be appreciated, enables rapid winding up of the estate.

It must be realized that where there are surviving children, as well as the surviving spouse, the above provisions operate in favour of this, his or her immediate family, to the *complete exclusion of all other relatives*.

(*c*) If the intestate leaves *no children*, but leaves a surviving spouse and a *surviving parent or parents or surviving brothers or sisters*, then the surviving spouse is at present entitled to receive *the sum of* £200,000 (variable by statutory instrument, free of duty and bearing interest until payment) and the *personal chattels*. Once more, of course, a smaller sum than this will normally exhaust the estate; but if there is any residue after these deductions have been made, then the spouse is entitled to *one half* of it *absolutely* (not merely to the *income* of this half, as (1)(*b*) above). As to the remaining half, see (3)(*b*), below. For deaths on or after 1 January 1996, the spouse must survive the intestate by 28 days.

(2)  *Surviving children* – The term 'children' here includes all children, whether legitimate, legitimated, adopted or (under the Family Law Reform

Act 1987) illegitimate. Their rights may be summarized under the following heads:

(*a*) Where there is a *surviving spouse as well as a surviving child or children*. The spouse will, as we have seen, be entitled to a 'statutory legacy' of £125,000, to the personal chattels, and also to a life interest in the income of one half of the remaining residue (if any). The other half of the remaining residue (if any) will be held on the 'statutory trusts' for the children. After the death of the surviving spouse the whole of the remaining residue will be held on the 'statutory trusts' for the surviving child or children; in the case of a child who survives the intestate, but dies before the surviving spouse, his share will pass to his estate.

(*b*) Where there is a *child or children, but not a surviving spouse* the residuary estate is held on the 'statutory trusts' for the child or children. Here 'residuary estate' means the entire residuary estate as above defined. All children, of either sex, are entitled to equal shares in it.

The following further points must be noted:

(*i*) Where a child dies *before the intestate*, leaving children of his own who survive the intestate, those children are entitled to 'represent' him, ie his share of the estate is divided between them. Thus, suppose that A dies intestate: he leaves children B and C. He had another child D, who predeceased him. D had two children $D^1$ and $D^2$, living at the death of A. A's estate will ultimately be divided (subject to deduction in favour of a surviving spouse, if any) in the proportions, B=1/3, C= 1/3, $D^1$ and $D^2$= 1/6 each.

(*ii*) Wherever anyone who is entitled to take upon intestacy is under the age of 18, the AEA provides that the statutory powers of 'maintenance' and 'advancement' conferred by the Trustee Act shall apply to his share. This means that the income of his share can either be spent on his maintenance or else accumulated and added to the capital of the share, and that up to one half of this capital can be applied for his 'advancement or benefit'; a phrase which by judicial interpretation may now be said to extend to practically any provision which can be considered to be for the long-term benefit of the child.

(*iii*) It sometimes happens that, during his life-time, an intestate who has more than one child has made an '*advancement*' to one or more of his children, or has paid him or her money for the purpose of marriage. These payments have to be taken into account in assessing the share, if any, to which the favoured child will be entitled upon the intestacy, unless the circumstances show that the intestate did not intend that result. In the technical phrase, the payments must be brought into *hotchpot*. This was abolished in relation to deaths on or after 1 January 1996.

(3) *Surviving parents of the deceased*:

(*a*) Where there are surviving *children* of the deceased his or her parents will receive nothing.

*(b)*  Where there is a *surviving spouse*, he or she will, as has been noted, be entitled to £200,000 and the personal chattels and to one half of any outstanding residue absolutely provided the spouse survives the intestate for the period of 28 days in respect of deaths on or after 1 January 1996. The surviving parents will be entitled to share the other half of this residue; or if only one parent survives, he or she will be absolutely entitled to all of it.

*(c)*  Where there is *no surviving spouse and there are no surviving children*, then the *entire* residuary estate will be divided equally between the surviving parents; or, if only one parent survives, he or she will be absolutely entitled to the whole.

Where there are surviving parents, brothers and sisters therefore have no claim.

(4)  *Brothers and sisters of the whole blood*:

*(a)*  Where there are *surviving children*, the surviving brothers and sisters will receive nothing.

*(b)*  Where there is *a surviving spouse and a surviving parent*, the surviving brothers and sisters will receive nothing.

*(c)*  Where there is *a surviving spouse, but no surviving children and no surviving parents*, subject to the right of the spouse to £200,000, the personal chattels, and half of the residue, the remaining half of the residue will be held on the statutory trusts for the surviving brothers and sisters.

*(d)*  Where there is *no surviving spouse, and there are no surviving children, and no surviving parents*, the surviving brothers and sisters will be entitled (upon the statutory trusts) to the entire residuary estate.

Provided that at least one of these brothers or sisters of the whole blood acquires a vested interest all other relatives will be excluded.

Nephews and nieces 'represent' brothers and sisters who predecease the intestate, in the same way that grandchildren represent children ((2)*(b)*(i) above).

(5)  *Surviving relations of remoter degree* – If any relatives included in categories (1)–(4), above, survive the deceased, provided that at least one of them takes a vested interest, he or they exclude all relatives of remoter degree. But failing the survival of relatives included in categories (1)–(4), then such relative are entitled to take according to their classes in the following order of priority (each class excluding other classes, according to that order):

*(i)*  Brothers and sisters of the half blood, upon the statutory trusts.

*(ii)*  Grandparents.

*(iii)*  Uncles and aunts who are brothers or sisters of the whole blood of a parent of the intestate.

*(iv)*  Uncles and aunts who are brothers or sisters of the half blood of a parent of the intestate.

In the case of class *(i)* nephews and nieces 'represent' the brothers and sisters, and in the case of classes *(iii)* and *(iv)* cousins 'represent' uncles and aunts in cases where the brother, sister, uncle or aunt predeceases the intestate.

No one can be entitled to benefit upon an intestacy unless he either falls directly within classes (1)–(5) above, or represents some person who would have done so had he or she lived.

The rules apply in cases of partial intestacy as well as in cases of total intestacy. Partial intestacy may arise where, for instance, a testator only disposes of part of his estate in his will, thus dying intestate as to the other part.

Where a person dies leaving no relatives within the prescribed categories *the estate passes to the Crown*; but, 'in accordance with the existing practice . . . the Crown . . . may . . . provide for dependants, whether kindred or not, of the intestate, and other persons for whom the intestate might reasonably have been expected to make provision . . . out of the property' (AEA, s 46(1)(*vi*)).

It must be added that in cases of divorce or judicial separation (provided in the latter case that the parties have not resumed cohabitation) where one spouse dies intestate the property will devolve as if the other party had been dead at the time of the intestate's decease (see the Matrimonial Causes Act 1973, s 18(2), Sch 1, para 13): this accords with the general policy of the AEA to give effect to presumed intention. The Inheritance (Provision for Family and Dependants) Act 1975 may, however, be invoked.

## 3   FAMILY PROVISION

Unlike Scots law and the civil law of the Continent, before the passing of the Inheritance (Family Provision) Act 1938 English law had no rules to ensure that testators should not leave all their property 'away' from their families. People were therefore free to cut off their children without a penny. That Act remedied this situation by permitting certain 'dependants' of deceased people to apply for an order of the court to make reasonable provision for them from the 'deceased's' estate if he, by his will, had failed to provide it.

The law on this matter is now governed by the Inheritance (Provision for Family and Dependants) Act 1975, and (s 1(1)) 'where . . . a person dies domiciled in England and Wales and is survived by . . . (a) a wife or husband . . . (b) a former (spouse) who has not remarried . . . (c) a child . . . (d) any person who was treated by the deceased as a child of the family (in relation to any marriage of his) . . . (e) any person . . . who immediately before the death of the deceased was being maintained . . . by the deceased . . . may apply to the court for an order . . . on the ground that the disposition of the deceased's estate effected by his *will* or the law relating to intestacy . . . is *not such as to make reasonable financial provision* for (that person).' It has been held that 'wife' includes a wife of a legally recognized polygamous union. Since 1 January 1996, a claim may be made by any person who during the whole period of two years ending immediately before the date when the deceased died was living (a) in the same household as the deceased and (b) as husband or wife of the deceased. 'Reasonable financial provision' means (s 1(2)), in the case of an application by a surviving *spouse* (unless a decree of judicial separation was in force at the time of the death or, in most circumstances, unless the relevant marriage was dissolved or annulled at the time of the death) such provision as is 'reasonable in all the circumstances', in the case of any other applicant only such provision as is required for his maintenance. The court may, *inter alia*, make an order for periodical or lump sum payments from the estate (s 2); and (s 3) in making the order it must have regard to a number of specified matters: eg the applicant's resources, the size of the estate and the applicant's conduct. By s 4 a time-limit of *six months* from the date of taking out of representation of the estate is (normally) imposed upon the making of applications. There are stringent provisions (including – s 11 – the avoidance of colourable contracts to leave property to others by will) designed to prevent the deceased from defeating the objects of the Act.

## B   THE ADMINISTRATION OF ESTATES

Having considered who is entitled to succeed to property on death we will now consider the practical problem of how the estate is administered. First, as to personal representatives.

### 1   PERSONAL REPRESENTATIVES

#### i   *The nature and purpose of representation*

Hitherto the deceased's estate has only been considered from the point of view of possible beneficiaries. Few of us, however, are without creditors in our lifetime and few of us die without debts. Hence our estates are usually subject to two principal classes of claims; the claims of beneficiaries on the one hand and of creditors on the other. These claims often conflict and yet they have, somehow or other, to be met. This might be done by permitting the property to pass direct to the beneficiaries and allowing the creditors to claim against them. That is what is done under some systems of law. English law, however, adopting its procedure ultimately from the ecclesiastical courts, interposes the *personal representatives* between the claimants. It is their duty to administer the estate by paying creditors, collecting debts and distributing the assets to the people entitled under the will or intestacy.

The general rule is that, since the AEA, all the property which the deceased owned at his death vests in these representatives. There is, however, an important exception to this. Sections 22–24 of the Act contain provisions designed to ensure that, on the death of a tenant for life under a settlement, the settled land (where the land remains settled) shall vest in the trustees of the settlement as '*special*' personal representatives. The settled land alone vests in them; the rest of the life tenant's property is administered by his ordinary or 'general' representatives. The duty of the trustees is to pass the legal estate in the land to the next tenant for life.

## ii The duties of personal representatives

The law which governs the duties of personal representatives, who are in a fiduciary position in many ways similar to trustees, is to be found partly in the Trustee Act 1925 ('TrA') but the essentials are now set out in the AEA 1971, s 9 – 'The personal representative of a deceased person shall be under a duty to: (a) collect and get in the . . . estate of the deceased and administer it according to law; (b) when required to do so . . . exhibit on oath in the court a full inventory of the estate and when so required render an account of the administration to the court; (c) when required to do so by the High Court, deliver up the grant of probate or administration to that court.' Like trustees, personal representatives may take advantage of s 23 of the TrA, and if they administer the estate properly they will incur no liability, and the expenses of administration will be borne by the estate.

## iii The classes of personal representatives

Personal representatives who are appointed by a *testator in his will* are called *executors*. They are usually appointed expressly; but sometimes an appointment may be implied, as where a testator nominates a particular person to pay his debts. In the latter event the executor is known technically as an executor *according to the tenor*.

The personal representatives of an *intestate* are called *administrators*: they derive their powers, as will appear, from the grant of *letters of administration*.

The matter is, however, somewhat more complicated than this, because even though there is a will, administrators may sometimes have to be appointed. Some examples of this situation may be given. In the first place, where there is a will but for some reason there are no executors, or the people named as such decline to act, someone must be appointed to act as personal representative. These people, when appointed, are known as *administrators cum testamento annexo* ('with the will annexed'). In the second place, minors cannot act as representatives, and it follows that if a minor is appointed by will there must be someone to act for him: such a person is known as an administrator *durante minore aetate* ('during minority'). In the third place, if there is a dispute about the validity of a will, clearly an executor appointed in the will cannot take office. In this case an *administrator pendente lite* ('during the litigation') has to be appointed. An administrator of this latter class may proceed with the administration of the estate, but he must not distribute the property.

Where an executor dies in the course of administration his own executor will take his place. If, however, he dies without appointing an executor there is no one to succeed him, and an admininstrator *de bonis non administratis* ('of the unadministered estate') must therefore be appointed. It should be noted that executors, and executors alone, are 'succeeded' in this way. Where an administrator of the estate of an intestate dies a new administrator must be specifically appointed.

A person who intermeddles in the estate (ie does some act, such as collecting the assets, normally done by a personal representative) is liable to account as personal representative even though he has never had any intention of becoming appointed; such a person is called an *'executor de son tort'*.

## iv Probate and letters of administration

Although an executor can enter upon his duties immediately after the death of the testator, his right to dispose of the estate is not fully established until he has obtained a grant of *probate* of the will. 'Probate' is official acceptance of the authenticity of the will and official sanction of the exectutor's right to act. It may be obtained in two ways; in *'common form'* or in *'solemn form'*. The former method is the more usual. The procedure is for the executor to apply either to the principal registry of the Family Division of the High Court at Somerset House or to a District Registry. He must produce the will, an affidavit called the 'executor's oath', and an Inland Revenue account. The 'oath' is in effect a promise by the executor to administer the estate according to law. The account contains particulars of the property comprised in the estate, which enable the Inland Revenue Commissioners to assess the estate duty payable. If these documents are in order, and estate duty is paid, 'probate' will be granted and a copy of the will will be handed to the executor; the original is retained at the Registry.

'Probate' in 'common form' is granted much as a matter of course. If, however, there is any serious dispute, for instance as to the validity of the will, probate in 'solemn form' will have to be obtained. This entails the hearing of evidence, and amounts in effect to an action, normally heard before a judge of the Chancery Division.

Letters of administration are granted in much the same way as probate. There is, however, one substantial difference in the procedure. An executor is a person in whom the testator has reposed confidence, an administrator is not. Formerly, therefore, administrators were usually required to enter into an 'administration bond' by which they undertook to pay the Principal Registrar double the gross value of the estate if they failed to administer it according to law and also they usually had to produce sureties against default. This rule has now, however, been altered by the AEA 1971, s 8 which only provides that the High Court may require one or more sureties (in practice usually insurance companies) to make good, within any limit imposed by the court, any loss which any person interested may suffer in consequence of a breach of his duties by the administrator. No action may be brought against the surety without leave of the court and in some circumstances a surety will not be required.

### v  Who may be appointed

Executors are appointed by the will. Nothing therefore need be mentioned about them under this head, beyond pointing out that probate will not be granted either to a minor or to more than four executors. It is usual, however, to appoint more than one, for it is open to an executor to refuse to act.

The appointment of administrators is within the discretion of the court, and Rules of Court prescribe an order of priority of choice. This order roughly follows the order of priority of persons entitled to take upon an intestacy; though sometimes – where for instance the estate is insolvent – a creditor may be appointed.

The maximum number of administrators is four. In certain cases, as where there is a minor beneficiary; there must normally be at least two, though even in these cases a trust corporation may act alone.

### vi  The powers and liabilities of personal representatives

Personal representatives are given absolute powers of disposing of the property for the purpose of administration. We have seen that in the case of a total intestacy an automatic trust for sale is imposed. By s 39 of the AEA the *powers* of trustees for sale are also conferred upon executors. This, of course, means that personal representatives have all the powers of a life tenant under the Settled Land Act 1925; in particular the power of selling land comprised in the estate. Even before that Act they were permitted to sell or pledge personal property comprised in the estate. All these powers, of course, come to an end when the administration is complete, the debts paid and the property vested in the beneficiaries.

By law personal representatives are officially allowed one year from the death in which to wind up the estate (AEA, s 44), but the courts will not tie them strictly to this period. Thus if any creditor or beneficiary complains that he has suffered on account of delay in distribution beyond the 'executor's year', he will have to prove that this delay was the result of some neglect on the part of the personal representatives.

The liability of personal representatives is in general limited by the value of the estate. They are, however, in a similar position to trustees, and if they do anything unlawful, eg distribute the assets of an insolvent estate to beneficiaries instead of to creditors, they may be personally liable. A personal representative is then said to have committed a *devastavit* ('he has wasted'). He can, however, take advantage of s 61 of the TrA.

## 2   ADMINISTRATION OF ASSETS

Having described the nature of personal representatives we are now in a position to consider their duties.

They generally administer the estate themselves (usually through a solicitor) without interference. If, however, someone interested in the estate – such as a beneficiary or a creditor – is dissatisfied with the administration he may, by an 'administration action', apply for administration by the court. If the estate is 'solvent' it will then be administered in the Chancery Division of the High Court. If it is 'insolvent' it may be administered either in the Chancery Division or in the Bankruptcy Court. Small estates, however, may sometimes be administered in a county court.

The four main duties of personal representatives are:

*(a)*   To collect all debts due to the estate.

*(b)*   To pay the debts and satisfy the liabilities of the estate.

*(c)*   To convert unauthorized investments into authorized ones; though they almost invariably have power to postpone this.

*(d)*   To distribute the remainder of the property according to the will or to the rules of intestacy.

Where personal representatives are in the happy position of administering an estate sufficiently large to satisfy all creditors and all beneficiaries their duties are comparatively simple. However, this is often not the case. On the other hand, the estate may be '*insolvent*', ie not large enough to satisfy all creditors in full: in this case, of course the beneficiaries can hope for nothing. On the other hand, though it is 'solvent' (ie the creditors can all be satisfied) it may be insufficient to meet the claims of all beneficiaries. In either case rules of law have had to be provided to govern the conflicting rights of claimants, so as to determine who will be paid and who will not. We will first consider the rules concerning 'insolvent' estates.

### i   Insolvent estates

Where the estate is insufficient to meet the claims of *creditors* in full the following rules apply (AEA, s 34(1) and first Sch 1, Part 1):

*(i)*   *Funeral expenses, testamentary expenses* and the *costs* of administration have first priority. They must, if possible, be paid in full.

*(ii)*   *Debts* have next priority. They have to be paid in a prescribed order. This order is the following:

*(a)*   *Preferred* debts rank first. Examples of these are arrears of rates and taxes for any one year and the wages of clerks, servants, and workmen due for a period of four months prior to the death.

*(b)*   *Ordinary* debts. These are any debts which are neither 'preferred' nor 'deferred'.

(c) *Deferred* debts. Examples of these are claims for money lent by a husband to his wife for business purposes and by a wife to her husband for any purposes; and loans made to a person for business purposes if the lender is to receive interest varying with the profits of the business.

Secured creditors are also entitled to special rights.

If the estate is insufficient to satisfy the claims of all creditors in any one class these claims must usually be cut down proportionately, according to their respective amounts. Thus suppose that when classes *(i)* and *(ii)(a)* claims have been satisfied, only £100 remains; then if A and B are ordinary creditors owed £1,500 and £500 respectively, they will receive £75 and £25 each.

By s 10 of the AEA 1971 a personal representative who, in good faith and at a time when he has *no reason to believe that the estate is insolvent*, pays the debt of any person (*including himself*) who is a creditor of the estate, is not to be liable to account to an unpaid creditor *of the same degree*. This rule does not, however, apply to a creditor who has been granted letters of administration solely because he is a creditor in respect of debts *due to himself*.

## ii Solvent estates

Even though an estate is '*solvent*' (ie there are enough funds available to meet all the claims of creditors) there may not be enough to pay the beneficiaries in full. The creditors must of course be paid somehow. It is therefore essential to know the order in which the beneficiaries are to lose their rights so that the creditors may be satisfied.

This order is laid down in s 34(3) and Part II of Sch 1 to the AEA. The funeral, testamentary and administration expenses and the debts are to be paid out of the following funds in the following order:

(a) First, resort is to be had to any property in the estate which is undisposed of by will, subject to the retention of a fund to meet pecuniary legacies.

(b) Next, to any property included in a 'residuary' gift, subject to the retention of a fund to meet the balance of the pecuniary legacies. A 'residuary' gift is a gift of anything that may remain of a testator's property after specific devises and bequests have been set aside.

(c) Next, to property specifically appropriated by the testator for the payment of debts.

(d) Next, to property left by the testator subject to a charge for the payment of debts.

(e) Next, to the fund, if any, retained to meet pecuniary legacies.

(f) Next, to property specifically devised or bequeathed, rateably, according to value.

(g) Finally, to property appointed by will under a general power (including the statutory power to dispose of entailed interests), rateably, according to value. This class of property comes last because, in a sense, it is not really the testator's 'own' to dispose of; though he is free to do so, it comes to him from elsewhere.

It is provided that this order of application may be varied by the will of the deceased. Thus if a testator shows a clear intention that a special fund of £x shall be set aside for payment of debts *in exoneration* of all other funds, this fund will be liable first, even before property in category *(a)*. The intention to exonerate must, however, appear clearly from the will; otherwise a fund which is merely set aside for the payment of debts will fall within category *(c)*.

Such then, is the order in which beneficiaries are liable to lose their interests. It only remains to be noticed that it may sometimes happen that an interest of a lower category (say, *(e)*) is disposed of in favour of creditors before an interest of a higher category (say, *(b)*). At one time this often occurred, because creditors were permitted, in certain circumstances, to proceed to satisfy their claims by direct resort to real property comprised in the estate. In this event the creditor would not concern himself with the 'priority' of the beneficiary entitled to the property attacked, so that a 'lower' beneficiary might lose his interest while 'higher' beneficiaries retained theirs. This cannot occur today because creditors may no longer proceed against the land directly. It is possible, however, that a personal representative may delve unnecesarily 'low' on the list in order to discharge liabilities. He may, for instance, dispose of property comprised in category *(e)* in favour of a creditor, intending to dispose of all the property in the 'higher' categories later. He may then discover that the estate is richer than he supposed, or that the liabilities are less than he supposed, so that he need never have attacked category *(e)* at all.

In such a situation the doctrine of *marshalling of assets* comes into play. This means that a beneficiary who loses property of a 'lower' category to which he is entitled may recoup his loss by claiming to be indemnified out of undisposed property to which someone else 'higher' on the list is entitled. The doctrine of marshalling is thus an application of the principle that, whatever the method of distribution, the prescribed order will always be observed. This principle is elementary. Suppose, for example, all property comprised in the estate, down to and including category *(d)* is disposed of in favour of creditors. Suppose that it is then discovered that the deceased had concealed certain property. Clearly category *(d)* beneficiaries will have first claim on this 'new' property.

3    TRANSFER OF PROPERTY TO BENEFICIARIES

When all testamentary and other expenses have been paid and all liabilities discharged, the final duty of personal representatives is to transfer the appropriate property to the appropriate beneficiaries.

The rule is that the representatives must assent to the transfer. In respect of any property other than land the assent requires no special formality; representatives may signify their intention to divest themselves of the property in favour of beneficiaries by any legally recognized method. Thus, a beneficiary may remove books which have been bequeathed to him with the consent, express or implied, of the executors. This will amount to an 'assent'. Shares may be transferred by executing a transfer to the beneficiary.

Where, however, it is desired to transfer the legal estate in land it is enacted by s 36(4) of the AEA that the assent '*shall be in writing, signed by the personal representative, and shall name the person in whose favour it is given*', and that '*an assent not in writing . . . shall not be effectual to pass a legal estate*'. This requirement must always be satisfied; and it is of cardinal importance in conveyancing. The reason for this is that s 36(7) provides that a written assent shall be taken, by a purchaser of the land for money or money's worth, to be sufficient evidence that the person in whose favour the assent is given is entitled to the legal estate. This means that a purchaser from the beneficiary who has obtained such an assent need not, and must not, examine the will in order to assume himself that the vendor is entitled to convey. All he needs to see is the assent. In two cases, however, he must not accept the bare evidence of the assent (the Act only provides that it is to be 'sufficient' evidence). First, if there is a memorandum of a previous assent endorsed upon the probate or letters of administration: this naturally makes the later assent suspect. Second, if, without examining the will, the purchaser actually has notice of a defect in the vendor's title, despite the assent. This might happen, for instance, where it appears from a recital in the assent itself that the vendor is not the person entitled to convey – that he is, for example, a beneficiary under a trust for sale – for it will be recalled that in this case it is the duty of the trustees, not of the beneficiary, to execute the conveyance.

This may be the proper place to remark that an apparent problem in the law of succession, testate or intestate, may sometimes arise where two or more people die or appear to have died simultaneously. Suppose, for example, that by his will X leaves Y a legacy and X and Y are both drowned in the same shipwreck, there being no evidence as to which of them died first. Can Y's representatives claim the legacy upon the assumption that X died first and that his will therefore operated in favour of Y, or is it to be assumed that Y died first so that the legacy 'lapsed' (Y being presumed dead before X died) and fell into residue so as to pass to X's intestate successors? This problem of '*commorientes*' (people dying together) is solved by the LPA, s 184 which provides that such deaths shall, subject to court order, be presumed to have occurred in order of *seniority*: thus, in the problem, Y's representatives would take if he were younger than X and X's intestate successors if X were younger than Y.

## 2   Bankruptcy

The law relating to bankruptcy is now governed by the Insolvency Act 1986, but bankruptcies prior to 29 December 1986 still fall under the Bankruptcy Act 1914.

The principal aims of the 1986 Act were to professionalize bankruptcy administration by ensuring that it is in the hands of the official receiver or of insolvency practitioners, to simplify bankruptcy procedure and to bring it into line with company insolvencies. Insolvency practitioners are people licensed to act as nominees or supervisors of voluntary arrangements, or as trustees in bankruptcy, by professional bodies which at present include the Law Society, the accountants' professional bodies, the Insolvency Practitioners Association or the Secretary of State. A further aim of the legislation was to encourage settlements by way of voluntary arrangements in order to avoid the complications of formal bankruptcy proceedings. It will thus be realized that there are two types of proceedings: voluntary arrangements, on the one hand and bankruptcy proceedings on the other. We will describe the former first.

### (a)   Voluntary arrangements

An insolvent debtor may, if he pleases, decide to make a voluntary arrangement; that is a composition with his creditors or a scheme of arrangement. A 'composition' has been defined as 'an agreement between the debtor and his creditors whereby the compounding creditors agree with the debtor and between themselves to accept from the debtor payment of less than the respective amounts due to them in full satisfaction of the whole of their claim'. The usual form of a 'scheme of arrangement' is an assignment by the debtor of his property (or a part of it) to a trustee for distribution of the proceeds of sale among the creditors, rateably or in agreed proportions.

The first step for a debtor who wishes to make a composition or scheme of arrangement of his affairs is to apply to the court for an *interim order*. This order has the effect of preventing a bankruptcy petition from being presented. In his application the debtor must state that he proposes to make a voluntary arrangement and must name a 'nominee' (an insolvency practitioner). Within 14 days the latter must submit a report to the court stating whether a meeting of the debtor's creditors should be called to consider the proposal. Upon receipt of this report, if satisfied that such a meeting should be held, the court will direct that the interim order be extended for a specified period. Thereafter the nominee must summon the meeting. The chairman of the meeting must report its deliberations to the court and, assuming that the court approves the proposal, every creditor who had notice of the meeting and was entitled to vote is bound by the arrangement whether or not he attended the meeting or voted in favour of the proposal. After the report to the court the interim order continues in being for a further 28 days. This is to allow the arrangement to be challenged by the debtor, any creditor entitled to vote, the nominee, or (where the debtor is a bankrupt) the trustee of his estate or the official receiver. After the 28 days no challenge is allowed. If the challenge is successful the period of the interim order will be extended. If there is no challenge, or the challenge is unsuccessful, after the 28 days the arrangement becomes binding and it is then for the nominee (thereafter known as a 'supervisor') to assume responsibility for the implementation of the arrangement.

All voluntary arrangements have to be registered in a register of individual voluntary agreements maintained by the Secretary of State.

## (b) Bankruptcy proceedings

### (1) Bankruptcy orders

**The bankruptcy petition** – Bankruptcy proceedings are initiated by a petition upon which the court may make a bankruptcy order. A petition may be presented by: (i) a creditor or creditors; (ii) the debtor; (iii) the supervisor of a voluntary arrangement or any person other than the debtor who is bound by the scheme; (iv) the official petitioner or any person specified by the court as having suffered loss where a criminal bankruptcy order has been made against the debtor. Where a petiton has been presented it can only be withdrawn by leave of the court. A petition may only be presented if, on the day upon which it was presented, the debtor: (i) is domiciled in England or Wales; or (ii) is personally present in England or Wales; or (iii) has been ordinarily resident or has had a place of residence in England or Wales during the previous three years; or (iv) has carried on business in England or Wales during the previous three years.

**Creditors' petitions** – A creditor's petition may only be presented subject to the following, amongst other, conditions: (i) the amount of the debt or aggregate amounts of the debts must at least come up to the 'bankruptcy level'; (ii) the debt, or debts, must be for a liquidated sum (ie a specific amount) and payable immediately or at some future time and must be unsecured; (iii) the debt, or debts, must be such that the debtor appears, either to be unable to pay or to have no reasonable prospect of doing so.

There must be a 'statutory demand'. That is to say, a written demand by the creditor for payment. This must be made in a prescribed form and must usually be served upon the debtor personally, allowing a period of at least three weeks for payment. Within 18 days of service of this demand the debtor may apply to the court to have it set side upon sufficient grounds.

**Debtors' petitions** – A debtor may present a petition to the court simply upon the ground that he is unable to pay his debts.

**Voluntary arrangements** – Where there has been a composition or a scheme of arrangement any creditor or the supervisor may present a petition for a bankruptcy order upon the following grounds: (i) that the debtor has failed to comply with his obligations under the scheme; (ii) either that the debtor's statement of affairs, or information given by him at a creditors' meeting, was false or misleading, or was subject to omissions; (iii) that the debtor has failed to comply with reasonable requirements of the supervisor.

## The bankruptcy order

A petition is presented in the High Court where: (i) the debtor has resided or carried on business within the London insolvency district for the greater part of six months immediately preceding the presentation of the petition; (ii) the debtor is not resident in England or Wales; (iii) the petitioning creditor is unable to ascertain the residence or place of business of the debtor; (iv) the petition is presented by a minister of the Crown or a government department. Otherwise petitions are presented in certain county courts having bankruptcy jurisdiction.

On a creditor's petition an order can only be made if the court is satisfied that the debt, or one of the debts, on which the petition was founded has not been paid, secured or compounded: or, in the case of a future debt, that there is no reasonable prospect that it will be paid when it falls due.

On a debtor's petition the court must not make an order if it appears that: (i) the total unsecured debts would be less than the 'small bankruptcy level', and (ii) the value of the estate would be equal to or more than the 'minimum amount', and (iii) during the five years prior to the presentation of the petition the debtor has not been adjudged bankrupt nor entered into a composition with his creditors or a scheme of arrangement of his affairs, and (iv) that it would be appropriate to appoint a person to prepare a report on the possibility of the debtor entering into voluntary arrangements. The 'small bankruptcy level' and the 'minimum amount' are amounts designated by statutory instrument from time to time.

As a general rule a *creditor's petition* must not be heard until at least 14 days after service. The debtor, the petitioning creditor and any other creditor who has given appropriate notice may appear at the hearing. And a debtor who wishes to oppose the petition must file a notice specifying his grounds of objection. On the hearing of the petition the court may make a bankruptcy order if it is satisfied that the statements in the petition are true and that the debt has not been paid, secured or compounded.

A *debtor's petition* must identify the debtor and admit insolvency and it must contain a statement of affairs. The bankruptcy order is settled by the court.

## (c)  Protection and investigation of the bankrupt's estate

*Protection of the estate*

**The receivership** – The court has power to appoint the official receiver as interim receiver of the debtor's property at any time after presentation of the petition before the bankruptcy order is made if such appointment is necessary for the protection of the property. After the bankruptcy order is made and before the estate becomes vested in a trustee the official receiver becomes automatically receiver and manager of the estate. The functions of the official receiver are to protect the estate and he has power to sell perishable goods or any goods the value of which is likely to diminish. However, a 'special manager' may be appointed – a person with particular expertise – where it appears to be advisable, when the official receiver has become interim receiver, after adjudication, or after the property has become vested in a trustee.

**Investigation** – Within 21 days of the bankruptcy order where the petition was presented by someone other than the debtor the latter must submit a *statement of affairs* to the official receiver and the official receiver must then send a summary of it to the creditors. A debtor who fails to submit a statement or does so incorrectly is guilty of contempt and certain other offences.

Thereafter the official receiver may apply to the court for a *public examination* of the bankrupt. At the public examination the persons invited to question the bankrupt are the official receiver, the trustee in bankruptcy, any special manager and any creditor who has tendered proof of a debt. The bankrupt must answer on oath. There is also provision for *private examination* of the bankrupt, his spouse or former spouse, of any person known or believed to have any property comprised in the bankrupt's estate in his possession or to be indebted to the bankrupt, and of any person appearing to the court to be able to give information concerning the bankrupt, his dealings, affairs or property.

**The bankrupt's estate**
The bankrupt's estate for the purposes of bankruptcy administration is defined as: (a) all property belonging to or vested in the bankrupt at the commencement of the bankruptcy; or (b) any property which is treated as being comprised in the estate, eg any property which has been acquired by, or has devolved upon, the bankrupt since the commencement of the bankruptcy.

But it must be noted that the following are *excluded* from the estate:

(*a*)  Such tools, books, vehicles and other equipment as are necessary to the bankrupt for personal use by him in his employment, business or vocation.

(*b*) Such clothing, bedding, furniture, household equipment and provisions as are necessary for satisfying the basic domestic needs of the bankrupt and his family.

(*c*) Property excluded from the bankrupt's estate by enactments other than the Insolvency Act 1986, eg social security payments and pensions.

(*d*) Property held by the bankrupt on trust for any other person.

(*e*) The right of nomination to a vacant ecclesiastical benefice.

(*f*) Damages awarded to the bankrupt for personal injury.

## The trustee

As a general rule, although at discretion he may himself retain the powers of administration, within 12 weeks of the making of the bankruptcy order, the official receiver will summon a general meeting of creditors to appoint a trustee ('trustee in bankruptcy' or 'trustee of the estate') who must be an insolvency practitioner. Once appointed, the trustee is responsible for the administration. He is obliged to have regard to any directions given to him by a general meeting of the creditors and, in particular, by vote at a general meeting of creditors, a 'creditors' committee' must be appointed to participate with the trustee. This committee must consist of not less than three, nor more than five, creditors. Further, there is an overall control of the trustee by the court. Any creditor may request the trustee to call a general meeting at any time. When he has completed the administration of the estate the trustee must call a final meeting of creditors for the purpose of obtaining his release. Where the official receiver has retained control of the administration he obtains his release from the Secretary of State. It should be added that in certain special circumstances the trustee may be appointed not by the general meeting of creditors but by the Secretary of State or the court.

## The administration of the estate

The estate vests automatically in the trustee upon his appointment. After acquired property (any property the debtor has acquired after the commencement of the bankruptcy) only vests in the trustee if he serves a written notice claiming it, and his title then relates back to the date upon which the bankrupt acquired it. But the trustee will have no title as against a purchaser of such property who has taken in good faith and for value, nor as against a banker who enters into a transaction in good faith and without notice of the bankruptcy. Any income earned by the bankrupt after the commencement of the bankruptcy may be subjected to an 'income payments order'; in which case it will form part of the estate and become vested in the trustee.

The trustee has wide powers in respect of the property comprised in the estate, some of which – such as the power of sale – he may exercise of his own accord. Some of which – such as carrying on a business of the bankrupt's – he may only exercise with the consent of his committee or of the court.

The trustee may, by giving prescribed notice, disclaim 'onerous property'; this, in the words of the Act, includes '(a) any unprofitable contract; and (b) any other property comprised in the bankrupt's estate which is unsaleable or not readily saleable, or is such that it may give rise to a liability to pay money or perform any other onerous act'. In particular, he may disclaim leasehold property which is unsaleable or not readily saleable. The effect of a disclaimer is to determine all the rights of the bankrupt in respect of the property disclaimed.

Any person claiming to be a creditor of the bankrupt must 'prove his debt', ie submit his claim in writing to the trustee (or to the official receiver, as the case may be) in a prescribed form, known as a 'proof of debt', and a secured creditor must give particulars of his security, including the value which he puts upon it. For this purpose a claim for unliquidated damages which has accrued before the commencement of the bankruptcy is now treated as a debt.

When he has sufficient funds the trustee must declare and distribute dividends with all convenient speed, subject to retention of sums necessary for the costs of administration.

Normally, of course, the estate will be insufficient to meet all claims. Consequently the Act prescribes an order of priority of payment. First come people entitled to payment of the bankruptcy costs and expenses. Second come preferential creditors. Third come ordinary creditors. Fourth comes interest due to both preferential and ordinary creditors. Fifth come any debt and interest owed to the bankrupt's spouse. If, within a class, such as preferential claims, there are insufficient funds for payment in full the claim must be abated in equal proportions between members of the class.

The *preferential* category is not now a large one: it includes, *inter alia*, deductions from emoluments made in respect of PAYE payments during 12 months preceding the bankruptcy order, VAT due within 6 months preceding the bankruptcy, employees' remuneration payable in a period of 4 months preceding the bankruptcy. *Ordinary* claims consist of all debts not falling within any other category.

In the unlikely event that the estate is sufficient to meet all claims in full any surplus must be distributed to the bankrupt himself.

## Voidable transactions

Certain transactions entered into by a bankrupt are voidable. There are quite a number of such transactions but the most important are 'transactions at an undervalue' and 'preferences'. These may be set aside by court order upon application by the trustee (or, as the case may be, the official receiver).

In the words of the Act 'an individual enters into a transaction with a person *at an undervalue* if: (a) he makes a gift to that person . . . (b) he enters into a transaction with a person in consideration of marriage, or (c) he enters into a transaction with that person for a consideration the value of which . . . is significantly less than the value . . . of the consideration provided by the individual'.

Such a transaction may be set aside if it took place within five years of the presentation of the petition, provided that the bankrupt was insolvent at the time of the transaction or became insolvent in consequence of it. If the transaction was with an 'associate' of the bankrupt there is a presumption that he was insolvent unless the contrary be proved. 'Associates' comprise a wide class of people including spouses, relatives and partners. Transactions entered into within two years of the presentation of the petition may be made the subject of an order irrespective of the bankrupt's solvency.

A *preference* includes anything the bankrupt does which puts a creditor or a guarantor, in the event of bankruptcy, in a better position than he would have been had the thing not been done. It is, however, essential that, in making the preference the bankrupt was influenced by a desire to prefer the creditor or guarantor should bankruptcy occur. Where the creditor or guarantor is an associate it is presumed that the bankrupt was so influenced. A preference may only be set aside where: (a) the bankrupt was insolvent at the time he made it or became insolvent in consequence of it; and (b) the preference was made within six months (two years in the case of associates) of the presentation of the bankruptcy petition.

Quite apart from these provisions relating specifically to bankruptcy it has long been the rule (now re-enacted and amended by the 1986 Act) that any transaction at an 'undervalue' may be set aside by the court where a debtor has entered into it for the purpose of putting assets beyond the reach of someone entitled to make a claim against him. But no such order may be made if it prejudices any interest in the relevant property (whether land or money) which was acquired by someone in good faith and without notice of the relevant circumstances.

### Discharge and annulment
Except in the case of criminal bankruptcies and where the bankrupt has been previously bankrupt within 15 years of his present bankruptcy (when a court order is required), the bankrupt is now, in general, automatically *discharged* – generally, after three years of the commencement of the bankruptcy. In the case of the two exceptional categories mentioned above the order cannot be obtained until the lapse of five years.

The effect of discharge is to release the bankrupt from all bankruptcy debts. This must not, however, be taken to mean that the bankruptcy creditors are not still entitled to all their rights under the administration. And the administration may well continue after discharge: so much so that a creditor may prove in after discharge.

*Annulment* is effected by an order of the court. Annulment differs in effect from discharge in that, after annulment, the bankrupt remains fully liable for the bankruptcy debts. There are various grounds upon which a bankruptcy order may be annulled. Amongst them are the fact that the bankruptcy order ought not to have been made, the fact that the bankruptcy debts and expenses have been paid, the fact that a composition has been approved by the creditors' meeting.

## Criminal bankruptcy

This concept was originally introduced by the Criminal Justice Act 1972. The purpose of criminal bankruptcy was to assist the financial victims of convicted criminals where the loss amounted, in aggregate, to more than a specified amount. (Financial loss arising from personal injury was not, however, included.) This was abolished by the Criminal Justice Act 1988 and replaced with provisions enabling confiscation orders to be made against offenders.

## Disqualifications

An undischarged bankrupt is subject to a number of disqualifications (which, however, now cease upon discharge). Amongst others, these include disqualification from: (a) the right of sitting in the House of Lords; (b) the right of election to or sitting in the House of Commons: and any member so disqualified must, after six months from adjudication, vacate his seat (discharge, however, removes this latter disqualification); (c) membership of a local authority; (d) holding a solicitor's practising certificate; (e) save with leave of the court, acting as a company director.

It should finally be noted that there are a number of bankruptcy offences and, in particular, it is an offence for an undischarged bankrupt to obtain credit without disclosing his status.

# Index

475